Pro ADO.NET 2.0

∎∎∎

Sahil Malik

Apress®

Pro ADO.NET 2.0

Copyright © 2005 by Sahil Malik

ISBN-13 (pbk): 978-1-59059-512-1
ISBN-10 (pbk): 1-59059-512-2

Printed and bound in the United States of America 9 8 7 6 5 4 3 2

Lead Editor: Jonathan Hassell
Technical Reviewers: Frans Bouma and Erick Sgarbi
Editorial Board: Steve Anglin, Dan Appleman, Ewan Buckingham, Gary Cornell, Tony Davis, Jason Gilmore,
    Jonathan Hassell, Chris Mills, Dominic Shakeshaft, Jim Sumser
Associate Publisher: Grace Wong
Project Manager: Emily K. Wolman
Copy Edit Manager: Nicole LeClerc
Copy Editor: Linda Marousek
Assistant Production Director: Kari Brooks-Copony
Production Editor: Ellie Fountain
Compositor: Kinetic Publishing Services, LLC
Proofreader: April Eddy
Indexer: Carol Burbo
Artist: Kinetic Publishing Services, LLC
Interior Designer: Van Winkle Design Group
Cover Designer: Kurt Krames
Manufacturing Manager: Tom Debolski

Distributed to the book trade worldwide by Springer-Verlag New York, Inc., 233 Spring Street, 6th Floor, New York, NY 10013. Phone 1-800-SPRINGER, fax 201-348-4505, e-mail orders-ny@springer-sbm.com, or visit http://www.springeronline.com.

For information on translations, please contact Apress directly at 2560 Ninth Street, Suite 219, Berkeley, CA 94710. Phone 510-549-5930, fax 510-549-5939, e-mail info@apress.com, or visit http://www.apress.com.

The source code for this book is available to readers at http://www.apress.com in the Source Code section.

I would like to dedicate this book to my parents.
Mom, for being extremely strict with me when I was a kid
and always very loving in all my years.
Pop, for saving me from Mom ;-),
and being the neverending source of inspiration and strength.
I love you both very much.

Contents at a Glance

Contents

▮CHAPTER 8   Sorting, Searching, and Filtering 213

▮CHAPTER 9   Updating Data 247

About the Author

SAHIL MALIK has been working as a consultant in Microsoft technology for about nine years now. He has worked for many top-notch clients across the globe, including many Fortune 100 companies and government organizations within the United States. Sahil started programming in a DOS world, moved to Win32 API, Borland C, MFC, VC /ATL, Visual Basic 6, and eventually to .NET in both Visual Basic .NET and C# worlds.

Sahil leads the office of Emerging Technologies at the National Cancer Institute, and is also currently helping architect a highly visible public website using ASP.NET 2.0/SQL Server 2005. He speaks frequently at local user groups and conferences. He was the lead author on *Pro ADO.NET with VB.NET 1.1*. For his community involvement and contribution, he has also been awarded the Microsoft MVP award.

About the Technical Reviewers

FRANS BOUMA started programming in 1986 on a Toshiba MSX-1, at the age of 16. After graduating with a bachelor's degree in Computer Science from the Hogeschool Enschede in the Netherlands in 1994, he started working with 4GL systems and post-relational databases, like uniVerse. In 1996, he founded Solutions Design, a company for database-driven web-application development. As the lead developer, he developed medium to large enterprise web applications using SQL Server, AS400, COM+, VC++, Visual Basic, and ASP.

In 2001, Solutions Design produced a content-management system completely based on Microsoft technologies like SQL Server 2000, COM+, VC++, Visual Basic 6, and ASP. The following year, Frans developed in C# his first .NET application, the open-source LLBLGen code generator for SQL Server stored procedures and .NET classes. Due to the worldwide success of LLBLGen, in 2003, Frans designed and developed for Solutions Design the O/R mapper and code generator LLBLGen Pro, which is currently one of the market-leading data-access solutions for .NET, C#, and VB.NET.

He now works full-time on LLBLGen Pro enhancements. For his community efforts, Frans received the MVP award for C# in 2004 and 2005.

ERICK SGARBI was introduced to the computing world in 1981, learned how to program Sinclair Basic on a ZX Spectrum, and by 1987 became a full-time AS400 COBOL programmer. He spent 1993 to 2001 working on several projects, mostly Java, C++, Visual Basic, and Delphi.

Erick attained a bachelor's degree in Information Systems from Australia Catholic University and acquired MCAD Charter membership in 2003. Since 2002, he has been involved in several senior development positions for .NET projects related to system's development and supplying contracts for Smart Clients and ASP.NET applications. Over the past few years, Erick has authored and performed technical reviews and edits on several .NET book titles.

Acknowledgments

No man is an island, and neither are his thoughts. I am merely the medium who wrote what I heard, read, and learned from various other well-accomplished individuals in my field or otherwise.

I would first like to thank my countless peers such as Bill Vaughn, Bill Ryan, Miha, Herfried Wagner, Jon Skeet, Carl Franklin, and countless other superb individuals who spend their time and effort disseminating what they know. They truly believe that a candle lighting another candle only creates more light. It is from their endless, tireless discussions, and countless, neverending community interaction that I was able to collect what I present in this book. None of these ideas is mine: I certainly didn't invent ADO.NET—I merely learned it from all these fine people.

I would then like to thank the two most critical, spit-in-the-face reviewers I could find. I was amazed at the thoroughness Frans Bouma and Erick Sgarbi exhibited in their work. They pored through the text and, thankfully, did not mince their words in helping solidify the content of this book. I'd like to thank them both, both as my reviewers and my well-meaning friends who have always wished the very best for me.

I would then like to thank the various Microsoft employees who graciously agreed to help with my neverending questions. I sit back and think why they agreed to help a complete stranger, thousands of miles away—and I cannot come up with a good explanation. These guys replied to e-mails that I sent at 3 a.m., within a matter of minutes. It is guys like these who truly love what they do and who are able to make such a fantastic programming platform. Of notable mention are Pablo Castro, Angel Saenz Badillos, Sushil Chordia, Andy Conrad, Mike Clark, Jim Johnson, Raphael Renous, Mark Ashton, Michael Rys, Chris Lee, Steve Lasker, and, of course, my MVP Lead Rafael Munoz. (And yet I think I must have missed a few names).

I would then like to thank my boss at work, who encouraged me and guided me much like a father would guide his son. I would like to thank Michael Arluk, who lent me his neverending support and encouragement in this rather difficult and time-consuming task of writing an entire book in such an aggressive duration and timeline. I have told him, and I will tell you, this book would not have been possible if it weren't for him.

Finally, I would then like to thank my parents for being the strictest and most loving parents one can pray for. They taught me discipline, they taught me dedication, they taught me focus, and they taught me endurance and constancy in tough times.

—Sahil Malik

Introduction

...Mission control to reader ... you are now nearing the ADO.NET planet in the .NET solar system of the Microsoft technology galaxy. Make sure no architectural mistake alien eats you up for dinner ...

Learning any new topic is like approaching a new planet. As you approach the planet from a distance, you first identify its place in the solar system, then the major geographical features on the surface, and finally you land on it and start digging deep and constructing buildings to finally call it your home. Then one day before you know it, you are married to a Mrs. Alien, have two kids, a mortgage, a car payment, and find yourself worrying about your kid's college education fund.

It is true!! Life is like a computer game, it keeps getting harder and then you die.

So why should learning ADO.NET be any different? Doesn't it make sense to start at the basics and then graduate to the complex?

This book begins with three rather short (about 50 pages combined) and simple chapters:

- The first chapter identifies where ADO.NET is located in the .NET solar system and its various major building blocks.

- The second chapter begins with identifying the major geographical features of the ADO.NET terrain. It serves very well as a map for the future chapters when you are on the ground digging deeper. Because this chapter is a map, you will be reminded to reference back to the various figures, class names, and namespaces presented in this chapter as you dig deeper in the terrain.

- The third chapter is when you land on the planet and start walking around and create four data-driven applications of increasing complexity.

Once you have landed on the planet, are armed with a map of the area, and have walked around a bit is when it's time to start digging deeper and do what we humans do so naturally—exploring (without exploding hopefully).

So let me ask you a question, When you hold a tool such as a hammer in your hand, what do you do with it? You bang things such as a nail with great force on its head, right?

Now what if someone started telling you, here is a hammer, it has two parts—the head and the handle. The handle is long and thus helps you exert torque because torque is directly proportional to the radius of the torque arm. The torque translates to a lot of momentum in a rather heavy hammer head. Now because momentum can neither be destroyed nor created per the equation

```
M1V1 = M2V2
```

and because the mass of the nail is so little, the momentum gets transferred to the nail, which results in a very high nail velocity thus driving it through the wood.

Oh my, I feel like hitting myself with the hammer when I hear such a complex description of a rather simple topic. Why can't we just say, "The hammer bangs the nail on its head so it is driven through the wood"? Simple, huh?

Then why can't learning ADO.NET be made as simple as that? There are some very basic things this data access architecture lets you do: connect with the database, fetch data, hold disconnected data, work with disconnected data, and save data back into the database. In writing this book, I have therefore tried to focus on the tasks you need to achieve and have tried to simplify ADO.NET's architecture in those terms.

Then there is the battle between C# and VB.NET, and different databases such as SQL Server and Oracle. Choosing between C# and VB.NET is a bit like choosing between democrats and republicans. No matter which side I pick, I lose half my friends, and it's not like either side is any better than the other. So I figured, why choose between these? All examples are presented both in C# and VB.NET. The examples written will work on a SQL Server 2005 database, but notable differences along with code snippets are presented for Oracle as well. A good example is MARS. It works both in SQL Server and Oracle, but what are the different implementation patterns? I will, however, say that, in a bid to prevent this book from looking like a soup of leftovers from the past week, I have tried to avoid the mish-mash effect by trying to concentrate more on SQL Server than on Oracle—though Oracle has not been ignored.

Thus, Chapters 4 through 11 are filled with content that is database agnostic. They are laid out in a simple task-oriented approach, which means instead of giving you a rote list of methods on DbCommand, in contrast I take the approach of "*You may need to query for a scalar, or a row, or maybe fill a DataSet instead, and this is how you would do that.*"

I could end the book there, but an ADO.NET book wouldn't be complete if I didn't mention SQL Server 2005–specific features such as SQLCLR (the CLR inside SQL Server) and XML features. Thus, Chapter 12 and Chapter 13 are specific to SQL Server 2005 and cover those topics.

Finally, architecture (especially data access) is a black art. There is no white or black, but plenty of gray. Okay, certain shades are definitely whiter than others, but you get the idea. The book ends with a discussion-oriented chapter that brings up the major debates that surround data access and application architecture in general.

I hope this book will arm you with enough knowledge to allow you to make informed day-to-day architectural decisions with confidence.

I hope you enjoy it.

. . . Mission control to reader . . . the ADO.NET planet is in sight, grab the steering, sit firm in the pilot's seat, tighten your seatbelts, pack your bags, and flip over to Chapter 1. The fun is about to begin . . .

CHAPTER 1

■■■

An Introduction to ADO.NET

A computer can be thought of as an information storage and processing machine. While not every application has a specialized program managing its store of information, it's hard to imagine a computer program that doesn't work with any kind of data. Certain applications, like Microsoft Word and Notepad, choose to manage their own data, while many other specialized applications, especially those that require vast amounts of data, choose a much more specialized program or architecture that runs on a separate machine, typically referred to as a *database*.

While some applications choose to use a server-based database architecture, like Oracle, Microsoft SQL Server, MySQL, DB2, and others, certain other applications might choose a file-based architecture instead, such as Microsoft Access or Excel.

Even various programs on a computer allow you to manage information effectively: programs that are designed specifically to handle information, such as databases that handle information quite differently than programs that sit between the user and the database. Most databases store their information as tables, which arrange data as a collection of rows and columns and values within them. Most modern databases will also let you specify relationships between these tables, which allow the database to keep data sanctity between various tables that have relationships between them.

However, programming languages have a different method of representing data. In particular, most modern-day object-oriented languages choose to represent data in hierarchical representations of objects.

In fact, one program could work with more than one data source at a time and it needs some sort of data access libraries to accomplish this task, as shown in Figure 1-1.

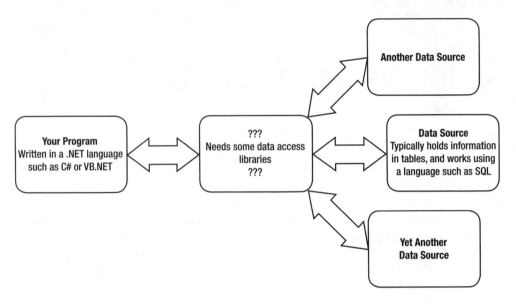

Figure 1-1. *A typical program and its data sources*

Therefore, there is a mismatch between how most databases handle information and how most programming languages handle information. It's at this very place where ADO.NET fits into the grand scheme of things.

But what is ADO.NET?

What Is ADO.NET?

Microsoft ADO.NET is part of the Microsoft .NET Framework: a set of tools and layers that allows your application to easily manage and communicate with its file-based or server-based data store. In the .NET Framework, the ADO.NET libraries appear under the System.Data name-space. These libraries include functionality to connect to these data sources, execute commands, and store, manipulate, and retrieve data. This is illustrated in Figure 1-2. For the sake of simplicity and discussion, only one data source is illustrated, but keep in mind that there could be more than one.

Figure 1-2. *What is ADO.NET and where does it fit in the picture?*

What sets ADO.NET apart from previous data access technologies is that it allows you to interact with your database in a completely disconnected data cache to work with data offline. While attempts have been made to achieve this in the past using technologies such as Remote Data Objects (RDO), those attempts were little more than patches on an existing technology. ADO.NET, on the other hand, is built from the ground up with this requirement in mind.

Disconnected data access is crucial for today's high-demand applications, as it's simply not possible to directly connect every single user or entity in a system to the database. Architecting your application for high-demand scenarios is covered in further depth from Chapter 4 onward.

An important element of disconnected data access is a database-agnostic container for tabular data. This database-agnostic disconnected container for tabular data is represented in the ADO.NET libraries by a `DataSet` or a `DataTable` object. These objects will be covered in a greater depth in Chapter 6.

It is important to understand, however, that ADO.NET succeeds a previous data access technology in the Microsoft world called ADO classic, or simply ADO. Even though ADO.NET and ADO are completely different data access architectures, it is important to understand where ADO falls short to appreciate what ADO.NET gives you.

What Is Wrong with ADO?

ActiveX Data Objects (ADO) was the premier data access technology under the Microsoft umbrella before ADO.NET was introduced as an integral part of the .NET Framework. An obvious question is "Why did Microsoft have to come up with a brand new data access technology when you had ADO serving this purpose?" As a matter of fact, this question could be broadened to "What is wrong with DAO, RDO, ODBCDirect, OleDb, and ADO?"

In short, over the years data access needs have changed, which necessitated a change in the premier data access technology. ADO was accessed primarily via unmanaged code, which in .NET would require you to write unmanaged code accessing ADO objects via a standard mechanism used to access COM objects called *interop*. Not only does unmanaged code accessed over interop pay a performance penalty in comparison with fully managed code, but a bigger disadvantage is that it doesn't conform to .NET security. Also, unmanaged code is subject to the old world problems of DLL Hell etc., and garbage collection doesn't quite work as well for interop-based objects either. As you may already know, garbage collection in .NET, to a great extent, alleviates the individual programs of cleaning up their freed memory. This facility was not available in COM, which relied on reference counting for memory management. If not architected correctly, it's possible that interoped COM components might not work well with the new garbage collection model, and might result in memory leaks. The last thing you want is memory leaks in your data layer, which is typically one of the most crucial parts of your application as far as performance and reliability goes.

Another big disadvantage of ADO was that it was really never designed to work with XML. XML was retrofitted into it after the fact, and (for those of you with previous ADO experience) while a `Recordset` could be converted to XML, the XML produced was hardly human readable and not as portable between various objects as you'd like it to be. On the other hand, ADO.NET has been designed from the ground up with these demands in mind.

Along the same lines, when ADO was written, web services and the entire concept of disconnected computing were still in their infancy. With the explosion of disconnected computing and extreme demands on a central database, it became evident that a new kind of data access architecture was required. The new data access architecture had to support better concurrency, pooling, XML support, and disconnected architecture in general. Thus, ADO.NET was born.

Meeting the Players: Important Objects in ADO.NET

Like any other architecture, there are certain important parts that make up ADO.NET. In this section, you'll look at the various objects that make up ADO.NET.

As you probably know, .NET classes can be grouped under namespaces. All ADO.NET-related functionality appears under the System.Data namespace. This doesn't mean that some other software developer cannot write libraries that don't belong to that namespace, but as the Microsoft .NET Framework ships, all ADO.NET-related functionality sits inside the System.Data namespace.

Also, like any other .NET component, ADO.NET doesn't live in isolation, and it can interact with various other parts of the .NET Framework such as the System.Web.UI.WebControls. Adapters.TableAdapter class or the System.Transactions namespace.

The ADO.NET architecture can be split into two fundamental spheres: the connected and the disconnected. The various classes that appear within ADO.NET can be categorized within the connected and disconnected spheres. The only major exception is the DataAdapter object, which acts as a sentry between the connected and disconnected spheres. Let's further examine the various details of each one of these spheres.

The Connected Objects

The connected part represents the objects that insist on having an open connection available for them to work and interact with the data source. Under the connected part of ADO.NET, there are the following main objects:

- Connection: This is the object that allows you to establish a connection with the data source. Depending on the actual .NET data provider involved, connection objects automatically pool physical database connections for you. It's important to realize that they don't pool connection object instances, but they try and recycle physical database connections. Examples of connection objects are OleDbConnection, SqlConnection, OracleConnection, and so on. These will be covered in further detail in Chapter 4.

- Transaction: There are times when you would want to execute a group of commands together as a group or as an atomic operation, as an "all-or-nothing" execution. An example might be a banking application where a credit must not occur if a corresponding debit cannot be done. Transaction objects let you group together such groups of commands and execute them atomically. Examples of transaction objects are OleDbTransaction, SqlTransaction, OracleTransaction, and so on. In ADO.NET 2.0, you also have the ability to run distributed transactions and enlist in nondatabase transactions via the System.Transactions namespace. In ADO.NET 1.0 and 1.1, this was possible as a less than ideal solution using the System.EnterpriseServices namespace. This comparison and further details will be covered in Chapter 11.

- DataAdapter: This object acts as a gateway between the disconnected and connected flavors of ADO.NET. It establishes the connection for you or, given an established connection, it has enough information specified to itself to enable it to understand a disconnected object's data and act upon the database in a prespecified manner. Examples of DataAdapters are SqlDataAdapter, OracleDataAdapter, and so on. DataAdapters will be covered in Chapter 7.

- Command: This object represents an executable command on the underlying data source. This command may or may not return any results. These commands can be used to manipulate existing data, query existing data, and update or even delete existing data. In addition, these commands can be used to manipulate underlying table structures. Examples of command objects are SqlCommand, OracleCommand, and so on. This will be covered in Chapter 5.

- Parameter: A command needs to be able to accept parameters. This allows commands to be more flexible and accept input values and act accordingly. These parameters could be input/output or return values of stored procedures, or "?" arguments passed to a SQL query, or simply named parameters to a dynamic query. Examples of parameters are SqlParameter, OracleParameter, and so on. This will be covered in Chapter 5.

- DataReader: The DataReader object is the equivalent of a read-only/forward-only firehose cursor that allows you to fetch data from a database at an extremely high speed but in a forward-only and read-only mode. This object will be covered in further detail in Chapter 5.

The Disconnected Objects

Constantly, connected applications alone don't fulfill the demands of modern-day distributed applications. Disconnected applications built using ADO.NET, however, take a different approach. Disconnected applications typically connect as late as possible and disconnect as early as they can. While they are working in a disconnected fashion, ADO.NET pools the actual physical connection between various requests. This is shown in Chapter 4 where an actual code demonstration clearly illustrates how an application can improve performance many times over by connection pooling in this fashion.

The various objects in consideration under the disconnected model of ADO.NET are as follows:

- DataSet: The DataSet is at the central core of the disconnected mode of ADO.NET data access. The best way to think of a DataSet is like having your own very mini relational database management system (RDBMS) completely represented in memory. While it isn't quite an RDBMS and should never be thought to replace an RDBMS, it helps to understand a DataSet if its various components are connected on a one-to-one basis with most major RDBMS objects. Also, it is important to realize that DataSets are available at System.Data.DataSet, i.e., above any .NET provider, thus making them .NET data provider–independent (more about .NET data providers in the next section). A DataSet can also be thought of as a logical collection of DataTables and DataRelations.

- DataTable: A DataTable is most similar to a table in a database. It consists of DataColumns, DataRows, and various constraints set upon them. It stores data in a row/column format. Starting with ADO.NET 2.0, a DataTable is fully convertible to XML and can be serialized just like a DataSet. For data access needs where your DataSet might contain only one DataTable, it may make more sense to use a DataTable instead. As you'll see in future chapters, this is not only more convenient, but it's also better performing.

- DataRow: One of the properties of DataTable is Rows of DataRowCollection type, which represents an enumerable collection of DataRow objects. As data is filled into a DataTable, the DataRowCollection gets new DataRow objects added to itself. The best logical equivalent of a DataRow in a database is a row in a table.

- DataColumn: A DataTable also contains a Columns property of DataColumnCollection type. Essentially, this represents the structure of a DataTable. The best logical equivalent of a DataColumn object in a database is an individual column in a given table in a database.

- DataView: A DataView is most similar to a view in a database. A DataView allows you to create a "view" on a DataTable and view a subset of the data based on a preset condition specified in its Filter property. You could also use the Sort property to sort the filtered subset of the DataTable's data. One DataTable can have multiple views defined on it.

- Constraint: A DataTable contains yet another property called Constraints of ConstraintsCollection type. This lets you create ForeignKeyConstraint or UniqueConstraint objects and associate various columns to certain conditions based on which data in the DataTable must pass for it to exist in the DataTable. The most logical equivalent of a ForeignKeyConstraint is a foreign key in a database, and UniqueConstraint specifies a Unique condition on a given column in a database.

- DataRelation: A DataSet, like a database, might contain various interrelated tables. A DataRelation object lets you specify relations between various tables that allow you to both validate data across tables and browse parent and child rows in various DataTables. Its most logical equivalent is a foreign key specified between two tables in a database. The difference between a ForeignKeyConstraint and a DataRelation is that a DataRelation, in addition to validating data, gives you a convenient mechanism to browse parent and child rows in a DataSet.

Figure 1-3 shows where the various connected and disconnected objects fit into the bigger picture.

Note that in Figure 1-3, your program talks with ADO.NET as a whole. In other words, it can choose to use the disconnected objects, the DataAdapter, the connected objects, or a combination thereof.

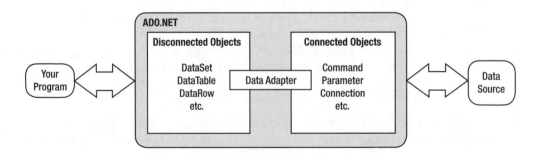

Figure 1-3. *ADO.NET connected objects, disconnected objects, and the DataAdapter*

All of these objects are covered in further depth in Chapter 6. When compared with ADO, the data holder object, which used to be Recordset, is now a DataSet. However, there is a critical difference. While a Recordset was also responsible for communicating with the database, a DataSet is not responsible for communicating with the database. Instead, it uses the gateway object between connected and disconnected modes—the DataAdapter. The disconnected data access model will be covered in Chapters 6 through 10.

Since the connected objects need to work directly with the underlying database, connected objects typically need to implement database-specific code. On the other hand, disconnected objects are meant to be database agnostic, thus it is logical to assume that they can be shared between different databases.

As it turns out, most connected objects are implemented inside what are referred to as .NET data providers.

.NET Data Providers

ADO.NET splits the connected objects as specific implementations for the underlying database. In other words, in order to connect with a Microsoft SQL Server database, there exists a specific class called SqlConnection. In fact, all such SQL Server–specific classes appear under the same System.Data.SqlClient namespace. Similarly, all Oracle-related classes would appear under the System.Data.OracleClient namespace.

These specific implementations for a specific database are referred to as .NET data providers. This can be seen in Figure 1-4.

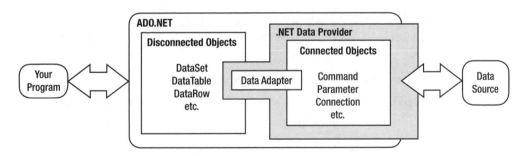

Figure 1-4. *A .NET data provider, and where it fits in the bigger picture*

The modern-day computing world offers us many popular databases to choose from. As described in the beginning of this chapter, these databases can be server- or file-based. While server-based databases tend to be more stable and are able to support multiple concurrent users better, file-based databases are easier to deploy and manage after your application has been installed on a wide client base. Do note, however, that this is a generalization; for instance, with Microsoft SQL Server 2005, you now have the capabilities of a full-fledged server-based database while being able to communicate with it with the ease of a file-based system.

Given the vast choice of data sources available, ADO.NET needs to be able to support a wide variety of data sources. Each data source might have its own peculiarities or set of features. Thus, ADO.NET supports a *provider* model. An ADO.NET provider for a particular data source can be defined as a set of classes within a namespace that are designed specifically to work with that particular data source.

In other words, for a specific data source, you need to have a specific .NET data provider. This distinction is a bit blurry in the case of OleDb and ODBC since, by their nature, they have been designed to work with any OleDb or ODBC compliant database, but even their specific implementations live inside a specific .NET data provider designed especially for them. This can be seen in Figure 1-5. Note that your program can use any of the objects inside the grey box in Figure 1-5. You can choose to use disconnected objects, data adapters, connected objects, or a combination thereof to architect your application.

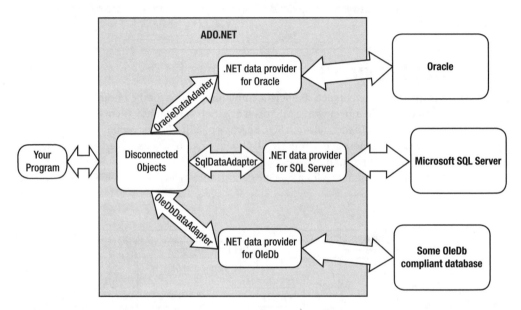

Figure 1-5. *The full picture: your program, ADO.NET, multiple data sources, and multiple data providers*

Now to set things in perspective for a moment, compare Figure 1-5 with Figure 1-1. The shaded block in Figure 1-5 represents a zoomed-in image of the middle block in Figure 1-1.

By convention, the providers that come with the .NET Framework can all be found in their own namespace under the System.Data namespace. Table 1-1 is a list of some common data providers that come with the .NET 2.0 Framework.

Table 1-1. *Various .NET Data Providers*

Data Source Name	Provider Namespace
Microsoft SQL Server 7.0 and above	System.Data.SqlClient
Oracle 8.1.6 and above	System.Data.OracleClient
SqlXml support in SQL Server	System.Data.SqlXml
Any ODBC data source	System.Data.ODBC
Any OleDb data source	System.Data.OleDb

As you may note from Table 1-1, Microsoft SQL Server 7.0 and Oracle 8.1.6 can also be accessed using the ODBC or OleDb data providers. Using the data source–specific data providers, such as `SqlClient` or `OracleClient`, gives you some distinct advantages over using generic data providers:

- Specialized data providers, such as `SqlClient` or `OracleClient`, give you much better performance than generic ones.

- Specialized data providers are better equipped for database-specific functionality.

- Specialized data providers give you the ability to work with database-specific data types. Doing so prevents boxing/unboxing costs in many instances, and it might alleviate data type precision errors that may arise inadvertently when saving an Int64 in an Int32 column.

There may be times, however, when you might not know the exact data source you need to interact with. ADO.NET provides you with a number of options in writing code that is provider agnostic. Specifically, ADO.NET 1.1 gave you two ways of writing code that was provider agnostic:

- *Using the nonspecialized data providers*: You could stick with a common minimum-base functionality between all data sources and use either the ODBC or the OleDb data providers. These data providers suffer performance, feature, and other disadvantages because they are not database specific. Nevertheless, they do provide you with one advantage—writing database-independent code. Depending on your exact need, you may choose to ignore the performance and feature-set issues and stick with one common .NET data provider.

- *Using interfaces and base classes*: ADO.NET provides standard interfaces and base classes for most commonly used objects. So, for example, the `System.Data.SqlClient.SqlConnection` object must implement `System.Data.IDbConnection` and inherit from `System.Data.Providerbase.DbConnectionBase`. By working with data types that are represented either by a base interface or an implemented interface, you can avoid runtime cast errors. The disadvantage of this approach is that you need to stick with the common minimum-base functionality even though now you might not pay the performance penalty that ODBC or OleDb data providers would have been subject to.

Either of these ways is not perfect. While the first method doesn't perform as well, the second method suffers from providing you a subset and, in many cases, a different set of functionality than the data source–specific provider would. To overcome these problems, ADO.NET 2.0 provides you with a convenient way to write code in a provider-agnostic method. For this purpose, ADO.NET 2.0 gives you a provider factory in which available providers can be instantiated as long as you know the correct provider name as a string variable. This is also referred to as the ProviderBase model.

Using the ProviderBase Model

This approach incorporates the best of both worlds. Any Windows machine might contain more than one data provider installed on it. In the .NET 2.0 Framework, there is a section in the Machine.Config file called DbProviderFactories. In that section, you can define various data providers that can be accessed using the ProviderBase model. Listing 1-1 shows a typical DbProviderFactories section in the Machine.Config file.

Listing 1-1. *The DbProviderFactories Section*

```
<system.data>
   <DbProviderFactories>
      <add name="Odbc Data Provider" invariant="System.Data.Odbc" support="BF"
description=".Net Framework Data Provider for Odbc"
type="System.Data.Odbc.OdbcFactory, System.Data, Version=2.0.3600.0,
Culture=neutral, PublicKeyToken=b77a5c561934e089" />
      <add name="OleDb Data Provider" invariant="System.Data.OleDb" support="BF"
description=".Net Framework Data Provider for OleDb"
type="System.Data.OleDb.OleDbFactory, System.Data, Version=2.0.3600.0,
Culture=neutral, PublicKeyToken=b77a5c561934e089" />
      <add name="OracleClient Data Provider" invariant="System.Data.OracleClient"
support="BF" description=".Net Framework Data Provider for Oracle"
type="System.Data.OracleClient.OracleClientFactory, System.Data.OracleClient,
Version=2.0.3600.0, Culture=neutral, PublicKeyToken=b77a5c561934e089" />
      <add name="SqlClient Data Provider" invariant="System.Data.SqlClient"
support="FF" description=".Net Framework Data Provider for SqlServer"
type="System.Data.SqlClient.SqlClientFactory, System.Data, Version=2.0.3600.0,
Culture=neutral, PublicKeyToken=b77a5c561934e089" />
      <add name="SQL Server CE Data Provider"
invariant="Microsoft.SqlServerCe.Client" support="3F7" description=".NET Framework
Data Provider for Microsoft SQL Server 2005 Mobile Edition"
type="Microsoft.SqlServerCe.Client.SqlCeClientFactory, Microsoft.SqlServerCe.Client,
Version=9.0.242.0, Culture=neutral, PublicKeyToken=89845dcd8080cc91" />
   </DbProviderFactories>
</system.data>
```

■**Note** Such information could be specified in any configuration file: Machine.Config, App.Config, Web.Config, and so on. Your custom data provider or a third-party data provider can be added to this collection by simply modifying the suitable configuration file.

You can easily enumerate through the available providers on your machine using the code shown in Listings 1-2 and 1-3.

Listing 1-2. *Enumerating Through Available Providers in C#*

```
DataTable factoryClassesTable = DbProviderFactories.GetFactoryClasses();
foreach (DataRow factoryClass in factoryClassesTable.Rows)
{
   Console.WriteLine("Name:"+ factoryClass["Name"]);
```

```
    Console.WriteLine("Description:"+ factoryClass["Description"]);
    Console.WriteLine("Invariant Name:"+ factoryClass["InvariantName"]);
    Console.WriteLine("\n");
}
```

Listing 1-3. *Enumerating Through Available Providers in Visual Basic .NET*

```
Dim factoryClassesTable As DataTable =  DbProviderFactories.GetFactoryClasses()
Dim factoryClass As DataRow
For Each factoryClass In factoryClassesTable.Rows
    Console.WriteLine("Name:" & factoryClass("Name"))
    Console.WriteLine("Description:" & factoryClass("Description"))
    Console.WriteLine("Invariant Name:" & factoryClass("InvariantName"))
    Console.WriteLine("")
Next
```

When this code is run, it produces output as shown here:

```
Name:Odbc Data Provider
Description:.Net Framework Data for Odbc
Invariant Name:System.Data.Odbc

Name:OleDb Data Provider
Description:.Net Framework Data for OleDb
Invariant Name:System.Data.OleDb

Name:OracleClient Data Provider
Description:.Net Framework Data for Oracle
Invariant Name:System.Data.OracleClient

Name:SQL Server CE Data Provider
Description:.NET Framework Data Provider for Microsoft SQL Server 2005 Mobile
Edition
Invariant Name:Microsoft.SqlServerCe.Client
```

If you wanted to actually use one of these data providers, you could use the code shown in Listings 1-4 and 1-5.

Listing 1-4. *Putting the ProviderBase Model to Work in C#*

```
//Select SQL Client factory - Can change to use any provider later
DbProviderFactory factory = DbProviderFactories.GetFactory("System.Data.SqlClient");

//Create Connection from the factory
SqlConnection testConnection = (SqlConnection)factory.CreateConnection();
testConnection.ConnectionString = "..."; //Specify connection string - See Chapter 4
testConnection.Open();

//Create Command from the factory
SqlCommand testCommand = (SqlCommand)factory.CreateCommand();
```

```
//Execute a command from the conneciton
testCommand.Connection = testConnection;
testCommand.CommandText = "...";
SqlDataReader reader = testCommand.ExecuteReader();
while (reader.Read())
{
    Console.WriteLine(reader.GetValue(0));
}
```

Listing 1-5. *Putting the ProviderBase Model to Work in Visual Basic .NET*

```
'Select SQL Client factory - Can change to use any provider later
Dim factory As DbProviderFactory = _
    DbProviderFactories.GetFactory("System.Data.SqlClient")

'Create Connection from the factory
Dim testConnection As SqlConnection = factory.CreateConnection()
testConnection.ConnectionString = "..." ' Specify connection string – See Chapter 4
testConnection.Open()

'Create Command from the factory
Dim testCommand As SqlCommand =  factory.CreateCommand()

'Execute a command from the conneciton
testCommand.Connection = testConnection
testCommand.CommandText = "..."
Dim reader As SqlDataReader =  testCommand.ExecuteReader()
While reader.Read()
    Console.WriteLine(reader.GetValue(0))
End While
```

One of the things you might note in Listings 1-4 and 1-5 is that the ProviderBase model allows you to retrieve strongly typed provider-specific objects such as SqlConnection and SqlCommand without knowing in advance which provider the user intends to work with. The user could have chosen "System.Data.SqlClient" through a drop-down on his UI, which is simply passed to the GetFactory method as a string parameter.

This is possible because the DbProviderFactory object always returns objects of data types that are actually base classes to various common objects in a .NET data provider. These common base objects contained in the System.Data.Common namespace can be inherited by any other class to create a third-party .NET data provider.

Third-Party .NET Data Providers

ADO.NET contains various base classes and interfaces that various third-party .NET data providers can derive or implement to create their own specific implementations of commonly used objects such as Connection, Command, and so on. One such example is the DbDataAdapter class that implements the IDbDataAdapter interface. Thus, the SqlDataAdapter that can be found in System.Data.SqlClient derives from DbDataAdapter, and hence implements the IDbDataAdapter interface. The most notable classes in this namespace are shown in Table 1-2.

Table 1-2. *Main System.Data.Common Classes*

Class Name	Description
DataAdapter	This class acts as a sentry between the connected and disconnected spheres of ADO.NET. It holds a set of data commands (DbCommand objects) and a data source connection (DbConnection object) that are used to fill the DataSet or DataTable and update the data source. This data source can be any type of data source, unlike the DbDataAdapter which is only used with relational data sources.
DbCommand	This class is used for executing SQL commands, such as SELECT queries against the data source.
DbCommandBuilder	This class is used to create the INSERT, UPDATE, and DELETE SQL statements for the command objects used by a data adapter. It can be used only with a single data source table, and only if the SELECT SQL statement has been specified and at least one unique column is returned as part of the row schema.
DbConnection	This class is the actual connection to the data source.
DbConnectionOptions	This class is used by the provider factory classes. It's used by the provider factory to create a connection; however, it can also be used manually for purposes such as splitting a connection string into key-value pairs. It has some properties and methods that can convert the string values in a key-value pair to integers and Booleans and check for the existence of a specific key, such as *Data Source*.
DbConnectionStringBuilder	This is a base class for creating connection strings, and it can be used in connection with a data provider factory to create a connection string, edit a connection string, read a connection string from a configuration file, and save a connection string to a configuration file. This is covered in Chapter 4.
DbDataAdapter	This class is an abstract helper class that is used with the IDbDataAdapter interface. The DbDataAdapter class is derived from the DataAdapter class, and it is used to create a data adapter for a relational database. This is done by creating a class that inherits the DbDataAdapter class and implements the IDbDataAdapter interface.
DbDataReader	This class reads a forward-only stream of rows from a data source, and the rows can be accessed one at a time. The connection must stay open while you're reading the rows from the DbDataReader because the rows are read directly from the data source when requested.
DbDataRecord	This class implements the IDataRecord and ICustomTypeDescriptor interfaces. This way it provides data-binding support for the DbEnumerator class. It is often used with data binding on ASP.NET pages instead of using the DataBinder.Eval method, which incurs a performance overhead by using reflection.
DbException	This is the generic data exception class, used for throwing data-related exceptions. This abstract class inherits from the ExternalException class.

Continued

Table 1-2. *(Continued)*

Class Name	Description
DbParameter	This class is used with parameters in your SQL commands to create dynamic queries that can change by supplying different values for the parameters.
DbProviderConfigurationHandler	This class is used to configure a DbProviderFactory using values from the application's configuration file.
DbProviderFactory	This class is used for creating provider-specific data-aware classes based on various input.
DbTransaction	This is the generic transaction class used to encapsulate SQL statements in an all-or-nothing transaction. It's used in conjunction with a connection object.

The System.Data.Design Namespace

The System.Data.Design namespace, which is the smallest of the ADO.NET namespaces, contains classes used to create typed DataSet classes, including code and parameters. This namespace is new to the .NET Framework 2.0, but the classes in this namespace were located in the System.Data namespace in previous versions of the .NET Framework.

The classes are mostly used internally by ADO.NET-related functionality that is exposed in the Visual Studio .NET IDE, such as creating a typed DataSet from a DataAdapter dragged from the toolbox and dropped on the designer. But it's there for your convenience if you need a way to create typed DataSets at runtime.

Summary

This chapter gave a brief introduction to the exciting world of ADO.NET. It introduced you to various important classes and their logical groupings within ADO.NET.

It touched upon the need for a new data access architecture and the problems it solves. It also showed how ADO.NET is logically grouped in the connected and disconnected parts and how various data sources are supported using the ProviderBase model. It outlined the challenges you can face when working with different providers available in ADO.NET as well as the various facilities ADO.NET provides to create a data source–agnostic data layer.

In the next chapter, you will build upon what you have already learned in this chapter and logically group the various classes into the namespace architecture that ADO.NET provides.

CHAPTER 2

■ ■ ■

The ADO.NET Object Model

Sir Isaac Newton, the British physicist who discovered gravity in the seventeenth century, was a brilliant man. But let's say that one day on his way to Cambridge he accidentally walked into a wormhole and somehow showed up in the twenty-first century. What would his reaction be?

Now imagine that he walks up to a large, painted, metal and glass box with four seats inside, four doors, four wheels, a place to pour fuel, and some kind of controls to direct the movement of that box. What would he consider that box to be?

If the last chapter was a little bit like explaining that the box is a car and it's controlled by using the pedals on the floor and the steering wheel on the dash, then this chapter is a bit like opening the hood of the car, looking inside at the machinery, and understanding how that liquid fuel makes this contraption move. Also, since you and I are engineers and engineers not only like to drive the car, but also to break it, repair it, and fully understand how the fuel makes the car move, it's imperative that we understand how to perform such operations on the ADO.NET car.

Before Sir Isaac Newton can learn how to rebuild an engine or change a timing belt, he first needs to understand what an engine is, what its purpose is, what it looks like, how it works, and where in that box the engine resides.

Chapter 1 introduced you to where ADO.NET fits into your architecture. You also saw how ADO.NET is split into two main parts, connected and disconnected, and how you can have various .NET data providers that allow you to work with different data sources.

This chapter takes the discussion away from logical block diagrams (learning how to drive the car) to a deeper insight into ADO.NET using class diagrams and class hierarchy (learning about the machinery). The purpose of understanding how various classes within ADO.NET are laid out is to enable you to reason how the commonality is enforced amongst diverse .NET data providers, and how the common disconnected parts of ADO.NET are able to perform a common role within ADO.NET.

This Is a Reference Chapter

As engineers, we like to understand what is under the hood before we sit behind the steering wheel; however, simply telling you what exists under the hood of ADO.NET without establishing practical groundwork underneath it all serves very little purpose.

This chapter introduces a lot of classes, interfaces, and namespaces that exist within ADO.NET. It makes no sense to memorize by rote every single class name, interface, or namespace presented in this chapter. Instead, concentrate on understanding the repeating inheritance pattern that appears within various classes in ADO.NET. By doing so, supplemented with referencing the various images, class names, and namespaces presented here, you'll retain the various names presented in this chapter. Eventually, you'll find no need to consult or memorize by rote the contents presented in this chapter.

Thus, as you read through the rest of the book, keep looking back upon the various class names and figures that appear in this chapter to settle the knowledge presented in the rest of the book.

Without any further delay, let us begin with a 10,000-ft. bird's-eye view of where and how ADO.NET appears in the .NET Framework.

10,000-Ft. View of ADO.NET

ADO.NET lives under the System.Data namespace within the .NET Framework. Like any other part of the .NET Framework, ADO.NET doesn't exist in a vacuum. There are classes under System.Windows.Forms, System.Xml, System.Web, and other namespaces within the .NET Framework that work with ADO.NET for operations such as drag-and-drop, transactions, and so on that interact with ADO.NET. An example of such a class is BindingSource that is contained under the System.Windows.Forms namespace, which is used to encapsulate a data source for data-binding purposes.

While Chapter 11 covers transactions, Chapter 3 covers the drag-and-drop method to create data-driven applications. A drag-and-drop operation in ADO.NET is a quick-and-easy way to create a data-driven application. It has its place in the overall scheme of things when it comes to creating prototypes or quick-and-easy applications when a full-scale enterprise-level architecture is not possible (due to time or budget restrictions); however, drag-and-drop operations are not nearly enough to have an enterprise-level application up and running—in most cases, you'll need to get your hands dirty with real code. For you to be able to code effectively, it's critical to understand the class structure within ADO.NET as well as the purpose and behavior of various distinct components of ADO.NET.

Another item mentioned in Chapter 1 was that the various connected portions of ADO.NET are data source–specific. The connected portions for a particular data source are collectively also referred to as the .NET data provider for that particular data source. Generally, by convention, the data providers are available under their own namespace under the System.Data namespace. For instance, a .NET data provider that allows you to connect to an Oracle database would generally be found at System.Data.OracleClient, just as the .NET data provider that allows you to connect with Microsoft SQL Server would be found at System.Data.SqlClient. This is, however, only a convention, so don't be surprised if you run into a data provider that doesn't follow this convention.

In fact, the various classes and interfaces that different classes under disparate .NET data providers either inherit from or implement can easily be implemented by any third-party .NET data provider. For instance, you could write your own .NET data provider by simply inheriting from the right classes and implementing the right interfaces. Obviously, then, your written .NET data provider could live in a namespace of your choice.

ADO.NET is a data access architecture. A few common operations such an architecture should allow you to perform are the following: establish a connection with the data source, execute a command, specify parameters to such a command, and fetch results back.

Let's examine each of these operations to understand what objects in ADO.NET allow you to perform these operations.

Establishing a Connection: DbConnection

In order to work with a data source, your program needs to establish a connection with it. Due to the variety of data sources available, the information required to connect to any given data source might be very different. For instance, you might need to supply a user ID and password along with the server and database name in order to connect to a Microsoft SQL Server database, but connecting to a Microsoft Access database would require a file-path location. Also, every data source might support a different set of operations; for instance, a Microsoft SQL Server database might allow you to change databases, which is an operation that's probably meaningless in Microsoft Access.

There are differences in each data source; however, at the end of the day, they are all data sources, thus there is a large degree of commonality between them as well. At the very least (just because the entity being discussed is a data source you can connect with), there must be some functionality to open a connection, close a connection, and also check the existing connection state.

Given the fact that there are differences and commonalities, it makes sense to have individual implementations for each data source's connection object, which all inherit from the same base class and implement the same interface.

What a coincidence, this is exactly what ADO.NET does! The connection object inherits from the DbConnection base class, which in turn implements the IDbConnection interface. Thus, the SqlConnection class, which appears at System.Data.SqlClient.SqlConnection, inherits from System.Data.Common.DbConnection, which in turn implements System.Data.IDbConnection. Similarly, the OracleConnection class, which appears at System.Data.OracleClient.OracleConnection, also inherits from DbConnection and implements IDbConnection.

This hierarchy can be seen in Figure 2-1.

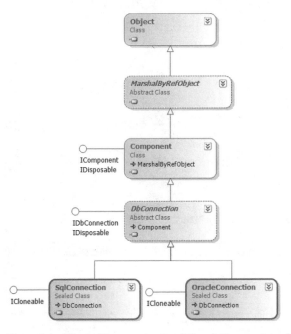

Figure 2-1. *The SqlConnection and OracleConnection classes and their base classes and interfaces*

As you can see, for a class to qualify as a valid connection object within the ADO.NET Framework, it must inherit from System.Data.Common.DbConnection. What's important about this class is that it implements IDbConnection, which in turn implements IDisposable. It's reasonable to expect that keeping a connection open is tantamount to holding valuable resources, thus the IDisposable interface requires you to implement the Dispose method where you are supposed to do any cleanup required by your object. Similarly, the IDbConnection interface establishes the common ground between various connection objects by enforcing a common set of methods and properties that they must implement to qualify as a valid connection object.

Thus, you can count on the fact that for the connection object of any .NET data provider you come across, the method to connect with its data source will be an Open method and not a Connect or EstablishConnection method. Such commonality also allows you to write data provider–independent code.

Another important thing to note in Figure 2-1 is that the DbConnection class inherits from the System.ComponentModel.Component class. This means that any ADO.NET connection object can be hosted at design time in an environment that implements the IContainer interface because a Component can be hosted inside a container that implements the IContainer interface. The place where this makes direct impact on you as a programmer is that you can host an ADO.NET connection object inside the component tray in Visual Studio .NET, as shown in Figure 2-2. This allows for an easy and convenient user interface that lets you specify various properties in a visual way at design time.

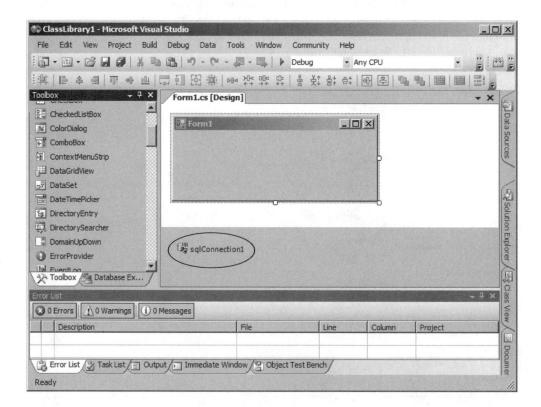

Figure 2-2. *Viewing a Connection object in the Visual Studio .NET component tray*

Once your application has the ability to establish a connection, the next important step is to be able to execute a command. A command has to be executed on a connection, and because a command can change the underlying data, it makes sense to have some kind of transactional semantics associated with the command object. Therefore, it makes sense to discuss commands in correlation with both connections and transactions. Let's look at that next.

Executing a Command: DbCommand and DbTransaction

Just like a connection object within the ADO.NET Framework requires commonality between its various implementations in different .NET data providers, the command object lives by the same rules. Just like a connection object needs to inherit from the System.Data.Common.DbConnection class, the command object needs to inherit from the System.Data.Common.DbCommand class, which in turn implements the IDbCommand interface. Thus, the Microsoft SQL Server–specific command object that appears under the SqlClient namespace, the SqlCommand object, inherits from DbCommand. This enforces the similar behavior and commonality between SqlCommand and any other command object within the framework, say OracleCommand.

Also, a command needs a connection to execute upon. For this reason, there exists a Connection property on the DbCommand object. The connection has to be of DbConnection type. Thus, because SqlConnection inherits from DbConnection and SqlCommand inherits from DbCommand, you can specify a SqlConnection object on the SqlCommand.Connection property.

Similarly, if the command needs a transaction, the DbCommand object has a property called Transaction, which is of DbTransaction type. DbTransaction is the base class that implements IDbTransaction, which enforces a common implementation and behavior between various Transaction implementations within different .NET data providers. Therefore, you can specify an OracleTransaction, which inherits from DbTransaction at the OracleCommand.Transaction property. This can be seen in Figure 2-3.

Another thing you may note in Figure 2-3 is that just like the DbConnection object, the DbCommand object also inherits from System.ComponentModel.Component, which in turn allows the command object to be visually edited inside a container such as Visual Studio .NET.

Commands are frequently written in a generic fashion. For instance, if you wish to have a command to update customer information, you probably want to write that command once and apply it to any customer that you may come across. This is achieved by specifying *parameters* to the command.

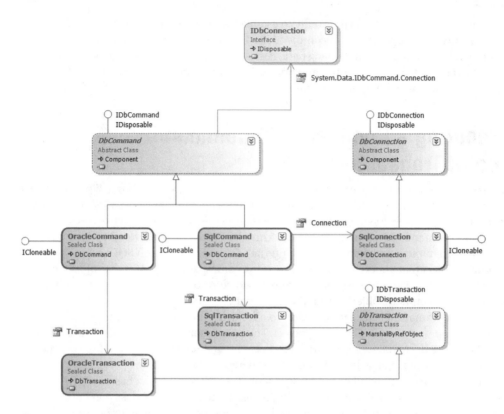

Figure 2-3. *The SqlCommand and OracleCommand objects, their Transaction and Connection properties, and their base class and interface implementations*

Creating Parameterized Commands: DbParameter

I am lazy. I don't want to write a new command for every single customer row that might appear in the Customers table. Fortunately, my boss agrees with me, because he doesn't want me wasting time where I shouldn't have to. And, fortunately, even most databases agree with me because they try to improve their performance by caching query plans when they see a command with the same repeating structure. Thus, it makes sense to create a parameterized query for every Customer row in the Customers table. Parameterized queries have other advantages too, like being more resistant to injection attacks, in general not requiring you to delimit single quote characters anytime you deal with a string parameter.

This can be achieved by specifying the command text once and using parameters to achieve the flexibility you may need for different Customer rows within the same table.

Thus, instead of writing a query that looks like

```
Update Customers Set FirstName = 'Sahil' where CustomerID = 1
```

you could, instead, write the query like

```
Update Customers Set FirstName = @FirstName where CustomerID = @CustomerID
```

Writing this query allows you to specify values for the two involved parameters, `@FirstName` and `@CustomerID`, and use the same command for customers other than `'Sahil'`.

Since a command is represented by the DbCommand object and every .NET data provider may need to have parameterized commands, this commonality is enforced at the DbCommand level by providing you with a property called Parameters. The Parameters property is of DbParametersCollection data type, which is nothing but a collection of DbParameter objects. This can be seen in Figure 2-4.

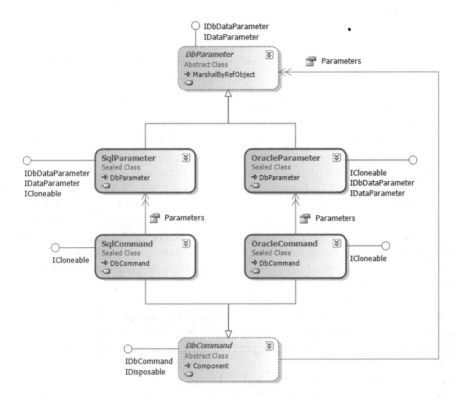

Figure 2-4. *Specifying Parameters to the SqlCommand and OracleCommand objects using SqlParameter and OracleParameter objects*

An important point to note in Figure 2-4 is that the association between SqlCommand's and OracleCommand's Parameters properties is represented by a double arrow instead of a single arrow, signifying that it is a collection and not a singular object. Also, as you can see from Figure 2-4, just as the DbCommand.Parameters property points to DbParametersCollection, the SqlCommand. Parameters property points to a SqlParameterCollection, which holds a number of SqlParameters. Similarly, the OracleCommand.Parameters property points to an object of OracleParameterCollection type, which is a collection of OracleParameters.

Thus, in this manner, every .NET data provider that must implement a command object must have a Parameters property that holds a variable of type that inherits from DbParametersCollection, which is a collection of DbParameter objects.

After executing commands over a connection, the data fetched needs to be held in some kind of object in .NET code. You could write up your own business objects to represent the data or you could use the standard object that comes as a part of the .NET Framework, the DataSet object, to act as the disconnected cache of your data. Let's examine the structure and purpose of the DataSet object briefly, though this object will be covered in depth in Chapter 6.

Holding Disconnected Data: DataSet

As you saw in Chapter 1, ADO.NET can be split into two major halves: the connected and the disconnected. The connection object, command object, transaction object, and parameter object along with a few others that form a .NET data provider are objects that need to be connected with the underlying data source to work.

Commands can be split into three major categories: Data Definition Language (DDL), which is used to define the structure of the database; Data Manipulation Language (DML), which is used to run queries such as UPDATE, INSERT, and DELETE; and Data Query Language (DQL), which is used to query data out of the database. An example of DQL is the SELECT command.

Once such a command is executed, frequently the results are not singular, but appear as a result set or maybe as a collection of result sets. A *result set* is simply tabular data that might contain one or more tables. The result set might be read in a connected fashion, using a DataReader object, which is described briefly later in this chapter and in detail in Chapter 5. Another way of reading the result set is to fill an object representation of the data and disconnect with the underlying data source. As you will see in Chapter 4, it's critical to open the connection as late as possible and close it as early as you can to facilitate better connection pooling. For now, it's enough to understand that *connection pooling* refers to the technique or process of sharing the valuable open connection with the data source between requests in an effort to significantly improve performance. Most providers in .NET will give you this facility by default; in other words, you don't have to write any code, but you need to follow the proper guidelines, as discussed in Chapter 4, to take advantage of connection pooling.

So, you need an object to hold disconnected data. Since the data is disconnected, its implementation doesn't have to be data source–specific, as long as there's some object in the middle acting as a bridge for you. In other words, the implementation of the object that holds disconnected data for you mustn't be specific to a particular underlying data source, such as Microsoft SQL Server or Oracle. This bridge, or the sentry between the connected and disconnected worlds, is the DataReader object described later in this chapter.

As mentioned before, to hold disconnected data, you could write your own business object. While that approach is certainly possible, it's also quite possible that there's some work involved in setting up the business objects, especially when you consider the fact that now you will be responsible for writing all the code to make operations such as data binding, state management, row versions history, etc. possible. (These are covered in further depth in Chapter 6.) It can be argued, however, that it's possible to create a business object–based architecture that saves you work in the long run or is simply a better architecture suited to your situation. There are various pros and cons to using a business object versus a DataSet, and these are covered in Chapter 14.

■**Note** What is a business object? A *business object* is an object that abstracts the entities in the domain that the program is written to represent. In other words, it's a representation of something logical in your architecture. Say you're designing a system for an insurance company. The customer will probably understand what a policy is, or what a premium is, but the concept of a DataSet or DataTable might be alien to him. The business objects would be representations of policy and premium rather than DataSets holding policy and premium information. The exact implementation of business objects is specific to your circumstance; however, good reference books for business objects are available: *Expert C# Business Objects* and *Expert One-on-One Visual Basic .NET Business Objects*, both by Rockford Lhotka (Apress, 2004/2003).

You can use business objects or you can use the DataSet object and its various constituents. The DataSet object acts as a ready-to-use disconnected cache of data that ships with the .NET Framework. Even though Chapter 6 discusses DataSets and their various constituents in detail, Figure 2-5 gives an overview of the major data provider–independent disconnected objects involved in the DataSet object structure.

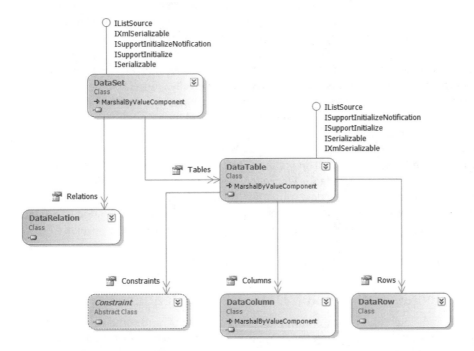

Figure 2-5. *The DataSet and its various constituents such as DataTable, DataRelation, DataColumn, DataRow, and Constraint*

The best way to understand a DataSet's structure is to draw a parallel with an RDBMS. However, I must point out that a DataSet is still an in-memory object. It shouldn't be confused or abused as an RDBMS. Its sole purpose is to do what an RDBMS cannot do—provide you with relational, structured data as a disconnected, portable, in-memory object.

So if a DataSet is the closest parallel to an RDBMS database, with tables and foreign-key relationships between them, then the DataTable object is the closest simile of a table and the DataRelation is the closest simile of a foreign-key constraint. Similarly, a column is the closest parallel to a DataColumn object and DataRow is the closest parallel to a row.

Thus, the DataSet object contains a collection of DataTable objects as a property called Tables, which is of DataTableCollection type. Also, it contains a property called Relations, which is of DataRelationCollection type that is a collection of DataRelation objects.

Similarly, the DataTable object has a property called Columns, which is a collection of DataColumn objects represented by the DataColumnCollection object. Also, it contains a DataRowCollection type property called Rows to represent the various rows as DataRow objects.

A DataTable may have constraints defined on itself (such as a UniqueConstraint), a collection of which is held by the Constraints property, which is of ConstraintCollection type that holds a collection of objects that are of Constraint type or inherit from the Constraint object.

Now that you have commands that can be executed to manipulate and fetch data, and objects to hold fetched data, next let's look at the two ways to fetch data from the underlying data source.

Fetching Data: Data Reader and Data Adapter

Now that you have an object to hold disconnected data and you have a bunch of objects to connect and execute transactional and parameterized commands, next you need to see the two ways to fetch data from the underlying data source. The two methods differ in their approaches of how long they keep the connection open.

The first approach is using a DataReader object, which insists upon an open and available connection in order to fetch results back. This approach typically works faster in a single-user scenario, but where you might need to do heavy processing between rows, it might have a significant impact on connection pooling. (This comparison and its various use cases have been further detailed in Chapter 14.)

The second approach is using a DataAdapter object. The data adapter takes a different approach by executing the command and filling out all the retrieved information in a disconnected cache—a DataSet or a DataTable. Once it's done filling out the information, it then disconnects itself from the underlying data source so the underlying physical connection can be reused by someone else. (See Chapter 4 for how an underlying physical connection is different from DbConnection and how this difference allows the physical connection to be reused by someone else.)

Let's examine these two approaches one by one, starting with the DataReader object.

The Connected Way to Fetch Data: DbDataReader

Some commands fetch data, some commands manipulate data, and some commands do both. For that reason, DbCommand contains various methods on it to execute the command. For instance, one of the methods is ExecuteNonQuery, which simply returns a sum of the total number of rows affected due to the command executed.

Another such method is the ExecuteReader method. The ExecuteReader method is used when you want to fetch the results of a query as a result set.

The ExecuteReader method returns an object that inherits from DbDataReader, which is a common abstract base class that any data reader implementation must inherit from. This can be seen in Figure 2-6.

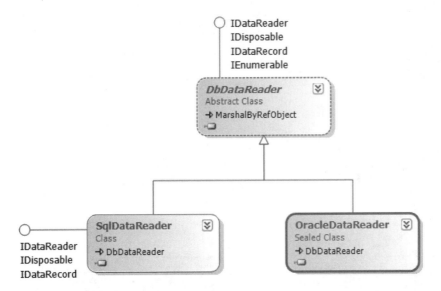

Figure 2-6. *SqlDataReader and OracleDataReader—both inherit from DbDataReader*

Once you have a DataReader object, you can use the various methods on it to iterate through the results and read the values of various columns of the row the data reader is currently positioned at.

It is important to realize, however, that a data reader is a read-only/forward-only, firehose cursor that insists on keeping an underlying physical database connection open while it's executing.

Data readers are covered further in Chapter 5.

The Bridge Between Connected and Disconnected: DbDataAdapter

The DataAdapter object is the sentry, or bridge, between the connected and disconnected worlds. Since the actual implementation of a data adapter is specific to the underlying data source, you have specific data adapters implemented as a part of the .NET data provider. For instance, Microsoft SQL Server requires a SqlDataAdapter and Oracle requires an OracleDataAdapter. If you need generic access via ODBC or OleDb, you have specific data adapters for the generic data access needs in the form of OdbcDataAdapter and OleDbDataAdapter.

Just like the rest of the connected-world ADO.NET objects, commonality between these various objects is enforced by a common base class—the DbDataAdapter class. This can be seen in Figure 2-7. If the number of crisscross arrows appears too overwhelming, try this little trick: Put your hand over the OracleCommand and OracleDataAdapter objects to view the relationship between SqlCommand/SqlDataAdapter and DbCommand/DbDataAdapter. Then repeat by putting your hand over SqlCommand and SqlDataAdapter to view the relationship between OracleCommand/OracleDataAdapter and DbCommand/DbDataAdapter.

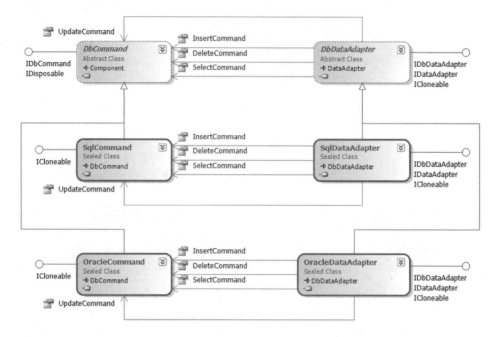

Figure 2-7. *SqlDataAdapter and OracleDataAdapter—both inherit from DbDataAdapter*

Also worth noting in Figure 2-7 are the two SqlCommand and OracleCommand classes, which both inherit from DbCommand. The data adapter needs various DbCommands to work. It can use up to four DbCommands as the InsertCommand, UpdateCommand, DeleteCommand, and SelectCommand properties for INSERT, UPDATE, DELETE, and SELECT operations. The base class for data adapters, DbDataAdapter, defines these four properties of DbCommand data type.

Following the trend of the rest of the ADO.NET connected objects, the specific data adapters, the SqlDataAdapter, OracleDataAdapter, etc., also provide you with four properties with the same names—InsertCommand, UpdateCommand, DeleteCommand, and SelectCommand, which take data provider–specific command objects such as SqlCommand and OracleCommand.

An important part of any programming architecture is error handling. .NET gives you a mechanism called *exception handling* to facilitate this task. ADO.NET, like any other architecture, contains a number of standard exceptions for various error conditions that may occur. Let's examine various exceptions available within ADO.NET that you should look out for.

Exceptions in ADO.NET

Errors happen. In the .NET Framework, they are thrown as exceptions that are segmented and protected callpaths, which allow developers to handle errors in a more robust manner. You can use a simple try...catch block to catch and act upon predefined possible error conditions. It is important to note, however, that exceptions are implemented as classes, and if your catch blocks are looking for a base-class exception before the specific inherited exception, you may never catch the specific exception. The specific or inherited exception will be masked by the base class.

For instance, in the .NET Framework, SqlTruncateException inherits from SqlTypeException, which inherits from System.Exception. So, if you were to write your exception-handling code as shown in Listings 2-1 and 2-2 and a SqlTruncateException occurs, it will be caught in the first System.Exception block and the code inside the catch block for SqlTruncateException will never be executed.

Listing 2-1. *Incorrect Way of Ordering Exception-Handling Blocks in C#*

```
try
{
    ...
}
catch (Exception ex)
{
    ...
}
catch (SqlTypeException sqlTypeEx)
{
    ...
}
catch (SqlTruncateException sqlTruncateEx)
{
    ...
}
```

Listing 2-2. *Incorrect Way of Ordering Exception-Handling Blocks in Visual Basic .NET*

```
Try
    ...
Catch ex as Exception
    ...
Catch sqlTypeEx as SqlTypeException
    ...
Catch sqlTruncateEx as SqlTruncateException
    ...
End Try
```

The correct way to order exception-handling blocks is shown in Listings 2-3 and 2-4.

Listing 2-3. *Correct Way of Ordering Exception-Handling Blocks in C#*

```
try
{
    ...
}
catch (SqlTruncateException sqlTruncateEx)
{
    ...
}
catch (SqlTypeException sqlTypeEx)
{
```

```
    ...
}
catch (Exception ex)
{
    ...
}
```

Listing 2-4. *Correct Way of Ordering Exception-Handling Blocks in Visual Basic .NET*

```
Try
    ...
Catch sqlTruncateEx as SqlTruncateException
    ...
Catch sqlTypeEx as SqlTypeException
    ...
Catch ex as Exception
    ...
End Try
```

Thus, to write effective exception-handling code, you have to understand the various exception classes that exist within ADO.NET and use them accordingly.

ADO.NET exceptions have been restructured in .NET 2.0. They can be categorized into four major categories:

- *Disconnected stack exceptions* inheriting from System.Data.DataException:

  The various exceptions that may occur when working with disconnected data caches are shown in Figure 2-8.

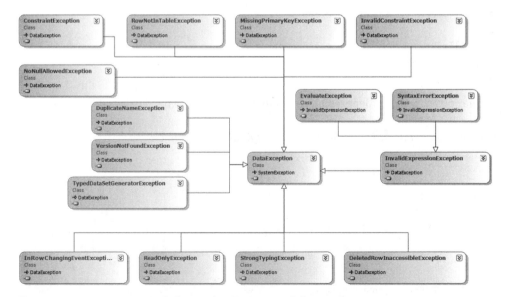

Figure 2-8. *Various exceptions thrown by disconnected data caches*

As you may note, all of these exceptions either directly or indirectly inherit from `System.Data.DataException`. Thus, if you have code that includes both ADO.NET and non-ADO.NET operations within your `try...catch` block, you can filter the ADO.NET exceptions that occur in disconnected data caches by looking for this exception type.

Most of the exceptions inherit directly from `System.Data.DataException` with the exception of `EvaluateException` and `SyntaxErrorException`. Both of these exceptions inherit from `InvalidExpressionException`, which, in turn, inherits from `System.Data.DataException`. The `InvalidExpressionException` acts as a catchall exception for all `DataColumn` expression-related exceptions.

- *Provider stack–specific exceptions* inheriting from `System.Data.Common.DbException`:

  These exceptions can be seen in the bottom left portion of Figure 2-9.

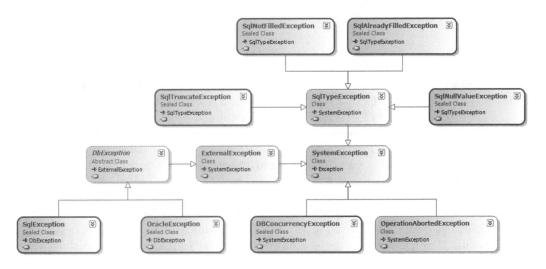

Figure 2-9. *Various other exceptions thrown by classes in ADO.NET*

These exceptions within ADO.NET are the ones that could be caused by third-party .NET data provider libraries and their underlying unmanaged code. These inherit from `System.Runtime.InteropServices.ExternalException`. Since `ExternalException` is a class common to the entire .NET Framework, ADO.NET puts another level of inheritance to segregate ADO.NET-specific external exceptions in the form of the `System.Data.Common.DbException`. Thus, any .NET data provider can now inherit from `DbException` and implement its own custom exception such as `SqlException` and `OracleException`.

- *SqlTypes-specific exceptions* inheriting from `System.Data.SqlTypes.SqlTypeException`:

  These exceptions inherit from `System.Data.SqlTypes.SqlTypeException`. As the name suggests, all exceptions that occur when working with `SqlTypes` inherit from this exception. The four exceptions that inherit from `SqlTypeException` are `SqlNotFilledException`, `SqlAlreadyFilledException`, `SqlTruncateException`, and `SqlNullValueException`. These can be seen in the top portion of Figure 2-9.

- *Other ADO.NET exceptions* inheriting directly from `System.Exception`:

    These exceptions comprise the group that inherits directly from `System.Exception`: `DBConcurrencyException` and `OperationAbortedException`. The `DbConcurrencyException` is thrown by the data adapter when it detects a concurrency violation. The data adapter deduces a concurrency violation when it has expected one row to be modified based upon the command it executed, but zero rows were modified at the time of execution. These can be seen in the bottom right portion of Figure 2-9.

    The `OperationAbortedException` is a new exception added in the .NET 2.0 Framework. This exception indicates that an operation has been aborted by the consumer of an API. In ADO.NET, this exception is thrown when the user aborts the `SqlBulkCopy` operations in the `SqlBulkCopy.SqlRowsCopied` event. `SqlBulkCopy` is a new introduction in .NET 2.0 and its purpose is to efficiently ferry large amounts of data between databases. This object is covered in Chapter 9.

Summary

This chapter gave you the essence of ADO.NET. It built upon the information presented in the first chapter, and took the discussion away from a logical placement of ADO.NET to a more physical placement with class structures and specific objects.

   While the figures showed Microsoft SQL Server–specific objects and Oracle-specific objects, it is important to realize that you could fire up Visual Studio .NET and create a new class library project that implements those very interfaces and inherits from those very base-class objects shown in this chapter and write your own .NET data provider.

   An example of a .NET data provider for Microsoft Message Queuing (MSMQ) was presented in my previous book titled *Pro ADO.NET with VB.NET 1.1* (Apress, 2004). Do note, however, that the information presented in that book pertains to .NET Framework 1.1, but the concepts are fairly similar. The big difference is the new provider factory, but you can look up an existing .NET data provider such as `SqlClient` using a tool such as Lutz Roeder's reflector and write up one for any data source of your choice.

   This chapter is probably the most concentrated theory chapter in this book. A lot of class names and interface names were introduced in this chapter. If you are feeling a bit overwhelmed because you can't remember all these names, that's perfectly all right. Even if you memorized all these names, your understanding will fade if not supplanted with practical examples. These names will begin to settle in your understanding as you move through this book and its various chapters. So, as you walk through the rest of the chapters in this book, keep referencing back to all the class names presented in this chapter.

   Subsequent chapters introduce these same objects to you in a practical, task-oriented approach. In the same spirit, the next chapter gets into writing some real code and creating a data-driven application.

CHAPTER 3

■■■

ADO.NET Hello World!

The first chapter explained the purpose of ADO.NET and where it fits in the overall architecture. It explained using common block diagrams, the very high-level structure of ADO.NET, the connected and disconnected portions of ADO.NET, and the .NET data provider model.

The second chapter took that discussion from a 30,000-ft. view to about a 10,000-ft. view where you saw the various objects, their inheritance layout within ADO.NET, the various namespaces, and the reasoning behind that structure.

It's now time to walk on the ground and write a few real data-driven applications. But before you deal with the intricacies and complexities of a true enterprise-level data-driven architecture, it makes sense to see a few simple applications first. This is in the spirit of "crawl before you walk, walk before you run." This chapter begins with extremely simple data-driven applications that require you to write absolutely no code at all. In fact, an entire working application is produced by only dragging and dropping. Then, this approach is taken forward to increasingly more involved examples where you'll blend some writing with dragging and dropping. You'll proceed to a small data-driven console application where you'll write every part of the code yourself.

Since all the examples presented in this chapter will be data driven, it is probably a good idea to set up the data source being used first. The examples presented in this book exemplify various ADO.NET concepts using a local Microsoft SQL Server 2005 instance. Any differences with Oracle or other major providers will be identified as they arise. For the purposes of this chapter, however, the examples are simple enough that there are no differences between the major data providers.

Setting Up the Hello World Data Source

The quintessential Hello World example serves as a simple introduction to any programming concept. Let's try and leverage that to our advantage by setting up a simplistic data source. As mentioned earlier, the data source will be a database on the local running instance of Microsoft SQL Server 2005. The database name will be Test, and it will contain one table called Demo. This table can be set up using the following script:

```
Create Table Demo
(
DemoID int identity primary key,
DemoValue varchar(200)
)
```

```
Go

Insert Into Demo (DemoValue) Values ('Hello World')
GO
```

The Demo table contains two columns, one of which is DemoID of int type, which is an identity column. Identity columns are specific to SQL Server; if you're working with Oracle, you'll have to modify your queries to use sequences instead. Thus, depending on the exact database you're working with, you'll have to leverage either an identity or a sequence. For instance, in IBM DB2 you have a choice of picking between a sequence and an identity.

The second column is DemoValue of VarChar(200) type, which stores a simple text value. You can download the previous script from the code samples for this chapter in the Downloads section of the Apress website (http://www.apress.com); it can be found under Chapter 3 in a file called Create Database.sql. This will enable you to set up such a data source for a local running instance of Microsoft SQL Server 2005.

Finally, there's one row inserted in the table—the Hello World row. You can run a simple SELECT query and find the contents of the underlying data source of your Hello World applications that you'll be writing in this chapter. Figure 3-1 shows the contents of the underlying data source.

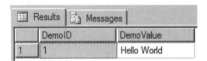

Figure 3-1. *Contents of the underlying data source for the examples in this chapter*

With the data source set up, let's begin by creating the first simplistic data-driven application.

Creating a Data-Driven Application: The Drag-and-Drop Approach

The purpose of this application is simple. All it needs to do is provide you with a user interface that lets you view the contents of the Demo table in the Test database. Also, it should give you some user interface that lets you modify the data.

Historically, developed applications have taken two diverse paths. One insists on being a monolithic, fat-client architecture that leverages the power of the desktop. Obviously, the advantage here is the flexibility you get by having the full power of the desktop and the local nature of the application. The disadvantages are deployment and maintenance issues.

The second kind of application is designed to work on various platforms through a browser. Typically, these applications are HTML-based, which leverage very little power of the end client, and most of the work is done at the server. The advantages are easy deployment and versioning, but the disadvantages include a colossal waste of the end client's computing power, and your application having to support various configurations at the end client that you cannot control.

In addition, there are some midway application architectures, such as ActiveX and ClickOnce. But for the purposes of this chapter, let's concentrate on the two major kinds of applications: web-based (ASP.NET) and Windows Forms–based.

Let's begin by looking at web-based applications first, or as they are referred to in the .NET platform, ASP.NET applications.

Drag and Drop in ASP.NET 2.0

The simplicity of creating an application using drag and drop in ASP.NET 2.0 is quite remarkable. The approach and underlying architecture are different from ASP.NET 1.1, which will not be discussed here.

The code for this example can be downloaded from the Downloads section for this chapter under DragDropWebsite, or you can easily create it yourself by following the steps here. Do note that because there's no code to write, the instructions are exactly the same for both C# and VB.NET:

1. Start by firing up Visual Studio 2005 and creating a new website. To do this, select File ➤ New ➤ WebSite.

2. Give it a name; I chose DragDropWebsite, which is demonstrated in Figure 3-2.

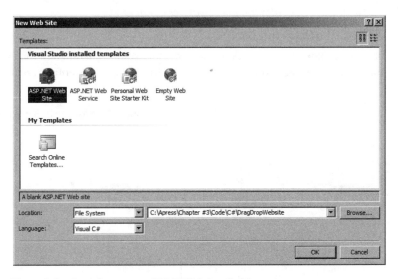

Figure 3-2. *Creating a new ASP.NET 2.0 website*

Take note that I am using C# in Figure 3-2 as my choice language. Since the steps are exactly the same for VB.NET, if you prefer, you can choose VB.NET as your choice language.

3. Click OK to create the website.

4. The created website should have one Default.aspx page created for you. If that page is not already open inside the Visual Studio IDE, double-click it to open it. At the bottom of that page, click Design to view a blank page.

5. Next, open the Database Explorer/Server Explorer window. If the window is not already visible, you can enable it by selecting View ➤ Server Explorer. This window should look similar to the one shown in Figure 3-3.

Figure 3-3. *The Database Explorer/Server Explorer window*

If your Database Explorer/Server Explorer window looks somewhat different than mine—don't panic. It's only because your Server Explorer already has a few entries and mine is blank.

6. Next, right-click on Data Connections and choose Add Connection as shown in Figure 3-4.

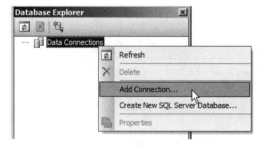

Figure 3-4. *Adding a connection to the Database Explorer/Server Explorer*

This should show a dialog box that prompts you to select the appropriate data source. At this point, you can go ahead and fill in the various values. When you click Test Connection, you should see a dialog box informing you that the connection is valid and the test succeeded, as shown in Figure 3-5.

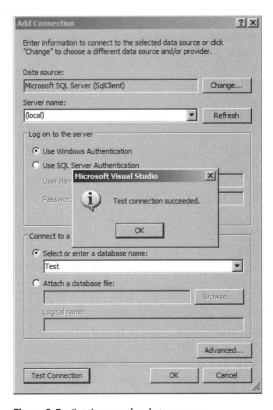

Figure 3-5. *Setting up the data source*

7. Click OK twice to accept the data source. At this point, you should be able to see a data source defined under the Data Connections node in the Database Explorer window.

8. Next, expand the Database Explorer's newly added data source until you see the Demo table. This can be seen in Figure 3-6.

Figure 3-6. *The Demo table—setting up the data source*

9. Now the fun starts! With your mouse, drag and drop the Demo table to the surface of Default.aspx. This should add two things on the surface of the .aspx page: a GridView control and a SqlDataSource. This can be seen in Figure 3-7.

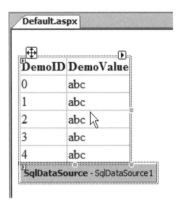

Figure 3-7. *The newly added GridView and SqlDataSource controls on the .aspx page*

Notice the small, black, arrow-like button facing to the right at the top-right edge of the GridView control. When you click it, you should see an editing pane that allows you to format the GridView control and set a few properties. Go ahead and enable editing and deleting, along with formatting the GridView to a scheme of your choice. This can be seen in Figure 3-8.

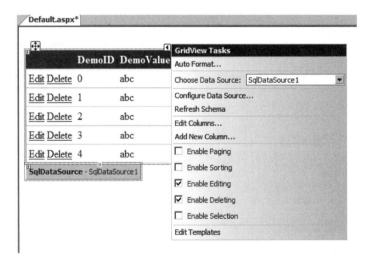

Figure 3-8. *Setting properties on the GridView*

10. That's it. Now compile and run the application. You might be prompted to start with or without debugging, just select the default choice. You should see your Hello World web-based application running, as shown in Figure 3-9.

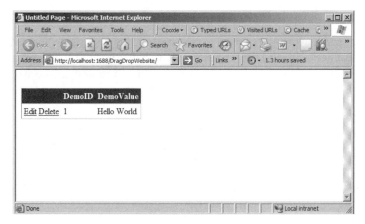

Figure 3-9. *Hello World in ASP.NET*

Try playing around with the application a bit. You'll notice that this is a fully functional application that even lets you modify the underlying data. If you do happen to modify the underlying data, you can easily restore it by running the script provided with this chapter again.

So you wrote absolutely no C# or VB.NET code and you have a data-driven web-based application ready. How did it all work? Well, the framework did all the work for you. It queried the underlying data source for you and encapsulated all that functionality within the various properties set on the `GridView` control and the `SqlDataSource` control.

If you view the source of the `.aspx` page and check out the listing for `SqlDataSource`, you'll see that it looks like the code shown in Listing 3-1.

Listing 3-1. *The SqlDataSource Control Defined on the Default.aspx Page*

```
<asp:SqlDataSource ID="SqlDataSource1" runat="server"
    ConnectionString="<%$ ConnectionStrings:TestConnectionString1 %>"
    DeleteCommand="DELETE FROM [Demo] WHERE [DemoID] = @original_DemoID"
    InsertCommand="INSERT INTO [Demo] ([DemoValue]) VALUES (@DemoValue)"
    ProviderName="<%$ ConnectionStrings:TestConnectionString1.ProviderName %>"
    SelectCommand="SELECT [DemoID], [DemoValue] FROM [Demo]"
    UpdateCommand=
      "UPDATE [Demo] SET [DemoValue] =
      @DemoValue WHERE [DemoID] = @original_DemoID">
    <InsertParameters>
      <asp:Parameter Name="DemoValue" Type="String" />
    </InsertParameters>
    <UpdateParameters>
      <asp:Parameter Name="DemoValue" Type="String" />
      <asp:Parameter Name="original_DemoID" Type="Int32" />
    </UpdateParameters>
    <DeleteParameters>
      <asp:Parameter Name="original_DemoID" Type="Int32" />
    </DeleteParameters>
</asp:SqlDataSource>
```

A few things are worth noting in Listing 3-1:

- The *connection string*, which is the information that tells the underlying libraries what data source to connect with and how to connect with it, has already been set up for you under ConnectionStrings:TestConnectionString1. This, as it turns out, has been specified in the Web.Config file under the ConnectionStrings section for you. This can be seen in Listing 3-2.

Listing 3-2. *The Connection String Defined for You in the Web.Config File*

```
<connectionStrings>
    <add name="TestConnectionString1"
    connectionString="Data Source=(local);Initial Catalog=Test;
        Integrated Security=True" providerName="System.Data.SqlClient"/>
</connectionStrings>
```

- The framework queried the underlying data source for you and prepared SQL statements for the various possible commands. This can be seen in Listing 3-1.

- Those commands are even parameterized with the right data types. All of this—written for you, by the framework. This also can be seen in Listing 3-1.

Next, let's turn our attention to the GridView control added for you by the framework. If you look in the source of the .aspx page, you should see code similar to that in Listing 3-3.

Listing 3-3. *The GridView Control Defined on the Default.aspx Page*

```
<asp:GridView ID="GridView1" runat="server" AutoGenerateColumns="False"
BackColor="White" BorderColor="#CCCCCC" BorderStyle="None" BorderWidth="1px"
CellPadding="4" DataKeyNames="DemoID" DataSourceID="SqlDataSource1"
EmptyDataText="There are no data records to display." ForeColor="Black"
GridLines="Horizontal">
    <FooterStyle BackColor="#CCCC99" ForeColor="Black" />
    <Columns>
        <asp:CommandField ShowDeleteButton="True" ShowEditButton="True" />
        <asp:BoundField DataField="DemoID" HeaderText="DemoID"
            ReadOnly="True" SortExpression="DemoID" />
        <asp:BoundField DataField="DemoValue"
            HeaderText="DemoValue" SortExpression="DemoValue" />
    </Columns>
    <PagerStyle BackColor="White" ForeColor="Black" HorizontalAlign="Right" />
    <SelectedRowStyle BackColor="#CC3333" Font-Bold="True" ForeColor="White" />
    <HeaderStyle BackColor="#333333" Font-Bold="True" ForeColor="White" />
</asp:GridView>
```

As you can see from Listing 3-3, the data source for the GridView control has been defined as the SqlDataSource1 object, which is what you see in Listing 3-1. This is what binds the GridView and the data source together. Then it's just a question of adding the relevant bound columns and the command buttons and your application is ready to run!

Thus, by a simple drag-and-drop operation, you're able to create a data-driven application from the ground up with very little code.

■**Caution** You just created a data-driven application. Why should you bother to read any further? At this point, I must goad you to continue. A little knowledge is a dangerous thing, and you should not leave your ADO.NET knowledge incomplete because you now have the power to create a data-driven application in a matter of minutes by a simple point-and-click operation. As you'll learn in future chapters, your application is just as good as the amount of effort you put into it. You can't expect drag-and-drop applications to help you create a well-architected enterprise-level application up and running; however, it's important to learn this approach and possibly leverage it to implement a fast track to your eventual goal.

Now, with the data-driven ASP.NET application set up, let's look at a Windows Forms–based application created in a similar fashion.

Drag and Drop in a Windows Forms Application

Similar to an ASP.NET data-driven application, let's go ahead and follow a few simple steps to create a data-driven Windows Forms application. You can download the necessary code for this application from the associated code download in DragDropWinApp; however, since it doesn't make much sense to look at the final code, because it is all autogenerated anyway, I recommend that you follow these steps:

1. Begin by creating a new Windows Forms application in the language of your choice. Call it DragDropWinApp. Open the Form1 form added for you in Design mode.

2. Next, within Visual Studio 2005, go to the Data Sources window. If this window is not visible by default, then select Data ➤ Show Data Sources, as shown in Figure 3-10.

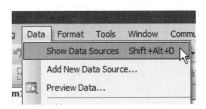

Figure 3-10. *The Show Data Sources menu item*

When you do see this window, as shown in Figure 3-11, click the Add New Data Source link.

Figure 3-11. *The Data Sources window*

3. When prompted to choose the Data Source type, select Database, as shown in Figure 3-12.

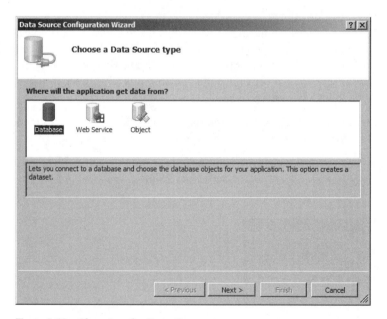

Figure 3-12. *Choosing the Data Source type*

4. When prompted to choose your data connection (see Figure 3-13), either choose the connection if it is already available in the list or click New Connection to add a new connection in a dialog box very much like Figure 3-5, which you saw in the ASP.NET drag-and-drop application.

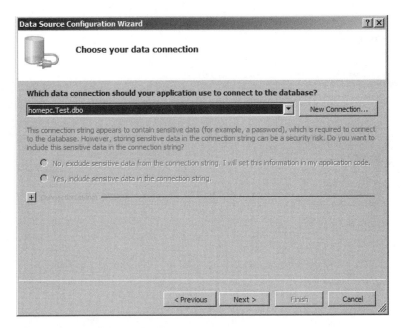

Figure 3-13. *Choosing the data connection*

5. When prompted, choose to save the connection string, as shown in Figure 3-14.

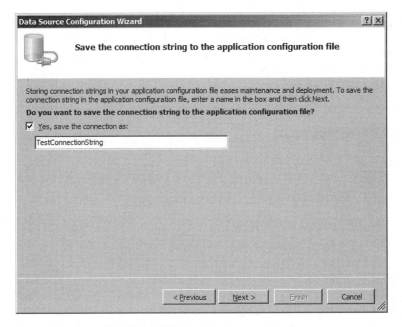

Figure 3-14. *Choosing to save the connection string*

6. When prompted to choose the database objects in your data source, choose the Demo table, as shown in Figure 3-15.

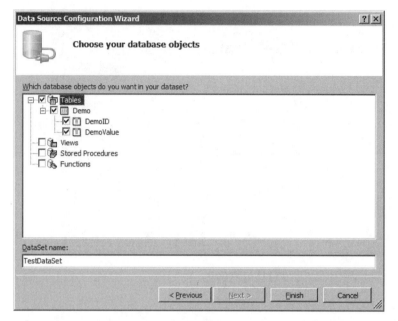

Figure 3-15. *Choosing the Demo table to be a part of your data source*

7. Click Next and Finish, which adds the TestDataSet data source to your application. At this point, you should see the TestDataSet data source added in the Data Sources window. If you select the Demo table under the data source, you can see a drop-down arrow next to it. For the purposes of this application, you can select DataGridView, as shown in Figure 3-16.

Figure 3-16. *Configuring the data source's Demo table*

8. Next, drag and drop the Demo table onto the surface of the form. This operation should add a number of controls to the surface of the form, as shown in Figure 3-17 (after rearranging them a bit).

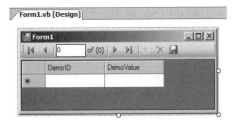

Figure 3-17. *The form in Design mode after rearranging the autogenerated controls*

This operation also adds a number of controls in the component tray under the form, as shown in Figure 3-18.

Figure 3-18. *Various controls added for you in the component tray*

9. That's it. Your data-driven application is ready. Compile and run it to see a fully operational window, as shown in Figure 3-19. You'll also see that you can edit the underlying data using this application. As an exercise to the reader, you can repeat this application by selecting something other than DataGridView in step 7.

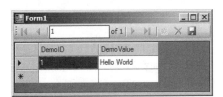

Figure 3-19. *A fully running data-driven Windows Forms application, created using drag and drop*

Again, you just created a fully functional data-driven application without actually having to write any code. As it turns out, in this case, the framework actually wrote some code for you. If you open the App.Config file, you'll see that the application has saved the connection string as an element, as shown in Listing 3-4.

Listing 3-4. *The Connection String in the App.Config File*

```
<connectionStrings>
    <add name="DragDropWinApp.Settings.TestConnectionString"
    connectionString=
    "Data Source=(local);Initial Catalog=Test;Integrated Security=True"
        providerName="System.Data.SqlClient" />
</connectionStrings>
```

Also, if you view the added form's code, you'll see the code as shown in Listings 3-5 and 3-6.

Listing 3-5. *Autogenerated Code in C#*

```csharp
private void bindingNavigatorSaveItem_Click(object sender, EventArgs e)
{
    if (this.Validate())
    {
        this.demoBindingSource.EndEdit();
        this.demoTableAdapter.Update(this.testDataSet.Demo);
    }
    else
    {
        System.Windows.Forms.MessageBox.Show(this, "Validation errors occurred.",
        "Save", System.Windows.Forms.MessageBoxButtons.OK,
        System.Windows.Forms.MessageBoxIcon.Warning);
    }

}


private void Form1_Load(object sender, EventArgs e)
{
    // TODO: This line of code loads data into the 'testDataSet.Demo' table.
    // You can move, or remove it, as needed.
    this.demoTableAdapter.Fill(this.testDataSet.Demo);

}
```

Listing 3-6. *Autogenerated Code in Visual Basic .NET*

```vbnet
Private Sub bindingNavigatorSaveItem_Click(ByVal sender As System.Object, _
    ByVal e As System.EventArgs) Handles bindingNavigatorSaveItem.Click
    If Me.Validate Then
        Me.DemoBindingSource.EndEdit()
        Me.DemoTableAdapter.Update(Me.TestDataSet.Demo)
    Else
        System.Windows.Forms.MessageBox.Show(Me, "Validation errors occurred.", _
        "Save", System.Windows.Forms.MessageBoxButtons.OK, _
        System.Windows.Forms.MessageBoxIcon.Warning)
    End If

End Sub


Private Sub Form1_Load(ByVal sender As System.Object, ByVal e As System.EventArgs) _
    Handles MyBase.Load
    'TODO: This line of code loads data into the 'TestDataSet.Demo' table.
    ' You can move, or remove it, as needed.
```

```
Me.DemoTableAdapter.Fill(Me.TestDataSet.Demo)
```

```
End Sub
```

This is not the only code generated for you. As you'll see in subsequent chapters, there is a lot of code generated in the `TestDataSet` strongly typed `DataSet` and in a hidden file called `Form1.Designer.cs` or `Form1.Designer.vb`. But for now, let's leave that for later.

Next, let's look at an application that gets a little bit more hands on as far as writing code yourself goes.

Hybrid Approach: Write Some Code, Do Some Drag and Drop

In the previous example, you saw how to easily create a data-driven Windows Forms application by simply dragging and dropping the various components onto the surface of the form. The important part to realize here is that the code that is autogenerated for you is "one size fits all." It's a lot of very generic code that is written in such a way that it will work in a logically correct manner for most applications; however, it might not be the most efficient code. Of course, when it works for most situations that implies that there will be that one odd situation where it won't work. Can you imagine your enterprise application having 500 tables? And then imagine having to drag and drop those 500 tables in a drag-and-drop architecture? It's just not maintainable. Plus, you can't customize that code to fit any situation that you may be faced with.

However, this approach does have its place in application architecture. Depending on your situation, you may decide that creating a full-fledged application using only a drag-and-drop application is a bad idea, but you could leverage the autogenerated code to your advantage by using the various generated objects as shortcuts and writing code similar to what has been shown in Listings 3-5 and 3-6 yourself.

Let's look at an example that demonstrates this very hybrid approach. You can download this application from the associated code download in `ConsoleApp`, or you can follow these steps to create such an application yourself:

1. Begin by creating a new console application. Call it `ConsoleApp`.

2. Follow steps 2 through 7 of the Windows Forms application to add a new data source. Since, in this exercise, you'll write code in a hybrid approach (drag-and-drop plus write code) as a part of a console application, it doesn't make sense to set the `Demo` table to `DataGridView` or anything else.

3. In the console application, write code as shown in Listings 3-7 and 3-8. This code will be used to fill in the contents of the `Demo` table into the `testDS.Demo` object, and then write out the value of the first row's `DemoValue` column.

Listing 3-7. *Code to Fill and Write Hello World from the Data Source in C#*

```
TestDataSet testDS = new TestDataSet();
TestDataSetTableAdapters.DemoTableAdapter tableAdapter =
    new TestDataSetTableAdapters.DemoTableAdapter();
tableAdapter.Fill(testDS.Demo);
```

```
TestDataSet.DemoRow demoRow =
    (TestDataSet.DemoRow)testDS.Demo.Rows[0];
Console.WriteLine(demoRow.DemoValue);
```

Listing 3-8. *Code to Fill and Write Hello World from the Data Source in Visual Basic .NET*

```
Dim testDS As TestDataSet = New TestDataSet()
Dim tableAdapter As TestDataSetTableAdapters.DemoTableAdapter = _
        New TestDataSetTableAdapters.DemoTableAdapter()
tableAdapter.Fill(testDS.Demo)

Dim demoRow As TestDataSet.DemoRow = _
    CType(testDS.Demo.Rows(0), TestDataSet.DemoRow)
Console.WriteLine(demoRow.DemoValue)
```

4. Compile and run the application. You should see an output as shown in Figure 3-20.

Figure 3-20. *The running hybrid application*

Thus, as you can see, you were able to write a few lines of code to leverage a lot of auto-generated code. Just as an exercise, read the code closely and try and understand what it does. There are really only four steps involved:

1. The first is to create an instance of TestDataSet:

C#
```
TestDataSet testDS = new TestDataSet();
```

VB.NET
```
Dim testDS As TestDataSet = New TestDataSet()
```

2. The second step is to create a new instance of the autogenerated `DemoTableAdapter` object. Note that this is an autogenerated object, which means this is a table adapter that is specific to your situation and the table you specified. As you'll see in Chapter 9, the framework actually wrote a lot of code for you to make this possible. In other words, this code is not a native part of the .NET Framework. Instead, it builds upon existing .NET Framework classes to provide you with a class, the `DemoTableAdapter` class, that is specific to your purpose and situation:

C#

```
TestDataSetTableAdapters.DemoTableAdapter tableAdapter =
    new TestDataSetTableAdapters.DemoTableAdapter();
```

VB.NET

```
Dim tableAdapter As TestDataSetTableAdapters.DemoTableAdapter = _
    New TestDataSetTableAdapters.DemoTableAdapter()
```

3. The third step is to use the `DemoTableAdapter` to fill in the `testDS.Demo` table. As you will see in Chapters 6 and 7, this fill operation is really being done by an underlying object called the `DataAdapter`, but in this case, the framework masks all these complexities from you. Obviously, if you needed deeper-level control (for instance, working with hierarchical data or other such situations), then this approach won't work for you. Chapter 10 covers an instance using hierarchical data where you could not possibly use this approach correctly enough to work with a relatively more complex data structure:

C#

```
tableAdapter.Fill(testDS.Demo);
```

VB.NET

```
tableAdapter.Fill(testDS.Demo)
```

4. And the final step is to query the filled object's first row's `DemoValue` column. This is very much like querying a `DataSet`. This is because `TestDataSet` is really nothing but a class that inherits from `DataSet`. It is also referred to as a strongly typed `DataSet`, which is covered in depth in Chapter 6:

C#

```
TestDataSet.DemoRow demoRow =
    (TestDataSet.DemoRow)testDS.Demo.Rows[0];
Console.WriteLine(demoRow.DemoValue);
```

VB.NET

```
Dim demoRow As TestDataSet.DemoRow = _
    CType(testDS.Demo.Rows(0), TestDataSet.DemoRow)
Console.WriteLine(demoRow.DemoValue)
```

This code gives you a little more flexibility than a pure drag-and-drop approach. But you still can't appreciate what is going on behind the scenes without actually diving deeper into the depths of ADO.NET.

For instance, *where is the SQL Query in the previous code?*

As you'll see in Chapter 9, the SQL Query is embedded deep inside the autogenerated code for TestDataSet. But let's leave that for Chapter 6. For now, let's look at a simple but purely write-yourself approach and create a simple application that connects to the data source and fetches the same results for you.

Data-Driven Application: The "Write Code Yourself" Approach

In the last example, I posed a question: Where is the SQL Query?

I gave the answer along with the question—it is embedded deep inside autogenerated code. But why should a simple query such as that have to be embedded in so much code? It really doesn't have to be. As a matter of fact, when you do see the autogenerated queries in the strongly typed DataSet in Chapter 9, you'll see that the queries take an extra-safe approach by comparing all columns and specifying highly inefficient, but accurate, UPDATE and DELETE queries. This is because the autogenerated code must work in all situations and can't make any assumptions as it is written in a one-size-fits-all approach.

Usually, in any application architecture, you'll have to make a choice between performance, flexibility, and initial effort. Application architecture is a black art. Unfortunately or fortunately, you can't fully automate the process: unfortunately because it means more work for you and me, and fortunately because you and I will have jobs for a very long time. There are many instances where you'll have to consciously decide and pick between various approaches. That's what this book intends to help you do—give you enough knowledge so you can make those decisions intelligently as an application architect. As a matter of fact, generally in a full-blown enterprise application, you'll see yourself doing more hands-on work writing code yourself, rather than dragging and dropping.

Thus, it's important that the underlying data-access architecture gives you the ability, or fine-level control, to selectively choose what you need. Luckily, ADO.NET does give you this ability.

Let's look at a quick example that achieves the same results as the previous console application example, but this time around with no drag-and-drop help. You can download the code for this exercise from the associated code download, or you can easily create it using the following steps:

1. Create a new console application. Call it ConsoleApp2.

2. Add the necessary using or Imports statements at the top of Program.cs or Module1.vb:

   C#
   ```
   using System.Data.SqlClient ;
   ```

   VB.NET
   ```
   Imports System.Data.SqlClient
   ```

3. Let's cheat here a bit. You need a connection string to connect to the data source. Connection strings have been mentioned briefly earlier in this chapter, but they will be covered in more detail in Chapter 4. For now just copy and paste the connection string from any of the previous examples. Create the connection string as a private string, so it is accessible to the rest of the code within the class, but not outside of it, like so:

C#

```
private static string connectionString =
    "Data Source=(local);Initial Catalog=Test;Integrated Security=True";
```

VB.NET

```
Private connectionString As String = _
    "Data Source=(local);Initial Catalog=Test;Integrated Security=True"
```

4. With the connection string added, write in the following code in the Main function or subroutine:

C#

```
SqlConnection testConnection = new SqlConnection(connectionString);
SqlCommand testCommand = testConnection.CreateCommand() ;
testCommand.CommandText = "Select DemoValue from Demo where DemoID = 1" ;
testConnection.Open() ;
string result = (string)testCommand.ExecuteScalar() ;
testConnection.Close();
Console.WriteLine(result) ;
```

VB.NET

```
Dim testConnection As SqlConnection = New SqlConnection(connectionString)
Dim testCommand As SqlCommand = testConnection.CreateCommand()
testCommand.CommandText = "Select DemoValue from Demo where DemoID = 1"
testConnection.Open()
Dim result As String = CType(testCommand.ExecuteScalar(), String)
testConnection.Close()
Console.WriteLine(result)
```

5. Compile and run the application. You should see output as shown in Figure 3-21, which is very much like the output shown in Figure 3-20.

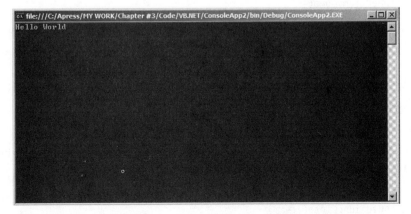

Figure 3-21. *The application that you wrote running in a hands-on way*

Here you were able to achieve the same results as the drag-and-drop approach in very few lines of code. By comparison, if you do actually browse the autogenerated code (see Chapter 9), you'll see that the autogenerated code can be hundreds or even thousands of lines of code.

Let's examine a bit more closely the code you just wrote. Some of it may not make sense yet (the necessary objects and methods involved are explained in Chapters 4 and 5), but let's look at the main steps involved:

1. First, *create an object that will hold the connection.* This is logical because to query the underlying data source you need a connection (this object is covered in detail in Chapter 4):

   C#
   ```
   SqlConnection testConnection = new SqlConnection(connectionString);
   ```

   VB.NET
   ```
   Dim testConnection As SqlConnection = New SqlConnection(connectionString)
   ```

2. Next, *create a command that will hold the SQL Query.* This could have even been a stored procedure, or it can even take parameters (the command object is covered in detail in Chapter 5):

   C#
   ```
   SqlCommand testCommand = testConnection.CreateCommand() ;
   testCommand.CommandText = "Select DemoValue from Demo where DemoID = 1" ;
   ```

   VB.NET
   ```
   Dim testCommand As SqlCommand = testConnection.CreateCommand()
   testCommand.CommandText = "Select DemoValue from Demo where DemoID = 1"
   ```

3. Next, in order to run the command, you need to *open the connection*:

   C#
   ```
   testConnection.Open() ;
   ```

   VB.NET
   ```
   testConnection.Open()
   ```

4. Now that the command is prepared and the underlying connection is open, you can *run the command* and fetch the results in a string variable:

   C#
   ```
   string result = (string)testCommand.ExecuteScalar() ;
   ```

   VB.NET
   ```
   Dim result As String = CType(testCommand.ExecuteScalar(), String)
   ```

5. Next, *close the connection.* This, as you will see in the next chapter, is extremely important to do. *Never fail to close an open connection*:

   C#
   ```
   testConnection.Close();
   ```

VB.NET
```
testConnection.Close()
```

6. With the results fetched in a string variable, you can now simply *show the results* using the `Console.Writeline` method:

C#
```
Console.WriteLine(result) ;
```

VB.NET
```
Console.WriteLine(result)
```

In brief, here are the steps you took to write a fully hand-written Hello World application:

1. Create a connection.

2. Create a command that holds the SQL Query.

3. Open the connection.

4. Run the command.

5. Close the connection.

6. Show the results.

When you see the steps without the objects involved, it seems like a fairly logical way to query your data source. Maybe the only curious thing to note is that the connection has been opened just before step 4—running the command—and closed immediately afterward. This golden rule of ADO.NET follows: "Open connections as late as possible and close them as early as you can."

This wraps up the last scenario presented in this chapter. In subsequent chapters, you'll come across the details of various objects involved that will help you create data-driven applications effectively.

Summary

Chapter 1 began by giving you a very high 30,000-ft. overview of what ADO.NET is, and where it fits into your general application architecture.

Chapter 2 got a little bit closer to the ground and took the discussion away from logical block diagrams and more toward class diagrams and the physical class structure layout of the various major objects and namespaces involved in ADO.NET. At this point, you should quickly glance back at Chapter 2 and compare the `SqlConnection` and `SqlCommand` objects involved in the last presented example in that chapter.

Chapter 3 was the first chapter in this book that presented you with true hands-on code, and you created four working data-driven applications.

So now that you have actually started walking on the ground of this new planet and have actually built some data-driven applications, it's time to start running by digging deeper into the framework. As an application architect and programmer, it's not only important to understand how to do something, but it's also important to understand how to do it right, and be able to reason between the various ways to achieve the same goal.

I can't tell you the one possible panacea simply because there isn't one that fits every single situation out there. This is because application architecture, especially ADO.NET, can't be zeroed down to black or white. There are too many scenarios to deal with and various shades of gray involved. However, certain things, such as not closing your database connections or abusing a `DataSet` as a database, are clearly bad.

Starting with Chapter 4, you'll see the various important objects involved in ADO.NET and the usage scenarios and best practices involved with them. As the book carries forward, the discussion will continue to visit various other important objects, their usage scenarios, and best practices involved.

Now that you have landed on this planet and have walked around a bit, tighten your seat belts, pack your bags, and hold onto your seat tightly, your magic carpet ride is about to begin with Chapter 4, "Connecting to a Data Source."

CHAPTER 4

■■■

Connecting to a Data Source

It's hard to imagine an application that doesn't have a data source. If a computer can be thought of as an information processing and storage machine, more often than not, the data storage for any serious application requires a dedicated data source. The data source could be as simple as a Microsoft Access database for a simple front-end point-of-sale application for your local convenience store, or it could be as complicated as a full-blown implementation of a leading commercial-quality database, such as Microsoft SQL Server or Oracle, for an e-commerce website.

Given the wide variety of applications that exist today, the demands on the database for a given application could range from a continuously connected user to multiple users seamlessly sharing connections using a connection pool.

Whether an application is simple or complicated, one fact remains: ADO.NET needs to be able to establish and manage a connection with a data source.

In this chapter, you'll examine the various methods available within ADO.NET to connect to a database. You'll learn how to create, open, and close connections. Since, in the modern Internet-driven world, it's far too common to see applications that require a vast number of users requesting real-time interaction with the system, and given that connecting to the database is one of the most expensive operations a server-based application might need to do, most modern-day data access architectures have implemented mechanisms like connection pooling to address this problem. In this chapter, you'll also examine how ADO.NET supports connection pooling and learn the proper way to close and destroy connection objects to take advantage of pooling.

The Ability to Connect

The need to connect to a data source is essential for any data access architecture. ADO.NET gives you the ability to connect to a data source by providing a suitable connection object, which is part of a data source–specific data provider. So the .NET Framework data provider for SQL Server would have a class by the name of SqlConnection that will allow you to establish a connection with a Microsoft SQL Server database, and the OracleClient data provider would have a class by the name of OracleConnection that will allow you to establish a connection to an Oracle database.

Whichever data source you are connecting to, there are a few common characteristics between connection implementations. Obviously, at the very least, you should be able to connect, or open, a connection. To open a connection, you need to specify what information is needed to open the connection, such as the name of the server, user ID, password, and so on. Since every target data source might need a different set of information for ADO.NET to connect to the data source, a flexible mechanism of specifying all these settings through a *connection string* is chosen.

A connection string tokenizes the minimum information needed to establish a connection in the form of string key-value pairs. The various key-value pairs in a connection string can also define certain configurable parameters defining the behavior of the connection. So a typical connection string takes the following form:

```
"parametername1=parametervalue1;parametername2=parametervalue2;..."
```

By virtue of being able to open a connection, it makes sense that you should also be able to close an open connection. In addition, for any communication you might need to do with the data source, you might need to check if the data source connection is currently open and available or not. So, you should also be able to retrieve the current state of the connection.

So, at the very least, you need two methods: Open and Close, and one State property on the class that allows you to establish a connection with the database. Let's create a connection object and write up a quick example that demonstrates the simple exercise of connecting to a database.

Creating Connection Objects

As you saw earlier, ADO.NET wraps the functionality of establishing connections with a given database in a typical connection class. Let's try creating an instance of the connection class: the connection object. Even though I'll demonstrate the examples using the SqlConnection class, the concepts for other kinds of connection objects in various providers remain the same. The various connection objects can simply be created by creating a new instance of their respective connection classes. This is shown here:

C#

```
SqlConnection testConnection = new SqlConnection();
```

VB.NET

```
Dim testConnection As New SqlConnection
```

Looks simple enough; however, as you might have already guessed, that's not enough because you haven't told your connection object which database to connect to, which access credentials to use, and so on. You need to specify these parameters using the ConnectionString property of the SqlConnection object, as shown here:

C#

```
SqlConnection testConnection = new SqlConnection();
string testConnectionString =
    "Data Source=(local);Initial Catalog=Test;Integrated Security=SSPI";
testConnection.ConnectionString = testConnectionString;
```

VB.NET

```
Dim testConnection As New SqlConnection
Dim testConnectionString As String = "Data Source=(local);" & _
    "Initial Catalog=Test;Integrated Security=SSPI"
testConnection.ConnectionString = testConnectionString
```

This code would prepare the connection object to open a connection to a SQL Server running on your local machine using Windows authentication and connect to a database called "Test". Alternatively, you could use one of the constructors of the SqlConnection class to give us a ready-to-use SqlConnection object, as shown here:

C#

```
SqlConnection testConnection=
    new SqlConnection(
    "Data Source=(local);Initial Catalog=Test;Integrated Security=SSPI");
```

VB.NET

```
Dim testConnection As New SqlConnection( _
    "Data Source=(local);Initial Catalog=Test;Integrated Security=SSPI")
```

Thus, as long as you know the ConnectionString, you could have a ready-to-use SqlConnection object in as little as one line of code. Also, with the connection object prepared here, all you need to do now is call the Open method to successfully open a connection to the specified database.

■Note Do note, however, that a connection object is not the same as a physical connection to the database. As you'll see later in this chapter, if you're using connection pooling, which is turned on by default for many providers, then calling Open on a connection object will either allow you to use an already open and unused physical connection, or open a brand new connection if sufficient open physical connections don't exist.

Using the connection strings shown in Listings 4-1 and 4-2, a quick example can be written that connects to a database called "Test" running on a local SQL Server instance. The examples use Windows authentication to connect to the database. They simply create the connection object, establish a connection, and check the state of the connection to verify if the connection was successfully opened or not, and finally they close the connection. The code can be seen in Listings 4-1 and 4-2 or can be downloaded as Exercise 4.1 from the Downloads section of the Apress website (http://www.apress.com).

Listing 4-1. *Working with a Connection Object in C#*

```
static void Main(string[] args)
{
    SqlConnection testConnection =
            new SqlConnection(
            "Data Source=(local);Initial Catalog=Test;Integrated Security=SSPI");
```

```
   try
   {
      testConnection.Open();
      if (testConnection.State == ConnectionState.Open)
      {
         Console.WriteLine("Successfully opened a connection");
      }
   }
   catch (Exception)
   {
      if (testConnection.State != ConnectionState.Open)
      {
         Console.WriteLine("Failed to open a connection");
      }
   }
   finally
   {
      // Closing a connection ensures connection pooling.
      if (testConnection.State == ConnectionState.Open)
      {
         testConnection.Close();
      }
      testConnection.Dispose();
   }
}
```

Listing 4-2. *Working with a Connection Object in Visual Basic .NET*

```
Sub Main()
   Dim testConnection As SqlConnection = _
      New SqlConnection( _
      "Data Source=(local);Initial Catalog=Test;Integrated Security=SSPI")
   Try
      testConnection.Open()
      If testConnection.State = ConnectionState.Open Then
         Console.WriteLine("Successfully opened a connection")
      End If
   Catch
      If testConnection.State <> ConnectionState.Open Then
         Console.WriteLine("Failed to open a connection")
      End If
   Finally
      ' Closing a connection ensures connection pooling.
      If testConnection.State = ConnectionState.Open Then
         testConnection.Close()
      End If
      testConnection.Dispose()
   End Try
End Sub
```

When the code in Listing 4-1 or 4-2 runs, assuming that you have a database called "Test" on your local machine and you have adequate access to it, the output should be either

```
"Successfully opened a connection"
```

or

```
"Failed to open a connection"
```

As you can see from Listings 4-1 and 4-2, the various key-value pairs in the connection string are how you pass various information to the connection object, which gives it sufficient information to connect to the database.

Usually, in order to connect to a given database, you'd need to specify more than one such key-value pair in a delimited string, as shown previously. So, as you saw in Listings 4-1 and 4-2, the connection string contains three such key-value pairs:

```
"Data Source=(local);Initial Catalog=Test;Integrated Security=SSPI"
```

Say that instead of Integrated Security=SSPI, a typo had crept in by entering *Itegrated* Security=SSPI; you wouldn't have been able to use the connection successfully. An industry-standard database, such as SQL Server or Oracle, could possibly support a lot of parameters inside a valid connection string. Remembering the exact names of the parameters, and maybe even parameter values, could get challenging at times. Fortunately, there is help!

Generating Provider-Specific Connection Strings

There are many parameters that could be specified in a connection string. Each of those parameter names needs to be spelled properly with a valid value in order for us to establish a connection to the database successfully. Not only could it get difficult to remember each parameter name and its spellings properly, but it is also easy to overlook the many configurable features for any data provider's connection object if you don't have an easy, intuitive way to construct your connection strings.

ADO.NET 2.0 tries to address this problem by providing a DbConnectionStringBuilder class. The DbConnectionStringBuilder object strongly types various connection string constituent values in order to avoid trivial programming errors as well as to make the connection string information more manageable.

Every .NET data provider is required to contain a class that inherits from DbConnectionStringBuilder to facilitate easy connection string building. So OracleClient would have an OracleConnectionStringBuilder class, and SqlClient would have a SqlConnectionStringBuilder class. We'll take a look at how this is done using the SqlConnectionStringBuilder class.

Let's say I stopped you in the middle of a hallway and asked, "Could you tell me about the database you wish to connect to?" Usually, instead of telling me the connection string, your answer would sound something like this:

The database I am interested in connecting to . . .

   . . . is on my local machine.

   . . . has the name "Test".

   . . . will allow me to connect using Windows authentication.

   . . . etc.

The SqlConnectionStringBuilder class is based around this paradigm, so instead of having to specify a connection string manually, you can specify the information using full intellisense inside the Visual Studio 2005 environment and derive a connection string from that instead. The sample code in Listings 4-3 and 4-4 demonstrates how to use the SqlConnectionStringBuilder class.

Listing 4-3. *Using the SqlConnectionStringBuilder Class in C#*

```csharp
static void Main(string[] args)
{
    SqlConnectionStringBuilder connstrBuilder = new SqlConnectionStringBuilder();
    connstrBuilder.DataSource = "(local)";
    connstrBuilder.InitialCatalog = "Test";
    connstrBuilder.IntegratedSecurity = true;

    using (SqlConnection testConnection =
        new SqlConnection(connstrBuilder.ToString()))
    {
        try
        {
            testConnection.Open();
            if (testConnection.State == ConnectionState.Open)
            {
                Console.WriteLine("Connection successfully opened");
                Console.WriteLine("Connection string used: " +
                    testConnection.ConnectionString);
            }
        }
        catch (Exception)
        {
            if (testConnection.State != ConnectionState.Open)
            {
                Console.WriteLine("Connection open failed");
                Console.WriteLine("Connection string used: "
                    + testConnection.ConnectionString);
            }
        }
    }
    // Automatic dispose call on conn ensures connection is closed.
    Console.WriteLine("Press any key to continue ..");
    Console.Read();
}
```

Listing 4-4. *Using the SqlConnectionStringBuilder Class in Visual Basic .NET*

```vbnet
Sub Main()
    Dim connstrBuilder As SqlConnectionStringBuilder = _
        New SqlConnectionStringBuilder()
```

```vbnet
connstrBuilder.DataSource = "(local)"
connstrBuilder.InitialCatalog = "Test"
connstrBuilder.IntegratedSecurity = True

Using testConnection As SqlConnection = _
    New SqlConnection(connstrBuilder.ToString())
    Try
        testConnection.Open()
        If testConnection.State = ConnectionState.Open Then
            Console.WriteLine("Connection successfully opened")
            Console.WriteLine("Connection string used: " & _
                testConnection.ConnectionString)
        End If
    Catch ex As Exception
        If testConnection.State <> ConnectionState.Open Then
            Console.WriteLine("Connection successfully failed")
            Console.WriteLine("Connection string used: " & _
                testConnection.ConnectionString)
        End If
    End Try
End Using
' Automatic Dispose Call on conn ensures connection is closed.
Console.WriteLine("Press any key to continue ..")
Console.Read()
End Sub
```

The execution results of this code are shown in Figure 4-1.

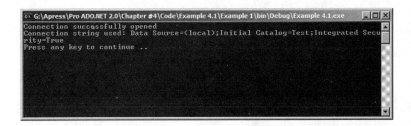

Figure 4-1. *Using a connection string generated by the SqlConnectionStringBuilder*

So, by using the `SqlConnectionStringBuilder` class you can easily create connection strings that would've otherwise required you to remember the various `ConnectionString` key-value pairs. As an exercise, you should examine the various properties available on the `SqlConnectionBuilderObject` and observe the various configurable parameters that can be communicated to the data source using the connection string.

Another good thing about the `SqlConnectionStringBuilder` and really any class that inherits from the `DbConnectionStringBuilder` class is that they can act as the bridge between a connection string and a description for the database. If you have an existing connection string that you wish to map to an instance of the `SqlConnectionStringBuilder` class, you could simply pass the existing connection string as a parameter to one of the constructor overloads for `SqlConnectionStringBuilder` or, alternatively, set the `SqlConnectionStringBuilder.ConnectionString` property. By doing so, all the relevant properties would be populated accordingly.

Even though the previous example demonstrated the use of connection builders using the `SqlConnectionStringBuilder` class, there's an equivalent class for each data provider. For example, `System.Data.OracleClient` has an `OracleClientConnectionStringBuilder` class, `System.Data.OleDb` has an `OleDbConnectionStringBuilder` class, and so on.

However, while this trick might work well for specialized data sources such as SQL Server or Oracle, the more generic data providers for OleDb and ODBC require you to specify keys such as Provider information. Again, it's quite possible to commit an error while spelling out the Provider information. And once again, fortunately, you are in luck!

The Easy Way to Any Connection String

The data provider–specific connection string builder classes allow you to easily create a connection string for their respective databases. For other data providers, though, the Microsoft universal data link (`.udl`) file offers a convenient, alternative method for creating and remembering complex connection strings. Here's how you create a simple connection string to connect to a Microsoft Access database located at `C:\Apress\MyDb.mdb`:

1. Create a new text file on your hard disk. Name it `myfile.udl`.

2. Double-click `myfile.udl` to bring up the Data Link Properties dialog box, as shown in Figure 4-2.

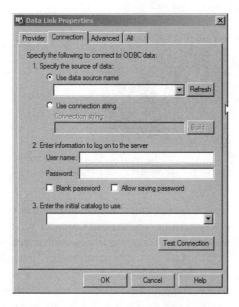

Figure 4-2. *The Data Link Properties dialog box*

3. Open the Provider tab and choose the Microsoft Jet 4.0 OLE DB Provider.

4. Open the Connection tab, specify the properties needed (if any), such as user ID and password, and click Test Connection to verify that everything works. A message box indicating the test result will now display.

5. Click OK twice: first to close the message box and then to close the Data Link Properties dialog box. Your changes are now saved.

The myfile.udl file can now be viewed in Notepad and it should look like Listing 4-5. Please note that the listing has been formatted for display purposes.

Listing 4-5. *myfile.udl File Content*

```
[oledb]
; Everything after this line is an OLE DB initstring
Provider=Microsoft.Jet.OLEDB.4.0;Password="";
Data Source=C:\Apress\Mydb.mdb;Persist Security Info=True
```

That's it. Now you can copy and paste the connection string into your code and begin connecting to the Microsoft Access database as shown here:

C#

```
OleDbConnection testConnection = new OleDbConnection
    ("Provider=Microsoft.Jet.OLEDB.4.0;" +
    "Data Source=C:\\Apress\\mydb.mdb;Persist Security Info=False");
```

VB.NET

```
Dim testConnection As New OleDbConnection( _
    "Provider=Microsoft.Jet.OLEDB.4.0;" & _
    "Data Source=C:\Apress\mydb.mdb;Persist Security Info=False")
```

Even better, you can be "lazy" and directly specify the .udl file as your connection string, like this:

C#

```
OleDbConnection testConnection = new OleDbConnection(
    "File Name=C:\\Apress\\myfile.udl");
```

VB.NET

```
Dim testConnection As New OleDbConnection( _
    "File Name=C:\Apress\myfile.udl")
```

While this technique works out of the box for OleDb or ODBC .NET data providers, there's one little nuance you need to be careful of when using this technique with a specific .NET data provider such as SqlClient or OracleClient: When accessing a data source through the OleDb or ODBC data providers, it's necessary to specify the Provider used in the connection string, such as *Microsoft.Jet.OLEDB.4.0*. When using the native .NET Framework data providers for SQL Server or Oracle, you don't need this piece of information, as the provider is fixed. Hence, you need to remove the Provider key-value pair from the generated connection string in order to use it with a SQL Server or Oracle database.

Securing Connection Strings

So far you've looked at the overall general architecture of the connection object. You saw how to create a connection object, and you saw a couple of easy ways to create a connection string.

While the examples shown so far work well, in a production application you would probably not want to hard code the connection string due to the following reasons:

- Connection strings often need to be changed after deployment. You don't want to recompile your application because someone changed a password or moved the database to a different server.

- .NET code can be disassembled and thus connection strings, including passwords, can be read.

- By storing the connection string in a common place, you ensure everyone uses exactly the same connection string. As you'll see later in this chapter, this ensures effective connection pooling. Effective connection pooling is critical to the performance of an application that needs to support multiple database requests. However, it's important to note that in ADO.NET physical connections are pooled at the client, not at the database server. Please see the "Connection Pooling" section later in this chapter for more information on this subject.

A common approach to this dilemma is to store the connection string in an XML-based configuration file instead, such as the Web.Config file for ASP.NET Web-based applications.

Using the .NET Framework 1.x, you could specify the connection string as an appSetting element, so your configuration file could look somewhat like this:

```
<?xml version="1.0" encoding="utf-8"?>
   <configuration>
      <appSettings>
         <add key="connectString" value="...." />
      </appSettings>
   </configuration>
```

While this certainly works, you're stuck with implementing your own encryption mechanisms to protect your connection strings from prying eyes.

The .NET Framework 2.0 includes a useful security enhancement. The engineers at Microsoft realized that one of the most common uses of a configuration file was to store connection strings, so not only did they create a separate section in the configuration file for connection strings, but they also created an infrastructure to support encryption of configuration file sections. There is a new protectedData section in configuration files specifically for this purpose.

The usage is fairly simple: You simply need to add a protectedData element to your configuration file and add the relevant sections you wish to protect as protectedDataSections elements inside the protectedData element. In the protectedDataSections, you can specify which provider you wish to use in order to encrypt the particular section of your configuration file.

■**Note** At the time of writing this book, the two provider choices you have are the
RSAProtectedConfigurationProvider and the DPAPIProtectedConfigurationProvider.

The relevant portion of your configuration file under .NET Framework 2.0 should look like
Listing 4-6. You'll note in Listing 4-6 that I'm using useMachineContainer="true". This is because
the RSA key container being used in this example is a machine-level key container.

Listing 4-6. *Configuration File with Encrypted Section*

```
<configuration>
    <connectionStrings>
        <EncryptedData/>
    </connectionStrings>

    <protectedData>
        <providers>
            <add name="MyProvider"
                type="System.Configuration.RsaProtectedConfigurationProvider"
                keyContainerName="MyKeys"
                useMachineContainer="true" />
        </providers>

        <protectedDataSections>
            <add name="connectionStrings"
                provider="MyProvider"
                inheritedByChildren="false"/>
        </protectedDataSections>
    </protectedData>
</configuration>
```

There's no connection string for the EncryptedData element. That makes sense since the
EncryptedData holding the connection string isn't something you want to type in by hand; you
have to resort to writing some code instead, as shown in Listings 4-7 and 4-8.

Listing 4-7. *Saving Encrypted Data to a Configuration File in C#*

```
Configuration config =
    ConfigurationManager.OpenExeConfiguration(ConfigurationUserLevel.None, "");
config.ConnectionStrings.ConnectionStrings.Add(
    new ConnectionStringSettings(
        "MyConnectionString",
        "Server=local; Database=Test; Password=myPassword; User Id=myUser;")
        );
config.Save();
```

Listing 4-8. *Saving Encrypted Data to a Configuration File in Visual Basic .NET*

```
Dim config as Configuration = _
   ConfigurationManager.OpenExeConfiguration(ConfigurationUserLevel.None, "")
config.ConnectionStrings.ConnectionStrings.Add( _
   New ConnectionStringSettings( _
     "MyConnectionString", _
     "Server=local; Database=Test; Password=myPassword; User Id=myUser;") _
     )
```

As you can see, yet another neat feature of .NET 2.0 is that configuration files can be edited directly through code. This was not possible to do in .NET 1.1 unless you resorted to editing the configuration file using an XmlDocument object. If you ran this code as is, it would probably throw an exception informing you that the KeySet was not found. What this means is that you first need to set up either a machine-level or user-level KeySet on the machine this code is being executed upon. The easiest way to do this would be to run the following at the command line:

```
aspnet_regiis -pc "MyKeys" -exp
```

Now with everything set up, if you ran the code shown in Listings 4-7 and 4-8 and opened the configuration file after execution, it would look like the code shown in Listing 4-9. Also note that if you're executing the code as a ConsoleApplication, these changes won't make it to App.Config but to ConsoleApplication1.exe.config, where ConsoleApplication1.exe is the name of the console application executable.

Listing 4-9. *Configuration File with Encrypted Section and Encrypted Data*

```
<configuration>
   <connectionStrings>
      <EncryptedData Type="http://www.w3.org/2001/04/xmlenc#Element"
         xmlns="http://www.w3.org/2001/04/xmlenc#">
   <EncryptionMethod Algorithm="http://www.w3.org/2001/04/xmlenc#tripledes-cbc" />
         <KeyInfo xmlns="http://www.w3.org/2000/09/xmldsig#">
            <EncryptedKey Recipient="" xmlns="http://www.w3.org/2001/04/xmlenc#">
      <EncryptionMethod Algorithm="http://www.w3.org/2001/04/xmlenc#rsa-1_5" />
               <KeyInfo xmlns="http://www.w3.org/2000/09/xmldsig#">
                  <KeyName>Rsa Key</KeyName>
               </KeyInfo>
               <CipherData>
                  <CipherValue>fquSeRPQvoa47qFzEys62yWC1VxNABD318DrCQc/hL6zLnuaG
                  GgQE6qxYSStHOccUntJ67HrDTjlpMOpRTxgXLLGzIq3vVLLMdKnRTE6eFAZcQe
                  pB7qBiK+PWuWTAcy4mFXfaHznPNiQNU4bDtkJCUO3j9FbLhUqeprSUCjOp1c=
                  </CipherValue>
               </CipherData>
            </EncryptedKey>
         </KeyInfo>
         <CipherData>
            <CipherValue>b/6ILwoFPKGop5jyGQfbHAuOoQ48M9JaHSYUJf1rTy4Tt1Kqr8qIYOx
            a7ufMFEXzdavBUE7V41+ul7oBQZK14UedkqvPPXXIRUNsqqJPkmtDDgombNPNaiAt2YV
```

```
        cL6339lw3NwNLAeRZlFOq5vqo9xvFAA//eyW13HkNvV14Bxm9rn7zNv4iQ5PCexOOi8T
        JJDMtUpetuYVccfYzuVwoK2LQTiqDJ/ILeVsiVfyGsRA=
        </CipherValue>
      </CipherData>
    </EncryptedData>
  </connectionStrings>

  <protectedData>
    <providers>
      <add name="MyProvider"
           type="System.Configuration.RsaProtectedConfigurationProvider"
           keyContainerName="MyKeys"
           useMachineContainer="true" />
    </providers>

    <protectedDataSections>
      <add name="connectionStrings"
         provider="MyProvider"
         inheritedByChildren="false"/>
    </protectedDataSections>
  </protectedData>
</configuration>
```

To retrieve the connection string, you merely have to use code that looks like this:

```
ConfigurationManager.ConnectionStrings["MyConnectionString"].ConnectionString
```

By doing so, the .NET Framework will automatically encrypt and decrypt the protected sections for you. Therefore, in .NET Framework 2.0, not only can you store connection strings in the configuration file in a separate dedicated section, you can also encrypt and decrypt them with almost no additional code. One important point to mention here is that the portion of your application that reads the connection strings (typically your main application) remains unchanged whether the connection strings are encrypted or not. What this means is that you could use unencrypted connection strings in development and encrypt them for production use—all this, without making any code changes!

So far, the examples you've seen demonstrate working with a SqlConnection object. However, all data providers have a valid connection object that works in a very similar fashion.

This would be a good time to refer back to Figure 2-1 and review the commonality between various connection objects in different .NET data providers.

Such common behavior and polymorphism, in the sense of object-oriented programming (OOP), between objects is good as it allows us to establish certain base classes and interfaces to wrap the common behavior or implementation in. It also allows us to program in a data provider–agnostic way, meaning that you, as a developer, don't care which data source you're connecting to. However, because every data source might have its own peculiarities, not only is different information needed to successfully establish a connection, but even when you do establish a connection successfully, each data source might, and often does, support different feature sets. These differences are not only applicable to connection objects, but also to other objects found in any data provider like the Command object, the Transaction object, and so on.

While the differences are handled in individual connection classes, such as SqlClient or OracleClient, the common behavior in ADO.NET 1.1 was enforced by the IDBConnection interface. The IDBConnection interface required any data provider's connection class to support a few basic minimum features such as ConnectionString, ConnectionTimeout, State, and so forth. Similarly, because all connection classes implement certain common logic, like the ability to dispose a connection after its use and perform a routine cleanup, ADO.NET 2.0 goes one step further and introduces the data provider factory model and a class called DbConnection, from which any connection class has to inherit. It also requires connection classes to implement the IDbConnection interface in order to maintain backward compatibility. As a matter of fact, the DbConnection class implements the IDbConnection interface. An additional advantage of implementing such base classes is the ability to query the system for all the data providers it might support and then hand the client the appropriate connection object for the selected data source.

The Common Behavior: IDbConnection

The common behavior of any connection object, like the ability to open a connection, close a connection, and determine its current state, is enforced by implementing the System.Data. IDbConnection interface. An ADO.NET connection object can be thought of as something that works with an external resource. What the connection object works with is not just an external resource; it's a resource that comes with an overhead in terms of performance, because connecting to a data source is one of the most overhead-enduring actions an application can perform. For this reason, it's important that a connection object implements IDisposable. IDisposable is the standard interface in .NET that defines a method named Dispose, which is used to release allocated resources—unmanaged ones in particular.

Note This is also enforced by the IDbConnection interface because it implements IDisposable.

The Dispose method on a connection object performs certain important cleanup jobs and is covered in greater detail later in this chapter.

The following is a list of various methods that IDbConnection requires the .NET data provider writer to implement:

- BeginTransaction: To ensure data consistency, most modern databases support the concept of transactions. Transactions define atomic operations, which operate in an all-or-nothing fashion. BeginTransaction is most commonly the function you need to call to begin a transaction on a database. This method is overloaded and one of its overloads allows you to specify the IsolationLevel this transaction will use. This transaction is different from the transactions implemented in the System.Transactions namespace. Transactions and isolation levels are covered in further depth in Chapter 11.

- ChangeDatabase: When connecting to a database server, one server might have multiple databases on it. The ChangeDatabase function allows you to change databases within the same server. Calling ChangeDatabase has less overhead than using a brand new connection object even with connection pooling turned on. The benefit, however, is limited to SQL Server since SQL Server uses a two-step connection process. The first step connects to the server and the second step connects to the requested catalog. By calling ChangeDatabase, you simply switch to another catalog.

- Open: The Open method is what opens a connection to the database and makes the connection ready to use. Open database connections cannot be pooled until they are explicitly closed or disposed, so it's important to open a database connection as late as possible and close it as early as you can.

- Close: Conversely, Close will close an open connection to the database. By calling Close, the underlying physical connection to the database is now ready to be pooled. Do note that disposing a connection object calls Close internally; but, in addition, it clears out the stateful information of the connection object, such as the connection string. What this means to you as an application developer is that, even though Close and Dispose both help in connection pooling, a closed connection can be reopened, whereas a disposed connection cannot be.

- CreateCommand: Interactions with the database are accomplished using Command objects. Command objects allow you to specify command text with various parameters. For a command to execute, it must know what database it will execute against. The CreateCommand method on a connection object will create a Command object that, when executed, will be executed on the connection object it was created from. Command objects are covered in depth in Chapter 5.

The following is a list of various properties that IDbConnection requires you to implement:

- ConnectionString: This property is used to specify various parameters that give sufficient information to the connection object to successfully open a connection to the database. You can also specify other information here to control the behavior of the connection object.

- ConnectionTimeout: Since the establishment of a connection is, at the very least, to a file and, in many cases, to a separate machine on the network, there could be issues such as timeouts or unsuccessful connection attempts due to network failures or other causes. ConnectionTimeout allows you to specify a number of seconds before the connection object gives up and throws an error. A value of 0 would indicate a limitless timeout and should be avoided. Do note, however, that CommandTimeouts are different from ConnectionTimeouts and, as of ADO.NET 2.0, CommandTimeouts cannot be configured at the connection level.

- Database: This property gets the name of the current database or the database to be used after the connection is opened.

- State: This allows the connection object to specify its current state. The most commonly used states are ConnectionState.Open and ConnectionState.Closed.

The Common Logic: DbConnection

The DbConnection class is a new class introduced in ADO.NET 2.0. It's marked abstract/MustInherit, which means you cannot instantiate it directly. A specific data provider's connection class is required to inherit from this class. The DbConnection class implements IDbConnection so you don't have to explicitly implement it. All this commonality allows you to develop applications that are somewhat agnostic to the exact data source type they might have to work with. The SQL will still be database specific though.

A .NET data provider's connection object would inherit from the DbConnection class and receive all the logic implemented in the base classes for free. It might decide to override a certain method's implementations to better suit its purposes, like the SqlConnection object overrides the Connection.Open method, whereas it builds upon the base class's SqlConnection.Dispose functionality.

High-Demand Applications

Sooner rather than later you'll find yourself writing ADO.NET code for a high-demand application. It could be a website or a highly concurrent system involving multiple real-time users. In a simpler single-user application, while keeping a connection open for an unwarranted long time might not have a serious impact on the database server performance, higher-demand applications pose different issues that you must consider within your architecture.

Earlier, I briefly touched on the fact that IDbConnection implements IDisposable. The IDisposable interface requires that the connection class implement the Dispose method where, by convention, all the cleanup of allocated resources happens.

In many complicated high-demand applications, you would probably want to use an industrial-strength database like SQL Server or Oracle as your backend data source. Under the wraps of data provider–specific connection objects like SqlConnection or OracleConnection, ADO.NET communicates with these databases across a network. Maintaining an open network connection and retrieving large amounts of data over the network is probably one of the most expensive operations a typical application needs to accomplish. Leading e-commerce websites and stock-trading applications typically have hundreds or even thousands of concurrent users requesting real-time interaction with a website or a server application. Most likely, it's not possible to let every individual connect to the database and keep his connection open for as long as he might need it. Thus, there is a problem.

Various data access architectures solve this dilemma by keeping a few ready-to-use open physical network connections and handing off currently not-in-use physical network connections to a request to open a database connection (like SqlConnection). In essence, this multiplexes fewer open physical connections over a number of DbConnection objects, via a mechanism called *connection pooling*, to create a facade of a highly available database while not using as many resources. Various data access architectures might even increase or shrink this pool of available open connections as the demands on the application change.

■Note It's important to realize that a SqlConnection or OracleConnection object instance isn't equivalent to having one physical connection to the database. The actual number of physically open connections is managed internally by ADO.NET using connection pooling. An actual physical connection is exposed to the end application for use through a specific DbConnection object, such as SqlConnection or OracleConnection.

In the next part of this chapter, you'll examine what connection pooling is and how it is implemented in ADO.NET. You'll see how to tweak connection pooling to fit your requirements and also understand the best practices about how to use connection pooling in a typical application.

Connection Pooling

In a highly concurrent/highly available–based application, it's important to realize that the majority of the time the user might hold an open connection and not actively use it because he is busy with other parts of the application. The application could essentially "time slice" his expensive resource—an open connection—and pool it between multiple users.

Using connection pooling with ADO.NET is really simple because you don't have to do anything to use connection pooling with the default settings; instead, you have to turn it off explicitly should you decide not to use it. For instance, for SqlClient, if you don't wish to pool your connections, you simply add the following key-value pair to your connection string:

```
Pooling=false;
```

Similarly, you can tweak connection-pooling settings by designating specific key-value pairs on the connection string. These are shown for SqlConnection in Table 4-1. As you saw earlier, in order to connect to a database, you need to specify a connection string. ADO.NET maintains a pool of open connections internally for each connection string. In other words, it maintains a collection of pools using the connection string as the key. When you request an open connection via the Open command on a connection object, ADO.NET internally checks to see if there's an unused physical database connection available. A physical database connection is ready to be pooled if no other user or portion of the application is actively using it. This means, for effective connection pooling, you must *open as late as possible, and close as early as you can.*

The real picture is a little more involved because ADO.NET makes decisions based on the application load and might maintain more than one open physical connection concurrently if it receives too many requests simultaneously. Alternatively, the number of open connections in a connection pool might decrease if the number of requested open connections is too low. There are default numbers set for these connection-pooling parameters, but they are configurable via the connection string. Table 4-1 shows the various connection-pooling parameters that can be set using the connection string.

Table 4-1. *SqlClient Connection Pooling Key-Value Pairs*

Name	Definition
Connection Lifetime	This parameter is useful in clustered environments. A value specified here will result in the connection being destroyed if the current time minus the creation time exceeds the connection lifetime specified. This allows a new server, brought online in a clustered environment, to start sharing the load immediately. The default value of 0 indicates an unlimited connection lifetime.
Connection Reset	This causes the connection to be reset every time it's pulled out of the pool for use. Specifically for Microsoft SQL Server 7.0, setting this to false avoids an extra database trip. In addition, the connection state itself is not reset. The default value is true.

(Continued)

Table 4-1. *(Continued)*

Name	Definition
Enlist	Setting this to true causes the pooler to automatically enlist the connection in the creating thread's current transaction context. The default value is true and other valid values are false, yes, and no.
Max Pool Size	This sets the upper limit beyond which if open connections are requested, they will have to wait for an existing connection to become available. The default value is 100.
Min Pool Size	This keeps a minimum number of connections available and ready to use. You might want to use this if you can incur the "always open" extra connection cost and you want to save the time it takes to connect to the database after a long period of inactivity. The default value is 0.
Pooling	As described before, this enables or disables pooling. The default value is true.

Let's play detective and verify the previous statements via a code example. The code shown in Listings 4-10 and 4-11 demonstrates a simple example of opening and closing the connection repeatedly with connection pooling turned off and on.

Listing 4-10. *Demonstrating Connection Pooling in C#*

```
SqlConnection testConnection =
   new SqlConnection
   ("Data Source=(local);Initial Catalog=Test;Integrated Security=SSPI;");
long startTicks = DateTime.Now.Ticks;

for (int i = 1; i <= 100; i++)
{
   testConnection.Open();
   testConnection.Close();
}

long endTicks = DateTime.Now.Ticks;
Console.WriteLine("Time taken : " + (endTicks - startTicks) + " ticks.");
testConnection.Dispose();
```

Listing 4-11. *Demonstrating Connection Pooling in Visual Basic .NET*

```
Dim testConnection As New SqlConnection( _
   "Data Source=(local);Initial Catalog=Test;Integrated Security=SSPI;")
Dim startTicks As Long = DateTime.Now.Ticks

For I As Integer = 1 To 100
   testConnection.Open()
   testConnection.Close()
Next
```

```
Dim endTicks As Long = DateTime.Now.Ticks
Console.WriteLine("Time taken : " & (endTicks - startTicks) & " ticks.")
testConnection.Dispose()
```

When the code runs, it produces output that looks like the following (the exact value will differ based on your machine's processing power and current running tasks):

```
Time taken : 400576 ticks.
```

Let's make a minor modification to this code and explicitly disable connection pooling like this:

C#

```
SqlConnection testConnection =
    new SqlConnection("Data Source=(local);Initial Catalog=Test;" +
    "Integrated Security=SSPI;Pooling=false");
```

VB.NET

```
Dim testConnection As New SqlConnection("Data Source=(local);" & _
    "Initial Catalog=Test;Integrated Security=SSPI;Pooling=false")
```

And now with no other modifications, when you run the code, the output looks like this:

```
Time taken : 7310512 ticks.
```

Even though the actual results will differ on your machine, the bottom line is that with connection pooling turned off, it took about 18 times longer to open and close 100 connections. This is so because with connection pooling explicitly turned off, every time you call the Open or Close method on the connection object, ADO.NET is actually opening and closing a database connection for you. With connection pooling turned on, it was barely pooling a handful of connections being used, probably as low as a single connection, to serve all the requests. This is because the application was making sure that it would close any unused connection as soon as it could. So, for the subsequent requests, ADO.NET could effectively pool the unused connections. As you can see, clearly this makes a big difference to the performance of your application!

So How Does It All Work?

Think of it this way: Beneath the DbConnection class, there's a broker class that maintains a pool of open connections. It has the responsibility of increasing or decreasing the actual number of open connections based on the demands of the application. To the broker class, every connection requested is uniquely identified by its corresponding connection string. So when any application on the same machine requests an open connection, it first checks its internal connection pool cache and if there is indeed an available connection, it hands it over. But if there isn't an available connection, it will create a new one (up to a configurable limit) and hand over the new connection.

Similarly, when any application is done using a connection and calls either Dispose or Close on the connection object, the broker class marks that connection as unused or unassigned but keeps it ready for a second user that might request it. The real implementation may be a little bit more complex, but this is the crux of the matter. The important part to realize here is that the caller of the Open method cannot possibly judge any difference between a pooled or unpooled connection, except maybe a much better performance.

The results of Listings 4-10 and 4-11 can also be verified by running the Performance Monitor. You can view the SQLServer:General Statistics\User Connections counter to verify how and how many actual connections are being established to the database. If you really want to shock yourself, you can create a new SqlConnection object, comment out the closing of the connection, and only open connections on newly created SqlConnection objects in rapid succession to view the connection usage of your application. You could even make it worse by not doing this in a loop so the created connection objects don't get garbage collected by falling out of scope at the end of the loop—which might be a scenario closer to a nonconnection-pooled high-demand application. Thus, it's *extremely* important that you close your connection as soon as possible and open as late as possible or the performance of your application will come grinding to its knees very quickly. Unfortunately, this is something that will happen only in load tests or in production, so it's important to architect your data access layer with this nuance in mind.

Deciding on the Right Pool Size

The right pool size depends on the kind of application you are working with. In most scenarios, it's wise to simply leave the default settings as they are. However, understanding that pools are maintained on individual client machines running ADO.NET, and not on the database server, is critical in making an informed decision about a pool size.

For ASP.NET applications, your pool is maintained on the web server. It makes absolutely no sense to disable connection pooling on an ASP.NET site. Though if you are running a large number of web heads over a Network Load Balanced architecture all connecting to the same database server, you must realize that the pool size, as far as the server is concerned, just got multiplied by the same number of web heads/web servers serving your website.

Similarly, if you have a number of application servers over a remoting connection or simply a web service, then the number of application servers will increase the number of active connections in the pool linearly.

■**Note** Too often I have seen a solution of a leaky application, i.e., an application that isn't responsibly closing the connections properly, being set a very large pool size. This isn't the right approach to a permanent acceptable solution. By doing so, you aren't fixing the actual problem, only giving yourself a little bit more time by masking the true problem. The true problem is to find the source of the leaky open connections and plug it.

This minor point of mention of "per client connection pool" becomes extremely important where you have a "cowboy-style" application (I just coined that word). A *cowboy-style application* is one that insists on connecting to the database directly, right from the user's desktop. There is no application server, web service, or website in the middle. In this circumstance, each client maintains a connection pool. This means, that with 1,000 clients, your database will suddenly come under 1,000 times the connection pool–size load. This situation will worsen rapidly, if you are unfortunate enough that your architecture is leaking open connections. It's for this reason that most .NET data providers that support connection pooling will give you fine-level control over the settings that dictate its behavior.

Now it may be tempting to hold one global DbConnection instance at each client and keep it open for the life of the application. The obvious problem with this is the inability of multiple threads to execute (at least reliably) multiple commands on that same connection at the same time. You can maintain Multiple Active Resultsets (MARS), but that is not quite the same thing as running parallel commands on one connection. This will become evident when you read about MARS in detail in Chapter 11.

Let's say that somehow you did architect a solution to the multiple parallel commands issue by implementing locks or semaphores on the one shared connection object; then it might be argued that a simple Windows Forms application could keep a connection open all the time, so, effectively, you could turn off connection pooling and live happily ever after.

While, in that specific situation, turning off connection pooling and actually holding an open connection object, and thus holding an open network or physical connection, might not make much of a performance difference, this locks you into an architecture where, as the needs of your application grow, you'll never be able to use an application server in order to access your database properly, via a data layer and connection pool. Not to mention, if your Windows Forms application crashes without explicitly closing a connection, it's now up to the garbage collector to do your cleanup for you. Unfortunately, the garbage collector fires its cleanup job on the basis of the unavailability of memory, and the SqlConnection object itself occupies very little memory. So the garbage collector blissfully ignores the fact that an open SqlConnection object is occupying significant system resources by holding onto an open connection.

This is something that you, as an architect or developer, will have to worry about. Or you could just not try and reinvent the wheel, and leave it all up to connection pooling to take care of it for you. Of course, remember to tweak the specific connection pool settings as needed if too many individual client pools seem to overload your server.

Corrupt Connection Pools

Now that you've seen the benefits of connection pooling, let's examine a complication that connection pools might introduce. Imagine a situation where an application has been running for a while. The application connects to a SQL Server database over the network. A nice and useful connection pool has been built with, say, 25 useful connections. Now some guy walks into the server room and trips over the power cord for the database server and accidentally reboots it. Quickly, he plugs it back in (and hopes nobody noticed a thing). There's now no way for the .NET CLR (Common Language Runtime), sitting on the application server or web server, to know that its connection pool is now corrupt. What's worse is that now when you request a connection to be opened, the connection pool broker class will simply hand you one of the connections because the connection pool broker class thinks what it's handing over to you is still a valid connection—little does it know that the connection no longer holds. Not only will the behavior from now on be unpredictable, but it's also probably occupying valuable system resources in the form of confused underlying network connections that are now actually dead. It's not until you execute a command on it that an exception will be thrown because the restarted SQL Server has no idea what connection you were on when the power failed. What's worse, this error will now be thrown at random on all of the remaining 24 connections in the corrupt connection pool.

In .NET 1.1, the only way to fix this would be to restart the application server. However, in .NET 2.0, two new static methods have been introduced for this purpose:

- `SqlConnection.ClearPool`: This method is used to clear a particular connection pool identified by the connection string passed as a parameter.

- `SqlConnection.ClearAllPools`: This method is used to clear all existing connection pools.

■Note It's important to note, however, that these two methods are not substitutes for closing all connections. Connections are just marked in an inconsistent state, and they are eventually garbage collected, but they are not explicitly closed. This mechanism shouldn't be used in place of properly disposing and closing your connections.

Closing Connections: Good Application Design

Earlier in this chapter you saw that a connection object must implement `IDisposable`. The `IDisposable.Dispose` method is, by convention, the method used for cleanup jobs for any object. While most good .NET programmers know to call `Dispose` if they see it, constructs exist in both C# and VB.NET, like the `using` block that automatically calls the `Dispose` method for you.

The ADO.NET connection object is no exception to the rule—it uses the `Dispose` method to clean up unallocated resources. In addition to cleaning up unallocated resources, `Dispose` calls `Close` on a connection object and makes it ready for reuse in a connection pool. In addition to calling `Close`, `Dispose` does a little more housekeeping work than `Close` might do. `Dispose` cleans the internal collections to clear out various settings, such as the connection string on a connection object, so it allows the garbage collector to reuse the memory used by the actual connection object; however, calling `Close` alone will make the actual underlying object available for reuse in a connection pool.

One of the most common ways to interact with a database is via a data access layer. A data access layer is nothing but a common set of classes that every portion of your application needs to go through in order to talk to the database. There are a few advantages of implementing a data access layer:

- The author of the data access classes ensures connections are disposed (and hence closed) as soon as possible.

- You can put performance metrics inside the data access layer.

- If there is, indeed, a connection leak (open connections being created without being closed) inside your data access layer, it can be traced and fixed easily.

An example of a data access layer is the Microsoft Data Access Application Block, which can be downloaded from Microsoft's website at `http://msdn.microsoft.com/library/en-us/dnbda/html/daab-rm.asp`. You might need to tweak it a little bit to suit your purposes, but it's a good starting point.

Within the data access layer, or outside if you choose not to implement one, you should use either `using` blocks or `try...catch...finally` constructs to always ensure your connections are disposed of properly.

Here's a description of the differences between calling the `Close` and `Dispose` methods, or none at all:

- Calling `Close` on a connection object enables the underlying connection to be pooled.

- Calling `Dispose` on a connection object alleviates the need for you to call `Close` on it explicitly. It not only ensures that the underlying connection can be pooled, but it also makes sure that allocated resources can now be garbage collected.

- Not calling either `Close` or `Dispose` will effectively kill your application performance by increasing the connection pool to a maximum limit, and then everyone will have to wait for the next available connection object. Not only that, but even when the open connections fall out of scope, they won't be garbage collected for a relatively long time because the connection object itself doesn't occupy that much memory—and the lack of memory is the sole criterion for the garbage collector to kick in and do its work.

In short, `Dispose` is the best option as it helps garbage collection and connection pooling, `Close` is second best option as it helps only connection pooling, and not calling either `Close` or `Dispose` is so bad that you shouldn't even go there.

Summary

In this chapter, you examined the various facets involved in being able to connect to a database through ADO.NET. You examined the class structure and learned how to establish a simple connection by specifying a connection string. Because it could be difficult to remember all those parameter name keywords, you looked at two alternate mechanisms for easily coming up with connection strings and a standard way of securing connection strings. Finally, you learned about connecting to the database in high-demand applications using connection pools. You saw an example of how using a connection pool could vastly affect application performance and what was necessary to do in applications to take advantage of connection pools.

Now that you know how to connect to a data source, in the next chapter you'll learn about how to execute commands and retrieve data from the data source in a connected mode.

Next, you'll look at data readers and commands in ADO.NET.

∎∎∎

CHAPTER 5

Retrieving Data in a Connected Fashion

The data source for an application is typically a dedicated external resource; it could be a file or server software like Microsoft SQL Server or Oracle running on a dedicated server, accessed over a network connection.

In the last chapter you read about establishing a connection with such an external resource. Even though the data itself might reside in an external resource, i.e., the data source, the data is eventually mapped into object representations of the entities/types of the data source, and the logic to process upon the object representations of the data resides within the application itself. Therefore, to process data, the application needs to retrieve the parts of the data from the data source, which the application should process.

As you saw in Chapters 1 and 2, ADO.NET is split into two main halves: the connected and disconnected. This chapter will concern itself with the connected fashion of retrieving data, which involves connecting to the data source over an ADO.NET connection, sending commands, and retrieving the results while remaining connected to the database or external data source.

The need for an external data source arises because applications tend to be better at storing the logic that will process the data rather than storing the actual data. It's not uncommon for an enterprise application's data to span several gigabytes, but usually, at a given time, the application is processing only a small subset of the data. Thus, the application needs a way to communicate with the data source requesting the subset of the data that it's interested in at a given time.

Communicating with the Data Source

After a connection has been made, communicating with the data source involves two operations:

1. Specifying what data the application is interested in.

2. Receiving results back.

Specifying what data the application is interested in involves sending a command/request via a predefined language or format. Even though ADO.NET doesn't limit you to a particular language or syntax, the most commonly accepted format of data source query language is a form of the Structured Query Language (SQL). Microsoft SQL Server supports T-SQL whereas Oracle chooses to support PL/SQL, but both are text-based and their syntaxes and purposes are similar, although not exactly the same.

In SQL, you have the ability to query your database by specifying some sort of selection logic via a SELECT command, or you can manipulate data using an INSERT, UPDATE, or DELETE command. If your database administrator has given you the appropriate access rights, you might also be allowed to manipulate data schema information or perform administrative tasks on your database. The textual strings comprise what is collectively referred to as *database* commands. In this chapter, however, we'll concentrate mostly on SELECT commands and leave the other Data Manipulation Language (DML) commands like INSERT, UPDATE, and DELETE for Chapter 9.

SQL is a powerful language and the command itself could take many shapes. The command sent to the database via ADO.NET could take any of the following forms:

```
-- Simple Select Command
SELECT useraddress, userphone FROM users WHERE username = 'John';
-- Parameterized command for reuse and flexibility
SELECT useraddress, userphone FROM users WHERE username = @UserName;
-- Stored Procedure Execution.
EXEC sp_getUserAddressPhone(@UserName);
```

ADO.NET supports the listed command forms, and you can execute them using an ADO.NET command object.

Let's get familiar with the command object by introducing an example in which you can query the database using a simple command.

Retrieving a Scalar Value

To query your database, you need to use a command object. The discussion in this chapter is mostly centered on using Microsoft SQL Server, but the concepts apply to any of the commonly found ADO.NET data providers. The generic command object in ADO.NET is represented by the DbCommand class, and the Microsoft SQL Server–specific command object is represented by the System.Data.SqlClient.SqlCommand class, which inherits from DbCommand. This would be a good time to quickly glance back at Figures 2-3 and 2-4 presented in Chapter 2. This will give you a visual understanding of the inheritance structure between SqlCommand, DbCommand, and other such classes.

Creating a command object is simple. You need to instantiate the object using any one of the four supported overloads. In its simplest form, the code can look like this:

C#

```
SqlCommand testCommand = new SqlCommand();
```

VB.NET

```
Dim testCommand As New SqlCommand()
```

Even though this code compiles, it doesn't really do anything. Now, let's take a step back and think about the minimum requirements for any command to execute successfully:

- It must execute against a database—but we didn't specify which connection this command will use to execute.

- We need to specify which action the command performs—but we didn't specify the command text (yet).

So at the very least, you need to specify the connection the command object should use and the action it should perform. Let's start with the first part of the information you must specify—the database the command will execute against.

Which Database to Execute Against

In the exercises in this chapter, you'll be connecting to a Microsoft SQL Server 2005 database named "Test" running on your local machine, using Windows authentication. This database will have one table called TestDemo with data, as shown in Figure 5-1.

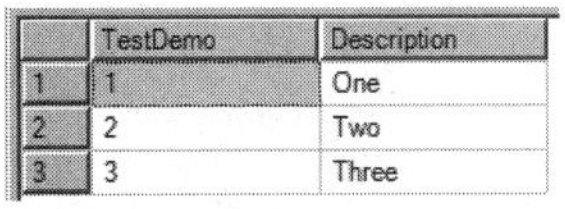

TestDemo	Description
1	One
2	Two
3	Three

Figure 5-1. *TestDemo for examples in this chapter*

Assuming that you have set up such a database on your machine, you can start writing your first exercise. You can either create the application by following the steps here, or you can find it in the Downloads section of the Apress website (http://www.apress.com) as Example 5.1:

1. Start up Visual Studio and create a new Console Application project named "Example 5.1."

2. Open the Program.cs class file (C#) or the Module1.vb module file (VB.NET).

3. Import the relevant disconnected and connected namespaces:

   C#

   ```
   using System.Data;
   using System.Data.SqlClient;
   ```

   VB.NET

   ```
   Imports System.Data
   Imports System.Data.SqlClient
   ```

4. Create and set up the SqlConnection object in the Main procedure:

   C#

   ```
   string connectionString =
       "Data Source=(local);Initial Catalog=Test;Integrated Security=SSPI;"
   using (SqlConnection testConnection = new SqlConnection(connectionString))
   {
       // Code will be added here
   }
   ```

VB.NET

```vbnet
Dim connectionString As String = _
    "Data Source=(local);Initial Catalog=Test;Integrated Security=SSPI;"
Using testConnection As New SqlConnection(connectionString)
    ' Code will be added here
End Using
```

Note that because you are making use of the using block, you don't need to explicitly call Close, because that will be called as a part of Dispose for you at the end of the using block. With the connection set up, you need to create a new SqlCommand object and specify the connection information. This can be done as shown in Listing 5-1 or 5-2 (within the using/Using block created in Example 5.1).

Listing 5-1. *Three Possible Ways of Instantiating the Command Object in C#*

```csharp
// Instantiate Command and specify Connection in two steps
SqlCommand testCommand = new SqlCommand();
testCommand.Connection = testConnection;
// Instantiate Comamnd and specify Connection in single step
SqlCommand testCommand = new SqlCommand("<<commandtext here>>", testConnection);
// Using CreateCommand method
SqlCommand testCommand = testConnection.CreateCommand();
```

Listing 5-2. *Three Possible Ways of Instantiating the Command Object in Visual Basic .NET*

```vbnet
' Instantiate Command and specify Connection in two steps
Dim testCommand As New SqlCommand()
testCommand.Connection = testConnection
' Instantiate Comamnd and specify Connection in single step
Dim testCommand As New SqlCommand("<<commandtext here>>", testConnection)
' Using CreateCommand method
testCommand = testConnection.CreateCommand()
```

Any of these three methods associate the testCommand SqlCommand object with the testConnection SqlConnection object. This is necessary since this is how you tell a command object which connection and, thus, which data source to use.

You might ask, "Why does ADO.NET even let me instantiate a command object without connection information?" This is so because it's not uncommon to wrap the command logic in various command objects and use them between various data sources. In other words, you might choose to reuse the same command object between different data sources. Of course, in doing so, you would have to disconnect and connect with various data sources, which emphasizes the disconnected flexibility that ADO.NET gives you.

Yet another method of creating a command object allows you to specify the transaction, in which you can wrap the commands executed using the command object:

```csharp
SqlCommand testCommand = new SqlCommand("...", connection, transaction);
```

This constructor overload will be discussed in further depth in Chapters 10 and 11.

As you might have figured out, we haven't actually specified which data to retrieve yet, and the first parameter in the second method of Listing 5-1 is an empty string with value "<<*commandtext here*>>". This is where the command text should be specified, which is sent to the data source once the command object is executed. So, no matter which of the three methods shown in Listing 5-1 you use to create the command object, you need to specify the command text. This is covered in the next section, "What to Execute."

What to Execute

The SELECT query your command object should hold is executed against the TestDemo table in the Test database. The command object should retrieve the number of rows in the TestDemo table using the SQL statement SELECT COUNT(*) FROM TestDemo, and it's done in any of the following ways:

C#

```
// Instantiate Command and specify command text in two steps
SqlCommand testCommand = new SqlCommand();
testCommand.CommandText = "SELECT COUNT(*) FROM TestDemo";
// Instantiate Command and specify command text in single step
SqlCommand testCommand = new SqlCommand("SELECT COUNT(*) FROM TestDemo");
```

VB.NET

```
' Instantiate Command and specify command text in two steps
Dim testCommand As New SqlCommand()
testCommand.CommandText = "SELECT COUNT(*) FROM TestDemo"
' Instantiate Command and specify command text in single step
Dim testCommand As New SqlCommand("SELECT COUNT(*) FROM TestDemo")
```

In addition, you can specify both the connection and the command text in a single line of code. This is what Example 5.1 in the code download uses:

C#

```
SqlCommand testCommand =
    new SqlCommand("SELECT COUNT(*) FROM TestDemo",testConnection);
```

VB.NET

```
Dim testCommand As New SqlCommand( _
    "SELECT COUNT(*) FROM TestDemo", testConnection)
```

Another piece of information you'd need to specify is the CommandType property on the command object. The default value is CommandType.Text, so in this case you don't need to worry about that. However, if, for instance, you were using a stored procedure instead, you'd then need to set CommandType to CommandType.StoredProcedure.

The code isn't complete until the command is actually executed and you see the results. Now that you have specified enough information for the command object, it's time to execute it and retrieve the results.

Executing a Command to Retrieve Results

As you saw in Chapter 4, the SqlConnection class inherits from the DbConnection class, which implements IDbConnection (see also Figure 2-1 from Chapter 2), and the most commonly used ADO.NET objects follow the same paradigm. So, the command class implements the IDbCommand interface and inherits from the DbCommand class. Actually, DbCommand implements IDbCommand (see Figures 2-2 and 2-3 from Chapter 2), which also means that the ExecuteScalar method is accessible using the SqlCommand class for executing a command that returns only a single result. The single result can only be a value, not a result set, so the ExecuteScalar method is what you need to retrieve the total number of rows in the TestDemo table.

Before you can call the ExecuteScalar method, the connection on which you execute the command must be open and available or else you'll get an exception. In this case, it means you need to open the connection, for which all you need to do is call the Open method on the connection object. The ExecuteScalar method returns a value of data type Object and should be called like this:

C#

```
int numResults = (int) testCommand.ExecuteScalar();
```

VB.NET

```
Dim numResults As Integer = CInt(testCommand.ExecuteScalar())
```

1. Add a call to the ExecuteScalar method to the code created in Example 5.1 so far.

2. Make sure you open the connection object before you execute the ExecuteScalar method, and close it afterwards.

3. Output the result of the ExecuteScalar method to the console, making the final code look like Listing 5-3 or 5-4.

Listing 5-3. *Executing a Simple Command in C#*

```
string connectionString =
    "Data Source=(local);Initial Catalog=Test;Integrated Security=SSPI;"

using (SqlConnection testConnection = new SqlConnection(connectionString))
{
    SqlCommand testCommand =
        new SqlCommand("SELECT COUNT(*) FROM TestDemo",testConnection);
    testConnection.Open();
    int numResults = (int) testCommand.ExecuteScalar();
    Console.WriteLine("Total number of rows in TestDemo: " + numResults);
    testConnection.Close();
}

Console.Read();
```

Listing 5-4. *Executing a Simple Command in Visual Basic .NET*

```
Dim connectionString As String = _
    "Data Source=(local);Initial Catalog=Test;Integrated Security=SSPI;"

Using testConnection As New SqlConnection(connectionString)
    Dim testCommand As New SqlCommand( _
        "SELECT COUNT(*) FROM TestDemo", testConnection)
    testConnection.Open()
    Dim numResults As Integer = CInt(testCommand.ExecuteScalar())
    Console.WriteLine("Total number of rows in TestDemo: " & numResults)
    testConnection.Close()
End Using

Console.Read()
```

When you compile and run the application, it produces the following output:

```
Total number of rows in TestDemo: 3
```

As expected, the application correctly reports the number of rows in the TestDemo table.

Even though Example 5.1 creates a fully functional ADO.NET application, it's obviously not very complex. Usually, in querying data sources, the results to a query are in the form of rows and columns, which is also commonly referred to as a *result set*.

So now, let's create an application that helps you retrieve a result set.

Retrieving a Result Set

As you saw in the previous section, ExecuteScalar is good for retrieving a single scalar value from a SELECT statement. So the natural question is, "What can you do to retrieve an entire result set?"

A full result set is obviously the result of a command such as SELECT * FROM TESTDEMO specified as the command text for a command object. For an object to qualify as a valid ADO.NET command object, it needs to implement the IDBCommand interface. One of the methods that the IDBCommand interface requires you to implement is the ExecuteReader method. ExecuteReader is the method that gives you access to the multiple rows in a result set. As you'll see later, ExecuteReader also gives you the ability to browse through multiple result sets using the NextResult method, which typically might be the result of a batched query (SQL Server) or multiple REF CURSORs (Oracle).

ExecuteReader returns an object of IDataReader data type, and IDataReader allows you to iterate through the various rows and columns in a result set in a read-only/forward-only fashion.

The IDataReader interface also implements IDataRecord and IDisposable interfaces. As mentioned in Chapter 4, IDisposable requires you to implement a method called Dispose that ensures the freeing, releasing, or resetting of unmanaged resources. On the other hand, the IDataRecord interface represents an individual record in ADO.NET. So you can safely assume that IDataRecord is the minimum functionality that any row representation in ADO.NET must implement. Here are a few important methods IDataRecord implements:

- Get[*DataType*]: Please note that the full name of the method, or rather methods, depends on the value you want to retrieve; say you wish to retrieve a Boolean value, you have a method called GetBoolean. If you wish to retrieve a Byte value, you have the GetByte method. In fact, there are methods for all intrinsic .NET data types. If you're unsure of the data type contained in a column, you have a generic GetValue method that would return an Object data type. All of the methods mentioned here accept an Int32 parameter. The Int32 value is the column ordinal, i.e., the number of the column within a row/record to retrieve a value from. Given that the ordering of the columns is zero-based, retrieving a value from the first column requires you specify 0 as the column ordinal.

- GetName: If you need the name of a specific column, you can use this method by passing the column ordinal. This method works conversely to the GetOrdinal method.

- GetOrdinal: If you need the ordinal of a specific column, you can use this method by passing the column name. This method works conversely to the GetName method.

- IsDbNull: Databases are different from .NET in that they can store null values in integers and other intrinsic types. Even though .NET 2.0 has introduced the concept of nullable value types, the IsDbNull method is used to check if a column value is represented as null/Nothing in the database. You'd still want to use this method instead of assigning the column value directly to a nullable value type because if the column holds a null value an exception is thrown. Due to performance reasons, a better alternative to using IsDbNull is to compare the retrieved value with System.DBNull.Value instead.

Now, given that you have an IDataRecord type of variable, you could access a given column using either the ordinal of the column you wish to query or specifying the name of the column you wish to query. So you could access a given column in the IDataRecord in either of the following two ways:

C#

```
IDataRecordInstance["MyColumn"]; // Using Column Name
IDataRecordInstance[0] ; // Using the column ordinal
```

VB.NET

```
IDataRecordInstance("MyColumn"); ' Using Column Name
IDataRecordInstance(0); 'Using the column ordinal
```

You might ask, "Why would you ever access a column value using the column ordinal, making your code look cryptic, instead of using the name of the column?" Well, only for performance reasons. Retrieving using the column ordinal performs far better than retrieving using the column name. That makes sense because the computer finds it easier to look through Int32 data types (4 bytes) rather than strings. In addition, since strings are immutable objects, every time you create a string it ends up eating a little bit more memory, thus a string indexer in a loop would consume all that much extra memory as many times as the loop might have run. This, of course, means that your code will look a bit more cryptic because you're using column ordinals rather than column names as strings.

In this situation specifically, the GetOrdinal method is especially useful. Given the name of a particular column, you can retrieve the column name at runtime and use that instead.

This is especially useful if you retrieve a collection of IDataRecord objects and you're iterating through them in a loop and all you know in advance is the column name, not the column ordinal. In the next section, you'll examine retrieving more than one row where all this will become clear—but more on that in just a bit.

▪Note For performance reasons, you should try and use the Int32 indexer in a loop instead of the string indexer. You can use the GetOrdinal and GetName methods to perform the conversion between column name and ordinal, and vice versa.

To fetch an entire result set, you need a method that gives you a collection of IDataRecord objects. The DbCommand.ExecuteReader method does exactly that. It returns a DbDataReader object.

So, given that you want to execute the query, SELECT * FROM TESTDEMO, you need to execute the ExecuteReader method.

To query for a result set instead of a scalar value, you also need a new SQL query command. The new SQL query command is the command text for the SqlCommand object, so you need new command text:

C#

```
SqlCommand testCommand =
    new SqlCommand("SELECT * FROM TESTDEMO",testConnection);
```

VB.NET

```
Dim testCommand As New SqlCommand( _
    "SELECT * FROM TESTDEMO", testConnection)
```

Now that you're getting back more than one row, an integer obviously won't be enough to hold the returned data. Instead of the integer, the object you'll use to read the data from the database is the SqlDataReader object, which implements IDataReader and inherits from DBDataReader. Accordingly, you need to make changes to your code. The following code can also be found as a part of the code download in Example 5.2:

C#

```
SqlDataReader sqlDr = testCommand.ExecuteReader(CommandBehavior.CloseConnection);
```

VB.NET

```
Dim sqlDr As New SqlDataReader(CommandBehavior.CloseConnection)
```

Now if you raised your eyebrows here and asked, "Why didn't ADO.NET just return a collection of IDataRecords instead?" that is, indeed, a very good question. There are mainly two reasons for that which will become clear as you read further, but I will mention them here briefly:

- First, the `SqlDataReader` is not a disconnected cache of `IDataRecords`. It does, however, give you the ability to return a disconnected cache (as you'll see shortly), but its default behavior is to read a little bit ahead of what you're requesting yet still remain connected to the database for any additional rows that might match the `SqlCommand` executed.

- Second, `SqlDataReader` is a lot more versatile than, say, a collection of `IDataRecords` would have been. Not only does it let you return multiple result sets, for larger data columns like blobs, it even supports a sequential access that allows you to read that particular row/column into a stream on demand. Pre-loading all that into an `IDataRecords` collection would have been less than ideal in many situations.

Also, you might notice that the code is passing a parameter to `ExecuteReader` here. Even though an overload exists that allows you to not pass this parameter, passing this parameter ensures that the underlying connection is closed once you are done with it and have closed the `SqlDataReader`. There are a few other options (command behaviors) you can specify to the `ExecuteReader` method. Here are the various command behaviors available:

- `Default`: Functionally the same as `ExecuteReader()`.

- `CloseConnection`: When the command is done executing, both the `DataReader` and the connection are closed. Now it's notable that `DataReader.Close` populates the final results of the query, like number of `RecordsAffected`, etc. So for complicated queries, the close process might take a while to execute. In such cases, you might want to call `DataReader.Cancel` instead and not use this parameter.

- `KeyInfo`: This parameter instructs the data reader to retrieve only column and primary-key information.

- `SchemaOnly`: This parameter returns only column information.

- `SequentialAccess`: This specifies that you'll read the data from the data reader sequentially. You might want to do this when you're reading large amounts of data like blobs or big XML chunks as varchars. The `OleDbDataReader`, however, will let you reread the column value until reading past it, whereas the `SqlDataReader` will not. Also, columns will need to be sequentially accessed.

- `SingleResult`: You can specify a batched query with multiple results and use the `NextResult` to move to the next result set. `SingleResult` returns only the first result set.

- `SingleRow`: This fetches only one row per result set. It's important to note, however, that this would block command execution and you would be responsible for calling `SqlDataReader.Close`.

Given that accessing a result set requires you to deal with `SqlDataReader`, which is a different kind of object, you need a new way of accessing and reading the `SqlDataReader`. Your reading logic would now look like Listing 5-5 or 5-6.

Listing 5-5. *Reading the Results from a SqlDataReader in C#*

```
if (sqlDr.HasRows)
{
    while (sqlDr.Read())
```

```
   {
      Console.WriteLine("TestDemo: " + sqlDr.GetInt32(0)
         + " and Description : " + sqlDr.GetString(1));
   }
}
```

Listing 5-6. *Reading the Results from a SqlDataReader in Visual Basic .NET*

```
If sqlDr.HasRows Then
   While sqlDr.Read
      Console.WriteLine("TestDemo: " & sqlDr.GetInt32(0) & _
         " and Description : " & sqlDr.GetString(1))
   End While
End If
```

In this code, using the HasRows property, you first check and see if the data reader returned any rows in the one result set you expect.

If, indeed, there are rows available, you start iterating through those rows in a forward-only fashion by calling the Read method. This is because the cursor in the result set is placed at the front of the first row, so to read that row you have to call the Read method.

And while your data reader object sqlDr is focused on a particular row, you can retrieve various column values out of that row by calling the GetInt32 and GetString methods.

When you compile and run the application, it produces the output shown in Figure 5-2.

Figure 5-2. *Results of using ExecuteReader to iterate through a result set*

It's important to note that the data reader gives you no way of going backward in the result set, nor does it give you any ability to edit the results. What you have is a *read-only/forward-only* method that is continuously connected to the database.

You might want to run a quick test on a larger result set being read into a SqlDataReader. Set a breakpoint after, say, the first execution of SqlDataReader.Read, and stop the underlying SQL Server and continue to iterate through the data reader. You might be surprised to learn that even with the database stopped, the SqlDataReader continues to retrieve results. Even though this behavior might appear surprising, it is, indeed, logical. The best way to imagine a data reader is as a hose with two ends. One end is in the application and the other is in the database. Even if someone turns the hose off at the database, for a short while results will continue coming in. If you increase the number of results returned by a few thousand rows, you'll notice that the data reader will eventually throw an exception informing you of the closed connection.

What this also means is that while a data reader is running, you are keeping a physical connection busy serving your request. So if you have logic that executes on every row, the physical connection will now remain open for the time the logic runs, plus the time it takes for you to retrieve the results out of the database.

As you saw in Chapter 4, the longer you keep your connections open, the worse your connection pooling performance will be. What you really need in such a situation is a disconnected cache of objects representing each row—you need a true collection of IDataRecords.

Such a collection might be useful if you want to pass the collected data to a data-binding UI, or do any other processing. This might be useful in the situation where you wish to read as fast as possible out of the database (hence, use a data reader), but the processing you might need to do on the results takes a long time and it keeps the connection object open for an inordinately long duration, thus nullifying any performance gains you might have achieved by using a data reader. You need a way to quickly iterate through a data reader's results and store them for processing purposes, and close the connection so someone else can use it.

Querying a Result Set for Storage

In the previous section, you saw how the data reader allows you to iterate through a collection of rows in a result set. What if you wanted to use this data for data-binding or number-crunching purposes? If it took you a long time to work on the data while in connected mode, you'd be forced to keep the connection open which would negatively impact connection pooling performance. Thus, when you might need to do significant processing between each iterated row, you should first try to read all the rows you can and close the underlying connection. Once you have the data, then you can start processing it.

The SqlDataReader class contains a method called GetEnumerator. What GetEnumerator allows you to do is use it in a foreach construct. In the foreach construct, the enumerator returns the objects sequentially that the enumerator holder is a collection of. In the case of SqlDataReader, the enumerator will return DbDataRecords one by one.

Let's examine this in Example 5.3 in the associated code download, or you can simply follow these steps:

1. Create a Windows Forms application.

2. Throw a DataGridView on the Form1 of the application, and name it myDataGrid. Also, format it to your favorite style.

3. Throw a button on the form and call it btnPopulate. Change the text to "Populate Arraylist".

4. If you wish, set various other "make the form pretty" properties, such as resize it properly, make it FixedSingle window style, disable the Maximize button, set the controls properly, etc. The form should look like Figure 5-3 in Design mode.

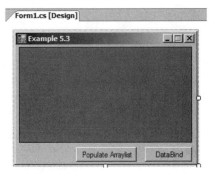

Figure 5-3. *Example 5.3's form in Design mode*

5. Double-click btnPopulate to open the code view with the cursor placed at the function that will be called when you click on the button when the form is running.

6. At this location, add the code shown in Listings 5-7 and 5-8.

Listing 5-7. *Creating a Disconnected Cache of DbDataRecords in C#*

```
string connectionString =
    "Data Source=(local);Initial Catalog=Test;Integrated Security=SSPI";
using (SqlConnection testConnection = new SqlConnection(connectionString))
{
    SqlCommand testCommand =
        new SqlCommand("SELECT * FROM TESTDEMO", testConnection);
    testConnection.Open();
    SqlDataReader sqlDr =
        testCommand.ExecuteReader(CommandBehavior.CloseConnection);

    if (sqlDr.HasRows)
    {
        foreach (DbDataRecord rec in sqlDr)
        {
            dbRecordsHolder.Add(rec); // dbRecordsHolder is an ArrayList
        }
    }
} // testConnection.Dispose is called automatically
```

Listing 5-8. *Creating a Disconnected Cache of DbDataRecords in Visual Basic .NET*

```
Dim connectionString As String = _
  "Data Source=(local);Initial Catalog=Test;Integrated Security=SSPI"
Using testConnection As SqlConnection = New SqlConnection(connectionString)
    Dim testCommand As SqlCommand = _
      New SqlCommand("SELECT * FROM TESTDEMO", testConnection)
    testConnection.Open()
    Dim sqlDr As SqlDataReader = _
```

```
            testCommand.ExecuteReader(CommandBehavior.CloseConnection)
    If sqlDr.HasRows Then
        For Each rec As DbDataRecord In sqlDr
            dbRecordsHolder.Add(rec) ' dbRecordsHolder is an ArrayList
        Next
    End If
End Using ' testConnection.Dispose is called automatically
```

7. Finally, add another button to the form, call it btnDataBind, change its text to DataBind, and double-click it to add the following code:

C#

```
myDataGrid.DataSource = dbRecordsHolder;
```

VB.NET

```
myDataGrid.DataSource = dbRecordsHolder
```

Let's examine what the code in Listings 5-7 and 5-8 does. It creates a command and fetches a data reader just like the console application you saw in Example 5.2; however, what is new this time around is that, instead of retrieving our data using the "Get" functions, you instead enumerated through various DbDataRecords and put those into an ArrayList called dbRecordsHolder. This ArrayList exists as a private variable in our class and is instantiated in the constructor as you can see in the associated code download. Since the ArrayList object is directly data-bindable, you can simply data bind it with myDataGrid as shown in step 7. Do note, however, that in an ASP.NET application, you can data bind the data reader directly.

Interestingly, if you now click Populate Arraylist, the ArrayList is filled up and the connection is closed because Dispose is called on the connection object. So at that point, you have all the data in the ArrayList, which is completely disconnected from the database. So what you're binding to the data grid is, indeed, disconnected from the database. The biggest advantage of this is that you didn't keep the SqlConnection open while your application was busy data binding with the UI.

The practical upshot of not having to keep the SqlConnection open while you were data binding is that you kept the connection open for as little time as possible. This results in much better connection pooling performance.`

Compile and run the application. Click Populate DataGrid first and then DataBind. The output looks like that shown in Figure 5-4.

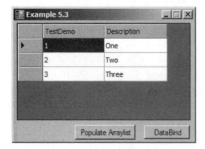

Figure 5-4. *A DbDataRecords ArrayList databound with a DataGridView*

Also note that, now as you try to update this data via the DataGridView, the DataGridView knows that this object is not editable and shows the data in read-only mode.

You've briefly brushed against the disconnected mode of storing data. You'll see a deeper disconnected data access mode discussion in Chapter 6, but for now let's return to the connected data retrieval mode discussion.

So far, the examples that you have seen in this chapter have involved querying the TestDemo table with two columns and three rows. However, it's not uncommon to see tables with tens of thousands of rows in them. As an experiment, you might want to try and change the command text to point to a larger table and run the code from Example 5.3 once again. You'll notice that while the command executes, the UI finds it difficult to even repaint itself because its main thread is busy executing the SqlCommand.

Getting back to this exercise and the discussion of retrieving data in a connected fashion, let's now pose the questions: "What if you had a large number of records (say 500,000) to retrieve? Will that freeze up your UI for the few seconds you're executing the command?" Or, "What if you had a report that takes 15 minutes to run? Could you execute the command that retrieves data for the report and alert the user when the results are available?" In other words, you wish to execute the command asynchronously, you wish to ask it to execute, and you wish to keep your main thread free for other requests—such as repainting itself, or responding to user input.

Before I talk about how to execute a SqlCommand asynchronously, let's be clear about what I mean by executing a command asynchronously.

Imagine that I am expecting an urgent courier package delivery today. One of my options is to sit at my doorstep and wait for the courier package. Another option is to go to work and ask my neighbor's teenager son to watch for the package for me and call me when it arrives.

In the first case, I will have to sit at the doorstep and do the very mundane task of sitting and waiting until the courier delivery driver shows up with my package. While it would work, it's a terrible waste of my day. This is the equivalent of *executing a task synchronously*. I'm continuously waiting for the driver and cannot do anything else in the meantime.

The second case is where I don't wait for results myself. Instead, I let someone else do that job for me, who will let me know (callback) when the package is there. In the meantime, I can concern myself with other important tasks. This is the equivalent of *executing a task asynchronously*.

Now, let's apply this paradigm to a long-running SqlCommand.

Querying Large Result Sets Asynchronously

In the previous two sections, you saw how to retrieve a result set using a data reader. The exercises ran very well because you had only three rows in your result set. But what if you had 100,000 rows? Could you use the previous code? Sure you could. The only problem is that the minute or two it will take for the previous command to get executed, the calling thread will be locked. If that thread happens to be the thread your UI was created on (say in a single threaded application like Example 5.3), your UI wouldn't even be able to repaint itself. The impression the user will get is that your application is "hung" and he might try and "End Task" your application.

In .NET 1.1, you could've gotten around this problem by firing off another thread, creating the data reader on that thread instead, and then having that thread notify the main thread that it was ready to retrieve the data. The right way to then show the data would be to use the Form.Invoke method to switch thread contexts and then data bind the fetched data on the UI in the context of the thread the UI was created upon.

If you didn't have to read the previous paragraph at least twice to understand what I just said, you are probably a really advanced .NET programmer. And if you did find yourself scratching your head a little bit, take heart because this was obviously a fairly complicated work-around to a situation that might occur much too often. Keeping that in mind, .NET 2.0 introduced asynchronous execution on many commands using the popular `Begin`/`End` methods and `IAsyncResult` data types.

■**Note** Never update the UI on a thread other than the thread the UI was created upon. This might cause the thread to update a textbox the user is typing data into. As a matter of fact, if you try doing this in .NET 2.0, you'll actually get a `System.InvalidOperationException`.

The code from Example 5.3 can be easily modified to use the asynchronous command execution method instead. But before you make any modifications to the code, first let's see what it will take to change the existing example to make it asynchronous, instead of the currently synchronous command execution.

First, you need a query that will take longer to execute. One quick way of ensuring that you have enough records that will take a while to retrieve is to simply execute the following SQL statement on your `TestDemo` table a few times:

```
INSERT INTO TESTDEMO (DESCRIPTION) (SELECT DESCRIPTION FROM TESTDEMO)
```

■**Note** In a production application, after such heavy insertion into the database, you might want to execute `UPDATE STATISTICS` on the given table to ensure fast selects.

Now that you have a query that takes longer to execute, your intention is that when the user clicks on Populate Arraylist, instead of blocking the UI, you instead use the `BeginExecuteReader` method of the `SqlCommand` object and pass it a callback method and the command object. The callback method is what will be called when the command execution completes. By doing so, we are telling the `BeginExecuteReader` method to "Go ahead and begin executing the method to get me a data reader, and when you are done, please call my callback, and also please remember to return this command object to me so I can remember what we were talking about."

Let's see how this looks in code. You can follow these four steps, or look at Example 5-4 in the associated code download for this chapter.

1. Starting with the code you have written for Example 5.3, replace the call to `ExecuteReader` with a call to `BeginExecuteReader` as shown here:

   C#

   ```csharp
   AsyncCallback callback = new AsyncCallback(DataReaderIsReady);
   IAsyncResult asyncresult =
       testCommand.BeginExecuteReader(callback, testCommand);
   ```

VB.NET

```
Dim callback as AsyncCallback = new AsyncCallback(DataReaderIsReady)
Dim asyncresult as IAsyncResult = _
  testCommand.BeginExecuteReader(callback, testCommand)
```

The biggest advantage of this approach is that since calling `BeginExecuteReader` is nonblocking (i.e., you'll be given the control of your thread back), you have the ability to continue processing on something else (like repainting your UI) while the command is being executed.

2. Add code for `DataReaderIsReady`, which is the method specified in the new `AsyncCallback` call. This is the method that's called when `BeginExecuteReader` is done processing. This code is shown in Listings 5-9 and 5-10.

Listing 5-9. *Callback Implementation for BeginExecuteDataReader in C#*

```csharp
private void DataReaderIsReady(IAsyncResult result)
{
    MessageBox.Show("Results Load Complete", "I'm Done");
    SqlCommand testCommand = (SqlCommand)result.AsyncState;

    SqlDataReader sqlDr = testCommand.EndExecuteReader(result);
    if (sqlDr.HasRows)
    {
        foreach (DbDataRecord rec in sqlDr)
        {
            dbRecordsHolder.Add(rec);
        }
    }
    sqlDr.Close();
    cmd.Connection.Dispose(); //Do not forget to at least close, if not dispose
}
```

Listing 5-10. *Callback Implementation for BeginExecuteDataReader in Visual Basic .NET*

```vbnet
Private Sub DataReaderIsReady(ByVal result As IAsyncResult)
    MessageBox.Show("Results Load Complete", "I'm Done")
    Dim testCommand As SqlCommand = CType(result.AsyncState, SqlCommand)
    Dim sqlDr As SqlDataReader = testCommand.EndExecuteReader(result)
    If sqlDr.HasRows Then
        For Each rec As DbDataRecord In sqlDr
            dbRecordsHolder.Add(rec)
        Next
    End If
    sqlDr.Close()
    cmd.Connection.Dispose()'Do not forget to at least close, if not dispose
End Sub
```

The `DataReaderIsReady` method is called once `cmd.BeginExecuteReader` is done with its processing. When you started the `BeginExecuteReader`, you passed in the command object. That object can now be retrieved using the `IAsyncResult.AsyncState` property. Once you have the `SqlCommand` object back, you can now get the prepared `SqlDataReader` by executing the `EndExecuteReader` method. From then on you can use the `SqlDataReader` as you had used it in the synchronous example you saw in Example 5.3.

The big difference, however, is that, while your underlying database (SQL Server in this case) is busy executing the query and preparing the results to send, your application is not tied up waiting to hear back from SQL Server. The framework lets you know when the results are ready, so you can begin listening at that time.

▦**Note** As you'll see in Chapter 13 when you write stored procedures in SQLCLR (the CLR inside SQL Server 2005), you have the option of sending the results in one shot (`SqlContext.Pipe.ExecuteAndSend`) or row by row (`SqlContext.Pipe.SendResultsStart`, `SqlContext.Pipe.SendResultsRow`, and `SqlContextPipe.SendResultsEnd`). This can be seen in the exercise `SqlServerStoredProc` in Chapter 13.

While `ExecuteAndSend` works as a blocking call [i.e., the caller client application (data reader or data adapter) has to wait for the entire result set to be ready before it can access the first row], the `SendResultsStart`, `SendResultsRow`, and `SendResultsEnd` methods allow your client application to begin reading the first row without having to wait for the entire result set to be ready first.

This technique, however, cannot be used when using T-SQL queries since SQL Server itself will not let `SendResultsRow` execute unless the entire query has finished executing first. This is because SQL Server tries to minimize the time you hold contentious resources.

Just remember to close the connection as a good coding practice in the end. Do note, however, that you don't have the `using` block or code limited to a single method's scope to do this for you here, so you need to remember to do this cleanup.

3. A rather thoughtful addition to ADO.NET 2.0 and SQL Server 2005 is that any features that could potentially be misused, thanks to bad architecture or simply little knowledge, need to be consciously allowed before they can be used. As mentioned earlier, asynchronous command execution, although essential to an application, has the possibility of being misused or improperly used. So to use asynchronous commands, you have to consciously make the decision to do so and tell ADO.NET to use them via your connection string. A change needs to be made to the connection string to allow your code to use asynchronous commands—thus, add the following to your connection string:

```
Asynchronous Processing=true
```

4. Let's compile and run the application now. The application looks exactly the same as Example 5.5 except now, when you click Populate Arraylist, your UI remains responsive. You could have even showed a nice animation while the data was being filled.

One thing you might want to do is show a progress bar as the results are being fetched. However, that's not possible because a progress bar has a minimum and a maximum. You know the minimum is zero, but you don't know the maximum until you have fully iterated through the data reader or at least have executed the command completely. The only way to show a truly accurate progress bar is to execute two commands and know the result count in advance, which might not be a very ideal situation. But you could show an animated UI informing the user of an impending action.

When you do click Populate Arraylist, eventually the application shows a Message Box (see Figure 5-5) informing the user that the command has finished executing. This means that your callback has just been called; you can now easily retrieve the SqlDataReader and start working with it. While you still spend the time retrieving the actual prepared rows from the underlying database, your main thread didn't get blocked while the query itself was executing and the results were being prepared.

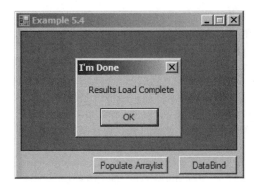

Figure 5-5. *Notification of the callback's execution*

After that message, you can click DataBind and get results similar to Example 5.5, only this time with many more results (see Figure 5-6).

TestDemo	Description
1	One
2	Two
3	Three
4	One
5	Two
6	Three

Figure 5-6. *Final databound UI with a large number of results*

Since your code is now split up between the method that calls BeginExecuteReader and the callback, one obvious downside is that you can't use the using block and close the connection while the data reader is being prepared. Instead, you'll need to close the connection after the callback execution has occurred. This is an important change since this could be a potential open connection leak, so you absolutely must remember to close the connection in the callback method yourself.

■**Note** Asynchronous commands are useful tools, but they should be used wisely. Not only have you now introduced the complexity of creating the connection in one place and closing at another—thus causing potential connection leaks—but also if the callback for some reason never gets executed, you now have an infinite thread, an open connection, and a non-garbage-collectable command object.

As an exercise, try and execute the code in Exercises 5-3 and 5-4 with a large number of records in the fetched result set and compare the UI's responsiveness across both code examples.

So far you have seen various methods of querying data from the database in a connected mode. You had a simple table to work with and you executed simple queries against it. Now let's consider a more real-world example.

Say you had two tables you wished to query instead of one and say that you were writing a UI for managing user permissions. You have predefined permissions in one table, and you have a list of users in the other table. There's no relationship between these two yet, and your desired UI would allow the user to match these in a many-to-many fashion.

There will be three parts to such an application. The first part will query the database for users and permissions. The second part will create a UI that allows the user to express his actions to a many-to-many relationship by introducing a third table, which will serve as a map between users and permissions. The third and final step will be to update the data back to the database.

For the scope of this chapter, let's focus our attention on the first step: querying multiple tables and retrieving multiple result sets.

Querying the Database for Multiple Result Sets

In the previously mentioned example, in order to query to independent result sets, one option is to make two roundtrips to the server and execute two distinct commands on the database. While that would certainly work, consider this scenario . . .

About 5 to 10 years back, when most of us were on dialup connections, it took a user located in the United States around half a second to ping a server in Tokyo. However, downloading a half megabyte file took the same user about half an hour on a paltry dialup connection. Today, he might have a fiber-optic cable running all the way to his computer, but when he tries pinging the same server in Tokyo, it still takes him about a half a second, but downloading half a megabyte now takes him just a few seconds. At the time of writing this book, scientists don't have an easy way of crossing the speed of light; so it is safe to assume that the ping time will probably not decrease much in the near future, although the download speeds will continue to rise.

Putting the previous paragraph in an ADO.NET perspective, the point is that multiple database hits for the same amount of data queried is much more expensive than a single database hit returning the same amount of data. It's for this reason we should attempt to make our conversations with the database chunky, not chatty.

■**Tip** In all disconnected computing scenarios, you should always try and make your communication chunky, not chatty.

So, you need an easy way to retrieve multiple result sets in one single database hit. For this let's see an exercise that will query two tables: UserBasicInformation and PermissionsTable from the TestDemo database on your local Test database. This exercise can be created in the following steps or can be downloaded in the associated code download under Example 5.5:

1. Starting with the code from Example 5.2 in the associated code download (this is the example that demonstrates a data reader with one result set), change the command text specified to the SqlCommand as shown here:

C#

```
SqlCommand cmd =
  new SqlCommand("SELECT * FROM USERBASICINFORMATION" + ";" +
  "SELECT * FROM PERMISSIONSTABLE", conn);
```

VB.NET

```
Dim cmd as SqlCommand = _
  New SqlCommand("SELECT * FROM USERBASICINFORMATION" & ";" & _
  "SELECT * FROM PERMISSIONSTABLE", conn)
```

As you can see, all that I did was concatenate the two command strings and put a ; character in the middle. This is commonly referred to as a *batched SQL command* in Microsoft SQL Server. In Oracle, even though batched queries are supported, they might be de-supported in the future. In Oracle, if you wish to return multiple result sets, instead you could create a stored procedure that returns multiple output REF CURSORs as shown here:

```
CREATE OR REPLACE PACKAGE UserPermsPkg AS
  TYPE ResultCurr IS REF CURSOR;
  PROCEDURE GetUserPerms (UserCur OUT ResultCurr,
                          PermsCur OUT ResultCurr);
END UserPermsPkg;

CREATE OR REPLACE PACKAGE BODY UserPermsPkg AS
  PROCEDURE GetUserPerms (UserCur OUT ResultCurr,
                          PermsCur OUT ResultCurr)
  IS
    LocalUserCur ResultCurr;
    LocalPermsCur ResultCurr;
  BEGIN
    OPEN LocalUserCur FOR
      SELECT * FROM USERBASICINFORMATION;
```

```
    OPEN LocalPermsCur FOR
        SELECT * FROM PERMISSIONSTABLE;

    UserCur := LocalUserCur;
    PermsCur := LocalPermsCur;
  END GetUserPerms;
END UserPermsPkg;
/
```

Thus, with a stored procedure such as this, you could use OracleDataReader and work with multiple result sets in one OracleDataReader that you can iterate over using the NextResult method.

2. The next change involves reading multiple result sets out of the SqlDataReader. The SqlDataReader object has a method called NextResult. The NextResult method allows you to move to the next result set. If there are no more result sets, it will return a false. This change is shown in Listings 5-11 and 5-12.

Listing 5-11. *Reading Multiple Result Sets Out of a Data Reader in C#*

```
if (sqlDr.HasRows)
{
    do
    {
        Console.WriteLine("                    ");
        while (sqlDr.Read())
        {
            Console.WriteLine(sqlDr.GetInt32(0)
                + " : " + sqlDr.GetString(1));
        }
    } while (sqlDr.NextResult());
}
```

Listing 5-12. *Reading Multiple Result Sets Out of a Data Reader in Visual Basic .NET*

```
If sqlDr.HasRows Then
    Do
        Console.WriteLine("                    ")
        While sqlDr.Read
            Console.WriteLine(sqlDr.GetInt32(0) _
                & " : " & sqlDr.GetString(1))
        End While
    Loop While sqlDr.NextResult()
End If
```

Note that I checked sqlDr.NextResult in a do...while/Do...Loop While loop. The main reason for that is because, by default, SqlDataReader points to the first result set in your collection. By calling NextResult, you would've moved to the next result set. This kind of loop lets you check for this condition *after* the first iteration.

3. Compile and run the application. The output shown in Figure 5-7 is produced.

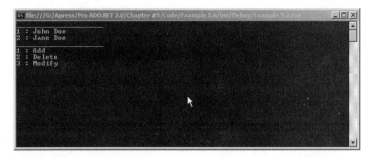

Figure 5-7. *Results of iterating through multiple result sets*

Thus, without executing multiple data readers, you have the ability to execute and fetch multiple data result sets in the same data reader. This is especially useful when working with disconnected data such as DataSets with more than one DataTable. That scenario will be covered in Chapters 6 and 7.

One interesting thing about all the examples you have seen so far is that the only data types you have fetched are the data types that are intrinsic to a given database. These are also referred to as *inbuilt scalar types*. You looked at querying a row, querying a result set, and querying multiple result sets, and in all these cases the data retrieved consisted of such inbuilt scalar types.

In object-oriented development (OOD), however, most business objects are represented via an object map representation. This hierarchical object map generally needs to be translated to and from a flat relational structure into a database, a process typically referred to as O/R mapping (object-relational mapping). While databases prefer to work with a relational structure, applications tend to prefer working with object representations of the data.

Thus, we have a mismatch.

Object-Oriented vs. Relational Representation

Let's assume a hypothetical situation: say you were creating a geographical-mapping application. Each point on a map is represented using an X,Y coordinate pair. How could you store this information in the database?

You could store this information as two integer columns in your database. But then you really don't have any good way of differentiating a coordinate with say, a kilometer-to-mile conversion lookup table, which also might store its data in a similar format. Not only that, any operations you may wish to do on the two coordinates would require you to read the two columns from the database and populate them into a business object or a class representation called XYCoOrdinate, in which you might implement commonly used functions such as distance from the center (0,0) coordinate.

But then, what if you wanted to execute a SQL query and find out which coordinate within a given set of coordinates is the furthest away from the center.

Another way of storing this data could be as a varchar column that stores the coordinates as X,Y, but again you would have to retrieve them from the database and convert them into an object representation if you really wanted to do any operation on it.

It would be rather nice if you could take the object and directly persist that into the database instead.

Storing Objects in the Database

Microsoft SQL Server 2005 allows you to extend its scalar type system by creating User-Defined Types (UDTs). UDTs allow you to create either a value-type or a reference-type representation of your object and store that directly into your database.

■**Note** UDTs are different from the `sp_addtype` stored procedure that SQL Server 2000 already gives you. Whereas UDTs let you represent object representations as a data type, `sp_addtype` allows you to create UDTs that are scalar data types based off the scalar data-type set supported in SQL Server.

Along with the object representation, you also have the ability to store logic in the class that represents the object. For example, you could write up a class that represents an `XYCoOrdinate`, and have one of the properties on it represent the distance from the center (0,0) coordinate.

SQL Server makes this possible by having the ability to host the CLR natively inside itself. Having the CLR inside SQL Server allows you to write stored procedures, UDTs, user-defined functions, triggers, etc. in any CLR-compliant language.

However, it is naive to think that the CLR running inside SQL Server runs in the same manner as it would run on your average Windows machine. The main difference is that SQL Server takes the responsibility and manages thread scheduling, synchronization, locking, and memory allocation.

THE CLR IS INSIDE OUT

An application generally interacts with the CLR by using `ICorRuntimeHost` or `CorBindToRuntimeEx`, which then calls `MSCOREE.DLL` which loads the runtime. Then, because of the fantastic .NET runtime, life becomes easier. This principle is followed by most applications except a few special cases—SQL Server being one of them.

SQL Server 2005 has a slightly different bootstrap mechanism. For one, it doesn't load the CLR unless asked to. This allows SQL Server to save a few MB of memory that the CLR would have occupied. Even when it does, instead of using `ICLRRuntimeHost` (the replacement for `ICorRuntimeHost` in .NET 2.0), and hence `ICLRRuntimeHost::SetHostControl`, SQL Server 2005 instead uses `IHostControl::GetHostManager`. What this means is a lot is now inside out. By doing so, the CLR has now delegated operations, like resource locking, thread management, etc. to SQL Server runtime instead (inside out).

Because the CLR inside SQL Server runs under different conditions than it runs on your desktop, it's subjected to different requirements, especially security. There are generally three categories of access security for managed code inside SQL Server:

- `SAFE`: This is the default.

- `EXTERNAL_ACCESS`: Certain external resources are accessible.

- `UNSAFE`: Effectively the same as an extended stored procedure.

Authoring your own UDTs is subject to similar security requirements.

In addition, the class or structure that might represent a UDT has to be understood by the SQL Server as easily convertible into a byte stream (thus be `Serializable`). It needs to show a logical textual representation when it's a part of the results of a simple `SELECT` statement (`ToString()`). And it needs to be easily insertable from a simple text-based SQL `INSERT` command (`Parse` method that accepts a `SqlString`). These methods and more will be covered in further depth in just a moment.

Note If you are unfamiliar with SQLCLR projects, you probably should read Chapter 13 before this next sample.

Visual Studio 2005 makes it simple for you by providing you a SQL Server Project wizard. Here's how you can easily create a UDT in Visual Studio 2005:

1. Create a new SQL Server project in Visual Studio.

2. Add a new UDT to that project. Call it "XYCoOrdinate".

3. The structure of the UDT is laid out for you. Modify the autogenerated UDT code to look like the code shown in Listing 5-13 or 5-14. (You can download the full UDT code from the Downloads section of the Apress website.)

Listing 5-13. *The XYCoOrdinate UDT in C#*

```csharp
[Serializable]
[StructLayout(LayoutKind.Sequential)]
[SqlUserDefinedType(Format.Native)]
public struct XYCoOrdinate : INullable
{
    private int x;
    private int y;

    public int X
    {
        get { return x; }
        set { x = value; }
    }
    public int Y
    {
        get { return y; }
        set { y = value; }
    }
```

```csharp
public override string ToString()
{
   return x.ToString() + "," + y.ToString();
}

public bool IsNull
{
   get
   {
      return false;
   }
}

public static XYCoOrdinate Null
{
   get
   {
      XYCoOrdinate h = new XYCoOrdinate();
      return h;
   }
}

public static XYCoOrdinate Parse(SqlString s)
{
   if (s.IsNull || s.Value.ToLower().Equals("null"))
   {
      return Null;
   }
   XYCoOrdinate u = new XYCoOrdinate();

   string str = s.ToString().Trim();
   int commaLocation = str.IndexOf(",");
   try
   {
      u.X = Convert.ToInt32(str.Substring(0, commaLocation));
      u.Y =
       Convert.ToInt32(
         str.Substring(commaLocation + 1, str.Length - commaLocation - 1));
   }
   catch (Exception ex)
   {
      throw new ApplicationException(
        "Error converting " + str + " to a co-ordinate.", ex);
   }
   return u;
}
}
```

Listing 5-14. *The XYCoOrdinate UDT in Visual Basic .NET*

```vbnet
<Serializable()> _
<StructLayout(LayoutKind.Sequential)> _
<SqlUserDefinedType(Format.Native)> _
Public Structure XYCoOrdinate
    Implements INullable

    Private m_x As Integer
    Private m_y As Integer

    Public Property X() As Integer
        Get
            Return m_x
        End Get
        Set(ByVal value As Integer)
            m_x = value
        End Set
    End Property

    Public Property Y() As Integer
        Get
            Return m_y
        End Get
        Set(ByVal value As Integer)
            m_y = value
        End Set
    End Property

    Public Overrides Function ToString() As String
        Return m_x.ToString() & "," & m_y.ToString()
    End Function

    Public ReadOnly Property IsNull() As Boolean Implements INullable.IsNull
        Get
            Return False
        End Get
    End Property

    Public Shared ReadOnly Property Null() As XYCoOrdinate
        Get
            Dim h As XYCoOrdinate = New XYCoOrdinate
            Return h
        End Get
    End Property

    Public Shared Function Parse(ByVal s As SqlString) As XYCoOrdinate
        If s.IsNull Or s.Value.ToLower().Equals("null") Then
```

```
            Return Null
        End If
        Dim u As XYCoOrdinate = New XYCoOrdinate()

        Dim str As String = s.ToString().Trim()
        Dim commaLocation As Integer = str.IndexOf(",")
        Try
            u.X = CInt(str.Substring(0, commaLocation))
            u.Y = CInt( _
                str.Substring(commaLocation + 1, str.Length - commaLocation - 1))
        Catch ex As Exception
            Throw New ApplicationException( _
                "Error converting " + str + " to a co-ordinate.", ex)
        End Try
        Return u
    End Function
End Structure
```

Let's quickly cover the basics that allow you to convert the autogenerated code to a working UDT. At a first glance, you'll notice the following method stubs created for you:

- ToString(): This is used when you use the UDT in a SQL query. The ToString() representation of the object is displayed in the SQL Server Management Studio results window.

- IsNull, Null: These help the mismatch of null handling between databases and .NET data types. You can write logic here to inform the database when your object should be interpreted as a null, or what its null representation means.

- Parse: This method is used to perform a translation between a scalar type and the UDT itself. This method is valuable because it allows you to insert into a UDT by specifying an instantiation scalar value via a simple SQL command.

An entire chapter could be written about UDTs alone, but since this is an ADO.NET book and not a SQL Server 2005 book we will not go into the depths of writing a UDT.

4. Once the UDT is compiled into a DLL, it can be easily registered into the SQL Server. You need to register the assembly in the SQL Server. This can be done using the following script:

```
Create Assembly XYCoOrdinate FROM 'C:\Apress\UDT.dll'
```

5. Once the assembly is added in SQL Server, you can register the UDT as a type from the previous registered assembly. This can be done using the following script:

```
Create Type XYCoOrdinate External Name UDT.XYCoOrdinate
```

6. With the UDT created, create a table that uses the previous UDT:

```
Create Table MyTest(
TestColumn XYCoOrdinate
)
```

7. And finally, you can insert data into the UDT column:

```
INSERT INTO MyTest Values('1,1') ;
```

Querying for UDT Data Using SQL

You can also very easily query the UDT column using a simple SQL command:

```
SELECT TESTCOLUMN FROM MYTEST
```

When you execute the previous SQL statement in the SQL Server Management Studio, you might get an error that looks like the following:

```
An error occurred while executing batch. Error message is: Could not load type
'System.Data.Sql.SqlUserDefinedTypeAttribute' from assembly
'System.Data, Version=2.0.0.0, Culture=neutral,
PublicKeyToken=b77a5c561934e089'.
```

This is because the SQL Server Management Studio is like any other .NET application. It queries the database using ADO.NET and when it cannot find a .NET class implementation to represent the object, it will throw an exception.

The work-around is to either put the UDT in GAC (Global Assembly Cache), or to put it in the same directory as the SQL Server Management Studio.

An easier work-around perhaps is to assume the presence of ToString() since everything in .NET inherits from System.Object, which the SQL Server Management Studio does have access to.

Thus the query could be written as

```
SELECT TESTCOLUMN.ToString() FROM MYTEST
```

but if your UDT implemented any custom methods, you'll need access to the assembly that implements the UDT.

Now that you have the ability to store objects, as objects in our database, let's return to the discussion of retrieving data in a connected fashion and see how a UDT can be fetched using a data reader.

Retrieving UDT Data in a Connected Fashion

There are multiple ways of retrieving a UDT from the database in a connected fashion. All of these involve the SqlCommand object and the SqlDataReader object. Even if you use a UDT in a disconnected fashion using a data adapter, internally the DataAdapter object will use a data reader.

The most straightforward way of doing so is simply to use command text that uses the ToString method:

C#

```
testCommand.CommandText = "SELECT TESTCOLUMN.ToString() FROM MYTEST";
```

VB.NET

```
testCommand.CommandText = "SELECT TESTCOLUMN.ToString() FROM MYTEST"
```

This method allows you to retrieve the textual representation of the UDT using the GetString method of the data reader, as shown here:

C#

```
string udtRepresentation = sqlDr.GetString(0) ;
```

VB.NET

```
string udtRepresentation = sqlDr.GetString(0)
```

Another equivalent of this code is to instead specify the SqlCommand's command text as

```
SELECT TESTCOLUMN FROM MYTEST
```

and to use the ToString() method on the object retrieved from the data reader instead:

```
string udtRepresentation = sqlDr[0].ToString() ;
```

However, the true value of UDTs shines when you're able to retrieve the data and represent them as objects, instead of string representations.

This can be easily achieved by casting the retrieved object as shown previously and, instead of using the ToString method, you could cast it to the object representation, like so:

C#

```
XYCoOrdinate xyc = (XYCoOrdinate) sqlDr[0] ;
```

VB.NET

```
Dim xyc as XYCoOrdinate = CType(sqlDr(0), XYCoOrdinate))
```

Now that you have the UDT available as a strongly typed object, you can either call the various implemented methods on this object directly or cast it to an appropriate class if your object model permits you to do so.

■**Note** At the time of this writing, in Visual Studio, UDTs by default are implemented as structs. You can just as easily change them to classes if you wish.

Pragmatic Use of UDTs

Like any technology, UDTs come with their own set of "Don't do's." It's important to realize that UDTs are not an O/R–mapping solution. It's unfair to expect UDTs to live up to the performance standards exhibited by scalar SQL Server data types. Although UDTs can be indexed, the sorting and indexing logic, especially in UDTs that are Format.UserDefined, is just as good as the implementer who implemented it.

It's important that UDTs be viewed as a tool to solve a specific problem in a specific case, and more as an ability to store objects directly into SQL Server rather than a replacement or panacea for relational scalar value to object mapping.

As you'll see in Chapter 12, yet another option ADO.NET 2.0 and SQL Server 2005 give you is to store data as Typed XML. Because Typed XML is schema based, you don't need to deploy separate assemblies representing the UDTs and you have the ability to store larger data chunks (UDTs are limited to 8K). But, in comparison, UDTs do give you better control over indexing than Typed XML does.

Note The correct usage of UDTs is dictated by the correct usage of SQLCLR. This topic is covered in further depth in Chapters 13 and 14.

Summary

In this chapter you examined retrieving data from a data source in a connected fashion using ADO.NET. You saw the DbCommand object, provided to you by ADO.NET, enable encapsulation of a text-based command and the various methods it provides you to access your data in a connected fashion. (One detail that was not covered in this chapter was the ExecuteXmlReader method on the SqlCommand object, which will be covered in depth in Chapter 12.) Finally you saw a new feature that SQL Server 2005 supports: storing objects directly into the database using UDTs.

Also in this chapter, one of the examples you saw concerned itself with creating a disconnected cache of your data using the data reader object. Even though a data reader is constantly connected to the database, we saw an example of where it would indeed make sense to be able to create such a disconnected cache of your data for further processing. In that example, you had to cook up your own solution to meet the desire for a disconnected paradigm of data. However, ADO.NET comes with a rich inbuilt collection of classes for this very purpose. This aspect of ADO.NET is examined in depth in the next chapter.

CHAPTER 6

DataSets

In the last chapter you examined the connected data access mode. You examined various objects and examples that comprise the connected portion of ADO.NET. That is the most logical method of data access, where you connect, interact, and disconnect.

In Chapter 4 where you also read about ADO.NET connections in depth, you also looked at the possibility of a high load, highly available system. Usually in such a system there are multiple users vying for the same valuable resource: the data source connection. You saw an example where such a valuable resource could be pooled in effect to give you as much as tens of times performance benefit in a multiuser, highly concurrent, highly available system.

For such pooling to work, individual users need to be respectful of a shared common resource, such as the data source connection, by releasing it as soon as they can and acquiring it as late as they can. As you'll see in this chapter, for such data access architecture to work you have to query as much data as you practically can, work in a disconnected fashion, and then reconnect to the data source and persist your changes while checking for concurrency at that time. You need to do this not only for connection pooling reasons, but also because disconnected data access is critical in scenarios such as distributed systems, low bandwidth connections, delegation of responsibility, etc.

In this chapter, you'll examine the centerpiece of ADO.NET's disconnected architecture, the DataSet. The DataSet is the object that allows you to load a portion of the data source and acts as the bucket of data that gives you a familiar relational structure of a disconnected nature and data source–independent data storage mechanism. While making it intuitive and easy to work on the data, the DataSet also maintains a history of up to one change per cell, thus making concurrency and persistence of changes back to the data source easier.

But first, let's see why it is critical to have a disconnected model.

The Case for the Disconnected Model

Everyone likes a bedtime story, so let me start this chapter with one.

Jon is a busy executive. Most of his work is on his desktop. His desktop is a powerful computer with lots of hard disk space. He has many Excel sheets and Word documents that he needs to work on. Frequently, Jon goes to the boardroom for meetings. The first time Jon went to such a meeting, he thought he could remain "connected" with his desktop and make frequent roundtrips to his desktop and bring any documents he might need to the meetings. In such a situation, Jon would begin discussing something, and frequently he would have to leave the meeting and run back to his desktop and fetch the documents he needed. While this certainly worked, Jon and his co-workers were quick to realize that this was not the most efficient use of everyone's time. Not only was Jon running a bit too much, but everyone ended up waiting for Jon while he was out getting the Word document or Excel sheet he needed. This was extremely wasteful of everyone's resources.

Thus, Jon bought a laptop. The laptop doesn't have as much disk space, or the processing power, or even such a big display or keyboard, but what the laptop does allow Jon to do is grab a subset of the Excel sheets and Word documents that he might need for his meeting, leaving the rest behind. The laptop isn't quite the same as the desktop, but it definitely prevents Jon from making frequent trips to his desktop. Jon can make changes on the fly to his Word documents and Excel sheets, and update his desktop when the meeting is over.

Now everyone is happy, Jon doesn't have to run as much, and his co-workers don't have to wait as much.

This example is very similar to any enterprise application. Jon had to run to a meeting room a few feet away, but typically on the Internet, you might have clients that are spread around the globe trying to connect with the database all too frequently. In a multiuser scenario when one client is working on the data and holding an open connection, other clients might have to open a brand new physical database connection to get their job done. What suffers in the end is the central database, which needs to juggle more physical connections at a given time than were needed. Especially, when most of the time, the underlying data source is simply waiting for the user to send an update or a query for more data.

This situation can be easily rectified just as Jon did. You could store all the data you need in a separate object (laptop, or DataSet). This object isn't quite as good as the database itself; it probably can't store as much data as the database and it probably doesn't have the same query flexibility and power as the underlying database does, but it works perfectly for disconnected scenarios.

For such an object to qualify as something that works well in disconnected scenarios, it should have the following desirable characteristics:

- It must be *serializable*: An object is considered to be serializable if it has the ability to save a memory (or data) state into a serial stream of bytes to be read later or to be sent across process and machine boundaries. Working in a disconnected scenario, you would find yourself sending the subset of the data across network, machine, and process boundaries. For this to work easily, it must be serializable.

- It must work *with XML*: Serializability of the object is good, but serialization could possibly be done to a binary form. Binary is not human readable. It's for this reason and more that XML is the lingua franca of the computer world—everyone understands it: humans and computers. It might not be ideal for some situations, such as wireless networks where the extra tags it comes with may make it unsuitable for work on a low bandwidth connection, but because it is text-based, and parsers exist for it on almost every platform, it makes sense that such an object that holds the subset of the data must work well with XML.

- It must *maintain a history of changes*: Querying for data is only half the story, persisting the changes back to the database, while taking care of concurrency issues, is usually the tougher half. It would be nice if the object had the ability to maintain a history of the changes done on it since its original fetch. That would allow the program you write to easily address issues such as concurrency as will be discussed in Chapters 9 and 10.

In Chapter 5, you saw an `ArrayList` being filled in with `DbDataRecords` in Examples 5.3 and 5.4. For the same amount of data involved, an `ArrayList` is much lighter weight than a `DataSet` is, but such an object does not satisfy the last two desirable characteristics just mentioned. In some situations, though, that might be a better choice. For example, if you don't need XML flexibility, or you're working with a read-only system [such as the presentation portion of a content management website, or maybe you intend to re-query the database at update to maintain concurrency checks (more on this in Chapters 9 and 10)], you might want to choose an `ArrayList` as your data object representation.

However, if an `ArrayList` does not satisfy the requirements of your architecture, you could create your own business object representation that satisfies all three conditions, or even more if your architecture demands it. Alternatively, you could use the `DataSet` object that comes as a part of ADO.NET that satisfies all three conditions and more.

As an example, when you're working with disconnected data, one of the things you'll need to worry about is being able to maintain an updated, refreshed copy of your data. The `DataSet` has inbuilt mechanisms, such as being able to extract changes or merge with another `DataSet`, that allow you to write code to avoid stale data. While it's possible to implement something like that in another object, such as an `ArrayList`, you would have to start from zero and put in relatively more work when compared with the `DataSet`.

The DataSet Object Model

Chapter 3 presented an abbreviated picture of the object model that springs from the `DataSet` object. Let's add some flesh to those bones and look at the bigger picture, shown in Figure 6-1. A more complete idea of the model will help you understand the power and usefulness of `DataSets`.

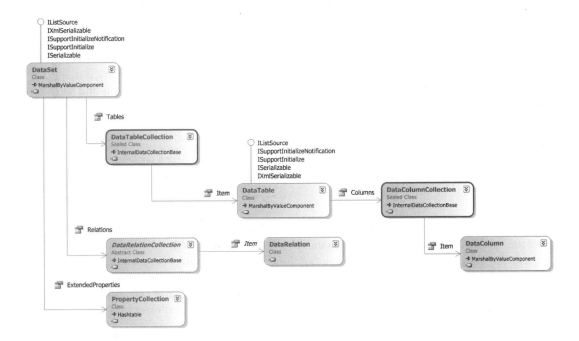

Figure 6-1. *A DataSet and its main constituents*

Table 6-1 shows the three collection properties that together make up the relational data structure of the DataSet: Tables, Relations, and ExtendedProperties.

Table 6-1. *DataSet and Its Main Constituents*

Property	Description
Tables	DataSet.Tables is an object of System.Data.DataTableCollection type that can contain zero or more System.Data.DataTable objects. Each DataTable represents a set of tabular data that's been extracted from a data source. In turn, each DataTable has collections called Columns and Rows, which can contain zero or more DataColumn or DataRow objects, respectively.
Relations	The DataSet.Relations property is a System.Data.DataRelationCollection object that can contain zero or more System.Data.DataRelation objects. A DataRelation object defines a parent-child relationship between two DataTables based on foreign-key values.
ExtendedProperties	DataSet.ExtendedProperties is a System.Data.PropertyCollection object that can contain zero or more user-defined properties. The ExtendedProperties collection can be used to store custom data related to the DataSet, such as the time when it was constructed.

To understand the DataSet fully then, you first need to understand the DataTable and its various constituents. For that reason, let's first dissect the DataTable class, understanding how it works and its role in a data-driven application. Once you have dealt with DataTables, you can start using them in DataSets, building DataRelations between them in the same way that you would have relationships between two tables in a database.

DataTable

Don't think that the DataTable class is in some way subservient to DataSet—it's central to the ADO.NET architecture, and DataTable objects can be used independently of DataSets, if that's what you need. This is even truer in .NET 2.0 where the DataTable is fully serializable and supports methods like Merge and GetChanges just as a DataSet does.

Note In .NET 2.0, the DataTable has all methods that a DataSet supports. For a single table use, for most purposes, you should try and use DataTable instead of DataSet because it's a smaller object.

As you can see from Figure 6-1, a DataTable implements the same standard interfaces as a DataSet does, thus in many cases giving it the same functionality that a DataSet has. As outlined previously, a DataTable contains (among other things) a Columns collection, a Rows collection, and a Constraints collection. The Columns and Constraints collections together define the schema for the DataTable (that is, the rules that govern what data the table can hold), while the Rows collection contains the data itself. Table 6-2 describes these various collections.

Table 6-2. *Various Collections in a DataTable*

Property	Description
Columns	The Columns collection is an instance of the System.Data.DataColumnCollection class, and is a container for zero or more DataColumn objects. The DataColumn objects define the properties of each DataTable column, such as their names, the type of data they store, and any primary key or seed and step information.
Rows	The Rows collection is an instance of the System.Data.DataRowCollection class, and is a container for zero or more DataRow objects. The DataRow objects contain the actual data in the DataTable, as defined by the DataTable.Columns collection. Each DataRow has one item for each DataColumn in the Columns collection.
Constraints	Constraints is an instance of the System.Data.ConstraintCollection class, and is a container for zero or more System.Data.ForeignKeyConstraint and/or System.Data.UniqueConstraint objects. The former define the action to be taken on a column in a primary key–foreign key relationship when a row is updated or deleted, while the latter are used to enforce the rule that all values in a given column should be unique.

DataColumn

As stated, a DataColumn is used to define the name and data type of a column in a DataTable. You can create a new DataColumn either by using the DataColumn constructor, or by invoking the Add() method of the DataTable.Columns collection property:

C#

```
// Adding a column using the constructor
DataColumn myColumn = new DataColumn("ID", typeof(System.Int32));
// Adding a column using a DataTable
productsTable.Columns.Add("ID", Type.GetType("System.Int32")) ;
```

VB.NET

```
' Adding a column using the constructor
Dim myColumn As New DataColumn("ID", GetType(System.Int32))
' Adding a column using a Datatable
productsTable.Columns.Add("ID", Type.GetType("System.Int32"))
```

The version of the DataTable.Columns.Add() method that you used here expects two arguments: the name of the new DataColumn and a Type object. (For the second of these, you used the typeof or GetType methods.) The Columns property is of DataColumnCollection data type and, in fact, there are four other overloaded versions of this method available on DataColumnCollection; here's how you might use them:

- Add(): Creates and adds a new DataColumn to the DataColumnCollection (and therefore, by implication, a new column to the table). In the absence of anything to specify otherwise, the new DataColumn object is given a default name ("Column1", "Column2", etc.).

- Add("ColumnName"): Creates and adds a DataColumn with the specified name to the table. The default data type of any column for which no type is specified is System.String.

- Add(myDataColumn): Adds the specified, preexisting DataColumn object to the DataColumnCollection.

- Add("SubTotal", Type.GetType("System.Single"), "Sum(Price)"): Creates and adds a DataColumn with the specified name, data type, and Expression property. The expression can be used to filter rows, to calculate the values in a column, or (as in this case) to create an aggregate column.

The following code snippet creates a new DataTable object through one of its three constructors (the other two allow for the creation of a table with a default name, and specify both a table name and a table namespace). Once created, it then defines the table's schema by creating three new columns in the Columns collection:

C#

```
// Create a new DataTable
DataTable productsTable = new DataTable("Products") ;
// Build the products schema
productsTable.Columns.Add("ID", typeof(System.Int32)) ;
productsTable.Columns.Add("Name", typeof(System.String)) ;
productsTable.Columns.Add("Category", typeof(System.Int32)) ;
```

VB.NET

```
' Create a new DataTable
Dim productsTable As New DataTable("Products")
' Build the Products schema
productsTable.Columns.Add("ID", GetType(System.Int32))
productsTable.Columns.Add("Name", GetType(System.String))
productsTable.Columns.Add("Category", GetType(System.Int32))
```

To build the schema for this new table, you can call the Add() method of the DataTable. Columns collection once for each column that you want to add to the DataTable. For each DataColumn, you can pass in arguments for the ColumnName and DataType properties. The result is a DataTable named "Products" that's made up of three columns named "ID", "Name", and "Category" of data types Int32, String, and Int32, respectively.

DataRow

With the DataTable constructed and the columns defined, you can now begin populating the DataTable with data. This process involves adding new DataRow objects to the DataTable.Rows collection, which is of DataRowCollection type. To create a new row in the DataTable, you need to first invoke the DataTable.NewRow() method, which returns a DataRow that conforms to the DataTable's current schema. Next, you can set the value of each column in the DataRow before calling the DataTable.Rows.Add() method and passing the new DataRow object as the only argument:

C#

```
// Create a new DataRow with the same schema as the DataTable
DataRow tempRow = productsTable.NewRow() ;
// Set Column Values
```

```
tempRow.Item["ID"] = 1 ;
tempRow.Item["Name"] = "Caterham Seven de Dion" ;
tempRow.Item["Category"] = 1 ;
// Add the DataRow to the DataTable
productsTable.Rows.Add(tempRow) ;
```

VB.NET

```
' Create a new DataRow with the same schema as the DataTable
Dim tempRow As DataRow = productsTable.NewRow()
' Set the column values
tempRow.Item("ID") = 1
tempRow.Item("Name") = "Caterham Seven de Dion"
tempRow.Item("Category") = 1
' Add the DataRow to the DataTable
productsTable.Rows.Add(tempRow)
```

This example is adding one row to productsTable. First, you create a new DataRow object (tempRow) using the schema from the DataTable by calling the productsTable.NewRow() method. Next, you set the value for each of the columns defined in the productsTable.Columns collection. Last, you invoke the productsTable.Rows.Add() method to add the new DataRow to the productsTable.Rows collection.

■**Note** The DataRow that's returned to you using the NewRow method is still detached from the DataTable. In other words, its RowState property is Detached. That row is not a part of the table until you have added it to the Rows collection by calling Rows.Add.

Constraints

Relational databases enforce data integrity with *constraints*—rules applied to a column or columns that define what action to take when data in a related column of a constituent row is altered. In ADO.NET, there are two types of constraints: ForeignKeyConstraints and UniqueConstraints. Let's take a quick look at constraints here, with one or two fairly straightforward examples. In Chapter 10, you'll see how you can leverage these constraints and relations to keep disconnected data clean and in accordance with the database rules.

ForeignKeyConstraint

A ForeignKeyConstraint is intended for use in enforcing referential integrity. In addition, you can define cascade behavior: When a value in a column in a parent table is changed or deleted, a ForeignKeyConstraint defines how the child table should react. For example, if a parent record is deleted, you could specify that all child records should be deleted too—or you could set the related field in the child records to null or default values, explicitly identifying orphaned records. This is known as a *cascading action*, because an action on the parent has consequences that travel down to affect the child as well.

The action to be taken on the child is defined in the `ForeignKeyConstraint.DeleteRule` and/or the `ForeignKeyConstraint.UpdateRule` property, and can be set to one of four possible `System.Data.Rule` enumerators, as shown in Table 6-3.

Table 6-3. *The System.Data.Rule Enumeration*

Value	Description
Cascade	Deletes or updates related rows. This is the default action. You have to be careful of this since, depending on the structure of your DataSet, it might not always be possible to enforce cascades.
SetNull	Sets values in related rows to DBNull.
SetDefault	Sets values in related rows to the value of their column's DefaultValue property.
None	No action is taken on related rows.

UniqueConstraint

A `UniqueConstraint` enforces that the values in a column or columns should be unique. This type of constraint is set automatically for primary-key columns, which I will discuss next. If a column has a `UniqueConstraint` defined, attempting to set the same value for that column in two different rows throws an exception of `System.Data.ConstraintException` type.

You can also set a `UniqueConstraint` over more than one column. In this case, setting the same values for every constrained column in two rows of the same table will throw an exception.

Setting a Primary Key: PrimaryKey Property

Since the `DataSet` and `DataTable` objects are designed to support most of the basic concepts of relational databases, a `DataTable` can and should have a *primary key*. In a `DataTable`, the primary key is defined as an *array* of `DataColumns` that together provide a unique identifier for a `DataRow` within the `DataTable`. To create a primary key, you need to set the `PrimaryKey` property of the `DataTable` to an array of `DataColumns`. When you define a primary key in this way, a `UniqueConstraint` is automatically applied to the `DataColumn` array:

C#

```
// Set up the ID column as the primary key
productsTable.PrimaryKey =
   new DataColumn[] { productsTable.Columns["ID"] };
```

VB.NET

```
' Set up the ID column as the primary key
productsTable.PrimaryKey = New DataColumn() {productsTable.Columns("ID")}
```

Dynamically Constructing a DataTable

Let's start to put together some of the things that you've looked at so far. In the following code example, which is an amalgam of the snippets you've seen so far, you create a `DataTable`, set the primary key, and then set the `AutoIncrement` and `ReadOnly` properties of the `DataColumn`, which signify that the column will not be directly modifiable and it will get its value automatically incremented as each row is added. This code example can be found in Example 6.1 in the code download for this chapter, which can be found in the Downloads section of the Apress website (http://www.apress.com). In addition, the DataColumn class exposes properties for setting up a read-only, auto-increment column, which is done here for the ID column. This can be seen in Listings 6-1 and 6-2.

Listing 6-1. *Setting Up the productsTable in C#*

```csharp
// Create the table
DataTable productsTable = new DataTable("Products") ;
// Build the Products schema
productsTable.Columns.Add("ID", typeof(System.Int32)) ;
productsTable.Columns.Add("Name", typeof(System.String)) ;
productsTable.Columns.Add("Category", typeof(System.Int32)) ;

// Set up the ID column as the primary key
productsTable.PrimaryKey =
    new DataColumn[] { productsTable.Columns["ID"] };

productsTable.Columns["ID"].AutoIncrement = true ;
productsTable.Columns["ID"].AutoIncrementSeed = 1 ;
productsTable.Columns["ID"].ReadOnly = true ;
```

Listing 6-2. *Setting Up the productsTable in Visual Basic .NET*

```vbnet
' Create the table
Dim productsTable As New DataTable("Products")

' Build the Products schema
productsTable.Columns.Add("ID", GetType(System.Int32))
productsTable.Columns.Add("Name", GetType(System.String))
productsTable.Columns.Add("Category", GetType(System.Int32))

' Set up the ID column as the primary key
productsTable.PrimaryKey = New DataColumn() {productsTable.Columns("ID")}

productsTable.Columns("ID").AutoIncrement = True
productsTable.Columns("ID").AutoIncrementSeed = 1
productsTable.Columns("ID").ReadOnly = True
```

Once the DataTable is constructed, you can fill it with DataRows. For this example, this exercise will populate the DataTable with alternating values by using the Math.IEEERemainder() method. In even-numbered rows, it will set the Name column of the DataRow to "Caterham Seven de Dion", and the Category value to 1. In odd-numbered rows, it will set the Name to "Dodge Viper" and the Category value to 2. This can be seen in Listings 6-3 and 6-4. Do note that in Listings 6-3 and 6-4 you're using the WriteXml method on a DataTable, which is a new feature available in .NET 2.0.

Listing 6-3. *Filling the productsTable in C#*

```csharp
DataRow tempRow;
// Populate the Products table with 10 cars
for (int i = 0; i < 10; i++)
{
   tempRow = productsTable.NewRow();
   // Make every even row Caterham Seven de Dion
   if (Math.IEEERemainder(i, 2) == 0)
   {
      tempRow["Name"] = "Caterham Seven de Dion #" + i.ToString();
      tempRow["Category"] = 1;
   }
   else
   {
      tempRow["Name"] = "Dodge Viper #" + i.ToString();
      tempRow["Category"] = 2;
   }
   productsTable.Rows.Add(tempRow);
}
productsTable.WriteXml("productsTable.xml") ;
```

Listing 6-4. *Filling the productsTable in Visual Basic .NET*

```vbnet
Dim tempRow As DataRow

' Populate the Products table with 10 cars
Dim i As Int32 = 0
For i = 0 To 9
  tempRow = productsTable.NewRow()

  ' Make every even row a Caterham Seven de Dion
  If Math.IEEERemainder(i, 2) = 0 Then
    tempRow("Name") = "Caterham Seven de Dion #" & i.ToString()
    tempRow("Category") = 1
  Else
    tempRow("Name") = "Dodge Viper #" & i.ToString()
    tempRow("Category") = 2
  End If

  productsTable.Rows.Add(tempRow)
Next i
productsTable.WriteXml("productsTable.xml")
```

The interesting thing about this code, compared to what you had earlier, is that you don't need to set a value for the ID column—it's a read-only, *auto-increment* column. This can be seen in the contents of productsTable.xml shown in Listing 6-5.

Listing 6-5. *productsTable in XML*

```xml
<?xml version="1.0" standalone="yes"?>
<DocumentElement>
  <Products>
    <ID>1</ID>
    <Name>Caterham Seven de Dion #0</Name>
    <Category>1</Category>
  </Products>
  <Products>
    <ID>2</ID>
    <Name>Dodge Viper #1</Name>
    <Category>2</Category>
  </Products>
  <Products>
    <ID>3</ID>
    <Name>Caterham Seven de Dion #2</Name>
    <Category>1</Category>
  </Products>
  <Products>
    <ID>4</ID>
    <Name>Dodge Viper #3</Name>
    <Category>2</Category>
  </Products>
  <Products>
    <ID>5</ID>
    <Name>Caterham Seven de Dion #4</Name>
    <Category>1</Category>
  </Products>
  <Products>
    <ID>6</ID>
    <Name>Dodge Viper #5</Name>
    <Category>2</Category>
  </Products>
  <Products>
    <ID>7</ID>
    <Name>Caterham Seven de Dion #6</Name>
    <Category>1</Category>
  </Products>
  <Products>
    <ID>8</ID>
    <Name>Dodge Viper #7</Name>
    <Category>2</Category>
  </Products>
  <Products>
    <ID>9</ID>
    <Name>Caterham Seven de Dion #8</Name>
    <Category>1</Category>
```

```
    </Products>
    <Products>
      <ID>10</ID>
      <Name>Dodge Viper #9</Name>
      <Category>2</Category>
    </Products>
  </DocumentElement>
```

DataTable Events

Like many of the objects in the .NET Framework, the DataTable exposes a set of events. In this case, the events can be captured and handled in order to update the user interface, or to validate edits or deletes before they are committed. Not including the event inherited from MarshalByValueComponent.Disposed, there are nine events in all, and they all work in more-or-less the same way, with similar arguments. They are listed in Table 6-4.

Table 6-4. *System.Data.DataTable Events*

Event	Description
ColumnChanging	Occurs when a value is being changed in the specified DataColumn in a DataRow.
ColumnChanged	Occurs after a value has been changed in the specified DataColumn in a DataRow.
RowChanging	Occurs when a DataRow is changing. This event will fire each time a change is made to the DataRow, after the ColumnChanging event has fired.
RowChanged	Occurs after a DataRow has been changed successfully.
RowDeleting	Occurs when a DataRow is about to be deleted.
RowDeleted	Occurs after a DataRow is successfully deleted from the DataTable.
TableClearing	Occurs when the table is being cleared.
TableCleared	Occurs after the table has been cleared.
TableNewRow	Occurs right after a new row has been generated.

Each of the DataTable events works in the same fashion. Handlers for the column-related events (ColumnChanging and ColumnChanged) receive a DataColumnChangeEventArgs object, which exposes three properties (see Table 6-5).

Table 6-5. *DataColumnChangeEventArgs Properties*

Property	Description
Column	Gets the DataColumn object with the changing value.
ProposedValue	Gets or sets the proposed value—that is, the new value being assigned to the column. In a ColumnChanging event handler, for example, you could evaluate the ProposedValue and make a decision on whether to accept or reject the change.
Row	Gets the DataRow object with the changing value.

The handlers for the row-related events other than the `TableNewRow` (i.e., `RowChanging`, `RowChanged`, `RowDeleting`, and `RowDeleted`) take a `DataRowChangeEventArgs` object, which exposes just two properties (see Table 6-6).

Table 6-6. *DataRowChangeEventArgs Properties*

Property	Description
Action	Gets the action (added, changed, deleted, etc.) that will occur/has occurred on the DataRow.
Row	Gets the DataRow object upon which the action will occur/has occurred.

The handlers for `TableCleared` and `TableClearing` receive a `DataTableClearTableEventHandler`, which exposes three properties (see Table 6-7).

Table 6-7. *DataTableClearTableEventHandler Properties*

Property	Description
Table	Gets the table being cleared as a property.
TableName	Gets the name of the table.
TableNamespace	Gets the table namespace for the given table. This is especially useful in XML conversions.

Finally, the handler for `TableNewRow` receives a `DataTableNewRowEventHandler`, which has only one property, `Row`, the row being added.

Practical Usage of DataTable Events

As you just saw, `DataTable` events can be split into three main categories:

- *Column-based*: `ColumnChanging`, `ColumnChanged`
- *Row-based*: `RowChanging`, `RowChanged`, `RowDeleting`, `RowDeleted`
- *Table-based*: `TableClearing`, `TableCleared`, `TableNewRow`

Generally, column-based and row-based events can be used to validate and control existing data. The `TableNewRow` event can be used to set values and such action items for any newly entered rows before they have been added to the table.

Let's first examine the sequence of events fired in the column-based and row-based events. The code for this can be found in Example 6.2 in the associated code download. This example starts where Example 6.1 left off. To keep the code cleaner, all the existing code for Example 6.1 has been moved into a method called `SetupAndPopulateDataTable` that simply returns the prepared `DataTable` that you can start working on.

Assuming now that you have the `productsTable` set up, you first need to set up the various event handlers. This can be seen in Listings 6-6 and 6-7.

Listing 6-6. *Setting Up Various Event Handlers on a DataTable in C#*

```
productsTable.ColumnChanged +=
    new DataColumnChangeEventHandler(productsTable_ColumnChanged);
productsTable.ColumnChanging +=
    new DataColumnChangeEventHandler(productsTable_ColumnChanging);
productsTable.RowChanged +=
    new DataRowChangeEventHandler(productsTable_RowChanged);
productsTable.RowChanging +=
    new DataRowChangeEventHandler(productsTable_RowChanging);
productsTable.RowDeleted +=
    new DataRowChangeEventHandler(productsTable_RowDeleted);
productsTable.RowDeleting +=
    new DataRowChangeEventHandler(productsTable_RowDeleting);
```

Listing 6-7. *Setting Up Various Event Handlers on a DataTable in Visual Basic .NET*

```
AddHandler productsTable.ColumnChanged, AddressOf productsTable_ColumnChanged
AddHandler productsTable.ColumnChanging, AddressOf productsTable_ColumnChanging
AddHandler productsTable.RowChanged, AddressOf productsTable_RowChanged
AddHandler productsTable.RowChanging, AddressOf productsTable_RowChanging
AddHandler productsTable.RowDeleted, AddressOf productsTable_RowDeleted
AddHandler productsTable.RowDeleting, AddressOf productsTable_RowDeleting
```

Next, you need to write implementations for the various event handlers though Visual Studio might have already created the stubs for you. This can be seen in Listings 6-8 and 6-9.

Listing 6-8. *Implementations for the Event Handlers in C#*[1]

```
private static void productsTable_ColumnChanged
    (object sender, DataColumnChangeEventArgs e)
{
    Console.WriteLine("productsTable_ColumnChanged");
    Console.WriteLine("   Value: " + e.Row["Name"].ToString());
    Console.WriteLine("   RowState: " + e.Row.RowState.ToString());
}

private static void productsTable_ColumnChanging
    (object sender, DataColumnChangeEventArgs e)
{
    Console.WriteLine("productsTable_ColumnChanging");
    Console.WriteLine("   Value: " + e.Row["Name"].ToString());
    Console.WriteLine("   RowState: " + e.Row.RowState.ToString());
}
```

---

1. Here and elsewhere in the book, the event handlers are marked static only because the main class Program in the case of C# runs through a `static void Main()`. This is not otherwise required.

```
private static void productsTable_RowChanged
   (object sender, DataRowChangeEventArgs e)
{
    Console.WriteLine("productsTable_RowChanged");
    Console.WriteLine("   Value: " + e.Row["Name"].ToString());
    Console.WriteLine("   RowState: " + e.Row.RowState.ToString());
}

private static void productsTable_RowChanging
   (object sender, DataRowChangeEventArgs e)
{
    Console.WriteLine("productsTable_RowChanging");
    Console.WriteLine("   Value: " + e.Row["Name"].ToString());
    Console.WriteLine("   RowState: " + e.Row.RowState.ToString());
}

private static void productsTable_RowDeleted
   (object sender, DataRowChangeEventArgs e)
{
    Console.WriteLine("productsTable_RowDeleted");
    Console.WriteLine("   RowState: " + e.Row.RowState.ToString());
}

private static void productsTable_RowDeleting
   (object sender, DataRowChangeEventArgs e)
{
    Console.WriteLine("productsTable_RowDeleting");
    Console.WriteLine("   RowState: " + e.Row.RowState.ToString());
}
```

Listing 6-9. *Implementations for the Event Handlers in Visual Basic .NET*

```
Private Sub productsTable_ColumnChanged(ByVal sender As Object, _
 ByVal e As DataColumnChangeEventArgs)
   Console.WriteLine("productsTable_ColumnChanged.")
   Console.WriteLine("Value: " & e.Row("Name").ToString())
   Console.WriteLine("RowState: " & e.Row.RowState.ToString())
End Sub

Private Sub productsTable_ColumnChanging(ByVal sender As Object, _
 ByVal e As DataColumnChangeEventArgs)
   Console.WriteLine("productsTable_ColumnChanging.")
   Console.WriteLine("Value: " & e.Row("Name").ToString())
   Console.WriteLine("RowState: " & e.Row.RowState.ToString())
End Sub

Private Sub productsTable_RowChanged(ByVal sender As Object, _
 ByVal e As DataRowChangeEventArgs)
```

```
      Console.WriteLine("productsTable_RowChanged.")
      Console.WriteLine("Value: " & e.Row("Name").ToString())
      Console.WriteLine("RowState: " & e.Row.RowState.ToString())
End Sub

Private Sub productsTable_RowChanging(ByVal sender As Object, _
  ByVal e As DataRowChangeEventArgs)
      Console.WriteLine("productsTable_RowChanging.")
      Console.WriteLine("Value: " & e.Row("Name").ToString())
      Console.WriteLine("RowState: " & e.Row.RowState.ToString())
End Sub

Private Sub productsTable_RowDeleted(ByVal sender As Object, _
  ByVal e As DataRowChangeEventArgs)
      Console.WriteLine("productsTable_RowDeleted.")
      Console.WriteLine("RowState: " & e.Row.RowState.ToString())
End Sub

Private Sub productsTable_RowDeleting(ByVal sender As Object, _
  ByVal e As DataRowChangeEventArgs)
      Console.WriteLine("productsTable_RowDeleting.")
      Console.WriteLine("RowState: " & e.Row.RowState.ToString())
End Sub
```

And finally with the DataTable setup, you can now modify some data using the following code. As you can see, in this case, you are modifying the column Name from the first row in the DataTable:

C#

```
productsTable.Rows[0]["Name"] = "Pinto";
```

VB.NET

```
productsTable.Rows(0)("Name") = "Pinto"
```

which produces output as shown here:

```
productsTable_ColumnChanging
    Value: Caterham Seven de Dion #0
    RowState: Unchanged
productsTable_ColumnChanged
    Value: Pinto
    RowState: Unchanged
productsTable_RowChanging
    Value: Pinto
    RowState: Unchanged
productsTable_RowChanged
    Value: Pinto
    RowState: Modified
```

If you try deleting a row using

```
productsTable.Rows[0].Delete() ;
```

the following output is produced:

```
productsTable_RowDeleting
    RowState: Modified
productsTable_RowDeleted
    RowState: Deleted
```

Hence, as you can see, the `ColumnChanging`, `RowChanging`, and `RowDeleting` events fire *before* the actual change has occurred, and these can be used to validate or even reject the proposed change. Whereas, the `ColumnChanged`, `RowChanged`, and `RowDeleted` events fire *after* the actual change has occurred and can thus be used for cleanup purposes.

■**Note** Do closely note, however, that there is a minute difference between the behavior of `ColumnChanging` and `RowChanging`. `ColumnChanging` occurs before the actual value change, and `RowChanging` occurs before the `RowState` change.

As an exercise, you could also add event handlers for `TableClearing` and `TableCleared` events, and run those with the `DataTable.Clear()` method. You'll see similar behavior there.

You could also try your hand at a new event introduced in .NET 2.0: the `TableNewRow` event. This is where you could include business logic in the creation of a new row. While all other events allow you to work on a row that is being added, deleted, or modified when currently in the Row collection of the table, this event allows you to modify its values based on custom business rules at its creation. A good practical use for such an event is a row generator class that inherits from `DataTable`. You might have written such a class to encapsulate your business logic, while generating a plain old `DataRow` that can be easily sent to the `DataLayer` as a part of the `DataTable`.

Relational Data

If a `DataSet` is like having a mini RDBMS in memory, a `DataTable` is the closest logical equivalent of a table in such a database. Most databases also support the concept of being able to create foreign-key constraints, which can be used to define relations between tables. As you can see in the object model in Figure 6-1, a `DataSet` consists of a `Tables` collection (`DataTableCollection`), and a `Relations` collection (`DataRelationCollection`). Thus, a `DataSet` can be referred to as a collection of `Tables` and `Relations`. The minimum number of either `Tables` or `Relations` that exist within a `DataSet` can be zero.

The Relations Collection

The `DataSet.Relations` property is an instance of the `DataRelationCollection` class. The `Relations` collection contains `DataRelation` objects, which are used to create parent-child relationships between `DataTables` in the `DataSet`. A primary key–foreign key relationship is an example of this type of relation.

We can create a relation between two tables in a DataSet by invoking the DataSet.Relations. Add() method. There are seven overloaded Add() methods:

- Add(DataRelation): Adds the specified DataRelation object to the collection.

- Add(DataColumn, DataColumn): Creates a DataRelation object in the collection based on the two DataColumns. The first argument is the parent column, and the second is the child column. The DataRelation is given a default name.

- *VB.NET*: Add(DataColumn(), DataColumn()) or *C#*: Add(DataColumn[], DataColumn[]): Creates a DataRelation object in the collection based on the two DataColumn arrays. The first argument is the parent column array, and the second is the child column array. The DataRelation is given a default name.

- Add(String, DataColumn, DataColumn) As DataRelation: Creates a DataRelation object in the collection with the specified string as the DataRelation.RelationName property.

- *VB.NET*: Add(String, DataColumn(), DataColumn()) or *C#*: Add(String, DataColumn[], DataColumn[]): Creates a DataRelation object in the collection with the specified string as the DataRelation.RelationName property.

- Add(String, DataColumn, DataColumn, Boolean): Creates a DataRelation object in the collection with the specified string as the DataRelation.RelationName property. The DataRelation is based on the two DataColumns. The Boolean argument indicates whether to create constraints (the default setting is True).

- *VB.NET*: Add(String, DataColumn(), DataColumn(), Boolean) or *C#*: Add(String, DataColumn[], DataColumn[], Boolean): Creates a DataRelation object in the collection with the specified string as the DataRelation.RelationName property. The DataRelation is based on the two DataColumn arrays. The Boolean argument indicates whether to create constraints.

You can create a relationship in a DataSet using any of these overloaded methods. Here's an example using the overload that accepts a relation name, and the two DataColumns that form the relation:

C#

```
//Create a relation between Customers and Orders.
myDataSet.Relations.Add("CustomersToOrders",
    myDataSet.Tables["Customers"].Columns["CustomerID"],
    myDataSet.Tables["Orders"].Columns["CustomerID"]) ;
```

VB.NET

```
' Create a relation between Customers and Orders
myDataSet.Relations.Add("CustomersToOrders", _
    myDataSet.Tables("Customers").Columns("CustomerID"), _
    myDataSet.Tables("Orders").Columns("CustomerID"))
```

This code invokes the Add() method of the myDataSet.Relations object to create a new DataRelation object in the myDataSet.Relations collection. As a result, a new UniqueConstraint is added to the Customers DataTable, and a ForeignKeyConstraint is added to the Orders

DataTable. The former (UniqueConstraint) ensures that all parent column values are unique in the table, and the latter (ForeignKeyConstraint) ensures that an invalid CustomerID never appears in the Orders table. By default, it also sets up cascading deletes and updates from Customers to Orders records.

It's also possible to construct the DataRelation object explicitly, and then add it to the Relations collection. This is done using the overload that accepts a DataRelation directly, and is demonstrated in the code here:

C#

```csharp
// Create two DataColumns
DataColumn parentColumn ;
DataColumn childColumn ;
// Set the two columns to instances of the parent and child columns
parentColumn = myDataSet.Tables["Customers"].Columns["CustomerID"] ;
childColumn = myDataSet.Tables["Orders"].Columns["CustomerID"] ;

// Create a new DataRelation object
DataRelation customersToOrders = New DataRelation("CustomersToOrders",
    parentColumn, childColumn) ;

// Add the DataRelation to the DataSet.Relations collection
myDataSet.Relations.Add(customersToOrders) ;
```

VB.NET

```vbnet
' Create two DataColumns
Dim parentColumn As DataColumn
Dim childColumn As DataColumn
' Set the two columns to instances of the parent and child columns
parentColumn = myDataSet.Tables("Customers").Columns("CustomerID")
childColumn = myDataSet.Tables("Orders").Columns("CustomerID")

' Create a new DataRelation object
Dim customersToOrders As New DataRelation( _
    "CustomersToOrders", parentColumn, childColumn)

' Add the DataRelation to the DataSet.Relations collection
myDataSet.Relations.Add(customersToOrders)
```

Also, as mentioned in the list, a DataRelation can be constructed using an *array* of DataColumns for both the parent and child columns. Imagine, for example, that there's a table of employees, and a table of managers. The Managers table contains data about the employees who are also managers (this example assumes that the names of such employees are duplicated in both the Employees table and the Managers table):

C#

```csharp
// Create arrays of DataColumns for the relevant columns
DataColumn[] parentArray = new DataColumn[2];
```

```
parentArray[0] = myDataSet.Tables["Employees"].Columns["FirstName"] ;
parentArray[1] = myDataSet.Tables["Employees"].Columns["LastName"] ;

DataColumn[] childArray = new DataColumn[2];
childArray[0] = myDataSet.Tables["Managers"].Columns["FirstName"] ;
childArray[1] = myDataSet.Tables["Managers"].Columns["LastName"] ;

DataRelation empToMngr = New DataRelation("EmployeesToManagers", parentArray,
    childArray) ;
myDataSet.Relations.Add(EmpToMngr) ;
```

VB.NET

```
' Create arrays of DataColumns for the relevant columns
Dim parentArray(2) As DataColumn
parentArray(0) = myDataSet.Tables("Employees").Columns("FirstName")
parentArray(1) = myDataSet.Tables("Employees").Columns("LastName")

Dim childArray(2) As DataColumn
childArray(0) = myDataSet.Tables("Managers").Columns("FirstName")
childArray(1) = myDataSet.Tables("Managers").Columns("LastName")

Dim empToMngr As New DataRelation( _
    "EmployeesToManagers", parentArray, childArray)
myDataSet.Relations.Add(EmpToMngr)
```

Here, you're constructing a DataRelation using a DataColumn array for the primary-key side columns and foreign-key columns of the relationship. When the relationship is constructed, a UniqueConstraint is added to the Employees table, enforcing a unique combination of first and last names, and a ForeignKeyConstraint is added to the Managers table, enforcing cascading deletes and updates across the relationship. Since adding a UniqueConstraint happens as a part of adding a DataRelation, an important thing to keep in mind is that if the values in the primary-key side table are not unique, you won't be able to successfully add a DataRelation. Instead, you'll get an exception.

Putting It All Together

So far you have looked at the various constituents of a DataSet shown in Figure 6-1. You looked at DataTables, DataRelations, and various Constraints. In Example 6.2, you saw that you can easily create an in-memory DataTable without the need of a database. Note that all the classes that have been discussed so far belong in the System.Data namespace. In other words, they are not specific to any particular data provider. This means that OracleClient and SqlClient use the same DataSet implementation. This goes inline with the disconnected nature of the DataSet. Thus, if you quickly glance back at Figure 1-5 in Chapter 1 to the block that says "Disconnected Objects," that is where the DataSet and all it's constituents introduced in this chapter sit.

Next, let's look at an example to solidify our understanding of DataSets and how relations and constraints work within them. The code can be found in the associated code download as Example 6.3.

The DataSet that will be created in this example has two tables in it. These are described in Tables 6-8 and 6-9.

Table 6-8. *The Animal Table*

Property	Description
AnimalID	This is the primary key.
AnimalName	String representation of the user's name.

Table 6-9. *The Pets Table*

Property	Description
PetID=	This is the primary key.
AnimalID	Has a foreign-key constraint with AnimalID.
PetName	The name of the pet.

As indicated, AnimalID serves as a primary key for the Animal table and as a foreign-key constraint between the Pets and Animal tables.

Example 6.3 provides you with a Windows Form that looks like what is shown in Figure 6-2.

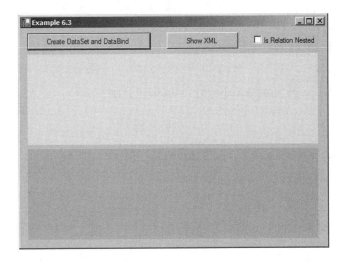

Figure 6-2. *Example 6.3's user interface*

As you can see, there are two buttons: Create DataSet and DataBind, and Show XML. Create DataSet and DataBind creates the bare DataSet schema, and binds the two tables to their individual DataGridViews. Such a DataSet can be set up using the code shown in Listings 6-10 and 6-11. You can find this code in the CreateSchema method in Example 6.3 of the associated code download.

Listing 6-10. *Setting Up the Schema for petsData in C#*

```csharp
DataTable AnimalTable = new DataTable("Animal");
DataColumn myDataColumn;

myDataColumn = new DataColumn("AnimalID", typeof(System.Int32));
myDataColumn.AutoIncrement = true;
AnimalTable.Columns.Add(myDataColumn);

myDataColumn = new DataColumn("AnimalName", typeof(System.String));
AnimalTable.Columns.Add(myDataColumn);

DataTable petsTable = new DataTable("Pet");

myDataColumn = new DataColumn("PetID", typeof(System.Int32));
myDataColumn.AutoIncrement = true;
petsTable.Columns.Add(myDataColumn);

myDataColumn = new DataColumn("AnimalID", typeof(System.Int32));
petsTable.Columns.Add(myDataColumn);

myDataColumn = new DataColumn("PetName", typeof(System.String));
petsTable.Columns.Add(myDataColumn);

DataSet toReturn = new DataSet("petsData");
toReturn.Tables.Add(AnimalTable);
toReturn.Tables.Add(petsTable);
toReturn.Relations.Add(
    new DataRelation("AnimalsPets",
    AnimalTable.Columns["AnimalID"], petsTable.Columns["AnimalID"]));

return toReturn;
```

Listing 6-11. *Setting Up the Schema for petsData in Visual Basic .NET*

```vbnet
Dim AnimalTable As DataTable = New DataTable("Animal")
Dim myDataColumn As DataColumn

myDataColumn = New DataColumn("AnimalID", GetType(System.Int32))
myDataColumn.AutoIncrement = True
AnimalTable.Columns.Add(myDataColumn)

myDataColumn = New DataColumn("AnimalName", GetType(System.String))
AnimalTable.Columns.Add(myDataColumn)

Dim petsTable As DataTable = New DataTable("Pet")
```

```
myDataColumn = New DataColumn("PetID", GetType(System.Int32))
myDataColumn.AutoIncrement = True
petsTable.Columns.Add(myDataColumn)

myDataColumn = New DataColumn("AnimalID", GetType(System.Int32))
petsTable.Columns.Add(myDataColumn)

myDataColumn = New DataColumn("PetName", GetType(System.String))
petsTable.Columns.Add(myDataColumn)

Dim toReturn As DataSet = New DataSet("petsData")
toReturn.Tables.Add(AnimalTable)
toReturn.Tables.Add(petsTable)
toReturn.Relations.Add( _
    New DataRelation("AnimalsPets", _
    AnimalTable.Columns("AnimalID"), petsTable.Columns("AnimalID")))

Return toReturn
```

It then data binds it with the appropriate grids, as shown in Listings 6-12 and 6-13.

Listing 6-12. *Data Binding petsData in C#*

```
petsData = CreateSchema();
petsGrid.DataSource = petsData.Tables["Pet"];
AnimalsGrid.DataSource = petsData.Tables["Animal"];
```

Listing 6-13. *Data Binding petsData in Visual Basic .NET*

```
petsData = CreateSchema()
petsGrid.DataSource = petsData.Tables("Pet")
AnimalsGrid.DataSource = petsData.Tables("Animal")
```

Show XML simply shows the contents of the DataSet as XML. This can be done using either WriteXml or GetXml. Since GetXml directly returns the DataSet as an XML string, let's use that instead:

C#
```
MessageBox.Show(petsData.GetXml(), "DataSet Contents");
```

VB.NET
```
MessageBox.Show(petsData.GetXml(), "DataSet Contents")
```

Finally, there is a checkbox that sets the nested property on the relation:

C#
```
if (petsData != null)
{
    petsData.Relations[0].Nested = nestedRelation.Checked;
}
```

VB.NET

```
If Not petsData Is Nothing Then
    petsData.Relations(0).Nested = nestedRelation.Checked
End If
```

Once this code is put together and the example is run, it produces a Windows Form as shown in Figure 6-2. Try adding some data as shown in Figure 6-3.

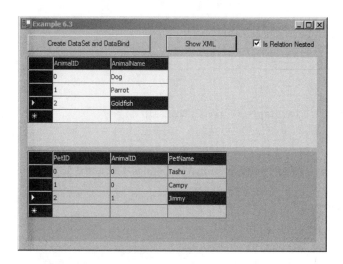

Figure 6-3. *Example 6.3 in action*

In editing the DataSet, you'll notice that

• The primary keys PetID and AnimalID are automatically generated for you.

• If you try to enter data that violates the relation set up for you, you'll get a System.Data. InvalidConstraint and the form will not let you enter the invalid data.

You can view the DataSet's contents at any time by clicking Show XML. One curious thing to note, however, is the difference between the XML generated when the relation's Nested property is set to true versus when it is set to false (see Listings 6-14 and 6-15).

Listing 6-14. *Contents of the DataSet with the Nested Property Set to false*

```
<petsData>
  <Animal>
    <AnimalID>0</AnimalID>
    <AnimalName>Dog</AnimalName>
  </Animal>
  <Animal>
    <AnimalID>1</AnimalID>
    <AnimalName>Parrot</AnimalName>
```

```
  </Animal>
  <Animal>
    <AnimalID>2</AnimalID>
    <AnimalName>Goldfish</AnimalName>
  </Animal>
  <petsTable>
    <PetID>0</PetID>
    <AnimalID>0</AnimalID>
    <PetName>Tashu</PetName>
  </petsTable>
  <petsTable>
    <PetID>1</PetID>
    <AnimalID>0</AnimalID>
    <PetName>Campy</PetName>
  </petsTable>
  <petsTable>
    <PetID>2</PetID>
    <AnimalID>1</AnimalID>
    <PetName>Jimmy</PetName>
  </petsTable>
</petsData>
```

Listing 6-15. *Contents of the DataSet with the Nested Property Set to true*

```
<petsData>
  <Animal>
    <AnimalID>0</AnimalID>
    <AnimalName>Dog</AnimalName>
    <petsTable>
      <PetID>0</PetID>
      <AnimalID>0</AnimalID>
      <PetName>Tashu</PetName>
    </petsTable>
    <petsTable>
      <PetID>1</PetID>
      <AnimalID>0</AnimalID>
    <PetName>Campy</PetName>
    </petsTable>
  </Animal>
  <Animal>
    <AnimalID>1</AnimalID>
    <AnimalName>Parrot</AnimalName>
    <petsTable>
      <PetID>2</PetID>
      <AnimalID>1</AnimalID>
      <PetName>Jimmy</PetName>
    </petsTable>
  </Animal>
```

```
<Animal>
  <AnimalID>2</AnimalID>
  <AnimalName>Goldfish</AnimalName>
</Animal>
</petsData>
```

The subtle difference between the two is that the XML representation actually nests the relation when the relation's Nested property is set to true. This way, by setting up a DataRelation, you can enforce referential integrity and also you can convert the structure of your data from a relational structure to a hierarchical XML structure with ease. A DataRelation has other uses besides data integrity, it also allows you to conveniently search through the various records in various DataTables of a DataSet. You'll see this using a many-to-many table relationship example in Chapter 8, and compare it with other alternatives, such as DataViews, etc.

You might note that in Example 6.3 only a DataRelation was set up, not a ForeignKeyConstraint, or for that matter even a UniqueKeyConstraint. As explained previously, the UniqueKeyConstraint is automatically set up for you when you marked a column as a PrimaryKey or set its AutoIncrement to True.

In a similar fashion, a ForeignKeyConstraint is added for you automatically when you set up a relation between the two tables. One of the things mentioned earlier was the ability to specify an UpdateRule or DeleteRule on a given constraint. By default these values are set to Cascade, so you could try changing the AnimalID for an Animal after a few Pet records have been associated with the Animal; you'll see that ADO.NET automatically cascades those changes for you. This way your data sanctity is maintained with very little effort required from you.

Obviously, this data sanctity is maintained only in memory. There is still a world of problems to be solved when you try saving this data back into the database. This is discussed in further depth in Chapter 10, but just as some food for thought, consider what would happen if while remaining disconnected you added rows that satisfy a given foreign-key constraint, but before you saved those rows in the database, some other user deleted the primary-key row out of the database. (Uh oh!!) This is a much broader topic commonly referred to as *concurrency*. While concurrency is discussed in depth in Chapters 9 and 10, always keep in mind while reading this chapter that the in-memory party you are having with the DataSet eventually needs to make it's way back into persisted relational storage, typically a database. More on that in Chapters 9 and 10, for the moment let's get back to the discussion of DataSets.

DataSets As Data Transfer Objects

Both DataSets and business objects have the ability to hold relational data. But there is one big difference. DataSets are data transfer objects, that is, they are dumb buckets of data that help you carry data from one point to another. They don't contain semantic behavior of the contents of the data; whereas, a business object is an object representation that abstracts logical entities in the specific business domain the program is being written for.

In other words, business objects hold data for you in a convenient enough representation. They allow you to view a typical database relational data structure as a more logical hierarchical object representation. These business objects could also have rules built inside of them for validation purposes. Chapter 14 gives a good comparison of a business object versus a DataSet, but it is wise to delay that discussion until you're fully familiar with all aspects of ADO.NET.

Earlier in this chapter, you looked at various desired characteristics of the object that would hold the responsibility of acting as the data carrier between various layers, processes, and machines. You saw that the DataSet object that comes bundled as a part of the Microsoft .NET Framework satisfies most of those requirements.

Frequently, you'd want to pass DataSets over Remoting or web-service boundaries. There is an important performance trick involved in sending DataSets over such boundaries. The problem is when DataSets are serialized—even if you use BinaryFormatter to serialize them, by default they will always be serialized as XML.

Note There are mainly two kinds of serialization in the .NET Framework. XML serialization and serialization done by a formatter that implements IFormatter. When I say a DataSet is serialized as XML, I mean to say that even if you didn't use XML serialization (hence you used BinaryFormatter which implements IFormatter), the resultant output is still XML.

That leads to not only performance issues, but when you send "Time" data types in strongly typed DataSets (covered later) over a Remoting interface that spans two time zones, the time zone translation actually might occur twice.[2]

This is obviously a problem. Let's see this using an example. The code for this example can be found in the associated code download as Example 6.4, but I will mention the important parts of the example here.

This example will create some sample data using a method called GiveMeFakeData() as shown in Listings 6-16 and 6-17. This DataSet has only one DataTable with two columns and a thousand rows.

Listing 6-16. *GiveMeFakeData() in C#*

```csharp
public static DataSet GiveMeFakeData()
{
    DataSet ds = new DataSet();
    DataTable dt = new DataTable("Animal");
    dt.Columns.Add(new DataColumn("AnimalID"));
    dt.Columns.Add(new DataColumn("AnimalType"));

    DataRow dr;
    for (int i = 0; i <= 999; i++)
    {
        dr = dt.NewRow();
        dr[0] = 1;
        dr[1] = "Rabbit";
        dt.Rows.Add(dr);
```

___

2. This discussion is bordering a discussion on Remoting. While this is not a Remoting book, you can refer to *Advanced .NET Remoting*, Second Edition by Ingo Rammer and Mario Szpuszta (Apress, 2005) for a good discussion on that topic.

```
            dr = dt.NewRow();
            dr[0] = 2;
            dr[1] = "Monkey";
            dt.Rows.Add(dr);

            dr = dt.NewRow();
            dr[0] = 3;
            dr[1] = "Donkey";
            dt.Rows.Add(dr);

            dr = dt.NewRow();
            dr[0] = 4;
            dr[1] = "Dog";
            dt.Rows.Add(dr);
        }

    ds.Tables.Add(dt);

    return ds;
}
```

Listing 6-17. *GiveMeFakeData() in Visual Basic .NET*

```
Function GiveMeFakeData() As DataSet
    Dim ds As New DataSet()
    Dim dt As New DataTable("Animal")
    dt.Columns.Add(New DataColumn("AnimalID"))
    dt.Columns.Add(New DataColumn("AnimalType"))

    Dim dr As DataRow
    Dim i As Integer
    For i = 0 To 999
        dr = dt.NewRow()
        dr(0) = 1
        dr(1) = "Rabbit"
        dt.Rows.Add(dr)

        dr = dt.NewRow()
        dr(0) = 2
        dr(1) = "Monkey"
        dt.Rows.Add(dr)

        dr = dt.NewRow()
        dr(0) = 3
        dr(1) = "Donkey"
        dt.Rows.Add(dr)
```

```
    dr = dt.NewRow()
    dr(0) = 4
    dr(1) = "Dog"
    dt.Rows.Add(dr)
Next i

ds.Tables.Add(dt)

Return ds
End Function
```

Next, this example attempts to Serialize and Deserialize this DataSet using the BinaryFormatter, which is a standard formatter that comes with the .NET Framework. In one case, it attempts to serialize it with the RemotingFormat set to SerializationFormat.Binary, and in the other case, you can simply comment out that line and leave it to the default value of SerializationFormat.Xml. In either case, the example does a rough performance count by counting the number of ticks it takes to Deserialize such a DataSet. This can be seen in Listings 6-18 and 6-19.

Listing 6-18. *Serialization and Deserialization of a DataSet in C#*

```
BinaryFormatter bf = new BinaryFormatter();
FileStream fs = new FileStream(
      System.Environment.CurrentDirectory.ToString() + "\\ds.dat",
      FileMode.OpenOrCreate);
DataSet ds = GiveMeFakeData() ;
ds.RemotingFormat = SerializationFormat.Binary;
bf.Serialize(fs, ds);
fs.Close();

// Check the deserialization performance.
fs = new FileStream(
      System.Environment.CurrentDirectory.ToString() + "\\ds.dat",
      FileMode.Open);
long nowTicks = DateTime.Now.Ticks;
DataSet ds2 = (DataSet)bf.Deserialize(fs);
long tickstotal = DateTime.Now.Ticks - nowticks ;
Console.WriteLine("Took me : " + tickstotal);
fs.Close();
```

Listing 6-19. *Serialization and Deserialization of a DataSet in Visual Basic .NET*

```
Dim bf As New BinaryFormatter()
Dim fs As New FileStream( _
   System.Environment.CurrentDirectory.ToString() & _
   "\ds.dat", FileMode.OpenOrCreate)
Dim ds As DataSet = GiveMeFakeData()
```

```
ds.RemotingFormat = SerializationFormat.Binary
bf.Serialize(fs, ds)
fs.Close()

' Check the deserialization performance.
fs = New FileStream( _
    System.Environment.CurrentDirectory.ToString() & _
    "\ds.dat", FileMode.Open)
Dim nowTicks As Long = DateTime.Now.Ticks
Dim ds2 As DataSet = CType(bf.Deserialize(fs), DataSet)
Dim tickstotal As Long = DateTime.Now.Ticks - nowticks
Console.WriteLine(("Took me : " & tickstotal))
fs.Close()
```

So first, run this example with RemotingFormat set to SerializationFormat.XML. This can be toggled by modifying the bolded line in Listings 6-18 and 6-19. When this example is run, it produces output that looks like

```
Took me : 1201728 ticks
```

Next, this example is run with RemotingFormat set to SerializationFormat.Binary. It produces output that looks like

```
Took me : 300432 ticks
```

The actual results may vary depending on the exact configuration of your machine and other processes running at the time of the test, but the comparison will be similar. As you can see the true binary serialization format is *much* faster than the default XML serialization format. Since the serialized stream is stored to a file on the disk, you may also note that the file size, hence the serialized stream size, is about 550KB in the case of default XML serialization, and about 55KB, or one-tenth in size, when using actual binary serialization enforced by SerializationFormat.Binary. So when such data is sent over a limited bandwidth connection, the difference will be even greater.

■Note The RemotingFormat property value defaults to SerializationFormat.XML. This is for backward compatibility with ADO.NET 1.1.

If you open the serialized file with SerializationFormat.XML in Notepad, it looks like what is shown in Figure 6-4.

Figure 6-4. *DataSet serialized as XML using the BinaryFormatter*

And when the DataSet is serialized with SerializationFormat.Binary and the file is opened in Notepad, it looks like what is shown in Figure 6-5.

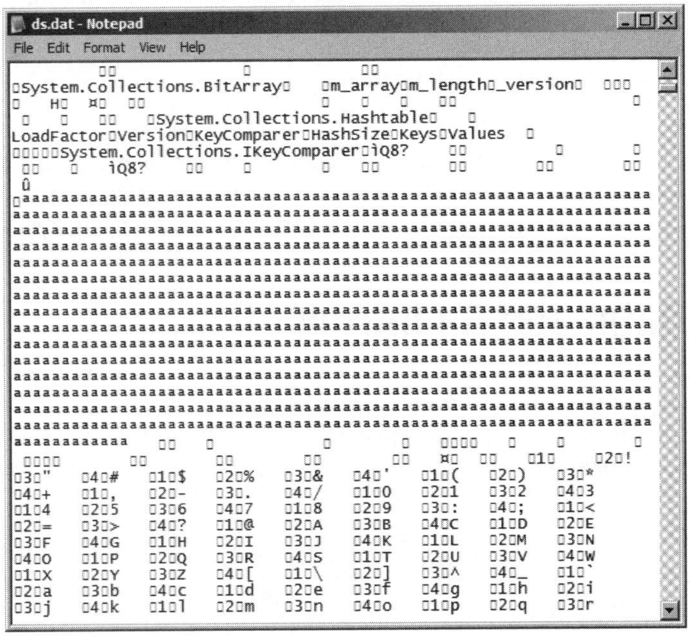

Figure 6-5. *DataSet serialized as true binary using the BinaryFormatter*

In ADO.NET 1.1, `SerializationFormat.XML` was the only choice, thus *even if you used* `BinaryFormatter`, *the* `DataSet` *would still be serialized as XML, and you would pay the associated performance penalties.*

■**Tip** A work-around for this problem exists for Framework 1.1 at `http://support.microsoft.com/default.aspx?scid=kb;en-us;829740`.

Now that serialization isn't such a problem with `DataSet`s anymore, there does exist another problem in `DataSet`s that make them less than ideal for all situations: `DataSet`s are not strongly typed.

What this means is that if you had a `DataSet` that stored customer information, you would have to access the customer row in a fashion similar to this:

C#
```
Int32 id = (Int32)customersDataset.Tables["Customers"].Rows[0]["CustomerId"] ;
```

VB.NET
```
Int32 id = CInt(customersDataset.Tables("Customers").Rows(0)("CustomerId"))
```

There are a few major problems with this approach:

- You need to remember the column names. Not only that but you need to spell them correctly every time and the compiler can't help you if you spell them incorrectly at certain places. Usually such an error would be caught at runtime.

- There is an associated boxing/unboxing or conversion cost because `DataSet` will always return values as an object. In this case, you had to convert the object to `Int32`.

- If, indeed, you get some data that doesn't conform to what you were expecting, there's no way the `DataSet` can do that check for you.

These problems are solved by strongly typed `DataSet`s. Specifically, the problem regarding boxing/unboxing or conversion isn't actually solved by strongly typed `DataSet`s, but actually masked because the generated code for strongly typed `DataSet`s takes care of those issues for you.

Strongly Typed DataSets: An Introduction

So far, you've looked at how to use the `DataSet` class provided by the `System.Data` namespace. You learned about the `Rows` collection and the `Columns` collection, and how to access individual rows and columns of data within the `DataSet`. For example, in a typical `DataSet`, you might access the first name of a customer like so:

C#

```
myRow = MyDataSet.Tables["Customers"].Rows[0];
Console.WriteLine(myRow["FirstName"]);
```

VB.NET

```
myRow = MyDataSet.Tables("Customers").Rows(0)
Console.WriteLine(myRow("FirstName"))
```

By the time you are done with this chapter, you'll be able to get access to your data in a much more programmer- and reader-friendly fashion:

C#

```
Console.WriteLine(CustomerDataSet.Customers[0].FirstName);
```

VB.NET

```
Console.WriteLine(CustomerDataSet.Customers(0).FirstName)
```

As you can see, the second method is much easier to understand and write. The functionality just described is made possible by a convention in the .NET Framework known as *strongly typed* DataSets: classes that inherit from a DataSet giving them a strongly typed nature based on an XSD structure you specify.

A typed DataSet is not a built-in member of the .NET Framework. As you will discover, it is a generated class that inherits directly from the DataSet class, and allows properties and methods to be customized from an XML schema that you specify. This class also contains other classes for DataTable and DataRow objects that are enhanced in similar ways. As a result, you can create schemas and classes for data that are customized precisely for *your* data, enabling you to write data-access code more efficiently. Do note, however, that even though your code will be up and running quicker, you will also be burdened eventually with keeping the structures of your strongly typed DataSets up to date as your system changes. A good comparison of strongly typed DataSets and DataSets is discussed in Chapter 14.

So, strongly typed DataSets need you to write XSD schemas. In fact, not every XSD schema qualifies to be a DataSet, so it may be argued that you need to know specifically what is allowed in an XML schema that controls what aspect of a DataSet.

The good news, however, is that for a majority of your needs, Visual Studio makes it extremely easy to author strongly typed DataSets. So as you add a new DataTable, it creates and maintains an XSD schema underneath for you.

However, it cannot hurt to learn what exactly the XSD under a strongly typed DataSet can contain. An XML schema provides a rich definition of the data types, relationships, keys, and constraints within the data it describes. There will be a discussion on how schemas and DataSets fit together and how to create strongly typed DataSets later in this chapter. First, let's have a brief overview of some of the basic elements of XSD.

Overview of XSD

Before I mire you in a discussion about XSDs, I must add that if you are already familiar with XSDs, you may feel free to skip this section and go directly to "DataSet Schemas." This is because Visual Studio makes it so easy to author strongly typed DataSets that for the most part you wouldn't need to know what is happening behind the scenes. However, just like anything, if you wish to complete this one missing piece of the jigsaw puzzle in your understanding, feel free to come back and read through this section.

If you did choose to stick with the XSD discussion, I should explain why I'm covering XSD here. Relational database servers like SQL Server and Oracle all have their own internal and proprietary formats for defining the structure of stored data. An Oracle table definition looks nothing like an internal SQL Server table definition. ADO.NET DataSets, on the other hand, need to work with every single database out there, and thus support a common set of features that can be defined in XSDs. It's important to note, however, that an in-memory DataSet does not store either it's structure or data as XML, it only supports easy conversion and compliance between itself and XML.

The *XML Schema Definition (XSD) language* is an application of XML for describing data structures. It's particularly useful to us here because it allows applications to read and use schema information when handling data. A strongly typed DataSet is a subclass of the (untyped) DataSet class, generated using an XML schema and, therefore, tailored to that particular XML schema.

The following overview of XSD should give you enough information to create and use strongly typed DataSets. However, this is only a small part of what XSD can do, but it's enough to understand strongly typed DataSets.

Simple Types

An XML schema is an XML document that defines the structure of other XML documents by specifying the structures and types of the elements that can be used in those documents. An XML schema also identifies the constraints on the content of those other XML documents, and describes the vocabulary (rules or grammar) that compliant XML documents must follow in order to be considered valid against the XML schema.

For instance, if you see an XML file without a schema, you have to assume that every single node's data type is string. Or any node can contain any other node, as long as it is valid XML. Thus, it's difficult to program against that XML or even use it as a data interchange vehicle, simply because the second party cannot definitely understand what data resides where. These rules can be enforced either by an XML schema (XSD), or by using a Document Type Definition (DTD).

One of the biggest disadvantages of using DTDs for constraining the behavior of instance documents was that the DTD syntax was not XML, so not only did the programmer have to learn a new syntax, but validating XML parsers had to know how to parse the DTD syntax as well as XML. XML schemas are actually a dialect of XML, so any XML parser can interpret schema information.

Putting all of this another way, the XSD elements in an XML schema control how various elements and attributes can appear in a related XML document. In this section, you will start a speedy overview of the XSD language by looking at the *simple types*—a part of XSD syntax that's used to define what types of data may appear in the content of an associated XML document.

Basic Data Types

The XSD standard defines several built-in data types, all of which are listed in Table 6-10.

Table 6-10. *Valid Data Types in an XSD Schema*

Primitive XML Data Type	Description
string	Represents a character string.
Boolean	Represents a true or false value.
decimal	Represents numbers of arbitrary precision.
float	Represents a single-precision, 32-bit floating point number.
double	Represents a double-precision, 64-bit floating point number.
duration	Represents a length of time.
dateTime	Represents a specific point in time.
time	Represents a given time of day.
date	Represents a calendar date.
gYearMonth	Represents a Gregorian month and Gregorian year.
gYear	Represents a Gregorian year.
gMonthDay	Represents a Gregorian month and Gregorian day. A specific date that occurs once a year.
gDay	Represents a Gregorian day of the month.
gMonth	Represents a Gregorian month.
hexBinary	Represents hex-encoded binary data.
base64Binary	Represents Base64-encoded arbitrary binary data.
anyURI	Represents any URI (as defined by RFC 2396)—may be absolute or relative.
QName	Represents a qualified name. Composed of a prefix and a local name, separated by a colon. The prefix must be a namespace that's been defined by a namespace declaration.
NOTATION	Represents a set of QNames.

To start making things a little clearer, the following is an example of an XSD file that (among other things) utilizes a couple of the primitive types described in Table 6-10. You might not understand all of the syntax at first, but the remainder will be described shortly. For now, just take a look at the attribute declarations and their associated data types (in bold):

```
<?xml version="1.0" encoding="utf-8" ?>
<xs:schema targetNamespace="http://tempuri.org/XMLSchema.xsd"
        elementFormDefault="qualified"
        xmlns="http://tempuri.org/XMLSchema.xsd"
        xmlns:xs="http://www.w3.org/2001/XMLSchema">
  <xs:element name="MyElement">
    <xs:complexType>
      <xs:attribute name="MyString" type="xs:string" />
      <xs:attribute name="MyTime" type="xs:time" />
      <xs:attribute name="MyBool" type="xs:boolean" />
      <xs:attribute name="MyDecimal" type="xs:decimal" />
    </xs:complexType>
  </xs:element>
</xs:schema>
```

This schema indicates that an element called `<MyElement>` can exist in an XML document associated with it, and that the element will have four attributes of varying data types. The following XML is part of a document that conforms to the previous schema:

```
<MyElement MyString="Hello"
           MyTime="12:00"
           MyBool="true"
           MyDecimal="3.851" />
```

You'll learn more about `<complexType>` and `<element>` elements later in this overview section.

Attributes

As shown previously, attributes provide additional information about a given element. Attributes can only exist within the context of an element that they give additional information about—they cannot contain child elements of their own. Attributes can be defined as being any of the primitive XML data types in Table 6-10, or derived types such as `positiveInteger`.

The syntax for declaring an attribute in XSD is

```
<xs:attribute default = (value)
    fixed = (value)
    form = (qualified | unqualified)
    id = ID
    name = Name
    ref = (reference qualified name)
    type = (data type, qualified name)
    use = (optional | prohibited | required)"
</xs:attribute>
```

The `<element>` element in the sample schema showed how you could nest attribute declarations in order to assign them to a given element. Without going into much more detail about the intricacies of attribute declarations here, let's look at a few of the more important attributes of the `<attribute>` element in XSD:

- `form`: Indicates whether the attribute needs to have a valid namespace prefix in the instance document.

- `type`: The name of one of the primitive data types, or a derived data type.

- `use`: Describes how the attribute can be used. The default value is `optional`, which indicates that the attribute is optional and can have any value (provided that the value doesn't contradict the `type`). You can also use this attribute to indicate that the attribute is `prohibited` in the instance document, or is `required` to appear.

Enumerations

Enumerations provide a way for you to restrict the values available for the XML document to those that you select. You can only provide enumerations for primitive data types, such as strings and integers. Primitive data types are not to be confused with the simple type and complex type that are defined in XML schemas. Primitive types can be compared with scalar variables in most programming languages. They stand in contrast with classes or structs.

You can create an enumeration by using an XSD `<simpleType>` element. Within the `<simpleType>`, you create a `<restriction>` with a base attribute.

The base attribute of the `<restriction>` tag is set with the primitive data type on which the restriction is placed. In the case of this sample, you're creating an enumeration of strings. So, at this point, your XSD fragment might look like this:

```
<xs:simpleType name="MyEnumeration">
  <xs:restriction base="xs:string">
  </xs:restriction>
</xs:simpleType>
```

From here, you can define any number of restrictions (placed inside the `<restriction>` element) on the value that this new simple data type can accept. Keep in mind that the previous XSD snippet is defining a new data type that you are going to want to use as the data type of an attribute later on.

As an example, let's define an enumeration restriction that looks like this: any attribute that's given this type will only be able to take on the values red, white, and blue:

```
<xs:enumeration value="red" />
<xs:enumeration value="white" />
<xs:enumeration value="blue" />
```

The final schema, which indicates that the XML document can contain a `<MyElement>` element with a MyEnum attribute and a MyString attribute, looks like this:

```
<?xml version="1.0" encoding="utf-8" ?>
<xs:schema targetNamespace="http://tempuri.org/XMLSchema.xsd"
           elementFormDefault="qualified"
           xmlns="http://tempuri.org/XMLSchema.xsd"
           xmlns:xs="http://www.w3.org/2001/XMLSchema">
  <xs:element name="MyElement">
    <xs:complexType>
      <xs:attribute name="MyEnum" type="MyEnumeration" />
      <xs:attribute name="MyString" type="xs:string" />
    </xs:complexType>
  </xs:element>
  <xs:simpleType name="MyEnumeration">
    <xs:restriction base="xs:string">
      <xs:enumeration value="red" />
      <xs:enumeration value="white" />
      <xs:enumeration value="blue" />
    </xs:restriction>
  </xs:simpleType>
</xs:schema>
```

So, if you attempted to validate the following XML against this schema, the validation would fail because the MyEnum attribute contains a value of purple, which isn't allowed by the enumeration you defined:

```
<MyElement MyEnum="purple" MyString="Hello" />
```

User-Defined Types

These are not to be confused with the User-Defined Types (UDTs) for SQL Server discussed in Chapter 5. In the context of an XML schema, a user-defined type is a restriction that's placed on the content of an element or an attribute. As you saw previously, enumerations can be used to create a kind of user-defined type, as they place a restriction on the values that primitive types can use. A user-defined simple type will always restrict the contents of the element or attribute to which it's applied to a subset of the base type from which it's derived. In other words, when you create a user-defined simple type, you create a restriction on a primitive type.

The way in which individual restrictions are placed on primitive types for the purpose of defining user-defined simple types is through XSD elements called *facets*.

Facets

Facets are elements that are used to define a legal set of values for a simple type (which can be a user-defined simple type, or a primitive type like string or float). Constraining facets appear as child elements of a <restriction> node, which is in turn a child of a <simpleType> node. Table 6-11 is a list of the constraining facets that can be applied to a simple type (either built-in or user-defined).

Table 6-11. *Constraining Facets*

Constraining Facet	Description
enumeration	As you have already seen, this facet constrains the value of a simple type to a specified list of values.
fractionDigits	Specifies the maximum number of allowable digits in the fractional portion of the value.
length	Specifies the number of units of length. The units are determined by the base type of the simple type to which the facet is being applied. All values must be *exactly* this length.
maxExclusive	Maximum value. All values must be *less than* this value to qualify.
maxInclusive	Maximum value. All values must be *less than or equal to* this value in order to qualify.
maxLength	Maximum number of units of length. Units are determined by data type.
minExclusive	Minimum value. All values must be *greater than* this value to qualify.
minInclusive	Minimum value. All values must be *greater than or equal to* this value to qualify.
minLength	Minimum allowed length of the value. Units of length depend on the data type.
pattern	Specifies a regular expression that all values must match. A favorite!
totalDigits	Value must have a specific maximum number of total digits.
whiteSpace	Indicates whether the element should preserve, replace, or collapse whitespace.

Complex Types

Complex types in XML schemas are used to declare the attributes that can be placed on an element. They can also be used to define the names, nature, and behavior of an element's child nodes (if any). If an element in the instance document is going to be anything other than simple (meaning that it contains no child elements, no attributes, and has only a basic data type as its contents), then you must declare it as a complex type in the schema.

Let's take a look at a fairly simple XML document with just a two-level hierarchy:

```
<Book>
  <Title>Pro ADO.NET</Title>
  <Publisher>Apress Ltd</Publisher>
</Book>
```

The top-level element [the DocumentElement, if you're used to DOM (Document Object Model) programming] is the <Book> element. It has two child elements: <Title> and <Publisher>. Based on the definition of a complex type, the <Book> element is complex, but both the <Title> and <Publisher> elements are simple (they are based on basic data types and have no attributes or child elements).

Let's create a portion of a schema that represents this hierarchy. Whenever you declare a complex type, you need to use the <complexType> XSD element:

```
<xs:element name="Book">
  <xs:complexType>
    <xs:sequence>
      <xs:element name="Title" type="xs:string" />
      <xs:element name="Publisher" type="xs:string" />
    </xs:sequence>
  </xs:complexType>
</xs:element>
```

The mixed Attribute

The <complexType> element's mixed attribute allows the content of a given element to contain a mixture of simple character data and child nodes. This attribute is extremely helpful in mixing markup tags with standard prose, such as defining reference links and information within the context of a magazine article, a book review, or any other form of content.

You could make a slight change to the previous schema and modify the <complexType> element to include the mixed="true" attribute, as follows:

```
<xs:element name="Book">
  <xs:complexType mixed="true">
    <xs:sequence>
      <xs:element name="Title" type="xs:string" />
      <xs:element name="Publisher" type="xs:string" />
    </xs:sequence>
  </xs:complexType>
</xs:element>
```

You could then write a valid XML document that contains mixed content, like this:

```
<Book>
  The title of this book is <Title>Pro ADO.NET</Title> and
  the publisher of the book is <Publisher>Apress Ltd</Publisher>.
</Book>
```

Mixed content is very often seen in business-to-business (B2B) document exchanges. For example, if a media provider supplied movie reviews to dozens of online movie retailers, they could provide those reviews with mixed content, marking up the portions containing data that could be accessed or searched for, such as the rating or the title of the movie. In general, however, mixed content is best avoided if possible, due to the complexities it adds to parsing code. This is because data tags are mixed with the data, and that can never be good.

Element Groups

There are only a few more things left to cover before you get into the specifics of how schemas affect DataSet objects. One of those things is *element groups*. Any time that a set of more than one element appears as a child of another element, it's considered to be an element group. There are four main XSD elements for defining the behavior of element groups:

- The `<all>` element
- The `<choice>` element
- The `<sequence>` element
- The `<group>` element

The <all> Element The `<all>` element indicates that all of the child elements declared beneath it can exist in the instance document, in any order. Here's how the book schema might change to accommodate such a thing:

```
<xs:element name="Book">
  <xs:complexType>
    <xs:all>
      <xs:element name="Title" type="xs:string" />
      <xs:element name="Publisher" type="xs:string" />
    </xs:all>
  </xs:complexType>
</xs:element>
```

The <choice> Element The `<choice>` element indicates that one *and only one* of its child elements can exist in the instance document. Therefore, if you modify the book schema to use a `<choice>` element, you can have either a `<Title>` element or a `<Publisher>` element in the instance document, but validation will fail if you have both:

```
<xs:element name="Book">
  <xs:complexType>
    <xs:choice>
```

```
    <xs:element name="Title" type="xs:string" />
    <xs:element name="Publisher" type="xs:string" />
  </xs:choice>
  </xs:complexType>
</xs:element>
```

The <sequence> Element The <sequence> element indicates that the order in which the child elements appear in an instance document must be the same as the order in which those elements are declared. The following is a modified book schema using the <sequence> element:

```
<xs:element name="Book">
  <xs:complexType>
    <xs:sequence>
      <xs:element name="Title" type="xs:string" />
      <xs:element name="Publisher" type="xs:string" />
    </xs:sequence>
  </xs:complexType>
</xs:element>
```

This means that if you try to validate the following XML document against this schema, the validation will fail, because the instance document contains the child elements in the wrong order:

```
<Book>
  <Publisher>Apress Ltd</Publisher>
  <Title>Pro ADO.NET</Title>
</Book>
```

The <group> Element The <group> element provides a method for naming a group of elements or attributes. This becomes exceedingly useful if the same grouping will appear in more than one place. For example, if you have an instance document that contains both customers and contacts, then you might want a reusable group of elements for the name, address, and phone number. The <group> element can contain an <all> element, a <choice> element, or a <sequence> element. Here's an example portion of a schema that utilizes a <group>:

```
<xs:group name="ContactInfo">
  <xs:all>
    <xs:element name="Address1" type="xs:string" />
    <xs:element name="Address2" type="xs:string" />
    <xs:element name="City" type="xs:string" />
    <xs:element name="State" type="xs:string" />
  </xs:all>
</xs:group>
<xs:element name="Contact">
  <xs:complexType>
    <xs:group ref="ContactInfo" />
    <xs:element name="Company" type="xs:string" />
```

```
    </xs:complexType>
  </xs:element>
  <xs:element name="Customer">
    <xs:complexType>
      <xs:group ref="ContactInfo" />
      <xs:element name="Status" type="xs:string" />
    </xs:complexType>
  </xs:element>
```

You can see how the ContactInfo grouping of elements was reused for two different parent elements, without having to retype the information.

Attribute Groups

This same idea of reusing groups can be applied to attributes just as easily as it can be applied to elements. If, for example, you wanted to convert the book description XML document so that the title and publisher become attributes of the <Book> element, you can group those attributes as follows, allowing them to be reused throughout the schema:

```
<xs:attributeGroup name="BookDetails">
  <xs:attribute name="Title" type="xs:string" />
  <xs:attribute name="Publisher" type="xs:string" />
</xs:attributeGroup>

<xs:element name="Book">
  <xs:attributeGroup ref="BookDetails" />
</xs:element>
```

So, the XML instance document for the new schema looks like this:

```
<Book Title="Pro ADO.NET" Publisher="Apress Ltd" />
```

XSD Annotation

One of the biggest benefits of XML schemas is that they are written in human-readable form. Compilers and applications can interpret them for use in data manipulation scenarios, while the programmers using those schemas can read them without recourse to a translator.

Sometimes, schemas will be sent to business partners to ensure that everyone is formatting their data properly. Other times, schemas are generated by an application architect and then provided to the programmers who write the actual code. No matter what the reason, it's extremely helpful to have the ability to embed documentation and additional information into the schema itself, rather than having the programmers search for it elsewhere.

XML schemas provide two ways of annotating a schema. You can either annotate your schema with documentation that's designed to be read by a human examining the schema, or you can use annotation that's designed to provide additional detailed information to the program or process that's interpreting the schema. In fact, all annotation for an XML schema occurs within the <annotation> element. The two different types of annotation occur as child elements of that parent. The <annotation> element itself should occur as the first child of the element to which the annotation applies.

The <documentation> Element

The <documentation> element contains human-readable information that's intended for the audience of the XML schema file. Here's a quick example of a modified schema for the book document that contains some documentation:

```
<xs:element name="Book">
  <xs:annotation>
    <xs:documentation>
      This book element contains information about a single book. It
      should contain the full title and the official name of the
      publisher.
    </xs:documentation>
  </xs:annotation>

  <xs:complexType>
    <xs:sequence>
      <xs:element name="Title" type="xs:string" />
      <xs:element name="Publisher" type="xs:string" />
    </xs:sequence>
  </xs:complexType>
</xs:element>
```

The <appinfo> Element

The <appinfo> element provides a way for the schema author to supply additional information to an application interpreting the schema. This kind of information might include script code, filenames, switches, or flags of some kind indicating parameters for processing. As with the <documentation> element, <appinfo> always occurs within an <annotation> element.

DataSet Schemas

Whether you read the previous "Overview of XSD" section or you decided that you could skip over that section because you were already familiar with XSDs, it's about time I started discussing how XSDs apply to DataSets.

This next section, then, is going to cover XML schemas as they apply to DataSet objects, covering the XSD elements and structures that relate directly to various DataSet behaviors and configurations.

Schema Translation

Before you get going, it's important to bear in mind that in previous examples, you have already manipulated and interrogated various DataSets' schemas without knowing anything at all about XSD, and you'll be doing more in the same vein later in the book. There are plenty of occasions when it's not necessary to know about the underlying XML schema in order to do useful work with ADO.NET.

Here, then, you'll read about how XML schemas are translated into the entities that DataSets expose to their clients: tables, rows, columns, relationships, keys, and constraints. While it's theoretically possible for you to accomplish everything you need by simply dragging a table from a database connection in Visual Studio .NET onto a new DataSet class and never looking at the underlying XSD, it may not be practical to do so. For example, there are many occasions when the structure in a database doesn't reflect the structure you want in your DataSet.

Having a thorough knowledge of which elements in XSD produce which behaviors in a DataSet can save you time, effort, redundant code, and the problem of Wizard-generated code getting *close* to your desired result, but not being exactly what you want. It's a good, defensive programming tactic to assume that a Wizard is just a starting point, and that any Wizard-generated code will have to be modified before it's ready to use. Dragging a table definition from SQL Server onto the design surface of the Visual Studio .NET DataSet designer might be sufficient to get the job done, but you can accomplish quite a bit more with some knowledge of the underlying details. However, try to limit changes done by hand to only the XSD portion. This is so because the C# or VB.NET code generated by MSDataSetGenerator (or XSD.exe) will end up overwriting your changes. Since strongly typed DataSets are implemented as partial classes, you should implement a parallel partial class that will not get overwritten every time the XSD schema changes.

Generating Tables and Columns

Here you are going to read about how to indicate tables, rows, and columns with XSD. In an XSD representation, every DataSet must have a single root element, which indicates the DataSet itself. It's beneath this root element that you can supply your definitions for the tables and columns of your DataSet.

Tables occur as complex elements beneath the root element. Columns appear as child elements of the complex elements indicating the tables.

Let's take the simple book schema from earlier in the chapter and make it into a DataSet schema. The first thing you need to do is define the outermost element—the DataSet itself. Let's call it <BookDataSet>. Beneath that, create an element called <Books>, and lower still beneath that create two elements: <Title> and <Publisher>. Let's take a look at the modified XSD to produce a working DataSet (BookDataSet.xsd):

```
<?xml version="1.0" encoding="utf-8" ?>
<xs:schema id="BookDataSet"
           targetNamespace="urn:apress-proadonet-chapter6-BookDataSet.xsd"
           elementFormDefault="qualified"
           xmlns="urn:apress-proadonet-chapter6-BookDataSet.xsd"
           xmlns:xs="http://www.w3.org/2001/XMLSchema"
           xmlns:msdata="urn:schemas-microsoft-com:xml-msdata">

  <xs:element name="BookDataSet" msdata:IsDataSet="true">
    <xs:complexType>
      <xs:choice maxOccurs="unbounded">
        <xs:element name="Books">
          <xs:complexType>
            <xs:sequence>
              <xs:element name="Title" type="xs:string" minOccurs="0" />
              <xs:element name="Publisher" type="xs:string" minOccurs="0" />
            </xs:sequence>
          </xs:complexType>
```

```
        </xs:element>
      </xs:choice>
    </xs:complexType>
  </xs:element>
</xs:schema>
```

There are a couple of new things here that might immediately jump out at you. The first is that an ID is assigned to the schema. Also, you'll see that there is an elementFormDefault attribute with the value qualified. This means that, by default, all elements within the schema must be qualified with their appropriate namespace prefix. You'll also notice that a target namespace has been defined for instance documents of this XML schema. While you could get away with leaving this blank, it's a good idea to give this information in order to avoid any potential collisions when transferring DataSets between domains, machines, or platforms.

Looking deeper into the schema, you'll notice that you can specify an unlimited number of <Books> elements, which then contain a sequence of elements called <Title> and <Publisher>, in that order. You could create a Books.xml document for our sample application to read that looks like this:

```
<BookDataSet xmlns="urn:apress-proadonet-chapter6-BookDataSet.xsd">
  <Books>
    <Title>Pro ADO.NET</Title>
    <Publisher>Apress Ltd</Publisher>
  </Books>
  <Books>
    <Title>Professional .NET Framework</Title>
    <Publisher>Apress Ltd</Publisher>
  </Books>
</BookDataSet>
```

Listings 6-20 and 6-21 demonstrate a part of a small console application that creates an ordinary DataSet, reads the XSD file (BookDataSet.xsd), loads the Books.xml file using the ReadXml method, and then prints the information in the XML file to the console, using the relational paradigm of tables, columns, and rows. This can be found in the associated code download as Example 6.5. The BookDataSet.xsd and Books.xml files are both in the bin directory beneath the project.

Listing 6-20. *Loading DataSet Data and Schema from XML and XSD in C#*

```
DataSet bookDataSet = new DataSet();
BookDataSet.ReadXmlSchema("BookDataSet.xsd");
BookDataSet.ReadXml("Books.xml");

Console.WriteLine("Recent Books:");
Console.WriteLine("-------------");

foreach (DataRow xRow in BookDataSet.Tables["Books"].Rows)
{
    Console.WriteLine("{0} by {1}", xRow["Title"], xRow["Publisher"]);
}
```

Listing 6-21. *Loading Dataset Data and Schema from XML and XSD in Visual Basic .NET*

```
Dim bookDataSet As DataSet = New DataSet()
BookDataSet.ReadXmlSchema("BookDataSet.xsd")
BookDataSet.ReadXml("Books.xml")

Console.WriteLine("Recent Books:")
Console.WriteLine("-------------")
For Each xRow as DataRow In BookDataSet.Tables("Books").Rows
    Console.WriteLine("{0} by {1}", xRow("Title"), xRow("Publisher"))
Next
```

When this code is run, it produces output that looks like

```
Recent Books:
-------------
Pro ADO.NET by Apress Ltd
Professional .NET Framework by Apress Ltd
```

Constraints

As you know, constraints are rules enforced on the contents of a DataSet. It's entirely possible to use nothing but the DataSet methods to create, modify, and enforce constraints, but you should also know what constraints look like in the underlying XSD that your DataSets work with. There are several constraint types that you can enforce on the data contained within a DataSet, via its associated schema.

Key Constraints

You can use the <key> element in an XML schema to enforce key constraints on data contained within the DataSet. A key constraint must be unique throughout the schema instance, and cannot have null values.

The following addition to the BookDataSet.xsd schema creates a key on the Title column:

```
<xs:key name="KeyTitle">
  <xs:selector xpath=".//Books" />
  <xs:field xpath="Title" />
</xs:key>
```

The <selector> element contains an xpath attribute, which indicates to the DataSet the XPath query to run in order to locate the table on which the key applies. The next element, <field>, also contains an XPath query, which indicates to the DataSet how to locate the field on which the key applies (relative to the table's element).

Unique Constraints

A unique constraint (<unique>) is slightly more forgiving and less strict than a key constraint. A unique constraint requires only that data should be unique, *if it exists*. Individual columns can specify whether or not they allow nulls, overriding some of the default behavior of the unique constraint. You could just as easily have indicated a unique constraint on the Title column with the following XSD fragment:

```
<xs:unique name="KeyTitle">
  <xs:selector xpath=".//Books" />
  <xsd:field xpath="Title" />
</xs:unique>
```

Foreign Keys (<keyref>) and Relationships

<keyref> elements within an XML schema provide a facility for declaring links within the document. The functionality they establish is similar in nature to that of foreign-key relationships in relational databases like SQL Server. If a DataSet encounters a <keyref> element when loading a schema, the DataSet will create an appropriate foreign-key constraint. It will also create a parent-child relationship (discussed shortly).

This example creates a new table in our DataSet called BookReviews. Then, the <keyref> element is used to create a foreign-key relationship between the BookReviews table and the Books table. To make things easier (and more realistic), a BookID column is also added. This code can be found in Example 6.6 of the associated code download.

Here's the new BookDataSet.xsd file for Example 6.6 (you'll have to find the BookDataSet.xsd on the file system as it is not added as a part of the project in Example 6.6):

```
<?xml version="1.0" encoding="utf-8" ?>
<xs:schema id="BookDataSet"
           targetNamespace="urn:apress-proadonet-chapter6-BookDataSet.xsd"
           elementFormDefault="qualified"
           xmlns="urn:apress-proadonet-chapter6-BookDataSet.xsd"
           xmlns:xs="http://www.w3.org/2001/XMLSchema"
           xmlns:msdata="urn:schemas-microsoft-com:xml-msdata">

  <xs:element name="BookDataSet" msdata:IsDataSet="true">
    <xs:complexType>
      <xs:choice maxOccurs="unbounded">
        <xs:element name="Books">
          <xs:complexType>
            <xs:sequence>
              <xs:element name="BookID" type="xs:integer" minOccurs="1" />
              <xs:element name="Title" type="xs:string" minOccurs="1" />
              <xs:element name="Publisher" type="xs:string" minOccurs="1" />
            </xs:sequence>
          </xs:complexType>
        </xs:element>
..... continued below
```

To this point, everything should look pretty familiar. You'll notice that the BookID column has been added. BookID is an integer column that must appear any time a <Books> element appears (minOccurs="1"). In other words, in the DataSet, this would be not nullable. Next, a new definition for a table is created. Remembering that a table in XSD is nothing more than an element that contains more elements, it's pretty easy to do:

```
..... continued from above
        <xs:element name="BookReviews">
```

```
        <xs:complexType>
          <xs:sequence>
            <xs:element name="BookID" type="xs:integer" minOccurs="1" />
            <xs:element name="Rating" type="xs:integer" minOccurs="1" />
            <xs:element name="Review" type="xs:string" minOccurs="0" />
          </xs:sequence>
        </xs:complexType>
      </xs:element>
    </xs:choice>
  </xs:complexType>
```

After that, some more familiar-looking code. You went over the <key> element earlier: the xpath attribute of the <selector> element indicates the Books table, while the xpath attribute for the <field> indicates the BookID column:

```
<xs:key name="KeyTitle">
  <xs:selector xpath=".//Books" />
  <xs:field xpath="BookID" />
</xs:key>
```

Finally, a <keyref> element is used to indicate that you're creating a foreign key originating from the BookID column of the BookReviews table, referring to the <key> element named KeyTitle:

```
    <xs:keyref name="KeyTitleRef" refer="KeyTitle">
      <xs:selector xpath=".//BookReviews" />
      <xs:field xpath="BookID" />
    </xs:keyref>
  </xs:element>
</xs:schema>
```

With the XSD file in place, you can next write the code to read the XSD and the XML into a DataSet. This code can be found in Listings 6-22 and 6-23.

Listing 6-22. *Loading Schema and Data for a Relational DataSet in C#*

```
DataSet bookDataSet = new DataSet();

BookDataSet.ReadXmlSchema("BookDataSet.xsd");
BookDataSet.ReadXml("Books.xml");

Console.WriteLine("Relations Created:");

foreach (DataRelation xRelation in BookDataSet.Relations)
{
    Console.WriteLine(xRelation.RelationName);
}

Console.WriteLine("Apress Books");
Console.WriteLine("----------");
Console.WriteLine();
```

Listing 6-23. *Loading Schema and Data for a Relational DataSet in Visual Basic .NET*

```
Dim BookDataSet As New DataSet()

BookDataSet.ReadXmlSchema("BookDataSet.xsd")
BookDataSet.ReadXml("Books.xml")

Console.WriteLine("Relations Created:")
Dim xRelation As DataRelation
For Each xRelation In BookDataSet.Relations
  Console.WriteLine(xRelation.RelationName)
Next

Console.WriteLine("Apress Books")
Console.WriteLine("----------")
Console.WriteLine()
```

Programmers like proof. To prove that a relationship in the DataSet has been created with exactly the same name as the <keyref> element in the XSD file, you can iterate through the Relations collection, printing out the name of the relationship. You'll see that there is indeed a relationship called KeyTitleRef in the DataSet immediately after the schema is loaded:

C#

```
foreach (DataRow xRow in BookDataSet.Tables["Books"].Rows)
{
    Console.WriteLine(xRow["Title"]);
......
}
```

VB.NET

```
For Each xRow as DataRow In BookDataSet.Tables("Books").Rows
    Console.WriteLine(xRow("Title"))
......
Next
```

So far, this is pretty straightforward: just iterate through each of the rows in the DataSet, and print out the value in the Title column for each of the rows:

C#

```
foreach (DataRow xRow in BookDataSet.Tables["Books"].Rows)
{
    Console.WriteLine(xRow["Title"]);
    // Obtain child rows using the KeyTitleRef relation
    foreach (DataRow zRow in xRow.GetChildRows("KeyTitleRef"))
    {
        Console.WriteLine("  {0}", zRow["Rating"]);
    }
}
```

VB.NET

```
For Each xRow as DataRow In BookDataSet.Tables("Books").Rows
   Console.WriteLine(xRow("Title"))
   ' Obtain child rows using the KeyTitleRef relation
   For Each zRow as DataRow In xRow.GetChildRows("KeyTitleRef")
      Console.WriteLine("  {0}", zRow("Rating"))
   Next
Next
```

The GetChildRows() method obtains a list of child rows of a given row, utilizing a relationship. You can specify either the name of the relationship or a DataRelation object. You can optionally specify a row version to further filter the results returned by querying the relation. In the source XML document, the information is stored flat, in two separate tables. With the use of GetChildRows(), you're actually forcing a hierarchical traversal of the information in the DataSet.

When you're all done, you're presented with console output like the following, showing each of the titles and the rating of each reviewer, indented to help display the hierarchy of the row relationships:

```
Relations Created:
KeyTitleRef

Apress Books
----------

Pro ADO.NET
  5
  1
Professional .NET Framework
  4
  2
```

So that you can see where the numbers are coming from, let's take a look at the updated Books.xml file that now contains information for the BookReviews table:

```
<BookDataSet xmlns="urn:apress-proadonet-chapter6-BookDataSet.xsd">
  <Books>
    <BookID>1</BookID>
    <Title>Pro ADO.NET</Title>
    <Publisher>Apress Ltd</Publisher>
  </Books>
  <Books>
    <BookID>2</BookID>
    <Title>Professional .NET Framework</Title>
    <Publisher>Apress Ltd</Publisher>
  </Books>
```

The Books table information should look pretty familiar. Next, however, the contents of the BookReviews table is listed. Each row in the latter table is defined by a <BookReviews> element:

```
<BookReviews>
   <BookID>1</BookID>
   <Rating>5</Rating>
   <Review>This book was by far one of the best books on .NET ever
          written!</Review>
</BookReviews>
<BookReviews>
   <BookID>1</BookID>
   <Rating>1</Rating>
   <Review>I'm not sure this could be classified as a technical manual. It
          is worth more as a paperweight</Review>
</BookReviews>
<BookReviews>
   <BookID>2</BookID>
   <Rating>4</Rating>
   <Review>Top Notch! Excellent book! I especially liked the chapter on
          strongly typed datasets and XSD schemas!</Review>
</BookReviews>
<BookReviews>
   <BookID>2</BookID>
   <Rating>2</Rating>
   <Review>I liked the introduction. That's it.</Review>
</BookReviews>
</BookDataSet>
```

Note Even though the presence of foreign keys and relationships in a DataSet's schema can indicate a hierarchical relationship, the data does not have to appear to be nested in the instance document. This can be controlled by the "nested" property on a DataRelation as seen before in Example 6.3.

Building Strongly Typed DataSets

So far, you've walked through some of the more commonly used features that are available to you in XSD, and you've learned how various elements in XML schemas affect the way in which DataSets behave. You've seen how to control the data types of individual columns, and how to represent multiple tables, columns, indexes, and constraints within a DataSet.

In truth, a lot of what you've covered with regard to XSD and DataSet schemas you could theoretically survive without, but knowing the internals of how your tools are working is always helpful. While most of the examples so far (and throughout this chapter) deal with using DataSets and XML data, all of this information can be applied to DataSets used in conjunction with relational databases, or DataTables used in conjunction with relational databases. The essential point to remember is that whether the data came from an XML document, a relational database, or some other provider, the schemas still have the same format. It's really immaterial *how the DataSet or DataTable was filled.*

In short, strongly typed `DataSets` let you turn the following lines of code:

C#

```
myRow = myDataSet.Tables["Customers"].Rows[0]
Console.WriteLine(myRow["FirstName"])
```

VB.NET

```
myRow = myDataSet.Tables("Customers").Rows(0)
Console.WriteLine(myRow("FirstName"))
```

into this short, easy-to-read line of code:

C#

```
Console.WriteLine(CustomerDataSet.Customers[0].FirstName) ;
```

VB.NET

```
Console.WriteLine(CustomerDataSet.Customers(0).FirstName)
```

This change is made possible by the strong support in the .NET Framework for inheritance and clear, logical object hierarchies. The essential concept behind a strongly typed `DataSet` is that a new class is created that derives from the `DataSet` class. This new class implements properties and methods that are strongly typed, based on the XSD schema that was used in order to generate it.

When this derived class is instantiated, it will provide logically named properties of integer type (if your schema called for integer columns), and further logically named properties that appear as arrays of strongly typed rows. So, rather than dealing with `DataRows` and `DataTables`, you end up dealing with task-specialized concepts such as a `CustomersRow` or a `CustomersTable`, which may contain columns called `FirstName` or `LastName`, rather than forcing you to employ difficult-to-use array indices/indexer accessors.

In .NET, there are two (equally valid) approaches to creating strongly typed `DataSets`. You can create them visually using a designer through the tools provided within Visual Studio .NET, or you can use command-line utilities and compiler arguments. Both approaches will be covered here, and you can pick the one that best fits your skills, style, and preferences.

Building Typed DataSets in Visual Studio .NET

Visual Studio .NET provides an incredibly easy, point-and-click approach to creating strongly typed `DataSets`. It's such a natural extension of Visual Studio .NET that if you're using it to develop your application, there's no sensible reason not to use it. To start out, let's take the concept from the "books and book reviews" example and develop a strongly typed `DataSet` for it in Visual Studio .NET:

1. As usual, start out by creating a new console application, this time named Example 6.7.

2. Next, right-click on the project name, select Add ➤ Add New Item, and then select the DataSet icon and type in **BookDataSet.xsd** as the filename.

3. From the Toolbox, drag two `DataTables` into open areas of the design surface. From there, you can use the visual interface to add columns to each `DataTable` you dropped onto the surface.

4. Create the columns according to the columns used in Example 6.7 (Books and BookReviews).

5. Then, finish it off by creating a primary key called KeyBookID on the BookID column in the Books table.

6. At this point, what you have is two completely disjointed and unrelated tables. Now for the fun stuff: the relationship. From the Toolbox, drag a Relation onto the designer, hovering over any of the elements (or whitespace) in the BookReviews element (table). When you let go, you'll see a dialog prompting you for more information about the relation (keyref). Change the name of the keyref to KeyBookIDRef. As there's already a key in one of the tables, and there are identically named columns in each table, the dialog comes populated with all of the information you need to form the parent-child relationship. You can confirm the dialog and generate the code. Your designer should look something like Figure 6-6.

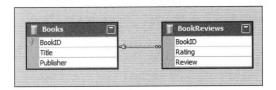

Figure 6-6. *Strongly typed XSD DataSet*

7. Finally, in the Properties window, change the targetNamespace property of the schema to urn:apress-proadonet-chapter6-BookDataSet.xsd, and attributeFormDefault to (Default).

Note One thing you should keep in mind is that the namespace of the data in the XML you're reading absolutely *must* be the same as the target namespace of this schema. Also, this namespace is case sensitive.

Now, take a look at the XSD for your visually designed, strongly typed DataSet (see Listing 6-24).

Listing 6-24. *XSD for the Visually Designed BooksDataSet Strongly Typed DataSet*

```
<?xml version="1.0" encoding="utf-8" ?>
<xs:schema id="BookDataSet"
        targetNamespace="urn:apress-proadonet-chapter6-BookDataSet.xsd"
        elementFormDefault="qualified"
        xmlns="urn:apress-proadonet-chapter6-BookDataSet.xsd"
        xmlns:mstns="urn:apress-proadonet-chapter6-BookDataSet.xsd"
        xmlns:xs="http://www.w3.org/2001/XMLSchema"
        xmlns:msdata="urn:schemas-microsoft-com:xml-msdata">
  <xs:element name="BookDataSet" msdata:IsDataSet="true">
```

```
    <xs:complexType>
      <xs:choice maxOccurs="unbounded">
        <xs:element name="Books">
          <xs:complexType>
            <xs:sequence>
              <xs:element name="BookID" type="xs:integer" minOccurs="0" />
              <xs:element name="Title" type="xs:string" minOccurs="0" />
              <xs:element name="Publisher" type="xs:string" minOccurs="0" />
            </xs:sequence>
          </xs:complexType>
        </xs:element>
        <xs:element name="BookReviews">
          <xs:complexType>
            <xs:sequence>
              <xs:element name="BookID" type="xs:integer" minOccurs="0" />
              <xs:element name="Rating" type="xs:integer" minOccurs="0" />
              <xs:element name="Review" type="xs:string" minOccurs="0" />
            </xs:sequence>
          </xs:complexType>
        </xs:element>
      </xs:choice>
    </xs:complexType>
    <xs:key name="KeyBookID">
      <xs:selector xpath=".//mstns:Books" />
      <xs:field xpath="mstns:BookID" />
    </xs:key>
    <xs:keyref name="KeyBookIDRef" refer="KeyBookID">
      <xs:selector xpath=".//mstns:BookReviews" />
      <xs:field xpath="mstns:BookID" />
    </xs:keyref>
  </xs:element>
</xs:schema>
```

It should come as no surprise that this looks remarkably similar to the document that you built manually during the schema overview. The only real difference is the use of the mstns namespace to link things together (tns is shorthand for "this namespace").

Now enter some code into the main class of the console application to generate the same output as our previous example, but fully utilizing the features of a class that you actually did nothing to generate, other than define the schema. This code can be found in Listings 6-25 and 6-26.

Listing 6-25. *Working with a Strongly Typed DataSet in C#*

```
BookDataSet myDataSet = new BookDataSet();
myDataSet.ReadXml("Books.xml");

Console.WriteLine("Relations Found:");
foreach (DataRelation xRelation in myDataSet.Relations)
```

```
{
   Console.WriteLine(xRelation.RelationName);
}

Console.WriteLine("Apress Books and Reviews");
Console.WriteLine("---------------------");
```

Listing 6-26. *Working with a Strongly Typed DataSet in Visual Basic .NET*

```
Dim myDS As New BookDataSet()
myDataSet.ReadXml("Books.xml")

Console.WriteLine("Relations Found:")
Dim xRelation As DataRelation
For Each xRelation In myDS.Relations
   Console.WriteLine(xRelation.RelationName)
Next

Console.WriteLine("Apress Books and Reviews")
Console.WriteLine("---------------------")
```

Notice here that you aren't instantiating a DataSet, but a class named BookDataSet. The Books.xml file you are using here is the same as the one you used in the last example, which should be copied to the bin (C#) or bin\debug (VB.NET) directory for this project. Just like last time, you dump the relationships defined in the DataSet to the console:

C#

```
foreach (BookDataSet.BooksRow book in myDataSet.Books.Rows)
```

VB.NET

```
For Each book As BookDataSet.BooksRow In myDataSet.Books.Rows
```

This is where it gets almost enjoyable to write the code. Instead of iterating through the rows of some table object that you reached through an ordinal or name, you can index through each of the BooksRow objects in the strongly typed DataSet's Books.Rows collection. It's much easier to read, and much easier for the programmer to write:

C#

```
Console.WriteLine(book.Title);

foreach (BookDataSet.BookReviewsRow review in book.GetBookReviewsRows())
{
   Console.WriteLine("  {0}", review.Rating);
}
```

VB.NET

```
Console.WriteLine(book.Title)

For Each review As BookDataSet.BookReviewsRow In book.GetBookReviewsRows()
   Console.WriteLine("  {0}", review.Rating)
Next
```

The code generator for the strongly typed DataSet will actually generate properly typed properties for each of the columns in a table. Here you can see that the example is printing out the value of Book.Title, rather than the following code or something similarly complex:

C#

```
Tables["Books"].Rows[0]["Title"] ;
```

VB.NET

```
Tables("Books").Rows(0)("Title")
```

Also note that instead of invoking the GetChildRows method, you are actually calling GetBookReviewsRows(), which the strongly typed DataSet implemented for you. This method returns an array of BookReviewsRow objects.

After you've placed all the code into your solution (or you've loaded the Example 6.7 project from the code download), rebuild it and then make sure that Show All Files is selected from the Project menu. You should see that the BookDataSet.xsd file has some child items. Expand them, and you'll see that a BookDataSet.Designer.cs/BookDataSet.Designer.vb file has been generated for you. This is the actual class definition that the example uses as the strongly typed DataSet.

If you open the BookDataSet.xsd file in Notepad, you would immediately notice that the Books table is represented by the following element:

```
<xs:element name="Books">
 <xs:complexType>
   <xs:sequence>
     <xs:element name="BookID" type="xs:integer" minOccurs="1" />
     <xs:element name="Title" type="xs:string" minOccurs="1" />
     <xs:element name="Publisher" type="xs:string" minOccurs="1" />
   </xs:sequence>
 </xs:complexType>
</xs:element>
```

Also, you would note that the BookReviews table is defined by the following element:

```
<xs:element name="BookReviews">
 <xs:complexType>
   <xs:sequence>
     <xs:element name="BookID" type="xs:integer" minOccurs="1" />
     <xs:element name="Rating" type="xs:integer" minOccurs="1" />
     <xs:element name="Review" type="xs:string" minOccurs="0" />
   </xs:sequence>
 </xs:complexType>
</xs:element>
```

And the relationship between the two is defined by the following xs:keyref and xs:key elements:

```
<xs:key name="KeyTitle">
   <xs:selector xpath=".//Books" />
   <xs:field xpath="BookID" />
 </xs:key>
 <xs:keyref name="KeyTitleRef" refer="KeyTitle">
   <xs:selector xpath=".//BookReviews" />
   <xs:field xpath="BookID" />
 </xs:keyref>
```

Let's take a look at the console output generated by this sample. It should look extremely similar to Example 6.6, but the key thing to remember is that this DataSet isn't generic—it has been derived and specialized to work *only* with Books and BookReviews, according to our schema:

```
Relations Found:
KeyBookIDRef
Apress Books and Reviews
---------------------
Pro ADO.NET
  5
  1
Professional .NET Framework
  4
  2
```

The code for BookDataSet.Designer.cs/BookDataSet.Designer.vb is too long to look at here in its entirety (though it's of course available in the code download for this chapter), but it's certainly worth taking a look at a few key points. The first thing you'll see is the Books property, which is a strongly typed wrapper around some inherent DataSet functionality. Here is the BookDataSet class's definition of the Books property:

C#

```
public BooksDataTable Books {
get {
   return this.tableBooks;
   }
}
```

VB.NET

```
Public ReadOnly Property Books() As BooksDataTable
   Get
       Return Me.tableBooks
   End Get
End Property
```

Like so many properties, this is just a wrapper around a private member variable. The key thing to note here is the data type of the property: it's actually a nested class called BooksDataTable, which is another dynamically generated class deriving from the DataTable class.

Now let's take a look at another piece of "magic" that the strongly typed DataSet is performing on your behalf: the invocation of GetChildRows() through the GetBookReviewsRows() method (a member of the BookDataSet.BooksRow class):

C#

```
public BookReviewsRow[] GetBookReviewsRows() {
   return
((BookReviewsRow[])(this.GetChildRows(this.Table.ChildRelations["KeyTitleRef"])));
}
```

VB.NET

```
    Public Function GetBookReviewsRows() As BookReviewsRow()
      Return CType(Me.GetChildRows( _
             Me.Table.ChildRelations("KeyBookIDRef")), BookReviewsRow())
    End Function
```

This function locates a DataRelation object by pulling the KeyBookIDRef item out of the ChildRelations collection. It then pulls the child rows by passing the relation object to the GetChildRows() function, changing the type of the resulting array of DataRow objects to an array of BookReviewsRow objects. As with all of the items in the strongly typed DataSet, this function is visible through intellisense in Visual Studio .NET, dramatically reducing your chances of mistyping the name of the child row's relation name.

One more useful feature of the typed DataSet is its strongly typed properties. Let's take a look at the Title property of the BooksRow class:

C#

```
public string Title {
      get {
         return ((string)(this[this.tableBooks.TitleColumn]));
      }
      set {
         this[this.tableBooks.TitleColumn] = value;
      }
}
```

VB.NET

```
    Public Property Title As String
      Get
        Try
          Return CType(Me(Me.tableBooks.TitleColumn), String)
        Catch e As InvalidCastException
          Throw New StrongTypingException( _
                       "Cannot get value because it is DBNull.", e)
        End Try
```

```
    End Get
    Set
        Me(Me.tableBooks.TitleColumn) = value
    End Set
End Property
```

This property is made possible by an override for the indexer (the Item property) in the DataRow class that BooksRow inherits from. It allows an actual column object to be supplied (specifically, a DataColumn object, or, as in this case, an object that inherits from DataColumn), rather than an ordinal or a string as a field identifier, on which to set and get values.

Building Typed DataSets Manually

Now that you have looked at how to make strongly typed DataSets through Visual Studio .NET, which automatically makes them available to the rest of the project, let's look at how to do it the "hard" way. Of course, that's a misnomer, because there's really nothing hard about using command-line tools to create your own strongly typed DataSets.

You shouldn't confuse "manually" with the process of writing all of the code for the DataSet class yourself. Even without Visual Studio .NET, there's still a tool called XSD.exe that automates generation of the class file. This approach is useful for batch code generation, typical in enterprise deployment or automated build environments. For the "manual" example, you will build the same example you have already built under Visual Studio .NET, though all of the compilation, code editing, and DataSet generation will be done from the command line and Notepad (or any other text editor).

The first thing that needs to be done is to create a new directory called Example 6.8. Into this, copy the BookDataSet.xsd file that you built containing the definitions for the Books table, the BookReviews table, the keys, and the keyref parent-child relationship.

Then, write a batch file to build a strongly typed DataSet. It's called BuildDS.cmd; the contents of this batch file are as shown:

C#

```
xsd /d /l:CS BookDataSet.xsd
```

VB.NET

```
xsd /d /l:VB BookDataSet.xsd
```

The batch file invokes a utility called XSD.exe, which is used to generate schema or class files from a given source. For this statement to work, you have to either run it from where xsd is in the same directory or where it is within the defined path. It can take a schema and either convert it to classes or create a typed DataSet from it (the /d argument). Also, it can create an XSD file from an XDR file to upgrade the schema definition. The /l version can specify the language to generate the strongly typed DataSet in.

Running the BuildDS.bat file creates a version of the strongly typed DataSet exactly the same as the one created through Visual Studio .NET. The same output for the Visual Basic version is as shown in Figure 6-7.

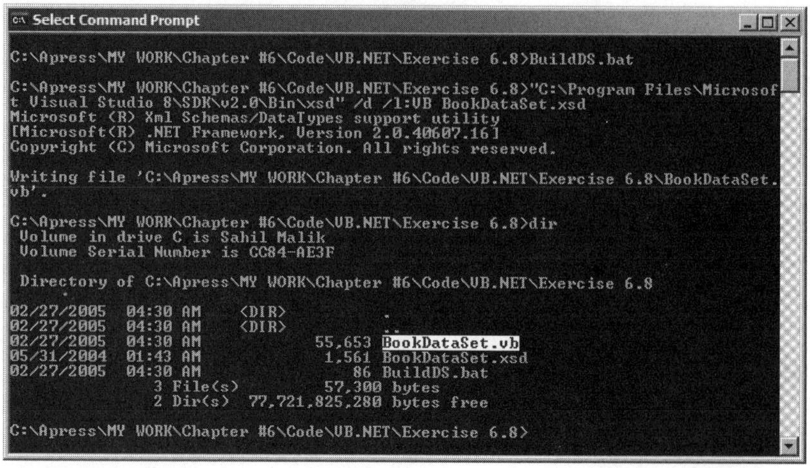

Figure 6-7. *Generating a strongly typed DataSet using command line*

Typed DataSet Performance

You have seen plenty of stuff demonstrating how strongly typed DataSets make the jobs of creating and consuming DataSets far easier. Typed DataSets are easier to maintain, have strongly typed accessors, provide rigid data validation, and, because they can still be serialized, can be exposed as the return types of web service function calls.

It would be reasonable to ask, however, whether these things are any faster or slower than regular DataSets. Unfortunately, the answer is far from clear. You may already know that throwing exceptions incurs a slight overhead from the runtime, as does typecasting. All of the properties and functions in a typed DataSet are wrapped in exception handling calls, and a great many are wrapped with typecasting code. This leads some people to believe that they are slightly less efficient than standard DataSets.

However, in any production application, you'll be wrapping your DataSet use in exception handling and typecasting code anyway, so the fact that the typed DataSet does this for you should be considered an advantage, and not a performance drain.

Plus, performance is about code performance *and* developer performance. Strongly typed DataSets make your code easier to develop and maintain. Those advantages are hard to ignore.

Annotating Typed DataSets

Earlier in the chapter, during the overview of some of the commonly used features of XSD, you read about covered schema annotation. You saw then that annotation could take two forms: the <documentation> element for human audiences, and the <appinfo> element. Here, you'll see another variety of (and use for) annotation that doesn't use the XSD <annotation> element.

As you've seen in the previous examples, when you create a strongly typed DataSet using the standard techniques, the names of that DataSet class's properties, methods, relations, and constraints will be created for you. If you're going to be using a lot of typed DataSets, or you plan on having them available for several other programmers or programming teams, you'll be pleased to know that you can obtain fine-grained control over the naming conventions and automated facilities of the code generator for typed DataSet classes.

This is accomplished by supplying attributes from two XML namespaces provided by Microsoft: the first is the `codegen` namespace (defined by `xmlns:codegen="urn:schemas-microsoft-com:xml-msprop"`) and the second is the `msdata` namespace (defined by `xmlns:msdata="urn:schemas-microsoft-com:xml-msdata"`).

codegen

The `codegen` namespace contains a set of attributes that directly affect the code generation of a `DataSet`. You can apply the `codegen` attributes to various elements of an XSD file, providing fine-grained instructions to either `XSD.exe` or the VS.NET compiler on exactly how to generate the new `DataSet`. There will be a sample of a Visual Studio .NET-annotated `DataSet` using these new attributes at the end of this section.

All of this functionality *can* be controlled by programmatically modifying the properties of the `DataSet` later on. However, if the functionality and control is built into the schema and the typed `DataSet` in human-readable form, there can be no mistake about how the class creator intended it to function.

typedName

The `typedName` attribute indicates the name of an object, as it will appear in the new `DataSet`. This attribute can be applied to `DataTables`, `DataRows`, properties, and `DataSet` events.

typedPlural

The `typedPlural` attribute will indicate the name of the object when a plurality of the object is needed, as in the `DataRowCollection` or the `DataTableCollection` object.

typedParent

The `typedParent` attribute indicates the name of the object when it is referred to in a parent relationship. Typed `DataSets` automatically generate accessor functions for retrieving parents and children. For example, in the previous example, the `GetBookReviewsRows()` function was a child accessor.

typedChildren

The `typedChildren` attribute indicates the name of the object when it is referred to in a child relationship. As stated previously, typed `DataSets` generate both parent and child accessors, usually with confusing or unwieldy names. Providing the `typedChildren` and `typedParent` attributes generally makes for a much easier user experience in your typed `DataSet`.

nullValue

The `nullValue` attribute is an incredibly useful one. It allows you to define what action will be taken in the `DataSet` when a `DBNull` value is encountered. The following is a list of the valid values for the `nullValue` attribute:

- `"replacement"`: Rather than indicating a behavior, you can simply indicate what value your `DataSet` will store instead of `DBNull`.

- `_throw`: Throws an exception any time a `DBNull` is encountered on the related element in the `DataSet`.

- _null: Returns a null (or throws an exception if a primitive type is encountered).

- _empty: Returns an object created from an empty constructor. For strings, it will return String.Empty. For any other primitive type, it will throw an exception.

msdata

The msdata namespace is another namespace used by Microsoft to control the behavior of a DataSet. It's primarily concerned with the definition, naming, and control of keys and constraints. The next five sections cover the attributes that it defines.

ConstraintName

This is the name of the constraint as it will appear in the DataSet. This can apply to any kind of constraint defined in XSD, such as a <key> or a <unique> constraint.

ConstraintOnly

The default behavior of the code generator is to create a relationship whenever a foreign-key constraint is found. You can override this behavior and *not* create the relationship automatically by using the ConstraintOnly flag. The syntax looks like this:

```
<element msdata:ConstraintOnly="true" />
```

UpdateRule

This attribute controls the behavior of related parent-child rows when an update is made to a row. If not supplied, the default is set to Cascade. Otherwise, it can be set to None, SetDefault, or SetNull, matching the settings as you earlier saw in this chapter:

- Cascade: Cascades the update across to all related rows.

- None: No action will be taken on related rows.

- SetDefault: All of the related rows affected by the update action will be set to their default values, as indicated by their DefaultValue property.

- SetNull: All related rows will be set to DBNull as a result of the update action.

DeleteRule

The available values for this attribute function identically to those for the UpdateRule attribute, with the exception that they are only applied when a delete action takes place.

Relationship

Like all good rules, there's an exception to the statement made earlier about these annotations not actually being in an <annotation> element. The <Relationship> element appears within an <appinfo> annotation element. If you wish, you can use <Relationship> to define a parent-child relationship as an alternative to using the key/keyref syntax. This is really a matter of preference, and many XSD purists prefer to use the key/keyref syntax. In any case, the syntax looks like this:

```
<xs:annotation>
  <xs:appinfo>
    <msdata:Relationship name="KeyBookIDRef"
                         msdata:parent="Books"
                         msdata:child="BookReviews"
                         msdata:parentkey="BookID"
                         msdata:childkey="BookID" />
  </xs:appinfo>
</xs:annotation>
```

Annotated Typed DataSet Example

Now that you've seen how to annotate a DataSet in order to control how its code is generated and to gain finer control over its behavior, constraints, and rules, let's take a look at one in action. For this example, we're going to create a Windows Forms application called Example 6.9. Add a new item to the project, choose DataSet as the type, and name it BookDataSet.xsd. Paste the following annotated XSD into your new DataSet class XSD file:

```
<?xml version="1.0" encoding="utf-8" ?>
<xs:schema id="BookDataSet"
          targetNamespace="urn:apress-proadonet-chapter6-BookDataSet.xsd"
          elementFormDefault="qualified"
          xmlns="urn:apress-proadonet-chapter6-BookDataSet.xsd"
          xmlns:mstns="urn:apress-proadonet-chapter6-BookDataSet.xsd"
          xmlns:xs="http://www.w3.org/2001/XMLSchema"
```

The next part is new. Visual Studio .NET puts the msdata namespace declaration into your DataSet schemas for you, but you have to enter the following one manually in order to gain access to the codegen namespace prefix:

```
          xmlns:codegen="urn:schemas-microsoft-com:xml-msprop"
          xmlns:msdata="urn:schemas-microsoft-com:xml-msdata">

  <xs:element name="BookDataSet" msdata:IsDataSet="true">
    <xs:complexType>
      <xs:choice maxOccurs="unbounded">
```

Here's a look at the first use of the codegen namespace. The following code is indicating that the typedName of the Books element (which matches <Books> tags in the XML instance document) is going to be called Book, and the typedPlural will be called Books:

```
      <xs:element name="Books" codegen:typedName="Book"
                              codegen:typedPlural="Books">
        <xs:complexType>
          <xs:sequence>
            <xs:element name="BookID" type="xs:integer" minOccurs="1" />
            <xs:element name="Title" type="xs:string" minOccurs="1" />
            <xs:element name="Publisher" type="xs:string" minOccurs="1" />
          </xs:sequence>
        </xs:complexType>
      </xs:element>
```

As with the `<Books>` tags, you are placing some logical naming conventions onto the individual items. A single row of the `BookReviews` table will now be considered a `BookReview`, rather than a `BookReviews`:

```
        <xs:element name="BookReviews" codegen:typedName="BookReview"
                                  codegen:typedPlural="BookReviews">
      <xs:complexType>
        <xs:sequence>
          <xs:element name="BookID" type="xs:integer" minOccurs="0" />
          <xs:element name="Rating" type="xs:integer" minOccurs="0" />
          <xs:element name="Review" type="xs:string" minOccurs="0" />
        </xs:sequence>
      </xs:complexType>
    </xs:element>
  </xs:choice>
</xs:complexType>

<xs:key name="KeyBookID">
  <xs:selector xpath=".//mstns:Books" />
  <xs:field xpath="mstns:BookID" />
</xs:key>
```

Finally, in the XSD file, there are a couple of really interesting things going on. The first is that the `DataGridView` control uses the name of the relationship to provide a visual link to the child tables. Therefore, you need to make sure now that this name will look good in the UI! Also, we've effectively renamed the `GetBookReviewsRows()` function that you saw earlier to `Reviews()`:

```
    <xs:keyref name="Reviews" refer="KeyBookID"
               codegen:typedParent="Book"
               codegen:typedChildren="Reviews">
      <xs:selector xpath=".//mstns:BookReviews" />
      <xs:field xpath="mstns:BookID" />
    </xs:keyref>
  </xs:element>
</xs:schema>
```

Next, let's come to the form for the application. Change the title of the form (the Text property) to Annotated Typed DataSet Binding Example. The form needs to contain two controls: a `DataGridView` control called `dgBooks`, and a button called `btnSumScores` with the text Sum Scores. You also need to add a private field to the form called Books, of `BookDataSet` type:

C#

```
private BookDataSet books;
```

VB.NET

```
Private books As BookDataSet
```

Now you have the constructor or the `Form_load` event of the form, which you need to modify to load the XML data for the form (the `Books.xml` file you saw earlier, which is copied to the root directory of the application):

C#

```csharp
public Form1()
{
    InitializeComponent();
    books = new BookDataSet();
    books.ReadXml("Books.xml");
    datagridBooks.DataSource = books.Books;
}
```

VB.NET

```vbnet
Private Sub Form1_Load( _
ByVal sender As System.Object, ByVal e As System.EventArgs) _
 Handles MyBase.Load
    books = New BookDataSet()
    books.ReadXml("Books.xml")
    datagridBooks.DataSource = books.Books
End Sub
```

Also, to show you how incredibly straightforward our new annotated class is, let's rig up the Sum Scores button to display a message box containing the sum of all of the scores of the reviews. You could just iterate through the `Reviews` table, but instead let's use the `For...Each` syntax to demonstrate just how close the code syntax is to how you might describe the functionality out loud to another programmer:

C#

```csharp
private void btnSumScores_Click(object sender, EventArgs e)
{
    int sum = 0;
...
}
```

VB.NET

```vbnet
Private Sub btnSumScores_Click(ByVal sender As System.Object, _
  ByVal e As System.EventArgs) Handles btnSumScores.Click
    Dim sum As Integer = 0
...
End Sub
```

This is the beauty of typed `DataSets`. Not only do you have accessors without (visibly) using array indices or collections, but also everything is named appropriately and everything is strongly typed, so if you attempt to use the wrong data type, an exception will be thrown. Iterating through a hierarchy of data has never been this easy:

C#

```csharp
foreach (BookDataSet.Book book in books.Books)
{
    foreach (BookDataSet.BookReview review in book.Reviews())
    {
        sum += Convert.ToInt32(review.Rating);
    }
}
MessageBox.Show(this, "Score Total: " + sum.ToString());
```

VB.NET

```vbnet
For Each Book as BookDataSet.Book In Books.Books
    For Each review as BookDataSet.BookReview In Book.Reviews()
        sum += CInt(review.Rating)
    Next
Next
MessageBox.Show(Me, "Score Total: " + sum.ToString())
```

Figure 6-8 shows just how much nicer everything looks when things have been annotated and given human- and programmer-readable names.

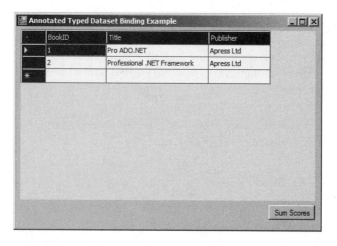

Figure 6-8. *Annotated typed DataSet binding example*

Summary

This chapter introduced you to the centerpiece of ADO.NET's disconnected architecture—the DataSet.

In this chapter, you then looked at various constituents of the DataSet object. You looked at DataTables, DataRows, DataColumns, DataRelations, etc. You saw many practical examples elucidating the usage of all of these objects. It was also noted that a lot of concepts mentioned for the DataSet are equally applicable to the DataTable object. This will become clearer as you subject the DataSet or DataTable to real-world scenarios that involve connecting to a data source.

Further on in this chapter, you saw a brief overview of the most common features of the XSD language. You read about the importance of this review of XSD as you delved into the structure of the DataSet and saw how it interprets XSD to form its internal data structure of columns, tables, constraints, keys, and relations.

After understanding how a DataSet interacts directly with XML schema information, you used such a schema to derive your own DataSet subclass that provided a strongly typed object model on top of a specific data structure.

Next, you learned how to provide additional information and instructions to the code generator, allowing you fine-grained control over the generation of the DataSet-derived classes. Finally, a strongly typed DataSet class was databound to a DataGridView demonstrating how the control handled the embedded hierarchical structure of the DataSet.

It may be notable, however, that none of the discussion presented in this chapter involved any sort of connection with any data source. This is critical to understand that a DataSet has nothing to do with any particular database, it lends itself to be equally useful to any specific data provider/data source.

Now that you have read about the connected part of ADO.NET in Chapters 4 and 5 and have been introduced to the centerpiece of the disconnected part of ADO.NET in this chapter, Chapter 6 will introduce you to the part of ADO.NET that acts as a gatekeeper between the disconnected and connected worlds: the DataAdapter.

After discussing filling a DataSet (or DataTable), the discussion will briefly return to the purely disconnected world and introduce an equally important object in ADO.NET, the DataView. This will be followed by a discussion of updating the data source in both connected and disconnected architectures addressing issues such as concurrency, etc.

CHAPTER 7

■■■

Fetching Data: The DataAdapter

So far you've been introduced to the various parts that make up ADO.NET. You read about how ADO.NET splits up data access between connected and disconnected portions and why it chooses to do so. In Chapters 4 and 5 you read about the connected part of ADO.NET. You read about how a connection is established, and how you can execute commands and fetch results out of the database in a connected fashion using a data reader.

Chapter 6 introduced you to the various objects, such as DataSet, DataTable, DataRow, DataRelation, and so on that comprise the purely disconnected data access part within ADO.NET. Various examples were given how DataSets can be used to hold a logical representation of your data model in both a strongly typed and non-strongly typed fashion.

Just as a data reader allows you to fetch data from a given data source, there exists an object in ADO.NET that acts as a bridge between the purely disconnected world of ADO.NET comprising the DataSet, DataTable, etc. and the connected world of the DBCommand objects that wrap various SQL statements: this object is the DataAdapter.

A DataAdapter not only lets you fill a DataSet or DataTable from the given data source, it also provides you with a convenient mechanism to persist, or save the changes back, into the database. This is usually achieved by specifying various command objects as properties on the DataAdapter object.

But before you look at updating the data source using a data adapter, first let's discuss *fetching data* using a data adapter.

What Is a DataAdapter?

As the name implies, a DataAdapter is the bridge between the connected and disconnected parts of ADO.NET. A DataAdapter is the object that lets you use connected objects, such as DbCommand, to fill and work with disconnected objects, such as the DataSet. As you have already seen in Chapters 4 and 5, in order to interrogate or interact with your data source, you need an object derived from DbConnection. Typically, this would be an instance of a SqlConnection, OracleConnection, or something similar. On an open and available object that is derived from DbConnection, you can send commands using an object that is derived from DbCommand. A DbCommand has the option of being able to retrieve the result set as a DbDataReader (such as SqlDataReader or OracleDataReader), or it may return a scalar value instead. Such commands may even be used to perform Data Manipulation Language (DML) on the database.

However, one of the things pointed out in Chapter 4 was the immense benefit of connection pooling in a multiuser, highly concurrent application environment. Since a data reader operates in a firehose read-only/forward-only manner, it ends up holding a connection open for its operation lifetime. Holding a connection open for an inordinately long time generally has a negative impact on connection pooling.

In Chapter 6, you read about various objects that form the disconnected architecture of ADO.NET. Objects such as DataSets, DataTables, DataRows, etc. help you hold a subset of the data in a relational form, similar to what you would find in the database. However, these objects, particularly the DataSet and DataTable, need to be *filled* using some mechanism.

ADO.NET employs the DbCommand object to abstract and hold the queries you wish to execute on the data source. The DbCommand object contains the information about what DbConnection it will employ in order to execute itself. The DataAdapter object is responsible for employing a DbCommand and acting as a gatekeeper/bridge between the connected world of DbCommand and DbConnection, and the disconnected world of DataTable and DataSet.

Structure of a DataAdapter

In Chapter 2 (specifically, Figure 2-7), you read about data adapters implementing the IDataAdapter and IDbDataAdapter interfaces without going into further detail. In fact, it's not the case that the various data adapters simply contain implementations of these interfaces' methods. Though that's effectively the outcome, there are a couple of stages in between.

The .NET Framework class hierarchy contains an abstract or MustInherit class that provider-specific data adapters inherit from called System.Data.Common.DbDataAdapter. It's the DbDataAdapter class that implements the IDbDataAdapter interface. The DbDataAdapter class provides the basic facilities for constructing a disconnected data-access mechanism to fill a DataSet or DataTable object and to update a data source.

The DbDataAdapter class in turn inherits from yet another class called the System.Data.Common.DataAdapter class, which in turn implements the IDataAdapter interface.

Figure 7-1 demonstrates the structure of two commonly used data adapters: the SqlDataAdapter and OracleDataAdapter in ADO.NET.

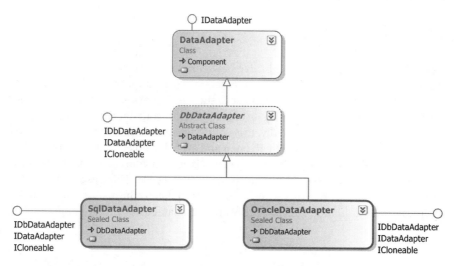

Figure 7-1. *Structure of SqlDataAdapter and OracleDataAdapter in ADO.NET*

In addition to Figure 7-1, you can also refer back to Figure 2-7 to understand how the various `DataAdapter` classes and various `DbCommand` classes work together.

It's also notable that the `DataAdapter` class in turn inherits from `System.ComponentModel.Component`. Therefore, the `DataAdapter`, by virtue of being a `Component`, can be hosted in any object that implements the `IContainer` interface. What this means is that a `DataAdapter` can be visually edited and worked upon in containers such as the Visual Studio IDE at design time, as you'll see later in this chapter.

Putting DataAdapters to Use

Now that you are familiar with the structure of `DataAdapters` in ADO.NET, rather than examining each method and property enforced by various interfaces that a `DataAdapter` implements, let's instead focus on the practical usage of `DataAdapters`.

`DataAdapters` can be used for both querying and/or updating the underlying data source. In this chapter, however, the main focus of discussion will be fetching data from the underlying data source. Once you have a good handle on fetching data, you can move on to working with it in disconnected mode in Chapter 8, followed by updating data, which is discussed in Chapters 9, 10, and 11.

Querying most major data sources involves the execution of a SQL query wrapped inside a `DbCommand` object. This has already been illustrated in Chapter 5, but first let's set up the database that the exercises of this chapter will run on.

Setting Up the Data Source

The exercises in this chapter, like the rest of the book, will demonstrate working examples running on a local instance of SQL Server 2005, or a local access database using the OleDb data provider. However, it's important to note that there are certain subtle differences between individual data providers. Specifically for the `OracleClient` .NET data provider, the relevant differences will be elucidated with the necessary code examples wherever applicable.

So for the examples in this chapter, the data source being used is a database called `Test` that can be easily created on your local instance of SQL Server 2005. To accomplish this, use the following script through SQL Server Management Studio:

```
Create Database Test
```

Next, you need to create a simple table structure that can be queried. For this purpose, you can create three tables with a many-to-many relationship between them: `UserTable`, `PermissionsTable`, and `UserPermissionsTable`. You can find the scripts for creating and populating them with data in the associated code download for this chapter in `CreateTestDatabase.Sql` (please see the Downloads section of the Apress website at `http://www.apress.com`), but the table structures are shown in Figure 7-2.

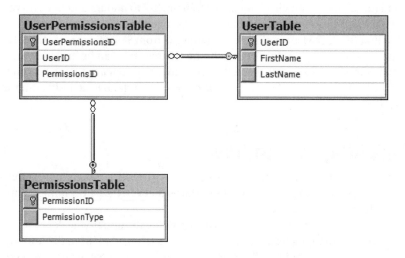

Figure 7-2. *Table structure for examples*

You can then fill the tables with some sample data.

Querying One Table: Point and Click

Now that you have data to query, let's write a quick sample as Exercise 7.1, which demonstrates getting the contents of one table in a disconnected fashion. For sample purposes, the discussion will concentrate on the UserTable:

1. Start by creating a Windows Forms project. Name it Exercise 7.1 and change the main form's text to Exercise 7.1.

2. Enable the Data Sources window for your project in Visual Studio 2005. If that window is not directly available, you can enable it using the Data ➤ Show Data Sources menu item as shown in Figure 7-3.

Figure 7-3. *Enabling the Data Sources window*

3. Once the Data Sources window is enabled, click the Add New Data Source icon on the top (or click the hyperlink in the window if available), and point the new database connection to the Test database on your local SQL Server 2005 instance. If you wish to use a SQL Server instance on the network, or an alternate data source such as Oracle, you need to use a different connection string and possibly different objects, but the overall pattern remains the same. Choosing the Test database on your local SQL Server 2005 instance is shown in Figures 7-4 and 7-5.

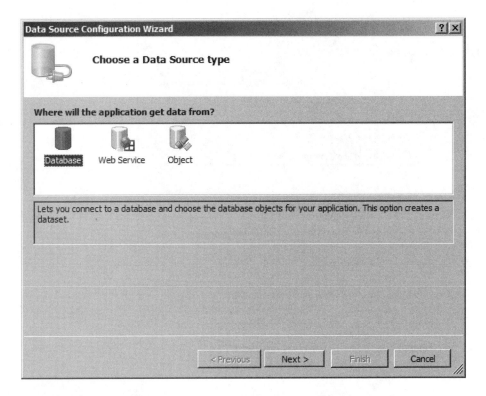

Figure 7-4. *Choosing the appropriate data source (in our case "Database")*

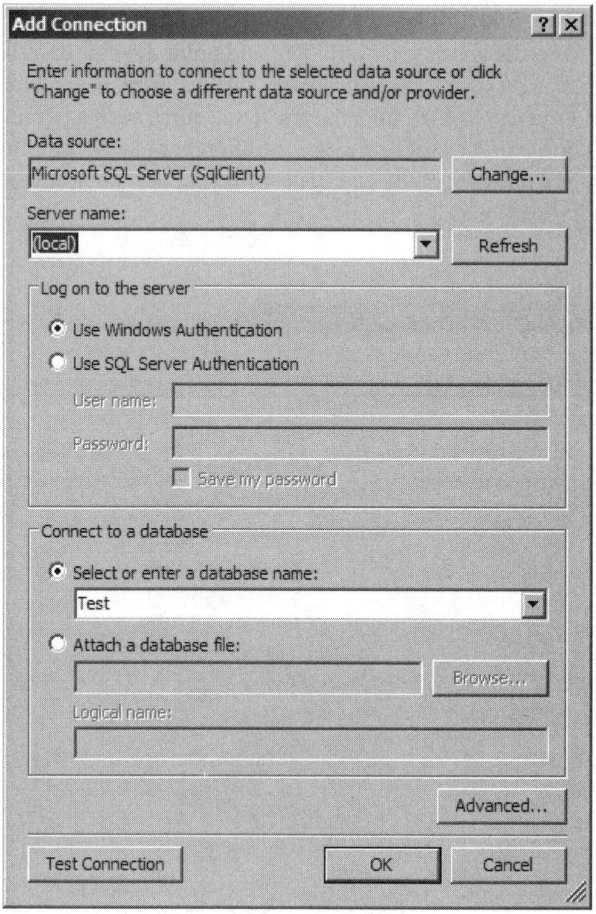

Figure 7-5. *Choosing the right database*

4. When prompted to "Choose your database objects," under `Tables` choose the `UserTable` as shown in Figure 7-6 and then click Finish.

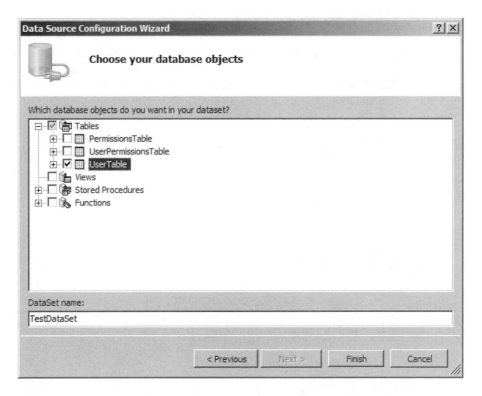

Figure 7-6. *Choosing the database objects*

5. You should now see the testDataSet and UserTable under the Data Sources window. At this point, you have the option of showing the UserTable in a DataGridView control, or as individual controls, or even in a custom control. This is shown in Figure 7-7.

Figure 7-7. *Choosing the display mode for UserTable*

For this example, we'll go with the Details mode. As an exercise, you can simply set the UserTable to DataGridView, then drag and drop the table to the form's surface.

6. Ensure that `UserTable` is set to `Details` mode as shown in Figure 7-7.

7. One by one, choose the relevant controls you wish to display—in this case, `FirstName` and `LastName`—then drag and drop them to the surface of the application's form. You'll notice that Visual Studio 2005 has added four objects in the component tray. These are shown in Figure 7-8.

Figure 7-8. *Objects added for you automatically in the component tray*

Also, after slight aesthetic resizing and positioning of various controls on the form, it now looks like as shown in Figure 7-9.

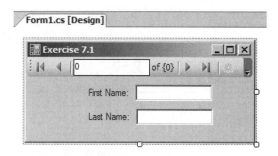

Figure 7-9. *The final form in Design mode*

8. Compile and execute the application. You should see output as seen in Figure 7-10.

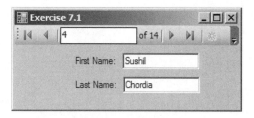

Figure 7-10. *The final running application*

But wait a minute. You didn't write any code!

Indeed you didn't. But Visual Studio did. If you enable Show All Files (Project ➤ Show All Files), you'll see a number of files that are maintained by Visual Studio for you. In this example, you'll notice that Visual Studio has added code for you mainly in the `Form1.Designer.cs` file and the

Form1.resx file. Also, it added an App.Config to save a connection string as you had instructed it to do so in steps 3 and 4. And in the code that you see in Form1.cs, Visual Studio added just one line of code to fill the DataTable.

Even though such an application can be developed using point and click, whenever you design an enterprise-level application, you might have to pass DataTables to various classes that might formulate XSD messages or business-object representations of your data. Thus, in many situations, you should be able to actually write code yourself and fill a DataTable or DataSet.

Querying One Table: Writing Code

In Exercise 7.2, you'll create functionality very similar to Exercise 7.1; where in Exercise 7.1 you created code by pointing and clicking, in Exercise 7.2 you'll actually write code yourself. You'll see that by writing such code, you have better control over how the database is queried and when the retrieved DataTable is databound to the UI. This is where you'll need to interact with a DataAdapter object instance. The code for this exercise can be found in the relevant code download for this chapter in Exercise 7.2. Or you can simply follow the steps here to create such an application:

1. Start by creating a Windows Forms application. Name it Exercise 7.2 and change the main form's text to Exercise 7.2.

2. On the main form for the newly added exercise, add a DataGridView and name it datagridView.

3. Next, add two buttons: buttonFillData with the text Fill Data, and buttonBind with the text DataBind. Your Windows Form, after a few resizing and control placement adjustments, should look like Figure 7-11.

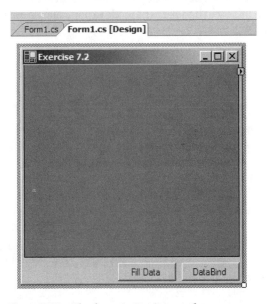

Figure 7-11. *The form in Design mode*

4. Now, go to the code for the form. To do this, right-click on the form and choose View Code. You'll see the partial class implementation for Form1.cs (or .vb). Over here, add using/Imports statements for System.Data and System.Data.SqlClient. Also, add a private variable to the class called userTable of type DataTable and instantiate it in the constructor, as shown here:

C#

```csharp
partial class Form1 : Form
{
    private DataTable userTable;

    public Form1()
    {
        InitializeComponent();
        userTable = new DataTable();
    }
...
}
```

VB.NET

```vbnet
Public Class Form1
    Private userData As New DataTable
...
End Class
```

5. Now, back to the form's designer: double-click Fill Data (buttonFillData) to create an event handler for its click event. In this event handler, write code to populate the DataTable. This is shown in Listings 7-1 and 7-2.

Listing 7-1. *Filling userTable Programmatically in C#*

```csharp
private void buttonFillData_Click(object sender, EventArgs e)
{
    // Never hard code connection strings.
    // Usually you would get this from a config file
    string connectionString =
    "Data Source=(local);Initial Catalog=Test;Integrated Security=SSPI;" ;

    using (SqlConnection testConnection = new SqlConnection(connectionString))
    {
        SqlCommand testCommand = testConnection.CreateCommand();
        testCommand.CommandText = "Select FirstName, LastName from userTable";
        SqlDataAdapter dataAdapter = new SqlDataAdapter(testCommand);
        dataAdapter.Fill(userTable);
    } // testConnection.Dispose called automatically.
}
```

Listing 7-2. *Filling userTable Programmatically in Visual Basic .NET*

```vb
Private Sub buttonFillData_Click( _
    ByVal sender As System.Object, ByVal e As System.EventArgs) _
        Handles buttonFillData.Click
    Dim connectionString As String
    connectionString = _
        "Data Source=(local);Initial Catalog=Test;Integrated Security=SSPI;"
    Using testConnection As SqlConnection = New SqlConnection(connectionString)
        Dim testCommand As SqlCommand = testConnection.CreateCommand()
        testCommand.CommandText = "Select FirstName, LastName from UserTable"
        Dim dataAdapter As New SqlDataAdapter(testCommand)
        dataAdapter.Fill(userData)
    End Using
End Sub
```

6. Again from the form's designer, double-click DataBind (buttonBind) to create an event handler for its click event. In this event handler, write code to data bind the DataGridView to the userTable. In this event handler, write the following code:

C#

```csharp
private void buttonBind_Click(object sender, EventArgs e)
{
    datagridView.DataSource = userTable;
}
```

VB.NET

```vb
Private Sub buttonBind_Click( _
    ByVal sender As System.Object, ByVal e As System.EventArgs) _
    Handles buttonBind.Click
    datagridView.DataSource = userData
End Sub
```

7. Compile and run the application. You should see a window similar to the one shown in Figure 7-12.

Figure 7-12. *The final running application*

8. As an exercise, change the `userTable` DataTable to a DataSet, and make suitable changes to the `DataBind` code. You'll note that the `DataAdapter` is able to `Fill` both a `DataTable` and a `DataSet`.

Unlike Exercise 7.1, this exercise involved writing some code. Let's dissect the code and try to understand what exactly was done.

The first part was obviously to set up the connection. This was done using the following code:

C#

```
using (SqlConnection testConnection = new SqlConnection(connectionString))
{
...
}
```

VB.NET

```
Using testConnection As SqlConnection = New SqlConnection(connectionString)
...
End Using
```

The next part was creating a `SqlCommand` for the underlying Microsoft SQL Server 2005 database (this has been extensively covered in Chapter 5):

C#

```
SqlCommand testCommand = testConnection.CreateCommand();
testCommand.CommandText = "Select FirstName, LastName from userTable";
```

VB.NET

```
Dim testCommand As SqlCommand = testConnection.CreateCommand()
testCommand.CommandText = "Select FirstName, LastName from UserTable"
```

The next step was to create a data adapter. This was done using the following statement:

C#

```
SqlDataAdapter dataAdapter = new SqlDataAdapter(testCommand);
```

VB.NET

```
Dim dataAdapter As New SqlDataAdapter(testCommand)
```

The SqlDataAdapter constructor supports four overloads. The overload used here (SqlDataAdapte(testCommand)) lets you specify a command with a connection setup in the constructor itself. The other three overloads available are as follows:

- SqlDataAdapter(): This sets up a bare instance of a SqlDataAdapter. The command with a valid connection now must be specified in the SelectCommand property. In Chapter 9, where updating data is discussed, you'll come across three more properties of a SqlDataAdapter object: the InsertCommand, DeleteCommand, and UpdateCommand properties, which also use SqlCommand type variables used for updating the data back to the data source. They cannot be specified via the constructor, but they can be specified as properties on the SqlDataAdapter object, once it is created.

- SqlDataAdapter(string commandText, SqlConnection connection): This overload lets you specify the command being used to fill the DataSet/DataTable as a string and the connection it will be filled from.

- SqlDataAdapter(string commandText, string connectionString): This overload lets you specify both the command and the relevant connection as strings; thus, you can specify all the necessary information in one line of code without instantiating any extra objects yourself.

And finally, with the data adapter ready, all the application had to do was fill the DataTable using the Fill method. This was done using the following code statement:

C#

```
dataAdapter.Fill(userTable);
```

VB.NET

```
dataAdapter.Fill(userTable)
```

Do note, however, that the data adapter's Fill method can be used to fill either a DataSet or a DataTable. So if, in a particular instance, your needs are met by a single DataTable, you should use that instead of a DataSet with one table in it because the single DataTable has a smaller memory footprint.

Another point to notice about this code is that *the underlying SqlConnection was never explicitly opened*. This is quite interesting because the SqlDataAdapter doesn't need an already open connection. As a matter of fact, as a part of the Fill operation, SqlDataAdapter would open the connection, fill the DataTable or DataSet, and close the connection as soon as possible.

This allows for the best connection pooling scenario (see Chapter 4) because the cardinal rule of connection pooling—"open as late as possible, close as early as you can"—was followed. If, indeed, for some reason you were to pass in an open connection instead, the SqlDataAdapter would have used the open connection, and left it open.

Thus, the SqlDataAdapter always leaves the connection in the same state it took it as.

As previously mentioned, the DataAdapter.Fill method has the ability to fill either a DataTable or a DataSet. You should try and use a DataTable when your design allows you to do so for single table operations.

However, not every database query operation can be a single result set. You might want to return more than one result set in one database hit. This was also discussed in context of a data reader in Chapter 5. Just as a data reader has the ability to fetch multiple result sets in one database hit,[1] the DataAdapter object also can fill an entire DataSet in one database hit.

Let's examine this using an example.

Filling DataSets: More Than One Table

As discussed in Chapter 6, just as a DataTable works for one single table, a DataSet has the ability to not only store multiple tables, but also relations between them. The magic occurs within the command text for the supplied relevant derived DbCommand. As a matter of fact, you can simply use Exercise 7.2's code and replace DataTable with a DataSet and make the appropriate change to the CommandText so you'd now be filling a DataSet with multiple tables instead of one. Obviously, you cannot simply bind a DataSet directly to a DataGridView kind of control, so the display logic would change too, but that will be discussed shortly. The code for filling the DataSet instead of a DataTable is shown in Listings 7-3 and 7-4. The userData variable now is of DataSet type.

Listing 7-3. *Filling a DataSet Programmatically in C#*

```
private void buttonFillData_Click(object sender, EventArgs e)
{
    // Never hard code connection strings.
    // Usually you would get this from a config file
    string connectionString =
    "Data Source=(local);Initial Catalog=Test;Integrated Security=SSPI;" ;

    using (SqlConnection testConnection = new SqlConnection(connectionString))
    {
        SqlCommand testCommand = testConnection.CreateCommand();
        testCommand.CommandText = "Select FirstName, LastName from userTable;" +
            " Select PermissionType from PermissionsTable";
        SqlDataAdapter dataAdapter = new SqlDataAdapter(testCommand);
        dataAdapter.Fill(userData);
    } // testConnection.Dispose called automatically.
}
```

1. This, in fact, depends on the actual .NET data provider and the underlying data source. So certain data readers might not allow you to fetch multiple result sets in one database hit; but for the sake of discussion, let's assume that they do let you fetch multiple result sets, as is the case in SQL Server or Oracle or any other "serious" database product.

Listing 7-4. *Filling a DataSet Programmatically in Visual Basic .NET*

```
Private Sub buttonFillData_Click( _
   ByVal sender As System.Object, ByVal e As System.EventArgs) _
      Handles buttonFillData.Click
   Dim connectionString As String
   connectionString = _
      "Data Source=(local);Initial Catalog=Test;Integrated Security=SSPI;"
   Using testConnection As SqlConnection = New SqlConnection(connectionString)
      Dim testCommand As SqlCommand = testConnection.CreateCommand()
      testCommand.CommandText = "Select FirstName, LastName from userTable;" & _
         " Select PermissionType from PermissionsTable"
      Dim dataAdapter As New SqlDataAdapter(testCommand)
      dataAdapter.Fill(userData)
   End Using
End Sub
```

Listings 7-3 and 7-4 are for the Microsoft SQL Server data provider. Even though they use dynamic SQL, you could have achieved the same thing using a stored procedure too. An example of such a stored procedure is shown in Listing 7-5.

Listing 7-5. *Microsoft SQL Server Stored Procedure Returning Multiple Results*

```
Create Procedure GetMultipleResults
As
Begin
   Select FirstName, LastName from userTable;
   Select PermissionType from PermissionsTable;
End
```

As already mentioned in Chapter 5 with regard to data readers, in Oracle you can achieve the same result using a stored procedure with multiple REF CURSORs. This is shown in Listing 7-6. Of course getting a single result back from an Oracle stored procedure would simply involve returning only one REF CURSOR.

Listing 7-6. *Oracle Package and Stored Procedure Returning Multiple Results*

```
CREATE OR REPLACE PACKAGE USERPERMSPKG AS
   TYPE RESULTCURR IS REF CURSOR;
   PROCEDURE GETUSERPERMS (USERCUR OUT RESULTCURR,
                           PERMSCUR OUT RESULTCURR);
END USERPERMSPKG;

CREATE OR REPLACE PACKAGE BODY USERPERMSPKG AS
   PROCEDURE GETUSERPERMS (USERCUR OUT RESULTCURR,
                           PERMSCUR OUT RESULTCURR)
   IS
      LOCALUSERCUR RESULTCURR;
      LOCALPERMSCUR RESULTCURR;
```

```
BEGIN
  OPEN LOCALUSERCUR FOR
      SELECT FIRSTNAME, LASTNAME FROM USERTABLE;
  OPEN LOCALPERMSCUR FOR
      SELECT PERMISSIONTYPE FROM PERMISSIONSTABLE;

  USERCUR := LOCALUSERCUR;
  PERMSCUR := LOCALPERMSCUR;
  END GETUSERPERMS;
END USERPERMSPKG;
/
```

So by simply swapping a DataTable for a DataSet, and the appropriate command text, you can now easily fill a DataSet instead of a DataTable. In Oracle, however, you have to perform an extra step of specifying additional parameters of OracleType.Cursor type to the relevant SelectCommand on the OracleDataAdapter. This can be easily done using the code shown here:

C#

```
dataAdapter.SelectCommand.Parameters.Add(
    new OracleParameter["USERCUR", OracleType.Cursor]);
dataAdapter.SelectCommand.Parameters[0].Direction = ParameterDirection.Output;
dataAdapter.SelectCommand.Parameters.Add(
    new OracleParameter["PERMSCUR", OracleType.Cursor]);
dataAdapter.SelectCommand.Parameters[1].Direction = ParameterDirection.Output;
```

VB.NET

```
dataAdapter.SelectCommand.Parameters.Add( _
    New OracleParameter("USERCUR", OracleType.Cursor))
dataAdapter.SelectCommand.Parameters(0).Direction = ParameterDirection.Output
dataAdapter.SelectCommand.Parameters.Add( _
    New OracleParameter("PERMSCUR", OracleType.Cursor))
dataAdapter.SelectCommand.Parameters(1).Direction = ParameterDirection.Output
```

But it gets even more interesting than this!

A DataSet might contain multiple DataTables filled in from different data sources. Or, you might not want to load all the data in one shot, but you might still want to maintain relationships between various DataTables while being disconnected. Since you cannot (easily at least) create DataRelations between two DataTables in different DataSets, you'd probably need a mechanism to fill in the DataSet using two different DbCommands, in two different database hits.

Let's examine this behavior using an example, Exercise 7.3. The code for this example can be found in the associated code download for Exercise 7.3:

1. Begin by creating a new Windows Forms application project. Name it Exercise 7.3 and change the main form's text to Exercise 7.3.

2. Place a combo box control called comboTables, a DataGridView control called datagridView, and two buttons called buttonUserData and buttonPermData with text properties set to Fill User Data and Fill Permissions Data, respectively. Your UI should look like Figure 7-13.

Figure 7-13. *DataSet UI fill example in Design mode*

The intention here is to be able to provide the user with a combo box full of various DataTables available in the DataSet. The DataGridView datagridView control shows the currently selected DataTable, and the two buttons allow you to fill in the DataSet one by one. Let's skip a Data Bind button here because the combo box will serve that purpose.

3. Add a private variable of DataSet type. Call it myData:

C#

```
partial class Form1 : Form
{
    private DataSet myData;

    public Form1()
    {
        InitializeComponent();
        myData = new DataSet();
    }
...
}
```

VB.NET

```
Public Class Form1
    Private myData As New DataSet
...
End Class
```

4. Now in the event handler for buttonUserData's click event, add the code shown in Listings 7-7 and 7-8.

Listing 7-7. *Filling a DataSet with the UserTable in C#*

```csharp
private void buttonUserData_Click(object sender, EventArgs e)
{
    // If there is a data source, remove it.
    datagridView.DataSource = null;
    // Never hard code connection strings.
    // Usually you would get this from a config file
    string connectionString =
    "Data Source=(local);Initial Catalog=Test;Integrated Security=SSPI;";

    using (SqlConnection testConnection = new SqlConnection(connectionString))
    {
        SqlCommand testCommand = testConnection.CreateCommand();
        testCommand.CommandText = "Select * from userTable";
        SqlDataAdapter dataAdapter = new SqlDataAdapter(testCommand);

        dataAdapter.Fill(myData, "UserTable");
    } // testConnection.Dispose called automatically.
    UpdateComboBox();
}
```

Listing 7-8. *Filling a DataSet with the UserTable in Visual Basic .NET*

```vbnet
Private Sub buttonUserData_Click( _
    ByVal sender As System.Object, ByVal e As System.EventArgs) _
    Handles buttonUserData.Click
    ' If there is a data source, remove it.
    datagridView.DataSource = Nothing
    ' Never hard code connection strings.
    ' Usually you would get this from a config file
    Dim connectionString As String = _
     "Data Source=(local);Initial Catalog=Test;Integrated Security=SSPI;"

    Using testConnection As SqlConnection = New SqlConnection(connectionString)
        Dim testCommand As SqlCommand = testConnection.CreateCommand()
        testCommand.CommandText = "Select * from userTable"
        Dim dataAdapter As New SqlDataAdapter(testCommand)

        dataAdapter.Fill(myData, "UserTable")
    End Using ' testConnection.Dispose called automatically.
    UpdateComboBox()
End Sub
```

This code loads the UserTable into the DataSet, and also calls a method named UpdateComboBox, which is responsible for keeping the DataSet and comboTables in sync. The code for UpdateComboBox is shown in Listings 7-9 and 7-10.

Listing 7-9. *Code to Keep the Combo Box and DataSet in Sync in C#*

```csharp
private void UpdateComboBox()
{
    comboTables.Items.Clear();
    foreach (DataTable tbl in myData.Tables)
    {
        comboTables.Items.Add(tbl.TableName);
    }
}
```

Listing 7-10. *Code to Keep the Combo Box and DataSet in Sync in Visual Basic .NET*

```vbnet
Private Sub UpdateComboBox()
    comboTables.Items.Clear()
    For Each tbl As DataTable In myData.Tables
        comboTables.Items.Add(tbl.TableName)
    Next
End Sub
```

5. In the event handler for buttonPermData's click event, add code exactly the same as that for buttonUserData's click event, but change the CommandText to

```
Select PermissionType from PermissionsTable
```

and the dataAdapter.Fill statement to

C#
```csharp
dataAdapter.Fill(myData, "PermissionsTable");
```

VB.NET
```vbnet
dataAdapter.Fill(myData, "PermissionsTable")
```

6. You're almost done. Now you need to hook up the combo box's SelectedIndexChanged event to toggle datagridView's current binding to a particular DataTable. This is shown in Listings 7-11 and 7-12.

Listing 7-11. *Binding the DataGridView with the Right Table in C#*

```csharp
private void comboTables_SelectedIndexChanged(object sender, EventArgs e)
{
    datagridView.DataSource = myData.Tables[comboTables.SelectedIndex];
}
```

Listing 7-12. *Binding the DataGridView with the Right Table in Visual Basic .NET*

```
Private Sub comboTables_SelectedIndexChanged( _
  ByVal sender As System.Object, ByVal e As System.EventArgs)  _
  Handles comboTables.SelectedIndexChanged
    datagridView.DataSource = myData.Tables(comboTables.SelectedIndex)
End Sub
```

7. Compile and run the application. Click the buttonUserData button. You'll see the combo box populated with one `DataTable`: the `UserTable`.

8. Click the buttonPermData button. You'll see that the `PermissionsTable` is also loaded into the `DataSet`. The final running application can be seen in Figure 7-14.

Figure 7-14. *DataSet UI fill example with tables filled*

One interesting thing to note in Exercise 7.3 is that if you click either of the two buttons repeatedly, the `DataAdapter` simply adds the rows over and over again. This is probably not what you would want in repeated "refreshes" of the `DataSet`.

To understand how you can prevent this from happening, you need to examine what causes this behavior in the first place. When the `DataAdapter` looks to fill an already full `DataSet`, it has no way of identifying which rows being filled are already present in the `DataSet`. There's no primary key to look up and verify with. The `DataSet` is missing the *schema* information.

Aha!! Thus to solve this issue, all you need to do is specify the schema, right?

Yes, that's all you need to do, but it gets easier than this; even though you could do it the hard way, you don't quite have to specify the full schema yourself. You can query the data source and *fill the schema instead.*

Querying Database Schema

In Exercise 7.3, you looked at an example that demonstrated filling a `DataSet` repeatedly from the underlying data source. One obvious problem was that with repeated "refreshes" of the data, the DataAdapter keeps adding more and more rows, i.e., it really doesn't refresh, it simply adds more rows.

The DataAdapter is unable to identify duplicate rows, because there is no schema information that clearly discerns primary keys and UniqueKeyConstraints in the DataTables within the DataSet.

This can be easily alleviated by having schema information in the DataTable. As a matter of fact, you don't really have to specify schema information; for simpler cases, you can just query the underlying schema information right from the database. Let's examine this in a code example in Exercise 7.4.

1. Begin by creating a new Windows Forms application project. Name it Exercise 7.4 and change the main form's text to Exercise 7.4. Also, add a private DataSet variable called myData.

2. On the main form, drop two buttons. Name them buttonSchema and buttonData with text properties set to Fill Schema and Fill Data, respectively. Also, drop a WebBrowser control. Name it xmlBrowser.

   In this example, buttonSchema will be used to query the database for the DataSet schema, and once the schema is loaded, buttonData will be used to fetch data from the database. Also, since the DataGridView control is unable to show us schema information, this example drops a notch by showing you the contents of the DataSet directly in XML. This allows you to view schema information and data information, i.e., entire DataSet information directly as XML loaded in the xmlBrowser control. Your form should look like what is shown in Figure 7-15.

Figure 7-15. *DataSet schema and data fill form in Design mode*

3. In the click event handler for buttonData, enter code as shown in Listings 7-13 and 7-14. This code is no different than what you have seen earlier for filling the data. Note that as compared to Exercise 7.3, a different overload of the Fill method is being used. You no longer need to explicitly *name* your table when doing a Fill. This is because the DataSet

has schema information in it, so you are no longer required to explicitly divide the data in two tables; the DataAdapter now can read the schema and channel the data properly into the correct DataTables. (As an exercise, you could replace Fill(myData,"UserTable") with Fill(myData) in Exercise 7.3 and notice that the example no longer works correctly.)

Listing 7-13. *Filling a DataSet in C#*

```csharp
private void buttonData_Click(object sender, EventArgs e)
{
    string connectionString =
    "Data Source=(local);Initial Catalog=Test;Integrated Security=SSPI;";

    using (SqlConnection testConnection = new SqlConnection(connectionString))
    {
        SqlCommand testCommand = testConnection.CreateCommand();
        testCommand.CommandText =
          "Select * from userTable; Select * from permissionsTable";
        SqlDataAdapter dataAdapter = new SqlDataAdapter(testCommand);

        dataAdapter.Fill(myData);
    } // testConnection.Dispose called automatically.
    DisplayContents() ;
}
```

Listing 7-14. *Filling a DataSet in Visual Basic .NET*

```vbnet
Private Sub buttonData_Click( _
  ByVal sender As System.Object, ByVal e As System.EventArgs) _
  Handles buttonData.Click
  Dim connectionString As String = _
    "Data Source=(local);Initial Catalog=Test;Integrated Security=SSPI;"

  Using testConnection As SqlConnection = New SqlConnection(connectionString)
      Dim testCommand As SqlCommand = testConnection.CreateCommand()
      testCommand.CommandText = _
        "Select * from userTable; Select * from permissionsTable"
      Dim dataAdapter As New SqlDataAdapter(testCommand)

      dataAdapter.Fill(myData)
  End Using
  ' testConnection.Dispose called automatically.
  DisplayContents()
End Sub
```

4. Similarly, in the click event handler for buttonSchema, add the code shown in Listings 7-15 and 7-16. Note that all you did was swap the Fill method call to FillSchema. The second parameter specified will be examined in further detail shortly, but for now it's enough to understand that the second parameter specifies the DataAdapter to use the table names as defined by the source, and not map them to something else (you can specify such mappings using the TableMappings property, but more on that in Exercise 7.6).

Listing 7-15. *Filling a DataSet Schema in C#*

```csharp
private void buttonSchema_Click(object sender, EventArgs e)
{
    string connectionString =
    "Data Source=(local);Initial Catalog=Test;Integrated Security=SSPI;";

    using (SqlConnection testConnection = new SqlConnection(connectionString))
    {
        SqlCommand testCommand = testConnection.CreateCommand();
        testCommand.CommandText =
            "Select * from userTable; Select * from permissionsTable";
        SqlDataAdapter dataAdapter = new SqlDataAdapter(testCommand);

        dataAdapter.FillSchema(myData, SchemaType.Source);
    } // testConnection.Dispose called automatically.
    DisplayContents() ;
}
```

Listing 7-16. *Filling a DataSet Schema in Visual Basic .NET*

```vbnet
Private Sub buttonSchema_Click( _
  ByVal sender As System.Object, ByVal e As System.EventArgs) _
  Handles buttonSchema.Click
  Dim connectionString As String = _
    "Data Source=(local);Initial Catalog=Test;Integrated Security=SSPI;"

  Using testConnection As SqlConnection = New SqlConnection(connectionString)
     Dim testCommand As SqlCommand = testConnection.CreateCommand()
     testCommand.CommandText = _
        "Select * from userTable; Select * from permissionsTable"
     Dim dataAdapter As New SqlDataAdapter(testCommand)

     dataAdapter.FillSchema(myData, SchemaType.Source)
  End Using
  ' testConnection.Dispose called automatically.
  DisplayContents()
End Sub
```

5. You might have noticed a call to a method named DisplayContents at the end of both the Fill and FillSchema listings. That method is responsible for displaying the contents of the DataSet as XML in the xmlBrowser control. The code for that can be seen in Listings 7-17 and 7-18.

Listing 7-17. *Displaying the Contents of a DataSet in C#*

```
private void DisplayContents()
{
    myData.WriteXml(Application.StartupPath + "\\myData.Xml",
      XmlWriteMode.WriteSchema) ;
    xmlBrowser.Navigate(Application.StartupPath + "\\myData.Xml") ;
}
```

Listing 7-18. *Displaying the Contents of a DataSet in Visual Basic .NET*

```
Private Sub DisplayContents()
    myData.WriteXml(Application.StartupPath & _
      "\myData.Xml", XmlWriteMode.WriteSchema)
    xmlBrowser.Navigate(Application.StartupPath & "\myData.Xml")
End Sub
```

6. Compile and run the application. Click Fill Schema and then Fill Data. Then click Fill Data repeatedly—you'll notice that unlike Exercise 7.3, because you have the schema information preloaded, the DataAdapter is able to discern duplicate rows and not add them. This can be seen in Figure 7-16. (Some of the elements have been collapsed to reduce the size of the image, but you can always run the associated example in the code download to view the full data.)

```
Exercise 7.4                                        _ □ ×
    <?xml version="1.0" standalone="yes" ?>
  - <NewDataSet>
    - <xs:schema id="NewDataSet" xmlns=""
        xmlns:xs="http://www.w3.org/2001/XMLSchema"
        xmlns:msdata="urn:schemas-microsoft-com:xml-msdata">
      - <xs:element name="NewDataSet" msdata:IsDataSet="true">
        + <xs:complexType>
        + <xs:unique name="Constraint1" msdata:PrimaryKey="true">
        + <xs:unique name="Table1_Constraint1"
            msdata:ConstraintName="Constraint1"
            msdata:PrimaryKey="true">
        </xs:element>
      </xs:schema>
    - <Table>
        <UserID>1</UserID>
        <FirstName>Sahil</FirstName>
        <LastName>Malik</LastName>
      </Table>
    - <Table>
        <UserID>2</UserID>
        <FirstName>Jonathan</FirstName>
        <LastName>Hassell</LastName>
      </Table>
    - <Table>
        <UserID>3</UserID>
        <FirstName>Angel-Saenz</FirstName>
        <LastName>Badillos</LastName>
      </Table>
    - <Table>
        <UserID>4</UserID>
        <FirstName>Sushil</FirstName>
        <LastName>Chordia</LastName>
      </Table>
    - <Table>
        <UserID>5</UserID>
        <FirstName>Pablo</FirstName>
        <LastName>Castro</LastName>
      </Table>
    - <Table>
        <UserID>6</UserID>
        <FirstName>William</FirstName>
        <LastName>Ryan</LastName>
      </Table>
    - <Table>
        <UserID>7</UserID>
        <FirstName>Frans</FirstName>
                                    [ Fill Schema ]  [ Fill Data ]
```

Figure 7-16. *DataSet schema and data example with the schema loaded*

7. Now re-run the application and instead of clicking Fill Schema, click Fill Data multiple times. What do you see? You'll notice that like Exercise 7.3, because the schema information is not loaded (since you didn't click Fill Schema), the DataAdapter keeps adding duplicate rows incorrectly. This can be seen in Figure 7-17. (Note that all nodes have been collapsed except one to demonstrate the repeated rows.)

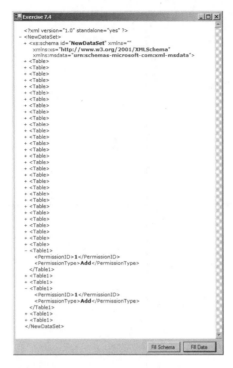

Figure 7-17. *DataSet schema and data example without the schema loaded*

8. Finally, run the application, click Fill Data twice (to load incorrect data), and now try and add a schema to the DataSet by clicking Fill Schema. You should see an exception as shown in Figure 7-18.

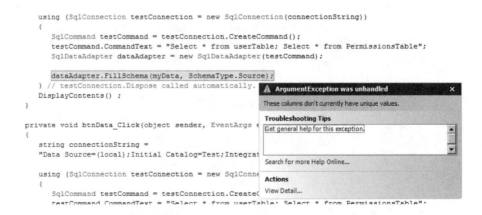

Figure 7-18. *The "Cannot load schema with incorrect data" exception*

For those of you with keen eyes, you might have noticed that the `CommandText` property of `testCommand` was changed. Instead of specifying column names or a batched query, the `CommandText` was changed to accept all columns *including the primary key* by specifying * for the columns. This is where the magic occurs. The primary key in the result set causes `FillSchema` to set a `UniqueConstraint` on the necessary column, and thus prevents the `DataAdapter` from filling in incorrect data. This can be seen in the schema in Listing 7-19.

Listing 7-19. *Primary Key Specified in the Schema*

```
<xs:unique name="Constraint1" msdata:PrimaryKey="true">
  <xs:selector xpath=".//Table" />
  <xs:field xpath="UserID" />
</xs:unique>
<xs:unique name="Table1_Constraint1" msdata:ConstraintName="Constraint1"
    msdata:PrimaryKey="true">
  <xs:selector xpath=".//Table1" />
  <xs:field xpath="PermissionID" />
</xs:unique>
```

Thus, you can see that `FillSchema` allows you to preserve your data sanctity by filling in a schema for you right from the database. It alleviates the need for you to write complex XSD schemas. It also makes your life easier by not requiring you to keep the XSDs in sync with the database, as the database structure might change with time. Though in a production application, you'd probably do better if you store/cache the schemas somewhere and not execute `FillSchema` for every new `DataSet` creation.

REFRESHING DATA IN A REAL-WORLD APPLICATION

So you're able to refresh your disconnected data cache by specifying a schema right? Well, this approach is simplistic, akin to a frictionless surface used in a physics book. Too bad in the real world a frictionless surface doesn't exist.

Before I start discussing a surface with friction in the real world, I should mention that the following paragraphs talk about updating data and concurrency. These topics are covered in Chapters 9, 10, and 11, so if this seems like too much information to digest at this point, you can come back and read this section later.

In the real world, between refreshes of data, you would have to worry about issues such as saving the data between refreshes, informing the user about specific rows that failed to be saved (due to concurrency violations or otherwise), and most importantly, it's quite possible that the user might have the `DataSet` databound with a UI. In this case, while it's certainly possible to fully refresh the `DataSet` and repopulate the UI, that might be an expensive operation for larger `DataSets` or, at the very least, the user might lose some of his changes. Another situation could be a web service on a low bandwidth connection where, due to bandwidth restrictions, ferrying the entire `DataSet` at every single request is just not an option.

The approach you should take instead in that circumstance is to extract only a subset of the entire `DataSet`. This subset can then be merged with the original `DataSet` using the `Merge` method. The subset will contain the changed rows that you were trying to save back to the database. These can be extracted using the `GetChanges` method at the client side before sending the `DataSet` to the `DataAdapter`. As you'll see in Chapters 9, 10, and 11, these rows come back from the `DataAdapter` with information regarding success or failure of their save operation.

This subset would also contain any new rows inserted or modified by any other user while your user was disconnected from the database and busy modifying his disconnected data cache. Given that your DataSet has a schema associated with itself, the added and modified rows are easily reconciled because *information regarding these rows is present in the subset* DataSet.

The information that the subset DataSet *will not, and cannot* possibly contain is information about deleted rows[2]—that is, rows that were fetched in your disconnected cache in the first request, but were subsequently deleted from the database by some other user while you were blissfully ignorant of the changes by virtue of being disconnected from the database.

It's for this purpose that you can leverage the IndexOf method on DataRowCollection to clearly identify if any DataRows have moved upward. Upward movement of a DataRow's index signifies that the DataRow immediately before itself has been deleted from the database; thus, you need to write code to remove them from your disconnected cache.

This way you can keep your disconnected data cache refreshed, including deleted records, without having to ferry huge amounts of data back and forth every time between your database and your DataSet. Or if your DataSet isn't too large, you could simply use a schema and keep reloading your entire DataSet every time, and avoid all this hassle.

In Exercise 7.4, one of the parameters specified to the FillSchema method was the mapping method used. You could specify either the mapping to be defined elsewhere, or you could instruct the DataAdapter to use the mapping specified in the source of the data. Next, let's examine mapping of various table and column names in detail.

Mapping

Frequently, the names that objects in a database have are inappropriate for a particular application. For example, you might want to provide a web service for English-speaking Americans using a database with a Spanish table and column names. You can map different names to one another—so that your code can refer to objects by the name you choose, regardless of the names they have in the database.

SQL has a built-in feature for mapping column names: the AS keyword. To be precise, that mechanism is referred to as *aliasing*, not mapping, but the end effect is the same. Many of you might already be familiar with this method, and in some cases it can be the simplest solution. Its use and shortcomings will be discussed shortly.

ADO.NET provides a built-in mapping solution using the DataTableMapping and DataColumnMapping objects, which provide a far more comprehensive solution.

Using the SQL AS Keyword

Before you look at the mapping facilities provided by ADO.NET, let's have a look at the traditional mapping (aliasing) methods provided by the SQL language.

---

2. Think about it, how can a DataSet contain information about DataRows that are not in the DataSet in the first place? Deleted rows are not a part of your result set, thus, they are absent from the DataSet.

In Exercise 7.5, you load a DataSet with data from an imaginary database with very terse column names. Then you can use the SQL AS keyword to alias these short names to longer, more meaningful names for use in your application. Then the rows are written to the console using these aliased names. The code for this example can be downloaded from Exercise 7.5.

1. Begin by creating a ConsoleApplication. Name it Exercise 7.5.

2. In the Sub Main or static void main, define a connection object. This time, let's be different and use the OleDb data provider interrogating an access database instead.

C#

```
OleDbConnection dbConn =
    new OleDbConnection(
      "Provider=Microsoft.Jet.OLEDB.4.0;Password=;" +
        "User ID=Admin;Data Source=..\\..\\db.mdb");
```

VB.NET

```
' Define a connection object
Dim dbConn As New _
    OleDbConnection("Provider=Microsoft.Jet.OLEDB.4.0;" & _
        "Password=;User ID=Admin;Data Source=..\db.mdb")
```

3. Next, create a data adapter to retrieve records from the database.

C#

```
// Create a data adapter to retrieve records from db
string selectQuery =
  "SELECT ID AS UserID, fn AS FirstName, " +
  "ln AS LastName, cty AS City, st AS State FROM tabUsers";
OleDbDataAdapter usersDataAdapter = new OleDbDataAdapter(selectQuery, dbConn);
```

VB.NET

```
' Create a data adapter to retrieve records from db
Dim selectQuery As String = _
    "SELECT ID AS UserID, fn AS FirstName, " & _
    "ln AS LastName, cty AS City, st AS State FROM tabUsers"
Dim usersDataAdapter As New OleDbDataAdapter(selectQuery, dbConn)
```

4. Fill the DataSet.

C#

```
DataSet usersDataSet = new DataSet("Users");
usersDataAdapter.Fill(usersDataSet);
```

VB.NET

```
Dim usersDataSet As New DataSet("Users")
usersDataAdapter.Fill(usersDataSet)
```

5. Finally, go through the rows one by one and print their values to `Console`.

C#

```
// Go through the records and print them using the aliased names
foreach (DataRow userRow in usersDataSet.Tables[0].Rows)
{
  Console.WriteLine(
     "ID: {0}, FirstName: {1}, LastName: {2}, City: {3}, State: {4}",
     userRow["UserID"], userRow["FirstName"],
     userRow["LastName"], userRow["City"], userRow["State"]);
}
```

VB.NET

```
' Go through the records and print them using the aliased names
For Each userRow As DataRow In usersDataSet.Tables(0).Rows
   Console.WriteLine( _
    "ID: {0}, FirstName: {1}, LastName: {2}, City: {3}, State: {4}", _
      userRow("UserID"), userRow("FirstName"), _
      userRow("LastName"), userRow("City"), userRow("State"))
Next
```

This method has succeeded in giving us new column names, which in many cases will be enough; however, it does not automatically map table names. You need to do that by using the `DataTable`'s `TableName` property.

The `Fill()` method provided by the `DataAdapter` object doesn't create mapping classes when it encounters the aliased column names. In fact, the database software, not .NET, handles the aliasing.

The ADO.NET Mapping Mechanism

Now let's take a look at the new mapping mechanisms provided by ADO.NET. The objects will be introduced by using mappings when filling a `DataSet`. The same concepts can be applied to using mappings when making updates to the data source, but those will be discussed in Chapters 9 and 10.

There is a big difference between the SQL aliasing method and the ADO.NET mapping method. For instance, the mapping objects allow developers to manage `DataSet` data and schemas that have been created using XML documents and XML schemas. With the SQL `AS` keyword, you can use the aliased column names only when you deal with the database and records.

In short, aliasing refers to renaming a column in the result set, whereas mapping refers to establishing a one-to-one translation between a result set's column name and a `DataColumn`'s name.

Using Mapping When Retrieving Data

When you fill a DataSet, the data adapter looks at its own TableMappings property to see if the developer has defined mapping rules. By default, the TableMappings property is empty, so the same column names used in the database are used in the relevant DataTables.

Let's take a look at how you can use the ADO.NET mapping mechanism to rename very terse column names in a DataSet to more meaningful alternatives. In Exercise 7.6, the same Microsoft Access database used in Exercise 7.5 will be used.

To use ADO.NET mappings, you need to create a DataTableMapping object. This object enables you to map between two names for the same table, and also contains the ColumnMappings property—a collection of DataColumnMapping objects that map between names of the column in the table. Once you have created this object and added all of the required column mappings, you can add it to the DataAdapter object's TableMappings property.

Let's look at an example that puts this into practice.

To keep the new code clear, a separate method will be used to handle the mapping: DoDataMappings. The code, which can be downloaded from Exercise 7.6, is extremely similar to Exercise 7.5, so only the outline of the code is shown in Listings 7-20 and 7-21.

Listing 7-20. *Using TableMappings in ADO.NET Using C#*

```
// Define a connection object
...
// Create a data adapter object to retrieve records from Db
DoDataMappings(usersDataAdapter);
// Fill the dataset
...
// go through the records and print them using the mapped names
...
```

Listing 7-21. *Using TableMappings in ADO.NET Using Visual Basic .NET*

```
' Define a connection object
...
' Create a data adapter to retrieve records from DB
...
DoDataMapping(usersDataAdapter)
' Fill the dataset
...
' Go through the records and print them using the mapped names
...
```

Notice the call to DoDataMappings, which comes before calling the data adapter's Fill method. This method means that although you have retrieved columns from the database with names like ln and cty, you can refer to them as LastName and City. Let's take a look at the DoDataMappings method now.

You start by declaring DataColumnMapping objects. Create a new DataColumnMapping object for each database column that you want to map to a DataSet column, as shown in Listings 7-22 and 7-23.

Listing 7-22. *Using C#: The DoDataMappings Method, Declaring DataColumnMapping Objects*

```csharp
public void DoDataMappings(OleDbDataAdapter dataAdapter)
{
    try
    {
        // Define each column to map
        DataColumnMapping userIDColumnMap = new DataColumnMapping("ID", "UserID");
        DataColumnMapping fNameColumnMap = new DataColumnMapping("fn", "FirstName");
        DataColumnMapping lNameColumnMap = new DataColumnMapping("ln", "LastName");
        DataColumnMapping cityColumnMap = new DataColumnMapping("cty", "City");
        DataColumnMapping stateColumnMap = new DataColumnMapping("st", "State");
```

Listing 7-23. *Using Visual Basic .NET: The DoDataMappings Method, Declaring DataColumnMapping Objects*

```vbnet
Public Sub DoDataMappings(dataAdapter As OleDbDataAdapter)
    Try
        ' Define each column to map
        Dim userIDColumnMap As New DataColumnMapping("ID", "UserID")
        Dim fNameColumnMap As New DataColumnMapping("fn", "FirstName")
        Dim lNameColumnMap As New DataColumnMapping("ln", "LastName")
        Dim cityColumnMap As New DataColumnMapping("cty", "City")
        Dim stateColumnMap As New DataColumnMapping("st", "State")
```

The DataColumnMapping object contains the relation between the column within the database and the column inside the DataSet. You can construct it by providing two strings: the first string specifies the column name in the data source; the second string defines the column name that will appear in the DataSet.

Once you have created these DataColumnMapping objects, you can create a DataTableMapping object and add the DataColumnMapping objects to it, as shown in Listings 7-24 and 7-25.

Listing 7-24. *Using C#: The DoDataMappings Method, Creating the usersMapping Object*

```csharp
        // Define the table containing the mapped columns
        DataTableMapping usersMapping = new DataTableMapping("Table", "tabUsers");
        usersMapping.ColumnMappings.Add(userIDColumnMap);
        usersMapping.ColumnMappings.Add(fNameColumnMap);
        usersMapping.ColumnMappings.Add(lNameColumnMap);
        usersMapping.ColumnMappings.Add(cityColumnMap);
        usersMapping.ColumnMappings.Add(stateColumnMap);
```

Listing 7-25. *Using Visual Basic .NET: The DoDataMappings Method, Creating the usersMapping Object*

```vbnet
        ' Define the table containing the mapped columns
        Dim usersMapping As New DataTableMapping("Table", "tabUsers")
        usersMapping.ColumnMappings.Add(userIDColumnMap)
        usersMapping.ColumnMappings.Add(fNameColumnMap)
```

```
usersMapping.ColumnMappings.Add(lNameColumnMap)
usersMapping.ColumnMappings.Add(cityColumnMap)
usersMapping.ColumnMappings.Add(stateColumnMap)
```

The DataTableMapping object has a constructor that takes two strings. The first specifies the name of the source table and is case sensitive. This name must correspond to the table name used during the filling or updating process accomplished by the DataAdapter object. If you don't specify a source table name, you must use the default name assigned by the DataAdapter object: Table.

The second parameter is the DataTable object's name in the DataSet. The DataTableMapping object exposes the ColumnMappings collection property that must contain every column you want to map from the database to the DataSet.

Finally, we add the DataTableMapping object to the TableMappings property of the data adapter. Now when we fill the DataSet, the data adapter will find the DataTableMapping in its TableMappings collection and use it, as shown in Listings 7-26 and 7-27.

Listing 7-26. *Using C#: The DoDataMappings Method, Adding the Table Mapping to the Data Adapter*

```
    // Activate the mapping mechanism
    dataAdapter.TableMappings.Add(usersMapping);
}
catch (Exception ex)
{
    // An error occurred. Show the error message
    Console.WriteLine(ex.Message);
}
}
```

Listing 7-27. *Using Visual Basic .NET: The DoDataMappings Method, Adding the Table Mapping to the Data Adapter*

```
    ' Activate the mapping mechanism
    dataAdapter.TableMappings.Add(usersMapping)
Catch ex As Exception
    ' An error occurred. Show the error message
    Console.WriteLine(ex.Message)
End Try
End Sub
```

This has taken quite a bit more code than just using the SQL AS keyword, but this approach works much better with disconnected data since this is an ADO.NET solution, not a SQL Server or an Oracle database solution. The good news is that there is a shorter way to use the data mapping objects—you just looked at the longer version to get a better idea of what is happening. The bad news is that it's still not quite as short as using the AS keyword. Let's look at a shortened version of the DoDataMappings method in Listings 7-28 and 7-29.

Listing 7-28. *Using TableMappings in ADO.NET Using C#: The Shortened DoDataMappings Method*

```csharp
private static void DoDataMappings(OleDbDataAdapter dataAdapter)
{
    try
    {
        // Define an array of columns to map.
        DataColumnMapping[] mappedColumns = {
            new DataColumnMapping("ID", "UserID"),
            new DataColumnMapping("fn", "FirstName"),
            new DataColumnMapping("ln", "LastName"),
            new DataColumnMapping("cty", "City"),
            new DataColumnMapping("st", "State")
        };

        // Define the table containing the mapped columns.
        DataTableMapping usersTableMapping = new DataTableMapping("Table", _
            "tabUsers", mappedColumns);

        // Activate the mapping mechanism.
        dataAdapter.TableMappings.Add(usersTableMapping);
    }
    catch (Exception ex)
    {
        Console.WriteLine(ex.ToString());
    }
}
```

Listing 7-29. *Using TableMappings in ADO.NET Using Visual Basic .NET: The Shortened DoDataMappings Method*

```vbnet
Sub DoDataMappings(ByVal dataAdapter As OleDbDataAdapter)
    Try
        ' Define an array of column to map
        Dim mappedColumns() As DataColumnMapping = { _
                New DataColumnMapping("ID", "UserID"), _
                New DataColumnMapping("fn", "FirstName"), _
                New DataColumnMapping("ln", "LastName"), _
                New DataColumnMapping("cty", "City"), _
                New DataColumnMapping("st", "State")}

        ' Define the table containing the mapped columns
        Dim usersTableMapping As New DataTableMapping("Table", "tabUsers", _
            mappedColumns)
```

```
        ' Activate the mapping mechanism
        dataAdapter.TableMappings.Add(usersTableMapping)
    Catch ex As Exception

        ' An error occurred. Show the error message
        Console.WriteLine(ex.Message)
    End Try
End Sub
```

This time you simply create an array of DataColumnMapping objects instead of declaring them all separately. You then use another DataTableMapping constructor that accepts an array of DataColumnMapping objects in the constructor, rather than adding each DataColumnMapping separately.

There are no substantial differences between using one method over the other. The first case requires more code, but it's slightly more readable than the second one; however, with a few clear comments, the shorter version is perfectly understandable.

MissingMappingAction and MissingSchemaAction

You just saw that when the data adapter fills a DataSet, it checks to see what table mappings have been specified. If none have been specified, then it uses the original names. However, this is only the default. You can also choose how you want the data adapter to react if it meets columns that you have no specified mappings for. The MissingMappingAction property of the data adapter has three settings:

- Passthrough *(the default)*: If a mapping is not specified, the data adapter will assume the name is the same in the data source and the DataSet.

- Error: If a mapping is not specified, the data adapter will raise a System.Exception.

- Ignore: If a mapping is not specified, the DataAdapter object will ignore that column.

Moreover, when the Fill() and the Update() methods are used, you can choose what the data adapter should do when a DataSet schema doesn't meet expectations. The MissingSchemaAction property of the data adapter can accept four values:

- Add *(default option)*: When the schema is missing for the current column, the data adapter will create it and add it to the DataSet object without creating information on primary keys or unique columns.

- AddWithKey: This is the same as the Add option, but with the difference that primary keys and unique columns will be created. Remember that the identity column will be created without identity seed and identity increment values. You should add them after the Fill() or the Update() calls.

- Ignore: When the schema is missing for the current column, the data adapter will ignore it and continue analyzing the other columns.

- Error: When the schema is missing for the current column, the data adapter will raise an exception.

These settings also apply when using the data adapter to update a data source, which will be discussed further in Chapters 9 and 10.

Summary

This chapter introduced you to the bridge between the connected and disconnected worlds within ADO.NET—the DataAdapter object. Just as Chapter 5 was concerned with fetching data in a connected mode, this chapter used DbCommand objects specified to the DataAdapter object to fill DataTables and DataSets.

You saw the various ways to fill either a DataSet or a DataTable. You also saw the importance of a schema present in a DataSet. You saw how the presence of a schema in a DataSet helps the DataAdapter make correct decisions when filling the data.

Finally, you saw how to use mapping to make code easier to read and modify, and how to map column and table names so that data can be passed easily between different data sources.

You saw how to use the AS keyword in SQL, which is a simple but inflexible way to achieve column mappings and really doesn't help you do table mappings, after which the ADO.NET mapping objects were discussed. The DataAdapter object's ColumnMappings property and the DataColumnMapping and DataTableMapping classes were demonstrated with a couple of examples.

Now that you have seen the objects required to hold disconnected data and how to fill data in those objects, the next chapter covers being able to work with the disconnected data objects once you have filled them from the data source. Our discussion will move to sorting, searching, and filtering disconnected data per your application's logic and requirements.

CHAPTER 8

■■■

Sorting, Searching, and Filtering

In the last two chapters, you examined various objects that allow you to fetch data from a data source and store it in a disconnected manner within your application. You saw how `DataSets` allow you to represent a disconnected cache of relational data in memory. If a `DataSet` is a relational representation of data, then `DataTables` along with various constraints provide you with a representation of tabular data extracted out of a data source, and `DataRelations` allow you to create relational structures between `DataTables`.

The other relational representation of data you'll frequently come across is any common modern-day relational database management system (RDBMS). However, a `DataSet` is not a database. It's merely a surrogate that allows you to keep data in a portable cache while remaining disconnected from the underlying data source. It's like a mini in-memory database represented by an object instance. What this means to you as an application developer is that instead of relying on some flavor of the popular structured query language (SQL), you have to rely upon a method of working with disconnected data using an object model instead.

ADO.NET allows you to perform several operations on these structures, such as sorting, searching, and filtering on this in-memory relational structure, using an object representation rather than a database engine. This chapter will discuss the various objects and facilities ADO.NET provides that allow you to sort, search, and filter disconnected data held in a `DataSet` or `DataTable` object.

The discussion will first focus on the `DataTable` and `DataSet` objects themselves, and will elucidate with examples of what facilities these objects provide for you to work with the data contained within them. Then a new object will be introduced, the `DataView` object, which is a view on a `DataTable` but has varied uses in a typical Windows Forms or ASP.NET application.

■**Note** It's tempting to think of the relationship between a `DataView` and a `DataTable` as the same as the relationship between a database view and a database table. That simile is close and helpful in understanding the concept, but it's not exactly the same. While a `DataTable` is simply tabular data which might be the result of a join between one or more tables from the underlying data source, a `DataView` lets you create a view on only one `DataTable` as a subset of the rows (and not columns), whereas a database view lets you create tabular data as a subset of both rows and columns from one or more tables. Therefore, a `DataTable` and a `DataView` aren't exactly like a Table or a View, but they are similar.

Finally to cap it off, this chapter will finish with a discussion on the best friend of DataSets—XML. A DataSet is easily convertible into XML and vice versa, and .NET does provide various objects to help the to-and-fro conversion and to help you leverage the power of both XML and DataSets in either.

Since this chapter concentrates on a purely disconnected discussion and, because disconnected objects once filled out of the data source are not specific to an individual data source anymore, it's not specific to any specific data provider or database (such as Oracle or MySQL), the concepts presented here can be easily applied verbatim to any data source.

As a matter of fact, to emphasize this point, the examples presented in this chapter don't use any specific data source. Instead, they use a hand-crafted disconnected DataSet, so let's begin by setting up that first.

Setting Up the Data Source

This chapter concerns itself with working with disconnected data, so ideally the disconnected data example being set up must be flexible and generic enough to prove itself as a basis for all examples concerning the various situations you might face in your programming experience.

The disconnected data being used in most of the examples in this book will use a simple Customers/Products scenario. There could be many products and there could be many customers. Also, there is a many-to-many mapping between the customers and products in another table called CustomerProducts, as shown in Figure 8-1.

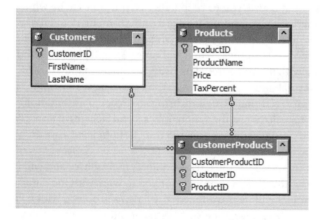

Figure 8-1. *Data structure for Customers/Products scenario*

Frequently, references will be made to a strongly typed DataSet implementation for this scenario, so you might want to set up both a strongly typed DataSet and a basic DataSet.

Also, as you have already learned in Chapter 6, this DataSet data structure can be easily filled with data in a disconnected mode. You can refer back to Chapter 6 on how to fill such a DataSet, but the code for filling the DataSet can be seen in Listings 8-1 and 8-2. The same code can also be used to fill the strongly typed DataSet. You can find this code, and the associated strongly typed DataSet, in the associated code download under the CreateDataSet class library project (see the Downloads section of the Apress website at http://www.apress.com). As you can see, instead of loading the DataSet line-by-line programmatically, all that the code does is simply read an XML file into the DataSet.

Listing 8-1. *Setting Up the DataSet in C#*

```csharp
public static DataSet FillDataset(string xmlFile)
{
    DataSet ds = new DataSet();
    ds.ReadXml(xmlFile);
    return ds;
}

public static CustProd FillStrongDataSet(string xmlFile)
{
    CustProd ds = new CustProd();
    ds.ReadXml(xmlFile);
    return ds;
}
```

Listing 8-2. *Setting Up the DataSet in Visual Basic .NET*

```vbnet
Public Shared Function FillDataset(ByVal xmlFile As String) As DataSet
    Dim ds As New DataSet()
    ds.ReadXml(xmlFile)
    Return ds
End Function

Public Shared Function FillStrongDataSet(ByVal xmlFile As String) As CustProd
    Dim ds As New CustProd()
    ds.ReadXml(xmlFile)
    Return ds
End Function
```

An easy way to create the loaded XML file would be to simply use another Windows application called EditData (that you can find in the code download as well); simply add in some values to the DataSet that has been set up. A sample of the data is shown in Figure 8-2. Even though the exercises in this chapter use the data presented here, you can enter any data you wish. This application is built upon the concepts you have learned in Chapter 6, but feel free to look through the code in the associated code download as well.

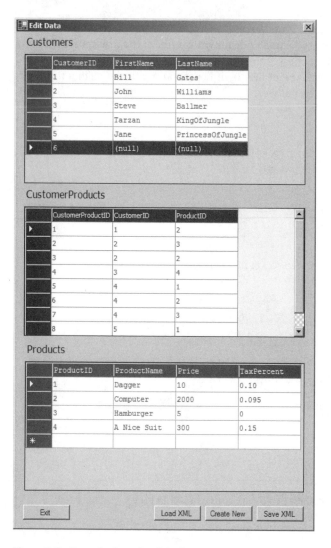

Figure 8-2. *Sample data for this chapter*

Now that the data source is set up, let's examine the various facilities the DataTable object provides that help you work with disconnected data easily.

Working in a DataTable

The DataTable object is an in-memory representation of tabular data. It can be filled as a result of a join between one or more tables in a database. What that means is that the data inside a DataTable is logically arranged with in-memory data structures that represent columns and rows. Also, there could be various constraints specified on the DataTable helping to keep the integrity of the data. Specifically, as you saw in Chapter 6, referential integrity is enforced using foreign-key constraints and data integrity is enforced using unique constraints.

Now another representation of tabular data is a table in an RDBMS. A table in a database will let you *find* a particular row using a syntax such as

```
Select * from products where productid = 1
```

Or, it might let you *select* a number of rows by specifying a query that looks like

```
Select * from products where productname like '%MP%'
```

Also, it could allow you to *sort the results* in a manner similar to

```
Select * from products where productname like '%MP%' order by price
```

Most databases will even let you *query calculated columns* such as

```
Select price + (price * tax) as totalprice from products
```

So essentially, a DataTable being the representation of tabular data in an in-memory object should allow you to find, select, sort, and determine calculated columns in a result set.

Also, because a DataTable works with disconnected data in an ASP.NET application or a Windows Forms application (or maybe a Windows service), it needs to do a little bit more than just what tabular data in a database, that is database tables, would provide. Because a DataTable is intended to be a disconnected cache of tabular data (with the ultimate goal of being able to persist changes that were done in a disconnected fashion back to the database), a DataTable also would need to *preserve row histories* for the changes done on it. And for certain situations, it must let you query for only the changed rows or for rows in a particular RowState (available as a property on a DataRow).

And finally, there are many events available on the DataTable object to facilitate your working with disconnected data.

Finding a Row

Frequently in typical application programming logic, you'd need to run a query against the database and fetch details for a particular ID or primary key: such as fetch details for a particular customer. This process is called *finding a row*. In the case of a database, you'd simply execute a SQL query, but a DataTable is not a table inside a database and cannot use a SQL query and a database engine to help itself do this job.

However, the DataTable.Rows or the DataRowCollection object provides you with a method called Find for this very purpose. One important thing to remember when using the Find method is that it allows you to find rows by operating only on the column that contains the primary-key values. So in a basic DataTable (not strongly typed), you would either need to load a schema or manually specify the primary key in code before Find can work. This is shown in Listings 8-3 and 8-4 or can be seen in the associated code download for this chapter in Exercise 8.1.

Listing 8-3. *Using Find to Identify One DataRow Using a Basic DataTable in C#*

```
// Base DataTable
DataTable myTable = DataSetFiller.FillDataset(dataFilePath).Tables[0] ;
// Set Primary Key
myTable.PrimaryKey = new DataColumn[] { myTable.Columns["CustomerID"] };
DataRow dr = myTable.Rows.Find("2");
```

```csharp
if (dr != null)
{
    Console.WriteLine("Find a row using a base DataSet");
    ShowDataRow(dr);
}
```

Listing 8-4. *Using Find to Identify One DataRow Using a Basic DataTable in Visual Basic .NET*

```vb
' Base DataTable
Dim myTable As DataTable = DataSetFiller.FillDataset(dataFilePath).Tables(0)
' Set Primary Key
myTable.PrimaryKey = New DataColumn() _
    {myTable.Columns("CustomerID")}

Dim dr As DataRow = myTable.Rows.Find("2")
If dr IsNot Nothing Then
    Console.WriteLine("Find a row using a base DataSet")
    ShowDataRow(dr)
End If
```

Also, once you do find the row, you can iterate through the contents of the row using the code shown in Listings 8-5 and 8-6.

Listing 8-5. *Displaying the Contents of One Row in C#*

```csharp
static void ShowDataRow(DataRow dr)
{
    foreach (DataColumn dc in dr.Table.Columns)
    {
        Console.Write(dr[dc] + " ");
    }
    Console.Write("\n\n");
}
```

Listing 8-6. *Displaying the Contents of One Row in Visual Basic .NET*

```vb
Sub ShowDataRow(ByVal dr As DataRow)
    For Each dc As DataColumn In dr.Table.Columns
        Console.Write(dr(dc) & " ")
    Next
    Console.WriteLine("")
End Sub
```

However, strongly typed DataSets make it a lot simpler. Not only do they provide you with a simpler way of accessing individual column values after a row has been found, but they also provide you with an easy way of finding the row by naming it in a familiar way that identifies the primary key. In our case, the method of concern would be FindByCustomerID, clearly telling you that this Find method will find using CustomerID. It gets even better; instead of specifying an object as a parameter to the Find method, you can simply specify in Int32 as shown in Listings 8-7 and 8-8.

Listing 8-7. *Using FindByCustomerID Using a Strongly Typed DataTable in C#*

```
// Strongly typed DataSet
CustProd.CustomersDataTable myStrongDataTable =
  DataSetFiller.FillStrongDataSet(dataFilePath).Customers;
CustProd.CustomersRow cr = myStrongDataTable.FindByCustomerID(2);
if (cr != null)
{
    Console.WriteLine("Find a row using a strongly typed DataSet");
    Console.WriteLine(cr.CustomerID + " " + cr.FirstName + " " + cr.LastName);
}
```

Listing 8-8. *Using FindByCustomerID Using a Strongly Typed DataTable in Visual Basic .NET*

```
' Strongly typed DataSet
Dim myStrongDataTable As CustProd.CustomersDataTable =_
    DataSetFiller.FillStrongDataSet(dataFilePath).Customers
Dim cr As CustProd.CustomersRow = myStrongDataTable.FindByCustomerID(2)
If cr IsNot Nothing Then
    Console.WriteLine("Find a row using a strongly typed DataSet")
    Console.WriteLine(cr.CustomerID & " " & cr.FirstName & " " & cr.LastName)
End If
```

However, being able to find one row using the primary key is clearly not enough. In many instances, you might need to find an entire collection of rows and the criteria specified as the filter for those rows, for example, might include a wildcard search.

Selecting a Number of Rows

In a database that allows you to query a number of rows from a given table, you'd generally include the search criterion as a where clause.

So, for instance, if you wished to query for all Customers whose name starts with Jo, you could write a query that looks something like this:

```
Select * from Customers where FirstName Like 'Jo%' ;
```

As it turns out, selecting from a DataTable is not much different. The DataTable object contains a method called Select, and all you really need to do is specify the where clause from the previous query as a parameter to the Select method. Thus, a call to the Select method would look like this:

C#
```
DataRow[] drs = myTable.Select("FirstName Like 'Jo%'");
```

VB.NET
```
Dim drs() As DataRow = myTable.Select("FirstName Like 'Jo%'")
```

The full code would look like as shown in Listings 8-9 and 8-10, or it can be found in Exercise 8.2.

Listing 8-9. *Using Select to Find Multiple Rows Matching a Criterion in C#*

```csharp
static void Main(string[] args)
{
    DataTable myTable = DataSetFiller.FillDataset(dataFilePath).Tables[0];
    DataRow[] drs = myTable.Select("FirstName Like 'Jo%'");
    if (drs != null)
    {
        Console.WriteLine("Find rows using a base DataSet");
        foreach (DataRow dr in drs)
        {
            ShowDataRow(dr);
        }
    }
}
```

Listing 8-10. *Using Select to Find Multiple Rows Matching a Criterion in Visual Basic .NET*

```vbnet
Sub Main()
    Dim myTable As DataTable = DataSetFiller.FillDataset(dataFilePath).Tables(0)
    Dim drs() As DataRow = myTable.Select("FirstName Like 'Jo%'")
    If drs IsNot Nothing Then
        For Each dr as DataRow In drs
            ShowDataRow(dr)
        Next
    End If
End Sub
```

Another thing that a database lets you do is return the results in a predefined sort order. You could query the data to find all matching rows where LastName ends with OfJungle, but say you want the results to be sorted by FirstName. This can be easily achieved by slightly modifying the code shown in Listings 8-11 and 8-12. All you need to do is replace the call to Select with a proper overload that allows you to specify a sort order. Also, you would have to replace the first parameter (the where clause passed to the Select method) with the appropriate search string. This can also be seen in Exercise 8.3 of the associated code download.

Listing 8-11. *Using Select to Find Rows and Specify a Sort in C#*

```csharp
static void Main(string[] args)
{
    DataTable myTable = DataSetFiller.FillDataset(dataFilePath).Tables[0];
    DataRow[] drs = myTable.Select("LastName Like '%OfJungle'","FirstName ASC");
    if (drs != null)
    {
        foreach (DataRow dr in drs)
        {
            ShowDataRow(dr);
        }
    }
}
```

Listing 8-12. *Using Select to Find Rows and Specify a Sort in Visual Basic .NET*

```
Sub Main()
    Dim myTable As DataTable = DataSetFiller.FillDataset(dataFilePath).Tables(0)
    Dim drs() As DataRow = _
        myTable.Select("LastName Like '%OfJungle'", "FirstName ASC")
    If drs IsNot Nothing Then
        For Each dr As DataRow In drs
            ShowDataRow(dr)
        Next
    End If
End Sub
```

If you run this code, the output produced will correctly fetch Tarzan and Jane as the KingOfJungle and PrincessOfJungle, respectively. Now let's say, Jane and Tarzan decide to marry each other and Jane changes her last name to QueenOfJungle. This can be easily achieved using the following code snippet:

C#

```
DataTable myTable = DataSetFiller.FillDataset(dataFilePath).Tables[0];
myTable.PrimaryKey = new DataColumn[] { myTable.Columns["CustomerID"] };
myTable.AcceptChanges();
DataRow janeRow = myTable.Rows.Find("5");
janeRow["LastName"] = "QueenOfJungle";
```

VB.NET

```
Dim myTable As DataTable = DataSetFiller.FillDataset(dataFilePath).Tables(0)
myTable.PrimaryKey = New DataColumn() _
    {myTable.Columns("CustomerID")}
myTable.AcceptChanges()
Dim janeRow As DataRow = myTable.Rows.Find("5")
janeRow("LastName") = "QueenOfJungle"
```

An important thing to note here is that as changes are done to a DataRow object, the DataRow maintains the previous values, and also maintains a RowState property as a DataRowState object. As will be discussed in the next two chapters, this built-in facility of a DataRow is immensely useful in working with disconnected data in the event of passing it over web services (or similar), and persisting it to the original data source while taking care of concurrency.

But more on that shortly. For now, the application just needs to find the rows that have changed. Hopefully, the only changed row would be the one that identifies Jane as the QueenOfJungle. This can be easily done using the following statement:

C#
```
DataRow[] drs = myTable.Select("", "", DataViewRowState.ModifiedCurrent);
```

VB.NET
```
Dim drs() As DataRow = myTable.Select("", "", DataViewRowState.ModifiedCurrent)
```

Thus, you pass in a DataViewRowState constant to identify the rows in a particular state that you're interested in querying. Even though DataViewRowState constants and DataRowState constants will be covered in greater depth in Chapters 9 and 10, for now it's sufficient to understand that the previous statement allows you to find the modified rows in the DataTable. You might also notice a call to AcceptChanges. This is important since when the DataSet or DataTable is read from XML, the default RowState for all those newly added rows is DataRowState.Added. By calling AcceptChanges, you effectively *accept the suggested changes* to the DataTable, and hence change all the RowStates to UnChanged. You can find the full code for this example in Exercise 8.4.

Frequently in a database, you might have a certain piece of information that can be derived definitively from a set of columns. In other words, you might need to calculate a certain column on the fly as a part or expression based on other columns in the result set.

Expressions: Calculating Columns on the Fly

Sometimes you may want to make calculations from columns of a tabular result set that produce values on the fly and appear as a column contained in the result. A real-world scenario would be to say that the Products table contains a price column and a tax column; what if you wanted to create a result set, with an additional column named "total price," as Price + Price * TaxPercent?

This can be easily achieved in the database with a SQL query that looks like

```
Select
    ProductID, Price, Tax, (Price + Price * TaxPercent) as TotalPrice
from Products;
```

Here, an expression is specified for TotalPrice. The database then calculates the TotalPrice for each row and includes that in the result set for you.

You can easily achieve the same result in a DataTable by specifying an expression on a new column you need to create. To emphasize the fact that this would be done on the fly for each column on the DataTable, this next example shall use a DataTable databound to a DataGridView on a Windows Forms application. This can be achieved in the following steps:

1. Start by creating a Windows Forms application. Name it Exercise 8.5. Also, change the text on the main form of the application to Exercise 8.5.

2. Drop a DataGridView on the form, make sure its Dock property is set to Dock.Fill. This will be named dataGridView1 by default.

3. In the Form1_Load event handler, which will be called when Form1 loads, add the code shown in Listings 8-13 and 8-14.

Listing 8-13. *Creating a Calculated Column in C#*

```
DataSet customerProducts =
CreateDataSet.DataSetFiller.FillStrongDataSet(dataFilePath);
DataTable productsTable = customerProducts.Tables[1];

DataColumn totalPrice = new DataColumn("Total Price");
totalPrice.Expression = "Price + Price * TaxPercent";
productsTable.Columns.Add(totalPrice);
dataGridView1.DataSource = productsTable;
```

Listing 8-14. *Creating a Calculated Column in Visual Basic .NET*

```
Dim customerProducts As DataSet = _
    CreateDataSet.DataSetFiller.FillStrongDataSet(dataFilePath)
Dim productsTable As DataTable = customerProducts.Tables(1)

Dim totalPrice As DataColumn = New DataColumn("Total Price")
totalPrice.Expression = "Price + Price * TaxPercent"
productsTable.Columns.Add(totalPrice)
dataGridView1.DataSource = productsTable
```

   4. Compile and run the application. You should see output as shown in Figure 8-3.

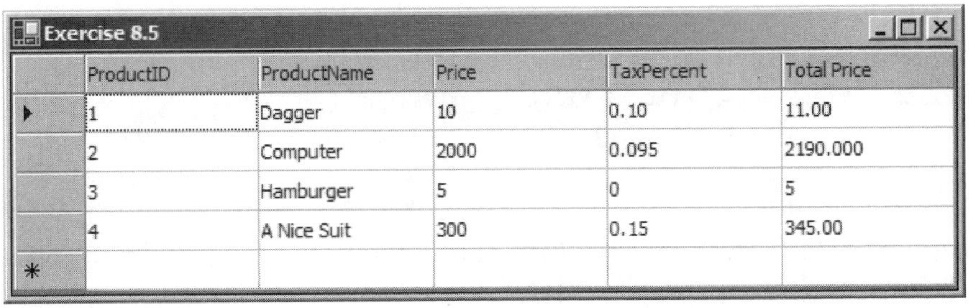

	ProductID	ProductName	Price	TaxPercent	Total Price
▶	1	Dagger	10	0.10	11.00
	2	Computer	2000	0.095	2190.000
	3	Hamburger	5	0	5
	4	A Nice Suit	300	0.15	345.00
*					

Figure 8-3. *Calculated columns using the Expression property*

As you can see in Figure 8-3, the column TotalPrice is calculated properly as per the expression you specified and is included in the DataTable. So what exactly is this code doing?

Well first of all, as you can see, the DataSet was filled using the FillStrongDataSet method instead of the FillDataSet method. This is critical since, for expressions to work, they need the data types set on the various columns. You cannot do a multiply operation using the * operand on two System.String column types, which is the default column type for a basic DataColumn. You could have instead chosen to specify the DataType property on a basic DataColumn; however, such an operation needs to be done *before* it's filled with data. This can be achieved easily using the following lines of code:

C#

```
productsTable.Columns["Price"].DataType = typeof(System.Int32);
// Fill Data here
```

VB.NET

```
productsTable.Columns("Price").DataType = GetType(System.Int32)
' Fill Data here
```

Or, you could simply implicit cast a basic DataSet back from a strongly typed DataSet, which is what is done in the following lines of code:

C#

```
DataSet customerProducts =
    CreateDataSet.DataSetFiller.FillStrongDataSet(dataFilePath);
```

VB.NET

```
Dim customerProducts As DataSet = _
    CreateDataSet.DataSetFiller.FillStrongDataSet(dataFilePath)
```

Note that implicit casting doesn't really require you to do anything, you can simply assign an inherited object instance back to the base. With the DataTable set up, the next three lines add a new column, totalPrice, set an expression on it, and add it to the DataTable:

C#

```
DataColumn totalPrice = new DataColumn("Total Price");
totalPrice.Expression = "Price + Price * TaxPercent";
productsTable.Columns.Add(totalPrice);
```

VB.NET

```
Dim totalPrice As DataColumn = New DataColumn("Total Price")
totalPrice.Expression = "Price + Price * TaxPercent"
productsTable.Columns.Add(totalPrice)
```

That's it! The next line simply data binds the DataTable to the DataGridView to display the results:

C#

```
dataGridView1.DataSource = productsTable;
```

VB.NET

```
dataGridView1.DataSource = productsTable
```

This approach works well for situations where you need to perform a calculation on every row in a DataTable. In certain situations, however, you might need to perform aggregate calculations on the entire DataTable. Luckily for such cases, the DataTable supports a method called Compute.

Performing Aggregate Calculations

Say you needed to perform a calculation over the rows of a table. In our case, say you needed to add the Price column for all rows and come up with a total of prices for all products.

If this were a database, you could simply write a query that looks like this:

```
Select Sum(Price) from Products
```

This query would go over all the rows and sum up their Price columns one by one to return a total. In a DataTable, however, you can achieve the same result using the Compute method. This is demonstrated in Listings 8-15 and 8-16. In this code, btnSumPrices is a button which, when clicked, computes the aggregate sum function on the Price column and puts the calculated value in a label called lblSumPrice.

Listing 8-15. *Using the Compute Method in C#*

```csharp
private void Form1_Load(object sender, EventArgs e)
{
   DataSet customerProducts =
      CreateDataSet.DataSetFiller.FillStrongDataSet(dataFilePath);
   // productsTable is defined as a private variable in the class.
   productsTable = customerProducts.Tables[1];

   DataColumn totalPrice = new DataColumn("Total Price");
   totalPrice.Expression = "Price + Price * TaxPercent";
   productsTable.Columns.Add(totalPrice);
   dataGridView1.DataSource = productsTable;
}

private void btnSumPrices_Click(object sender, EventArgs e)
{
   string price = productsTable.Compute("Sum(Price)", "").ToString();
   lblSumPrice.Text = "The total price is : " + price;
}
```

Listing 8-16. *Using the Compute Method in Visual Basic .NET*

```vb
Private Sub Form1_Load( _
  ByVal sender As System.Object, ByVal e As System.EventArgs) _
  Handles MyBase.Load
   Dim customerProducts As DataSet = _
      CreateDataSet.DataSetFiller.FillStrongDataSet(dataFilePath)
   ' productsTable is defined as a private variable in the class.
   productsTable = customerProducts.Tables(1)

   Dim totalPrice As DataColumn = New DataColumn("Total Price")
   totalPrice.Expression = "Price + Price * TaxPercent"
   productsTable.Columns.Add(totalPrice)
   dataGridView1.DataSource = productsTable
End Sub

Private Sub btnSumPrices_Click( _
  ByVal sender As System.Object, ByVal e As System.EventArgs) _
  Handles btnSumPrices.Click
   Dim price As String = _
      productsTable.Compute("Sum(Price)", "").ToString()
   lblSumPrice.Text = "The total price is : " & price
End Sub
```

You can easily modify this code to include only a subset of rows based on a condition. For instance, if instead you wished to calculate the Sum of all prices, where price was less than 500, you could modify the previous code to include the following code:

C#

```
string price = productsTable.Compute("Sum(Price)", "Price < 500").ToString();
```

VB.NET

```
Dim price as String = _
    productsTable.Compute("Sum(Price)", "Price < 500").ToString();
```

The final running application with the filter for a price less than 500 can be seen in Figure 8-4, or can be found in the associated code download under Exercise 8.6.

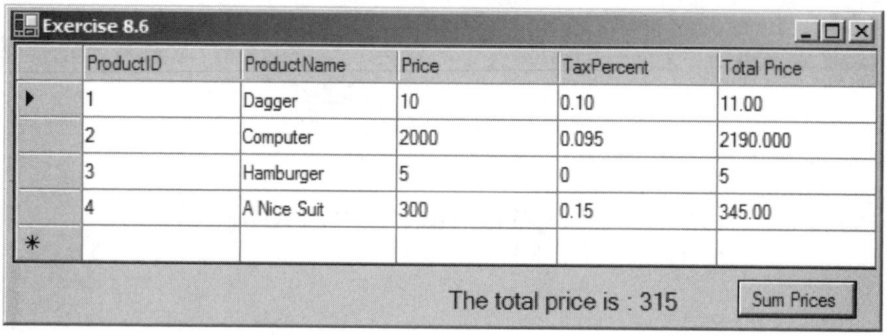

Figure 8-4. *Aggregate values using the Compute method*

Another important thing databases let you do is specify foreign-key constraints between sets of fields in various tables. In many cases, in a database, you would specify joins to extract result sets that are an aggregate between multiple tables based upon existing or assumed relationships. As already mentioned, if a DataTable is the representation of in-memory tabular data, and thus a simile to a table in a database, then the closest simile to a relation would be the DataRelation object.

Working with the DataRelation Object

Databases let you specify SQL queries with joins between tables. A DataSet does allow you to define DataRelations between various tables, but doesn't quite allow you to specify joins between DataTables using a SQL query–like syntax. What it does allow you to do, however, is leverage specified DataRelations to find child rows for a parent row, or the parent row for any given child row.

Given the database structure that is being worked with in this chapter, one of the most common problems you might need to solve is "Which customer ordered what products?" Even though that could be done as a JOIN in the database, what if you had to do that in a DataSet when you cannot use SQL along with the power of a database engine?

As far as setting up relations goes, this can be mapped using a many-to-many relationship in the DataSet, which is exactly what the CustProd strongly typed DataSet does. Refer back to Figure 8-1; there is a table in the middle of Customers and Products called CustomerProducts which, with the help of two many-to-one relationships, helps you map one many-to-many relationship.

So for a given `CustomerID`, if you wished to find out what products have been ordered by the customer, you could find that out in two steps:

1. Find the child rows for the particular `CustomerID` in the `CustomerProducts` table.

2. For each one of those child rows, find the relevant parent row from the `Products` table.

Let's examine this in an example:

1. Create a new Windows Form application. Name it Exercise 8.7. Also, change the text on the main form of the application to Exercise 8.7.

2. On this form drop three listboxes, which will be used to show the relevant rows from each of the three tables. Name them `lbCustomers`, `lbCustomerProducts`, and `lbProducts`. Also, drop two buttons to perform the two row-filtering steps mentioned previously. Name these two buttons `btnFilter1` and `btnFilter2`. Set their text properties to "GetChildRows >>" and "GetParentRow >>", respectively. The form should look like as shown in Figure 8-5.

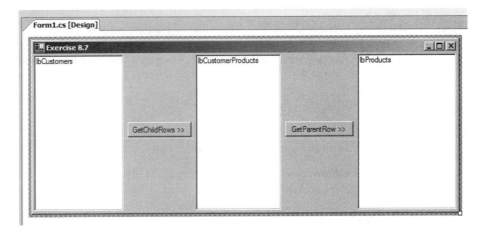

Figure 8-5. *Many-to-many relationship mapping example form in Design view*

3. In the `Form1_Load` event handler, add the following code:

C#

```csharp
private void Form1_Load(object sender, EventArgs e)
{
    customerProducts =
        CreateDataSet.DataSetFiller.FillStrongDataSet(dataFilePath);
    foreach (DataRow dr in customerProducts.Tables["Customers"].Rows)
    {
```

```
        lbCustomers.Items.Add(
            dr["CustomerID"] + ":" + dr["FirstName"] + " " + dr["LastName"]);
    }
}
```

VB.NET

```
Private Sub Form1_Load( _
  ByVal sender As System.Object, ByVal e As System.EventArgs) _
  Handles MyBase.Load
    customerProducts = _
        CreateDataSet.DataSetFiller.FillStrongDataSet(dataFilePath)
    For Each dr As DataRow In customerProducts.Tables("Customers").Rows
        lbCustomers.Items.Add( _
          dr("CustomerID") & ":" & dr("FirstName") & " " & dr("LastName"))
    Next
End Sub
```

This code loads the customerProducts DataSet as usual. You might note that once again the code is using the FillStrongDataSet method instead. This is because it gives a convenient way to get a DataSet with preestablished relationships. If you didn't have relationships defined in the DataSet, you could easily add them using a code snippet similar to the one shown here (the … signifies actual parameters you would need to pass in):

C#

```
customerProducts.Relations.Add(new DataRelation(...));
```

VB.NET

```
customerProducts.Relations.Add(new DataRelation(...))
```

4. Next, for a selected row in the lbCustomers listbox, if btnFilter1 is clicked, the application needs to find out the child rows and populate those in the lbCustomersProducts listbox. This is achieved using the GetChildRows method on the DataRow object. This is shown in Listings 8-17 and 8-18.

Listing 8-17. *Finding Child Rows for a Given Selected Row in C#*

```
private void btnFilter1_Click(object sender, EventArgs e)
{
    if (lbCustomers.SelectedIndex < 0)
    {
        return;
    }
    DataRow selectedRow =
      customerProducts.Tables["Customers"].Rows[lbCustomers.SelectedIndex];
    DataRow[] childRows =
      selectedRow.GetChildRows(customerProducts.Relations[1]);
    lbCustomerProducts.Items.Clear();
    foreach (DataRow dr in childRows)
```

```
    {
        lbCustomerProducts.Items.Add(dr["CustomerProductID"]);
    }
}
```

Listing 8-18. *Finding Child Rows for a Given Selected Row in Visual Basic .NET*

```
Private Sub btnFilter1_Click( _
  ByVal sender As System.Object, ByVal e As System.EventArgs) _
  Handles btnFilter1.Click
    If lbCustomers.SelectedIndex < 0 Then
        Return
    End If
    Dim selectedRow As DataRow = _
        customerProducts.Tables("Customers").Rows(lbCustomers.SelectedIndex)
    Dim childRows() As DataRow = _
        selectedRow.GetChildRows(customerProducts.Relations(1))
    lbCustomerProducts.Items.Clear()
    Dim dr As DataRow
    For Each dr In childRows
        lbCustomerProducts.Items.Add(dr("CustomerProductID"))
    Next
End Sub
```

As you can see in Listings 8-17 and 8-18, the first thing the code does is identify the selected row using the following code:

C#

```
DataRow selectedRow =
  customerProducts.Tables["Customers"].Rows[lbCustomers.SelectedIndex];
```

VB.NET

```
    Dim selectedRow As DataRow = _
        customerProducts.Tables("Customers").Rows(lbCustomers.SelectedIndex)
```

Once the selected row is identified, it then uses the GetChildRows method and a DataRelation object, and is easily able to identify the child rows as a DataRow array. This is shown in the following code:

C#

```
DataRow[] childRows = selectedRow.GetChildRows(customerProducts.Relations[1]);
```

VB.NET

```
    Dim childRows() As DataRow = _
        selectedRow.GetChildRows(customerProducts.Relations(1))
```

5. Just as you were able to find ChildRows, you can easily find the ParentRow for any DataRow using the GetParentRow method. That is what the application does when you click the btnFilter2 button. For each identified row in the lbCustomerProducts listbox, it finds the relevant ParentRow for each such row, and populates those into the lbProducts listbox. The code for this can be seen in Listings 8-19 and 8-20.

Listing 8-19. *Finding Parent Rows for Various Rows in C#*

```
private void btnFilter2_Click(object sender, EventArgs e)
{
    DataRow custProdRow;
    DataRow prodRow;
    DataTable custProdTable = customerProducts.Tables["CustomerProducts"] ;
    lbProducts.Items.Clear();
    foreach (object item in lbCustomerProducts.Items)
    {
        int custProdId = (int)item;
        custProdRow = custProdTable.Rows.Find(custProdId);
        prodRow = custProdRow.GetParentRow(customerProducts.Relations[0]);
        lbProducts.Items.Add(ProdRow["ProductName"]);
    }
}
```

Listing 8-20. *Finding Parent Rows for Various Rows in Visual Basic .NET*

```
Private Sub btnFilter2_Click( _
  ByVal sender As System.Object, ByVal e As System.EventArgs) _
  Handles btnFilter2.Click
    Dim custProdRow As DataRow
    Dim ProdRow As DataRow
    Dim custProdTable As DataTable = _
        customerProducts.Tables("CustomerProducts")
    lbProducts.Items.Clear()
    Dim item As Object
    For Each item In lbCustomerProducts.Items
        Dim custProdId As Integer = CType(item, Integer)
        custProdRow = custProdTable.Rows.Find(custProdId)
        ProdRow = custProdRow.GetParentRow(customerProducts.Relations(0))
        lbProducts.Items.Add(ProdRow("ProductName"))
    Next
End Sub
```

6. Compile and run the application. Select "Tarzan KingOfJungle" from lbCustomers and click btnFilter1; you should see output as shown in Figure 8-6.

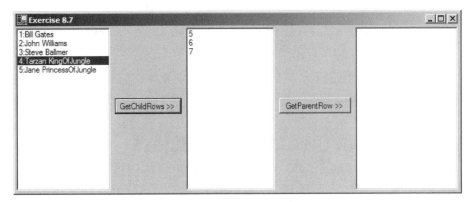

Figure 8-6. *Filtered out rows identified as child rows of Tarzan*

7. Next click `btnFilter2` to filter out parent rows for all the rows identified as related to Tarzan in `lbCustomerProducts`. Thus Tarzan has ordered the Dagger, Computer, and Hamburger products. You can see this in the output shown in Figure 8-7.

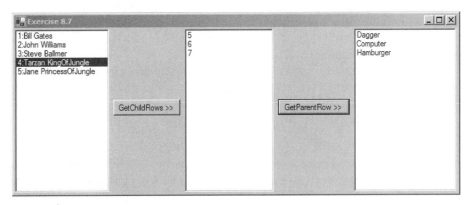

Figure 8-7. *Finding parent rows for all identified rows to get product details such as ProductName*

So as you can see, `DataRelations` not only help you ensure referential integrity across various `DataTables`, they also let you easily browse through rows across various `DataTables` in a `DataSet`. Another interesting use of `DataRelations` is that they allow you to control the nesting properties of the generated XML, if the nested property on a relation is set to `true`. (This is explained in detail in Example 6.3 of Chapter 6 and won't be covered here.)

Earlier in this chapter you saw the `Select` method on a `DataTable` that allows you to get a subset of `DataRows` in a `DataTable` based on a specified criterion or predicate. Yet another way (and possibly a much more flexible and useful way) of extracting a subset of rows from a `DataTable` is the `DataView` object. Not only is the `DataView` object directly data bindable, but it also allows you an easy mechanism to search, sort, and filter through records; however, what a DataView gives you in addition to what a DataTable provides is the ability *to restrict* (based on a specified criterion) your result set to a view that contains a subset of the total number of rows in the DataTable.

As an exercise, you could try and build an application that answers the question "What other customers ordered the products that Tarzan ordered?"

Working with the DataView Object

The DataView object is more than a replacement for the DataTable's Select method. Not only are the results of the Select method on a DataTable not directly data bindable, but it is also not a very efficient method to query rows.

As has been mentioned, if a DataSet lets you represent in-memory relational data, then a DataTable lets you represent in-memory tabular data, and a DataRelation lets you specify relations between the tabular data. Carrying that simile forward, it's tempting to think that the DataView object, being a view on a DataTable object, is very much like a view on a table in the database.

They are definitely similar, but there is a big difference. Views in a database will let you specify any arbitrary SQL query that serves as the basis for the view. That SQL query has the ability to provide you with a subset of columns, or even any arbitrary combination of columns from any arbitrary number of tables based upon a join. The big difference, however, is that DataViews will only let you work on a DataTable—they will not let you select a subset of columns. All the columns will be visible in the resulting DataView.

Also, just as a DataTable consists of DataRows, representing various rows in the DataTable, a DataView consists of DataRowViews. You can reach the underlying table using the DataView.Table property and the underlying row using the DataRowView.Row property.

Creating a DataView

A DataView can be created using any of the three constructor overloads it supports. The first constructor overload allows you to create a DataView but not specify any information. It looks like this:

C#
```
DataView myView = new DataView() ;
```

VB.NET
```
Dim myView as DataView = New DataView()
```

The second constructor directly ties the DataView to a DataTable. Once you have created such a DataView, you can then set various other properties on the DataView to create a "view" of the DataTable's data. This looks like the following code snippet:

C#
```
DataView myView = new DataView(myTable) ;
```

VB.NET
```
Dim myView as DataView = New DataView(myTable)
```

The third and final constructor of DataViews allows you to specify all that information in one line of code. It lets you specify not only the table, but also the sort, search, and RowState filter criteria. This looks like the following code snippet:

C#

```
DataView dv =
   new DataView(
   productsTable, "ProductID = 1", "ProductName", DataViewRowState.Unchanged);
```

VB.NET

```
DataView dv = _
   new DataView( _
   productsTable, "ProductID = 1", "ProductName", DataViewRowState.Unchanged)
```

Thus, you can either use the third overload to specify all the necessary information in one line of code, or you can use the following properties on the DataView object to convey the necessary information:

- RowFilter: This property allows you to specify a selection criteria, similar to the one passed in DataTable's Select method, and allows you to filter the returned rows. For instance, CustomerID =4 will return Tarzan per our data.

- Sort: This property allows you to specify a sort order on the returned results.

- RowStateFilter: As you are making changes to the DataTable, the DataTable maintains a history of the changes you have done to one step in history. This property allows you to specify a DataViewRowState and identify versions of data.

Other ways to search through the DataRowViews contained inside a DataView object are by the Find and FindRows methods.

- Find: Works in a similar way as the DataTable.Rows.Find method, but not exactly the same. It allows you to specify a criterion or predicate for searching over the columns mentioned in the Sort property of the DataView. Sort and Find work hand in hand because the value you specify as a filter to the Find method is evaluated against the sorted column only. It allows you to identify the one row that matches that specified criterion. The one row identified, however, is returned as an index of the row that matched the criterion.

- FindRows: Allows you to return a number of DataRowView objects that match a specified search criterion. There are two major differences between FindRows and Find. First, FindRows can return multiple DataRowView objects. Second, FindRows returns an array of DataRowView objects, whereas Find would return an index integer.

Let's solidify our understanding of the these concepts using an example. You can download the final code for this example in the associated code download in Exercise 8.8, or you can simply follow these steps and create one yourself. The intention here is fairly simple:

1. As usual, start by creating a Windows Forms application. Name it Exercise 8.8, and change the text on the main form of the application to Exercise 8.8.

2. Put a `DataGridView` control on it (`dgView`) and four buttons. Set the names and text properties of the buttons as follows:

- `btnLoad`, Load Data

- `btnSort`, Sort Data

- `btnFilter`, Filter Data

- `btnFindRows`, Find Rows

The form in Design view should look like as shown in Figure 8-8.

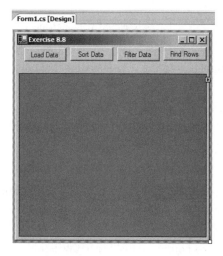

Figure 8-8. *DataView example's main form in Design view*

3. In this example, `dgView` will be databound to a `DataView` called `CustomerView`, which will be based on the `DataTable CustomerTable`. The `CustomerView` will be loaded in the event handler for the Load Data button. In the event handler for `btnLoad`, enter the following code:

C#

```csharp
private void btnLoad_Click(object sender, EventArgs e)
{
    CustomersTable =
CreateDataSet.DataSetFiller.FillDataset(dataFilePath).Tables["Customers"];
    CustomersView = new DataView(CustomersTable);
    dgView.DataSource = CustomersView;
}
```

VB.NET

```vbnet
Private Sub btnLoad_Click( _
  ByVal sender As System.Object, ByVal e As System.EventArgs) _
```

```
Handles btnLoad.Click
  CustomersTable = _
  CreateDataSet.DataSetFiller.FillDataset(dataFilePath).Tables("Customers")
  CustomersView = New DataView(CustomersTable)
  dgView.DataSource = CustomersView
End Sub
```

Compile and run the application. When you click Load Data, the application should successfully load the data of the `Customers` table and display it in the `dgView` `DataGridView` control as shown in Figure 8-9.

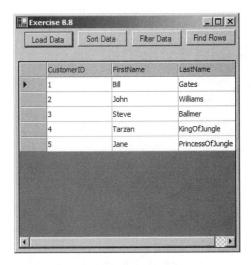

Figure 8-9. *Data loaded in CustomersView DataView and databound to a DataGridView control*

4. Next, the application will try and sort the data on the `FirstName` column in ascending order. In the event handler for `btnSort`, add the following code:

C#

```csharp
private void btnSort_Click(object sender, EventArgs e)
{
    CustomersView.Sort = "FirstName ASC";
}
```

VB.NET

```vbnet
Private Sub btnSort_Click( _
  ByVal sender As System.Object, ByVal e As System.EventArgs) _
  Handles btnSort.Click
    CustomersView.Sort = "FirstName ASC"
End Sub
```

Compile the application and run it. First click Load Data and then click Sort Data. When you click Sort Data, you'll note that dgView now shows you the various rows sorted in ascending order. This should look like as shown in Figure 8-10.

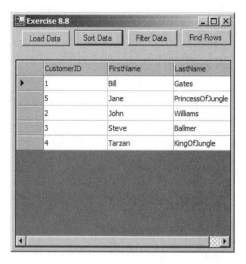

Figure 8-10. *Data loaded and sorted in CustomersView DataView and databound to a DataGridView control*

5. Next, click Filter Data. The application will try and filter out the rows where the last name ends in OfJungle. So as you saw before, the RowFilter you need to specify is "LastName Like '%OfJungle'". This can be done in the following code snippet:

C#

```
private void btnFilter_Click(object sender, EventArgs e)
{
    CustomersView.RowFilter = "LastName like '%OfJungle'" ;
}
```

VB.NET

```
Private Sub btnFilter_Click( _
  ByVal sender As System.Object, ByVal e As System.EventArgs) _
  Handles btnFilter.Click
    CustomersView.RowFilter = "LastName like '%OfJungle'"
End Sub
```

Well since only Tarzan and Jane prefer to live in the jungle, the application correctly shows you only two rows that matched the row filter specified. This can be seen in Figure 8-11.

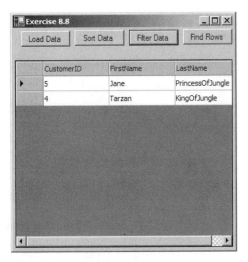

Figure 8-11. *Data loaded, sorted, and filtered in CustomersView DataView and databound to a DataGridView control*

6. Finally, the application will find the rows based on the sort key. Since our sort key is FirstName, let's try and find the names of customers who match the FirstName "Tarzan". This can be done using the following code snippet:

C#

```csharp
private void btnFindRows_Click(object sender, EventArgs e)
{
    DataRowView[] drvs = CustomersView.FindRows("Tarzan");
    foreach (DataRowView drv in drvs)
    {
        MessageBox.Show(
            drv.Row["FirstName"] + " " + drv.Row["LastName"], "Selected Item");
    }
}
```

VB.NET

```vbnet
Private Sub btnFindRows_Click( _
  ByVal sender As System.Object, ByVal e As System.EventArgs) _
  Handles btnFindRows.Click
    Dim drvs() As DataRowView = CustomersView.FindRows("Tarzan")
    Dim drv As DataRowView
    For Each drv In drvs
        MessageBox.Show( _
            drv.Row("FirstName") & " " & drv.Row("LastName"), "Selected Item")
    Next
End Sub
```

Compile and run the application. Click the Load Data, Sort Data, Filter Data, and Find Rows buttons in succession; you should see a message box that looks like Figure 8-12.

Figure 8-12. *Finding the customer whose first name is Tarzan*

7. Now just for giggles, run the application again. Load the data using the Load Data button, *do not* sort the data, filtering is optional, and try running FindRows *without* the data sorted. You should see an exception as shown in Figure 8-13. VB.NET should show you a similar exception.

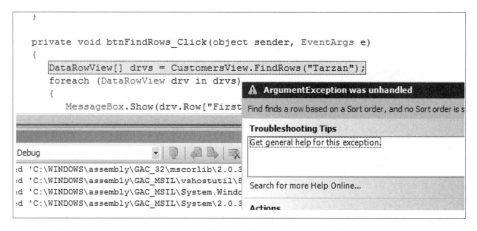

Figure 8-13. *Attempting to execute FindRows without a sort specified—gives an exception*

Thus, as you can see, it's critical that a sort order be specified on the columns that either Find or FindRows will execute on.

8. As an exercise, you can easily replace FindRows with Find and get similar results. You could also specify multiple columns in the sort order and specify multiple Find or FindRows criteria using a different overload.

Both the DataTable and DataView objects also let you update the data referenced in them akin to the ability to do so in a database using INSERT, UPDATE, and DELETE SQL DML statements. This ability of DataView and DataSet objects will be covered in further depth in Chapter 9 where updating data is introduced in both connected and disconnected scenarios.

Converting a DataView to a DataTable

A notable enhancement introduced in .NET 2.0 is that a method has been added to the DataView object that easily lets you create a new DataTable based on the rows available in a DataView. This is incredibly helpful in extracting a smaller set of the rows in a DataTable as a brand new DataTable. The usage is fairly simple and is shown here:

C#

```
DataTable custProdTable = DataSetFiller.FillDataset(dataFilePath).Tables(2) ;
DataView view = new DataView[custProdTable];
view.RowFilter = "ProductID > 2";
DataTable subsetTable = view.ToTable[];
// or
DataTable subsetTable = view.ToTable["TableName"];
```

VB.NET

```
Dim custProdTable As DataTable = _
   DataSetFiller.FillDataset(dataFilePath).Tables(2)
Dim view as DataView = New DataView(custProdTable)
view.RowFilter = "ProductID > 2"
Dim subsetTable as DataTable = view.ToTable()
' or
Dim subsetTable as DataTable = view.ToTable("TableName")
```

Either of these result in a DataTable with the same number of columns as the original DataTable. There is, however, another overload that lets you limit the number of columns you get back in the result set.

Where this method is incredibly useful is in finding distinct result sets, akin to the DISTINCT keyword in SQL. For instance, if you wanted to find distinct ProductIDs in the CustomerProducts table, you could easily achieve that using the following code snippet (note that the first parameter to the ToTable method signifies that you want the resulting DataTable to contain distinct rows):

C#

```
DataTable custProdTable = DataSetFiller.FillDataset(dataFilePath).Tables(2) ;
DataView view = new DataView[custProdTable];
view.RowFilter = "ProductID > 2";
DataTable subsetTable = view.ToTable[true,"ProductID"];
```

VB.NET

```
Dim custProdTable As DataTable = _
   DataSetFiller.FillDataset(dataFilePath).Tables(2)
Dim view as DataView = New DataView(custProdTable)
view.RowFilter = "ProductID > 2"
Dim subsetTable as DataTable = view.ToTable(True,"ProductID")
```

Of course, as you can see, this overload can also be used in extracting a DataTable with fewer numbers of columns than the original. This can be done by changing the first parameter to false and indicating that you are not requesting distinct rows, as shown here:

C#

```csharp
DataTable custProdTable = DataSetFiller.FillDataset(dataFilePath).Tables(2) ;
DataView view = new DataView[custProdTable];
view.RowFilter = "ProductID > 2";
DataTable subsetTable = view.ToTable[false, "CustomerID", "ProductID"];
```

VB.NET

```vbnet
Dim custProdTable As DataTable = _
    DataSetFiller.FillDataset(dataFilePath).Tables(2)
Dim view as DataView = New DataView(custProdTable)
view.RowFilter = "ProductID > 2"
Dim subsetTable as DataTable = view.ToTable(False, "CustomerID", "ProductID")
```

Within the computer sphere of the world, the commonly accepted data interchange language that most platforms and programming languages use is XML. XML can also be referred to as the lingua franca of the computer world. As already explained in previous chapters, the disconnected data objects, specifically the DataSet and DataTable objects, offer easy workability with XML.

Leveraging XML to Work with Disconnected Data

DataSet and DataTable objects are good friends with XML. Earlier in Chapter 6, you reviewed that one of the desirable features of the objects that might hold disconnected data for us is that they are easily workable with XML. Indeed both the DataSet and DataTable are easily convertible to and from XML. You have already seen some of this functionality in the form of the ReadXml, WriteXml, ReadXmlSchema, WriteXmlSchema, and the GetXml (DataSet only) methods on these objects. As a matter of fact, the data for all examples in this chapter is stored in an XML file and we simply read it using the ReadXml method.

There is yet another interesting method on the DataSet object that has not been covered so far: the InferXmlSchema method. You should avoid using this method in a production application; InferXmlSchema will scan every value in your DataSet and come up with a schema that *it thinks* fits your data. For maximum compatibility, InferXmlSchema will assume every column to be a string, so not only won't you get the schema you want, but it's also a rather inefficient way of generating schemas. Instead, you should prefer to specify your own schemas. If you cannot specify your own schema, you could instead rely on the FillSchema method, but in a high-demand application, you should avoid using the FillSchema method directly in production. Instead, you could prepare a set of schemas ready to be read into the appropriate DataSets.

■**Tip** Schemas on DataSets are great, but you should specify them only if you need them. If you must specify one, your first preference for performance reasons should be to specify them yourself and use the ReadXmlSchema method. The second preference should be to use the FillSchema method, and third preference should be to use InferXmlSchema method.

Another thing you saw was how the nested property on the DataRelation object affects the XML generated by these methods.

Even though a much deeper coverage will be given to the facilities ADO.NET provides in working with XML data in Chapter 12, there's one object in the .NET Framework that allows you to specifically work with disconnected data and XML: the XmlDataDocument object.

XmlDataDocument

Okay, so on one hand you have the DataSet object that is easily convertible into XML, and on the other hand you have the XMLDocument object that has the ability to hold XML, which if in the right format can be easily imported into a DataSet. So frequently you would end up with two entirely disparate objects with really no common ground between them. You'd have doubling up of your data and they will eventually get out of sync.

The object that has the ability to store both a DataSet and it's XML representation, and keep them both in sync for you, is the XmlDataDocument object. The XmlDataDocument object has the ability to hold the data and expose it as an XmlDocument or a DataSet—whichever you prefer.

Let's examine how XmlDataDocument works with the help of an example:

1. Start by creating a Window Forms application. Name it Exercise 8.9 and change the text on the main form of the application to Exercise 8.9.

2. Add a DataGridView control and call it dgView. This will be used to display the contents of the Customers DataTable.

3. Next, add a WebBrowser control, name it xmlViewer. This will be used to display the data in the XML document represented by the XmlDataDocument. Your form should look like Figure 8-14 in Design mode.

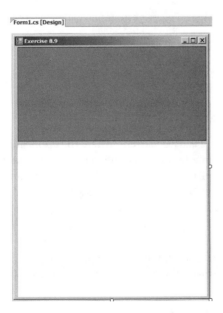

Figure 8-14. *XmlDataDocument exercise main form in Design mode*

4. In Form1_Load, add the following code:

C#

```csharp
private void Form1_Load(object sender, EventArgs e)
{
   CustomersTable =
 CreateDataSet.DataSetFiller.FillDataset(dataFilePath).Tables["Customers"];
   xdd = new XmlDataDocument(CustomersTable.DataSet);
   dgView.DataSource = CustomersTable;
   xdd.Save(Application.ExecutablePath + "_xdd.xml");
   xmlViewer.Navigate(Application.ExecutablePath + "_xdd.xml");
   CustomersTable.RowChanged +=
      new DataRowChangeEventHandler(CustomersTable_RowChanged);
}
```

VB.NET

```vbnet
Private Sub Form1_Load( _
  ByVal sender As System.Object, ByVal e As System.EventArgs) _
  Handles MyBase.Load
   CustomersTable = _
 CreateDataSet.DataSetFiller.FillDataset(dataFilePath).Tables("Customers")
   xdd = New XmlDataDocument(CustomersTable.DataSet)
   dgView.DataSource = CustomersTable
   xdd.Save(Application.ExecutablePath & "_xdd.xml")
   xmlViewer.Navigate(Application.ExecutablePath & "_xdd.xml")
End Sub
```

As you can see, this code creates a new XmlDataDocument instance called xdd using the
following line of code:

C#

```csharp
xdd = new XmlDataDocument(CustomersTable.DataSet);
```

VB.NET

```vbnet
xdd = New XmlDataDocument(CustomersTable.DataSet)
```

Also, it subscribes to the CustomersTable.RowChanged event, where the application can
easily use that as a mechanism to act upon any changes done to the data contained
inside CustomersTable. In the case of VB.NET, however, the explicit subscription is
taken care of by the language keyword WithEvents, which is mentioned in the declaration of CustomersTable as shown here:

```
Private WithEvents CustomersTable As DataTable
```

This code also uses simple data binding to display the results of the CustomersTable
DataTable and it uses the WebBrowser control to display the results of the XmlDataDocument
as XML.

5. In the event handler for the CustomersTable.RowChanged event, add the following code
to refresh the contents of XmlViewer:

C#

```
void CustomersTable_RowChanged(object sender, DataRowChangeEventArgs e)
{
    xdd.Save(Application.ExecutablePath + "\xdd.xml");
    xmlViewer.Navigate(Application.ExecutablePath + "\xdd.xml");
}
```

VB.NET

```
Private Sub CustomersTable_RowChanged( _
  ByVal sender As Object, ByVal e As System.Data.DataRowChangeEventArgs) _
  Handles CustomersTable.RowChanged
    xdd.Save(Application.ExecutablePath & "_xdd.xml")
    xmlViewer.Navigate(Application.ExecutablePath & "_xdd.xml")
End Sub
```

6. Compile and run the application. You should see output as shown in Figure 8-15.

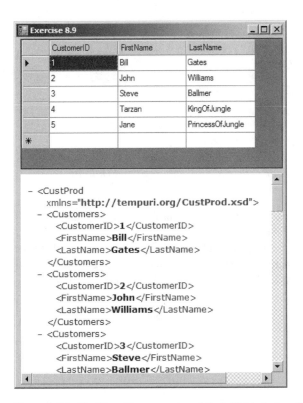

Figure 8-15. *XmlDataDocument and DataTable being displayed concurrently*

7. Now go ahead and make some change to the DataTable. For instance, change the name Bill to Chill; you'll see that the XmlDataDocument automatically understands the change and the resultant XML reflects the contents of the DataTable without any additional plumbing. This is shown in Figure 8-16.

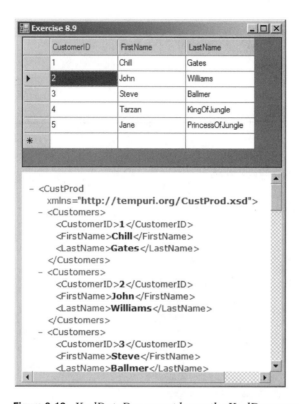

Figure 8-16. *XmlDataDocument keeps the XmlDocument and DataSet in sync*

In addition to this, you can leverage standard XML features such as XPath queries to query across the DataSet's data.

ADO.NET itself contains a lot of other XML-related functionality. Some of this functionality is around the new XML data type introduced in Microsoft SQL Server 2005, or there are functions such as ExecuteXmlReader on the SqlClient .NET data provider. Finally, there is a .NET data provider at System.Data.SqlXml, which is primarily used to leverage the XML features available in the Microsoft SQL Server database. These will be covered in further depth in Chapter 12, where XML and ADO.NET are discussed.

Summary

In this chapter, you looked at sorting, searching, and filtering over disconnected data. This is quite an important part of ADO.NET. A good handle on these concepts will allow you to write effective applications.

This chapter discussed the various methods of working with disconnected data using DataTables, DataViews, DataRelations, and, finally, using the XmlDataDocument. Typically, in an application built around disconnected architecture, you would query the data and fill a disconnected cache—such as a DataTable or a DataSet. Then, based upon the user's requests, you would make updates to that data.

While this chapter presented you with the concepts of being able to find the right rows to make updates to, the next two chapters will discuss the process of making the updates and persisting them into a data source. What you have learned in this chapter will be very useful in the next chapter, which discusses updating data.

CHAPTER 9

■■■

Updating Data

Updating data back into the data source is probably one of the most interesting parts of any application. This is because updating data back into the data source requires you, as an architect, to make many decisions usually guided between a balance of effort, level of concurrency support, performance, and data sanctity. It's also one of the most critical pieces of your application as far as efficiency and the right design are concerned. Before architecting the updating part of your application, you need to ask yourself a few questions.

These questions will basically be centered on *what kind of data sanctity or integrity you require out of your data layer in a highly concurrent environment*. Based upon that you could decide on the concurrency management scheme to use. When you do decide on the concurrency management scheme, you'll then have to evaluate how exactly you wish to build the concurrency detection and conflict resolution features in your data layer. And to build such concurrency features, you'll need to decide what built-in ADO.NET features you wish to leverage.

After you decide on the concurrency management schemes, the next big questions to ask yourself regard *the performance you wish to garner out of the data layer*. Do you wish to rely on autogenerated commands, which might be designed in a one-size-fits-all approach? Do you wish to cache commands? Or command parameters? Do you want to design specific supplied commands that take the specific table structures and business case into cognizance at the risk of a higher management hassle for all the commands? Or do you wish to use database-specific features and pass the data in bulk forms to the database server, in such a way that the solution is the least portable between databases, but the most efficient?

Finally, one of the most important questions you need to ask yourself while architecting the data layer is *"What am I designing this data layer for, and how much effort am I willing to put in it?"* Is coming up with the best and most efficient way to persist data really worth it for a single-user desktop application?

This chapter and the next don't give you a panacea for all your updating needs; I wish there were such a thing. The exact solution really depends on your needs. These chapters, however, do give you enough information for you to intelligently decide what might suit your needs the best.

As it turns out, just like in real life, ADO.NET has no freebies. Like anything else, the more effort you put in, the better your data layer will perform and the cleaner your data will be. Given that you might have many choices at each step as far the previous three questions go, it will pay off well if you know what choices you have, and how much work each one of those choices will entail.

Knowing about the various methods ADO.NET provides to update changes or new data into your database will allow you to make intelligent decisions regarding these three questions—and that is what this chapter and the next are all about.

These two chapters focus on a "crawl before you walk, walk before you run" approach. The examples presented start with the simplest and increase in complexity and real-life application. In each case, the various pros and cons of any approach will be discussed that will allow you to intelligently decide if a given approach is right for you to use in your application architecture.

Another important point to mention before you start your journey is that this is where significant differences begin to show up between individual databases and .NET data providers. The examples presented here will run on a local instance of SQL Server 2005 on a database called Test. You can find the relevant SQL scripts in the associated code download (see the Downloads section of the Apress website at http://www.apress.com); however, any specific differences with Oracle will be pointed out as the discussion moves along.

Starting with simplest first, let's examine how ADO.NET updates data.

Updating a Table: The Easy Drag-and-Drop Approach

In Chapter 3, you saw a simple example created using drag and drop demonstrating a full-fledged application that queries data from the database and updates the changes back into it. It all seemed to work like magic, but there really was more to it than that. ADO.NET actually wrote a lot of code for you behind the scenes. Let's quickly go over such an example again and see exactly what ADO.NET does behind the scenes:

1. First, set up a database called Test on your local SQL Server 2005 instance and create a table called Animals in it using the following script:

   ```
   Create Database Test
   GO
   USE Test
   GO
   CREATE TABLE Animals(
       AnimalID int NOT NULL,
       AnimalName varchar(50) NOT NULL,
      CONSTRAINT PK_Animals PRIMARY KEY (AnimalID)
   )
   GO
   ```

2. Once this table is set up, start up Visual Studio and create a Windows Forms application. Change its main form's text to Exercise 9.1.

3. From the Visual Studio menu, select Data ➤ Add New Data Source. As already described in Chapter 7, add a new data source for the Test database running on the local instance of SQL Server 2005. When prompted to choose your database objects, choose the Animals table.

4. Again, in the Data Sources window (select Data ➤ Show Data Sources window), select Animals, and choose the DataGridView option. This has also been seen in Figure 7-7 of Chapter 7.

5. Finally, drag and drop Animals to the main application form. After a little rearrangement, your main application form should look like Figure 9-1.

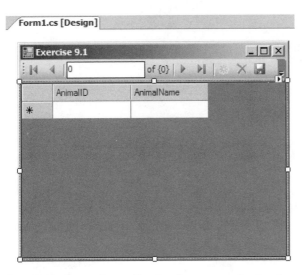

Figure 9-1. *The main application form created using drag and drop in Design view*

6. You'll notice that Visual Studio, by virtue of a simple drag-and-drop operation, added a number of objects as shown in Figure 9-2.

Figure 9-2. *Objects added for you by Visual Studio*

7. In the animalsBindingNavigator control, make sure that the Save button (i.e., the bindingNavigatorSaveItem control) has its enabled property set to true.

8. Compile and run the application. Add a few rows as shown in Figure 9-3. Click Save. You can now run a Select * from Animals query on the local database to verify that your results were indeed saved to the database.

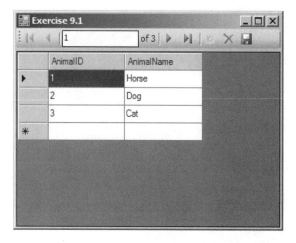

Figure 9-3. *A few rows added and saved to the database*

What just happened? How did a single line of code end up doing so much work? To discover the answers, let's examine the objects added for us one by one.

To get into the real meat of the matter, select Show All Files in your Visual Studio IDE, as shown in Figure 9-4.

Figure 9-4. *The Show All Files button*

The first object added is the `testDataSet`. If you double-click it, you'll see that it contains two objects: the Animals `DataTable` and the `AnimalsTableAdapter` `TableAdapter`. If you right-click the `AnimalsTableAdapter` and choose Configure, as shown in Figure 9-5, you'll see a dialog box as shown in Figure 9-6.

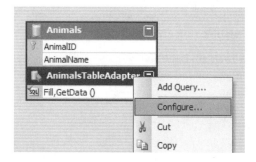

Figure 9-5. *Configuring the TableAdapter*

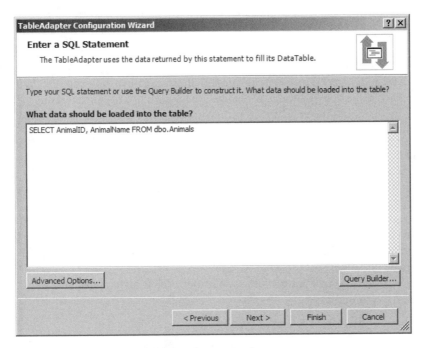

Figure 9-6. *TableAdapter Configuration dialog box*

In this dialog box, you can easily configure the SELECT query being used to fill the testDataSet at runtime. Not only that, but by clicking Advanced Options you can see a dialog box as shown in Figure 9-7.

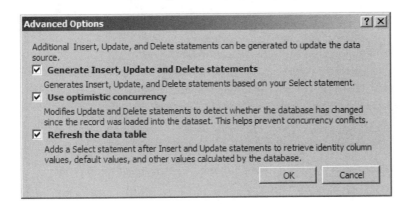

Figure 9-7. *TableAdapter Configuration dialog box—Advanced Options*

In the Advanced Options dialog box, you are presented with three options. The exact underlying behavior of these three options will become clear as you progress through this and the next chapter, but for now it is sufficient to understand that these checkboxes allow you to do the following:

- Specify that you are interested in a `TableAdapter` that lets you `INSERT`, `UPDATE`, and `DELETE`.

- Use optimistic concurrency.

- Refresh the data table. After an update to the underlying data source, refreshes the data presented to the user, to demonstrate any changes or concurrency resolution results that might occur due to another user updating the same table at the same time. (Covered in detail in the next chapter.)

The first checkbox is self explanatory, by checking it, you receive the ability to use the `TableAdapter` and update the underlying data source.

The second and third checkboxes have to do with the disconnected nature of this application and the ensuing concurrency problems that it might create. For instance, between your filling the `DataSet`, someone else could have changed the data. Not only would you want to resolve such conflicts which arise due to the disconnected nature of a `DataSet`, but you also want to refresh your disconnected data cache (`DataSet` or `DataTable`) whenever you reestablish the connection with the underlying data source.

To understand the disconnected nature of this application, delete all rows from the data source using the following SQL query:

```
Delete from Animals
```

Now once again, let's start at the beginning. Imagine a situation where two users are simultaneously adding information to the database. To simulate that, start two instances of the application and add some data as shown in Figure 9-8. It's important to note that at this stage, neither of the application instances has saved the data.

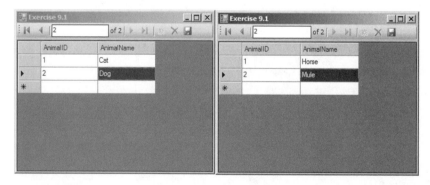

Figure 9-8. *Two users using the same application concurrently—with a concurrency problem*

For those of you with keen eyes, you might have noticed that both the users ended up using the *same primary key values* for the newly entered rows. Why would they do that? This is because neither of the users knew the primary keys being used by the other user. This happens because both users are completely disconnected from the underlying database and don't have that common policeman—the database—telling them what keys to use. There's no common entity that connects them and tells them what primary keys should be used. What's important to realize at this point is that the users *were able to enter data* incorrectly *but not save it* because they are disconnected from the database. This might appear incorrect on the surface, but the data isn't really saved in the database yet, so no damage has been done. The only changes done so far are in their local copies of the in-memory disconnected data cache, in this case the DataTable. The database is untouched and still sober.

The users have no way of knowing what the right value of the primary keys should be because they don't have a centrally connected database doing this job for them. You did have the option of remaining centrally connected to the database and locking the rows being edited by individual users but, as covered in Chapter 4, this would require you to keep a connection open and hence degrade the system performance significantly. More than just connection pooling, by implementing such pessimistic row locking, you would effectively make other users wait until one user is done with his changes. Depending on your situation, maybe that is the solution you wish to go with. Row, page, or table-level locks for extremely long durations, however, are not advised in most situations.

Without going too deep into the rather interesting topic of concurrency just yet, try saving the data in the application on the left (Dog and Cat), and then try saving the data in the application on the right (Horse and Mule) only *after* the Dog and Cat application has saved its data. You will get an exception as shown in Figure 9-9.

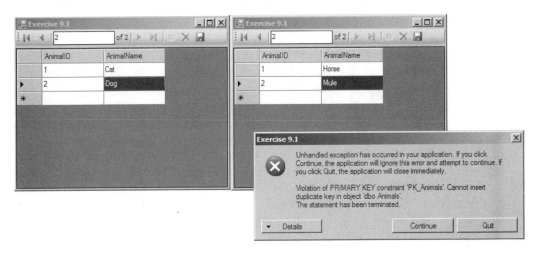

Figure 9-9. *Our simple point-and-click application even checks for concurrency.*

The application clearly tells you that the primary key PK_Animals was violated.

■**Note** This error was really thrown by the database. Throwing such exceptions is expensive, especially when going over a Remoting layer. A better approach would have been to have the ability to detect such conflicts and convey to the user a remedial approach instead. Throwing an exception after a well-meant update attempt is somewhat like going to the hospital after an accident. Obviously, a better approach would be to design a better traffic system that prevents an accident in the first place. That is covered in detail in the next chapter.

So basically, the second user cannot save his data unless he uses the correct keys. But how will the second user know *what keys to use* unless he refreshes the data?

This can be achieved by refreshing the data from the data source *after* an attempted update has failed. As a matter of fact, it makes sense to refresh the data from the underlying data source even if an update succeeds because the user might wish to add further rows or edit any existing rows, including the ones entered by another user. Also, by refreshing data you get the latest snapshot including the last generated primary key, and your next generated disconnected primary key in the DataTable has a lower probability of being incorrect—this way, you save yourself the pain of an exception and yet another refresh.

As it turns out, ADO.NET does give you enough control to automatically resolve such conflicts. This will become clearer as you read through the various examples in this chapter and the next. For now it's sufficient to understand that the disconnected model introduces some interesting new issues that usually wouldn't arise with a constantly connected application.

How Does It All Work?

This is such an obvious question especially since you didn't write even one line of code.

How could just dragging and dropping possibly take care of generating various queries for you for updates, inserts, and deletes; deciding between updates, inserts, and deletes on various rows in a DataTable; and, at the same time, even take care of concurrency issues?

Note What you are just about to do is degut a lot of autogenerated code. This comes with good news and bad news. The bad news first: there is a lot of code to look at—almost like a wall of ASCII, so my intention in this section is to give you a guided tour through this jungle of code. The good news is that you don't have to memorize every little bit of this code, just view it conceptually to try and understand what it does functionally.

Earlier in Figure 9-4 you enabled the Show All Files button. By doing so, under the Solution Explorer window, you would notice a file created for you by Visual Studio, which contains the actual code for the strongly typed DataSet. This file is the testDataSet.Designer.cs/testDataSet.Designer.vb file. In addition to testDataSet and AnimalsDataTable definitions, something you have already seen in Chapter 7, there lies a definition for AnimalsTableAdapter. The various methods in AnimalsTableAdapter are shown in Listings 9-1 and 9-2.

Listing 9-1. *Various Methods in AnimalsTableAdapter in C#*

```
public interface IAnimalsTableAdapter {
    int Fill(testDataSet.AnimalsDataTable dataTable);
    testDataSet.AnimalsDataTable GetData();
    int Delete(int Original_AnimalID, string Original_AnimalName);
    int Insert(int @AnimalID, string @AnimalName);
    int Update(int @AnimalID, string @AnimalName, int @Original_AnimalID);
    int Update(testDataSet dataSet);
    int Update(testDataSet.AnimalsDataTable dataTable);
    int Update(System.Data.DataRow[] dataRows);
    int Update(System.Data.DataRow dataRow);
}
```

Listing 9-2. *Various Methods in AnimalsTableAdapter in Visual Basic .NET*

```
Public Interface IAnimalsTableAdapter
    Function Fill(ByVal dataTable As testDataSet.AnimalsDataTable) As Integer
    Function GetData() As testDataSet.AnimalsDataTable
    Function Delete(ByVal Original_AnimalID As Integer, _
      ByVal Orignal_AnimalName as String) As Integer
    Function Insert(ByVal AnimalID As Integer, ByVal AnimalName As String) _
      As Integer
    Function Update(ByVal AnimalID As Integer, ByVal AnimalName As String, _
      ByVal Original_AnimalID As Integer) As Integer
    Function Update(ByVal dataSet As testDataSet) As Integer
    Function Update(ByVal dataTable As testDataSet.AnimalsDataTable) As Integer
    Function Update(ByVal dataRows() As System.Data.DataRow) As Integer
    Function Update(ByVal dataRow As System.Data.DataRow) As Integer
End Interface
```

Inside the AnimalsTableAdapter class, you have a definition for each one of these methods. First, let's focus our attention on the Fill method, which fills the AnimalsDataTable. The code for a sample Fill method is shown in Listings 9-3 and 9-4.

Listing 9-3. *AnimalsTableAdapter.Fill Method in C#*

```csharp
public virtual int Fill(testDataSet.AnimalsDataTable dataTable) {
    this.Adapter.SelectCommand =
        ((System.Data.SqlClient.SqlCommand)(this.CommandCollection[0]));
    if ((this.m_clearBeforeFill == true)) {
        dataTable.Clear();
    }
    int returnValue = this.Adapter.Fill(dataTable);
    return returnValue;
}.
```

Listing 9-4. *AnimalsTableAdapter.Fill Method in Visual Basic .NET*

```
Public Overloads Overridable Function Fill( _
  ByVal dataTable As testDataSet.AnimalsDataTable) As Integer _
  Implements IAnimalsTableAdapter.Fill
  Me.Adapter.SelectCommand = _
    CType(Me.CommandCollection(0),System.Data.SqlClient.SqlCommand)
  If (Me.m_clearBeforeFill = true) Then
    dataTable.Clear
  End If
  Dim returnValue As Integer = Me.Adapter.Fill(dataTable)
  Return returnValue
End Function
```

Upon closer examination of this code, it looks very similar to the code you have already seen in various listings of Chapter 7. This is a simple case of specifying a SelectCommand to a SqlDataAdapter object and calling the Fill method on it. But what is this.CommandCollection[0]?

Interestingly, if you browse through the code for AnimalsTableAdapter a little bit, you'll find that this command is a SqlCommand representation of the command text you specified in Figure 9-5. The code for setting up such commands can be found in the InitCommandCollection method. This can be seen in Listings 9-5 and 9-6.

Listing 9-5. *AnimalsTableAdapter.InitCommandCollection Method in C#*

```csharp
private void InitCommandCollection() {
    this.m_commandCollection = new System.Data.SqlClient.SqlCommand[1];
    this.m_commandCollection[0] = new System.Data.SqlClient.SqlCommand();
    this.m_commandCollection[0].Connection = this.Connection;
    this.m_commandCollection[0].CommandText =
        "SELECT AnimalID, AnimalName FROM dbo.Animals";
    this.m_commandCollection[0].CommandType = System.Data.CommandType.Text;
}
```

Listing 9-6. *AnimalsTableAdapter.InitCommandCollection Method in Visual Basic .NET*

```vbnet
Private Sub InitCommandCollection()
    Me.m_commandCollection = New System.Data.SqlClient.SqlCommand(0) {}
    Me.m_commandCollection(0) = New System.Data.SqlClient.SqlCommand
    Me.m_commandCollection(0).Connection = Me.Connection
    Me.m_commandCollection(0).CommandText = _
        "SELECT AnimalID, AnimalName FROM dbo.Animals"
    Me.m_commandCollection(0).CommandType = System.Data.CommandType.Text
End Sub
```

CommandCollection is an array because one TableAdapter can hold multiple commands. Next, look up the code for the definition of the Delete(int Original_AnimalID, string Original_AnimalName) overload. This is shown in Listings 9-7 and 9-8.

Listing 9-7. *AnimalsTableAdapter.Delete(int Original_AnimalID, string Original_AnimalName) Method in C#*

```csharp
public virtual int Delete(int Original_AnimalID, string Original_AnimalName) {
    this.Adapter.DeleteCommand.Parameters[0].Value = ((int)(Original_AnimalID));
    if ((Original_AnimalName == null)) {
        throw new System.ArgumentNullException("Original_AnimalName");
    }
    else {
        this.Adapter.DeleteCommand.Parameters[1].Value =
            ((string)(Original_AnimalName));
    }
    System.Data.ConnectionState previousConnectionState =
        this.Adapter.DeleteCommand.Connection.State;
    this.Adapter.DeleteCommand.Connection.Open();
    try {
        return this.Adapter.DeleteCommand.ExecuteNonQuery();
    }
```

```
    finally {
        if ((previousConnectionState == System.Data.ConnectionState.Closed)) {
            this.Adapter.DeleteCommand.Connection.Close();
        }
    }
}
```

Listing 9-8. *AnimalsTableAdapter.Delete(int Original_AnimalID, string Original_AnimalName) Method in Visual Basic .NET*

```
Public Overloads Overridable Function Delete( _
    ByVal Original_AnimalID As Integer, _
    ByVal Original_AnimalName As String) As Integer
    Me.Adapter.DeleteCommand.Parameters(0).Value = _
        CType(Original_AnimalID,Integer)
    If (Original_AnimalName Is Nothing) Then
        Throw New System.ArgumentNullException("Original_AnimalName")
    Else
        Me.Adapter.DeleteCommand.Parameters(1).Value = _
            CType(Original_AnimalName,String)
    End If
    Dim previousConnectionState As System.Data.ConnectionState = _
        Me.Adapter.DeleteCommand.Connection.State
    Me.Adapter.DeleteCommand.Connection.Open
    Try
        Return Me.Adapter.DeleteCommand.ExecuteNonQuery
    Finally
        If (previousConnectionState = System.Data.ConnectionState.Closed) Then
            Me.Adapter.DeleteCommand.Connection.Close
        End If
    End Try
End Function
```

Again, this code takes an AnimalID and AnimalName as parameters to the function, sets a parameter on a command (DeleteCommand), and simply uses the ExecuteNonQuery method to execute the command. If you look up the definition of DeleteCommand, you can find that it is the InitAdapter private method. Its definition looks like as shown in Listings 9-9 and 9-10.

Listing 9-9. *DeleteCommand in C#*

```
this.m adapter.DeleteCommand = new System.Data.SqlClient.SqlCommand();
this.m adapter.DeleteCommand.Connection = this.Connection;
this.m adapter.DeleteCommand.CommandText =
 "DELETE FROM [dbo].[Animals] WHERE ((([AnimalID] = @Original_AnimalID) AND ([Animal"
 + "Name] = @Original_AnimalName))";
this.m adapter.DeleteCommand.CommandType =
    System.Data.CommandType.Text;
this.m adapter.DeleteCommand.Parameters.Add(
```

```
    new System.Data.SqlClient.SqlParameter("@Original_AnimalID",
    System.Data.SqlDbType.Int,
    0, System.Data.ParameterDirection.Input,
    0, 0, "AnimalID", System.Data.DataRowVersion.Original,
    false, null, "", "", ""));
this.m_adapter.DeleteCommand.Parameters.Add(
    new System.Data.SqlClient.SqlParameter("@Original_AnimalName",
    System.Data.SqlDbType.VarChar, 0,
    System.Data.ParameterDirection.Input, 0, 0,
    "AnimalName", System.Data.DataRowVersion.Original,
    false, null, "", "", ""));
```

Listing 9-10. *DeleteCommand in Visual Basic .NET*

```
Me.m_adapter.DeleteCommand = New System.Data.SqlClient.SqlCommand
Me.m_adapter.DeleteCommand.Connection = Me.Connection
Me.m_adapter.DeleteCommand.CommandText = _
    "DELETE FROM [dbo].[Animals] WHERE (([AnimalID] = @Original_AnimalID) " & _
    " AND ([Animal" & _
     "Name] = @Original_AnimalName))"
Me.m_adapter.DeleteCommand.CommandType = System.Data.CommandType.Text
Me.m_adapter.DeleteCommand.Parameters.Add( _
    New System.Data.SqlClient.SqlParameter("@Original_AnimalID", _
    System.Data.SqlDbType.Int, 0, System.Data.ParameterDirection.Input, 0, 0, _
    "AnimalID", System.Data.DataRowVersion.Original, false, Nothing, "", "", ""))
Me.m_adapter.DeleteCommand.Parameters.Add( _
    New System.Data.SqlClient.SqlParameter("@Original_AnimalName", _
    System.Data.SqlDbType.VarChar, 0, _
    System.Data.ParameterDirection.Input, 0, 0, _
     "AnimalName", System.Data.DataRowVersion.Original, _
    false, Nothing, "", "", ""))
```

As a matter of fact, if you look through the code of InitAdapter, the various table mappings, adapters, and commands are set up within this private method. The full code for InitAdapter is shown in Listings 9-11 and 9-12.

Listing 9-11. *InitAdapter in C#*

```
private void InitAdapter() {
    this.m_adapter = new System.Data.SqlClient.SqlDataAdapter();
    System.Data.Common.DataTableMapping tableMapping =
        new System.Data.Common.DataTableMapping();
    tableMapping.SourceTable = "Table";
    tableMapping.DataSetTable = "Animals";
    tableMapping.ColumnMappings.Add("AnimalID", "AnimalID");
    tableMapping.ColumnMappings.Add("AnimalName", "AnimalName");
    this.m_adapter.TableMappings.Add(tableMapping);
    this.m_adapter.DeleteCommand = new System.Data.SqlClient.SqlCommand();
    this.m_adapter.DeleteCommand.Connection = this.Connection;
```

```
this.m_adapter.DeleteCommand.CommandText =
    "DELETE FROM [dbo].[Animals] WHERE (((([AnimalID] = @Original_AnimalID) AND"
    + "([Animal" + "Name] = @Original_AnimalName))";
this.m_adapter.DeleteCommand.CommandType = System.Data.CommandType.Text;
this.m_adapter.DeleteCommand.Parameters.Add(
    new System.Data.SqlClient.SqlParameter("@Original_AnimalID",
    System.Data.SqlDbType.Int, 0, System.Data.ParameterDirection.Input, 0, 0,
    "AnimalID", System.Data.DataRowVersion.Original,
    false, null, "", "", ""));
this.m_adapter.DeleteCommand.Parameters.Add(
    new System.Data.SqlClient.SqlParameter("@Original_AnimalName",
    System.Data.SqlDbType.VarChar, 0, System.Data.ParameterDirection.Input, 0,
    0, "AnimalName", System.Data.DataRowVersion.Original, false, null,
    "", "", ""));
this.m_adapter.InsertCommand = new System.Data.SqlClient.SqlCommand();
this.m_adapter.InsertCommand.Connection = this.Connection;
this.m_adapter.InsertCommand.CommandText =
"INSERT INTO [dbo].[Animals] ([AnimalID], [AnimalName]) " +
" VALUES (@AnimalID, @Animal" +
"Name);\r\nSELECT AnimalID, AnimalName FROM Animals WHERE " +
" (AnimalID = @AnimalID)";
this.m_adapter.InsertCommand.CommandType = System.Data.CommandType.Text;
this.m_adapter.InsertCommand.Parameters.Add(
    new System.Data.SqlClient.SqlParameter("@AnimalID",
    System.Data.SqlDbType.Int, 0, System.Data.ParameterDirection.Input, 0, 0,
    "AnimalID", System.Data.DataRowVersion.Current, false, null, "", "", ""));
this.m_adapter.InsertCommand.Parameters.Add(
    new System.Data.SqlClient.SqlParameter("@AnimalName",
    System.Data.SqlDbType.VarChar, 0, System.Data.ParameterDirection.Input, 0,
    0, "AnimalName", System.Data.DataRowVersion.Current,
    false, null, "", "", ""));
this.m_adapter.UpdateCommand = new System.Data.SqlClient.SqlCommand();
this.m_adapter.UpdateCommand.Connection = this.Connection;
this.m_adapter.UpdateCommand.CommandText =
"UPDATE [dbo].[Animals] SET [AnimalID] = @AnimalID, [AnimalName] = " +
" @AnimalName WHE" +
    "RE (([AnimalID] = @Original_AnimalID) AND ([AnimalName] = " +
    "@Original_AnimalName))" +
    ";\r\nSELECT AnimalID, AnimalName FROM Animals WHERE " +
    "(AnimalID = @AnimalID)";
this.m_adapter.UpdateCommand.CommandType = System.Data.CommandType.Text;
this.m_adapter.UpdateCommand.Parameters.Add(
    new System.Data.SqlClient.SqlParameter("@AnimalID",
    System.Data.SqlDbType.Int, 0, System.Data.ParameterDirection.Input, 0, 0,
    "AnimalID", System.Data.DataRowVersion.Current, false, null, "", "", ""));
this.m_adapter.UpdateCommand.Parameters.Add(
    new System.Data.SqlClient.SqlParameter("@AnimalName",
    System.Data.SqlDbType.VarChar, 0, System.Data.ParameterDirection.Input, 0,
```

```
            0, "AnimalName", System.Data.DataRowVersion.Current,
            false, null, "", "", ""));
    this.m_adapter.UpdateCommand.Parameters.Add(
        new System.Data.SqlClient.SqlParameter("@Original_AnimalID",
        System.Data.SqlDbType.Int, 0, System.Data.ParameterDirection.Input, 0, 0,
        "AnimalID", System.Data.DataRowVersion.Original,
        false, null, "", "", ""));
    this.m_adapter.UpdateCommand.Parameters.Add(
        new System.Data.SqlClient.SqlParameter("@Original_AnimalName",
        System.Data.SqlDbType.VarChar, 0, System.Data.ParameterDirection.Input, 0,
        0, "AnimalName", System.Data.DataRowVersion.Original,
        false, null, "", "", ""));
}
```

Listing 9-12. *InitAdapter in Visual Basic .NET*

```
Private Sub InitAdapter()
    Me.m_adapter = New System.Data.SqlClient.SqlDataAdapter
    Dim tableMapping As System.Data.Common.DataTableMapping = _
        New System.Data.Common.DataTableMapping
    tableMapping.SourceTable = "Table"
    tableMapping.DataSetTable = "Animals"
    tableMapping.ColumnMappings.Add("AnimalID", "AnimalID")
    tableMapping.ColumnMappings.Add("AnimalName", "AnimalName")
    Me.m_adapter.TableMappings.Add(tableMapping)
    Me.m_adapter.DeleteCommand = New System.Data.SqlClient.SqlCommand
    Me.m_adapter.DeleteCommand.Connection = Me.Connection
    Me.m_adapter.DeleteCommand.CommandText = _
    "DELETE FROM [dbo].[Animals] WHERE " & _
    " (([AnimalID] = @Original_AnimalID) AND ([Animal"& _
    "Name] = @Original_AnimalName))"
    Me.m_adapter.DeleteCommand.CommandType = System.Data.CommandType.Text
    Me.m_adapter.DeleteCommand.Parameters.Add( _
    New System.Data.SqlClient.SqlParameter("@Original_AnimalID", _
    System.Data.SqlDbType.Int, 0, System.Data.ParameterDirection.Input, 0, 0, _
    "AnimalID", System.Data.DataRowVersion.Original, _
    false, Nothing, "", "", ""))
    Me.m_adapter.DeleteCommand.Parameters.Add( _
    New System.Data.SqlClient.SqlParameter("@Original_AnimalName", _
    System.Data.SqlDbType.VarChar, 0, System.Data.ParameterDirection.Input, 0, _
    0, "AnimalName", System.Data.DataRowVersion.Original, _
    false, Nothing, "", "", ""))
    Me.m_adapter.InsertCommand = New System.Data.SqlClient.SqlCommand
    Me.m_adapter.InsertCommand.Connection = Me.Connection
    Me.m_adapter.InsertCommand.CommandText = _
    "INSERT INTO [dbo].[Animals] ([AnimalID], " & _
    " [AnimalName]) VALUES (@AnimalID, @Animal"& _
    "Name);"&Global.Microsoft.VisualBasic.ChrW(13)& _
```

```
Global.Microsoft.VisualBasic.ChrW(10)& _
"SELECT AnimalID, AnimalName FROM Animals WHERE (AnimalID = @AnimalID)"
 Me.m_adapter.InsertCommand.CommandType = System.Data.CommandType.Text
 Me.m_adapter.InsertCommand.Parameters.Add( _
New System.Data.SqlClient.SqlParameter("@AnimalID", _
System.Data.SqlDbType.Int, 0, System.Data.ParameterDirection.Input, 0, 0, _
 "AnimalID", System.Data.DataRowVersion.Current, false, Nothing, "", "", ""))
 Me.m_adapter.InsertCommand.Parameters.Add( _
New System.Data.SqlClient.SqlParameter("@AnimalName", _
System.Data.SqlDbType.VarChar, 0, System.Data.ParameterDirection.Input, 0, _
 0, "AnimalName", System.Data.DataRowVersion.Current, _
false, Nothing, "", "", ""))
 Me.m_adapter.UpdateCommand = New System.Data.SqlClient.SqlCommand
 Me.m_adapter.UpdateCommand.Connection = Me.Connection
 Me.m_adapter.UpdateCommand.CommandText = _
"UPDATE [dbo].[Animals] SET [AnimalID] = " & _
" @AnimalID, [AnimalName] = @AnimalName WHE"& _
"RE (([AnimalID] = @Original_AnimalID) AND " & _
" ([AnimalName] = @Original_AnimalName))"& _
";"&Global.Microsoft.VisualBasic.ChrW(13)& _
Global.Microsoft.VisualBasic.ChrW(10)& _
"SELECT AnimalID, AnimalName FROM Animals WHERE (AnimalID = @AnimalID)"
 Me.m_adapter.UpdateCommand.CommandType = System.Data.CommandType.Text
 Me.m_adapter.UpdateCommand.Parameters.Add( _
New System.Data.SqlClient.SqlParameter("@AnimalID", _
System.Data.SqlDbType.Int, 0, System.Data.ParameterDirection.Input, 0, 0, _
 "AnimalID", System.Data.DataRowVersion.Current, false, Nothing, "", "", ""))
 Me.m_adapter.UpdateCommand.Parameters.Add( _
New System.Data.SqlClient.SqlParameter("@AnimalName", _
System.Data.SqlDbType.VarChar, 0, System.Data.ParameterDirection.Input, 0, _
 0, "AnimalName", System.Data.DataRowVersion.Current, _
 false, Nothing, "", "", ""))
 Me.m_adapter.UpdateCommand.Parameters.Add( _
New System.Data.SqlClient.SqlParameter("@Original_AnimalID", _
System.Data.SqlDbType.Int, 0, System.Data.ParameterDirection.Input, 0, 0, _
 "AnimalID", System.Data.DataRowVersion.Original, _
 false, Nothing, "", "", ""))
 Me.m_adapter.UpdateCommand.Parameters.Add( _
New System.Data.SqlClient.SqlParameter("@Original_AnimalName", _
System.Data.SqlDbType.VarChar, 0, System.Data.ParameterDirection.Input, 0, _
 0, "AnimalName", System.Data.DataRowVersion.Original, _
 false, Nothing, "", "", ""))
End Sub
```

Now before I drown you in any more code, if you look through Listings 9-11 and 9-12, the SQL query that gets executed finally for deletion of a record identified by AnimalID and AnimalName looks like this:

```
DELETE FROM [dbo].[Animals]
WHERE
(([AnimalID] = @Original_AnimalID) AND ([AnimalName] = @Original_AnimalName))
```

If you look through the code, you'll see the same pattern repeat for UpdateCommand and InsertCommand. These commands, as you have already seen in Chapter 5, are the purely connected method of executing a prepared SQL command on the database.

Finally, look up the definition of Update(testDataSet dataSet). As you might expect, this overload is responsible for taking whatever changes a DataSet might have and persisting them to the database. This is shown in Listings 9-13 and 9-14.

Listing 9-13. *AnimalsTableAdapter.Update(testDataSet dataSet) Method in C#*

```
public virtual int Update(testDataSet dataSet) {
    return this.Adapter.Update(dataSet, "Animals");
}
```

Listing 9-14. *AnimalsTableAdapter.Update(testDataSet dataSet) Method in Visual Basic .NET*

```
Public Overloads Overridable Function Update(ByVal dataSet As TestDataSet) _
    As Integer
    Return Me.Adapter.Update(dataSet, "Animals")
End Function
```

So the code for updating the entire DataSet, going through each table, each row, and making decisions for what needs to be done to each row (add/insert/delete/leave alone) is done by Listings 9-13 and 9-14. Why is the code so simple? Just a call to SqlDataAdapter.Update? As you'll see later in this chapter, the Update method does all that work for you. It does this by looking at the RowState on each row, one by one, and then calling the necessary SqlCommand specified as properties InsertCommand, UpdateCommand, and DeleteCommand on the SqlDataAdapter.

That brings up another interesting point. You never specified an InsertCommand, UpdateCommand, or DeleteCommand. All you did was specify a SelectCommand, and based upon the first checkbox you checked in Figure 9-7, these commands were *"automagically" generated for you*. These commands were generated by the SqlCommandBuilder object.

Next, let's look at the SqlCommandBuilder object and see how you can leverage it to generate commands for you, in a slightly non-drag-and-drop approach.

Using the Command Builder Object

In the previous example, you saw how a drag-and-drop operation on a single table allows you to create various commands and a fully functional application with very little code. You also saw how the SelectCommand is really the only command you specify yourself, all other commands are generated for you behind the scenes. These commands are generated by theSqlCommandBuilder object.

Upon closer examination, the command generated for you is probably not the most efficient command, an instance of which can be seen in the UpdateCommand.CommandText here:

```
UPDATE
   [dbo].[Animals] SET [AnimalID] = @AnimalID,
   [AnimalName] = @AnimalName
WHERE
   (([AnimalID] = @Original_AnimalID) AND ([AnimalName] = @Original_AnimalName))
   ;
SELECT AnimalID, AnimalName FROM Animals WHERE (AnimalID = @AnimalID)
```

This generated SQL query is simply awful! It not only tries to update the primary key, so you need to be very sure that you don't mess that up, but also it compares every single column in your WHERE clause. As you can see, in this case, you had only two columns involved, but on UPDATE, just to be *very sure* that concurrency conflicts are taken care of, the autogenerated code takes the extra-safe approach of comparing *every column* during an update with the original values. Obviously, you can specify your own command text values in the properties of the TableAdapter. As a matter of fact, for complicated queries involving multiple tables, you'll have to specify these commands yourself.

The SqlCommandBuilder object uses the SelectCommand specified to retrieve the metadata from the database directly. If the SelectCommand changes, you should call the RefreshSchema method on the SqlCommandBuilder object to refresh the rest of the commands. The criteria for the command builder to work is that the SelectCommand specified must act against only one table, and at least the primary key or a unique column must be a part of the retrieved results. If these conditions are not met, you will get an InvalidOperationException. Obviously, there is no free trip in life, nor in ADO.NET, so generating these queries is going to require some extra work, typically an extra query on the database schema.

By default the CommandBuilder does not generate very efficient queries, but it takes a super safe approach by comparing all columns during an UPDATE, INSERT, or DELETE operation. This is probably the safest and most database-portable approach as it doesn't use any database-specific features (such as a timestamp in Microsoft SQL Server). At the same time, however, it's also probably the most inefficient approach simply because the WHERE clause is too complicated.

As it turns out, you can specify to the CommandBuilder object that you do not wish to use such a safe and inefficient approach using the ConflictOption property. This is a new feature in .NET 2.0. Let's see this using an example. The code for this example can be downloaded as a Console application in the associated code download under Exercise 9.2 or it may be created by following these steps:

1. Begin by creating a Console application. Name it Exercise 9.2. Also create a table called Animals2, with structure similar to the one used in Exercise 9.1, but with an additional Timestamp column. You can find the SQL script to create such a table in the associated code download under Exercise 9.2.

2. The purpose of this exercise is to experiment with the CommandBuilder object. There are two ways to instantiate a CommandBuilder object: the first is by using the default constructor followed by setting the DataAdapter as a property. The second is by specifying the DataAdapter as a parameter to the constructor. For this example, to save us some typing, let's go with the second approach as shown in the following code:

C#

```
SqlDataAdapter myDataAdapter =
    new SqlDataAdapter("Select * from Animals2", connectionString);
SqlCommandBuilder cmdBldr = new SqlCommandBuilder(myDataAdapter) ;
```

VB.NET

```
Dim myDataAdapter As SqlDataAdapter = _
    New SqlDataAdapter("Select * from Animals2", connectionString)
Dim cmdBldr As SqlCommandBuilder = New SqlCommandBuilder(myDataAdapter)
```

3. That's it. All you need to do now is check the various commands generated by the command builder. As an example, let's look at the update command, which can be seen in the following code:

C#

```
Console.WriteLine("Update Command = ");
Console.WriteLine(cmdBldr.GetUpdateCommand().CommandText);
```

VB.NET

```
Console.WriteLine("Update Command = ")
Console.WriteLine(cmdBldr.GetUpdateCommand().CommandText)
```

4. Compile and run the application. Note the command text generated by the GetUpdateCommand method. Your results should look similar to those shown here:

```
UPDATE [Animals2] SET [Animal2ID] = @p1, [AnimalName] = @p2
WHERE (([Animal2ID]= @p3) AND ([AnimalName] = @p4))
```

5. As you can see in parameters p3 and p4, the data adapter is supposed to substitute the original column values, thus the generated command checks for all columns during an update, just to be very sure there is no concurrency conflict. Now, go ahead and modify the code, and add an additional line to set a value for the command builder's ConflictOption property. Also set the ConflictOption's value from the default value of CompareAllSearchableValues to CompareRowVersion. The full code is now shown here:

C#

```
SqlDataAdapter myDataAdapter =
    new SqlDataAdapter("Select * from Animals2", connectionString);
SqlCommandBuilder cmdBldr = new SqlCommandBuilder(myDataAdapter) ;

cmdBldr.ConflictOption = ConflictOption.CompareRowVersion;
```

```
Console.WriteLine("Update Command = ");
Console.WriteLine(cmdBldr.GetUpdateCommand().CommandText);
```

VB.NET

```
Dim myDataAdapter As SqlDataAdapter = _
    New SqlDataAdapter("Select * from Animals2", connectionString)
Dim cmdBldr As SqlCommandBuilder = New SqlCommandBuilder(myDataAdapter)
```

cmdBldr.ConflictOption = ConflictOption.CompareRowVersion

```
Console.WriteLine("Update Command = ")
Console.WriteLine(cmdBldr.GetUpdateCommand().CommandText)
```

6. Compile and run the application, and examine the value of the update command's text once again. You should receive results as shown here:

```
UPDATE [Animals2] SET [Animal2ID] = @p1, [AnimalName] = @p2
WHERE (([Timestamp] = @p3))
```

Note that if you had not used a table with a Timestamp data type, you would have gotten an exception. The Timestamp data type column in SQL Server is a special column that changes its value every time the row's value changes; therefore, it's a great way to check for concurrency conflicts in an efficient manner.

7. Now change the ConflictOption to OverwriteChanges, and examine the generated update command's command text. It should look like as shown here:

```
UPDATE [Animals2] SET [Animal2ID] = @p1, [AnimalName] = @p2
WHERE (([Animal2ID] = @p3))
```

In this case, you're instructing the command builder to not worry about concurrency and overwrite the previous values; therefore, the statement checks only for the primary key in its WHERE clause.

8. Thus, you can see how to leverage the CommandBuilder object to generate queries for you, plus you get some extra flexibility by using the ConflictOption property that you do not get in a pure drag-and-drop operation. This reinforces the notion that your data layer is as efficient and clean as the amount of effort you are willing to put into it. The more-effort approach of getting down and dirty and writing all your SQL yourself might be the best choice in a high-demand enterprise application anyway. Needless to say, 500 monkeys dragging and dropping 2,000 tables in an enterprise application will not necessarily be a good solution.

Now for a moment look at Listings 9-13 and 9-14 again. Specifically, this part:

C#

```
this.Adapter.Update(dataSet, "Animals");
```

VB.NET

```
Me.Adapter.Update(dataSet, "Animals")
```

As you have already seen, in Chapter 7, the `DataAdapter` object acts as the gatekeeper between the connected world and the disconnected world. Also you saw in Chapter 6 how the `DataSet` and `DataTable` objects not only hold data for you in a disconnected cache, but also maintain some history of the changes being done to the data. It's that historical change information that lets the previous simple one-line statement decide what action needs to be taken on each row in each table of the `DataSet`.

State Management in a DataRow and Its Use in Updating Data

A `DataSet` allows you to store data fetched from an underlying data source or otherwise in a disconnected fashion. You have already been introduced to `DataSet`s and fetching data into a `DataSet`.

But fetching data from the data source and holding it in a disconnected fashion is only half the story. Your application will probably make numerous changes to the data while keeping it disconnected from the underlying data source and finally reconnect using a data adapter via the `Update` method call. Also, just by calling `Update` on the data adapter, the application will also expect the underlying data adapter to magically understand which rows need to be updated, inserted, or deleted and expect the changes be persisted properly.

In this scenario of connect, fetch, disconnect, modify, reconnect, and persist changes, a number of things might need to be taken care of:

- You might need to figure out what rows were inserted, deleted, or updated.

- Other users could have saved their changes in the meantime, and the queried data you hold in a disconnected cache might not be valid anymore.

- The key values generated by you for newly inserted records might not be correct.

- After you do manage to do an update properly, you would probably need to fetch a refresh of the current data back to the application.

As it turns out, the `DataSet`, `DataTable`, and other objects that compose the disconnected part of ADO.NET do support a number of features that allow you to address all these issues appropriately.

At the heart of it all is the `DataRow.RowState` property. The `DataRow.RowState` property is of type `DataRowState` enumeration. Table 9-1 shows you various values for the `DataRowState` enumeration.

Table 9-1. *The DataRowState Enumeration*

Constant	Value	Description
Detached	1	A `DataRow` can be connected to a maximum of one `DataTable` at any given time. If it is not connected to any `DataTable`, then the row's state is detached.
UnChanged	2	This row was fetched from the data source and no changes have been done to it.

Constant	Value	Description
Deleted	8	This row was fetched from the data source and then deleted from the DataTable. During an Update, the data adapter will execute a DeleteCommand on it.
Added	4	This row was not fetched from the data source, it was added in the DataTable. During an Update, the data adapter will execute an InsertCommand on it.
Modified	16	This row was fetched from the data source but has been modified since. During an Update, the data adapter will execute an UpdateCommand on it.

As you can see from Table 9-1, ADO.NET can identify what happened to each row by examining its RowState. Also, you can see from Table 9-1 how the data adapter's Update command is able to discern between *what it needs to do to a row* based upon the RowState property of the DataRow.

Let's examine this using an exercise that demonstrates all five row states. In this exercise, the database already contains some data as shown in Figure 9-10.

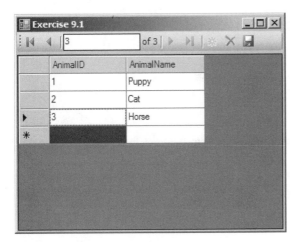

Figure 9-10. *Current data in the database*

This provides the application with enough use cases to simulate any of the row states in Table 9-1. In this exercise, the data shown in Figure 9-10 is fetched into a DataTable inside a Console application and various row states are examined. After that is done, the following changes will occur:

- The first row identifying a Puppy is changed to "Dog".

- The second row identifying a Cat is deleted.

- The third row identifying a Horse is left untouched.

- A fourth row is added that identifies a Camel.

- And a fifth row is created using the NewRow method, but it's not added to the DataTable.

Without much further delay, let's start writing an application that will perform these operations on various DataRows in a DataTable:

1. Begin by creating a new Console application. Name it Exercise 9.3.

2. Add a helper function to help you display the row states for the AnimalsTable. This can be seen in Listings 9-15 and 9-16.

Listing 9-15. *Displaying the Row States in C#*

```csharp
private static void DisplayRowStates(string Message, DataTable table)
{
    Console.Clear();
    Console.WriteLine("\n");
    Console.WriteLine(Message);
    Console.WriteLine("-------------------------------------------");

    foreach (DataRow dr in table.Rows)
    {
        Console.WriteLine(dr.RowState.ToString());
    }

    Console.WriteLine("\nPress Enter to Continue ..") ;
    Console.Read() ;
}
```

Listing 9-16. *Displaying the Row States in Visual Basic .NET*

```vbnet
Private Sub DisplayRowStates( _
  ByVal Message As String, ByVal table As DataTable)
    Console.Clear()
    Console.WriteLine(vbCrLf)
    Console.WriteLine(Message)
    Console.WriteLine("-------------------------------------------")

    Dim dr As DataRow
    For Each dr In table.Rows
        Console.WriteLine(dr.RowState.ToString())
    Next

    Console.WriteLine(vbCrLf + "Press Enter to Continue ..")
    Console.ReadLine()
End Sub
```

3. Write code to fill in a DataTable and display the row states. This has been covered in depth in Chapter 7. The code can be seen in Listings 9-17 and 9-18.

Listing 9-17. *Filling a DataTable and Displaying the Row States in C#*

```csharp
static void Main(string[] args)
{
    using (SqlConnection testConnection = new SqlConnection(connectionString))
    {
        SqlCommand testCommand = testConnection.CreateCommand();
        testCommand.CommandText = "Select * from Animals";
        SqlDataAdapter sqlDa = new SqlDataAdapter(testCommand);
        DataTable animalsTable = new DataTable("Animals");
        sqlDa.Fill(animalsTable);

        DisplayRowStates(
            "Row states for a freshly filled DataTable:",animalsTable);
    }
}
```

Listing 9-18. *Filling a DataTable and Displaying the Row States in Visual Basic .NET*

```vbnet
Sub Main()
    Using testConnection As SqlConnection = New SqlConnection(connectionString)
        Dim testCommand As SqlCommand = testConnection.CreateCommand()
        testCommand.CommandText = "Select * from Animals"
        Dim sqlDa As SqlDataAdapter = New SqlDataAdapter(testCommand)
        Dim animalsTable As DataTable = New DataTable("Animals")
        sqlDa.Fill(animalsTable)

        DisplayRowStates( _
            "Row states for a freshly filled DataTable:", animalsTable)
    End Using
End Sub
```

4. Compile and run the application. You should see output as shown in Figure 9-11.

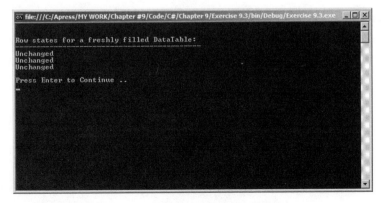

Figure 9-11. *Row states for a freshly filled DataTable*

Well, that makes sense. So far you haven't made any changes to the rows, so all the rows correctly report the row states as unchanged.

5. Next, do the following changes:

• The first row identifying a Puppy is changed to "Dog".

• The second row identifying a Cat is deleted.

• The third row identifying a Horse is left untouched.

• A fourth row is added that identifies a Camel.

These changes can be seen in Listings 9-19 and 9-20.

Listing 9-19. *Making Changes to the DataTable in C#*

```csharp
DataRow rowInQuestion;
// Make Changes - Modify the puppy
rowInQuestion = animalsTable.Rows[0];
rowInQuestion["AnimalName"] = "Dog";
// Make Changes - Delete the cat
rowInQuestion = animalsTable.Rows[1];
rowInQuestion.Delete();
// Leave the Horse untouched.
// Make Changes - Insert a camel
rowInQuestion = animalsTable.NewRow();
rowInQuestion["AnimalID"] = 4;
rowInQuestion["AnimalName"] = "Camel";
animalsTable.Rows.Add(rowInQuestion);

DisplayRowStates("Row states for a modified DataTable:", animalsTable);
```

Listing 9-20. *Making Changes to the DataTable in Visual Basic .NET*

```vbnet
Dim rowInQuestion As DataRow
' Make Changes - Modify the puppy
rowInQuestion = animalsTable.Rows(0)
rowInQuestion("AnimalName") = "Dog"
' Make Changes - Delete the cat
rowInQuestion = animalsTable.Rows(1)
rowInQuestion.Delete()
' Leave the Horse untouched.
' Make Changes - Insert a camel
rowInQuestion = animalsTable.NewRow()
rowInQuestion("AnimalID") = 4
rowInQuestion("AnimalName") = "Camel"
animalsTable.Rows.Add(rowInQuestion)

DisplayRowStates("Row states for a modified DataTable:", animalsTable)
```

6. Compile and run the application. You should see output that looks like Figure 9-12.

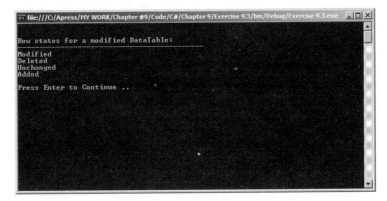

Figure 9-12. *Row states for a modified DataTable*

As you can see, the rows appear to have the correct row states clearly identifying which rows have been Modified, Deleted, and Added, and which ones that have been left Unchanged.

7. Now similar to the Camel row, create a new row, but don't add it to the animalsTable DataTable. Then check the row state of this new row:

C#

```
rowInQuestion = animalsTable.NewRow();
rowInQuestion["AnimalID"] = 5;
rowInQuestion["AnimalName"] = "Monkey";
```

VB.NET

```
rowInQuestion = animalsTable.NewRow()
rowInQuestion("AnimalID") = 5
rowInQuestion("AnimalName") = "Monkey"
```

When you compile and run the application, you can see the output the previous line produces as Monkey row's RowState: Detached. Thus, when a DataRow is not associated or a part of any DataRowCollection as a Rows property of a DataTable, its RowState is Detached. Indeed, if you were to iterate through the various rows in animalsTable after this code executes, you would note that the rowInQuestion with AnimalName = "Monkey" is not a part of the animalsTable.

8. Next comes being able to update these changes back into the database. When the code calls sqlDa.Update and passes the animalsTable as a parameter, the data adapter will iterate through each row and call the InsertCommand for DataRowState.Added, UpdateCommand for DataRowState.Modified, and DeleteCommand for DataRowState.Deleted. The detached rows are not a part of the DataTable so they will be ignored, and the modified rows don't need any action, so they will be ignored too.

For the rest of the rows, depending on the exact nature of the change, the RowState of the DataRow gets the appropriate value. Depending upon the RowState, the appropriate command as a property of the data adapter executes. The properties that hold the necessary commands are DeleteCommand, InsertCommand, and UpdateCommand.

But first you have to specify the DeleteCommand, UpdateCommand, and InsertCommand properties. Now you could specify any valid SQL command here, including stored procedures, but for the sake of simplicity, let's just go ahead and use the SqlCommandBuilder object covered in the previous section. The code can be seen in Listings 9-21 and 9-22.

Listing 9-21. *Setting Various Commands in C#*

```csharp
// Update the changes back to the database.
SqlCommandBuilder cmbldr = new SqlCommandBuilder(sqlDa);

// Setup Update Command
sqlDa.UpdateCommand = cmbldr.GetUpdateCommand();
Console.WriteLine("Update Command: " + sqlDa.UpdateCommand.CommandText);

// Setup Insert Command
sqlDa.InsertCommand = cmbldr.GetInsertCommand();
Console.WriteLine("Insert Command: " + sqlDa.InsertCommand.CommandText);

// Setup Delete Command
sqlDa.DeleteCommand = cmbldr.GetDeleteCommand() ;
Console.WriteLine("Delete Command: " + sqlDa.DeleteCommand.CommandText);

sqlDa.Update(animalsTable);
```

Listing 9-22. *Setting Various Commands in Visual Basic .NET*

```vbnet
' Update the changes back to the database.
Dim cmbldr As SqlCommandBuilder = New SqlCommandBuilder(sqlDa)

' Setup Update Command
sqlDa.UpdateCommand = cmbldr.GetUpdateCommand()
Console.WriteLine("Update Command: " + sqlDa.UpdateCommand.CommandText)

' Setup Insert Command
sqlDa.InsertCommand = cmbldr.GetInsertCommand()
Console.WriteLine("Insert Command: " + sqlDa.InsertCommand.CommandText)

' Setup Delete Command
sqlDa.DeleteCommand = cmbldr.GetDeleteCommand()
Console.WriteLine("Delete Command: " + sqlDa.DeleteCommand.CommandText)

sqlDa.Update(animalsTable)
```

9. Before you compile and run the application, set up a trace on the local SQL Server (or whatever database server you are running against). The purpose of the trace is to be able to capture all queries being sent to the database.

10. With the trace running, compile and run the application. The application will report that it has set the UpdateCommand to

```
UPDATE [Animals]
SET [AnimalID] = @p1, [AnimalName] = @p2
WHERE (([AnimalID] = @p3) AND ([AnimalName] = @p4))
```

the InsertCommand to

```
INSERT INTO [Animals] ([AnimalID], [AnimalName]) VALUES (@p1, @p2)
```

and the DeleteCommand to

```
DELETE FROM [Animals] WHERE (([AnimalID] = @p1) AND ([AnimalName] = @p2))
```

As per the Profiler/SQL trace results, the following SQL statements were executed:

```
UPDATE [Animals]
SET [AnimalName] = @p1
WHERE
(([AnimalID] = @p2) AND
([AnimalName] = @p3))',N'@p1 varchar(3),@p2 int,
@p3 varchar(5)',@p1='Dog',@p2=1,@p3='Puppy'
```

So, as per these SQL statements, the Dog row, whose DataRowState you changed to Modified, had the UpdateCommand run on it with the appropriate parameter values specified.

```
DELETE FROM [Animals]
WHERE
(([AnimalID] = @p1) AND
([AnimalName] = @p2))',N'@p1 int,@p2 varchar(3)',@p1=2,@p2='Cat'
```

As per these SQL statements, the Cat row was deleted from the database. For rows with DataRowState = Deleted, the command specified in the DeleteCommand property was executed.

```
INSERT INTO [Animals] ([AnimalID], [AnimalName])
VALUES (@p1, @p2)',N'@p1 int,@p2 varchar(5)',@p1=4,@p2='Camel'
```

And finally as per these SQL statements, the command specified in the InsertCommand gets executed for DataRowState = Added, in our case the Camel row.

11. Next, check the final row states of the updated DataTable using the following code snippet:

C#

```
DisplayRowStates("Final Row States:", animalsTable);
```

VB.NET

```
DisplayRowStates("Final Row States:", animalsTable)
```

The output should look like as shown in Figure 9-13.

Figure 9-13. *Final row states after a successful update*

Thus, you can see from Figure 9-13 that after a successful update, the data adapter not only acts upon the right rows with the right commands, but it also changes the row states to Unchanged.

12. There is one big drawback of this code. For three updates, you ended up making three database trips. There are multiple ways to get around this issue. One approach could be to use XML or a comma-delimited string passed directly into a stored procedure. But a rather easy quick-fix approach would be to use the UpdateBatchSize property on the SqlDataAdapter. Just before the Update statement, add the UpdateBatchSize as follows:

C#

```
sqlDa.UpdateBatchSize = 3;
```

VB.NET

```
sqlDa.UpdateBatchSize = 3
```

Now restore the Animals table in the database to the original three rows and rerun the application to view similar results. If you were, however, expecting to see one single batched SQL statement being sent to the database per the SQL Profiler trace, you might be in for a surprise. In fact, the SQL Profiler does not report any difference, but network roundtrips are still saved. Instead of implementing batched support in SQL, ADO.NET prefers to implement batching at the TDS (Tabular Data Stream) protocol level.

WHY IS BATCHING IMPLEMENTED IN TDS AND NOT IN SQL?

Batch updating works in a rather interesting fashion. Say your INSERT command's text looks like this:

```
INSERT INTO Customer (id, name) VALUES (@id, @name);
```

and the update command's text looks like this:

```
UPDATE Customer SET name = @name WHERE id=@id;
```

Now, the logical way to think is that maybe the DataAdapter, at least in the case of SqlClient, should just batch these two commands together as shown here:

```
INSERT INTO Customer (id, name) VALUES (@id, @name);
UPDATE Customer SET name = @name WHERE id=@id;
```

The problem is immediately apparent: the same parameter name is used multiple times. Now maybe the DataAdapter could parse through the query contents and rename the parameters, but not only is that a lot of work that requires a lot of code (which means it is prone to a lot of bugs), but also there is an upper limit of 2,100 parameters that a SqlCommand can have. Because individual commands may have a varying number of parameters, batching the commands is not the answer. Another significant disadvantage is that the query structure can change with the DataTable changes, which means that the query plans cache will not be used optimally in the database.

Instead, by setting a BatchSize on the SqlDataAdapter object, it uses a much simpler approach at the TDS protocol level. For batched statements, instead of executing one command and putting an end marker on the communication, ADO.NET simply puts another command start marker and executes another command. This way it saves on multiple roundtrips in a simple and elegant manner behind the scenes.

In order to see batching work, the only difference you'll notice as a programmer is a significant performance gain. If you wanted to delve behind the scenes, you would have to use a network sniffer such as Snort to examine the packets, as SQL Profiler will still show you individual commands being executed one by one.

Exercise 9.3 demonstrated editing a simple example of a handwritten piece of code (as opposed to one generated using drag and drop) that has the ability to perform various updates on a single table. As it turns out, when you have other real-world issues to take care of, such as multiple tables and concurrency issues, the situation gets a bit more *not so straightforward*. Those scenarios will be covered in the next chapter.

One big downside of using a DataAdapter is the fact that it treats every single row as an individual entity and insists on executing a SQL command for each row modification—add, modify, or delete. In .NET 1.1, this would have caused a network roundtrip for each changed row; however, .NET 2.0 provides you with an UpdateBatchSize property that alleviates the situation to some extent, but it is nowhere close to being suitable for data transfer operations between multiple databases.

Again, fortunately for this specific purpose, a new class has been introduced in .NET Framework called the SqlBulkCopy class.

Moving Large Amounts of Data: SqlBulkCopy

If you ask your local database administrator how he moves massive amounts of data between databases, the answer you'll get will probably be either by BCP (Bulk Copy) or DTS (Data Transformation Services). This is for a good reason. BCP and DTS both work much faster than a row by row SQL statement insert would be.

In .NET Framework 1.1, if you wanted to implement the functionality of copying over vast amounts of data between databases, the DataSet or data adapter would have been a very poor choice. This is because filling the DataSet, sending it across, changing all row states, iterating over each single row, and executing one SQL command per row would take so long that it would be simply impractical (though I have seen applications that try that anyway, and, of course, that is clearly bad architecture).

Even in .NET Framework 1.1, the better approach would be to export a DTS package as Visual Basic 6.0 code and convert it to .NET using some interop for the COM objects involved, or maybe even just save it as a DTS package in SQL Server and start it through SQL executed via ADO.NET. That approach would work screamingly faster than a DataSet/data adapter approach.

However, that is not a fully managed solution. Not only that, if your primary language of choice is C#, you would have to perform the additional step of converting from VB.NET to C#.

.NET 2.0, however, has introduced a new class specifically for this purpose: the SqlBulkCopy class. Put simply, SqlBulkCopy copies data from one table to another over two different open SqlConnections. The two different open SqlConnections can also point to the same database if that is what you prefer, or they may point to different databases. Let's review this concept using a code example.

You can download the code for this sample in the associated code download under the SqlBulkCopy example, or you may simply follow these steps:

1. Start by adding a new Console application, and name it SqlBulkCopy.

2. The purpose of this application is to demonstrate the rather fast copying of data between two tables of identical structure. So naturally the first step is to create two tables of identical structure. You can easily achieve this with the following SQL statement:

   ```
   Create Table AnimalsCopy as Select * from Animals where 1 = 2
   ```

3. Since the application works with the same database, you'll need only one connection string; however, you'll need two different SqlConnections: one for the data reader that the SqlBulkCopy will read from, and one for SqlBulkCopy itself. So let's start by creating the data reader that will read from the Animals table. This can be seen in the following code:

   C#

   ```csharp
   using (SqlConnection firstConnection = new SqlConnection(connectionString))
   {
       SqlCommand cmdAnimals = firstConnection.CreateCommand();
       cmdAnimals.CommandText = "Select * from Animals";
       firstConnection.Open();
       SqlDataReader dr = cmdAnimals.ExecuteReader();
       ...
   ```

```
    ...
} // Dispose is called on firstConnection
```

VB.NET

```
Using firstConnection As SqlConnection = New SqlConnection(connectionString)
   Dim cmdAnimals As SqlCommand = firstConnection.CreateCommand()
   cmdAnimals.CommandText = "Select * from Animals"
   firstConnection.Open()
   Dim dr As SqlDataReader = cmdAnimals.ExecuteReader()
   ...
   ...
End Using ' Dispose is called on firstConnection
```

4. The second part of the application uses the SqlBulkCopy object instance to insert data read from the created data reader into the AnimalsCopy table. This can be done easily using the bold sections of the following code:

C#

```
using (SqlConnection firstConnection = new SqlConnection(connectionString))
{
    SqlCommand cmdAnimals = firstConnection.CreateCommand();
    cmdAnimals.CommandText = "Select * from Animals";
    firstConnection.Open();
    SqlDataReader dr = cmdAnimals.ExecuteReader();

    using (SqlConnection secondConnection =
       new SqlConnection(connectionString))
    {
       SqlBulkCopy bc = new SqlBulkCopy(secondConnection);
       bc.DestinationTableName = "AnimalsCopy";
       bc.WriteToServer(dr);
       bc.Close();
       dr.Close();
    } // Dispose is called on firstConnection
}
```

VB.NET

```
Using firstConnection As SqlConnection = New SqlConnection(connectionString)
   Dim cmdAnimals As SqlCommand = firstConnection.CreateCommand()
   cmdAnimals.CommandText = "Select * from Animals"
   firstConnection.Open()
   Dim dr As SqlDataReader = cmdAnimals.ExecuteReader()
```

```
Using secondConnection As SqlConnection = _
   New SqlConnection(connectionString)
   Dim bc As SqlBulkCopy = _
      New SqlBulkCopy(secondConnection)
   bc.DestinationTableName = "AnimalsCopy"
   bc.WriteToServer(dr)
   bc.Close()
   dr.Close()
End Using ' Dispose is called on secondConnection
End Using ' Dispose is called on firstConnection
```

5. That's it. Compile and run the application to copy rows from one table to another in a screamingly fast manner. As an exercise, connect to a larger table and write up an equivalent application leveraging DataSets and data adapters, and notice the time it takes in comparison with SqlBulkCopy. You'll see that SqlBulkCopy is hundreds to thousands of times faster.

So far you have seen the ability to persist the changes back into the database once you have made changes to the disconnected data cache. An important facet Exercise 9.3 touched upon was the ability to edit and update a disconnected data cache, such as a DataTable. In Exercise 9.3, you saw examples of adding, modifying, and deleting existing data in a DataTable. Before going any further, let's strengthen our foundation by discussing the various methods available to you, as an application developer, to edit data in a disconnected form.

Editing Disconnected Data

The various objects in ADO.NET that compose the disconnected part of ADO.NET offer the ability to make edits or modifications to themselves, while remembering to some extent the various edits done on themselves. As on a database, there are mainly three kinds of modification operations you could perform on disconnected data:

- Add new rows

- Modify existing rows

- Delete existing rows

As it turns out, ADO.NET gives you more than one option and more than one object to achieve this goal.

Add New Rows

There are two ways to add a *new* row to a DataTable, and two ways to add *existing* rows (from other DataTables or Detached rows) to a DataTable.

Let's look at adding new rows first. The first way assumes that you have a schema or at least a structure preloaded to the DataTable. This is usually a shortcut way to generate a new row with all the relevant columns and their various properties set. This can be seen in the code here:

C#

```
rowInQuestion = animalsTable.NewRow();
rowInQuestion["AnimalID"] = 4;
rowInQuestion["AnimalName"] = "Camel";
animalsTable.Rows.Add(rowInQuestion);
```

VB.NET

```
rowInQuestion = animalsTable.NewRow()
rowInQuestion("AnimalID") = 4
rowInQuestion("AnimalName") = "Camel"
animalsTable.Rows.Add(rowInQuestion)
```

If, instead, you're working with a DataView object attached to a DataTable, you can use the AddNew method on DataView to achieve the same results.

The second method to add a new DataRow into a DataTable is to use the LoadDataRow method. This method allows you to add a new DataRow and set its various values in one convenient method call. This is shown here:

C#

```
object[] rowVals = {"4", "Camel"} ;
animalsTable.LoadDataRow(rowVals, false);
```

VB.NET

```
Dim rowVals() As Object = {"4", "Camel"}
animalsTable.LoadDataRow(rowVals, False)
```

An interesting difference between these two methods is that the first method will add the new row and set its RowState property to DataRowState.Added. You can, at this point, call AcceptChanges to change the row state to DataRowState.Unmodified for all such rows in the DataTable or DataSet. The second method, however, allows you to pass in a second parameter, which if set to true, will not only add the row, but also set its RowState to DataRowState.Unmodified.

In addition, two methods exist for adding existing DataRows to a DataTable. The first is the ImportRow method, which simply takes a DataRow as a parameter, and the second is the Merge method, which merges two sets of disconnected data (DataSet, DataTable, DataRow array, etc.). The Merge method will be covered in detail later in this chapter.

Modify Existing Rows

Modifying existing rows is easy. You just find the right row and the right column and assign it a value. This is shown in the code snippet here:

C#

```
rowInQuestion = animalsTable.Rows[0];
rowInQuestion["AnimalName"] = "Dog";
```

VB.NET

```
rowInQuestion = animalsTable.Rows(0)
rowInQuestion("AnimalName") = "Dog"
```

The DataRowState at the end of this edit would be Modified. By now you might already know this, but I must reiterate, modifying a row as shown in an in-memory disconnected cache *does not mean that the underlying database got modified too.* The database does not get modified unless you successfully call an Update on the relevant data adapter.

There is another way of modifying rows. The DataRow object has a method called BeginEdit, and a matching method called EndEdit. You can modify the rows between these two method calls. The difference here is that all the changes are buffered until you call EndEdit. If, in case you change your mind, you call CancelEdit instead, all the changes are rolled back. This can be seen in the following code snippet:

C#

```
rowInQuestion = animalsTable.Rows[0];
rowInQuestion.BeginEdit();
rowInQuestion["AnimalName"] = "Dog";
rowInQuestion.EndEdit() ; // This could have been rowInQuestion.CancelEdit() also
```

VB.NET

```
rowInQuestion = animalsTable.Rows(0)
rowInQuestion.BeginEdit()
rowInQuestion("AnimalName") = "Dog"
rowInQuestion.EndEdit()'This could have been rowInQuestion.CancelEdit() also
```

Finally, there is yet another way of modifying rows. You can modify a row by simply loading an object array into the ItemArray property of a DataRow as shown here:

C#

```
rowInQuestion = animalsTable.Rows[0];
rowInQuestion.ItemArray = new object[] {null, "Dog"} ;
```

VB.NET

```
rowInQuestion = animalsTable.Rows(0)
rowInQuestion.ItemArray = New Object() {Nothing, "Dog"}
```

When using the ItemArray property, by specifying certain columns as null or Nothing, those values are not changed.

If, instead, you are working with a DataView object, you can identify the individual DataRowView object you are interested in, and then use the BeginEdit/EndEdit methods just as you would on a DataRow. In addition, you could access the DataRow directly using the Row property on the DataRowView object. This makes sense since a DataRowView object is working with the relevant DataRow object behind the scenes.

There are, however, two interesting properties on the DataRowView object: the IsEdit and IsNew properties. These two properties can be used to identify if a row is being edited, and if the row being edited is new or not.

Delete Existing Rows

Deleting a row is really straightforward. You just call the DELETE method on it as shown here:

C#

```
rowInQuestion = animalsTable.Rows[1];
rowInQuestion.Delete();
```

VB.NET

```
rowInQuestion = animalsTable.Rows(1)
rowInQuestion.Delete()
```

This statement will mark the row's RowState as Deleted; however, the row still remains in the DataTable until you do an Update using a DataAdapter or an AcceptChanges on the DataTable. Thus, this approach is useful when sending information about deleted rows to the database via the data adapter. If the rows were *actually* removed from the DataTable, the data adapter would have no clue which rows to execute delete queries upon.

Another way of removing a row is by using either the Remove or RemoveAt method on the DataRowCollection object (DataTable.Rows is of DataRowCollection type). This is shown here:

C#

```
animalsTable.Remove(rowInQuestion) ;
// or
animalsTable.RemoveAt(1) ;
```

VB.NET

```
animalsTable.Remove(rowInQuestion)
' or
animalsTable.RemoveAt(1)
```

Or you can use the nuclear option and call DataRowCollection.Clear() to completely remove all rows from the DataTable's Rows collection.

However, the Remove, RemoveAt, and Clear methods are not available on a DataView. If you are using a DataView, you'd need to either access the underlying table using the DataView.Table property, or you could call DataRowView.Delete to mark a row as deleted (but not actually removed) from the DataTable.

Once again, in any of these three cases (Add, Modify, Delete), it's critical to understand that *only the disconnected cache of data is edited.* With any of these statements, *the underlying database is not modified.* As a matter of fact, the underlying database remains untouched until you call a relevant data adapter's Update command with the appropriate command objects set.

So while the changes are being made, you can still look at the history of the DataRow to some extent. This is done using the following code:

C#

```
rowInQuestion = animalsTable.Rows[0];
rowInQuestion.BeginEdit();
rowInQuestion["AnimalName"] = "Dog";
Console.Write(rowInQuestion["AnimalName", DataRowVersion.Proposed]);
rowInQuestion.EndEdit() ;

Console.Write(rowInQuestion["AnimalName", DataRowVersion.Original]);
Console.Write(rowInQuestion["AnimalName", DataRowVersion.Current]);
```

VB.NET

```
rowInQuestion = animalsTable.Rows(0)
rowInQuestion.BeginEdit()
rowInQuestion("AnimalName") = "Dog"
Console.Write(rowInQuestion("AnimalName", DataRowVersion.Proposed))
rowInQuestion.EndEdit()

Console.Write(rowInQuestion("AnimalName", DataRowVersion.Original))
Console.Write(rowInQuestion("AnimalName", DataRowVersion.Current))
```

Thus, you can specify a DataRowVersion along with the column name and get various versions of the DataRow by specifying what version you want. Table 9-2 lists various values you can use for DataRowVersion.

Table 9-2. *The DataRowVersion Enumeration*

Constant	Description
Current	This constant will give you the current value stored inside a column.
Original	This constant allows you to fetch the original value stored inside a column.
Proposed	This constant allows you to fetch the proposed value after a BeginEdit and update, but before an EndEdit.
Default	This constant retrieves the value as if the constant wasn't specified.

You can write up a few quick samples to verify the various cases and permutations of the various DataRow versions under different editing scenarios, and understand the exact behavior of each. It's important to realize that not all of these constants apply to every editing situation. If you request for a DataRow version that doesn't exist, you will get an exception.

A Real-World Example

In the previous example, you saw how an application can edit a DataTable or DataSet while remaining disconnected from the data source; however, imagine that you have more than one user concurrently working with the database. This presents some interesting new situations to take care of.

For instance, imagine the following scenarios . . .

Erick wishes to add a new row to the database. He queries the database and gets the rows shown in Table 9-3.

Table 9-3. *Erick's View of animalsTable*

AnimalID	AnimalName
1	Puppy
2	Cat
3	Horse

Now after Erick has added in his rows, Frans wants to add yet another row. He comes by, queries the database, and gets the same rows as shown in Table 9-3.

While Frans is still working on the database, Erick makes an update and inserts his row. So the content of the database looks like Table 9-4.

Table 9-4. *Contents of the Database After Erick Calls DataAdapter.Update*

AnimalID	AnimalName
1	Puppy
2	Cat
3	Horse
4	Emu

Meanwhile, Frans is completely disconnected from the data source. He adds a fourth row in his disconnected cache of data and, not knowing any better, his new row looks like this:

4   Camel

Now, when Frans reconnects to the data source, he will get an exception because the primary key 4 has already been used by Erick.

You saw an instance similar to this in Exercise 9.1, but what Exercise 9.1 didn't let you do was recover from that gracefully.

Wouldn't it be nice if Frans was at least told that the latest data in the database has a primary key value of 4, not 3, so Frans should add his row with a value of 5? Wouldn't it be even nicer if this decision of automatically getting the next primary key value is done automatically for Frans, and he is simply informed of the newly generated primary key?

This would certainly be possible, but one premise behind this approach is that the primary key generated for Frans while he was disconnected was simply a dummy. Only after he makes an update is the new primary key value generated from the database and returned to him.

There's one requirement for this approach to work: you shouldn't use columns that mean something in business logic as primary keys; for instance, each of the animals had unique account numbers that never repeated and two new animals come along to be entered into the system—the Camel and the Emu.

While from a database sanctity point-of-view using the account number as a primary key would certainly work, the challenge that this presents is that the account number would be generated while two users are disconnected from the central database, and thus might be inaccurate. So the Camel and Emu might get overlapping account numbers or would simply not be able to store the data correctly.

Think about it: You certainly don't want to show an inaccurate account number on the user interface and then try to explain to a non-techie user the complications of disconnected data and why he or she shouldn't read out the data to the customer until he or she has clicked Save, thus calling Update on the underlying data adapter (or equivalent). So just don't use a primary key that has a meaning in your business logic. Columns that have a meaning in your business logic should be shown a clear dummy or null value, which is populated only by the central entity in control that can act as a policeman—your database. This way, you can keep the primary key behind the scenes on the UI and the dummy account number shown as something obvious like "Dummy Account Number #1" or simply "–1". It's much easier to tell the user that negative account numbers are invalid—don't use them.

■**Tip** It's recommended that you not use primary keys that have a meaning in your business logic. Such database design generally gives you more flexibility in disconnected scenarios.

So, given that you are disconnected, a better way to solve this situation would be to generate a dummy AnimalID and allow the database to generate a social security number or account number during the update. And after an update, the DataTable could be *refreshed* with the latest data in the database to inform the end user of the newly generated values.

Let's cover all of these instances using an example.

■**Note** It's critical that you understand this example thoroughly. The concepts presented in this example and this chapter in general are all centered around a single DataTable—which is a simplistic view of a real-world application. In the next chapter, there is a deeper discussion on concurrency in light of hierarchical multitable scenarios, and that is where you will build upon these concepts. Also note that the next example illustrates a Seed Generator table, mentions SQLCLR, uses @@IDENTITY, and SCOPE_IDENTITY(). The intention here is to show every possibility and discuss each approach's pros and cons. So get a coffee and make sure your eyes and mind aren't tired before you continue from here.

First, the underlying table needs a modification. The full SQL script for this example can be found in the associated code download under the SQL folder in a file called Exercise 9.4.sql.

The SQL script re-creates the Animals table, this time with a new column called AccountNumber of data type int. This is a not null column that will hold unique values for AccountNumbers. To enforce this, as you can see in Exercise 9.4, there is a Unique constraint specified on it. It then inserts three rows to get us started. The data should look like as shown in Figure 9-14. The script also creates the relevant stored procedures and calls the necessary SQL statements to get you started.

	AnimalID	AnimalName	accountnumber
1	1	Puppy	1
2	2	Cat	2
3	3	Horse	3

Figure 9-14. *Original data in the DataTable*

This exercise uses stored procedures. There are numerous advantages and disadvantages of using inline SQL over stored procedures. For the purpose of this book, it's sufficient to say that this exercise could be done using either inline SQL or stored procedures.

So let's get started with the exercise:

1. This application will be done in a Windows Forms application since it's easier to see the contents of an entire DataTable in it. Start by creating a Windows Forms application, call it Exercise 9.4, and change its main form's text to Exercise 9.4.

2. Start by dragging a DataGridView control on the form (call it dgView). Add two buttons (call them btnLoad and btnSave) and change their text properties to Load and Save, respectively. As the name suggests, Load will load the animalsTable and Save will save it back to the database. Your form should look like as shown in Figure 9-15 in Design view.

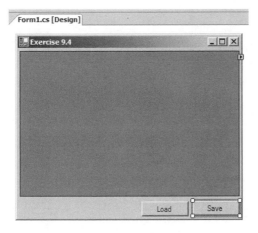

Figure 9-15. *The main form of the application in Design view*

3. Now with the form set up, let me present the logic for you before I delve too deeply into the actual code. The basic idea here is to generate dummy IDs for the AnimalID column when disconnected from the database. The real IDs will be generated in the database because the AnimalID column is an Identity column. Second, the AccountNumber column is not intended to be entered by the user, so the code can simply mark it as read only. The AccountNumber column is the column that I mentioned before—it's a column that has meaning in your business logic, therefore not a good candidate for a primary key in disconnected scenarios. Thus, the first thing you need to do is set up the animalsTable DataTable structure in Form1's constructor. This is shown in Listings 9-23 and 9-24. While you are setting up the DataTable's schema, also go ahead and data bind the animalsTable to dgView.

Listing 9-23. *Setting Up the Empty Table's Schema in C#*

```csharp
public Form1()
{
    InitializeComponent();

    // Setup the schema for the Table.
    animalsTable = new DataTable("Animals");
    DataColumn dc = null;

    dc = new DataColumn("AnimalID");
    dc.Unique = true;
    dc.AutoIncrement = true;
    dc.AutoIncrementSeed = -1;
    dc.AutoIncrementStep = -1;
    dc.DataType = typeof(System.Int32);
    animalsTable.Columns.Add(dc);

    dc = new DataColumn("AnimalName");
    animalsTable.Columns.Add(dc);

    dc = new DataColumn("AccountNumber");
    dc.ReadOnly = true;
    animalsTable.Columns.Add(dc);

    // DataBind it, even though it has no rows in it yet.
    dgView.DataSource = animalsTable;
}
```

Listing 9-24. *Setting Up the Empty Table's Schema in Visual Basic .NET*

```vbnet
Private Sub Form1_Load( _
  ByVal sender As System.Object, ByVal e As System.EventArgs) _
  Handles MyBase.Load
    ' Setup the schema for the Table.
    animalsTable = New DataTable("Animals")
```

```
        Dim dc As DataColumn

        dc = New DataColumn("AnimalID")
        dc.Unique = True
        dc.AutoIncrement = True
        dc.AutoIncrementSeed = -1
        dc.AutoIncrementStep = -1
        dc.DataType = Type.GetType("System.Int32")
        animalsTable.Columns.Add(dc)

        dc = New DataColumn("AnimalName")
        animalsTable.Columns.Add(dc)

        dc = New DataColumn("AccountNumber")
        dc.ReadOnly = True
        animalsTable.Columns.Add(dc)

        ' DataBind it, even though it has no rows in it yet.
        dgView.DataSource = animalsTable
    End Sub
```

In this bold code, it makes sense to set the `AccountNumber` to read only because clearly that will be generated in the database and repopulated in the `DataTable` during an `Update` operation as you'll see shortly. But why in the world would I set up the `AutoIncrement = True`, `AutoIncrementSeed = -1`, and `AutoIncrementStep = -1` for the `AnimalID` column? Well, this is because in the database that column is set up as an identity. So the database has the responsibility of generating them—*not* your disconnected application. I, as a disconnected user, cannot accurately determine the next identity because you, as another disconnected user, could have used up the next identity value that was sequentially next in my `DataTable`.

If this appears confusing, write two numbers (1 and 2) on two sheets of paper. Give each to two of your friends and ask them to write the next number in sequence. Both of them will say it is 3; but you need to maintain one set of numbers, so whose 3 do you accept? What if the first friend wanted to add two numbers in sequence? What if you didn't know how many numbers either friend will add in advance? So how about this, just ask your friends to tell you *how many rows* they intend to add and you, as the central policeman, tell them the accurate IDs generated. Whoever comes in first gets the next IDs, and you simply tell them *after the update* what IDs were generated for them.

So let's get rid of the confusion and set up our `DataTable` in such a way that *unsaved key values appear as negative, and they are generated in a sequence of –1, –2, –3, and so on.* This way, because each row is inserted one by one (`InsertCommand` on data adapter), your stored procedure can send back the autogenerated key and the data adapter can put it back in the `DataRow` for you.

4. Now with the empty `DataTable` set up and databound to the `DataGridView` control, you can go ahead and write the code to load the `DataTable` in the event handler for btnLoad's click event. This is shown here:

C#

```csharp
private void btnLoad_Click(object sender, EventArgs e)
{
    SqlDataAdapter sqlDA =
        new SqlDataAdapter("Select * from Animals", connectionString);
    animalsTable.Rows.Clear();
    sqlDA.Fill(animalsTable);
}
```

VB.NET

```vbnet
Private Sub btnLoad_Click( _
  ByVal sender As System.Object, _
  ByVal e As System.EventArgs) Handles btnLoad.Click
    Dim sqlDA As SqlDataAdapter = _
      New SqlDataAdapter("Select * from Animals", connectionString)
    animalsTable.Rows.Clear()
    sqlDA.Fill(animalsTable)
End Sub
```

5. With the DataTable loaded, if you run the application and click Load, you should see the data loaded in the DataGridView. If you now try and add a new row, you'll see a negative ID generated in the DataTable as shown in Figure 9-16.

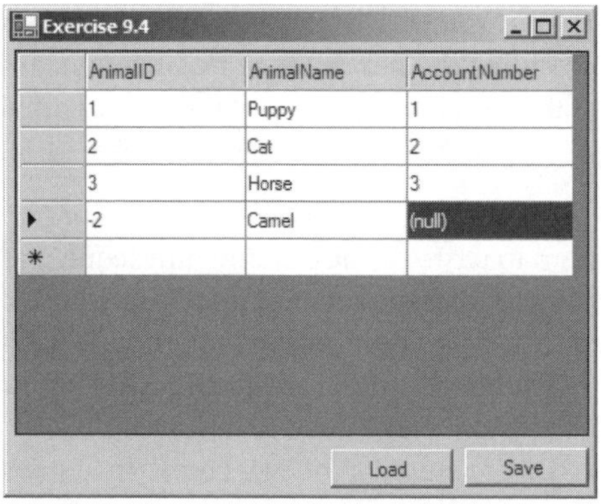

Figure 9-16. *Adding a new row*

6. Since you haven't written any implementation for btnSave yet, exit the application.

7. Now that you have tested the loading portion, you can begin writing the code for inserting the data, that is, saving the added DataRows to the data source. As you saw in the previous example, the InsertCommand is what will get called for a newly inserted row because its DataRowState is Added. So you need to write the implementation of the

InsertCommand. This is done in the implementation of btnSave. In addition, btnSave also calls Update on the relevant SqlDataAdapter it creates. The btnSave's click event handler's implementation in code looks like Listings 9-25 and 9-26.

Listing 9-25. *Setting Up the InsertCommand and Saving in C#*

```csharp
private void btnSave_Click(object sender, EventArgs e)
{
    SqlCommand insertCommand = new SqlCommand();
    insertCommand.CommandType = CommandType.StoredProcedure;

    SqlParameter param = null;

    param = new SqlParameter("@AnimalID", SqlDbType.Int);
    param.Direction = ParameterDirection.Output;
    param.SourceColumn = "AnimalID";
    insertCommand.Parameters.Add(param);

    param = new SqlParameter("@AnimalName", SqlDbType.VarChar);
    param.SourceColumn = "AnimalName";
    insertCommand.Parameters.Add(param);

    param = new SqlParameter("@AccountNumber", SqlDbType.Int);
    param.SourceColumn = "AccountNumber";
    param.Size = 40;
    param.Direction = ParameterDirection.Output;
    insertCommand.Parameters.Add(param);

    insertCommand.CommandText = "UP_ANIMALINSERT";
    SqlDataAdapter sqlDA = new SqlDataAdapter(
        "Select * from Animals", connectionString);
    insertCommand.Connection = new SqlConnection(connectionString);
    insertCommand.UpdatedRowSource = UpdateRowSource.Both;
    sqlDA.InsertCommand = insertCommand;

    sqlDA.Update(animalsTable);
}
```

Listing 9-26. *Setting Up the InsertCommand and Saving in Visual Basic .NET*

```vbnet
Private Sub btnSave_Click( _
  ByVal sender As System.Object, ByVal e As System.EventArgs) _
  Handles btnSave.Click
    Dim insertCommand As SqlCommand = New SqlCommand()
    insertCommand.CommandType = CommandType.StoredProcedure

    Dim param As SqlParameter
```

```
        param = New SqlParameter("@AnimalID", SqlDbType.Int)
        param.Direction = ParameterDirection.Output
        param.SourceColumn = "AnimalID"
        insertCommand.Parameters.Add(param)


        param = New SqlParameter("@AnimalName", SqlDbType.VarChar)
        param.SourceColumn = "AnimalName"
        insertCommand.Parameters.Add(param)


        param = New SqlParameter("@AccountNumber", SqlDbType.Int)
        param.SourceColumn = "AccountNumber"
        param.Size = 40
        param.Direction = ParameterDirection.Output
        insertCommand.Parameters.Add(param)


        insertCommand.CommandText = "UP_ANIMALINSERT"
        Dim sqlDA As SqlDataAdapter = _
         New SqlDataAdapter("Select * from Animals", connectionString)
        insertCommand.Connection = New SqlConnection(connectionString)
        insertCommand.UpdatedRowSource = UpdateRowSource.Both
        sqlDA.InsertCommand = insertCommand

        sqlDA.Update(animalsTable)
End Sub
```

Since the application has been written to demonstrate only adding a row, only an InsertCommand has been specified. If you wanted to, you could have easily specified a DeleteCommand and an UpdateCommand as well; however, whatever this application achieves using a stored procedure can be easily done using inline SQL instead.

One important thing to note is that three parameters have been added that match the parameter names for the UP_ANIMALINSERT stored procedure parameters. It's also important to specify the parameter sizes and the SourceColumn from the relevant DataTable or DataSet in order to guide the data adapter to use the correct values from the correct columns when it calls the command.

Finally, you'll notice that two of the parameters, the primary key AnimalID and the AccountNumber, are actually output parameters. Their values are generated in the database and are passed back to the application. So this is in line with what has been discussed so far, these keys are generated by the central policeman—the database. The application simply listens to the database (out parameters) and, with the help of the data adapter, overwrites its "fake" values with the "real" values supplied by the database.

Next, let's see what the stored procedure does.

The stored procedure implementation does mainly three things. First, it calculates an AccountNumber, which for our purposes is simply a number that increases sequentially (much like an Oracle sequence emulated in SQL Server).

The second thing it does is insert the new row.

And the third thing it does is extract the newly entered row's primary key value using the @@IDENTITY[1] SQL Server keyword.

The stored procedure code can be seen in Listing 9-27

Listing 9-27. *UP_ANIMALINSERT Stored Procedure Used to Insert a New Row and Send Back Autogenerated Values*

```
CREATE PROCEDURE UP_ANIMALINSERT
   @AnimalID INT OUTPUT,
   @AnimalName VARCHAR,
   @AccountNumber INT OUTPUT
AS
   BEGIN TRANSACTION
      INSERT INTO SEEDGENERATOR DEFAULT VALUES
      SET @AccountNumber = SCOPE_IDENTITY()
   ROLLBACK TRANSACTION

   INSERT INTO ANIMALS (ANIMALNAME, ACCOUNTNUMBER) VALUES (@AnimalName,
      @AccountNumber)

   SELECT @AnimalID = @@IDENTITY
GO
```

It's interesting to note how the sequential account number is created is using an emulation of sequences in SQL Server, which is simply a table that looks like this:

```
CREATE TABLE [SeedGenerator]
   ( [SeedGenerator] [bigint] IDENTITY(1,1) NOT NULL )
ON [PRIMARY]
```

■**Note** This technique works, and my intention here was to demonstrate an alternative to using Globally Unique Identifiers (GUIDs) if you wanted to establish unique values that may not necessarily be tied together in one table. In this example, however, you could have easily used identity instead because AccountNumbers needed to be unique within one table. But what if you wanted unique IDs generated to be unique between various tables? Yes, you could use GUIDs, but GUIDs occupy more space and they suffer from performance issues. So you can use the previous script to generate number (int, bigint) unique values. However, a quick word of caution is also in order here. The previous code will have problems in transactional scenarios because to SQL Server the seed generation will appear as a nested transaction (Chapter 11 talks about transactions in depth). An alternative in that scenario is to use SQLCLR to generate throw-away seed values.

---

1. A little knowledge is a dangerous thing, so I must mention there is a big difference between SCOPE_IDENTITY() and @@IDENTITY. More on that in a couple of pages, for now let's stay with the flow of this exercise.

Now if you begin a transaction, insert, and then roll back while getting the latest generated seed using SCOPE_IDENTITY(), this effectively works as a nonblocking sequence number generated in SQL Server.

Tip This trick of generating sequences using a rolled back transaction and SCOPE_IDENTITY can be used to generate seeds akin to sequences in Oracle. Oracle sequences have an additional buffering mechanism: they buffer the next 20 sequences for performance reasons, so it isn't quite *exactly* the same because these numbers will be a strict sequence, but its close enough for most applications. Also, you can easily retrieve the current value using CurVal on a sequence after it has been generated.

---

8. Finally, compile and run the application. When you click Load and add a row, you should see output similar to Figure 9-16. Now after adding the row, go ahead and click Save. You should see an output similar to Figure 9-17.

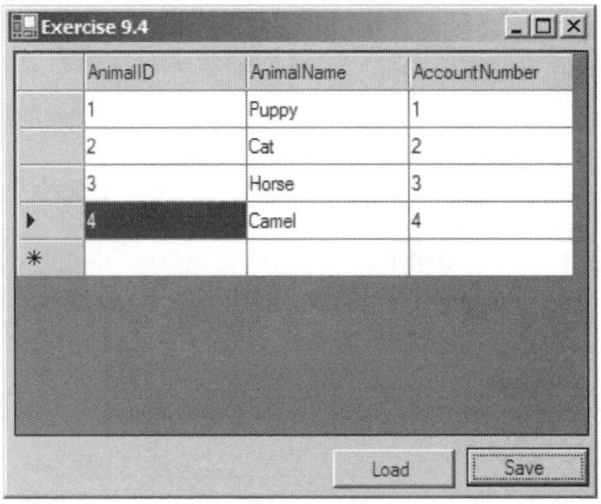

Figure 9-17. *New row added and latest keys fetched from the database*

In Exercise 9.4, if you examine SQL Profiler, the query that was sent to the database looked somewhat like this:

```
UP_ANIMALINSERT @AnimalID=@p1 output,@AnimalName='Camel',@AccountNumber=@p3 output
```

Thus, as you can see, the newly generated IDs were fetched from the central database. Now if Frans and Erick try to execute the same application at the same time, they won't run into primary-key and unique-constraint errors. This is because the true unique IDs are being generated by the entity that is central and know-all in your architecture—the database. Their respective Windows Forms applications generate fake keys or no keys, and simply overwrite their in-memory values when they get reliable values from the central policeman—the database.

There is, however, more than one way to achieve these results. An obvious second option is to use inline SQL instead of stored procedures to do the job, but that is not what I'm talking about.

Another way of doing it is using the DataAdapter.RowUpdated event. The RowUpdated event is called every time the DataAdapter updates a new row in the database. This event call occurs after the row has been updated. There's an equivalent event called RowUpdating, which is called before the row has been updated.

The RowUpdated event gets a SqlRowUpdatedEventArgs passed into it (in the case of OleDb or Oracle data providers, it is OleDbRowUpdatedEventArgs or OracleRowUpdatedEventArgs, respectively). Using the RowUpdatedEventArgs (the base class for SQL/Oracle/OleDbRowUpdatedEventArgs), you can easily identify the row that was updated last and execute an ExecuteNonQuery method to retrieve the key values.

As you might have guessed, due to the second database hit and event call, this method is significantly slower than the stored procedure or batched SQL methods. However, say if you were working with an Access database using the OleDb .NET data provider, you don't quite have the ability to create stored procedures with output parameters.

In that case, you would have to use the RowUpdated event on OleDbDataAdapter and use the OleDbUpdatedEventArgs.Row property to identify the row and act accordingly. You can also find the exact nature of the statement executed using OleDbUpdatedEventArgs.StatementType to differentiate between INSERTs, UPDATEs or DELETEs.

Now, again in Exercise 9.4, you might have noticed that at one point the code uses @@IDENTITY and at another point it uses SCOPE_IDENTITY(). Why is that?

As a footnote, I mentioned that there is a big difference between the two. The difference is more in the realm of SQL Server rather than ADO.NET, but since it might be used regularly in ADO.NET, I will mention the two briefly.

@@IDENTITY returns the last identity value generated on your connection. In other words, if your insert caused a trigger to fire that did *another* insert (say in an audit table), you'd end up getting the identity value of the audit table, not the table you did an insert in. That is obviously incorrect for our purposes. Thus, SCOPE_IDENTITY(), which is supported by SQL Server 2000 onward, should be used (which returns the last ID generated on the particular scope). Scope can be a stored procedure, trigger, function, or batch.

The *only case* where you still might have to use @@IDENTITY instead of SCOPE_IDENTITY() is where your scope is a batch or stored procedure, and you wish to retrieve the last generated value *after* the stored procedure or batch is done executing. In such a case, SCOPE_IDENTITY() will return a null.

Writing This Application in Oracle

Exercise 9.4 has been demonstrated using SQL Server 2005. It's notable, however, that the same ADO.NET concepts apply to any other database. The idea is to get the key values back and emulate the same behavior using database-specific features.

One key difference with Access was mentioned in which you would have to use the RowUpdated event to fill in key values. Similarly in Oracle, there are a few differences. You don't quite have to resort to the RowUpdated event for OracleDataAdapter, but since you don't have identity type columns in Oracle, you would need to use an Oracle-specific feature called sequences to generate and query identity values. An Oracle *sequence* is simply a database object that gives you a convenient way to generate sequential numbers for use in situations such as primary keys to a table. They aren't always strictly sequential, but they are unique (unless you reset a sequence).

A sequence can be created using the following PL/SQL statement:

```
Create Sequence seq_animals start with 1 increment by 1
```

This sequence could be used to generate primary key values for the Animals table. Now if the account numbers need to be strictly sequential (i.e., with no gaps), you would need to disable the cache for a sequence using a statement that looks like this:

```
Create Sequence seq_accountnumber start with 1 increment by 1 nocache.
```

The default value of cache is 20. Thus, if the system is shut down, or for any reason the sequence is not queried for a while, up to the next 20 sequences will be lost.

To generate the next key, you can simply use a SQL statement like this:

```
Select seq_animals.nextval from dual ;
```

And to select the last generated value on a sequence you can use a SQL statement that looks like this:

```
Select seq_animals.curval from dual;
```

That's it. The rest of the concepts (with the exception of using PL/SQL to write your stored procedures instead of T-SQL in Oracle) are the same between SQL Server and Oracle.

■Note This application could have been made a lot less complicated by simply using GUIDs as primary keys. Again, it depends on your exact situation, and GUIDs just might be a better solution for your purposes. It's important to note, however, that GUIDs occupy a lot of space in indexes and the key itself. They cannot be as efficient as an int data type can be. An int occupies 4 bytes, whereas a GUID occupies 16. For a single database scenario, you should use int or long data types as primary keys if performance is a key criterion; however, for applications involving multiple databases, where the generated keys should be mutually unique, or where simplicity is the guiding factor and not performance, the GUID might present an easy implementation.

There is yet another way to make this application better. Imagine a situation where the end users were actually modifying data while connecting to a server over a low bandwidth connection. Or maybe they, in fact, call a web service to persist their changes.

Now, if the DataTable had hundreds of rows and at any given point either user modifies only a few of those rows, it seems to be a terrible waste of bandwidth to actually send the full DataSet or DataTable over. It would be nice if the rows that the DataAdapter will simply ignore (i.e., the rows with DataRowStates = Unchanged) could be simply filtered out.

Both the DataSet and the DataTable provide a method for this very purpose: the GetChanges method. Another method that goes hand in hand with GetChanges is the Merge method, which, as the name suggests, merges two DataSets or DataTables.

Optimizing Your Application: GetChanges and Merge

One upshot of working with disconnected architecture is that you have a disconnected cache of your data. Actually, you might have more than one disconnected cache of data. Two users, or parts of your application, might need to modify the cache based upon their roles and you, as an application architect, might be left with the responsibility of reconciling those changes. Not only that, if there is indeed one entity that holds all the data, it seems like a terrible waste of bandwidth and resources to pass around an entire DataSet or DataTable when only a few rows have actually changed.

ADO.NET provides you with two methods for this very quandary on both the DataSet and DataTable objects.

The first method is GetChanges, which lets you filter out a DataTable or DataSet with only the changes. Using an appropriate overload, you also have the ability to create a DataTable or DataSet with rows in a specified RowState.

■**Note** The resultant DataSet created by DataSet.GetChanges might contain a few rows with DataRowState. Unchanged to maintain referential integrity based upon the existing relations present in the DataSet.

The second method is the Merge method, which allows you to merge a specified DataSet, DataTable, or an array of DataRow objects into a DataSet.

You can quickly write an example to examine the behavior of these methods:

1. Create a new Windows Forms application project. Name it Exercise 9.5 and change its main form's text property to Exercise 9.5.

2. Add a new strongly typed DataSet called CustProd (this is the same DataSet used in Chapter 8). The structure of this DataSet is shown in Figure 9-18.

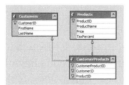

Figure 9-18. *Structure of the strongly typed DataSet*

3. Add three DataGridView controls on the form, which will be databound with individual tables within the DataSet. Name these three dgCustomers, dgProducts, and dgCustomerProducts. Also, add two buttons: btnClose with text property set to Exit, and btnGetChanges with text property set to Get Changes. The form should look like Figure 9-19 in Design view.

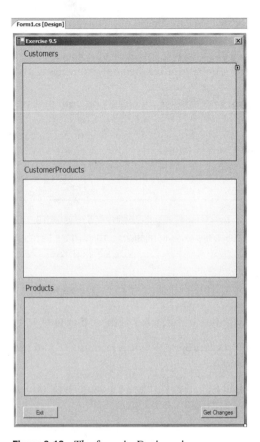

Figure 9-19. *The form in Design view*

4. In the constructor of the form, set up, load, and data bind the DataSet from an XML file sitting on the disk. This XML file can be found in the associated code download and it is the same XML file used in Chapter 8. The code for the constructor is shown in Listings 9-28 and 9-29.

Listing 9-28. *Loading and Data Binding the DataSet in the Constructor in C#*

```csharp
public Form1()
{
    InitializeComponent();

    myDataSet = new CustProd();
    dgCustomers.DataSource = myDataSet.Customers;
    dgCustomerProducts.DataSource = myDataSet.CustomerProducts;
    dgProducts.DataSource = myDataSet.Products;

    myDataSet.ReadXml("Data.xml");
    myDataSet.AcceptChanges();
}
```

Listing 9-29. *Loading and Data Binding the DataSet in the Constructor in Visual Basic .NET*

```
Private Sub Form1_Load( _
  ByVal sender As System.Object, _
  ByVal e As System.EventArgs) Handles MyBase.Load
  myDataSet = New CustProd()
  dgCustomers.DataSource = myDataSet.Customers
  dgCustomerProducts.DataSource = myDataSet.CustomerProducts
  dgProducts.DataSource = myDataSet.Products

  myDataSet.ReadXml("Data.xml")
  myDataSet.AcceptChanges()
End Sub
```

5. In the event handler for btnClose, add the following code to ensure the form is closed when the user clicks the Exit button.

C#

```csharp
private void btnClose_Click(object sender, EventArgs e)
{
    this.Close();
}
```

VB.NET

```
Private Sub btnClose_Click( _
  ByVal sender As System.Object, ByVal e As System.EventArgs)( _
  Handles btnClose.Click
  Me.Close()
End Sub
```

6. Finally, in the btnGetChanges OnClick event handler, add the following code:

C#

```csharp
private void btnGetChanges_Click(object sender, EventArgs e)
{
    CustProd changedDS = (CustProd)myDataSet.GetChanges();
    dgCustomers.DataSource = changedDS.Customers;
    dgCustomerProducts.DataSource = changedDS.CustomerProducts;
    dgProducts.DataSource = changedDS.Products;
}
```

VB.NET

```
Private Sub btnGetChanges_Click( _
  ByVal sender As System.Object, ByVal e As System.EventArgs) _
```

```
    Handles btnGetChanges.Click
      Dim changedDS As CustProd = CType(myDataSet.GetChanges(), CustProd)
      dgCustomers.DataSource = changedDS.Customers
      dgCustomerProducts.DataSource = changedDS.CustomerProducts
      dgProducts.DataSource = changedDS.Products
    End Sub
```

As you can see, this code performs a GetChanges on the DataSet and rebinds the newly retrieved DataSet to the UI.

7. Compile and run the application. You should see the application running as shown in Figure 9-20. The current data with all rows is shown. Because myDataSet.AcceptChanges was called in the constructor, all row states at this point are UnChanged.

8. Change the CustomerID column of the first row in the CustomerProducts table. So let's say, given the structure of the DataSet, the CustomerID was changed from 1 (Bill Gates) to 2 (John Williams). Click the Get Changes button. You should see an output as shown in Figure 9-20.

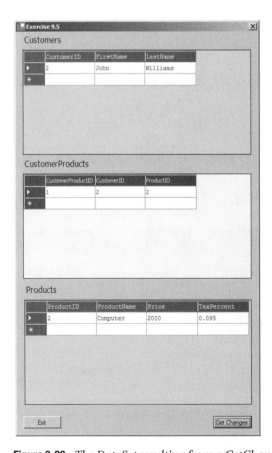

Figure 9-20. *The DataSet resulting from a GetChanges operation*

Interestingly enough in Exercise 9.5, even though the RowState of the modified row in CustomerProducts is DataRowState.Modified, the other relevant rows shown in the result have their RowStates set to DataRowState.Unchanged. This is an important point to consider since GetChanges takes a safe approach and returns all rows that satisfy the current existing relations defined in the DataSet. Obviously, DataTable.GetChanges is a lot simpler as it does not have to worry about relations.

Another point to note here is that most of the exercises presented in this chapter concern themselves with a single table in a DataSet or a DataTable. This greatly simplifies the discussion as the concepts can be carried over to a multiple table scenario. In a multiple table scenario, though, where you have to deal with generating valid keys in a disconnected scenario over multiple relations, the commands and logic required to update the DataSet back into the database can get a bit more involved. It's in that situation where the ability of GetChanges to retrieve all affected rows—including the ones with RowStates Unchanged–is invaluable. This will be demonstrated in the next chapter where multiple table hierarchies will be discussed.

Tip Like anything, GetChanges has its own set of Don't Do's. One important point to consider is that the time required to perform a GetChanges on a DataSet might increase exponentially with the size of the DataSet. If you have a rather large DataSet, then consider doing a GetChanges on individual tables instead. It's hard to say what might be the upper limit on the number of tables on which doing GetChanges is considered okay. The actual time taken depends on the number of tables, size of tables, number of rows, and various relations.

EXTRACTING CHANGES AS AN XML DIFFGRAM

GetChanges offers you a convenient method to extract changes as a DataSet or a DataTable in the same structure as the original DataSet or DataTable. However, ADO.NET gives you yet another convenient mechanism to clearly identify the changes in a DataSet or DataTable using a diffgram.

A diffgram is nothing but an XML representation of the disconnected cache with a node that clearly identifies the changes done. As a matter of fact, in the btnGetChanges OnClick event handler mentioned previously, you can easily add a single line of code that looks like this:

C#

```
myDataSet.WriteXml("diffgram.xml", XmlWriteMode.DiffGram);
```

VB.NET

```
myDataSet.WriteXml("diffgram.xml", XmlWriteMode.DiffGram)
```

This line will allow you to extract the diffgram, which is shown in Figure 9-21 with the original data node compressed for easier viewing.

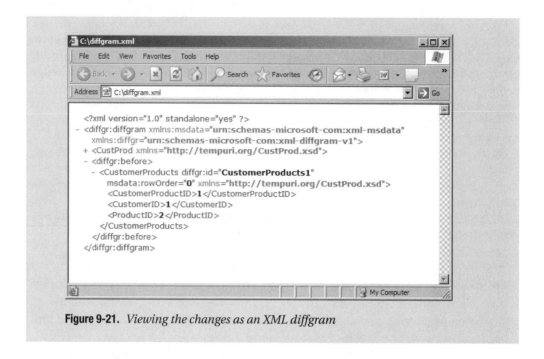

Figure 9-21. *Viewing the changes as an XML diffgram*

Now that you have the changes extracted out as a mini DataSet with the same structure as the original DataSet, you can use a second method called Merge to integrate those changes with an existing DataSet elsewhere. The use of Merge is rather simple. It looks something like this:

C#

```
Table1.Merge(Table2) ;
```

VB.NET

```
Table1.Merge(Table2)
```

A DataSet also has a Merge method on it, so this discussion can be applied to both a DataSet and a DataTable.

Now I wish I could tell you Merge was as simple as the previous single line of code; however, because the Merge method could be presented with a number of unique cases, it has to take decisions on all of those cases. This is best explained by presenting a few sample cases. The one common theme to remember is that *whenever it comes to making a decision, Table1 will override Table2*. I know this doesn't make much sense yet, but this will become clear in the following cases.

The code for this exercise can be downloaded in Exercise 9.6 in the associated code download. Since you have seen examples of DataSets and DataTables being created and filled many times over now, I will skip creating the example step by step and present only the pertinent parts. You can, however, see the entire code in the associated code download.

In this exercise, as usual, the strongly typed DataSet provides us with a convenient aid in creating the table structures needed to demonstrate various possible cases. This exercise contains a strongly typed DataSet that defines four tables as shown in Figure 9-22.

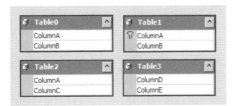

Figure 9-22. *Various DataTables for Exercise 9.6*

With the strongly typed DataSet set up, next add two DataGridView controls to the form, which will be used to demonstrate the results of the two tables being merged. Also add various buttons, the purposes of which are clear by their text properties. The form in Design view can be seen in Figure 9-23.

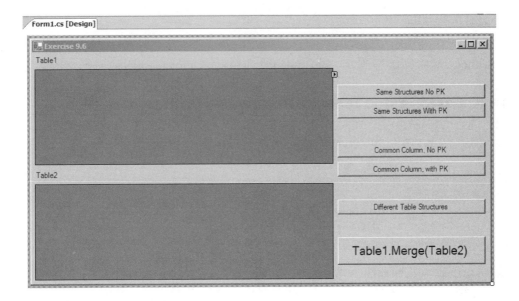

Figure 9-23. *The application's main form in Design view*

The way this exercise works is that you can click on various buttons on the right and populate the two DataGridView controls with two DataTables satisfying either of our cases. When you click the Merge button (Table1.Merge(Table2)), it does exactly what its caption suggests: it will call Table1.Merge(Table2). The results of the merge will be viewable in the DataGridView that displays Table1 (that is the DataGridView on the top).

The code for the Merge method is as shown here:

C#

```csharp
private void btnMerge_Click(object sender, EventArgs e)
{
    DataTable table1 = (DataTable)dgView1.DataSource;
    DataTable table2 = (DataTable)dgView2.DataSource;
    table1.Merge(table2);
}
```

VB.NET

```vbnet
Private Sub btnMerge_Click( _
  ByVal sender As System.Object, ByVal e As System.EventArgs) _
  Handles btnMerge.Click
    Dim table1 As DataTable = CType(dgView1.DataSource, DataTable)
    Dim table2 As DataTable = CType(dgView2.DataSource, DataTable)
    table1.Merge(table2)
End Sub
```

Without much further ado (no pun intended), let's jump into the various cases.

Merge Case 1: Same Table Structures, No Primary Key

In the strongly typed DataSet, Table0 can be used as a sample table that has no primary keys defined on it. The two instances of these tables can be loaded as per the following code:

C#

```csharp
VariousTables.Table0DataTable table1 = new VariousTables.Table0DataTable();
table1.LoadDataRow(new object[] { "1", "One" }, true);
table1.LoadDataRow(new object[] { "2", "Two" }, true);

VariousTables.Table0DataTable table2 = new VariousTables.Table0DataTable();
table2.LoadDataRow(new object[] { "2", "Monkey" }, true);
table2.LoadDataRow(new object[] { "3", "Donkey" }, true);

dgView1.DataSource = table1;
dgView2.DataSource = table2;
```

VB.NET

```vbnet
Dim table1 As VariousTables.Table0DataTable = _
   New VariousTables.Table0DataTable()
table1.LoadDataRow(New Object() {"1", "One"}, True)
table1.LoadDataRow(New Object() {"2", "Two"}, True)

Dim table2 As VariousTables.Table0DataTable = _
```

```
        New VariousTables.Table0DataTable()
table2.LoadDataRow(New Object() {"2", "Monkey"}, True)
table2.LoadDataRow(New Object() {"3", "Donkey"}, True)

dgView1.DataSource = table1
dgView2.DataSource = table2
```

When you run the application, the data in the two tables is as shown in Figure 9-24.

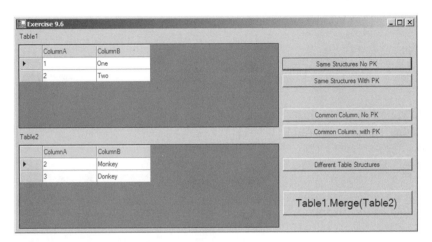

Figure 9-24. *Original data before Merge*

When you click the Merge button, the tables are merged as shown in Figure 9-25.

ColumnA	ColumnB
1	One
2	Two
2	Monkey
3	Donkey

Figure 9-25. *Data after Merge*

Thus as you can see, with no primary keys defined, the Merge method simply adds the rows—just because it doesn't know any better. Defining a primary key on the DataTable fixes the situation somewhat.

Merge Case 2: Same Table Structures, with Primary Key

In the strongly typed DataSet, Table1 can be used as a sample table that has primary keys defined on it. The two instances of these tables can be loaded as per the following code:

C#

```
VariousTables.Table1DataTable table1 = new VariousTables.Table1DataTable();
table1.LoadDataRow(new object[] { "1", "One" }, true);
table1.LoadDataRow(new object[] { "2", "Two" }, true);

VariousTables.Table1DataTable table2 = new VariousTables.Table1DataTable();
table2.LoadDataRow(new object[] { "2", "Monkey" }, true);
table2.LoadDataRow(new object[] { "3", "Donkey" }, true);

dgView1.DataSource = table1;
dgView2.DataSource = table2;
```

VB.NET

```
Dim table1 As VariousTables.Table1DataTable = _
    New VariousTables.Table1DataTable()
table1.LoadDataRow(New Object() {"1", "One"}, True)
table1.LoadDataRow(New Object() {"2", "Two"}, True)

Dim table2 As VariousTables.Table1DataTable = _
    New VariousTables.Table1DataTable()
table2.LoadDataRow(New Object() {"2", "Monkey"}, True)
table2.LoadDataRow(New Object() {"3", "Donkey"}, True)

dgView1.DataSource = table1
dgView2.DataSource = table2
```

When you run the application, the data in the two tables is as shown in Figure 9-26.

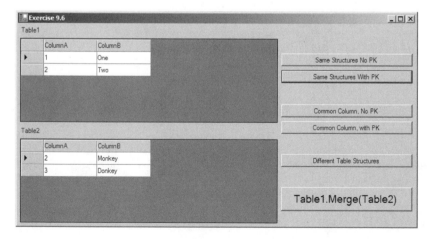

Figure 9-26. *Original data before Merge*

When you click the Merge button, the tables are merged as shown in Figure 9-27.

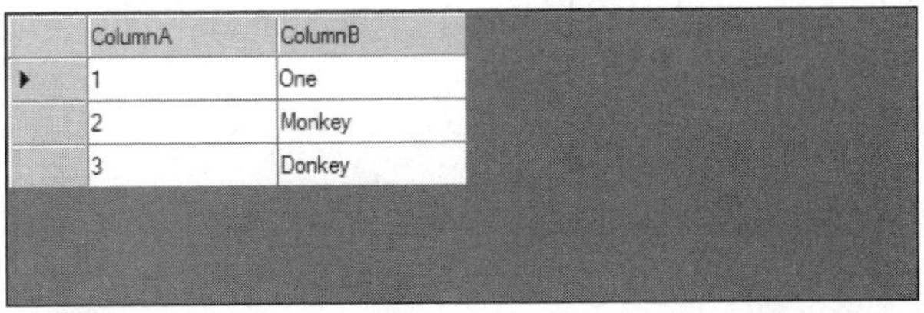

	ColumnA	ColumnB
▶	1	One
	2	Monkey
	3	Donkey

Figure 9-27. *Data after Merge*

So, with primary keys defined, the Merge evaluates the primary keys and whenever it notices a difference it lets Table1's rows override those of Table2. So, effectively, you have *merged* Table2 into Table1.

Merge Case 3: Common Column, No Primary Key

In the strongly typed DataSet, the two tables that satisfy this case can be Table0 and Table2. They have a common ColumnA, but no primary keys. The two instances of these tables can be loaded as per the following code:

C#

```
VariousTables.Table0DataTable table1 = new VariousTables.Table0DataTable();
table1.LoadDataRow(new object[] { "1", "One" }, true);
table1.LoadDataRow(new object[] { "2", "Two" }, true);

VariousTables.Table2DataTable table2 = new VariousTables.Table2DataTable();
table2.LoadDataRow(new object[] { "2", "Monkey" }, true);
table2.LoadDataRow(new object[] { "3", "Donkey" }, true);

dgView1.DataSource = table1;
dgView2.DataSource = table2;
```

VB.NET

```
Dim table1 As VariousTables.Table0DataTable = _
    New VariousTables.Table0DataTable()
table1.LoadDataRow(New Object() {"1", "One"}, True)
table1.LoadDataRow(New Object() {"2", "Two"}, True)

Dim table2 As VariousTables.Table2DataTable = _
    New VariousTables.Table2DataTable()
table2.LoadDataRow(New Object() {"2", "Monkey"}, True)
table2.LoadDataRow(New Object() {"3", "Donkey"}, True)
```

```
dgView1.DataSource = table1
dgView2.DataSource = table2
```

When you run the application, the data in the two tables is as shown in Figure 9-28.

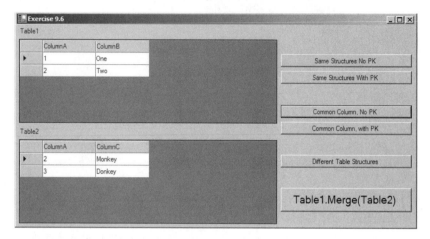

Figure 9-28. *Original data before Merge*

When you click the Merge button, the tables are merged as shown in Figure 9-29.

ColumnA	ColumnB	ColumnC
1	One	(null)
2	Two	(null)
2	(null)	Monkey
3	(null)	Donkey

Figure 9-29. *Data after Merge*

So, with no primary keys defined, and a different column, the Merge method will end up combining the common column and simply substitute null wherever it cannot find the appropriate values.

Merge Case 4: Common Column, with Primary Key

In the strongly typed DataSet, the two tables that satisfy this case can be Table1 and Table2. They have a common ColumnA with a primary key defined on Table1. The key on Table2 is optional as I mentioned before; in this merge, Table1 is what really matters. The two instances of these tables can be loaded as per the following code:

C#

```csharp
VariousTables.Table1DataTable table1 = new VariousTables.Table1DataTable();
table1.LoadDataRow(new object[] { "1", "One" }, true);
table1.LoadDataRow(new object[] { "2", "Two" }, true);

VariousTables.Table2DataTable table2 = new VariousTables.Table2DataTable();
table2.LoadDataRow(new object[] { "2", "Monkey" }, true);
table2.LoadDataRow(new object[] { "3", "Donkey" }, true);

dgView1.DataSource = table1;
dgView2.DataSource = table2;
```

VB.NET

```vbnet
Dim table1 As VariousTables.Table1DataTable = _
  New VariousTables.Table1DataTable()
table1.LoadDataRow(New Object() {"1", "One"}, True)
table1.LoadDataRow(New Object() {"2", "Two"}, True)

Dim table2 As VariousTables.Table2DataTable = _
  New VariousTables.Table2DataTable()
table2.LoadDataRow(New Object() {"2", "Monkey"}, True)
table2.LoadDataRow(New Object() {"3", "Donkey"}, True)

dgView1.DataSource = table1
dgView2.DataSource = table2
```

When you run the application, the data in the two tables is as shown in Figure 9-30.

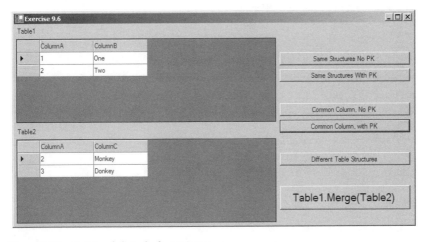

Figure 9-30. *Original data before Merge*

When you click the Merge button, the tables are merged as shown in Figure 9-31.

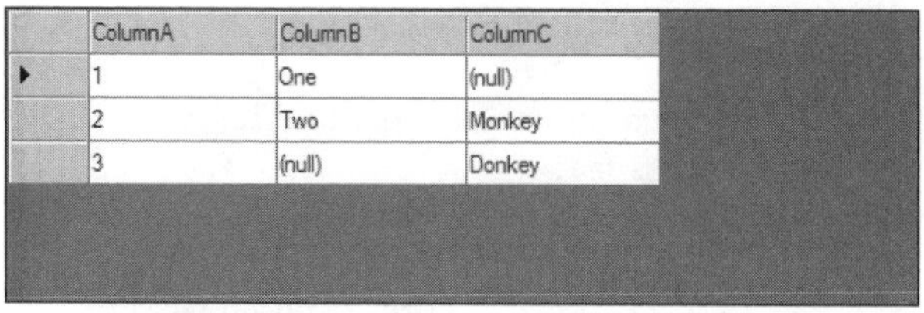

ColumnA	ColumnB	ColumnC
1	One	(null)
2	Two	Monkey
3	(null)	Donkey

Figure 9-31. *Data after Merge*

So, with a primary key defined, and a different column, the `Merge` method will end up combining the common column and substituting `null` wherever it cannot find the appropriate values. But wherever there is a conflict, Table2's row is thrown out the window and Table1's row is kept. Therefore, if there were a third column in either table, which wasn't the primary key, and a differing value between Table1 and Table2 existed, you would see Table1 overriding Table2.

Merge Case 5: Absolutely Different Table Structures

In this case, the two table structures have nothing in common. All the columns differ. The code for loading such `DataTables`[2] can be seen here:

C#

```
DataTable table1 = new DataTable();
table1.Columns.Add(new DataColumn("ColumnA"));
table1.Columns.Add(new DataColumn("ColumnB"));
table1.LoadDataRow(new object[] { "1", "One" }, true);
table1.LoadDataRow(new object[] { "2", "Two" }, true);

VariousTables.Table3DataTable table2 = new VariousTables.Table3DataTable();
table2.LoadDataRow(new object[] { "3", "Monkey" }, true);
table2.LoadDataRow(new object[] { "4", "Donkey" }, true);

dgView1.DataSource = table1;
dgView2.DataSource = table2;
```

VB.NET

```
Dim table1 As DataTable = New DataTable()
table1.Columns.Add(New DataColumn("ColumnA"))
table1.Columns.Add(New DataColumn("ColumnB"))
table1.LoadDataRow(New Object() {"1", "One"}, True)
table1.LoadDataRow(New Object() {"2", "Two"}, True)
```

2. Why is Table1 not a strongly typed DataTable here? Because the final merge results do not satisfy the unique constraint. As you can see in Figure 9-33, two rows have ColumnA as null, which has a UniqueConstraint defined on it. See the code download for a detailed explanation of comments in code.

```
Dim table2 As VariousTables.Table3DataTable = _
    New VariousTables.Table3DataTable()
table2.LoadDataRow(New Object() {"2", "Monkey"}, True)
table2.LoadDataRow(New Object() {"3", "Donkey"}, True)

dgView1.DataSource = table1
dgView2.DataSource = table2
```

When you run the application, the data in the two tables is as shown in Figure 9-32.

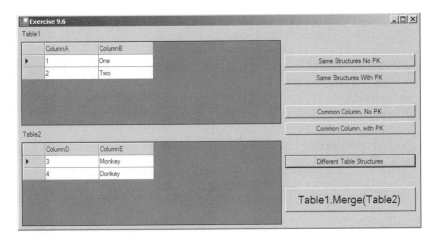

Figure 9-32. *Original data before Merge*

When you click the Merge button, the tables are merged as shown in Figure 9-33.

ColumnA	ColumnB	ColumnD	ColumnE
1	One	(null)	(null)
2	Two	(null)	(null)
(null)	(null)	3	Monkey
(null)	(null)	4	Donkey

Figure 9-33. *Data after Merge*

Thus as you can see, with no common columns, the two tables are merged by simply slapping them together and substituting null wherever a value isn't found.

Other Ways of Merging DataTables

DataTable.Merge supports three overloads. Exercise 9.6 demonstrates only one of them. The other two are as follows:

- Merge(DataTable, Boolean): Merges a DataTable into the calling DataTable, preserving changes according to the Boolean argument. A value of True indicates that any changes to the calling DataTable should be maintained. A value of False indicates that such changes should be discarded.

- Merge(DataTable, Boolean, MissingSchemaAction): Merges a DataTable into the calling DataTable, preserving changes according to the Boolean argument and handling an incompatible schema according to the MissingSchemaAction argument. The MissingSchemaAction enumerator is discussed in just a moment.

Merging DataSets

The DataSet class also exposes a Merge() method that's used to merge one DataSet into another, a DataTable into a DataSet, or an array of DataRows into a DataSet. This type of action is useful when you have data for the same purpose coming from two separate sources—say, inventory data coming from multiple remote locations. Each location can pass a DataSet object to a centralized application where the DataSets can be merged. The critical difference between DataSet merging and DataTable merging is that DataSet merging takes into consideration the defined relations, as well as columns and data in various DataTables.

The DataSet class has the following overloaded Merge() methods:

- Merge(DataRow()): Merges an array of DataRow objects into the calling DataSet.

- Merge(DataSet): Merges a DataSet into the calling DataSet.

- Merge(DataTable): Merges a DataTable into the calling DataSet.

- Merge(DataSet, Boolean): Merges a DataSet into the calling DataSet, preserving changes according to the Boolean argument. A value of True indicates that any changes to the calling DataSet should be maintained. A value of False indicates that such changes should be discarded.

- Merge(DataRow(), Boolean, MissingSchemaAction): Merges an array of DataRow objects into the calling DataSet, preserving changes to the DataSet according to the Boolean argument, and handling an incompatible schema according to the MissingSchemaAction argument.

- Merge(DataSet, Boolean, MissingSchemaAction): Merges a DataSet into the calling DataSet, treating the other two arguments as mentioned previously.

- Merge(DataTable, Boolean, MissingSchemaAction): Merges a DataTable into the calling DataSet, treating the other two arguments as mentioned previously.

The MissingSchemaAction argument is an enumerator that specifies how to handle the merge operation if the object being merged has a different schema from the calling DataSet. This scenario would occur if, say, a new DataColumn were added to the schema in the merging DataSet. We'll have a closer look at this possibility in a moment.

Merging Two DataSets/DataTables with Different Schemas

As described previously, you can merge two DataSets with different schemas and specify how the schema differences should be handled:

```
MyDataSet.Merge(myOtherDataSet, True, MissingSchemaAction.Add)
```

The MissingSchemaAction enumeration is used to specify how schema differences should be handled. The possible enumerators are shown in Table 9-5.

Table 9-5. *MissingSchemaAction Enumeration Values*

Value	Description
Add	Indicates that additional columns defined in the source DataSet (myOtherDataSet) should be added to the schema of the target DataSet (myDataSet).
AddWithKey	Indicates that additional columns defined in the source DataSet should be added to the target DataSet along with any primary key information.
Error	Indicates that a System.SystemException will be thrown if the target schema and source schema do not match.
Ignore	Indicates that any additional columns in the source DataSet should be ignored when it is merged into the target DataSet.

Updating Records Using Mapped Names

Until now, our discussion has focused on updating the data source by specifying commands with hard-coded column names or relying on the fact that column names defined in our commands match the ones defined in the database.

In Chapter 7, you looked at how TableMappings and ColumnMappings help you bridge this translation gap of different column/table names in fetching data. The same concepts can be applied to other database operations, such as inserting a new record or updating an existing one. As a matter of fact, after mapping column names, you can use them throughout your code to accomplish every kind of database task. Let's see an example of adding a new record inside the Microsoft Access DB.MDB database (see Listings 9-30 and 9-31).

Listing 9-30. *Example of Adding a Record Using C#*

```
#region Using directives

using System;
using System.Collections.Generic;
using System.Text;
using System.Data.OleDb;
using System.Data.Common;
using System.Data;

#endregion

namespace Exercise_9_7
{
    class Program
    {
        static void Main(string[] args)
```

```
        {
            DataSet dsUsers = new DataSet("Users");

            try
            {
                // Define a connection object
                OleDbConnection dbConn = new OleDbConnection(
                    "Provider=Microsoft.Jet.OLEDB.4.0;" +
                    "Password=;User ID=Admin;Data Source=db.mdb");

                // Create a data adapter to retrieve records from DB
                OleDbDataAdapter daUsers =
                    new OleDbDataAdapter("SELECT ID,fn,ln,cty,st" +
                    " FROM tabUsers", dbConn);

                // Define each column to map
                DataColumnMapping dcmUserID =
                    new DataColumnMapping("ID", "UserID");
                DataColumnMapping dcmFirstName =
                    new DataColumnMapping("fn", "FirstName");
                DataColumnMapping dcmLastName =
                    new DataColumnMapping("ln", "LastName");
                DataColumnMapping dcmCity =
                    new DataColumnMapping("cty", "City");
                DataColumnMapping dcmState =
                    new DataColumnMapping("st", "State");

                // Define the table containing the mapped columns
                DataTableMapping dtmUsers = new DataTableMapping("Table", "User");
                dtmUsers.ColumnMappings.Add(dcmUserID);
                dtmUsers.ColumnMappings.Add(dcmFirstName);
                dtmUsers.ColumnMappings.Add(dcmLastName);
                dtmUsers.ColumnMappings.Add(dcmCity);
                dtmUsers.ColumnMappings.Add(dcmState);

                // Activate the mapping mechanism
                daUsers.TableMappings.Add(dtmUsers);

                // Fill the dataset
                daUsers.Fill(dsUsers);

                // Declare a command builder to create SQL instructions
                // to create and update records.
                OleDbCommandBuilder cb = new OleDbCommandBuilder(daUsers);

                // Insert a new record in the DataSet
                DataRow r = dsUsers.Tables["User"].NewRow();
                r["FirstName"] = "Eddie";
```

```
                r["LastName"] = "Robinson";
                r["City"] = "Houston";
                r["State"] = "Texas";
                dsUsers.Tables["User"].Rows.Add(r);

                // Insert the record in the database
                daUsers.Update(dsUsers.GetChanges());

                // Align in-memory data with the data source ones
                dsUsers.AcceptChanges();

                // Print successfully message
                Console.WriteLine("A new record has been"
                    + " added to the database.");
            }
            catch (Exception ex)
            {
                // Reject DataSet changes
                dsUsers.RejectChanges();

                // An error occurred. Show the error message
                Console.WriteLine(ex.Message);
            }
        }
    }
}
```

Listing 9-31. *Example of Adding a Record Using Visual Basic .NET*

```
Imports System.Data.OleDb
Imports System.Data.Common

Module Module1
    Sub Main()
        Dim dsUsers As New DataSet("Users")

        Try
            ' Define a connection object
            Dim dbConn As New _
        OleDbConnection("Provider=Microsoft.Jet.OLEDB.4.0;" & _
        "Password=;User ID=Admin;Data Source=db.mdb")

            ' Create a data adapter to retrieve records from DB
            Dim daUsers As New OleDbDataAdapter("SELECT ID,fn,ln,cty,st" & _
                " FROM tabUsers", dbConn)

            ' Define each column to map
            Dim dcmUserID As New DataColumnMapping("ID", "UserID")
            Dim dcmFirstName As New DataColumnMapping("fn", "FirstName")
```

```vb
        Dim dcmLastName As New DataColumnMapping("ln", "LastName")
        Dim dcmCity As New DataColumnMapping("cty", "City")
        Dim dcmState As New DataColumnMapping("st", "State")

        ' Define the table containing the mapped columns
        Dim dtmUsers As New DataTableMapping("Table", "User")
        dtmUsers.ColumnMappings.Add(dcmUserID)
        dtmUsers.ColumnMappings.Add(dcmFirstName)
        dtmUsers.ColumnMappings.Add(dcmLastName)
        dtmUsers.ColumnMappings.Add(dcmCity)
        dtmUsers.ColumnMappings.Add(dcmState)

        ' Activate the mapping mechanism
        daUsers.TableMappings.Add(dtmUsers)

        ' Fill the dataset
        daUsers.Fill(dsUsers)

        ' Declare a command builder to create SQL instructions
        ' to create and update records.
        Dim cb As New OleDbCommandBuilder(daUsers)

        ' Insert a new record in the DataSet
        Dim r As DataRow = dsUsers.Tables("User").NewRow()
        r("FirstName") = "Eddie"
        r("LastName") = "Robinson"
        r("City") = "Houston"
        r("State") = "Texas"
        dsUsers.Tables("User").Rows.Add(r)

        ' Insert the record in the database
        daUsers.Update(dsUsers.GetChanges())

        ' Align in-memory data with the data source ones
        dsUsers.AcceptChanges()

        ' Print successfully message
        Console.WriteLine("A new record has been" & _
          " added to the database.")
    Catch ex As Exception
        ' Reject DataSet changes
        dsUsers.RejectChanges()

        ' An error occurred. Show the error message
        Console.WriteLine(ex.Message)
    End Try
  End Sub
End Module
```

In the bolded snippet of code in Listings 9-30 and 9-31, a new row has been created and filled using the mapped column names. In Listings 9-32 and 9-33, a column is updated using a mapping mechanism.

Listing 9-32. *Example of Updating a Record Using ColumnMappings Using C#*

```csharp
#region Using directives

using System;
using System.Collections.Generic;
using System.Text;
using System.Data.OleDb;
using System.Data.Common;
using System.Data;

#endregion

namespace Exercise_9_8
{
    class Program
    {
        static void Main(string[] args)
        {
            DataSet dsUsers = new DataSet("Users");
            try
            {
                OleDbConnection dbConn =
                    new OleDbConnection("Provider=Microsoft.Jet.OLEDB.4.0;" +
                    "Password=;User ID=Admin;Data Source=db.mdb");

                // Create a data adapter to retrieve records from db
                OleDbDataAdapter daUsers =
                    new OleDbDataAdapter("SELECT ID,fn,ln,cty,st" +
                    " FROM tabUsers", dbConn);

                // Define each column to map
                DataColumnMapping dcmUserID =
                    new DataColumnMapping("ID", "UserID");
                DataColumnMapping dcmFirstName =
                    new DataColumnMapping("fn", "FirstName");
                DataColumnMapping dcmLastName =
                    new DataColumnMapping("ln", "LastName");
                DataColumnMapping dcmCity =
                    new DataColumnMapping("cty", "City");
                DataColumnMapping dcmState =
                    new DataColumnMapping("st", "State");
                // Define the table containing the mapped columns
                DataTableMapping dtmUsers =
```

```
          new DataTableMapping("Table", "User");
      dtmUsers.ColumnMappings.Add(dcmUserID);
      dtmUsers.ColumnMappings.Add(dcmFirstName);
      dtmUsers.ColumnMappings.Add(dcmLastName);
      dtmUsers.ColumnMappings.Add(dcmCity);
      dtmUsers.ColumnMappings.Add(dcmState);

      // Activate the mapping mechanism
      daUsers.TableMappings.Add(dtmUsers);

      // Fill the dataset
      daUsers.Fill(dsUsers);

      DataColumn[] dcaKey = { dsUsers.Tables["User"].Columns["UserID"] };
      dsUsers.Tables["User"].PrimaryKey = dcaKey;

      // Declare a command builder to create SQL instructions
      // to create and update records.
      OleDbCommandBuilder cb = new OleDbCommandBuilder(daUsers);

      // Update an existing record in the DataSet
      DataRow r = dsUsers.Tables["User"].Rows.Find(8);

      if (r != null)
      {
         r["FirstName"] = "Venus";
         r["LastName"] = "Williams";
         r["City"] = "Houston";
         r["State"] = "Texas";

         // Update the record in the database
         daUsers.Update(dsUsers.GetChanges());

         // Align in-memory data with the data source ones
         dsUsers.AcceptChanges();

         // Print success message
         Console.WriteLine("The record has been updated " +
            "successfully.");
      }
      else
      {
         Console.WriteLine("No record found...");
      }
   }
   catch (System.Exception ex)
   {
      // Reject DataSet changes
```

```
            dsUsers.RejectChanges();

            // An error occurred. Show the error message
            Console.WriteLine(ex.Message);
        }
    }
  }
}
```

Listing 9-33. *Example of Updating a Record Using ColumnMappings Using Visual Basic .NET*

```
Imports System.Data.Common
Imports System.Data.OleDb

Module Module1
    Sub Main()
        Dim dsUsers As New DataSet("Users")

        Try
            ' Define a connection object
            Dim dbConn As New _
        OleDbConnection("Provider=Microsoft.Jet.OLEDB.4.0;" & _
        "Password=;User ID=Admin;Data Source=db.mdb")

            ' Create a data adapter to retrieve records from db
            Dim daUsers As New OleDbDataAdapter("SELECT ID,fn,ln,cty,st" & _
                " FROM tabUsers", dbConn)

            ' Define each column to map
            Dim dcmUserID As New DataColumnMapping("ID", "UserID")
            Dim dcmFirstName As New DataColumnMapping("fn", "FirstName")
            Dim dcmLastName As New DataColumnMapping("ln", "LastName")
            Dim dcmCity As New DataColumnMapping("cty", "City")
            Dim dcmState As New DataColumnMapping("st", "State")
            ' Define the table containing the mapped columns
            Dim dtmUsers As New DataTableMapping("Table", "User")
            dtmUsers.ColumnMappings.Add(dcmUserID)
            dtmUsers.ColumnMappings.Add(dcmFirstName)
            dtmUsers.ColumnMappings.Add(dcmLastName)
            dtmUsers.ColumnMappings.Add(dcmCity)
            dtmUsers.ColumnMappings.Add(dcmState)

            ' Activate the mapping mechanism
            daUsers.TableMappings.Add(dtmUsers)

            ' Fill the dataset
            daUsers.Fill(dsUsers)
```

```
                ' Set the primary key in order to use the Find() method
                ' below.
                Dim dcaKey() As DataColumn = _
            {dsUsers.Tables("User").Columns("UserID")}
                dsUsers.Tables("User").PrimaryKey = dcaKey

                ' Declare a command builder to create SQL instructions
                ' to create and update records.
                Dim cb as OleDbCommandBuilder = New OleDbCommandBuilder(daUsers)

                ' Update an existing record in the DataSet
                Dim r As DataRow = dsUsers.Tables(0).Rows.Find(3)

                If Not r Is Nothing Then
                    r("FirstName") = "Venus"
                    r("LastName") = "Williams"
                    r("City") = "Houston"
                    r("State") = "Texas"

                    ' Update the record in the database
                    daUsers.Update(dsUsers.GetChanges())

                    ' Align in-memory data with the data source ones
                    dsUsers.AcceptChanges()

                    ' Print success message
                    Console.WriteLine("The record has been updated " & _
                        "successfully.")
                Else
                    Console.WriteLine("No record found...")
                End If
            Catch ex As Exception
                ' Reject DataSet changes
                dsUsers.RejectChanges()

                ' An error occurred. Show the error message
                Console.WriteLine(ex.Message)
            End Try
        End Sub
End Module
```

In Listings 9-32 and 9-33, you can see how the Find method retrieves the DataRow object reference that is used in the updating process. The code has to define a primary key within the DataSet in order to use the Find method, which needs a valid primary key value as a parameter to retrieve the correct record.

Summary

This chapter was your first introduction to the updating side of ADO.NET. Until this chapter, you had examined various facilities ADO.NET provides as far as retrieving data and working with it in a connected or disconnected mode. This chapter completes the circle by enabling you to write a complete application from querying to working to updating.

Updating data consists of three operations: add, modify, and delete. In this chapter, you saw how the `DataAdapter` object uses various information from `DataSets` or `DataTables` and executes the necessary queries. You saw an easy way to build those queries using the `CommandBuilder` object and the pros and cons of that approach; and you saw how you could specify your own queries if you needed to.

You also saw the various methods available for editing data in `DataSet`, `DataTable`, and `DataView` objects. Knowing such methods allows you to effectively work on the disconnected cache of data with ease. Along the same lines, you saw various facilities such as `GetChanges`, `Merge`, and mappings that allow you to create an updating logic for your application that suits your needs the best.

In this chapter, among others, Exercise 9.4 was concerned with being able to work reliably in a multiuser scenario. You saw how the disconnected nature of the application leads to situations where you need to think about concurrency and conflict resolution. Another curious thing about all the exercises involving interaction with the database in this chapter was that almost all of them dealt with the simple case of one single `DataTable` or one table in a `DataSet`.

The one-table scenario makes it easier to explain the basic concepts, but frequently in your architecture you'll be required to save changes from a hierarchical `DataSet`. The hierarchical `DataSet` introduces interesting problems when you think about concurrency, key generation, and passing back the necessary data per the various relationships.

Chapter 10 continues this discussion and presents more complex and real-world scenarios involving hierarchical `DataSets` in a multiuser environment. It takes the discussion on concurrency further and explains the various cross-database concurrency management specifics.

CHAPTER 10

■ ■ ■

Updating Data: Advanced Scenarios

In the last chapter, you were introduced to the concept of updating in ADO.NET. This chapter takes the same discussion a step further by introducing more real-world scenarios and other real-world problems.

ADO.NET is different from previous data access architectures in the sense that it allows you to retrieve a purely disconnected cache of records in an object representation of a database called a DataSet. The DataSet resembles the database, but isn't quite a database. It allows you to search, sort, and filter through the records it contains, works with various relations, and leverages the power of both an object representation and XML representation to allow you to easily update its contents.

But a DataSet isn't a database, and it shouldn't be abused as one either; this statement will become very clear in the contents of this chapter. In a fully connected environment, you can easily update, insert, or delete various relational data; however, when you are working with disconnected data, the mundane tasks of fetching the latest generated keys and managing concurrency issues on the same hierarchical relational data can get quite complex.

Because a DataSet is completely disconnected, all the changes done to it while it's disconnected are then saved back to the database, typically when the user clicks the Save button, or when some other part of the application architecture does the equivalent of a save. When this happens, the operation ultimately calls a data adapter's Update method or something similar. In most cases, data adapters support updating single tables or row arrays; if you need anything more complex, it's generally up to you to write the commands for that.

Now you could modify the DataSet as much as you wish, the only thing that would have been changed so far would be the in-memory disconnected cache. Until you click Save (by virtue of which you will start a process that will insert, modify, or delete various changes to the database), the database is untouched. And even when you do click Save, because of the fact that you had queried a snapshot of the database as a DataSet some time in history, that snapshot might be out of date when you do a save. There could be a number of other users who might be working on the same data, and you need to be mindful of the changes they might have done between your querying for the data and your attempting to save the changes.

Between querying and saving, a number of things could have happened that you might need to take care of at save time, including the following:

- The row you are trying to update could have been deleted by another user.

- The row you are trying to insert has a foreign-key relationship with another row, which could have been deleted in the meantime by another user.

- The row you are trying to update has already been updated by another user, but he didn't update the particular column you are interested in. Should your update be done or should it be rejected?

- You are trying to perform a hierarchical insert. One of the rows you need to insert is a foreign key in another table that you need to do an update or insert in—which may or may not be a part of your DataSet.

Oh my! That is a lot of questions and scenarios. The first thing you, as an architect, need to do when designing your update logic is to list various scenarios (like those just mentioned), and decide which approach will work the best for your particular situation. You need to be concerned about a conflict detection methodology and a concurrency resolution strategy.

Conflict Detection and Concurrency Resolution

The central policeman of a disconnected architecture, the database, is somewhat like a busy traffic intersection. The bad way to architect would be to arrange for ambulances to carry patients to the hospital once an accident has occurred. The right and better way to architect would be to instead put in traffic lights to regulate the traffic better, thus preventing an accident in the first place. So, via proper application and database design, the first step should be to sit back and think about the possible cases that might cause a conflict, and see if those can be resolved using a proper database design.

Preventing Conflicts: Traffic Lights

You should try and design the database in such a way that conflicts do not occur. This might be too tall of an order to fit most situations, but certain cases can be clearly addressed. For example, to prevent primary-key conflicts, you could use GUID primary-key columns. GUIDs are always unique so the issue of overlapping primary keys will never occur.

■Note Remember that GUIDs are not a good candidate for a clustered key in the database, not to mention that the columns themselves and the indexes on them occupy a lot more space, and don't perform quite as well as an int identity column. But for using keys in a distributed system where the key can be generated either by the application or by the database, a GUID might be a wise choice. Plus, not every database has a uniqueidentifier data type.

Another method to avoid primary-key conflicts is, in the case of inserts, to let the user request a number of keys beforehand. In other words, the UI of the application can be designed in such a manner that it first asks the user how many rows he wishes to insert. Once he communicates that he wishes to enter, say, 5 rows, then 5 keys are generated for him in the database and sent across the wire to the application, which are then added to his DataTable. Now should the user choose to discard those primary keys and not save them, you would simply end up wasting those 5 possible keys, but in many cases that is a better solution than checking for the existence of a key or throwing an exception. Even if you use Int32, you have quite a few keys to waste before you start running short, and even when you do run short of keys, by then we'll all be wearing silver jumpsuits communicating to a database perhaps on Uranus. Perhaps by then the world will have moved to 64-bit computing.

This approach perhaps works better for Oracle where you have sequences; however, as demonstrated in Chapter 9, you can easily emulate a sequence in SQL Server using a Seed Generator table.

Another approach could be to use a journaling database, which keeps saving your changes incrementally, rather than updating a particular row all the time. The advantage of this approach is that conflicts never occur; the downside, obviously, is that at times querying data out of the database can prove to be challenging.

Depending on your situation and creativity, you could come up with other scenarios and solutions. But as you can clearly see, none of the approaches is a panacea, which is what makes it so important that the needs of the application be clearly evaluated before any particular scheme is sought after.

With the right database design, you can minimize conflicts but you cannot completely eliminate them. Because of this, you need a conflict detection and concurrency resolution strategy.

Handling Conflicts: Going to the Hospital After an Accident

There might be certain situations where you can't help but let a conflict occur. For example, you might decide that you don't wish to use GUIDs for extreme performance needs, you don't want to use any homegrown sequence generation mechanism because you want to rely on SQL Server to generate the identities for you. You might decide that a journaling or staging database doesn't quite meet your needs. Even when you do use GUIDs, you probably won't have any conflicts on inserts, but you'll still have updates on other columns in the table that are not GUIDs that might conflict with each other.

Let's think of a real-world example. Say you have a distributed, disconnected system that allows you to view and update patient information. In this case, say one user is updating the patient's bills with his current address and a clerk sitting at a desk somewhere else in the world is updating the patient's address because the patient happened to call in at that very moment. Here you need to come up with a scheme that allows the system to automatically make decisions about what it needs to do in these types of situations.

It's generally a bad idea to prompt the user with a conflict situation and ask the user what needs to be done. The reason behind this is because by the time the user decides what needs to be done, the data could have changed yet again. It's best to prompt the user with a failure message and the refreshed data, and request that he try again.

So how does one go about building a data layer that makes decisions about saving data in a highly concurrent environment? As it turns out, there is more than one way to do so.

Pessimistic Concurrency

The best way to prevent a conflict with a row you are updating is to ensure nobody else messes with it while you are working with it. All you need to do is lock the row you wish to update and anyone who wishes to update that row, while you still haven't updated it, simply waits, times out, or is given an error. That sounds like a great idea, but it has some serious drawbacks.[1]

First, by locking rows you are creating a serious contention with the one central piece of architecture in your system—the database. This goes against ADO.NET's general philosophy, which emphasizes connecting as late as possible and disconnecting as soon as you can. Now, not only does the database have to do the "row protection" (or page or table protection) for you, but it also has to constantly listen to your request if you decide to unlock that row.

Second, this approach goes against another ADO.NET philosophy, which encourages connection pooling by reducing the actual time you need and keeping the connection open and reserved for yourself. ADO.NET will allow you to do this should you choose this as your solution, but it's not a recommended approach. Rightfully so, ADO.NET encourages you to use a disconnected architecture, which just doesn't go hand in hand with resource locking at the database level. It's true, however, that you could execute a database-specific command using the DbCommand object, like the one shown here (a SQL Server command):

```
Select * from Customers HOLDLOCK where CustomerID = 1093
```

By using such a command in a transaction, you'd essentially end up locking the rows and prevent any other user from updating those rows until you commit or abort the transaction.

This creates some interesting problems. The end user could have locked the row by one of his actions and then, let's say, that he left for lunch and left the screen open leaving that row locked. Now while he is out to lunch, nobody else can update that row. Not only that, but you have the serious contention issue of a lock causing another lock. If it gets bad enough, you might end up with deadlocks in the database, which will require the intervention of a database administrator to clean up and kill those transactions for everyone else in a concurrent system—clearly something you'd rather not deal with in a highly concurrent application. So now you have to worry about implementing a timeout mechanism on the user interface, but what if the application crashes?

Let's say the application didn't crash, but given that application logic can get complex, what if you had Resource A waiting for Resource B, Resource B waiting for Resource C, and Resource C waiting for Resource A? You'd have a deadlock, and even though some databases can detect such a situation, it's still quite expensive for the one central resource involved.

Since ADO.NET lets you execute commands directly at the database level (using DbCommand), another way of implementing a solution slightly better than transaction-based row locking is to create a scrollable, updateable server-side cursor. This can be implemented in ADO.NET by simply wrapping the CREATE CURSOR command inside a DbCommand. The server-side cursor can then be positioned to the particular row you wish to work with—hence, apprising your application of the latest changes at any given point in time. This does not, however, solve the problem of having to create and keep an open connection for the life of the cursor, but if you must do pessimistic locking this might be a better approach.

Yet another method could be to build in a check-in/check-out functionality of rows in the application. Thus, using some clever application logic, a checked-out row is left alone by other

---

1. As you will see shortly, a better way to implement locking, without explicitly using pessimistic concurrency, is to implement locking in the logic that surrounds the database. This way, a user is informed in advance that the 10 minutes he is about to spend updating a particular screen of information shouldn't be done now because another user is busy working with the data at this very moment. Also, in this approach, you don't keep a database connection open or overload the central policeman more than you absolutely need to.

requests. This can be implemented easily by adding a Boolean column to a table. In this manner you remain disconnected but you still have to worry about timeouts and unexpected application crashes.

For these reasons, pessimistic locking in general is highly discouraged in high-demand applications. This approach, however, is completely safe, which is perhaps why it is called pessimistic concurrency—it simply assumes the worst case and plans accordingly.

Even though ADO.NET encourages you to write applications that do not leverage pessimistic concurrency, ADO.NET doesn't prevent you from using pessimistic concurrency in situations where that is the only answer. Toward the end of this chapter, I will demonstrate a situation where, in lieu of a complete database restructure, pessimistic concurrency is the only good answer.

Optimistic Concurrency

Put simply, *optimistic concurrency* assumes that locking a resource to prevent data corruption is not necessary; instead, it relies on various schemes of checking the validity of data before performing the actual update, delete, or insert. If the row has changed, the update or delete fails and must be tried again. It might lock the row for the short duration of executing the command, but it's not quite as bad as pessimistic locking, which tends to lock the rows between the first select and the last update/insert/delete.

There are various optimistic concurrency options.

Last-In Wins

As the name suggests, whoever updates last is what the database remembers. This is probably the simplest optimistic concurrency scheme, and you really don't have to do anything to implement it. This is how it works.

Say the row you have to update looks like Table 10-1.

Table 10-1. *Updateable Row*

AnimalID	AnimalType	AnimalWeight
1	Puppy	3 lbs

Now say Frans and Erick come by and query this row. The row is now contained in a disconnected cache, probably a `DataRow` inside a `DataTable` somewhere. While Frans was still updating his row, Erick updates the row to `AnimalType` = `Dog`. So the contents of the table now look like Table 10-2.

Table 10-2. *Updated Row*

AnimalID	AnimalType	AnimalWeight
1	Dog	50 lbs

Frans thinks that the row in the database still contains "Puppy" and chooses to update it to "Mutt". Under the last-in wins situation, he will simply update the row to Puppy with complete disregard of Erick's changes. So the row in the table will finally end up looking somewhat like Table 10-3.

Table 10-3. *Final Updated Row Per Last-In Wins*

AnimalID	AnimalType	AnimalWeight
1	Mutt	50 lbs

Typically, this is done by using a sequence of SQL queries that looks like this:

```
-- Erick's Select query
Select AnimalID, AnimalType, AnimalWeight from Animals
-- Frans'ss Select query
Select AnimalID, AnimalType, AnimalWeight from Animals
-- Erick's update query
Update Animals Set AnimalType = 'Dog', AnimalWeight = '50 lbs' where AnimalID = 1
-- Frans's update query
Update Animals Set AnimalType = 'Mutt', AnimalWeight = '50 lbs' where AnimalID = 1
```

Since the row lookup was done using only the primary key, which is probably indexed, and only the columns changed were updated, this performs fairly well because Frans never checked for any concurrency/conflicts and saved the time to run those queries.

Check All Columns Before an Update

The problem with the previously mentioned approach is that Erick thinks he's still working with a Dog. It's not until Erick fully refreshes his user interface that he'll see that Frans changed the row in the database to Mutt. And when he does do a refresh, by then he might have updated another pets table using the Dog animal row just because he didn't know the latest name for the animal in the database. (Prevent such accidents: using the right database design, you would obviously not copy the name of the animal, but only the key, i.e., AnimalID).

Perhaps a better approach in this scenario would have been for Frans to check for Erick's or any other user's updates between the time he fetched the data and the time he wished to update his changes back to the database. So, instead of issuing an UPDATE command that contains only the primary key in the WHERE clause, the UPDATE command's WHERE clause could instead contain a check for all values queried in the first place.

In other words, the sequence of commands the database will work with would look like this:

```
-- Erick's Select query
Select AnimalID, AnimalType, AnimalWeight from Animals
-- Frans's Select query
Select AnimalID, AnimalType, AnimalWeight from Animals

-- Erick's update query
Update Animals
    Set AnimalType = 'Dog', AnimalWeight = '50 lbs'
where
    AnimalID = 1 and AnimalWeight = '3 lbs' and AnimalType = 'Puppy'
-- Frans's update query
Update Animals
    Set AnimalType = 'Mutt', AnimalWeight = '50 lbs'
where
    AnimalID = 1 and AnimalWeight = '3 lbs' and AnimalType = 'Puppy'
```

These queries take a slightly safer approach; instead of issuing only the primary key as part of the WHERE clause to identify the one row to be changed, a WHERE clause is constructed out of *all the values in the disconnected data cache that were queried in the first place*. By doing so, at the end of Erick's UPDATE query, the data in the table looks like as shown in Table 10-4. Now at this time, when Frans comes and queries for a row based on his original data, he will simply not update any rows. This can be easily caught using the return value of the ExecuteNonQuery method on the DbCommand object which will tell you that no rows changed, when you had expected one row to be changed.

Table 10-4. *Updated Row*

AnimalID	AnimalType	AnimalWeight
1	Dog	50 lbs

This is a one-size-fits-all approach and is what the previous data access architectures, such as Recordsets in ADO classic, used.

Obviously, you don't corrupt data using this approach. In this approach, once a conflict has been detected because ExecuteNonQuery returned 0 modified rows (whereas the expected number was 1), Frans will know that a conflict has occurred. At this point the application should inform Frans of the conflict by refilling his data cache and asking him to save his changes again if he wishes to.

This approach is used by classic data access platforms such as the Recordset in ADO classic and CommandBuilder in .NET Framework 1.1. As a matter of fact, as you saw in Chapter 9, to ensure backward compatibility, the CommandBuilder object still uses this approach by default.

But, what if one of the columns involved in this comparison was a blob? It would take a lot to compare a blob, which could even be in megabytes of data. Thankfully, the query generation engine used in SqlCommandBuilder or OracleCommandBuilder is smart enough to exclude the blob data types, which has a negative side that blobs will not be checked for this kind of concurrency check done by various common command builder objects. The query generation engine still, however, must query the database for the structure of the table and various data types involved. That query could not only be expensive, but also it might not work if you do not have the proper access rights. Even if you were able to run this query, and generate a query that contains every single column in the WHERE clause, simply executing such a generated query might be quite a bit more expensive than other approaches.

The biggest advantage of this approach, however, is that setting up this kind of optimistic concurrency model requires very little effort (for a single table at least). If your performance needs aren't that severe, given the lesser code maintenance you would have to do in this solution, maybe this would be the better approach for you.

Check Only Modified Columns and Primary Keys Before an Update

Checking all columns has its downsides: it will not work with blobs, it's too expensive to generate such a query, and it takes too long to execute. Plus, if you decide that the programmatic ease of generating such a query is not worth the performance you might need out of the system, you may choose a midway approach.

The midway approach involves checking only the modified columns plus the primary key. So let's say that Frans and Erick have already queried the table as per Table 10-1. Now Erick updates the table as per Table 10-2. At this point, Frans agrees that he doesn't wish to rename Puppy to Mutt; rather, he wishes to update the Puppy to Dog. But let's say Frans has a heavier dog; his dog is 60 lbs not 50 lbs. So the sequence of queries would look somewhat like this:

```
-- Erick's Select query
Select AnimalID, AnimalType, AnimalWeight from Animals
-- Frans's Select query
Select AnimalID, AnimalType, AnimalWeight from Animals

-- Erick's update query
Update Animals
    Set AnimalType = 'Dog', AnimalWeight = '50 lbs'
where
    AnimalID = 1 and AnimalWeight = '3 lbs' and AnimalType = 'Puppy'
-- Frans's update query, this will now fail.
Update Animals
    Set AnimalWeight = '60 lbs'
where
    AnimalID = 1 and AnimalWeight = '3 lbs'
```

This query sequence will succeed for Erick, but it will fail for Frans. At this point, however, Frans will have the ability to refresh the data back from the database. He will intelligently decide that, indeed, Erick has already done half the work by updating Puppy to Dog, but Frans doesn't quite agree that the dog is only 50 lbs. So Frans will reexecute a set of queries as shown here, to update *only the Dog's weight*:

```
-- Frans's Select query
Select AnimalID, AnimalType, AnimalWeight from Animals

-- Frans's update query
Update Animals
    Set AnimalWeight = '60 lbs'
where
    AnimalID = 1 and AnimalWeight = '50 lbs'
```

This query will now succeed. So in this approach, Frans was prevented from making changes to a row that had changed. He was rightfully informed that another user had modified the row. Given such a meaningful message and the latest data on his screen, he could now easily update the Animal row and change only its weight.

Obviously, this approach has the plus of not having a very complex WHERE clause. Also, such a WHERE clause would generally be specified by you in advance, instead of being queried from the database. This would generally lead to better performance in comparison with a query that compares every single column in the WHERE clause, though query plans could change much too frequently to be effectively cached.

There are still a few problems with this approach, though.

Checking for Timestamps

In our pursuit to find the best concurrency management scheme, the last approach discussed updating the database by specifying only the primary key and the modified columns.

The first obvious downside of this approach is that you would need to reformulate the query every time. While that could be done, it would involve string manipulation either in the database or in the application logic—not to mention that because the query structure would change, the database will not cache the execution plan, thus leading to lower performance.

Another sinister, but not as obvious, problem is that a hole exists in the previous logic.

Let's say that in the second pass of queries that Frans was executing, he queried a Dog that weighed 50 lbs and now he wishes to update the Dog to 60 lbs. In the meantime, a third user, Sushil, comes between the query and update that Frans did. Sushil changes the Dog to a Monkey. So the sequence of queries in the second pass would now look somewhat like this:

```
-- Frans's Select query
Select AnimalID, AnimalType, AnimalWeight from Animals
-- Sushil's Select query
Select AnimalID, AnimalType, AnimalWeight from Animals

-- Sushil's Update query
Update Animals
    Set AnimalType = 'Monkey'
where
    AnimalID = 1 and AnimalType = 'Dog'
-- Frans's update query
Update Animals
    AnimalWeight = '60 lbs'
where
    AnimalID = 1 and AnimalWeight = '50 lbs'
```

So at the end of the execution of these queries

- Sushil thinks he has a Monkey that weighs 50 lbs.

- Erick thinks he has a Dog that weighs 50 lbs.

- Frans thinks he has a Dog that weighs 60 lbs.

But when Pablo (a fourth user) requests for `AnimalID = 1`, he gets back a Monkey that weighs 60 lbs.

Naturally, this is not the best approach—even though it's the best performing approach that is most easily portable between databases.

The Microsoft SQL Server database offers the `Timestamp` column. The `Timestamp` column is a column on a table that changes every time a DML operation is done to it.

An `UPDATE` query that makes use of the `Timestamp` column looks like this:

```
Update Animals
    AnimalWeight = '60 lbs'
where
    AnimalID = 1 and TimeStamp = 0x00000000000007D1
```

It's important to note that if you choose to use transactional updates (as described in the next chapter) for optimistic concurrency as implemented in the application to work properly, the application must use a low transaction level such as `ReadCommitted`. As you'll also see in the next chapter, as you raise isolation levels your concurrent performance goes down. In the previously described situation for instance, you gain no advantage by choosing a higher isolation level such as Serializable, so you should try and keep it as low as possible. In this case, ReadCommitted would be ideal. The one lower isolation level, ReadUncommitted, should be avoided if you want any kind of data sanctity. But before I confuse you with too many new words, let's reserve a deeper discussion on that in the next chapter.

Another important point to note is that the T-SQL timestamp data type is not the same as the timestamp data type defined in the SQL-92 standard. The SQL-92 timestamp data type is equivalent to the T-SQL datetime data type. A future release of Microsoft SQL Server may modify the behavior of the T-SQL Timestamp data type to align it with the behavior defined in the standard. At that time, the current timestamp data type will be replaced with a RowVersion data type.

For you to be able to use a Timestamp column in a table, you have to specify it during the table creation:

```
CREATE TABLE SomeTable (identifier int PRIMARY KEY, timestamp)
```

The column name in this case would be "timestamp". RowVersion on the other hand requires you to specify a column name.

Which Concurrency Model Do You Choose: Pessimistic or Optimistic?

So this is weird, while pessimistic concurrency models require you to implement more checks at the server end (or the logic that surrounds the server), optimistic concurrency models cause more user frustration where *someone* (either Erick or Frans) will lose their work.

So what do you do? Well, here are two cardinal rules to follow when architecting your data access strategy in highly concurrent environments:

1. Given the transactional nature of databases and your operations, you *have to lock resources for some time at some point*. The idea is to lower the contention, the time duration, and the amount of resources you lock. This is achieved by not keeping the connection open for too long and keeping user interaction out of the time duration the resources are locked at the database level. In other words, *database resources should be locked for the least amount of time possible*.

2. Keep the user in the forefront of your thoughts. A screen that takes 10 minutes to fill needs a pessimistic logical model wrapped around the logic that sits next to the database. This is because you don't want to tell the user that his 10 minutes of careful hard work is lost!

   But you shouldn't break rule 1 either. That is, you cannot lock database resources for 10 minutes at a particular user's whim. In other words, rows that need to be modified, but take 10 minutes to specify the modifications, need to implement a check-in/check-out functionality. Now the actual check-in process, the actual check-out process, and—once you have the changes ready—the actual update are small, low-contention operations that don't involve interactive user inputs. Those can then be wrapped within a single transaction with implicit resource locking as a result—but only for a very short duration, and on as little resources as possible.

Many interesting design patterns arise out of this; for instance, here are a few real-world applications:

- A concert ticket booking website can implement functionality to lock your seats for 2 minutes. This way, the seats are checked out to you for 2 minutes, so no explicit clean-up logic is needed. If another user requests the same seats after 2 minutes, you lose the seats; that is, your records are implicitly checked in due to time lapse.

- A payment application to an insurance account would need you to first open a batch, enter checks, and then close a batch before you can apply the batch. Of course, the user would also request the identity keys in advance for the checks they are about to enter.

- An e-commerce site may decide that checking inventory every time an order is placed for a popular item is too expensive to do at every order placement. Instead, it may choose to inform the last five or ten users that their orders cannot be fulfilled or, when the inventory drops below a certain number, it may show a message informing that their orders may be delayed.

- When editing a complex screen full of information about a patient, you would first need to take it out of read-only mode (check out), then do your changes, and finally save (check in your changes).

The common underlying theme is to avoid situations that lock too many resources for too long at a given point in time and implement as many optimistic checks to keep the system more maintainable. But in a real-world application, that is never completely unavoidable. In those instances, you need to decide on the right combination of approaches that have been mentioned here.

Implementing Concurrency: Practical Concerns

Per the previous academic discussion, you could probably come up with a concurrency mechanism that suits you best. In most cases, you would probably want to go with optimistic concurrency. As a matter of fact, even where you need strict row locking, you could use alternate mechanisms such as check-in/check-out logic and not create actual row locks in the database.

When you have selected an appropriate concurrency management strategy, there are a few things you need to consider when implementing concurrency in your data layer.

Null Values

.NET 1.x doesn't allow nullable value types like databases or languages such as C++ may allow you to have. .NET 2.0 did introduce nullable value types, but they are not quite the same as the nullable value types that may exist in the context of databases or C++; thus, those don't go all the way in helping you deal with the null mismatches between databases and .NET. It's for this purpose that .NET provides you with various facilities to work with nullable columns in the database.

A database null is represented by the `System.DBNull` structure in .NET. Usually, this can be easily retrieved using the `System.Convert.DBNull` constant to assign null values to a column. Alternatively, on reads you can use the `DbDataReader.IsNull` method to check if a particular column is null or not. As a better performing alternative, you could also compare the result of `GetValue` with `DBNull.Value` inside a data reader loop.

Strongly typed `DataSets` make it even easier for you by allowing you to set a particular column to null using the syntax as shown in the following code:

C#

```
rowAnimal.IsAnimalTypeNull();
rowAnimal.SetAnimalTypeNull() ;
```

VB.NET

```
rowAnimal.IsAnimalTypeNull()
rowAnimal.SetAnimalTypeNull()
```

If this were not a strongly typed DataSet, your code would look something like this:

C#

```
if (rowAnimal.IsNull("AnimalType")) { ... }
// And
rowAnimal("AnimalType") = Convert.DBNull ;
```

VB.NET

```
If rowAnimal.IsNull("AnimalType") Then
...
End If
' And
rowAnimal("AnimalType") = Convert.DBNull
```

Specifically for concurrency concerns, if you do need to check for null values in a SQL query, your query's WHERE clause must include

```
Where AnimalType IS NULL
```

instead of

```
Where AnimalType = NULL
```

If the query needs to adjust for both null and not null values, you could write the WHERE clause like so:

```
Where (AnimalType = ? OR ((AnimalType IS NULL) AND (? IS NULL)))
```

The ? character represents a configurable parameter.

Number of Rows Affected and Triggers

A *trigger* is a piece of code in your database that gets executed after a certain operation occurs. Typically, you might want to implement a trigger for auditing purposes on inserts on a table.

The issue triggers create is that, in SQL Server Management Studio, if you inserted a row into a table that has such a trigger set on it, SQL Server Management Studio would return output that looks like this:

```
(1 row(s) affected)
(1 row(s) affected)
```

This output is correct since the first row is due to the insert you did and the second is probably an insert into the log table—thanks to the trigger. The problem is this: when you run ExecuteNonQuery on such a command, ExecuteNonQuery will tell you that it ended up modifying two rows. Since concurrency management schemes depend on checking how many rows did get modified, such an approach would create a problem.

The work-around for this is to use SQL Server's NOCOUNT setting. By setting NOCOUNT ON and NOCOUNT OFF at appropriate places inside the trigger, you can ensure that you do not confuse your application logic by reporting changed rows that might not be important from a concurrency check point of view.

Similarly, if you have a batched SQL statement, or a stored procedure which has multiple statements modifying rows, then you need to execute SELECT @@ROWCOUNT to find the exact number of rows modified at each specific given statement.

Multiple Rows Being Updated

This is a tricky one. You have a DataTable with three rows changed. One is inserted, another is modified, and the third is deleted. Now, assuming that you have specified an InsertCommand, UpdateCommand, and DeleteCommand on the DataAdapter, the appropriate commands will get called one by one based upon the various RowStates.

Say the InsertCommand succeeds, but the modified (UpdateCommand) fails; should you then

- Go ahead and execute the DeleteCommand?

- Stop execution right there?

- Roll back the InsertCommand?

Well, technically per your application logic, you should be able to choose any of these three. The exact situation might demand that you handle each scenario per its specific requirements. It's for this reason that you have the ContinueUpdateOnError property on a DataAdapter. The behavior is actually quite simple: By leaving ContinueUpdateOnError on false (the default value), if an error occurs during the execution of a command for a particular changed row, you should get a DbConcurrencyException. At that point, the DataAdapter will stop executing any further commands and return.

If you set the ContinueUpdateOnError property to true, the DataAdapter would continue executing commands. Its default value is false because by setting this property to false, you complete or fail an entire update operation and report success only on a complete success. That is, if one row fails the whole operation fails; thus, making the update atomic in nature if indeed you did wrap it in a transaction.

However, it's important that, in this case, ADO.NET should somehow inform us of the rows that have errors in them. This can be easily found out using the DataRow.HasErrors property to verify if a particular row has errors in it or not. If it does have errors, then you can get the exact error description using the DataRow.RowError property. Similarly, the DataSet and DataTable also have the HasErrors property, which lets you easily identify any errors at a global level. If a DataRow does have an error when it's databound to a DataGridView control, the particular row shows an exclamation mark indicating an error, and the tool tip indicates the error description (you can see this in action in Exercise 9.1).

Also, once all the errors have been reconciled, you can use the `ClearErrors` method to clear all errors on a `DataRow`, `DataTable`, or `DataSet`.

Finally, on an error condition, in certain cases, you not only want to stop execution, but you also want to roll back anything you have done so far. This can be done using transactions, which will be covered in Chapter 11.

Working with Hierarchical Data

So far in this chapter and in Chapter 9, you have covered all the fundamentals that would allow you to deal with various updating scenarios including concurrency in most practical settings. Strangely enough, most of the examples shown deal with only one `DataTable`, or a `DataSet` with one `DataTable`. As a matter of fact, drag-and-drop operations, command builders, etc., all work well with only one table. If you need something more complex, you will need to implement your own queries.

Alas, the answer is usually never as simple as "implement your own queries"!

It's quite probable that in working with `DataSets` you might have hierarchical updates that might need to be saved into the database. These hierarchical changes pose interesting challenges.

This is best demonstrated using an example. So far the examples have used the `Animals` table, which allows you to enter different animal types. Go ahead and add another table to that `DataSet`. This is the `Pets` table, and because each pet is an Animal, there is a foreign-key relationship between the `Pets` table and the `Animals` table using the `AnimalID` as the foreign key. Also, to make things even more interesting, go ahead and add a third table called `PetBelonging`. This table will be used to save the belongings of a pet you might have. So a Dog called Tashu might have a collar, a bowl, and a bone. The database table layout diagram can be seen in Figure 10-1.

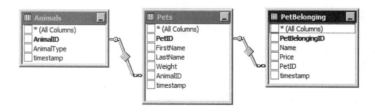

Figure 10-1. *A sample hierarchical database*

You can download the code for this discussion in Exercise 10.1, and you can download the database setup script in setup `database.sql` from the associated code download (see the Downloads section of the Apress website at `http://www.apress.com`).

As you can see in the code download, to make our lives easier the exercise uses a strongly typed DataSet. The strongly typed DataSet contains three tables as shown in Figure 10-2, which mimic the database table structure.

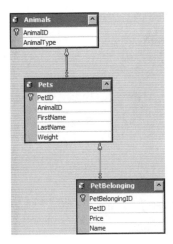

Figure 10-2. *The strongly typed DataSet*

Because the strongly typed DataSet is intended to store a disconnected cache, some of the concepts learned in this chapter are used to set up primary keys, seed, and increment values in the three tables. Thus, in Exercise 10.1 you can see Animals.AnimalID, Pets.PetID, and PetBelonging.PetBelongingID have been set up as primary keys with AutoIncrementSeed = 0, and AutoIncrementStep = -1 in the strongly typed DataSet.

Finally, again to mimic the database, two relationships are set up between the three DataTables representing the foreign keys that exist in the database. The first is FK_Animals_Pets between Animals.AnimalID and Pets.AnimalID, and the second is FK_Pets_PetBelonging between Pets. PetID, and PetBelonging.PetID. These relationships have their update rule and delete rule set to cascade by default.

With the DataSet set up, the three tables can be easily bound to three DataGridViews to generate columns at design time. Also, just to make sure the user doesn't meddle with the autogenerated keys, the primary columns in all three tables, Animals.AnimalID, Pets.PetID, and PetBelonging.PetBelongingID, have been marked as read only.

The final UI in design time looks like as shown in Figure 10-3.

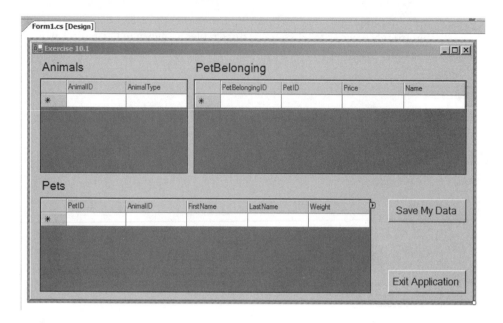

Figure 10-3. *The user interface for Exercise 10.1 in Design view*

As you can see, there are only two buttons: One exits the application, which simply calls a this.Close/Me.Close. The other button is quite interesting; it just says Save My Data, which is typically the level of complexity you should expect the user to deal with. Behind Save My Data it should take care of all various issues a disconnected cache might create.

Finally, in the form's constructor or load event, with the UI set up as mentioned previously, you can simply use some TableMappings magic to fill the data in the right tables. The DataSet being filled is animalsData, which is a private member variable at the form level. This is shown in Listings 10-1 and 10-2. The FillData/Sub method is called from either the form's constructor or from the form's load event.

Listing 10-1. *Filling the DataSet and Data Binding It to the Right DataGridViews in C#*

```
private void FillData()
{
    animalsData = new AnimalsDataSet();
    SqlDataAdapter sqlDa = new SqlDataAdapter(
        "Select * from Animals; Select * from Pets; Select * from PetBelonging",
        connectionString);
    sqlDa.TableMappings.Add("Table", "Animals");
    sqlDa.TableMappings.Add("Table1", "Pets");
    sqlDa.TableMappings.Add("Table2", "PetBelonging");
    sqlDa.Fill(animalsData);
```

```
   dgAnimals.DataSource = animalsData.Tables["Animals"];
   dgPets.DataSource = animalsData.Tables["Pets"];
   dgPetBelonging.DataSource = animalsData.Tables["PetBelonging"];
}
```

Listing 10-2. *Filling the DataSet and Data Binding It to the Right DataGridViews in Visual Basic .NET*

```
Private Sub FillData()
   animalsData = New AnimalsDataSet()
   Dim sqlDA As SqlDataAdapter = New SqlDataAdapter( _
      "Select * from Animals; Select * from Pets;" & _
      "Select * from PetBelonging", _
   connectionString)
   sqlDa.TableMappings.Add("Table", "Animals")
   sqlDa.TableMappings.Add("Table1", "Pets")
   sqlDa.TableMappings.Add("Table2", "PetBelonging")
   sqlDa.Fill(animalsData)

   dgAnimals.DataSource = animalsData.Tables("Animals")
   dgPets.DataSource = animalsData.Tables("Pets")
   dgPetBelonging.DataSource = _
   animalsData.Tables("PetBelonging")
End Sub
```

Now if you run the application, you should see the data populated as shown in Figure 10-4.

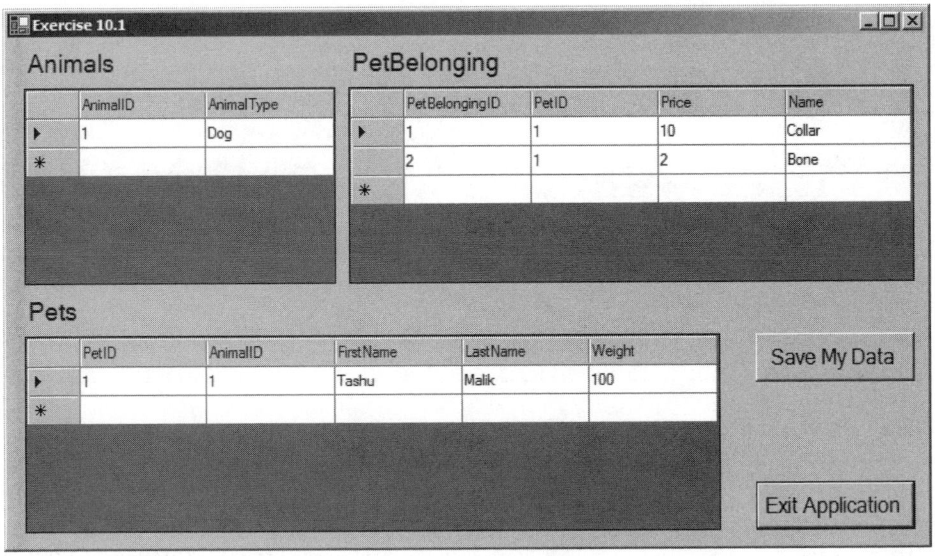

Figure 10-4. *The application allowing the user to edit data at runtime*

Great, now that the application is able to display the data, this is where the fun begins!

The disconnected cache will maintain a certain level of data sanctity by virtue of the various relationships set up. So it's safe to assume that in this application, the three cases you would have to deal with are INSERTs, UPDATEs and DELETEs.

Let's look at INSERTs first.

Inserting Hierarchical Data

The DataSet schema defined in the application will maintain some level of data sanctity. Specifically, it will ensure the data types, presence of required fields, and foreign-key values (or referential integrity).

Given that we have three tables, any data that is inserted into the database will have to be inserted in a top-down approach. In other words, let's assume that you want to make the following changes to the database:

- Add a new animal type: Monkey.

- Add a new pet of type "monkey": Jimmy Malik.

- Jimmy Malik has a "pet belonging": swing, which costs 25 dollars.

The changes that you must make to the data are shown in Figure 10-5.

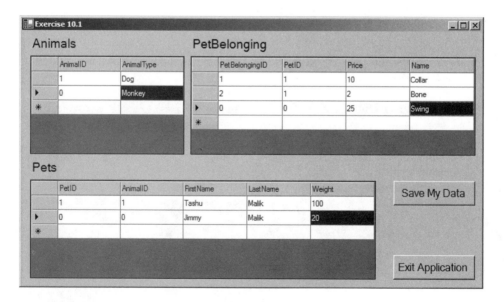

Figure 10-5. *Newly added data in the application*

So sit back and think, what is the piece of data that you absolutely need, but do not have yet in order to save the swing that cost 25 dollars into the PetBelonging table? Naturally, it's the pet that the swing belongs to. The pet being Jimmy who cannot be saved into the Pets table unless an Animal exists that identifies Jimmy as a Monkey.

So the first table that needs to be saved is the `Animals` table, followed by the `Pets` table using the key received from the `Animals` table, and finally the `PetBelonging` table—thus, a "top-down" approach. The insert command for the `Animals` table, `insertAnimalCommand`, is shown in Listings 10-3 and 10-4.

Listing 10-3. *Setting Up the insertAnimalCommand in C#*

```
SqlCommand insertAnimalCommand = new SqlCommand();
insertAnimalCommand.Connection = testConnection;
insertAnimalCommand = new SqlCommand("UP_ANIMALINSERT");
insertAnimalCommand.CommandType = CommandType.StoredProcedure;

param = new SqlParameter("@AnimalID", SqlDbType.Int, 4, "AnimalID");
param.Direction = ParameterDirection.Output;
insertAnimalCommand.Parameters.Add(param);

param = new SqlParameter("@AnimalType", SqlDbType.VarChar, 50, "AnimalType");
param.Direction = ParameterDirection.Input;
insertAnimalCommand.Parameters.Add(param);

insertAnimalCommand.Transaction = trans;
```

Listing 10-4. *Setting Up the insertAnimalCommand in Visual Basic .NET*

```
Dim insertAnimalCommand As SqlCommand = New SqlCommand()
insertAnimalCommand.Connection = testConnection
insertAnimalCommand = New SqlCommand("UP_ANIMALINSERT")
insertAnimalCommand.CommandType = CommandType.StoredProcedure

param = New SqlParameter("@AnimalID", SqlDbType.Int, 4, "AnimalID")
param.Direction = ParameterDirection.Output
insertAnimalCommand.Parameters.Add(param)

param = New SqlParameter("@AnimalType", SqlDbType.VarChar, 50, "AnimalType")
param.Direction = ParameterDirection.Input
insertAnimalCommand.Parameters.Add(param)

insertAnimalCommand.Transaction = trans
```

Curiously enough, look at the last statement in these two listings. What is effectively being done is a transaction is being set up. Even though transactions will be covered in depth in the next chapter, at this point it's sufficient to understand that the commands executed upon the three tables must lie within a transaction because if for some reason an insert on the `PetBelongings` table fails, you don't want to leave orphan rows in either the `Pets` table or the `Animals` table. A transaction will ensure that all the rows will either insert and be committed, or will not insert and will be rolled back together. Setting up a transaction is fairly easy and can be achieved with the following code:

C#

```
testConnection.Open();
SqlTransaction trans = testConnection.BeginTransaction();
```

VB.NET

```
testConnection.Open()
Dim trans As SqlTransaction = testConnection.BeginTransaction()
```

One immediately apparent downside of setting up a command like this is that you need to open the connection and keep it open until the transaction is either rolled back or committed. So this goes back to the two rules previously specified, and necessitates that you keep user input out of the transaction itself because the user, based on his whim, could now keep the transaction running and the connection open for an unnecessarily long time.

Also, you may notice that in Listings 10-3 and 10-4, the AnimalID parameter is an "OUT" parameter; in other words, using the concepts you learned in Chapter 9, as the data adapter calls the INSERT command for each row added in the data table one by one, the respective AnimalID has to be fetched back into the Animals DataTable. This is where it gets really interesting. Because the UpdateRule on FK_Animals_Pets has been set to cascade, these newly fetched AnimalIDs are then automatically copied to the Pets DataTable.

The stored procedure for inserting an animal into the Animals database is shown in Listing 10-5.

Listing 10-5. *Stored Procedure for Inserting an Animal into the Database*

```
CREATE PROCEDURE UP_ANIMALINSERT
  @AnimalID INT OUTPUT,
  @AnimalType VARCHAR(50)
AS
    INSERT INTO ANIMALS
       (AnimalType)
    VALUES
       (@AnimalType)

    SELECT @AnimalID = SCOPE_IDENTITY()
GO
```

Similarly, the commands for the Pets table and the PetBelonging table can be set up in .NET code as per Listings 10-6 and 10-7.

Listing 10-6. *Setting Up the insertPetCommand and insertPetBelongingCommand in C#*

```
// Moving down the hierarchy - the Pets Table
#region insertPetCommand
SqlCommand insertPetCommand = new SqlCommand();
insertPetCommand.Connection = testConnection;
```

```csharp
insertPetCommand = new SqlCommand("UP_PETSINSERT");
insertPetCommand.CommandType = CommandType.StoredProcedure;

param = new SqlParameter("@PetID", SqlDbType.Int, 4, "PetID");
param.Direction = ParameterDirection.Output;
insertPetCommand.Parameters.Add(param);

param = new SqlParameter("@FirstName", SqlDbType.VarChar, 50, "FirstName");
param.Direction = ParameterDirection.Input;
insertPetCommand.Parameters.Add(param);

param = new SqlParameter("@LastName", SqlDbType.VarChar, 50, "LastName");
param.Direction = ParameterDirection.Input;
insertPetCommand.Parameters.Add(param);

param = new SqlParameter("@Weight", SqlDbType.Int, 4, "Weight");
param.Direction = ParameterDirection.Input;
insertPetCommand.Parameters.Add(param);

// This parameter will be retrieved from the first command insertAnimalCommand
param = new SqlParameter("@AnimalID", SqlDbType.Int, 4, "AnimalID");
param.Direction = ParameterDirection.Input;
insertPetCommand.Parameters.Add(param);

insertPetCommand.Transaction = trans;
#endregion

// Finally moving to the end of the hierarchy - PetBelonging
#region insertPetBelongingCommand
SqlCommand insertPetBelongingCommand = new SqlCommand();
insertPetBelongingCommand.Connection = testConnection;

insertPetBelongingCommand = new SqlCommand("UP_PETBELONGINGINSERT");
insertPetBelongingCommand.CommandType = CommandType.StoredProcedure;

param = new SqlParameter("@PetBelongingID", SqlDbType.Int, 4, "PetBelongingID");
param.Direction = ParameterDirection.Output;
insertPetBelongingCommand.Parameters.Add(param);

param = new SqlParameter("@Name", SqlDbType.VarChar, 50, "Name");
param.Direction = ParameterDirection.Input;
insertPetBelongingCommand.Parameters.Add(param);

param = new SqlParameter("@Price", SqlDbType.Float, 8, "Price");
param.Direction = ParameterDirection.Input;
insertPetBelongingCommand.Parameters.Add(param);
```

```
// This parameter will be retrieved from the first command insertPetCommand
param = new SqlParameter("@PetID", SqlDbType.Int, 4, "PetID");
param.Direction = ParameterDirection.Input;
insertPetBelongingCommand.Parameters.Add(param);

insertPetBelongingCommand.Transaction = trans;
#endregion
```

Listing 10-7. *Setting Up the insertPetCommand and insertPetBelongingCommand in Visual Basic .NET*

```
' Moving down the hierarchy - the Pets Table
'   insertPetCommand
Dim insertPetCommand As SqlCommand = New SqlCommand()
insertPetCommand.Connection = testConnection

insertPetCommand = New SqlCommand("UP_PETSINSERT")
insertPetCommand.CommandType = CommandType.StoredProcedure

param = New SqlParameter("@PetID", SqlDbType.Int, 4, "PetID")
param.Direction = ParameterDirection.Output
insertPetCommand.Parameters.Add(param)

param = New SqlParameter("@FirstName", SqlDbType.VarChar, 50, "FirstName")
param.Direction = ParameterDirection.Input
insertPetCommand.Parameters.Add(param)

param = New SqlParameter("@LastName", SqlDbType.VarChar, 50, "LastName")
param.Direction = ParameterDirection.Input
insertPetCommand.Parameters.Add(param)

param = New SqlParameter("@Weight", SqlDbType.Int, 4, "Weight")
param.Direction = ParameterDirection.Input
insertPetCommand.Parameters.Add(param)

' This parameter will be retrieved from the first command insertAnimalCommand
param = New SqlParameter("@AnimalID", SqlDbType.Int, 4, "AnimalID")
param.Direction = ParameterDirection.Input
insertPetCommand.Parameters.Add(param)

insertPetCommand.Transaction = trans

' Finally moving to the end of the hierarchy - PetBelonging
'   insertPetBelongingCommand
Dim insertPetBelongingCommand As SqlCommand = New SqlCommand()
insertPetBelongingCommand.Connection = testConnection
```

```
insertPetBelongingCommand = New SqlCommand("UP_PETBELONGINGINSERT")
insertPetBelongingCommand.CommandType = CommandType.StoredProcedure

param = New SqlParameter("@PetBelongingID", SqlDbType.Int, 4, "PetBelongingID")
param.Direction = ParameterDirection.Output
insertPetBelongingCommand.Parameters.Add(param)

param = New SqlParameter("@Name", SqlDbType.VarChar, 50, "Name")
param.Direction = ParameterDirection.Input
insertPetBelongingCommand.Parameters.Add(param)

param = New SqlParameter("@Price", SqlDbType.Float, 8, "Price")
param.Direction = ParameterDirection.Input
insertPetBelongingCommand.Parameters.Add(param)

' This parameter will be retrieved from the first command insertPetCommand
param = New SqlParameter("@PetID", SqlDbType.Int, 4, "PetID")
param.Direction = ParameterDirection.Input
insertPetBelongingCommand.Parameters.Add(param)

insertPetBelongingCommand.Transaction = trans
```

The respective stored procedures can be set up using the code shown in Listing 10-8.

Listing 10-8. *Stored Procedures for Inserting a Pet and a PetBelonging into the Database*

```
CREATE PROCEDURE UP_PETSINSERT
  @PetID INT OUTPUT,
  @FirstName VARCHAR(50),
  @LastName VARCHAR(50),
  @Weight INT,
  @AnimalID INT
AS
    INSERT INTO PETS
                        (FirstName, LastName, Weight, AnimalID)
    VALUES
                        (@FirstName, @LastName, @Weight, @AnimalID)

    SELECT @PetID = SCOPE_IDENTITY()
GO


CREATE PROCEDURE UP_PETBELONGINGINSERT
  @PetBelongingID INT OUTPUT,
  @Name VARCHAR(50),
  @Price FLOAT,
  @PetID INT
```

```
AS
   INSERT INTO PETBELONGING
                         (Name, Price, PetID)
   VALUES
                         (@Name, @Price, @PetID)

   SELECT @PetBelongingID = SCOPE_IDENTITY()
GO
```

Once the commands are set up, the actual work can be started. As mentioned earlier, the insertions need to be done in a top-down approach. So, first, an insert is done into the Animals table, followed by the Pets table, followed by the PetBelonging table.

As you can see in Listings 10-9 and 10-10, an interesting point to note is the transaction. If any of these INSERT commands throws an exception, it's important to roll back all the changes, which can typically be done in the catch block of a try...catch...finally block. Since the finally block will get executed irrespective of the fact that the transaction commits or rolls back, it's a perfect candidate for putting in a call to close the connection and to fill the DataSet again with the latest data from the database.

Listing 10-9. *Persisting Inserts Back into the Database Using Three New Instances of DataAdapter for Three Tables in C#*

```csharp
// .. Start the work
try
{
    sqlDa = new SqlDataAdapter("Select * from Animals", testConnection);
    sqlDa.InsertCommand = insertAnimalCommand;
    sqlDa.InsertCommand.Connection = testConnection;
    sqlDa.Update(animalsData.Animals.Select("", "", DataViewRowState.Added));

    sqlDa = new SqlDataAdapter("Select * from Pets", testConnection);
    sqlDa.InsertCommand = insertPetCommand;
    sqlDa.InsertCommand.Connection = testConnection;
    sqlDa.Update(animalsData.Pets.Select("", "", DataViewRowState.Added));

    sqlDa = new SqlDataAdapter("Select * from PetBelonging", testConnection);
    sqlDa.InsertCommand = insertPetBelongingCommand;
    sqlDa.InsertCommand.Connection = testConnection;
    sqlDa.Update(animalsData.PetBelonging.Select("", "", DataViewRowState.Added));

    // All good, let's commit.
    trans.Commit();
}
```

```
catch (System.Exception)
{
   trans.Rollback();
}
finally
{
   FillData();
   testConnection.Dispose();
}
```

Listing 10-10. *Persisting Inserts Back into the Database Using Three New Instances of DataAdapter for Three Tables in Visual Basic .NET*

```
' .. Start the work
Try
   sqlDa = New SqlDataAdapter("Select * from Animals", testConnection)
   sqlDa.InsertCommand = insertAnimalCommand
   sqlDa.InsertCommand.Connection = testConnection
   sqlDa.Update(animalsData.Animals.Select("", "", DataViewRowState.Added))

   sqlDa = New SqlDataAdapter("Select * from Pets", testConnection)
   sqlDa.InsertCommand = insertPetCommand
   sqlDa.InsertCommand.Connection = testConnection
   sqlDa.Update(animalsData.Pets.Select("", "", DataViewRowState.Added))

   sqlDa = New SqlDataAdapter("Select * from PetBelonging", testConnection)
   sqlDa.InsertCommand = insertPetBelongingCommand
   sqlDa.InsertCommand.Connection = testConnection
   sqlDa.Update(animalsData.PetBelonging.Select("", "", DataViewRowState.Added))

   ' All good, let's commit.
   trans.Commit()
Catch
   trans.Rollback()
Finally
   FillData()
   testConnection.Dispose()
End Try
```

After this code is done executing, you can see the retrieved data back in the application as shown in Figure 10-6. Notice that the newly generated keys correspond with the hierarchical relationships.

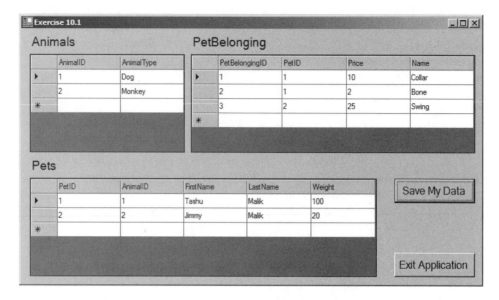

Figure 10-6. *Added data, after clicking the Save button. Notice the Key values.*

As you can see in Listings 10-9 and 10-10, a special overload of the DataAdapter's Update method was used. DbDataAdapter.Update supports a few other overloads as shown in Table 10-5.

Table 10-5. *DbDataAdapter.Update Overloads*

Constant	Description
DbDataAdapter.Update(DataRow[])	Calls INSERT, UPDATE, DELETE on various changed rows specified in the data row array.
DbDataAdapter.Update(DataSet)	Calls INSERT, UPDATE, DELETE on various changed rows in the first table of the DataSet. Note that previous MSDN documentation versions specify that the commands will be called on all rows in the DataSet; that is incorrect.
DbDataAdapter.Update(DataTable)	Calls INSERT, UPDATE, DELETE on various changed rows in the specified DataTable.
DbDataAdapter.Update(DataRow[].DataTableMapping)	Calls INSERT, UPDATE, DELETE on various changed rows in the specified DataRow array, while taking care of various mappings.
DbDataAdapter.Update(DataSet, String)	Calls INSERT, UPDATE, DELETE on various changed rows in one DataTable of a DataSet identified by the second parameter.

The overload used is DbDataAdapter.Update(DataRow[]). The DataRow array is filtered out for only the added rows using the DataTable.Select method. The reason this was necessary was because, in hierarchical updates, inserted rows might need a different logic than updated (DataViewRowState.ModifiedCurrent) or deleted (DataViewRowState.Deleted) rows.

Let's look at those cases next.

Updating Hierarchical Data

Updating data is actually simpler—you simply call UpdateCommand using the data adapter one by one on all involved tables. Obviously, like the InsertCommand, it would make sense to wrap all such interactions in a transaction.

Generally, you should also put in a suitable concurrency check, like in this application's table structure case, you can simply check for timestamps. So the UPDATE SQL query could look something like this:

```
Update Animals
Set AnimalName = @AnimalName
Where AnimalID = @AnimalID and timestamp = @timestamp
```

The only complication that might arise would be if you decided to update a row that involved a change in the data of a hierarchical relationship. Even though the DataSet will maintain foreign-key sanctity, you might end up in a situation where a child table is being updated to a foreign-key value *before the foreign-key value is saved.* In other words, if you decided to change Tashu Malik to a Monkey instead of a Dog but if the Monkey hadn't been saved yet, then you'd get an error.

Therefore, it makes sense to do updates in a top-down approach, but make sure that updates are done *after* insert commands have been executed.

Deleting Hierarchical Data

Deleting hierarchical data is probably the most different. As you saw earlier, inserts should be done in a top-down approach; updates must be done after inserts, but in a top-down approach; and deletions are actually upside down.

Deletes must be done in a down-top approach. This is so because, say for instance, after having saved Jimmy Malik as a Monkey that has a Swing for a belonging, in the next transaction you wish to delete Jimmy the Monkey, his Swing, and the animal Monkey.

If you were to go in a top-down approach, you'd first delete the animal Monkey. Right at that moment, you'd get an error informing you that related rows (namely the row that identifies Jimmy Malik) depend on the row you are trying to delete, thus you cannot delete Monkey. The exact error would look something like this:

```
DELETE statement conflicted with REFERENCE constraint
FK__Pets__AnimalID__7F60ED59'.
The conflict occurred in database 'Test', table 'Pets', column 'AnimalID'
```

Therefore, it's important that the PetBelonging row that holds a Swing should be deleted first, followed by the Pets row, and finally by the Animal row.

Putting It All Together: Saving Hierarchical Data

The previous discussion showed you how to segregate the relevant rows and what order you would operate SQL queries on them in order to save them in the database, while taking care of concurrency. So here are the conclusions of saving hierarchical data:

- Do inserts first in a top-down approach.

- Then do updates in a top-down approach.

- Finally, do deletes in a down-top approach.

Note These are not cardinal, unbreakable rules. They just make sense in most cases, though depending on the exact structure of your DataSet you might come up with a different approach. It's important to understand how a DataAdapter works, and then understand the previous discussion that concludes with these three points, rather than just memorizing them.

The final "Save My Data" code for the given DataSet in Exercise 10.1 would look somewhat like Listings 10-11 and 10-12. Obviously, this is just an outline. Generally, you would put such transactional code in either using blocks or in try...catch constructs.

Listing 10-11. *Insert, Update, Delete Code for a Hierarchical DataSet in C#*

```
// First inserts and updates in a top-down approach.
sqlDa = new SqlDataAdapter("Select * from Animals", testConnection);
sqlDa.InsertCommand = insertAnimalCommand;
sqlDa.InsertCommand.Connection = testConnection;
sqlDa.Update(animalsData.Animals.Select("", "", DataViewRowState.Added));

sqlDa = new SqlDataAdapter("Select * from Animals", testConnection);
sqlDa.UpdateCommand = updateAnimalCommand;
sqlDa.UpdateCommand.Connection = testConnection;
sqlDa.Update(animalsData.Animals.Select("", "", DataViewRowState.ModifiedCurrent));

sqlDa = new SqlDataAdapter("Select * from Pets", testConnection);
sqlDa.InsertCommand = insertPetCommand;
sqlDa.InsertCommand.Connection = testConnection;
sqlDa.Update(animalsData.Pets.Select("", "", DataViewRowState.Added));

sqlDa = new SqlDataAdapter("Select * from Pets", testConnection);
sqlDa.UpdateCommand = updatePetCommand;
sqlDa.UpdateCommand.Connection = testConnection;
sqlDa.Update(animalsData.Pets.Select("", "", DataViewRowState.ModifiedCurrent));

sqlDa = new SqlDataAdapter("Select * from PetBelonging", testConnection);
sqlDa.InsertCommand = insertPetBelongingCommand;
sqlDa.InsertCommand.Connection = testConnection;
sqlDa.Update(animalsData.PetBelonging.Select("", "", DataViewRowState.Added));

sqlDa = new SqlDataAdapter("Select * from PetBelonging", testConnection);
sqlDa.UpdateCommand = updatePetBelongingCommand;
sqlDa.UpdateCommand.Connection = testConnection;
```

```
sqlDa.Update(animalsData.PetBelonging.Select("", "",
    DataViewRowState.ModifiedCurrent));

// Finally deletes in a down-top approach.
sqlDa = new SqlDataAdapter("Select * from PetBelonging", testConnection);
sqlDa.DeleteCommand = deletePetBelongingCommand;
sqlDa.DeleteCommand.Connection = testConnection;
sqlDa.Update(animalsData.PetBelonging.Select("", "", DataViewRowState.Deleted));

sqlDa = new SqlDataAdapter("Select * from Pets", testConnection);
sqlDa.DeleteCommand = deletePetCommand;
sqlDa.DeleteCommand.Connection = testConnection;
sqlDa.Update(animalsData.Pet.Select("", "", DataViewRowState.Deleted));

sqlDa = new SqlDataAdapter("Select * from Animal", testConnection);
sqlDa.DeleteCommand = deleteAnimalCommand;
sqlDa.DeleteCommand.Connection = testConnection;
sqlDa.Update(animalsData.Animal.Select("", "", DataViewRowState.Deleted));
```

Listing 10-12. *Insert, Update, Delete Code for a Hierarchical DataSet in Visual Basic .NET*

```
' First inserts and updates in a top-down approach.
sqlDa = New SqlDataAdapter("Select * from Animals", testConnection)
sqlDa.InsertCommand = insertAnimalCommand
sqlDa.InsertCommand.Connection = testConnection
sqlDa.Update(animalsData.Animals.Select("", "", DataViewRowState.Added))

sqlDa = New SqlDataAdapter("Select * from Animals", testConnection)
sqlDa.UpdateCommand = updateAnimalCommand
sqlDa.UpdateCommand.Connection = testConnection
sqlDa.Update(animalsData.Animals.Select("", "", DataViewRowState.ModifiedCurrent))

sqlDa = New SqlDataAdapter("Select * from Pets", testConnection)
sqlDa.InsertCommand = insertPetCommand
sqlDa.InsertCommand.Connection = testConnection
sqlDa.Update(animalsData.Pets.Select("", "", DataViewRowState.Added))

sqlDa = New SqlDataAdapter("Select * from Pets", testConnection)
sqlDa.UpdateCommand = updatePetCommand
sqlDa.UpdateCommand.Connection = testConnection
sqlDa.Update(animalsData.Pets.Select("", "", DataViewRowState.ModifiedCurrent))

sqlDa = New SqlDataAdapter("Select * from PetBelonging", testConnection)
sqlDa.InsertCommand = insertPetBelongingCommand
sqlDa.InsertCommand.Connection = testConnection
sqlDa.Update(animalsData.PetBelonging.Select("", "", DataViewRowState.Added))
```

```
sqlDa = New SqlDataAdapter("Select * from PetBelonging", testConnection)
sqlDa.UpdateCommand = updatePetBelongingCommand
sqlDa.UpdateCommand.Connection = testConnection
sqlDa.Update(animalsData.PetBelonging.Select("", "",
    DataViewRowState.ModifiedCurrent))

' Finally deletes in a down-top approach.
sqlDa = New SqlDataAdapter("Select * from PetBelonging", testConnection)
sqlDa.DeleteCommand = deletePetBelongingCommand
sqlDa.DeleteCommand.Connection = testConnection
sqlDa.Update(animalsData.PetBelonging.Select("", "", DataViewRowState.Deleted))

sqlDa = New SqlDataAdapter("Select * from Pets", testConnection)
sqlDa.DeleteCommand = deletePetCommand
sqlDa.DeleteCommand.Connection = testConnection
sqlDa.Update(animalsData.Pet.Select("", "", DataViewRowState.Deleted))

sqlDa = New SqlDataAdapter("Select * from Animal", testConnection)
sqlDa.DeleteCommand = deleteAnimalCommand
sqlDa.DeleteCommand.Connection = testConnection
sqlDa.Update(animalsData.Animal.Select("", "", DataViewRowState.Deleted))
```

So what if you had a hierarchical relationship set up that didn't allow you to come up with such a clean top-down approach? It can still be done, but only as long as your single table fundamentals are clear and you understand the reasoning presented in this example.

Let me explain what I mean using a short description of how this argument could be applied to a many-to-many approach.

Say you have a Customers table, a Products table, and a CustomerProducts table that acts as a map between Customers and Products since there exists a many-to-many relationship between the two.

In such a case, there are two tables at the top (Customers and Products) and only one table at the bottom (CustomerProducts).

But you could still start at any one of the two tables at the top, say the Customers table, and get your inserts right first. This could be done by creating the DataRow array using GetChildRows instead of the Select method. Similarly, you could then use the Products table and, using a similar technique, insert all the newly entered products. At this point, you could then execute GetChildRows again to find all the relevant rows from the mapping table.

This leaves you with the newly inserted CustomerProducts rows. So how do you find the newly inserted CustomerProducts rows? Well, you could find them as all rows with RowState = Added from the relevant DataTable; but remember that in isolating inserts before updates before deletes, you need to find them as a union of the two sets of GetChildRows DataRow arrays you got from the Products table and Customers table. Thus, you would need to perform the extra step of removing duplicates between the two DataRow arrays that you prepared by calling the two GetChildRows methods.

Then, as usual, updates can follow inserts, and deletes can take a down-top approach.

This Code Just Won't Work!

Surprise, surprise! This code won't work. That's the bad news; the good news is that you are very close to the true solution.

Exercise 10.1 has one problem. It might work in a single-user scenario, but not for multiple users in a highly concurrent system. Consider this: Say Frans started updating Animals, followed by Pets, followed by PetBelongings. Right at that very moment, Erick decides to start deleting the very same animal Frans had been working on—this time in the direction of PetBelongings, then Pets, and then Animals. In fact, why even the same animal? Let's just say that Erick's rows were on the same page that ends up getting locked because Frans's row happened to be right there as well. Or maybe Frans is making such heavy-duty inserts to the tables that he starts locking a lot of pages, and SQL Server simply locks the entire table for Frans. Then Erick, who is going in the reverse direction as Frans, will be deadlocked.

As it must happen in real life and by Murphy's law, as soon as you put this application in production, Frans and Erick end up locking each other, thus creating a deadlock.

What Is the Solution?

One solution is to use only row-level locks. Another solution is to use cascading deletes that wrap every affected row in multiple tables in one transaction immediately. Both of these solutions will require you to tinker with your production database and make changes you'd rather not make because of other reasons. But there exists a third solution that doesn't require you to change your database structure, but does require some extra hard work in writing additional code.[2]

This is the one rare situation that I mentioned at the beginning of the chapter where pessimistic concurrency is your friend. Assuming that the AnimalID both Frans and Erick were contending upon was AnimalID = 2, first you could execute a query to lock the rows being updated in all three tables ahead of time using a SQL query shown here:

```
SELECT * FROM ANIMALS WITH (HOLDLOCK)
    INNER JOIN PETS ON PETS.ANIMALID = ANIMALS.ANIMALID
    INNER JOIN PETBELONGING ON PETBELONGING.PETID = PETS.PETID
WHERE ANIMALS.ANIMALID = 1
```

By doing so, you have effectively locked all the rows that you *will be* updating ahead of time. The scope of such an operation should be kept as minimal as possible, thus the correct place for such code will be inside the scope of a single stored procedure inside the database wrapped by a Begin Transaction/Rollback/Commit block. This will ensure that rows are not left locked inadvertently.

In such a case, the correct approach would not be to find all "inserted" rows in the Animals table and then work on them in one shot, but to work on each inserted Animal row one by one,

---

2. Remember when I said you need to sit back and think "How much work are you willing to put into this data layer?" I wasn't kidding. This is the utmost ideal solution in a highly transactional system with many updates and inserts happening concurrently. It also requires the most work. Much like a Ferrari costs more and is a better car, but still Honda sells more cars—which one do you want? And if you want a Ferrari, are you willing to pay for one?

deal with its children Pet rows and PetBelonging rows, and then commit that one single transaction. The children rows can be found using the relations defined in the DataSet using the GetChildRows method. Then for the next set of rows, start a new transaction.

Similarly, updated rows could follow the same approach by segregating not only by row states, but also by segregating out child rows in a manner similar to inserted rows.

And finally for deleted rows, you could use the GetParentRow to find the affected rows up the chain.

Now if you are raising your eyebrows, eager to point out that a deadlock might still occur only its probability is reduced, you are absolutely right! A deadlock still might occur, but the good news is that most advanced database management systems, such as Oracle or SQL Server, will be able to resolve this contention using deadlock detection mechanisms.

Hierarchical Updates: Conclusion

The logic you need to write to reliably save hierarchical data back into the database needs you to craft rules around the exact structure of the hierarchy you are dealing with. The basic rules remain the same: inserts first, updates next, and deletes last. Also, in order to reduce the contention on the hardworking central policeman of your architecture—the database—it makes sense to segregate such an operation into a number of smaller atomic transactions. Obviously, these are guidelines more than unbendable rules. But given these guidelines, your exact database structure, and concurrency requirements, you would be able to come up with a reliable data persistence mechanism.

So you just looked at an entire chapter devoted to saving three tables correctly, while taking care of concurrency. Needless to say, this translates into a lot of code and a lot of conditions you need to be careful of. While previous data access architectures had problems in even letting you express such logic, at least ADO.NET provides you with a straightforward, albeit long drawn, solution.

Even then, it's quite apparent that in saving hierarchical data you have to write a lot more code, and you have to worry about a lot more scenarios. Not to mention, you can't use straightforward update and delete methodologies. Thus, don't put too many tables in a DataSet. To finish up, let me reiterate the first rule about DataSets: *A DataSet is not a database, and it shouldn't be abused as one.*

At this point, I would encourage you to come up with a few database structures yourself and decide how you would update such disconnected in-memory data back into the database. Here's a problem statement to get you started: Think of a database structure for an e-commerce website that sells books, CDs, and DVDs. Each one of these has a price, quantity, and certain specific attributes (such as books have ISBNs and DVDs have running times). How would you design such a database? How would you query such a database? And how would you write the persistence logic for such a database?

Summary

This chapter built upon what you learned in Chapter 9: the basics of updating data in a database. You took the simple update discussion to a more practical real-world scenario and introduced issues such as concurrency, handling errors, and hierarchical updates.

You saw the reason why concurrency management is important and how you can prevent situations where a conflict might occur by using the right database design. You saw the most logical and straightforward, but not advised, method of concurrency management: pessimistic locking. You read that pessimistic locking is a bad choice for a multiple-user scenario, and how you can emulate pessimistic locking–like results by using a mechanism other than actual locks on the database such as a check-in/check-out functionality in the logic. As a better approach, optimistic concurrency was discussed. You saw the various methods of implementing optimistic concurrency including a SQL Server–specific implementation. You saw the pros and cons of each approach allowing you to decide clearly which approach you'd rather take in your data layer design.

Finally, you saw an example of managing updates from a hierarchical DataSet. You saw how you need to filter out the right rows and execute them in the right sequence to get your inserts, updates, and deletes into the database as the user had expected them to be saved. You saw how you need to filter out the right rows and persist them in the right order so your changes are stored properly and you are not thrown an exception from the database. You saw how much code you need to write in such a situation, which merits simplifying data representation in your application to simplistic cases.

An interesting thing you saw in this example was the usage of transactions. Updating the database and, to some extent, reading from it go hand in hand with transactions. Transactions give you the ability to run a batch of statements together or roll them all back together. The next chapter drives the discussion forward by delving into the depths of managing transactional scenarios in ADO.NET.

CHAPTER 11

■ ■ ■

Transactions

Databases hold information. ADO.NET helps you interact with that information. Information is critical in today's information age, and its sanctity is required to be guarded closely.

In a multiuser scenario, or even within a single-user scenario, as multiple processes, threads, and entities make changes to the database, there is a danger of stepping over someone else's changes. In addition, in certain situations, even within the same logical process, you may wish to execute a number of statements together.

For example, when you walk to an ATM (automated teller machine), pop in your card, and request some cash to be withdrawn, there are a distinct number of steps that occur in such a transaction. A request is made to check if you have the necessary funds, the funds are disbursed, and the account balance is reduced accordingly.

It's necessary that no other operation be done between checking the funds and disbursing them, because if that weren't the case, someone could hack the system while checking the funds once and withdraw a number of times on the same reported balance.

Also it is critical that the account balance be reduced accordingly as cash is dispensed, and vice versa if a deposit is made. For example, not only would it be really bad if you didn't get the cash, but also if your account balance was reduced.

Thus, all these steps must happen together as if they were one unified step—that is, they must all commit or all roll back together. The operation that will commit or roll back all of these steps together is commonly referred to as a transaction.

There are a number of systems involved in this transaction: the database, the ATM, and who knows how many computers in the middle.

Since a transaction could lock contentious resources for a finite time and also because it doesn't come for free, as is logical to expect, wrapping these distributed steps into one transaction costs system resources, and at times you might decide *not to implement* a transaction but rather implement checks and boundary conditions around a failed condition. This is, in fact, what most disconnected ATMs would do—add sanity checks at the beginning and ending of various distributed commands, and limit the maximum damage that can be done. Thus, if a command sequence fails, you have a recourse action and limited damage.

Therefore, the next time you use an ATM in a shady bar that is not actively connected over a connection to the bank's computer, you will have a daily withdrawal limit set on your card (limiting damage), and there will be a camera watching you (recourse action). Also, the bank's computers will maintain enough information for a recourse action to correct the data, if need be.

Thus, it's important to understand where you can and should leverage transactions to avoid the need for such checks and recourse, and where you should rely on a potential recourse action where a transaction mishap might occur. In most cases, however, it makes sense to use the rich framework provided to you to wrap up transactions, but as it turns out, even within that realm there are many choices and flavors to pick from.

This chapter delves into the basics of transactions as it applies to ADO.NET and databases, while giving sufficient coverage to distributed transactions using the new System.Transactions namespace in .NET 2.0. You'll see the various pros and cons of each approach that will help you make wise choices applicable to your system architecture.

Also discussed in this chapter is a SQL Server 2005–specific feature—MARS (Multiple Active Resultsets) and its support in ADO.NET. In short, MARS lets you execute multiple statements and maintain their results on the same connection. It's important to note that, in reality, the statements are not executing in parallel, they are only executing on the same connection. However, simultaneously, active result sets are being maintained.

This makes me sit back and scratch my head and wonder, what if those two commands include a select command and an update command? What if there is another insert command in the mix? What happens if there is a transaction in the mix? MARS gets especially interesting when viewed within transactional semantics and deserves sufficient attention in this context, as will be discussed in this chapter.

But first things first, what is a transaction?

What Is a Transaction?

A *transaction* is a set of operations where either all of the operations must be successful or all of them must fail to ensure consistency and correct behavior within a system. Let's look at the traditional example of a transaction.

Suppose you need to transfer $1,000 from account A to account B. This operation involves two steps:

1. $1,000 should be deducted from account A.

2. $1,000 should be added to account B.

Say that you successfully completed step 1, but due to some error step 2 failed. If you do not undo step 1, then the entire operation will be faulty. Transactions help to avoid this. Operations in the same transaction will only make changes to the database if *all* the steps are successful. So in this example, if step 2 fails, then the changes made by step 1 will not be committed to the database.

Transactions usually follow certain guidelines known as the ACID properties, which ensure that even complex transactions will be self-contained and reliable.

ACID Properties

Transactions are characterized by four properties popularly called ACID properties. To pass the ACID test, a transaction must be *Atomic, Consistent, Isolated,* and *Durable.* While this acronym is easy to remember, the meaning of each word is not obvious. Here is a brief explanation:

- *Atomic*: All steps in the transaction should succeed or fail together. Unless *all* the steps from a transaction complete, a transaction is not considered complete.

- *Consistent*: The transaction takes the underlying database from one stable state to another.

- *Isolated*: Every transaction is an independent entity. One transaction should not affect any other transaction running at the same time.

- *Durable*: Changes that occur during the transaction are permanently stored on some media, typically a hard disk, before the transaction is declared successful. For instance, logs could be maintained on a drive so, should a failure occur, the database can be reconstructed so as to retain transactional integrity.

Note that these are ideal characteristics of a transaction. In the real world, you may choose to tweak some behavior to suit your requirements. In particular, you can alter the isolation behavior of a transaction, which will be discussed shortly. Also, constructs, such as nested transactions that will also be looked at later, allow you to control the atomicity of a transaction.

However, you should only change from these behaviors after careful consideration. The following sections include discussion of when and how to change them.

Database Transactions

Transactions are frequently used in many business applications because they lend robustness and predictability to a system. Typically, when you develop a software system, some data source is used to store the data. In order to apply the concept of transactions in such software systems, the data source must support transactions. Modern databases, such as Microsoft SQL Server 2005 and Oracle 9*i*, provide strong support for transactions. For instance, SQL Server 2005 provides support for T-SQL statements such as BEGIN TRANSACTION, SAVE TRANSACTION, COMMIT TRANSACTION, and ROLLBACK TRANSACTION.

Data access APIs, such as ODBC, OleDb, and ADO.NET, enable developers to use transactions in their applications. Typically, RDBMSs and data access APIs provide transaction support as long as you are working with a single database. In many large applications, where more than one database is involved, you may need to use the Microsoft Distributed Transaction Coordinator (MSDTC).

Microsoft Transaction Server (MTS) and COM+, which are popular middlewares, also use MSDTC internally to facilitate multidatabase transactions, or even transactions between different transaction-aware entities, commonly referred to as *resource managers*. It should be noted that .NET 1.1 provides access to COM+ functionality via the System.EnterpriseServices namespace, and in .NET 2.0 you can use the System.Transactions namespace to control distributed transactions as a better alternative to System.EnterpriseServices.

Local and Distributed Transactions

Transactions can be split into local and distributed categories:

- *Local transaction*: Uses a transaction-aware data resource (for example, SQL Server) and has the scope of a single transaction. When a single database holds all of the data involved in a transaction, it can enforce the ACID rules on its own. This means that on a single database server, such as SQL Server, you can even use local transactions across databases, as long as you are using the same connection.

- *Distributed transaction*: Spanning multiple transaction-aware data resources, distributed transactions may need to read messages from a Message Queue Server, retrieve data from a SQL Server database, and write to other databases.

Many software packages (such as MSDTC) are available to assist with programming distributed transactions, which help ensure integrity by controlling commit and rollback behavior across all data resources, using mechanisms such as a two-phase commit and rollback.

MSDTC can only be used with applications that have compatible interfaces for transaction management. MSMQ, SQL Server, Oracle, Sybase, and several others are such applications, referred to as resource managers, which are currently available.

Manual and Automatic Transactions

Another way to slice and dice different kinds of transactions is as manual or automatic transactions.

A *manual transaction* model

- Allows you to use explicit instructions to begin and end the transaction to control the transaction boundary.

- Allows you to start a new transaction from within an active transaction (it supports nested transactions).

A set of objects, such as `SqlConnection`, `SqlTransaction`, etc., are provided by the ADO.NET data providers to help create a connection to the data source; begin, commit, or roll back the transaction; and finally close the connection manually.

An *automatic transaction* model wraps around a statement or a number of statements implicitly. In other words, additional statements simply enlist automatically in the current running transaction. If your transaction spans multiple transaction-aware resource managers (such as SQL Server or MSMQs), an *automatic transaction* is your best option. `System.Transactions` or COM+ will do all of the coordination work, causing extra overhead, but the application design will be much simpler, reducing coding requirements.

MSDTC is used to manage transactions in a distributed environment, which allows a .NET application to run a transaction that combines a number of diverse activities such as the following:

- Retrieving data from a SQL Server database

- Inserting an order into an Oracle database

- Writing a message to a Microsoft Message Queue

Transaction Vocabulary

There are some commands that are used frequently in the context of database transactions; they are `BEGIN`, `COMMIT`, `SAVE`, and `ROLLBACK`. These are the basic building blocks used in implementing transactions. Before going any further, let's take a quick look at what these commands do:

- `BEGIN`: Before executing any statements under a transaction, a transaction must be initiated; to do this, you use `BEGIN`.

- `COMMIT`: A transaction is said to be committed when all the changes that occurred during the transaction are written successfully to the underlying persistent store such as the database; you achieve this with the `COMMIT` command.

- SAVE: SAVE allows you to set a marker, or a savepoint, within a transaction where you can roll back to. This is discussed later in the chapter.

- ROLLBACK: A ROLLBACK occurs when all changes made by the transaction need to be undone because some part of the transaction has failed. Some architectures, such as MTS, have a method to abort the transaction by the name of SetAbort, and others might simply refer to it as Abort.

Now that you know the basics of transactions, let's see how ADO.NET provides support for them.

ADO.NET Transaction Support

ADO.NET provides strong support for database transactions. ADO.NET in itself supports single database transactions, which are tracked on a per-connection basis. It may leverage System.Transactions to involve cross-database transactions or transactions involving more than one resource manager.

The transaction functionality is provided with the connection object of ADO.NET. There are some differences in the implementation of transaction support in ADO.NET and in ADO.

If you have worked with ADO, you'll recall that it provides methods such as BeginTrans, CommitTrans, and RollbackTrans for the connection object itself. In the case of ADO.NET, the connection object is used simply to start a transaction. The commit or rollback of the transaction is taken care of by a dedicated object, which is an implementation of the transaction class. This enables you to associate different command objects with a single transaction object, so that those commands participate in the same transaction.

ADO.NET provides connected as well as disconnected data access, and provides support for transactions in both of these modes. In connected mode, the typical sequence of operations in a transaction will be as follows:

1. Open a database connection.

2. Begin a transaction.

3. Fire queries directly against the connection via the command object.

4. Commit or roll back the transaction.

5. Close the connection.

Figure 11-1 shows how transactions are handled in connected mode.

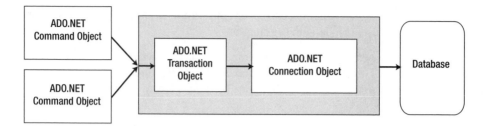

Figure 11-1. *Transactions in a connected mode*

In disconnected mode, generally, data is fetched first (usually one or more tables) into a DataSet object, the connection with the data source is closed, the data is manipulated as required, and then the data is updated back into the database. In this mode, the typical sequence of operations will be as follows:

1. Open a database connection.

2. Fetch the required data in a DataSet object.

3. Close the database connection.

4. Manipulate the data in the DataSet object.

5. Again, open a connection with the database.

6. Start a transaction.

7. Assign the transaction object to the relevant commands on the data adapter.

8. Update the database with changes from the DataSet.

9. Close the connection.

Figure 11-2 illustrates this sequence of events.

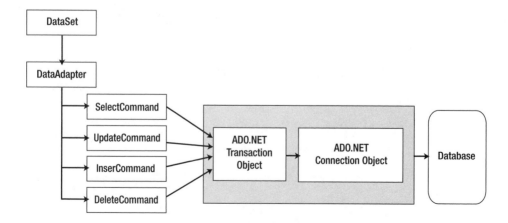

Figure 11-2. *Transactions in a disconnected mode*

Implementing transactions in connected mode is relatively simple, as we have everything happening live; however, in disconnected mode, while updating the data back into the database, some care should be taken to account for concurrency issues. Also, depending on your architecture, it might be necessary to roll back any changes made to the DataSet that might have been done in a partially successful, but rolled back update.[1] An example demonstrating that can be seen in Chapter 10's Exercise 10.1.

The following section will discuss the transaction class. It will also look at the commonly used methods of the transaction class and typical ways of using these methods.

Transaction Class

The various .NET-managed providers available in the .NET Framework, like OleDb, SqlClient, OracleClient, and ODBC, etc., each has its own implementation of the transaction class: the OleDb data provider has the OleDbTransaction class, which resides in the System.Data.OleDb namespace; the ODBC data provider has the OdbcTransaction class, which resides in the System.Data.Odbc namespace, and so on for the other providers (SqlTransaction class and OracleTransaction class).

All of these classes implement the IDbTransaction interface from the System.Data namespace. Most of the properties and methods of these classes are identical; however, each has some specific methods of its own, as shall be discussed shortly.

This would be a good time to flip back to Chapter 2 and look at Figure 2-3 to examine the parallelism that various IDbTransaction implementations exhibit, such as SqlTransaction and OracleTransaction.

Methods of the Transaction Class

Commit and rollback were discussed earlier in this chapter. The transaction classes have two methods that will be used frequently that reflect these:

- Commit: This method identifies a transaction as successful. Once you call this method, all the pending changes are written permanently to the underlying database once this method returns without an error. The exact implementation depends on the data provider, but typically this translates to executing a COMMIT on the underlying database.

- Rollback: This method marks a transaction as unsuccessful, and pending changes are discarded. The database state remains unchanged.

Typically, both of these methods are used together. The following code snippet shows how they are used in the most common way:

C#

```
using (SqlConnection myConnection = new SqlConnection(connectionString))
{
    myConnection.Open();
    myTransaction = myConnection.BeginTransaction();
```

---

1. Of notable mention here are the AcceptChangesDuringUpdate and ContinueUpdateOnError properties on the data adapter object. These were discussed in Chapter 9.

```
   myCommand1.Transaction = myTransaction;
   myCommand2.Transaction = myTransaction;
   try
   {
      myCommand1.ExecuteNonQuery();
      myCommand2.ExecuteNonQuery();
      myTransaction.Commit();
   }
   catch
   {
      myTransaction.Rollback();
      throw;
   }
   finally
   {
      myConnection.Close();
   }
}
```

VB.NET

```
Using myConnection As SqlConnection = New SqlConnection(connectionString)
   myConnection.Open()
   myTransaction = myConnection.BeginTransaction()
   myCommand1.Transaction = myTransaction
   myCommand2.Transaction = myTransaction
   Try
      myCommand1.ExecuteNonQuery()
      myCommand2.ExecuteNonQuery()
      myTransaction.Commit()
   Catch ex As Exception
      myTransaction.Rollback()
      Throw ex
   Finally
      myConnection.Close()
   End Try
End Using
```

The command object has a Transaction property that you must set in order to execute your command within a transaction. The transaction classes also have other properties and methods, which will be looked at later in the chapter.

Let's solidify our understanding and develop an application that uses the transactional features of ADO.NET.

Writing Transactional Database Applications

Implementing a basic transaction using ADO.NET in an application can be fairly straightforward. The most common sequence of steps that would be performed while developing a transactional application is as follows:

1. Open a database connection using the Open method of the connection object.

2. Begin a transaction using the BeginTransaction method of the connection object. This method provides a transaction object that can be used later to commit or roll back the transaction. Note that the changes caused by any queries executed before calling the BeginTransaction method will be committed to the database immediately after they execute.

3. Set the Transaction property of the command object to the transaction object mentioned in step 2.

4. Execute the SQL commands using the command object. More than one command object may be used for this purpose as long as the Transaction property of all the objects is set to a valid transaction object.

5. Commit or roll back the transaction using the Commit or Rollback method of the transaction object.

6. Close the database connection.

Note that once you have started a transaction on a certain connection, all the queries that use that particular connection must fall inside the boundary of the transaction. For example, two INSERT queries and one UPDATE query can be executed inside a transaction. In the midst, if you were to execute a SELECT query without the transaction, you'd get an error indicating that a transaction is still pending. Also, one connection object can have only one pending transaction at a time.

In other words, once you call the BeginTransaction method on a connection object, you cannot call BeginTransaction again, until you commit or roll back that transaction. In such situations, you will get an error message stating that parallel transactions are not supported. To overcome this error, you may use another connection to execute the query.

There is, however, a new SQL Server 2005–specific feature called MARS that lets you maintain multiple active result sets on one connection, *but not multiple transactions*. Now because you can execute multiple interleaved command batches at the same time, it gets especially interesting in transactional scenarios. Essentially in MARS, nondeterministic transaction scenarios that involve multiple interleaved commands are disallowed. But that will be discussed in detail later in this chapter.

Implementing Transactions

So without much further ado, let's get our hands dirty and write an actual application demonstrating single database/nondistributed transactions using ADO.NET.

For the purposes of this application, a small Console application will suffice. As usual, let's begin with setting up the database for various examples in this chapter.

The database is a simple customers/products database with three tables: Customers, which holds the customer details; Products, which holds the products details; and CustomerProduct, which holds the many-to-many mapping between the Customers table and the Products table. The schema for the database is shown in Figure 11-3, or it may be created using the CreateDatabase.SQL file in the associated code download for this chapter (see the Downloads section of the Apress website at http://www.apress.com).

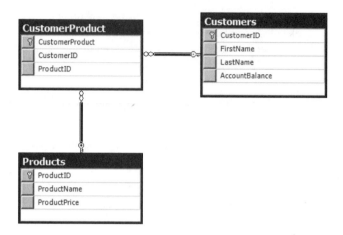

Figure 11-3. *Sample database for a transactional application*

To get started, go ahead and populate the Customers table with the rows as shown in Figure 11-4.

	CustomerID	FirstName	LastName	AccountBalance
1	1	Capt.	Kirk	100
2	2	Super	Man	100

Figure 11-4. *Sample rows for the Customers table*

Also, go ahead and add the rows for the Products table as shown in Figure 11-5.

	ProductID	ProductName	ProductPrice
1	1	Cape	4
2	2	Phasor Gun	9

Figure 11-5. *Sample rows for the Products table*

As you can see, both of our customers start with an account balance of 100 dollars. What this application will try to do is place an order for Superman. Superman will purchase a cape, and because a cape is worth 4 dollars, his account balance will reduce from 100 to 96 dollars. This operation will involve two SQL queries. The first query to place an order for Superman will look like this:

```
Insert into CustomerProduct
   (CustomerID, ProductID)
Values
   (2, 1)
```

The second query to update his account balance to 96 will look like this:

```
Update Customers
   Set AccountBalance = 96²
Where
   CustomerID = 2
```

One way to make this work would be to wrap up the two queries in a single transaction at the database level. This can be done easily using a group of statements that look like this:

```
Begin Transaction
Insert into CustomerProduct
   (CustomerID, ProductID)
Values
   (2, 1)
Update Customers
   Set AccountBalance = 96
Where
   CustomerID = 2
Commit
```

This can be wrapped as inline SQL or as a stored procedure call. What is interesting in this approach is that it doesn't let you have fine-grained control (at least not in .NET code) between the insert and update. That kind of control is especially important when dealing with disconnected DataSets. For instance, if between the insert and update someone else placed an order for Superman for a product that costs 100 dollars, then per the previous commands, without a concurrency check built in, your issued commands would result in a negative balance for Superman (which should not be allowed). That is obviously not the right thing to do. It corrupts your database and makes Superman mad at you—you don't want either to happen.

Thus, a better way to implement this scenario would be to have concurrency checks and transactions based upon individual ADO.NET commands wrapped up in DbTransaction objects. In code, this would look like Listings 11-1 and 11-2. (You can find the code for Listings 11-1 to 11-6 in the associated code download for this chapter under Exercise 11.1.)

Listing 11-1. *Transactional Command Execution in C#*

```
static void Main(string[] args)
{
    using (SqlConnection testConnection = new SqlConnection(connectionString))
```

---

2. Bonus points for you if you immediately jumped in your seat and thought, "A better way to write this query would be Set AccountBalance = AccountBalance - 4." You are right, but I wanted to exemplify the query as is because what if the query was the result of a disconnected DataSet with the value "96" simply substituted as a parameter by the data adapter?

```csharp
    {
        SqlCommand myCommand = testConnection.CreateCommand();
        SqlTransaction myTransaction = null;
        try
        {
            testConnection.Open();
            myTransaction = testConnection.BeginTransaction();
            myCommand.Transaction = myTransaction;
            myCommand.CommandText =
                "Insert into CustomerProduct (CustomerID, ProductID) Values (2, 1)";
            myCommand.ExecuteNonQuery();
            myCommand.CommandText =
                "Update Customers Set AccountBalance = 96 Where CustomerID = 2";
            myCommand.ExecuteNonQuery();
            myTransaction.Commit();
        }
        catch (System.Exception)
        {
            myTransaction.Rollback();
            throw ex;
        }
        finally
        {
            testConnection.Close();
        }
    }
}
```

Listing 11-2. *Transactional Command Execution in Visual Basic .NET*

```vbnet
Sub Main()
    Using testConnection As New SqlConnection(connectionString)
        Dim myCommand As SqlCommand = testConnection.CreateCommand()
        Dim myTransaction As SqlTransaction = Nothing

        Try
            testConnection.Open()
            myTransaction = testConnection.BeginTransaction()
            myCommand.Transaction = myTransaction
            myCommand.CommandText = _
                "Insert into CustomerProduct (CustomerID, ProductID) Values (2, 1)"
            myCommand.ExecuteNonQuery()
            myCommand.CommandText = _
                "Update Customers Set AccountBalance = 96 Where CustomerID = 2"
            myCommand.ExecuteNonQuery()
            myTransaction.Commit()
        Catch ex As Exception
```

```
      Try
          myTransaction.Rollback()
      Catch ex1 As SqlException
          Throw ex1
      End Try
   Finally
       testConnection.Close()
   End Try
  End Using
End Sub
```

This is extremely similar to Exercise 10.1 shown in Chapter 10. In a real-world application, you could enhance this code to include concurrency checks or nondatabase operations as well.

■**Note** This method can be used to wrap commands in a transaction only within one database server. If commands need to be run between servers and databases (not using linked servers or linked databases), or involve nondatabase entities, then you have to resort to distributed transactions discussed later in this chapter.

In the next code example, the transaction begins by calling the BeginTransaction method of the connection object. The BeginTransaction method returns an instance of the transaction object, which is held in a SqlTransaction variable called myTransaction. This transaction object can then be assigned to the transaction property of the SqlCommand object:

C#

```
testConnection.Open();
myTransaction = testConnection.BeginTransaction();
myCommand.Transaction = myTransaction;
```

VB.NET

```
testConnection.Open()
myTransaction = testConnection.BeginTransaction()
myCommand.Transaction = myTransaction
```

If this transaction were to run against an Oracle database, you would have simply used the OracleTransaction object. The important thing to realize is that the underlying database must support transactions for this approach to work.

Once the transaction is set up, it's simply a question of executing various SQL queries using the command object. This is done as shown in Listings 11-3 and 11-4.

Listing 11-3. *Running Various Queries Using the SqlCommand Object in C#*

```
myCommand.CommandText =
    "Insert into CustomerProduct (CustomerID, ProductID) Values (2, 1)";
```

```
myCommand.ExecuteNonQuery();
myCommand.CommandText =
    "Update Customers Set AccountBalance = 96 Where CustomerID = 2";
myCommand.ExecuteNonQuery();
```

Listing 11-4. *Running Various Queries Using the SqlCommand Object in Visual Basic .NET*

```
myCommand.CommandText = _
    "Insert into CustomerProduct (CustomerID, ProductID) Values (2, 1)"
myCommand.ExecuteNonQuery()
myCommand.CommandText = _
    "Update Customers Set AccountBalance = 96 Where CustomerID = 2"
myCommand.ExecuteNonQuery()
```

You may change the CommandText property of the same object to fire different queries or create new command objects. Remember that if you use new command objects, their Transaction property needs to be set. Typically, you could place the appropriate code in a try...catch block, so that if an error occurs, the transaction can be rolled back. You may also carry out any business validations here, and decide whether to commit or roll back the transaction.

Once the application is done with the various operations, it must call either the Commit or Rollback method of the transaction object as shown in Listings 11-5 and 11-6.

Listing 11-5. *Committing or Rolling Back the Changes in C#*

```
catch (System.Exception)
{
    myTransaction.Rollback();
}
finally
{
    myTransaction.Commit();
    testConnection.Close();
}
```

Listing 11-6. *Committing or Rolling Back the Changes in Visual Basic .NET*

```
Catch ex As Exception
    myTransaction.Rollback()
Finally
    myTransaction.Commit()
    testConnection.Close()
End Try
```

Thus, as you can see, transactions enable you to wrap a number of commands into one logical command execution unit that follows the ACID rules described earlier in this chapter.

It's worth noting, however, that in the event you did not call Rollback yourself, the framework will take care of it for you. But this doesn't mean that you should be lazy and not call Rollback simply because the framework might not do it immediately, and thus keep resources busy for longer than necessary. In case you forget to call `Rollback`, `Rollback` will be called when the underlying physical connection is closed or reused. This is immediate if you are using the API directly, or when connection pooling is disabled. If connection pooling is enabled, then this would happen when the physical connection is pruned from the pool, or when the same physical connection is reused by another `SqlConnection` instance. Since this might take an unpredictable amount of time to occur, it is wise to call `Rollback` yourself.

There are a couple of notable things about Listings 11-1 and 11-2 versus a nontransactional code update.

First and foremost is the fact that you had to open a connection to the database a few statements before the command execution. In fact, you cannot do a `BeginTransaction` without calling an `Open` on the database connection first. This means you tie up the physical connection resource for a longer than usual duration. This has a negative impact on performance in connection-pooled environments. Also, because the database has to act as the sentry, which manages the various transactions it has to accept from various concurrent clients, the database is probably working harder as well.

But do realize that even for statements executed on a database such as SQL Server in auto commit mode, there is still an implicit transaction that surrounds each statement. Thus, if you had a number of rows to insert, and each one of them was wrapped in their own implicit transaction by virtue of being in auto commit mode, instead of a `BEGIN TRANSACTION` block specified by you, you would get *lower* performance on such a big batch by explicitly *not using* transactions. This is because, when modifying data inside a transaction, all data gets written to a temporary log, and on commit it is very efficiently copied over to the database. In the case of auto commit mode, each statement needs to be persisted individually.

Therefore, the first direct impact of transactional code is on performance. In single or lesser statements, transactions may be slower, but in larger sets of data they would generally be faster. As you shall see later in this chapter, the lowered performance is even more pronounced in the case of distributed transactions. Thus, you should use transactions especially on smaller statement sets only if you have a compelling need to do so. However, it is important to emphasize that you shouldn't skimp on using transactions when the situation truly demands one—just be aware that everything comes at a price. Saving milliseconds or even microseconds of execution time, at the cost of corrupting your database, is never the right answer.

Now if you were to run the code in debug mode, pause between the two DML statements, and run a `SELECT` query querying the account balance for Superman from the database (or the products he has ordered) *while the transaction has not yet been committed*, what state of data should others see if the table is queried at this time?

If the locks have not yet been placed, you would still see the state of data before any DML statements had been executed. Is this what you wanted? What if the locks were actually placed? In certain cases you might want to customize this behavior. You might want to have other parts of the application wait until you are done with your transaction, thus ensuring that, at the risk of running at a lower response time (because the subsequent requests had to wait for the transactions to finish), the database provides the latest and greatest state of the data after the transaction completes. Or in fact, with the latest databases, you might want (while a transaction is pending) other requests to the same data to actually return a snapshot of the data as it existed *before the transaction began*.

It turns out, such level of customizability can be provided by specifying isolation levels on transactions.

Examining the Effect of Isolation Levels

Now that you know how to implement basic transactions, let's go into some more detail and look at how you can control the behavior of a transaction, and how a transactional batch of queries affects other queries running on the same resource. This is typically done by specifying an isolation level on your transactions.

This section will cover isolation levels and how they affect your application. In doing so, you'll encounter some terms that are frequently used while discussing isolation levels. In addition, you'll see how to set isolation levels in your code.

What Are Isolation Levels?

An *isolation level* is a measure of the extent to which changes made outside a transaction are visible inside that transaction. It determines how sensitive your transaction is to changes made by other transactions.

For example, by default in SQL Server, if two transactions are running independently of one another, then records inserted by one transaction are not visible to the other transaction, unless the first transaction is committed.

The isolation level concept is closely related to the locks concept, because by determining isolation levels for a given transaction you can determine how long the given transaction must hold locks on resources to protect them against changes that may be made by others.

You may wish to alter the behavior of the transactions so that the second transaction can view records inserted by the first one. This may amount to reading invalid data (because it isn't committed yet), which is typically referred to as a *dirty read*. But, if you wish to shoot yourself in the foot by reading invalid data, ADO.NET does give you the facility to do so.[3] You can achieve this through setting isolation levels appropriately. For an ADO.NET programmer, the isolation level can be set via isolation level enumerated values.

Some Related Terms

Before going any further, it's important to understand some terms that are used frequently when discussing isolation levels:

- *Dirty read*: A dirty read is a condition when a transaction reads data that has yet to be committed. Consider a case where transaction A inserts some records into a table, but is pending. Transaction B reads these records. Now, if transaction A rolls back, transaction B will refer to data that is invalid.

- *Nonrepeatable read*: Consider a case where transaction A reads a record from a table. Transaction B then alters or deletes the records and commits the changes. Now, if transaction A tries to re-read the record, it will either be a different version or it will not be available at all. Such a condition is called a nonrepeatable read.

---

3. "Shoot yourself in the foot" may be a very strong term, but in certain instances, it might be necessary to do this. If you have a rather busy table (lots of inserts and updates), and some part of the application doesn't care about 100 percent data accuracy, but does care about response time for its selects, then this would be a possible way out of that scenario. Though, the Snapshot isolation takes care of many of those scenarios.

- *Phantom read*: Suppose that transaction A has some criteria for record selection. Initially, transaction A has, say, 100 rows matching these criteria. Now transaction B inserts some rows that match the selection criteria of transaction A. If transaction A executes the selection query again, it will receive a different set of rows than in the previous case. The rows added in this way are called phantom rows.

Possible Isolation Levels in ADO.NET

Let's now look at the different isolation level values that you can implement with ADO.NET. These values are accessible via the `IsolationLevel` enumeration:

- `Chaos`: The pending changes from more highly isolated transactions cannot be overwritten. This setting is not supported by SQL Server or Oracle.

- `ReadUncommitted`: In this case, a dirty read is possible. This means that no shared locks are placed, and no exclusive locks are honored. This type of isolation level is appropriate when you want to work with all the data matching certain conditions, irrespective of whether it's committed or not.

  Generally, you would use this isolation level where the application doesn't require guaranteed accuracy in the data it queries, and where the priority is performance over accuracy. If performance is the chief criterion in your application design, you should prefer this isolation level over others, but do understand that it comes at the cost of possibly inaccurate data. Note that the `Snapshot` isolation level described shortly provides a much better alternative than `ReadUncommitted` in doing nonblocking `SELECT` queries. Even though you don't get the latest data, at least you get committed data. A good, practical use of `ReadUncommitted` is data monitoring by an administrator. I recommend that you use this isolation level sparingly.

  In this scenario, there is no concurrency model being followed, unless you implement your own homegrown concurrency check model such as `Timestamps`, `RowVersions`, etc. These have been discussed in depth in the last chapter. This isolation level is not supported in Oracle.

- `ReadCommitted`: Shared locks are held while the data is being read by the transaction. This avoids dirty reads, but the data can be changed before a transaction completes. This may result in nonrepeatable reads or phantom rows. This type of isolation level is appropriate when you want to work with all the data that matches certain conditions, and is committed.

  Shared locks are locks that are placed when a transaction wants to read data from the database, and no exclusive lock is already held on that data item. No other transactions can modify the data while shared locks exist on a table or tables. Exclusive locks are the locks that prevent two or more transactions modifying data simultaneously. An *exclusive lock* is issued when a transaction needs to update a table or tables, and no other locks are already held on the respective tables. Because an exclusive lock is needed, this would qualify as pessimistic locking on the database.

  This isolation level can be used where you need transactional consistency for long running queries, but you do not care if you may get nonrepeatable reads. This isolation level is supported in Oracle. Also, this is the default isolation level for both `SqlTransaction` and `OracleTransaction`.

- RepeatableRead: In this case, shared locks are placed on all data that is used in the predicate (criterion) of a query. This prevents others from modifying the data and also prevents nonrepeatable reads. However, phantom rows are possible. This type of isolation level is appropriate when you want the records that are read to retain the same values for future reads.

  This kind of transaction ensures that all other modifications to the data are stopped until the transaction completes. Thus, this kind of transaction lends itself well to situations where you need consistency within the transaction *at the cost* of poor concurrent performance of the system. However, phantom reads are still possible, and this technically qualifies as pessimistic concurrency and should be avoided in a disconnected scenario if possible. This isolation level is not supported in Oracle.

- Snapshot: This type of isolation level reduces the probability of having a lock placed on the rows by storing a version of the data that one application can read while another is modifying the same data. In other words, if transaction A is modifying the data, then transaction B will not be able to see the changes being done. What's important is transaction B will not get locked and will read the snapshot of the data before transaction A had begun. So this type of isolation level is ideal for applications that need integrity of data in long running queries, but that do not plan on modifying the data. This, again, can be used in an optimistic concurrency model.

  In SQL Server 2005, the Snapshot isolation must be enabled at the database level first before it can be used. This can be done using the following command:

  ```
  ALTER DATABASE <<TheDataBaseName>> SET ALLOW_SNAPSHOT_ISOLATION ON
  ```

- Serializable: In this case, a lock is placed on the data preventing other users from updating or inserting rows into the DataSet until the transaction is complete. This lock could be placed on the row, the page, or the table depending on a lot of factors specific to the underlying database. This type of isolation level is appropriate when you want all the data you're working with in your predicate to be exactly the same until you finish the processing. This isolation level is supported in Oracle.

  Generally, this isolation level is useful when the application works on sets of rows, and needs absolute consistency between all operations it may do within a transaction. This ensures the cleanest data, but will result in the most database locks and must be used only when you need pessimistic locking and absolute control over your data. This is obviously at the cost of performance in a highly concurrent system.

- Unspecified: In this type, a different isolation level from the one specified is being used; however, the level cannot be determined.

These isolation level values can be supplied while initiating a transaction through the BeginTransaction method of the DBConnection object. It's important to note, however, that whether or not an isolation level will work for a given data provider depends on the underlying database. You also may read the current value of isolation level using the IsolationLevel property of the transaction object.

Changing Isolation Levels

To solidify our understanding of isolation levels, let's develop a small application that changes the default isolation level of a SQL Server database from ReadCommitted to ReadUncommitted (see Exercise 11.2 in the associated code download). The application works in the following way:

1. Open a connection to the local Test database and begin a transaction. The isolation level for this transaction will be the default: ReadCommitted.

2. Open another connection with the database and begin another transaction. However, the isolation level for this transaction will be set to ReadUncommitted.

3. From the first transaction, a row is inserted into the Customers table.

4. Without committing the first transaction, this row is fetched from the second transaction with isolation level ReadUncommitted. The results will be shown in the console. This will prove that, even though the first transaction is yet to be finished, the second transaction reads records inserted by it, which is evil and the equivalent of the spawn of Satan in data sanctity and transactional world, but as mentioned before, if you want to shoot yourself in the foot, feel free.

5. The first transaction will be rolled back and the same query for the second transaction will be run to fetch the newly inserted (now rolled back) customer again, in order to show that the results for the very same query are now different, thus proving that ReadUncommitted is not a reliable transaction isolation level as far as data consistency goes.

So let's examine the code for this exercise step by step. The first step is to set up two connections and individual transactions on those connections. The transaction isolation level for the first transaction is left at the default value of ReadCommitted, and the second is set to ReadUncommitted. This can be seen in Listings 11-7 and 11-8.

Listing 11-7. *Setting Up Two Transactions with Isolation Levels ReadCommitted and ReadUncommitted in C#*

```
SqlConnection connection1 = new SqlConnection(connectionString);
SqlConnection connection2 = new SqlConnection(connectionString);

SqlCommand command1 = connection1.CreateCommand();
SqlCommand command2 = connection2.CreateCommand();

connection1.Open();
connection2.Open();
SqlTransaction transaction1 = connection1.BeginTransaction();
command1.Transaction = transaction1;
SqlTransaction transaction2 =
    connection2.BeginTransaction(IsolationLevel.ReadUncommitted);
command2.Transaction = transaction2;
```

Listing 11-8. *Setting Up Two Transactions with Isolation Levels ReadCommitted and ReadUncommitted in Visual Basic .NET*

```
Dim connection1 As SqlConnection = New SqlConnection(connectionString)
Dim connection2 As SqlConnection = New SqlConnection(connectionString)

Dim command1 As SqlCommand = connection1.CreateCommand()
Dim command2 As SqlCommand = connection2.CreateCommand()

connection1.Open()
connection2.Open()
Dim transaction1 As SqlTransaction = _
   connection1.BeginTransaction()
command1.Transaction = transaction1
Dim transaction2 As SqlTransaction = _
   connection2.BeginTransaction(IsolationLevel.ReadUncommitted)
command2.Transaction = transaction2
```

Also note that in this code, two commands are created that will enlist in the specified transactions. The next step is to set up command text for both commands—the first that will insert a row and the second that will check for the existence of the inserted row.

These commands are then executed and results are shown. The transaction is then rolled back and the results are shown. This can be seen in Listings 11-9 and 11-10.

Listing 11-9. *Working with Two Commands on the Same Table, in Two Transactions on Different Isolation Levels in C#*

```
SqlDataReader myReader;
try
{
    command1.CommandText =
        "INSERT INTO CUSTOMERS (FIRSTNAME, LASTNAME, ACCOUNTBALANCE) "
            + "VALUES ('Bat', 'Man', 100)";
    command1.ExecuteNonQuery();

    command2.CommandText =
        "SELECT FIRSTNAME, LASTNAME from CUSTOMERS where FIRSTNAME = 'Bat'";
    myReader = command2.ExecuteReader();

    Console.WriteLine("Results when the transaction is midway:");
    if (!myReader.HasRows)
    {
        Console.WriteLine("No Rows Found");
    }
    while (myReader.Read())
    {
        Console.WriteLine(
            "FirstName: " + myReader[0] + " and LastName: " + myReader[1]);
    }
```

```
    myReader.Close();

    transaction1.Rollback();

    command2.CommandText =
        "SELECT FIRSTNAME, LASTNAME from CUSTOMERS where FIRSTNAME = 'Bat'";
    myReader = command2.ExecuteReader();

    Console.WriteLine("Results when the transaction is rolled back:");
    if (!myReader.HasRows)
        Console.WriteLine("No Rows Found");
    while (myReader.Read())
    {
        Console.WriteLine(
            "FirstName: " + myReader[0] + " and LastName: " + myReader[1]);
    }
    myReader.Close();
}
catch (System.Exception ex)
{
    Console.WriteLine(ex.ToString());
}
finally
{
    connection1.Dispose(); // Dispose will also close the connection
    connection2.Dispose();
}
```

Listing 11-10. *Working with Two Commands on the Same Table, in Two Transactions on Different Isolation Levels in Visual Basic .NET*

```
Dim myReader As SqlDataReader
Try
    command1.CommandText = _
        "INSERT INTO CUSTOMERS (FIRSTNAME, LASTNAME, ACCOUNTBALANCE) " & _
        " VALUES ('Bat', 'Man', 100)"
    command1.ExecuteNonQuery()

    command2.CommandText = _
        "SELECT FIRSTNAME, LASTNAME from CUSTOMERS where FIRSTNAME = 'Bat'"
    myReader = command2.ExecuteReader()

    Console.WriteLine("Results when the transaction is midway:")

    If Not myReader.HasRows Then
        Console.WriteLine("No Rows Found")
    End If
```

```
    While myReader.Read()
        Console.WriteLine("FirstName: " + myReader(0) + " and LastName: " + ➡
myReader(1))
    End While

    myReader.Close()

    transaction1.Rollback()

    command2.CommandText = _
        "SELECT FIRSTNAME, LASTNAME from CUSTOMERS where FIRSTNAME = 'Bat'"
    myReader = command2.ExecuteReader()

    Console.WriteLine("Results when the transaction is rolled back:")
    If Not myReader.HasRows Then
        Console.WriteLine("No Rows Found")
    End If
    While myReader.Read()
        Console.WriteLine("FirstName: " + myReader(0) + " and LastName: " + ➡
myReader(1))
    End While
    myReader.Close()
Catch ex As System.Exception
    Console.WriteLine(ex.ToString())
Finally
    connection1.Dispose() ' Dispose will also close the connection
    connection2.Dispose()
End Try
```

Next, compile and run the application. As you can see, even though the first transaction had not been committed, the results are still visible in the second transaction. The problem with this is that, obviously, the person who queried the second query's results for his purposes now assumes that the row that was a *dirty read* actually exists in the database. The results are as shown in Figure 11-6.

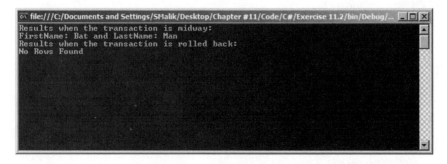

Figure 11-6. *Dirty read demonstration using ReadUncommitted isolation level*

If you were to make a slight modification and change the isolation level of the first transaction to Serializable and then run the code again, you'd notice that the code will simply hang at the SELECT command execution. This is because isolation level Serializable will block any further reads from the underlying data source (row, page, or table) until the first transaction has either rolled back or committed.

Now try another experiment. Set the isolation level on both transactions to Snapshot and run the application again. You should probably see an exception as shown in Figure 11-7.

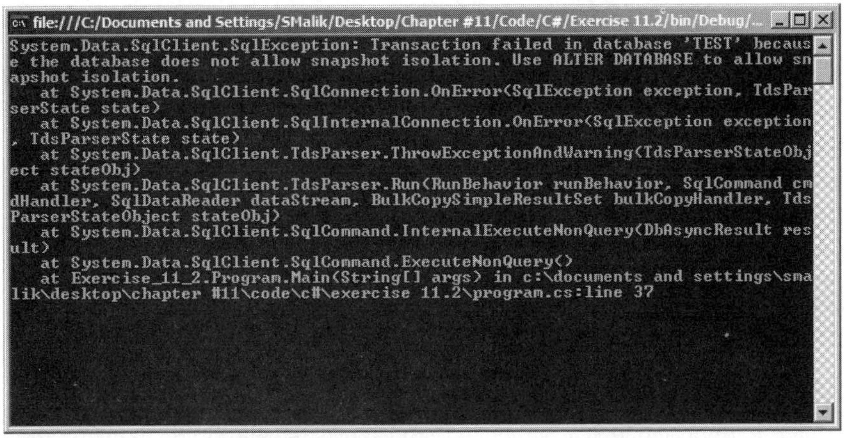

Figure 11-7. *Running the example with IsolationLevel = Snapshot without enabling them in the database first*

You get this error because this isolation level is disabled by default. To enable it, simply run the following command:

```
ALTER DATABASE TEST SET ALLOW_SNAPSHOT_ISOLATION ON
```

Run the application again and you should see the results shown in Figure 11-8.

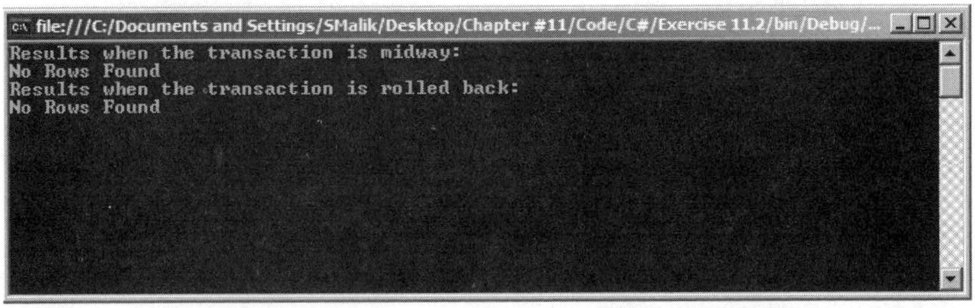

Figure 11-8. *Running the example with IsolationLevel = Snapshot after enabling them in the database*

Thus, as you can see, by playing with the isolation level you can customize the exact behavior of your transactions.

■**Note** Changing the default isolation level is a tricky issue that depends on the level of consistency and concurrency you want. Generally, you'll find that the higher the isolation level, the higher the consistency, but the lower the concurrency, the lower the performance.

The need to run multiple commands on a particular database concurrently brings up yet another interesting discussion. Say, for example, you had a unique situation where you wanted to open a connection and lock the rows you were interested in reading from. While the data is locked, you needed to update the locked data, using a data reader *under the same transaction and isolation level*. Because only one command can execute on a connection at a given time, the locks held by the first connection would prevent the second connection from updating.

This is, however, not true in the case of SQL Server 2005. SQL Server 2005 provides you with the ability to run multiple commands on the same connection—an ability referred to as Multiple Active Resultsets, or MARS.

Multiple Active Resultsets

MARS is a new feature supported in SQL Server 2005 and above that allows you to maintain multiple, simultaneously active result sets in parallel on the same connection.

Oracle has a similar ability of being able to support multiple result sets on the same connection by using a stored procedure with more than one REF CURSOR. Once you have a command set up with multiple REF CURSOR parameters, you can simply add parameters of OracleDbType.RefCursor type with ParameterDirection set to output to the OracleCommand. Then you can use the following code snippet to access multiple parallel data readers in Oracle:

C#

```
OracleDataReader firstDataReader =
    ((OracleRefCursor)twoRefCursorCommand.Parameters[0].Value).GetDataReader();
OracleDataReader secondDataReader =
    ((OracleRefCursor)twoRefCursorCommand.Parameters[1].Value).GetDataReader();
```

VB.NET

```
Dim firstDataReader as OracleDataReader = _
(CType(twoRefCursorCommand.Parameters(0).Value,OracleRefCursor)).GetDataReader()
Dim secondDataReader as OracleDataReader = _
(CType(twoRefCursorCommand.Parameters(1).Value,OracleRefCursor)).GetDataReader()
```

On the other hand, SQL Server 2005 requires you to simply execute two SqlCommands on the same SqlConnection. This can be seen in the partial code snippet shown here:

C#

```
cmd1.Connection = myConnection ;
cmd2.Connection = myConnection ;

SqlDataReader firstReader = cmd1.ExecuteReader() ;
SqlDataReader secondReader = cmd2.ExecutReader() ;
```

VB.NET

```
cmd1.Connection = myConnection
cmd2.Connection = myConnection

Dim firstReader As SqlDataReader = cmd1.ExecuteReader()
Dim SqlDataReader As SqlDataReader = cmd2.ExecutReader()
```

The implications of MARS on a transactional scenario are quite profound, but before I discuss those, let me quickly discuss a short primer on how MARS works. It's important to note that MARS in SQL Server works only in SQL Server 2005[4] and above, and in SQL Server 2000 and below you are still restricted to running one command per connection.

SQL Server is queried using the SQL SELECT command. By executing the SELECT command, results are copied into prereserved network buffers, which are then sent to the caller. Network write operations will succeed and free up used buffers as long as the client is reading from the buffers. If, for some reason, the client is unable to read, the network buffers will fill up and be unusable, and either the server will force a timeout or the client will catch up. This is typically referred to as "default result sets" or firehose cursors, a.k.a. data readers.

Now that you have the ability to read the results of a SQL query, you could write up code as shown in Listings 11-11 and 11-12 that attempt to run two firehose cursors at the very same time.

Listing 11-11. *Attempting to Run Two Data Readers on the Same Open Connection Concurrently in C#*

```
SqlCommand cmd = conn.CreateCommand();
SqlCommand cmd2 = conn.CreateCommand();

cmd.CommandText=
    "select * from customers";
cmd2.CommandText=
    "Update Customers set FirstName='Tarzan' where CustomerId = @CustomerID";

SqlParameter custID=cmd2.Parameters.Add("@CustomerID", SqlDbType.Int);
```

---

4. As you'll see later in this chapter, you also need to be using the SqlClient from ADO.NET 2.0 or the SQL Native Client.

```
reader=cmd.ExecuteReader();
while (reader.Read())
{
   ProcessOperation(); // Some dummy function

   custID.Value=reader.GetInt32(0); // CustomerID
   cmd2.ExecuteNonQuery();
}
```

Listing 11-12. *Attempting to Run Two Data Readers on the Same Open Connection Concurrently in Visual Basic .NET*

```
Dim cmd As SqlCommand = conn.CreateCommand()
Dim cmd2 As SqlCommand = conn.CreateCommand()

cmd.CommandText=
   "select * from customers"
cmd2.CommandText=
   "Update Customers set FirstName='Tarzan' where CustomerId = @CustomerID"

Dim custID As SqlParameter = cmd2.Parameters.Add("@CustomerID",SqlDbType.Int)

reader=cmd.ExecuteReader()
While reader.Read()
   ProcessOperation() ' Some dummy function

   custID.Value=reader.GetInt32(0) ' CustomerID
   cmd2.ExecuteNonQuery()
End While
```

By attempting to execute this code, you would get an InvalidOperationException as shown here:

```
InvalidOperationException, There is already an open DataReader associated with this
 Connection which must be closed first.
```

Okay, so when you executed ExecuteNonQuery, cmd2 tried to execute a command and attempted to maintain a parallel result set to the reader SqlDataReader, and because that is not permissible, by default you get an error.

But the code in Listings 11-11 and 11-12 can be made to work in SQL Server 2005 using MARS, all you need to do is add MultipleActiveResultsets = true[5] in the connection string. By doing so, you instruct ADO.NET that you are interested in keeping multiple active result sets open on this connection.

---

5. This is SqlClient-specific. MARS can be made to work with the latest versions of OleDb and ODBC, but the connection keyword used is different. For OleDb, the keyword is MarsConn; for ADO (and OleDb if connecting using service components), it is Mars Connection; and for ODBC, it is MARS_Connection.

MARS, however, is not a parallel execution of commands; the commands execute in an interleaved fashion, and only simultaneously active result sets can be maintained.

Interleaved Command Execution

As just mentioned, MARS does not involve running parallel commands; instead, it interleaves the commands. In other words, within the execution of a batch, other commands can be run. The MARS infrastructure allows multiple batches to execute in an interleaved fashion, however, the execution can switch at only well-defined points. As a matter of fact, you can group all commands in two major groups.

The first group consists of commands that are allowed interleaved execution before completion. These include the SELECT, FETCH, READTEXT, RECEIVE, BULK INSERT, and asynchronous cursor population commands.

The second group consists of all other commands, such as INSERT or UPDATE, that must execute as a complete batch before any other command can be executed.

What this means is that, if there is an Update statement running, and a second batch is submitted, that batch will be executed only after the Update statement completes.

On the other hand, an UPDATE statement can freely interleave a SELECT command's execution. However, because an UPDATE statement interjected the SELECT command, no results are produced from the SELECT command until the UPDATE command completes. This makes sense from a data sanctity point of view. Keep in mind that the Update statement could have interleaved in the middle of the SELECT query, which means some of the results could have already been sent to the client, only the rest of the results are held back until the UPDATE statement finishes.

MARS When Not Using SqlClient

Listings 11-11 and 11-12 were demonstrated using the SqlClient .NET data provider. It's important to note, however, that OleDb has had MARS-like behavior for quite some time now. There is one big difference, however.

Previous versions of OleDb make it look like they are supporting parallel result sets on the same connection; whereas, in reality, they were using implicit connections. This has two significant downsides:

- At a given point, you may have more connections than you realize. Connection pooling performance will degrade and this problem will typically raise its head under heavy load in production.

- As the isolation levels of various transactions are raised, you might get deadlocks. SQL Server will resolve the deadlocks, but that is still not what you were trying to achieve.

The SQL Native Client OleDb provider and ODBC driver that ship with SQL Server 2005, however, do support MARS. This means that as long as you have the latest OleDb provider and ODBC driver installed on your system, you can still use MARS with System.Data.OleDb and System.Data.Odbc.

One point to mention is that the connection string keyword you need to specify to enable MARS is different for OleDb and ODBC than it is for SqlClient. In order to use MARS with OleDb, you need to add the following to your connection string:

```
MarsConn=yes
```

Or, if you are connecting using OleDb service components, add

```
MARS Connection=True
```

For ODBC, you need to add

```
MARS_Connection=yes
```

If you forget to add these keywords, the behavior will revert to what it was like for previous versions of OleDb providers and ODBC drivers. That is, you will start using implicit connections.

MARS and Transactions

In a MARS-enabled world, you can run multiple interleaved commands and maintain parallel result sets, but you cannot run multiple transactions at the same time on the same connection.

This means that you have to be careful when mixing older versions of OleDb with transactions of a high isolation level. As mentioned earlier, it might appear on the surface with older versions of OleDb that multiple commands are, indeed, working in the same transaction and same connection; however, previous versions of OleDb will simply use a new connection and you might end up in a deadlock. Older versions of ODBC, on the other hand, respond with a "connection busy" error.

Let's say that you tried doing the same in a MARS-enabled world. This could include `SqlClient` connecting with SQL Server 2005, or OleDb or ODBC connecting with the SQL Native Client for SQL Server 2005.

In a MARS-enabled world, a transaction on multiple commands including a transaction with a higher isolation level can be made to work. This is *not because* MARS can handle multiple parallel transactions; in fact, you *cannot have multiple parallel transactions* on one connection that enables multiple interleaved commands and parallel result sets. But because all those commands are indeed working on one single connection, and maintaining their result sets in parallel while remaining on *one single transaction* at the same isolation level on the same connection, is how you are able to run multiple interleaved commands on the same transaction and on the same connection. And once you achieve multiple interleaved commands in one transaction on one single connection, the isolation level could be whatever you wish.

This raises interesting questions and possibilities about how transactions work in a MARS-enabled world.

If you attempt to[6] run two commands on the same transaction, then the regular interleaving rules apply. So what are the interleaving rules?

If the command being executed is reading results and belongs to one of the commands that allows interleaving (`SELECT`, `FETCH`, `READTEXT`), and another operation attempts to modify the data (`INSERT/UPDATE`, etc.), then, as per the interleaving rules, the DQL (Data Query Language) statement will need to yield to the DML statement. Once the read operation has been blocked, the read operation ensues after the changes have been completed by the DQL command.

---

6. You may not be able to, because MARS will not allow nondeterministic transactions.

In this scenario, however, you cannot accurately predict if this will happen or not. This is due to several factors, like if the client is keeping up with the server, the network packet size, etc. Also, the DQL statement can yield to the DML statement at only specific well-defined points that depend on many factors. Therefore, whether or not the client would see the changes in his select statement, done as a result of the update statement, depends on if the update statement was run before the select statement finished or not. In other words, whether the client sees the changes or not, depends on the position of the changes in the result set and if the changed rows have already been "put on the wire" or not—and that is impossible to predict.

If two commands attempt to modify the same data, then the commands are serialized in order, and are run one after another. The final results depend on the command order execution, which is always sequential and never parallel (even in multithreaded environments).

If the command being run is a BULK INSERT command, then other DDL, DML, or read operations are not allowed on the target object of a bulk insert. In such a case, an error is generated telling that there are conflicting pending requests under the same transaction.

Always remember, though, that these scenarios occur under a single connection/single transaction situation. Multiple transactions on one SqlConnection under MARS do not work.

MARS and Transaction Savepoints

Savepoints, as discussed later in this chapter, are a technique that allow you to set flags within a transaction's lifetime, which allow you to roll back to a savepoint instead of rolling back all the work. Because MARS allows only one running transaction, multiple command batches running in an interleaved fashion in MARS would completely confuse each other's logic.

Because you cannot run multiple transactions in MARS, and because you cannot have more than one set of savepoints in one transaction, by rolling back to a particular savepoint in one batch of commands, you might end up rolling back some of another batch's work.

It is for this reason that if serialized commands are executing, then MARS will allow you to set savepoints; but if commands begin to get interleaved, then savepoints cannot be set. In fact, such nondeterministic transactions will be explicitly disallowed in MARS. This means, if you have a result set already active, and a BEGIN TRANSACTION is requested on the same connection that already has a result set in parallel, then such a request would fail.

But how can you be sure that a parallel result set exists? That depends on a lot of circumstances. Before you request your Insert command to be executed, it is quite possible that the Select command result has already been consumed by the client. In this case, your transaction savepoint will succeed. But if the client was busy doing something else, the network was crowded, or for any other reason there still existed a parallel result set, then the savepoint will fail. So how can you be sure that a clearly interleaved command operation will, or will not, let you set a savepoint on the transaction? The answer is you cannot be sure of this, and thus you shouldn't base your architecture on it. The only way to be completely sure that there are no active result sets is to close all your readers.

MARS—A LITTLE PRACTICAL WORD OF ADVICE

You might wonder why I chose to mention the very specific details of MARS such as interleaving rules, serialized commands versus interleaved commands, and their effect on transactions. It is extremely important that you understand all of these rules before you decide to use MARS in your application architecture.

As mentioned previously, whether a command will be interleaved or serialized cannot be accurately determined. This is because it depends on a lot of features, stemming from the fact that you cannot accurately predict when the full result set for a query has been put on the wire for the client to consume. So what does this mean? Well, consider the code shown here:

C#

```csharp
using (SqlConnection testConnection = new SqlConnection(marsConnectionString))
{
    testConnection.Open();
    SqlCommand myCommand = testConnection.CreateCommand();
    myCommand.CommandText = "exec sp_who";
    SqlDataReader myDataReader =
     myCommand.ExecuteReader(CommandBehavior.Default);
    Boolean flag = myDataReader.Read();
    try
    {
        SqlTransaction myTran = testConnection.BeginTransaction();
    }
    catch(Exception e){
        Console.WriteLine(e);
    }
}
```

VB.NET

```vbnet
Using testConnection As SqlConnection = _
     new SqlConnection(marsConnectionString)
    testConnection.Open()
    Dim myCommand As SqlCommand =  testConnection.CreateCommand()
    myCommand.CommandText = "exec sp_who" 'this does not repro the problem.
    Dim myDataReader As SqlDataReader = _
     myCommand.ExecuteReader(CommandBehavior.Default)
    Dim flag As Boolean =  myDataReader.Read()
    Try
        Dim myTran As SqlTransaction =  testConnection.BeginTransaction()
    Catch e As Exception
        Console.WriteLine(e)
    End Try
End Using
```

This code will work fine because there is just one result set being maintained and a transaction in this scenario should not cause a problem. But now go ahead and change the CommandText of myCommand to

```
exec sp_who;exec sp_who;exec sp_who;exec sp_who;exec sp_who;➡
exec sp_who;exec sp_who;exec sp_who;
```

In this scenario, when BeginTransaction is called, SQL Server will determine whether or not a new transaction can be created deterministically or not. If it can be, then you don't get an error. But just because chances are that the client has not yet caught up with the multitude of results the server produced (i.e., a parallel result set exists when BeginTransaction was called), you end up getting an exception that says

```
The transaction operation cannot be performed because there are other
threads working on this transaction.
```

While this might not seem such a big deal on the face of it, what this means in practical terms is that when the application is working with a small amount of data (development environment), everything will work just fine. But when the size of the database grows, you will start seeing this error intermittently.

So just be careful when using MARS and try to understand exactly what happens behind the scenes.

MARS Deadlocks Within One Transaction

This is a situation you need to be careful of when using MARS. Imagine that you are running an Update command on a particular table. Within the Update command, you have a trigger specified on the table, which then runs a Select command to return certain results.

This sounds quite harmless until you consider the fact that the Select command in the trigger will run once every time the Update command changes a row. So, in a MARS scenario, where an Update command (or any other DML command) does not allow a Select command to execute (unless the interleaved Update command has executed fully), you would have a dead-lock situation where the Select command in the trigger cannot execute until the Update command is done executing, and the Update command cannot execute because a trigger action (the Select command) is still pending execution.

Thus, you have a deadlock. Luckily for us, SQL Server 2005's deadlock monitor will detect this and it will fail the Select statement—alleviating us from the deadlock. You will still, however, not get the results you were expecting.

■**Tip** As a general rule when using MARS, always remember that all you're doing is running seemingly parallel, but in practice interleaved, command-execution blocks.

Advanced Single Database Techniques

Up till now, you have seen how to implement transactions using ADO.NET. You've also seen how to change a transaction's isolation level. Now it's time to move on to some advanced topics: savepoints, nested transactions, and using transactions with disconnected data access techniques.

Savepoints

Whenever you roll back a transaction, it nullifies the effects of every statement from that transaction. In some cases, you may not want to roll back each and every statement, so you need a mechanism to roll back only part of a transaction. You can implement this through the use of savepoints.

Savepoints are markers that act like a bookmark: you may mark a certain point in the flow of a transaction and then roll back up to that point, rather than completely rolling back the transaction. The Save method of the transaction object accomplishes this. Note that the Save method is available only for the SqlTransaction class, and not for the OleDbTransaction or the System.Data.OracleClient.OracleTransaction classes. The Oracle Data Provider for .NET (ODP.NET), however, does allow you to implement savepoints. If you, however, wanted to implement savepoints using OracleTransaction under System.Data.OracleClient, you could always execute direct queries using the OracleCommand object, or you could simply wrap it up in a package or stored procedure.

Let's develop a simple example that illustrates the use of the Save method. This example will focus on the SqlTransaction object since it supports savepoints right out of the box (see Exercise 11.3 in the associated code download).

The code for this example can be seen in Listings 11-13 and 11-14.

Listing 11-13. *Implementing Savepoints in ADO.NET Using C#*

```
static void Main(string[] args)
{
    using (SqlConnection testConnection = new SqlConnection(connectionString))
    {
        SqlCommand testCommand = testConnection.CreateCommand();
        testConnection.Open();

        SqlTransaction myTransaction = testConnection.BeginTransaction();
        testCommand.Transaction = myTransaction;

        try
        {
            testCommand.CommandText =
                "Insert into Customers (FirstName, LastName, AccountBalance) " +
                    " Values ('Bat','Man',100)";
            testCommand.ExecuteNonQuery();
            myTransaction.Save("firstCustomer");

            testCommand.CommandText =
                "Insert into Customers (FirstName, LastName, AccountBalance) " +
                    " Values ('The','Joker',100)";
            testCommand.ExecuteNonQuery();

            myTransaction.Rollback("firstCustomer");
```

```csharp
        testCommand.CommandText =
            "Insert into Customers (FirstName, LastName, AccountBalance) " +
                " Values ('Robin','Sidekick',100)";
        testCommand.ExecuteNonQuery();
        myTransaction.Commit();

        testCommand.CommandText = "Select * from Customers";
        SqlDataReader sqlDa = testCommand.ExecuteReader();

        while (sqlDa.Read())
        {
            Console.WriteLine(
                " FirstName: " + sqlDa["FirstName"] +
                " LastName = " + sqlDa["LastName"] +
                " AccountBalance = " + sqlDa["AccountBalance"]);
        }
        sqlDa.Close();
    }
    catch (System.Exception ex)
    {
        Console.WriteLine(ex.ToString());
    }
    testConnection.Close();
} // testConnection.Dispose is called automatically.
}
```

Listing 11-14. *Implementing Savepoints in ADO.NET Using Visual Basic .NET*

```vbnet
Sub Main()
    Using testConnection As SqlConnection = New SqlConnection(connectionString)
        Dim testCommand As SqlCommand = testConnection.CreateCommand()
        testConnection.Open()

        Dim myTransaction As SqlTransaction = testConnection.BeginTransaction()
        testCommand.Transaction = myTransaction

        Try
            testCommand.CommandText = _
                    "Insert into Customers (FirstName, LastName, AccountBalance)" _
                    & " Values ('Bat','Man',100)"
            testCommand.ExecuteNonQuery()
            myTransaction.Save("firstCustomer")

            testCommand.CommandText = _
                    "Insert into Customers (FirstName, LastName, AccountBalance)" _
                    & " Values ('The','Joker',100)"
            testCommand.ExecuteNonQuery()
```

```
        myTransaction.Rollback("firstCustomer")

        testCommand.CommandText = _
            "Insert into Customers (FirstName, LastName, AccountBalance)" _
            & " Values ('Robin','Sidekick',100)"
        testCommand.ExecuteNonQuery()
        myTransaction.Commit()

        testCommand.CommandText = "Select * from Customers"
        Dim sqlDa As SqlDataReader = testCommand.ExecuteReader()

        While sqlDa.Read()
           Console.WriteLine( _
               " FirstName: " + sqlDa("FirstName") + _
               " LastName = " + sqlDa("LastName") + _
               " AccountBalance = " + sqlDa("AccountBalance"))
        End While
        sqlDa.Close()
      Catch ex As System.Exception
        Console.WriteLine(ex.ToString())
      End Try
      testConnection.Close()
    End Using
End Sub
```

Here, the application executed a total of three queries that insert customers. After inserting the first customer, the application issued a savepoint by using the following statement:

```
mytransaction.Save("firstCustomer")
```

The application then inserts one more row and rolls back up to the savepoint called firstCustomer. Note how the same Rollback method is used with the savepoint name as a parameter (to roll back the whole transaction just don't use the parameter). The application then inserts another row and, finally, commits the transaction. Then the customers are displayed to confirm that the effect of the first insert is, indeed, committed to the database.

Figure 11-9 shows the execution results of this application.

Figure 11-9. *Example of savepoints*

Note that the missing customer IDs are due to the fact we rolled back some inserts.

There are a couple of things that can make savepoints messy. One of the common mistakes programmers make while working with savepoints is they forget to call either `Commit` or `Rollback` after rolling back to a certain savepoint. Savepoints can be thought of as bookmarks: you still need to explicitly call `Commit` or `Rollback`. Another point to note is that once you roll back to a savepoint, all the savepoints defined after that savepoint are lost. You must set them again if they are needed.

Nested Transactions

As you saw in the previous section, savepoints allow a transaction to be arranged as a sequence of actions that can be rolled back individually. Nesting, on the other hand, allows a transaction to be arranged as a hierarchy of such actions. In cases of nested transactions, one transaction can contain one or more other transactions. To initiate such nested transactions, the `Begin` method of the transaction object is used. This method is available only for the `OleDbTransaction` class, and not for the `SqlTransaction` or the `OracleClientTransaction` class. The following code snippet illustrates the usage of the `Begin` method:

C#

```
Mytransaction = myconnection.BeginTransaction() ;
myanothertransaction = mytransaction.Begin() ;
```

VB.NET

```
Mytransaction = myconnection.BeginTransaction()
myanothertransaction = mytransaction.Begin()
```

The `Begin` method returns an instance of another transaction object, which we can use just like the original transaction object. However, rolling back this transaction simply rolls back the current transaction, and not the entire transaction.

■Note Savepoints and nested transactions provide a means of dividing a transaction into multiple "sub-transactions." The `SqlClient` data provider and ODP.NET support savepoints with the `Save` method of the transaction object, whereas the OleDb data provider supports nested transactions with the `Begin` method of the transaction object.

Using Transactions with a DataSet and Data Adapter

In the exercises presented thus far in this chapter, you used the command object directly to fire queries against the database. However, you can also use the `DataSet` and `DataAdapter` objects. You might want to do this, for instance, if you had bound data in a `DataSet` to controls and wanted to implement batch updates.

You would first fetch all the records needed, place them in the DataSet, and then manipulate them as required. Finally, you might send new values back to the database. Since the data adapter uses command objects internally to update changes back to the database, you would, essentially, be using the same techniques as discussed previously.

There is, however, one important point to be careful of when working with a DataSet. Say you had a DataTable with four rows that you needed to save (update, delete, or insert) back to the database. The first logical approach would be to use transactions with a DataAdapter and DataSet and wrap the four ensuing commands in one transaction, as shown in the following code:

C#

```
testConnection.Open();
SqlTransaction myTransaction = testConnection.BeginTransaction();
myUpdateCommand.Transaction = myTransaction;
sqlDA.UpdateCommand = myUpdateCommand;
try
{
    sqlDA.Update(customersTable);
    myTransaction.Commit();
}
catch (Exception ex)
{
    myTransaction.RollBack();
}
finally
{
    testConnection.Close();
}
```

VB.NET

```
testConnection.Open()
Dim myTransaction as SqlTransaction = testConnection.BeginTransaction()
myUpdateCommand.Transaction = myTransaction
sqlDA.UpdateCommand = myUpdateCommand
Try
    sqlDA.Update(customersTable)
    myTransaction.Commit()
Catch
    myTransaction.RollBack()
Finally
    testConnection.Close()
End Try
```

Unfortunately, this code snippet has a major problem. Let's say that as your application was executing commands for the four rows one by one, the first row's command executed fine, the second worked fine, and the third threw an exception. In this case, while the database would roll back the first and second executed command's changes, in the DataSet itself, the row states for the first two rows would have changed back to UnModified. Thus, at this point, you would have no easy recourse of setting the row states back to what they should have been.

In .NET 1.1, the solution for this problem would be to extract a smaller DataSet with only the changes using the GetChanges method, and work with that smaller DataSet instead. In the event of a successful transaction, you could then refresh the data and Merge the new and fresh data back from the database into the DataSet.

There are, however, numerous problems with this approach. One big problem is that Merge and GetChanges are potentially expensive commands to run. In .NET 1.1, the time required to run Merge or GetChanges increases exponentially with the increase in complexity in the DataSet. In .NET 2.0, the internal logic is vastly improved and the decrease in performance is linear, but they are still expensive commands to run. A bigger problem is that if you were using any of the events, such as RowUpdated, to set error values in your DataSet (which in this case would be the smaller DataSet extracted using GetChanges), then all your user-friendly errors will now have to be "hand merged" back to the original DataSet, or they will simply be lost. Then there are other issues surrounding the fact that you might have specified autoincrement primary keys in your original DataSet, and an automated merge will simply mess up all the primary-key values extracted out of the database. In fact, I am sure there are even more scenarios you could think of where this approach would cause problems.

It is for this purpose that .NET 2.0 has introduced a new property, called AcceptChangesDuringUpdate, on the DataAdapter object. Setting AcceptChangesDuringUpdate to true instructs the data adapter that it should not change row states on rows as it is executing the commands on various rows. Instead, you will have to call AcceptChanges on the DataSet as a whole at the end of your update. This can be seen in the associated code download under the AccChanges code sample, or in the following code snippet:

C#

```
testConnection.Open();
SqlTransaction myTransaction = testConnection.BeginTransaction();
sqlDA.UpdateCommand.Transaction = myTransaction;
sqlDA.AcceptChangesDuringUpdate = false;

try
{
    sqlDA.Update(ds);
    myTransaction.Commit()
    ds.AcceptChanges();
}
catch (Exception ex)
{
    MessageBox.Show(ex.ToString());
}
```

VB.NET

```
testConnection.Open()
Dim myTransaction as SqlTransaction = testConnection.BeginTransaction()
myUpdateCommand.Transaction = myTransaction
sqlDA.UpdateCommand = myUpdateCommand
sqlDA.AcceptChangesDuringUpdate = false;
Try
   sqlDA.Update(customersTable)
   myTransaction.Commit()
Catch
   myTransaction.RollBack()
Finally
   testConnection.Close()
End Try
```

In this code snippet, the application updates the data source using the myDataAdapter data adapter. The important thing to note here is that, by doing so, you can roll back the entire transaction. Therefore, if you had four changes to persist, and the third change gave you an error, not only could you now stop at the third change, but you could also roll back the first and second changes.

As you saw in the previous chapter, this is incredibly useful in persisting relational data. Especially since this gives you the ability to span multiple data adapters and various commands executed on them, or just multiple command objects, across multiple changed rows using the same transaction object, or a finite set of command objects.

Distributed Transactions

As you have seen in this chapter so far, the DBTransaction object can be used to group together various commands on one database and execute them all as one unitary transaction. But let's say that one of our customers wishes to make a transfer between his checking and savings account using an ATM.

This could be achieved using two command objects: one that inserts a debit into his savings account, and another that makes a credit of an equal amount to his checking account. If you specify the same DbTransaction object on either command's transaction property, both the commands would then be a part of the same transaction.

This statement, however, is not completely true. This statement holds true *only if* both of the tables lie within the same database. If the checking and savings accounts exist in different databases, you need a different approach to enlist both these operations, involving two separate databases in one transaction.

Such a transaction that can span multiple resources is referred to as a *distributed transaction*.

Important Players in Distributed Transactions: RMs and DTCs

In a distributed transaction, you could have units that perform the actual work and report a success or a failure. These units can be referred to as resource managers (RMs). In addition to the RMs, you need an application that listens to and coordinates between RMs, which is typically referred to as the Distributed Transaction Coordinator (DTC)[7] also referred to as the transaction manager.

The transaction coordinator that ships with Windows is the Microsoft Distributed Transaction Coordinator (MSDTC). MSDTC is a Windows service that provides transactional coordination for distributed applications.

Here is a typical flow of a distributed transaction:

1. An application begins a transaction requesting one from the MSDTC. This application is commonly also referred to as the *initiator*.

2. The application then asks the RM to do its work as a part of the same transaction (this is actually configurable), and the RMs register with the transaction manager as a part of the same transaction. This is commonly referred to as *enlisting in a transaction*.

3. If all goes well, the application commits the transaction.

4. If something fails, either step can issue a rollback.

5. In either case, the transaction coordinator coordinates with all the RMs to ensure that they all either succeed and do the requested work, or they all roll back their work.

MSDTC is used by MTS/COM+, `System.EnterpriseServices`, and, starting with .NET 2.0, in the new `System.Transactions` namespace. In fact, you can bypass both COM+ and .NET and simply use the MSDTC proxy `msdtcprx.dll`.

Two-Phase Commits

In a distributed transaction scenario, various RMs need to implement a reliable commit protocol, the most common implementation of which is known as a two-phase commit.

In a two-phase commit, the actual commit for the work is split into two phases. The first phase involves preparing the changes required for the commit. At this point, the RM communicates to the transaction coordinator that it has its changes prepared and ready to be committed, but not actually committed yet.

Once all the RMs give the green flag to the transaction coordinator, the transaction coordinator then lets everyone know that it is okay to go ahead and commit their changes.

This picture is obviously oversimplified, and entire books have been written on transaction coordinators and RMs, but that discussion is beyond the scope of this book.

This brings up an interesting question: *Who can participate in a distributed transaction?* It's not just the database, or a number of databases that can participate in a distributed transaction. In fact, anything that has the ability to enlist itself in an MSDTC transaction can enlist itself in a distributed transaction managed by the MSDTC. For instance, MSMQ can enlist in a transaction that has two other `SqlConnection` objects that connect to two different databases.

Implementing a Distributed Transaction: The .NET 1.1 Way

To appreciate the beauty of .NET 2.0's distributed transactions implementation, it's first necessary to become familiar with the ugly duckling of .NET 1.1's implementation. So let's look at that

---

7. DTC is a Microsoft-specific name.

first. If you are already familiar with this, or not interested in becoming friends with the ugly duckling, you may jump directly to the "Implementing a Distributed Transaction: The .NET 2.0 Way" section.

In .NET 1.1, distributed transactions can be implemented using the System. EnterpriseServices namespace, which provides you with a convenient method to access MSDTC functionality.

To do so, your project must be a class library. This is so because Component Services is designed to run without a UI. The class that will enlist itself in an MSDTC transaction needs to inherit from ServicedComponent and it will need to be in the Global Assembly Cache (GAC). Because it needs to be in the GAC, you will also need to strongly name it, using the sn.exe tool that comes with the .NET SDK.

Finally, you need to specify the TransactionAttribute at the top of the class specifying its behavior when it encounters an MSDTC transaction. This is done using the TransactionOption enumeration. The various TransactionOption enumeration values are shown in Table 11-1.

Table 11-1. *TransactionOption Enumeration Values*

Constant	Description
Disabled	This component does not participate in transactions. This is also the default value.
NotSupported	This component runs outside the context of a transaction.
Supported	This component participates in a transaction if one exists, but does not require a transaction or creates one for itself.
Required	This component must have a transaction. If no transaction exists, one will be created. If one exists, it will participate in the transaction.
RequiresNew	This component requires a transaction and will create a brand new transaction for itself.

Thus, in this manner, you could create a number of components that enlist themselves in an MSDTC transaction via Enterprise Services. Each of these calls SetComplete upon success or SetAbort upon failure. By calling SetComplete, you are notifying the transaction coordinator that you are ready and willing with your changes, pending others. If anyone else in the chain calls SetAbort, then all bets are off and no changes are committed.

You can see example code for such a component in Listings 11-15 and 11-16.

Listing 11-15. *ODP.NET Component with the Ability to Enlist Itself in a Distributed Transaction Using Enterprise Services in C#*

```
using System;
using System.EnterpriseServices;
using System.Data;
using Oracle.DataAccess.Client;
using Oracle.DataAccess.Types;
using System.Runtime.CompilerServices;
using System.Reflection;

// returns the name of Assembly, that is used by CLR to bind the Assembly
[assembly: ApplicationName("DistributedTransaction")]
```

```
// Name of a file containing the strong name key
[assembly: AssemblyKeyFile(@"DistributedTransaction.snk")]

namespace DistributedTransactionExample
{
    // Apply a Transaction Attribute class to this class
    [Transaction(TransactionOption.Required)]

    // Inherit from ServicedComponent class.
    public class DistributedTransaction : ServicedComponent
    {
        public static void updateAmounts(int id, float amount)
        {
            OracleCommand debitCommand ;
            OracleCommand creditCommand ;
            try
            {
                string cmdTxt =
        "UPDATE Credit SET CreditAmount =" + amount + " WHERE CreditID =" + id;

                // OracleCommand for credit database
                creditCommand =
                    new OracleCommand(cmdTxt, creditConnectionString);

                // OracleCommand for debit database
                debitCommand = new
                    OracleCommand(cmdTxt, debitConnectionString);

                // Executes the Oracle Commands
                creditCommand.ExecuteNonQuery();
                debitCommand.ExecuteNonQuery();
            }
            finally
            {
                // Release all resources held by OracleCommand objects
                creditCommand.Dispose();
                debitCommand.Dispose();
            }
        }
    }
}
```

Listing 11-16. *ODP.NET Component with the Ability to Enlist Itself in a Distributed Transaction Using Enterprise Services in Visual Basic .NET*

```
Imports System
Imports System.EnterpriseServices
Imports System.Data
```

```
Imports Oracle.DataAccess.Client
Imports Oracle.DataAccess.Types
Imports System.Runtime.CompilerServices
Imports System.Reflection

' returns the name of Assembly that is used by CLR to bind the Assembly
<assembly: ApplicationName("DistributedTransaction")> _

' Name of a file containing the strong name key
<assembly: AssemblyKeyFile("DistributedTransaction.snk")> _


Namespace DistributedTransactionExample
    ' Apply a Transaction Attribute class to this class
    ' Inherit from ServicedComponent class.
    <Transaction(TransactionOption.Required)> _
    Public Class DistributedTransaction Inherits ServicedComponent
        Public Shared  Sub updateAmounts(ByVal id As Integer, ByVal amount As single)
            Dim creditCommand As OracleCommand
            Dim debitCommand As OracleCommand
            Try
                Dim cmdTxt As String =
        "UPDATE Credit SET CreditAmount =" & amount & " WHERE CreditID =" & id

                ' OracleCommand for credit database
                creditCommand =
                    New OracleCommand(cmdTxt, creditConnectionString)

                ' OracleCommand for debit database
                debitCommand = New
                    OracleCommand(cmdTxt, debitConnectionString)

                ' Executes the Oracle Commands
                creditCommand.ExecuteNonQuery()
                debitCommand.ExecuteNonQuery()
            Finally
                ' Release all resources held by OracleCommand objects
                creditCommand.Dispose()
                debitCommand.Dispose()
            End Try
        End Sub
    End Class
End Namespace
```

This is the old way of doing things and, as you can see, it requires considerable effort as far as strong naming and splitting your transactional components into neatly segregated units that can be registered in Component Services is concerned. Another way of doing this in .NET 1.1

(only Windows 2003 or Windows XP Service Pack 2) is by using the ServiceConfig class as shown in the following code sample:

C#

```
ServiceConfig config = new ServiceConfig();
config.Transaction = TransactionOption.Required;
ServiceDomain.Enter(config);
try
{
    // Do your transactional code here, SqlConnections will auto enlist.
}
catch(Exception e)
{
    Console.WriteLine(e.Message);
    // Exception - abort abort abort !!
    ContextUtil.SetAbort();
}
finally
{
    ServiceDomain.Leave();
}
```

VB.NET

```
Dim config As ServiceConfig =  New ServiceConfig()
config.Transaction = TransactionOption.Required
ServiceDomain.Enter(config)
Try
    ' Do your transactional code here, SqlConnections will auto enlist.
Catch e As Exception
    Console.WriteLine(e.Message)
    ' Exception - abort abort abort !!
    ContextUtil.SetAbort()
Finally
    ServiceDomain.Leave()
End Try
```

But even this requires either Windows 2003 or Windows XP Service Pack 2. But this is a relatively cleaner method of dealing with distributed transactions in .NET 1.1.

Rightfully so, .NET 2.0 came up with a better architecture leveraging the System.Transactions namespace.

Implementing a Distributed Transaction: The .NET 2.0 Way

Distributed transactions can be easily implemented in .NET 2.0 using the System.Transactions namespace. The best way to see this is to look at an example.

The application you are going to see involves two databases. The first database is the Credits database, with one table "Credits". Credits simply has a CreditID and a CreditAmount. Similarly, there is a second table called the "Debits" table. The Debits table has a DebitID and a DebitAmount. You can find the relevant SQL script to set up these databases in the associated code download under the CreateDistributedDatabase.sql file in Exercise 11.4.

The code you are going to see attempts to wrap the two matching insert operations into one transaction. In other words, if a debit fails, the previously inserted credit must also be rolled back.

The code for this example is really simple. It can be seen in Listings 11-17 and 11-18. There is no need for strong names, segregating your code into separate assemblies, or putting them in the GAC. All of that mess is simply replaced by the code you see here:

Listing 11-17. *Implementing a Distributed Transaction in .NET 2.0 Using C#*

```csharp
static void Main(string[] args)
{
    try
    {
        using (TransactionScope myTransaction = new TransactionScope())
        {
            using (SqlConnection connection1 = new SqlConnection(connectionString1))
            {
                connection1.Open();
                SqlCommand myCommand = connection1.CreateCommand();
                myCommand.CommandText =
                    "Insert into Credits (CreditAmount) Values (100)";
                myCommand.ExecuteNonQuery();
            }

            Console.WriteLine(
                "The first connection transaction has done its work" +
                ", moving on to the second.");
            Console.ReadLine();

            using (SqlConnection connection2 = new SqlConnection(connectionString2))
            {
                connection2.Open();
                SqlCommand myCommand = connection2.CreateCommand();
                myCommand.CommandText = "Insert into Debits(DebitAmount) Values (100)";
                myCommand.ExecuteNonQuery();
            }
            myTransaction.Complete() ;
        }
    }
    catch (System.Exception ex)
    {
        Console.WriteLine(ex.ToString());
    }
}
```

Listing 11-18. *Implementing a Distributed Transaction in .NET 2.0 Using Visual Basic .NET*

```vb
Sub Main()
    Try
        Using myTransaction As TransactionScope = New TransactionScope()
            Using connection1 As SqlConnection = New SqlConnection(connectionString1)
                connection1.Open()
                Dim myCommand As SqlCommand = connection1.CreateCommand()
                myCommand.CommandText = _
                    "Insert into Credits (CreditAmount) Values (100)"
                myCommand.ExecuteNonQuery()
            End Using

            Console.WriteLine( _
            "The first connection transaction has done its work," & _
            " moving on to the second.")
            Console.ReadLine()

            Using connection2 As SqlConnection = New SqlConnection(connectionString2)
                connection2.Open()
                Dim myCommand As SqlCommand = connection2.CreateCommand()
                myCommand.CommandText = _
                    "Insert into Debits(DebitAmount) Values (100)"
                myCommand.ExecuteNonQuery()
            End Using
            myTransaction.Complete()
        End Using
    Catch ex As System.Exception
        Console.WriteLine(ex.ToString())
    End Try
End Sub
```

As you can see, the transaction is contained with the help of a using block. The application creates a new instance of a TransactionScope, which identifies the portion of code that will enlist itself in the transaction. Thus, all code that appears between the constructor of TransactionScope and the Dispose call on the created TransactionScope instance will fall in the created transaction.

Another thing one of the constructors on TransactionScope allows you to do is *suggest* an isolation level to the individual RMs inside the transaction. I say suggest, and not define, an isolation level because the RM can choose to ignore that request and implement a higher isolation level should it be necessary to do so.

Then, within the using block, various RMs come into play—in our case, two SqlConnection objects connecting to two different databases. Let's go ahead and dissect the running of this application bit by bit.

When you compile and run the application, set a breakpoint at the end of the first connection's command ExecuteNonQuery execution. If, at that point, you go to SQL Server Management Studio and run the SQL command:

```
SET TRANSACTION ISOLATION LEVEL READ UNCOMMITTED
BEGIN TRANSACTION
SELECT CREDITAMOUNT FROM CREDITS
COMMIT
```

you'll notice that SQL Server 2005 reports that one row has been inserted so far, as shown in Figure 11-10. Do note, however, that since this insert is contingent upon the second connection's insert, this is a dirty read. But because, in this instance, you are interested in peeking beneath the action and you do intend to do a dirty read, you can use the uncommitted isolation level to actually read the halfway modified row. Just for fun, can you guess what would happen if you were to remove the isolation level and then run only the `Select` statement? Try it!! Here is a hint: the distributed transaction is executing the transaction at a high isolation level, such as `Serializable`.

Figure 11-10. *Dirty read as a result of the first part of a distributed transaction*

Another thing to note here is that if you go to the Control Panel ➤ Administrative Tools ➤ Component Services applet and navigate through the tree on the left side to view the transaction list (as shown in Figure 11-11), nothing appears under the Distributed Transaction Coordinator's Transaction List, *as long as* `SqlConnection` `connection2` doesn't come into the picture.[8]

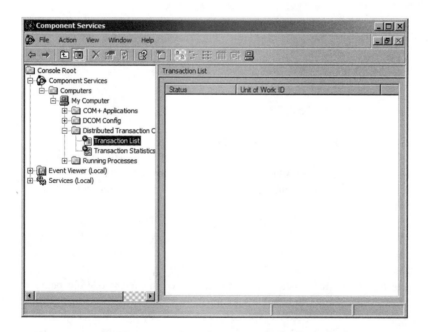

Figure 11-11. *The Transaction List does not show any transactions until a second RM comes into the picture.*

---

8. This example assumes that the first connection was connected to SQL Server 2005.

Now, step through the code in debug mode. As soon as you trip over the `connection2.Open` line in code, you'll notice that a transaction appears in the DTC's list of transactions. This is shown in Figure 11-12.

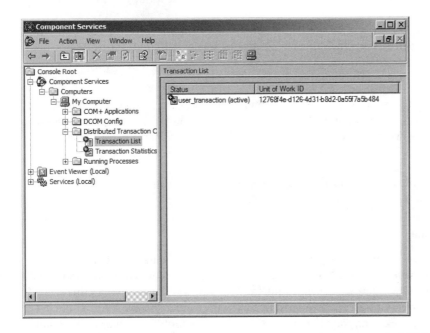

Figure 11-12. *The Transaction List shows a transaction only when a second RM comes into the picture.*

This is quite an important concept that is typically referred to as *promotable enlistment* of transactions. Do note, however, that of the currently implemented .NET data providers shipping with .NET 2.0, promotable enlistment is supported only by `SqlConnection` connecting with SQL Server 2005. Other scenarios, such as `SqlClient` connecting with SQL Server 2000, `OracleConnection`, etc., do work with distributed transactions, but they are handled exclusively by MSDTC.

Promotable Enlistment: A Quick Primer

MSDTC is expensive. It generates a lot of network traffic[9] and it possibly could run into network issues, such as firewalls, etc. Thus, it's unfair that every single transaction, whether or not it needs full distributed support, should pay the price of MSDTC. For instance, depending on your logic, your database transaction might be limited to a single database. In that instance, it would be overkill to involve MSDTC.

It's for situations like these that a new facade layer called the Lightweight Transaction Manager (LTM) has been introduced in .NET 2.0. The LTM is what manages a transaction, as long as it doesn't need MSDTC.

---

9. To be specific, MSDTC generates a lot of network roundtrips. The actual data transferred isn't that much, but too many roundtrips kill application performance.

The important part to realize is that LTM is not something you write. In fact, you write an RM to take advantage of the LTM. In the case of ADO.NET 2.0, the SqlConnection object is an example of an RM that is already written for you, which takes advantage of the LTM and promotable enlistment. The only thing you have to do to take advantage of LTM is to use SqlConnection.

Before I can explain the specific conditions under which a transaction escalates from an LTM to an MSDTC, I need to explain a few other basic concepts revolving around System.Transactions.

Volatile Enlistment

An RM that deals with resources that are not permanent in nature, such as an in-memory cache, is a good candidate for *volatile enlistment*. This means that the RM can go ahead and perform the first phase of the two-phase commit process, but if it is unable to perform the second phase, it does not need to explicitly recover the first phase. In other words, it does not need to provide a recovery contract.

RMs that intend to use volatile enlistment generally do so by using the Transaction.EnlistVolatile method.

Durable Enlistment

A *durable enlistment*, on the other hand, has permanent (durable) data that depends on the transaction for consistency. A good example of durable enlistment could be a transactional file system. Say, for instance, you are copying a file from one location to another. In this case, if you happen to be overwriting an already existing file, in the event of an abort you would need to restore the already existing state (i.e., restore the previous file). Thus, in case of a failure, a durable transaction will have logged transactions that it is participating in and it will recover those transactions with the help of the transaction manager to get the final rolled back outcome. When it is done recovering the transaction, it responds to the transaction manager to let it know that it has completed recovery, so the transaction manager can report a successful recovery/rollback.

RMs that intend to use durable enlistment generally do so by using the Transaction.EnlistDurable method.

Promotable Enlistment

Promotable enlistment refers to the process where a remote durable resource, located in a different appdomain/process/machine, participates in an LTM transaction without causing it to escalate to an MSDTC transaction. In other words, where performance is a criterion, you might choose to enlist the transaction as promotable enlistment using Transaction.EnlistPromotableSinglePhase, indicating that if certain conditions are met, then the transaction would then escalate to MSDTC. The SqlConnection object is a good example of an object that makes use of promotable enlistment.

So what are the conditions that lead to the escalation of a transaction being managed by the LTM to the MSDTC? A transaction will be escalated to MSDTC when any of the following occurs:

- At least one durable resource that doesn't support single-phase notifications is enlisted in the transaction

- At least two durable resources that support single-phase notifications are enlisted in the transaction

- A request to marshal the transaction to a different appdomain or different process is done

Being able to limit transactions within the LTM significantly reduces the overload of creating and managing a transaction. The good news is that as long as the RM is promotable enlistment–aware, you (as a user of that RM) get this performance benefit for free. You do, however, have to understand how promotable enlistment works, should you choose to implement your own RMs.

This, as you can tell, has a significant positive impact on performance; however, in the case of SQL Server 2005, it gets even better.

Usually in distributed transactions involving databases, the isolation level of such transactions is Serializable. This ensures the best database consistency, at the cost of expensive locks and poor concurrent performance. However, with SQL Server 2005, as long as there is only one RM involved, you can still get away with a lower isolation level, such as ReadCommitted. As soon as the second RM comes into picture, the isolation level could be[10] bumped up to Serializable.

Do note, however, that by using one of the overloads of TransactionScope's constructor, you can specify the *desired or suggested* isolation level that the RMs should use. Which isolation level the RMs choose to use depends on their implementation.

System.Transactions: Manually Enlisting and Multithreaded Environments

So how would you use System.Transactions.Transaction in a multithreaded environment? An instance of System.Transactions.Transaction, which can be accessed using Transaction.Current, is stored at thread-level storage. This means if you had, say, two instances of SqlConnection on different threads (or any other RM for that matter), in order for them to enlist within the same distributed transaction, you'd need to come up with a thread-safe approach.

Let me kill two birds with one stone with an example that demonstrates manual enlisting in a distributed transaction and a thread-safe approach of letting RMs in multiple threads enlist in the same transaction (see Exercise 11.5 in the associated code download).

Here are the two tricks I am going to use. In order for a SqlConnection instance to enlist itself in a transaction, it needs to use the following code snippet:

C#

```
connection2.EnlistTransaction(tran);
```

VB.NET

```
connection2.EnlistTransaction(tran)
```

---

10. Why "could be"? Because the final decision rests on the RM—SqlConnection. In certain instances, it might still keep the isolation level to, say, ReadCommitted in a distributed transaction.

In this code, connection2 is an instance of a SqlConnection and tran is an instance of System.Transactions.Transaction.

So how do you get an instance of that transaction? Well, first of all, you cannot instantiate it directly. You could either create a new instance of System.Transactions.CommittableTransaction or you have to use System.Transactions.Transaction.Current to access the currently running transaction. Once you access it, a thread-safe approach would be to clone that transaction by calling Transaction.Clone. This is shown here:

C#

```
Transaction tran = Transaction.Current.Clone();
```

VB.NET

```
Transaction tran = Transaction.Current.Clone()
```

Once your transaction is cloned, you can pass it to a thread's entry point as shown here:

C#

```
Thread myThread;
myThread =
    new System.Threading.Thread(new ParameterizedThreadStart(ThreadEntryPoint));
Transaction tran = Transaction.Current.Clone();
myThread.Start(tran);
```

VB.NET

```
Dim myThread As Thread
myThread =
    New System.Threading.Thread(New ParameterizedThreadStart(ThreadEntryPoint))
Dim tran As Transaction = Transaction.Current.Clone()
myThread.Start(tran)
```

The ThreadEntryPoint is nothing but a method that serves as the entry point for the thread. In this method you can manually enlist a SqlConnection instance into the currently running transaction. This is shown in the following code:

C#

```
private static void ThreadEntryPoint(object transactionInstance)
{
    isThreadRunning = true ;
    Transaction tran = (Transaction)transactionInstance;
    using (SqlConnection connection2 = new SqlConnection(connectionString2))
    {
        connection2.Open();
        connection2.EnlistTransaction(tran);
```

```
      // Do something here - this connection is manually enlisted.
      tran.Rollback(); // ok to do
   }
   isThreadRunning = false ;
}
```

VB.NET

```
Private Sub ThreadEntryPoint(ByVal transactionInstance As Object)
   isThreadRunning = true
   Dim tran As Transaction = CType(transactionInstance, Transaction)
   Using connection2 As SqlConnection = New SqlConnection(connectionString2)
      connection2.Open()
      connection2.EnlistTransaction(tran)
      ' Do something here - this connection is manually enlisted.
      tran.Rollback() ' ok to do
   End Using
   isThreadRunning = false
End Sub
```

Take note in this code that one of the comments says that it is okay to Rollback. This means that a cloned transaction can Rollback, but it cannot Commit. The full code can be seen in Listings 11-19 and 11-20.

Listing 11-19. *Thread-safe and Manual Enlistment in a System.Transactions.Transaction Using C#*

```
private static string connectionString1 = "...";
private static string connectionString2 = "...";
private static bool isThreadRunning = false;
static void Main(string[] args)
{
   try
   {
      using (TransactionScope myTransaction = new TransactionScope())
      {
         Thread myThread;
         myThread =
            new System.Threading.Thread(new
               ParameterizedThreadStart(ThreadEntryPoint));
         Transaction tran = Transaction.Current.Clone();
         myThread.Start(tran);

         using (SqlConnection connection1 = new SqlConnection(connectionString1))
         {
            connection1.Open();
            // Do something here - this connection will auto-enlist
         }
```

```csharp
            // Wait for the other thread to finish
            while (isThreadRunning)
            {
               Console.Write("\rWaiting for thread to finish .. ");
            }
            myTransaction.Complete();
         }
      }
   catch (System.Exception ex)
   {
      Console.WriteLine(ex.ToString());
   }
}

private static void ThreadEntryPoint(object transactionInstance)
{
   isThreadRunning = true;
   Transaction tran = (Transaction)transactionInstance;
   using (SqlConnection connection2 = new SqlConnection(connectionString2))
   {
      connection2.Open();
      connection2.EnlistTransaction(tran);
      // Do something here - this connection is manually enlisted.
      tran.Rollback(); // ok to do
   }
   isThreadRunning = false;
}
```

Listing 11-20. *Thread-safe and Manual Enlistment in a System.Transactions.Transaction Using Visual Basic .NET*

```vbnet
Private connectionString1 As String = "..."
Private connectionString2 As String = "..."
Private isThreadRunning As Boolean = False

Sub Main()
   Try
      Using myTransaction As TransactionScope = New TransactionScope()
         Dim myThread As Thread
         myThread = _
            New System.Threading.Thread( _
               New ParameterizedThreadStart(AddressOf ThreadEntryPoint))
         Dim tran As Transaction = Transaction.Current.Clone()
         myThread.Start(tran)

         Using connection1 As SqlConnection = _
            New SqlConnection(connectionString1)
            connection1.Open()
```

```
            ' Do something here - this connection will autoenlist
          End Using
          ' Wait for the other thread to finish
          While (isThreadRunning)
             Console.Write("\rWaiting for thread to finish ..")
          End While
          myTransaction.Complete()
       End Using
    Catch ex As System.Exception
       Console.WriteLine(ex.ToString())
    End Try
End Sub

Private Sub ThreadEntryPoint(ByVal transactionInstance As Object)
    isThreadRunning = True
    Dim tran As Transaction = CType(transactionInstance, Transaction)
    Using connection2 As SqlConnection = New SqlConnection(connectionString2)
       connection2.Open()
       connection2.EnlistTransaction(tran)
       ' Do something here - this connection is manually enlisted.
       tran.Rollback() ' ok to do
    End Using
    isThreadRunning = False
End Sub
```

Now, much like Exercise 11.4, if you put a breakpoint on the following line:

C#

```
connection2.EnlistTransaction(tran);
```

VB.NET

```
connection2.EnlistTransaction(tran);
```

you would note that the transaction appears in the DTC as soon as this line is executed. This confirms that, indeed, the second connection is now listed in the transaction and the transaction has been promoted to the DTC; whereas before, this line's execution (connection2) was not enlisted, thus manual enlistment is working. Also, because the transaction has executed a rollback in the subsequent line of code, you'll note that in the original thread the transaction will not successfully commit and you'll get an exception as shown here:

```
System.Transactions.TransactionAbortedException: The transaction has aborted.
```

Thus, in this case, the application creates a clone of a Transaction object instance and you can use that to enlist the SqlConnection instance in a distributed transaction when you consider it necessary to do so. Once you have a Transaction instance, you can then enlist SqlConnection objects inside the current transaction.

There is yet another class that you could use for manual enlistment: System.Transactions. CommittableTransaction. Even though you can create a new instance of CommittableTransaction, only the creator of the distributed transaction can commit the transaction. In other words, copies of a `CommittableTransaction` obtained through `System.Transactions.Transaction.Clone` cannot be committed.

Note that in .NET 1.1, you could achieve the same using `System.EnterpriseServices` using the `EnlistDistributedTransaction` method. Also, it is important to note that once a connection is enlisted, it cannot be unenlisted.

These examples using `System.Transactions` will also work for other databases, such as Oracle. However, promotable enlistment works only for `SqlConnection` connecting with SQL Server 2005.

Judicious Use of Transactions

Even though ADO.NET provides good support for transactions, it's not always necessary to use transactions. A more accurate statement perhaps could be that you should use transactions when you can, but not overuse them. Every time you use a transaction, you carry some overhead. Plus, transactions may involve some kind of locking of table rows. Thus, unnecessary use of transactions will cause performance penalties. As a rule of thumb, use a transaction only when your operation *requires* one. For example, if you are simply selecting records from a database, or firing a single query, then most of the time you will not need an explicit transaction because your statement is already wrapped in an implicit transaction. However, as mentioned previously, it's important to note that in multistatement updates, transactions can actually make the operation faster, rather than slower. Also, if it comes down to a choice between a few milliseconds saved versus compromising your data sanctity, the right answer is to not worry about the milliseconds and keep your data clean.

This effect is even more pronounced when using distributed transactions involving MSDTC. Because true distributed transactions (involving more than one RM in different appdomains or durable RMs) involve running the underlying ADO.NET transactions in `IsolationLevel. Serializable`, and because you could run into network issues, and finally because MSDTC generates a lot of network traffic,[11] distributed transactions are typically extremely expensive and problematic.

As a matter of fact, in a database scenario or ADO.NET world, you should prefer to use distributed transactions only when you have a nondatabase entity, such as an RM that you wrote yourself enlisting itself in the transaction, or when you cannot wrap the multidatabase transaction inside the database using SQL. For instance, in many scenarios, you can get away with using linked tables or linked servers.

If you do have nondatabase RMs involved, or you cannot get away with wrapping up distributed transactions inside the database itself, then you could apply sanctity checks at the end of a transaction so incorrectly committed transactions can be recovered from in a nontransactional form.

But if that is not a suitable solution, then you should try and use the `System.Transactions` namespace–based transactions. However, always remember to limit the scope of your transaction to as little as possible.

---

11. Actually MSDTC will cause a lot of roundtrips with small payloads, and a lot of roundtrips is what really kills performance. (See "Querying the Database for Multiple Result Sets" in Chapter 5.) Even though MSDTC isn't querying the database, the same principles apply—too many roundtrips affect performance negatively.

Transactional features are provided by the underlying RDBMS, ADO.NET, or MSDTC. The choice between these actually depends on what you want to accomplish:

- *RDBMS transactions* offer the best performance as they only need a single roundtrip to the database. They also provide the flexibility associated with explicitly controlling the transaction boundary. The negative side to RDBMS transactions is that you also need code in T-SQL (which may be not as easy as using VB.NET or C#) and that your code is separated into two locations (in the .NET project and also on SQL Server).

- *ADO.NET transactions* are easy to code and provide the flexibility to control the transaction boundary with explicit instructions to begin and end the transaction. To achieve this ease and flexibility, a performance cost is incurred for extra roundtrips to the database to complete the transaction.

- *MSDTC transactions* will be the only choice if your transaction spans multiple transaction–aware RMs, which could include more than one database, MSMQ, and so on. They greatly simplify the application design and reduce coding requirements. However, since the MSDTC service does all of the coordination work, it may have some extra performance overhead.

Transactions and Performance

Always keep in mind that a lengthy transaction that performs data modification to many different tables can effectively block the work of all other users in the system. This may cause serious performance problems. While implementing a transaction, the following practices can be followed in order to achieve acceptable results:

- Keep transactions as short as possible.

- Avoid returning data with a SELECT in the middle of a transaction, unless your statements depend on the data returned.

- If you use the SELECT statement, select only the rows that are required so as not to lock too many resources and to keep performance as good as possible. If your architecture permits you to do so, simply move the selects out of the transaction.

- Try to write transactions completely in either T-SQL or in the API. Mixing and matching will only cause confusion. Also, try and give preference to wrap transactions from the client using the API rather than T-SQL. There could be instances where you may need to wrap a transaction completely within T-SQL; if that is what you need, it is perfectly acceptable. What you want to avoid is beginning a transaction using SqlTransaction and rolling back or committing from within the stored procedure or the other way around.

- Avoid transactions that combine multiple, independent batches of work. Put such batches in individual transactions.

- Avoid large updates if at all possible. Of course this doesn't mean that you should give up transactional robustness to avoid a large update. If you can't avoid it, then don't— just don't unnecessarily increase the size of your transaction as it will cause more resources to lock.

Default Behavior for Transactions

One point to note is the default behavior of transactions. By default, if you do not explicitly commit the transaction, then the transaction is rolled back. Even though default behavior allows the rolling back of a transaction, it's always a good programming practice to explicitly call the Rollback method. This will not only release any locks from data, but also make code much more readable and less error-prone.

Transactions and User Confirmation

When developing applications that deal with transactions interactively, some care must be taken to avoid locking issues. Consider a case in which you are developing an application that transfers money from one account to another. You develop a user interface, in the form of a typical message box, which requires confirmation about the money transferred. Now, consider that your application conforms to the following sequence of operations:

1. Open a connection.

2. Begin a transaction.

3. Execute various queries.

4. Ask for user confirmation about the transaction by prompting a message box.

5. Upon confirmation, commit the transaction.

6. In the absence of a confirmation, roll back the transaction.

If, after step 4, the user is unable to confirm the transaction (perhaps they leave for a meeting), the locks will still be maintained on the rows under consideration. Also, a live connection is maintained with the database. This might cause problems for other users. In such cases, we can instead perform steps 1, 2, and 3 *after* getting confirmation from the user.

In general, you should avoid such scenarios where there is the need for user action in the middle of a transaction. If you don't know exactly how long an action within a transaction lasts, then you should try and get enough information that allows you to fully commit or roll back the transaction in one code sequence.

Simultaneous ADO.NET and RDBMS Transactions

Although rare, you might encounter cases where you use ADO.NET transactions as well as RDBMS transactions. Suppose that you have one stored procedure that uses transactions internally, and you call this stored procedure as a part of your own ADO.NET transaction. In such cases, both the transactions work as if they are nested. In such cases, the ADO.NET commit or rollback decides the outcome of the entire process. However, there are chances of getting into errors if you roll back from the stored procedure or place improper nesting levels (see the "Nested Transactions" section earlier in this chapter).

Mixing T-SQL and API transactions is a bad idea. It will only cause confusion. If you begin a transaction in T-SQL, then end it in T-SQL; if you begin a transaction in the API (ADO.NET), then end it in the API.

Summary

This chapter completes a series of three chapters that allows you to judiciously decide the best possible way to update data back into the data source while maintaining data sanctity. While Chapters 9 and 10 dealt with just updating as well as updating in advanced scenarios by taking care of hierarchy and concurrency issues, this chapter introduced you to the powerful topic of transactions.

You were introduced to transactions within one database, the various nuances of transactions in light of savepoints, nested transactions, and a new SQL Server 2005–specific feature called MARS. In addition, this chapter discussed the various possible ways to enforce distributed transactions along with the pros and cons of each approach, so you are armed with knowledge to design your data layer correctly per your application needs.

The concepts presented in these three chapters are essential since there is no silver bullet for data access and data layer design. It's difficult to outline a particular practice as a one-size-fits-all best practice, so the concepts presented in these chapters allow you to judiciously decide where and how to use what mix of data source updates, concurrency checks, transactions, or distributed transactions.

While ADO.NET deals mostly with databases, and handling and working with data stored in such data sources, another popular method of storing and transmitting data as chunks is XML. It's quite logical to think that XML would have profound implications on ADO.NET's architecture. You have already seen some XML features in DataSets, etc., but ADO.NET's XML support is far richer.

The next chapter adds icing to the cake because it explains the various XML facilities available in ADO.NET, and SQL Server 2005 in general. By understanding and leveraging various XML features available to data access, you can truly create a well-architected data access architecture.

CHAPTER 12

■ ■ ■

XML and ADO.NET

Lingua franca: A common language used by speakers of different languages

It wouldn't be a stretch of imagination to say that if English is the lingua franca of the world, XML is probably the lingua franca of the computer world. XML by the very nature of it allows you to create a structured and hierarchical representation of your data. Because it is text-based, it can flow freely from one platform to another; and because parsers and standard schema exist on most platforms for its validation, it is the almost de facto choice for transferring data between different applications on different platforms.

Since ADO.NET is a data access architecture, and XML is a popular method to hold and move data, it is quite reasonable to expect that ADO.NET has significant interoperability with XML built in it. As a matter of fact, in the .NET Framework itself, there is the System.XML namespace that is entirely devoted to working with data in XML form.

In Chapter 6, you have already seen some interoperability within the DataSet object and XML. You saw how easy it is to convert both a DataSet and a DataTable to XML and vice versa. You also saw how XSD schemas, which are XML, dictate the structure and data validity of a strongly typed DataSet.

This chapter and the next present concepts specific to SQL Server. This chapter carries that discussion forward and introduces you to the ability of leveraging the XML features built in SQL Server. This chapter also looks into the new XML data type in SQL Server 2005 and how you can use that to build better architected applications.

Finally, this chapter looks at the SqlXml data provider that has been included as a part of the .NET Framework 2.0, but was also available in a previous version as a part of Microsoft Data Access Components (MDAC) and could be used in .NET 1.1 and before.

But first, let's start with the basics and examine how you can leverage the XML features built in the Microsoft SQL Server database.

SQL Server Native XML Support

Given that XML lends you the ability to hold islands of data without a dedicated database, and given the fact that most of your data will reside in a database somewhere, it's critical that there should be a method to extract XML data out of a relational database such as SQL Server. Also, when programming with such data islands of XML, frequently you'll be manipulating, transmitting, or receiving them using a language such as C# or VB.NET. It is critical that the data access block of such platforms, ADO.NET, should provide you with an easy way to leverage such XML features of SQL Server. But before discussing how to use the XML support that SQL Server provides, it's critical to understand what kind of native XML support that SQL Server provides.

The introduction of SQL Server 2000 heralded a suite of new XML-related features that could be readily exploited by an ADO.NET application. SQL Server 2005 took the picture one step further by introducing the XML data type that could be stored in a prevalidated, preindexed form as XML in the database. But first, let's investigate three of the key SQL Server 2005 XML features:

- *FOR XML*: The FOR XML clause of a SQL SELECT statement allows a row set to be returned as an XML document. The XML document generated by a FOR XML clause is highly customizable with respect to the document hierarchy generated, per-column data transforms, representation of binary data, XML schema generated, and a variety of other XML nuances.

- *OPENXML*: OPENXML in T-SQL allows a stored procedure call to manipulate an XML document as a row set. Subsequently, this row set can be used to perform a variety of tasks including SELECT, INSERT, DELETE, and UPDATE.

- *The new XML data type*: With the introduction of SQL Server 2005, SQL Server now contains a new native data type to represent XML documents. This data type is different from the other two methods of interacting with the database in the sense that it acts on a new native data type "xml", which can be prevalidated against a schema stored along with the table definition in the database.

For example, SELECT queries containing FOR XML clauses could be used to generate an XML document using tables such as Doctors, Pharmacies, and Medications. The results of such a query (an XML document) could correspond with a properly formed medical prescription, and could be used by both an insurance company and the pharmacy that will ultimately dispense the prescription. In such a case, the XML document is immediately generated in the appropriate format using FOR XML, and therefore doesn't require the kind of programmatic massaging that's supported by the classes in System.Xml.

As suggested previously, where FOR XML generates XML, OPENXML is utilized in the consumption of XML. Imagine a pharmacy that receives prescriptions in the form of XML documents. These prescriptions could be used to update an underlying SQL Server database, in conjunction with SQL INSERT, UPDATE, and DELETE commands. There is no need to parse the XML document and generate the appropriate SQL command from that process. Instead, the XML document is included as part of the SQL command. What's elegant about the XML-specific features of SQL Server is that no intricate steps are required by ADO.NET in order to exploit them. Queries containing a FOR XML clause, for example, require no extra ADO.NET coding in order to execute them. However, you do need to be aware that a query contains a FOR XML clause when it's executed, because you have to execute it using the ExecuteXmlReader method of the SqlCommand class.

In this part of the chapter, you'll look at the construction of two console applications that demonstrate these SQL Server XML features being exploited using ADO.NET:

- Exercise 12.1 demonstrates a method to use the various styles of the FOR XML query (RAW, AUTO, PATH, and EXPLICIT).

- Exercise 12.2 demonstrates using OPENXML to INSERT, DELETE, and UPDATE in a table using data provided in an XML document.

You'll also look at a variety of ways to construct SQL script files that demonstrate FOR XML and OPENXML. In some instances, these scripts must be run before sample applications can be run.

FOR XML

The T-SQL extension to the SELECT statement, FOR XML, is defined in the following way:

```
FOR XML mode [, XMLDATA][, ELEMENTS][, BINARY BASE64]
```

The permissible FOR XML modes are RAW, AUTO, PATH, and EXPLICIT, listed in order from the least sophisticated to the most sophisticated. These modes generate SQL as follows:

- RAW: Generates a two-dimensional XML grid, where each row returned by the query is contained in an element named <row>. The values of the column returned by the query are represented by attributes in the <row> elements.

- AUTO: Generates a potentially hierarchical XML document, where the value returned for every column is contained in an element or an attribute.

- PATH: Generates a potentially hierarchical XML document and gives you a much simpler way than cumbersome EXPLICIT queries to describe a hierarchical structure of elements and attributes. This mode is new in SQL Server 2005, and you should try to use this instead of FOR XML EXPLICIT whenever you can.

- EXPLICIT: Allows you to specify the precise form used to contain the value of each column returned by the query. The values of columns can be returned as attributes or elements, and this distinction can be specified on a per-column basis. The exact data type used to represent a column can also be specified, as can the precise XML document hierarchy generated by the query.

Note The optional components of a FOR XML query (XMLDATA, ELEMENTS, and BINARY BASE64) will be discussed in conjunction with the detailed overview of each mode.

FOR XML Queries: A Quick Overview

A FOR XML RAW query is the most basic form of a FOR XML query. As stated previously, the XML document generated contains one type of element, named <row>. Each <row> element corresponds to a row returned by the query. This simplicity can lead to a great deal of replicated data, since there is no hierarchy within the generated XML document.

An example of a FOR XML RAW query, to be executed against SQL Server's AdventureWorks database, is as follows:

```
SELECT
    Loginid, Title,
    Humanresources.Department.Departmentid, Humanresources.Department.Name
FROM
```

```
    Humanresources.Employee
    INNER JOIN Humanresources.Department ON
    Humanresources.Employee.Departmentid = Humanresources.Department.Departmentid
WHERE Humanresources.Department.Departmentid = 7
FOR XML RAW
```

The XML document generated by this query contains *a lot of* elements named <row>—one per row of data returned. True to form, the FOR XML RAW query generates duplicate data, since every element shown contains the attribute DepartmentID, but the value of the DepartmentID attribute is the same for many different <row> elements:

```
<row LOGINID="adventure-works\guy1" TITLE="Production Technician - WC60"
DEPARTMENTID="7" NAME="Production" />
<row LOGINID="adventure-works\jolynn0" TITLE="Production Supervisor - WC60"
DEPARTMENTID="7" NAME="Production" />
<row LOGINID="adventure-works\ruth0" TITLE="Production Technician - WC10"
DEPARTMENTID="7" NAME="Production" />
<row LOGINID="adventure-works\barry0" TITLE="Production Technician - WC10"
DEPARTMENTID="7" NAME="Production" />
...
```

A FOR XML query of AUTO type exploits the hierarchical nature of certain SQL queries. Each table associated with a FOR XML AUTO query is represented as an XML element. To demonstrate that, reword the previously mentioned query as shown here:

```
SELECT
    Humanresources.Department.Departmentid, Humanresources.Department.Name,
    Humanresources.Employee.Loginid, Humanresources.Employee.Title
FROM
    Humanresources.Department
    INNER JOIN Humanresources.Employee On
    Humanresources.Department.Departmentid = Humanresources.Employee.Departmentid
WHERE Humanresources.Department.Departmentid = 7
FOR XML AUTO
```

When you run this query, SQL Server will take advantage of the fact that there is only one DepartmentID, and logically it will nest various employees that appear under this department ID. The results are as shown here:

```
<HUMANRESOURCES.DEPARTMENT DEPARTMENTID="7" NAME="Production">
  <HUMANRESOURCES.EMPLOYEE LOGINID="adventure-works\guy1" TITLE="Production
Technician - WC60" />
  <HUMANRESOURCES.EMPLOYEE LOGINID="adventure-works\jolynn0" TITLE="Production
Supervisor - WC60" />
  <HUMANRESOURCES.EMPLOYEE LOGINID="adventure-works\ruth0" TITLE="Production
Technician - WC10" />
  ...
  ...
  ...
```

```
<HUMANRESOURCES.EMPLOYEE LOGINID="adventure-works\olinda0" TITLE="Production
Technician - WC20" />
<HUMANRESOURCES.EMPLOYEE LOGINID="adventure-works\tom0" TITLE="Production
Technician - WC10" />
</HUMANRESOURCES.DEPARTMENT>
```

The criterion SQL Server follows is that the columns mentioned first are attempted to be grouped together first. For example, this query takes advantage of the fact that there is only one DepartmentID and, hence, it uses the FOR XML AUTO directive to specify that all results should be grouped under the particular DepartmentID. If you had written the query like so:

```
SELECT
    Humanresources.Employee.Loginid, Humanresources.Employee.Title,
    Humanresources.Department.Departmentid, Humanresources.Department.Name
FROM
    Humanresources.Department
    INNER JOIN Humanresources.Employee On
    Humanresources.Department.Departmentid = Humanresources.Employee.Departmentid
WHERE Humanresources.Department.Departmentid = 7
FOR XML AUTO
```

then the results you'd receive would be in the form of

```
...
<HUMANRESOURCES.EMPLOYEE LOGINID="adventure-works\guy1" TITLE="Production Technician
- WC60">
    <HUMANRESOURCES.DEPARTMENT DEPARTMENTID="7" NAME="Production" />
</HUMANRESOURCES.EMPLOYEE>
...
```

FOR XML EXPLICIT is the most advanced and customizable form of the FOR XML query. Using this form, a specific position within the XML data hierarchy can be specified for each table-column pairing. FOR XML EXPLICIT queries use per-column directives to control the form of the XML data generated, so that one column from a table may generate an XML element, while another column may generate an attribute. The following snippet from a FOR XML EXPLICIT query's SELECT clause demonstrates how the DepartmentID and Name from the AdventureWorks HumanResources.Department table can be specified as either an attribute or an element within the same XML document:

```
SELECT
    1 As Tag,
    Null As Parent,
    Departmentid As [Department!1!Departmentid],
    Name As [Department!1!Name!Element]
FROM
    Humanresources.Department
FOR XML EXPLICIT
```

Ignoring the Tag and Parent parts of this query for now, the alias following the first instance of DepartmentID contains no directive, so it's treated as an attribute (the default).

However, the element directive in the alias following the second Name column causes that column to be represented as an element. I'll go into more detail later on, but a portion of the XML generated by the previous SQL is as follows:

```
<DEPARTMENT DEPARTMENTID="12">
  <NAME>Document Control</NAME>
</DEPARTMENT>
<DEPARTMENT DEPARTMENTID="1">
  <NAME>Engineering</NAME>
</DEPARTMENT>
<DEPARTMENT DEPARTMENTID="16">
  <NAME>Executive</NAME>
</DEPARTMENT>
...
```

FOR XML PATH is a new addition to SQL Server 2005. As you'll see shortly, with multiple tables and multiple levels of hierarchy, FOR XML EXPLICIT queries get rather cumbersome to manage. In fact, most of what FOR XML EXPLICIT lets you do can be done using FOR XML PATH. There are very few scenarios such as CDATA sections where you may still need to use FOR XML EXPLICIT. These are discussed later in this chapter.

For example, if you wished to write the previous query in FOR XML PATH, it could easily be written like so:

```
SELECT
    DepartmentID "Department/@DepartmentID",
    NAME "Department/Name"
FROM
    HumanResources.Department
FOR XML PATH ('')
```

As you can see, this is a simple SELECT query with some XPath-looking syntax after each column. The first "Department/@DepartmentID" specifies that DepartmentID should appear as an attribute under the department node, and the second "Department/Name" specifies that Name should appear as an element under Department. The results of this query look exactly like the FOR XML EXPLICIT query and are shown here:

```
<Department DepartmentID="12">
  <Name>Document Control</Name>
</Department>
<Department DepartmentID="1">
  <Name>Engineering</Name>
</Department>
<Department DepartmentID="16">
  <Name>Executive</Name>
</Department>
```

Thus, as you can see, the various modes of FOR XML allow you to easily render a relational and tabular structure into a hierarchical XML structure.

FOR XML's Optional Arguments

The following optional arguments can be used in conjunction with a FOR XML query:

- ELEMENTS is only applicable to a FOR XML AUTO query, and specifies that the value of each column returned will be represented as an element within the XML document, rather than as an attribute (the default).

- BINARY BASE64 causes any binary data within the XML document to be represented in base-64 encoding. Such data is found in columns of BINARY, VARBINARY, or IMAGE type. The BINARY BASE64 option must be specified in order for FOR XML RAW and FOR XML EXPLICIT queries to retrieve binary data.

  By default, a FOR XML AUTO query handles binary data by creating a reference within the XML document to the location of the binary data. The disadvantage of doing this, however, is that it limits an XML document's portability. When BINARY BASE64 is specified for a FOR XML AUTO query, the generated XML document will contain the binary data.

- XMLDATA generates a schema for the XML document generated by the FOR XML query. This schema is placed at the start of the XML document.

The following SQL is identical to one of our earlier examples, save that it contains the optional XMLDATA argument:

```
SELECT
    Humanresources.Employee.Loginid, Humanresources.Employee.Title,
    Humanresources.Department.Departmentid, Humanresources.Department.Name
FROM
    Humanresources.Department
    INNER JOIN Humanresources.Employee On
    Humanresources.Department.Departmentid = Humanresources.Employee.Departmentid
WHERE Humanresources.Department.Departmentid = 7
FOR XML AUTO, XMLDATA
```

A portion of the XML document generated by this query (including the schema) is as follows:

```
<Schema name="Schema1" xmlns="urn:schemas-microsoft-com:xml-data"
xmlns:dt="urn:schemas-microsoft-com:datatypes">
  <ElementType name="HUMANRESOURCES.EMPLOYEE" content="eltOnly" model="closed"
order="many">
    <element type="HUMANRESOURCES.DEPARTMENT" maxOccurs="*" />
    <AttributeType name="LOGINID" dt:type="string" />
    <AttributeType name="TITLE" dt:type="string" />
    <attribute type="LOGINID" />
    <attribute type="TITLE" />
  </ElementType>
  <ElementType name="HUMANRESOURCES.DEPARTMENT" content="empty" model="closed">
    <AttributeType name="DEPARTMENTID" dt:type="i2" />
    <AttributeType name="NAME" dt:type="string" />
    <attribute type="DEPARTMENTID" />
```

```
      <attribute type="NAME" />
   </ElementType>
</Schema>
```

FOR XML RAW

Let's start looking more closely at SQL Server's FOR XML queries. Another example of a FOR XML RAW query is

```
SELECT Thumbnailphoto
FROM Production.Productphoto
FOR XML RAW, BINARY BASE64
```

The presence of the BINARY BASE64 argument here causes the binary data (the Photo column of IMAGE type) to be encoded and placed within the XML-generated document. In fact, although BINARY BASE64 is classified as an "optional" argument, it's *required* for queries of RAW and EXPLICIT type when the query contains a column of binary type. A portion of the output generated by this query, with the data in Photo truncated for clarity, is as follows:

```
<row FirstName="Steven" LastName="Buchanan" Photo="FRwv ... atBf4=" />
<row FirstName="Laura" LastName="Callahan" Photo="FRwvA ... +tBf4=" />
<row FirstName="Nancy" LastName="Davolio" Photo="FRwvAA ... StBf4=" />
<row FirstName="Anne" LastName="Dodsworth" Photo="FRwv  ... 6tBf4=" />
...
```

Had you not specified BINARY BASE64 here, the previous query would have produced a very clear error message:

```
Msg 6829, Level 16, State 1, Line 1
FOR XML EXPLICIT and RAW modes currently do not support addressing binary data as
URLs in column 'THUMBNAILPHOTO'. Remove the column, or use the BINARY BASE64 mode,
or create the URL directly using the 'dbobject/TABLE[@PK1="V1"]/@COLUMN' syntax.
```

FOR XML AUTO

FOR XML's AUTO mode supports the use of BINARY BASE64, but doesn't require it. When the BINARY BASE64 option *isn't* specified, *references* to any binary data will be included in the generated XML document. In order to demonstrate such references, consider the following SQL query:

```
SELECT Productphotoid, Thumbnailphoto
FROM Production.Productphoto
FOR XML AUTO
```

Here, the ProductPhotoID column has been deliberately included as it is the primary key, and it will be used to generate an XPath reference to the Product's thumbnail photo. This is the kind of thing you get:

```
<PRODUCTION.PRODUCTPHOTO ProductPhotoID="1" THUMBNAILPHOTO=
"dbobject/PRODUCTION.PRODUCTPHOTO[@ProductPhotoID='1']/@ThumbNailPhoto" />
<PRODUCTION.PRODUCTPHOTO ProductPhotoID="69" THUMBNAILPHOTO=
"dbobject/PRODUCTION.PRODUCTPHOTO[@ProductPhotoID='69']/@ThumbNailPhoto" />
```

```
<PRODUCTION.PRODUCTPHOTO ProductPhotoID="70" THUMBNAILPHOTO=
"dbobject/PRODUCTION.PRODUCTPHOTO[@ProductPhotoID='70']/@ThumbNailPhoto" />
<PRODUCTION.PRODUCTPHOTO ProductPhotoID="72" THUMBNAILPHOTO=
"dbobject/PRODUCTION.PRODUCTPHOTO[@ProductPhotoID='72']/@ThumbNailPhoto" />
...
```

Referencing XML data is clearly more readable than including binary data. Since the binary data itself is not contained in the XML document, copying the document to another location results in references that can no longer be resolved—references to binary data are not portable. Microsoft-specific references to binary data should be avoided unless the deployment environment is Microsoft-homogeneous.

Moving on, the `Production.ProductPhoto` table of the `AdventureWorks` database contains a primary key called `ProductPhotoID`, which is also the name of a foreign key in the `Production.ProductProductPhoto` table (mapping table between product and product photo). An example of a `FOR XML AUTO` query that accesses the `ProductProductPhoto` and `ProductPhoto` is shown here:

```
SELECT
    PP.Productphotoid, PP.Thumbnailphoto, PPP.Modifieddate
FROM
    Production.Productphoto PP
INNER JOIN
    Production.Productproductphoto PPP On
    PP.Productphotoid = PPP.Productphotoid
FOR XML AUTO
```

A portion of the output generated by this query is as follows:

```
...
<PP PRODUCTPHOTOID="111" THUMBNAILPHOTO=
"dbobject/PRODUCTION.PRODUCTPHOTO[@ProductPhotoID='111']/@ThumbNailPhoto">
  <PPP MODIFIEDDATE="2001-06-01T00:00:00" />
  <PPP MODIFIEDDATE="2001-06-01T00:00:00" />
  <PPP MODIFIEDDATE="2001-06-01T00:00:00" />
  <PPP MODIFIEDDATE="2001-06-01T00:00:00" />
  <PPP MODIFIEDDATE="2001-06-01T00:00:00" />
</PP>
<PP PRODUCTPHOTOID="113" THUMBNAILPHOTO=
"dbobject/PRODUCTION.PRODUCTPHOTO[@ProductPhotoID='113']/@ThumbNailPhoto">
  <PPP MODIFIEDDATE="2003-06-01T00:00:00" />
  <PPP MODIFIEDDATE="2003-06-01T00:00:00" />
  <PPP MODIFIEDDATE="2003-06-01T00:00:00" />
  <PPP MODIFIEDDATE="2003-06-01T00:00:00" />
</PP>
...
```

This document exploits the relationship between `ProductPhoto` and `ProductProductPhoto`. Each `ProductPhotoID` (element `<PP>`) contains subelements corresponding to itself (element `<PPP>`). Instead of this, you could also specify the `ELEMENTS` option and modify the query as shown here:

```
SELECT
    PP.Productphotoid, PP.Thumbnailphoto, PPP.Modifieddate
FROM
    Production.Productphoto PP
INNER JOIN
    Production.Productproductphoto PPP ON
    PP.Productphotoid = PPP.Productphotoid
FOR XML AUTO, ELEMENTS
```

This will produce output as shown here:

```
<PP>
  <PRODUCTPHOTOID>78</PRODUCTPHOTOID>
  <THUMBNAILPHOTO>
    dbobject/PRODUCTION.PRODUCTPHOTO[@ProductPhotoID='78']/@ThumbNailPhoto
  </THUMBNAILPHOTO>
  <PPP>
    <MODIFIEDDATE>2002-06-01T00:00:00</MODIFIEDDATE>
  </PPP>
  <PPP>
    <MODIFIEDDATE>2002-06-01T00:00:00</MODIFIEDDATE>
  </PPP>
...
</PP>
<PP>
...
</PP>
```

As you can see, as a consequence of doing this, the attributes used to contain per-column data in the generated document would be replaced by elements.

This ability to choose between elements and attributes is useful, but there's no way to indicate that *some* columns should have their data contained in attributes, while *other* columns have their data contained in elements. What's lacking is the ability for each column to declare its own representation within the XML document (attribute or element, the level of the hierarchy at which it is to be placed, etc.). The FOR XML EXPLICIT mode, which I will discuss next, will address that shortcoming.

FOR XML EXPLICIT

The EXPLICIT mode of FOR XML provides a tremendous amount of flexibility when it comes to the generation of XML documents, but the tradeoff is a fair amount of complexity with respect to the writing of such queries. To understand this fully, let's experiment with a FOR XML EXPLICIT query that will be executed against the set of tables shown in Figure 12-1. This can also be created in your local SQL Server instance using the ForXmlExplicit.SQL that can be found in the associated code download for this chapter.

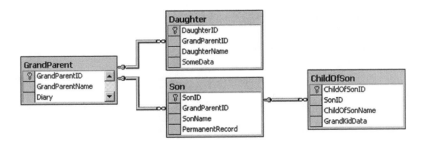

Figure 12-1. *Schema for the FamilyDB database*

These tables are not meant to be realistic; rather, they're intended to demonstrate how to represent a relational hierarchy as an XML hierarchy. The subsequent code examples will also make use of this database called FamilyDB. However, you can create them in any database you like, so long as you make the appropriate changes to the code. The tables are related as follows:

- GrandParent contains a primary key called GrandParentID.

- Daughter contains a primary key called DaughterID and a foreign key called GrandParentID that refers to an entry in the GrandParent table.

- Son contains a primary key called SonID and a foreign key called GrandParentID that refers to an entry in the GrandParent table.

- ChildOfSon contains a primary key called ChildOfSonID and a foreign key called SonID that refers to an entry in the Son table.

Using FOR XML EXPLICIT and this hierarchy of relational database tables, you could generate an XML document with the following format:

- A root element named <GrandParent>, which will contain each row of the GrandParent table and all of the grandparent's children and grandchildren. This root element will contain the data retrieved from the GrandParent table by the FOR XML EXPLICIT query.

- Directly below the <GrandParent> element will exist elements named <Daughter> and <Son>. Each of these elements will contain the data retrieved from their respective tables, Daughter and Son.

- At the level below the <Son> element will exist the <ChildOfSon> element. This will contain the data retrieved from the ChildOfSon table.

The mechanism that FOR XML EXPLICIT uses to support the generation of a specific hierarchy is to assign a *tag* to each element within the XML hierarchy. Every element declares a tag value, and the value of its *parent*. For our proposed hierarchy, this is as shown in Table 12-1.

Table 12-1. *Hierarchy Description for Our Query*

Level	Tag	Parent
GrandParent	1	0
Son	2	1
Daughter	3	1
ChildOfSon	4	2

The GrandParent has a tag value of 1, and a parent value of 0. (When the parent of a level in the XML hierarchy is set to zero, this indicates that the element is at the root of the XML document.) Notice that both Son (tag 2) and Daughter (tag 3) have a parent value of 1 (the GrandParent level of the XML hierarchy). Daughter is at the second, rather than the third, level of the hierarchy because its parent's value is 1. The ChildOfSon is assigned a tag value of 4, and is associated with a parent whose tag value is 2 (a Son).

Each column of a FOR XML EXPLICIT query specifies a per-column encoding that includes a tag value. The form that this per-column encoding takes is as follows:

```
columnName AS [ContainedElementName!Tag!AttributeOrElementName!Directive]
```

The subcomponents that make up the explicit declaration of a column are

- ContainedElementName: The name of the element in which this column returned by the query will be contained. For example, each column of the GrandParent table will be contained in the <GrandParent> element, whether as an element or an attribute.

- Tag: The tag value associated with a column. For example, each column of the Son table is associated with a tag value of 2, while each column of the Daughter table is associated with a tag value of 3.

- AttributeOrElementName: The name of the element or attribute that will contain this returned column's data.

  - If no Directive is specified, then this is the name of the attribute (for example, [Son!2!SonID] where the attribute containing the data is named SonID).

  - If the Directive specified is xml, element, or CDATA, then AttributeOrElementName specifies the name of the element that will contain this column's data (for example, [GrandKid!4!GrandKidData!xml], where the element containing the data is named GrandKidData).

  - If a Directive is specified, then AttributeOrElementName is optional.

  - If no AttributeOrElementName is specified, then the column's data is included as child content of the element specified by ContainedElementName.

- Directive: Used to specify the format that data should take (hide, element, xml, xmltext, or CDATA), and to specify references between columns. Supplying a directive for a column is optional. We will review the directives in full a little later on.

FOR XML EXPLICIT: Two-Level Example

Before things get out of hand, let me demonstrate a query that works with only two levels of the three-level database that you just created. This query is designed to demonstrate how a FOR XML EXPLICIT hierarchy can be created, by using UNION ALL to combine the results of multiple queries:

```
SELECT 1 as Tag,
       NULL as Parent,
       G.GrandParentID as [GrandParent!1!GrandParentID],
       NULL      as [Son!2!SonName]
FROM   GrandParent G
WHERE  G.GrandParentID IN (Select GrandParentID from Son)
UNION ALL
SELECT 2 as Tag,
       1 as Parent,
       S.GrandParentID,
       LTRIM(RTRIM(S.SonName))
FROM   GrandParent G, Son S
WHERE  G.GrandParentID = S.GrandParentID
ORDER BY [GrandParent!1!GrandParentID], [Son!2!SonName]
FOR XML EXPLICIT , ROOT('XML')
```

Here you can see two subqueries: SubQuery1 and SubQuery2. The first of these retrieves columns from the GrandParent table—on this occasion, just GrandParentID. Specifying a tag of 1 and a parent of 0 means that the data retrieved will be at the root of the XML document. The children of this <GrandParent> element will use the tag value in order to indicate it as their parent in the XML hierarchy.

SubQuery2 retrieves the SonID column from the Son table, and by specifying a tag value of 2 and a parent of 1 dictates that the elements of this subquery are to be stored in a subelement of a <GrandParent> element.

The subqueries of our FOR XML EXPLICIT query are combined using UNION ALL. Using a SQL union means that every subquery must retrieve the same columns as every other subquery. Notice that SubQuery1 returns a value for the Son table's SonID:

```
0 AS [Son!2!SonName]
```

The value for SonID in each row returned by SubQuery1 is 0, but the value isn't displayed because its tag value is specified as 2. In other words, the data associated with this column only appears at tag level 2. Similarly, the Son's subquery, SubQuery2, contains a 0 representing the GrandParentID column. This value is never displayed either, because the data displayed for the Son table is at tag level 2, and GrandParentID is at tag level 1.

It's extremely important to note that this query is not the same as the regular row/column result T-SQL query that you might be used to. For instance, try removing the ORDER BY clause specified in the previous query, and compare the results. You'll notice that the element grouping is completely incorrect if the ORDER BY clause is missing.

The XML document generated by the previous query is as follows:

```
<XML>
  <GrandParent GrandParentID="1">
    <Son SonName="Han" />
```

```
    </GrandParent>
    <GrandParent GrandParentID="2">
      <Son SonName="Darth" />
      <Son SonName="Luke" />
    </GrandParent>
</XML>
```

Entity Encoding

Before delving further into the tantalizing world of FOR XML EXPLICIT directives, let's look at an equally important concept: *entity encoding*. Entity encoding is the means by which XML special characters can be included in data. What are special characters? The "less-than" character (<) is special because it's used to start each element within an XML document. For example, how would an XML parser handle data of the following form?

<CompareThis> MassOfEarth < MassOfJupiter </CompareThis>

This is not actually well-formed XML, because the < character inside the element's data leads to a parsing error. In this XML-like snippet, the less-than character indicates the start of each tag, and is also part of the data associated with the element: MassOfEarth < MassOfJupiter. The previous snippet could be made well-formed by using entity encoding to change how the less-than character is represented:

<CompareThis> MassOfEarth < MassOfJupiter </CompareThis>

< is the entity encoded form of the less-than character, so there is no ambiguity for XML parsers here. The characters deemed as special by XML include &, ', >, <, and ". When you need them, they should by written within an XML document using the alternative representations shown in Table 12-2.

Table 12-2. *Various Entity Encoding Representations*

Character Name	Character Literal	Entity Encoding Representation
Ampersand	&	&amp;
Apostrophe	'	&apos;
Greater-than	>	&gt;
Less-than	<	&lt;
Quotation mark	"	&quot;

This concept of entity encoding is pertinent to the next section's discussion of the FOR XML EXPLICIT directives.

Directives

The short SQL query you just saw demonstrated how the FOR XML EXPLICIT clause in T-SQL can be used to generate a specific hierarchy. However, real-life situations will present you with loftier goals where you might need to exercise what you will see next: "directives" for the FOR XML EXPLICIT clause. The FOR XML EXPLICIT directives presented in this section include what you see in Table 12-3.

Table 12-3. *FOR XML EXPLICIT Directives*

Directive	Description
element	Causes a particular column in the query to be represented by an element rather than an attribute.
hide	Causes a column in the SELECT clause of the query not to generate XML, and therefore not to be included in the XML document generated.
xml	Causes the data associated with a column to be included in the XML document, but not to be entity encoded.
xmltext	Causes the data associated with a column to be included in the XML document as XML. A column can contain XML, and this will be placed in the generated XML document.
CDATA	Causes the data associated with a column to be included in the generated XML document as CDATA data type.
ID	Causes the data associated with a column to be included in the generated XML document as ID data type.
IDREF	Causes the data associated with a column to be included in the generated XML document as IDREF data type.
IDREFS	Causes the data associated with a column to be included in the generated XML document as IDREFS data type.

Just before I get to the main example, let's take a closer look at a few of these directives. For a start, the data associated with a column specified using the element directive is contained within an XML element in the generated document. An example of this is as follows:

```
[GrandKid!4!ChildOfSonName!element]
```

The data associated with a column that's been configured like this will be contained in an element called <ChildOfSonName>, like this:

```
<GrandKid>
  <ChildOfSonName>Kyle</ChildOfSonName>
  ...
</GrandKid>
```

Next, the xml directive causes the data in the column to which it applies not to be entity encoded when placed in the XML document. This means, for example, that any < characters are not converted to <. An example of such a specification is

```
[GrandKid!4!GrandKidData!xml]
```

The XML generated by this directive is as follows, where quote and question-mark characters are not entity encoded, even though they are classified as special characters within XML:

```
<GrandKid>
  <GrandKidData>"/?%#</GrandKidData>
  ...
</GrandKid>
```

Moving on, when the `xmltext` directive is specified for a column, the data associated with this column is assumed to be well-formed XML, and is included in the document at the beginning of the child content of the element containing it. An example of using the `xmltext` directive is

```
Diary AS [GrandParent!1!!xmltext]
```

The output generated by this part of a SQL query is completely dependent on the data contained in the `Diary` column. For the case of the `GrandParent` named Olivia, the `Diary` column contains XML corresponding to the chapters of a diary. The `<Chapter>` elements in the following XML snippet are not generated by SQL Server, but rather extracted as data from the `Diary` column of the `GrandParent` table, courtesy of the `xmltext` directive:

```
<GrandParent GrandParentName="Olivia">
  <Chapter>ChapNum="1" Body="It was the best of times"</Chapter>
  <Chapter>ChapNum="2" Body="It is a far, far"</Chapter>
```

Finally for now, when the `hide` directive is specified for a column, the column is not included in the generated XML document. Such hidden columns can be used to affect the overall architecture without having their data appearing in the XML document. These columns will ultimately be included in an `ORDER BY` clause, because they are typically used to order data.

An example of specifying a hidden column is

```
[GrandParent!1!OrderByGrandParentName!hide]
```

Each subquery of the large `FOR XML EXPLICIT` query that you'll look at next contains a column corresponding to `GrandParentName`, aliased to `OrderByGrandParentName`. This column is not displayed because of the hide directive. In fact, the `ORDER BY` clause of our sample query looks like this—a total of four hidden columns are used to specify the order of the data generated:

```
ORDER BY [GrandParent!1!OrderByGrandParentName!hide],
         [Son!2!OrderBySonName!hide],
         [Daughter!3!OrderByDaughterName!hide],
         [GrandKid!4!OrderByChildOfSonName!hide]
```

It's worth bearing in mind that the directives are not the only controllers of per-column encoding. To understand this, consider the following portion of a query:

```
GrandParentID AS [GrandParent!1!],
GrandParentName AS [GrandParent!1!OrderByGrandParentName!hide],
RTRIM(GrandParentName) AS [GrandParent!1!GrandParentName],
Diary AS [GrandParent!1!!xmltext],
```

Here, the values retrieved from the `GrandParent` table will all be contained in the XML element, `<GrandParent>`. The data associated with the `GrandParentName` column is contained in the attribute `GrandParentName` (third line). For the `GrandParentID` column, however, there is no attribute name specified, and therefore there is no attribute to contain this column's data. Under these circumstances, the data associated with the `GrandParentID` column is contained directly in the `<GrandParent>` element. A sample of the XML generated by this portion of our query is as follows:

```
<GrandParent GrandParentName="Jeb">
  <Chapter> ChapNum="1" Body="They call me Ishmael"</Chapter>
  <Chapter> ChapNum="2" Body="Whale sinks"</Chapter>

</GrandParent>
```

The <Chapter> elements and their corresponding attributes are again retrieved from the Diary column, but notice that in this snippet of XML, the "1" is not associated with an attribute. This "1" is the value of the GrandParentID column.

FOR XML EXPLICIT: Three-Level Example

So far, each directive has been presented in piecemeal fashion, but all of the pieces you have seen so far have actually been part of a larger query—a query that generates a three-level XML hierarchy in the following form:

```
<GrandParent> contains Son and Daughter elements
  <Son> contains GrandKid elements
    <GrandKid> </GrandKid>
  </Son>
  <Daughter> </Daughter>
</GrandParent>
```

The query in question is a union of four separate queries combined using UNION ALL. These subqueries perform the following tasks in generating the XML document:

- Retrieve the grandparent data at level 1 of the hierarchy

- Retrieve the son data at level 2 of the hierarchy

- Retrieve the daughter data at level 2 of the hierarchy

- Retrieve the grandchild (child of son) data at level 3 of the hierarchy

The query itself looks like as shown in Listing 12-1

Listing 12-1. *Putting Everything Together: Hierarchical FOR XML EXPLICIT Query with Various Directives*

```
-- Generate the Grandparent level of the hierarchy
SELECT 1 AS Tag,
       0 AS Parent,
       GrandParentID AS [GrandParent!1!],
       GrandParentName AS [GrandParent!1!OrderByGrandParentName!hide],
       RTRIM(GrandParentName) AS [GrandParent!1!GrandParentName],
       Diary AS [GrandParent!1!!xmltext],
       0 AS [Son!2!SonID],
       '' AS [Son!2!OrderBySonName!hide],
       '' AS [Son!2!SonName],
       '' AS [Son!2!!CDATA], -- PermanentRecord
       0 AS [Daughter!3!DaughterID!element],
```

```
                '' AS [Daughter!3!OrderByDaughterName!hide],
                '' AS [Daughter!3!DaughterName!element],
                '' AS [Daughter!3!SomeData!element],
                0 AS [GrandKid!4!ChildOfSonID!element],
                '' AS [GrandKid!4!OrderByChildOfSonName!hide],
                '' AS [GrandKid!4!ChildOfSonName!element],
                '' AS [GrandKid!4!GrandKidData!xml]

FROM GrandParent

UNION ALL

-- Generated the Son level of the hierarchy
SELECT 2 AS Tag,
        1 AS Parent,
        0, -- GrandParent.GrandParentID
        G.GrandParentName AS [GrandParent!1!OrderByGrandParentName!hide],
        '', -- GrandParent.Name
        '', -- GrandParent.Diary
        SonID,
        RTRIM(SonName),
        RTRIM(SonName),
        PermanentRecord,
        0, -- Daughter.DaughterID
        '', -- Daughter.OrderByDaughterName
        '', -- Daughter.DaughterName
        '', -- Daughter.SomeData,
        0, -- ChildOfSon.ChildOfOnID,
        '', -- ChildOfSon.OrderByChildOfSonName
        '', -- ChildOfSon.ChildOfSonName
        '' -- ChildOfSon.GrandKidData
FROM GrandParent AS G, Son AS S
WHERE G.GrandParentID = S.GrandParentID

UNION ALL

-- Generate the Daughter level of the hierarchy
-- that is in the same level as the Son's data
SELECT 3 AS Tag,
        1 AS Parent,
        0, -- GrandParent.GrandParentID
        G.GrandParentName AS [GrandParent!1!OrderByGrandParentName!hide],
        '', -- GrandParent.Name
        '', -- GrandParent.Diary
        0, -- Son.SonID
        '', -- Son.SonName (hidden)
        '', -- Son.SonName
        '', -- Son.PermentRecord
```

```
        DaughterID,
        RTRIM(DaughterName),
        RTRIM(DaughterName),
        SomeData,
        0, -- ChildOfSon.ChildOfOnID,
        '', -- ChildOfSon.OrderByChildOfSonName
        '', -- ChildOfSon.ChildOfSonName
        '' -- ChildOfSon.GrandKidData

FROM GrandParent AS G, Daughter AS D
WHERE G.GrandParentID = D.GrandParentID

UNION ALL

-- Execute grandchild (child of son) level of the query
SELECT 4 AS Tag,
        2 AS Parent,
        0, -- GrandParent.GrandParentID
        G.GrandParentName AS [GrandParent!1!OrderByGrandParentName!hide],
        '', -- GrandParent.Name
        '', -- GrandParent.Diary
        0, -- Son.SonID
        RTRIM(S.SonName),
        '', -- Son.SonName
        '', -- Son.PermentRecord
        0, -- Daughter.DaughterID
        '', -- Daughter.OrderByDaughterName
        '', -- Daughter.DaughterName
        '', -- Daughter.SomeData,
        CS.ChildOfSonID,
        RTRIM(CS.ChildOfSonName),
        RTRIM(CS.ChildOfSonName),
        CS.GrandKidData

FROM GrandParent AS G, Son AS S, ChildOfSon AS CS
WHERE G.GrandParentID = S.GrandParentID AND S.SonID = CS.SonID

ORDER BY [GrandParent!1!OrderByGrandParentName!hide],
        [Son!2!OrderBySonName!hide],
        [Daughter!3!OrderByDaughterName!hide],
        [GrandKid!4!OrderByChildOfSonName!hide]

FOR XML EXPLICIT, ROOT('XML')
```

The ROOT keyword is new to SQL Server 2005, and it allows you to wrap the whole output in one node, in our case the node will be named "XML". The output for the sizable query shown in Listing 12-1 can be seen in Figure 12-2.

```
XML_F52E2B61...49916B29.xml*    SQLQuery1.sql-HOMEPC.test*
<XML>
   <GrandParent GrandParentName="Jeb">
      <Chapter> ChapNum="1" Body="They call me Ishmael"</Chapter>
      <Chapter> ChapNum="2" Body="Whale sinks"</Chapter>
      1
      <Daughter>
         <DaughterID>1</DaughterID>
         <DaughterName>Sade</DaughterName>
         <SomeData>abcd&lt;&gt;'</SomeData>
      </Daughter>
      <Son SonID="3" SonName="Han">
         <![CDATA[<Book><Chapter> ChapNum="1" Body="Bye, Bye Yoda"</Chapt
         <GrandKid>
            <ChildOfSonID>3</ChildOfSonID>
            <ChildOfSonName>Kyle</ChildOfSonName>
            <GrandKidData>?????"""???</GrandKidData>
         </GrandKid>
      </Son>
   </GrandParent>
   <GrandParent GrandParentName="Olivia">
      <Chapter> ChapNum="1" Body="It was the best of times"</Chapter>
      <Chapter> ChapNum="2" Body="If is a far, far"</Chapter>2<Daughter>
         <DaughterID>2</DaughterID>
         <DaughterName>Avril</DaughterName>
         <SomeData>efg&gt;&lt;''&amp;&amp;&amp;"...</SomeData>
      </Daughter><Daughter>
         <DaughterID>3</DaughterID>
         <DaughterName>Sonya</DaughterName>
         <SomeData>&lt;&gt;&lt;&gt;&lt;&gt;&lt;&gt;&lt;&gt;</SomeData>
      </Daughter>
      <Son SonID="2" SonName="Darth">
         <![CDATA[<Book><Chapter> ChapNum="1" Body="Bye, Bye ice planet"<
      </Son>
      <Son SonID="1" SonName="Luke">
         <![CDATA[<Book><Chapter> ChapNum="1" Body="A new hope"</Chapter>
         <GrandKid>
            <ChildOfSonID>1</ChildOfSonID>
            <ChildOfSonName>Jasmine</ChildOfSonName>
            <GrandKidData>$$$$$$$$$$$</GrandKidData>
         </GrandKid><GrandKid>
            <ChildOfSonID>2</ChildOfSonID>
            <ChildOfSonName>Sophia</ChildOfSonName>
            <GrandKidData>"/?%#</GrandKidData>
         </GrandKid>
      </Son>
   </GrandParent>
   <GrandParent GrandParentName="Rex">
      <Chapter> ChapNum="1" Body="Dad takes over spice world"</Chapter>
      <Chapter> ChapNum="2" Body="Revenge"</Chapter>3
   </GrandParent>
</XML>
```

Figure 12-2. *Output of the FOR XML EXPLICIT*

Sizable query indeed. The query is HUGE! Typing it is one story, getting it right is a whole other story, and understanding it, yet another story. Thankfully, SQL Server 2005 has introduced a new FOR XML PATH syntax that allows you to write queries with relative ease, which you would have to otherwise write using FOR XML EXPLICIT.

SQL Server 2005 and FOR XML PATH

So the query used in Listing 12-1 was huge. Specifically, it reads from four tables, and based upon the relationships between those four tables, you had to split the query into four separate SQL statements tied together with a UNION ALL clause.

Actually, it's more complex than that. A UNION ALL clause in regular T-SQL (not using FOR XML) would simply require you to make sure that the column sets match, both logically and physically. However, when working with XML data, and FOR XML EXPLICIT queries, you have to logically make sure that all your "tags" match, and that you specify the correct ORDER BY clause in the very end.

Obviously, this is a fairly complex routine to achieve something rather straightforward. Luckily for this very reason, SQL Server 2005 has introduced the new FOR XML PATH syntax.

The usage is fairly simple. Consider the following query:

```
SELECT 1 as Tag,
       NULL as Parent,
       G.GrandParentID as [GrandParent!1!GrandParentID],
       NULL       as [Son!2!SonName]
FROM   GrandParent G
WHERE  G.GrandParentID IN (Select GrandParentID from Son)
UNION ALL
SELECT 2 as Tag,
       1 as Parent,
       S.GrandParentID,
       LTRIM(RTRIM(S.SonName))
FROM   GrandParent G, Son S
WHERE  G.GrandParentID = S.GrandParentID
ORDER BY [GrandParent!1!GrandParentID], [Son!2!SonName]
FOR XML EXPLICIT , ROOT('XML')
```

If you wanted to write this same query using the FOR XML PATH syntax, it would look like this:

```
SELECT
   RTRIM (G.GRANDPARENTNAME) [@GRANDPARENTNAME],
   (
      SELECT
         RTRIM (S.SONNAME) [@SONNAME]
      FROM
         DBO.SON    S
      WHERE
         S.GRANDPARENTID = G.GRANDPARENTID
      FOR XML PATH('SON'), TYPE
   )
FROM
   DBO.GRANDPARENT G
WHERE EXISTS
(
   SELECT
      *
```

```
    FROM
        DBO.SON S2
    WHERE
        S2.GRANDPARENTID = G.GRANDPARENTID
)
ORDER BY
    G.GRANDPARENTNAME
FOR XML PATH ('GRANDPARENT'), ROOT ('XML')
```

Is this query any simpler? Maybe not. After all, it's just about as long as the FOR XML EXPLICIT query. Though, when you read through the query it seems easier to understand. The difference is even more apparent when there are more than two tables involved. So you were able to write a simple-to-understand query using FOR XML PATH rather than using FOR XML EXPLICIT, but you produced the same results.

Nevertheless, the previous query can be simplified further, producing almost the same results:

```
Select
    G.GrandParentID "GrandParent/@GrandParentID",
    RTRIM(S.SonName) "GrandParent/Son/@SonName"
FROM
    GrandParent G INNER JOIN SON S ON G.GrandParentID = S.GrandParentID
For Xml Path('GrandParent'), Root('XML')
```

This query is definitely much simpler than the initial FOR XML EXPLICIT query and its exact replacement FOR XML PATH query. The difference, however, lies in the results. The minor difference this query will produce is that if a grandparent has more than one son, instead of listing all sons under one XML node, they will each be listed under their parent grandparent node. This issue is, however, easily solved in .NET code using an XSL transform or similar mechanism. For larger blocks of XML this might be slower, but for smaller blocks of XML, the simplicity may warrant a better solution under certain conditions.

This way, for most FOR XML EXPLICIT cases, you can replace them with FOR XML PATH queries instead. However, do note that not everything is possible to do using FOR XML PATH, for instance, the xmltext directive is not easily emulated in a FOR XML PATH query.

For instance, if you had a varchar column that actually contained XML data inside of it, you could emulate the xmltext directive in FOR XML PATH queries by casting that data to xml data type first. While that approach would work, you would pay the overhead of the cast involved.

One thing that cannot be done in FOR XML PATH queries is CDATA sections, but for most other cases, you should try and use FOR XML PATH queries instead of FOR XML EXPLICIT queries. Also, given the fact that between the various flavors of FOR XML available, you can generate any desired XML structure based on your underlying data and relationships using one mechanism or other.

Okay, so now you can pretty much generate any kind of XML structure from relational data. But that is only half the story. The other half is reading these FOR XML queries from ADO.NET.

Using FOR XML Queries with ADO.NET

Now that you have seen the various ways to write FOR XML queries, next let's look at an example that tests the use of a FOR XML query with ADO.NET. You can use any of the queries used previously; for instance, let's use the query shown here:

```
SELECT
    Loginid, Title,
    Humanresources.Department.Departmentid, Humanresources.Department.Name
FROM
    Humanresources.Employee
    INNER JOIN Humanresources.Department On
    Humanresources.Employee.Departmentid = Humanresources.Department.Departmentid
WHERE Humanresources.Department.Departmentid = 7
FOR XML RAW, XMLDATA
```

Here the XMLDATA option has been used in order to generate a schema for the XML document.

To execute this query, a SqlCommand instance is created and associated with an instance of SQL Server containing an AdventureWorks database. At the same time, the query is specified as command text to the SqlCommand. This is demonstrated in Exercise 12.1 in the associated code download (see the Downloads section of the Apress website at http://www.apress.com) or can also be seen in Listings 12-2 and 12-3.

Listing 12-2. *Setting Up a FOR XML Query Command in C#*

```
SqlCommand testCommand = testConnection.CreateCommand();
testCommand.CommandText =
    "SELECT " +
    "LOGINID, TITLE, " +
    "   HUMANRESOURCES.DEPARTMENT.DEPARTMENTID, HUMANRESOURCES.DEPARTMENT.NAME " +
    "FROM " +
    "   HUMANRESOURCES.EMPLOYEE " +
    "   INNER JOIN HUMANRESOURCES.DEPARTMENT ON " +
 HUMANRESOURCES.EMPLOYEE.DEPARTMENTID = HUMANRESOURCES.DEPARTMENT.DEPARTMENTID " +
    "WHERE HUMANRESOURCES.DEPARTMENT.DEPARTMENTID = 7 " +
    "FOR XML RAW, XMLDATA";
```

Listing 12-3. *Setting Up a FOR XML Query Command in Visual Basic .NET*

```
Dim testCommand As SqlCommand = testConnection.CreateCommand()
testCommand.CommandText = _
    "SELECT " & _
    "LOGINID, TITLE, " & _
"   HUMANRESOURCES.DEPARTMENT.DEPARTMENTID, HUMANRESOURCES.DEPARTMENT.NAME " & _
    "FROM " & _
    "   HUMANRESOURCES.EMPLOYEE " & _
    "   INNER JOIN HUMANRESOURCES.DEPARTMENT ON " & _
    "   HUMANRESOURCES.EMPLOYEE.DEPARTMENTID = " & _
    " HUMANRESOURCES.DEPARTMENT.DEPARTMENTID " & _
    "WHERE HUMANRESOURCES.DEPARTMENT.DEPARTMENTID = 7 " & _
    "FOR XML RAW, XMLDATA"
```

Once the SqlCommand instance has been created and the connection opened, the SqlCommand object's ExecuteXmlReader method can be called. ExecuteXmlReader executes a query containing a FOR XML clause, and returns an instance of System.Xml.XmlReader type. The XmlReader can then be read in a fashion very similar to a data reader. This is shown in Listings 12-4 and 12-5.

Listing 12-4. *Reading Up an XmlReader in C#*

```
testConnection.Open();
XmlReader xrdr = testCommand.ExecuteXmlReader();
StreamWriter sw = new StreamWriter("Output.xml");
sw.WriteLine("<xml>");

while (xrdr.Read())
{
    sw.WriteLine(xrdr.ReadOuterXml());
}

sw.WriteLine("</xml>");
sw.Close();
xrdr.Close();
testConnection.Close();
```

Listing 12-5. *Reading Up an XmlReader in Visual Basic .NET*

```
testConnection.Open()
Dim xrdr As XmlReader = testCommand.ExecuteXmlReader()
Dim sw As StreamWriter = New StreamWriter("Output.xml")

sw.WriteLine("<xml>")
While xrdr.Read()
    sw.WriteLine(xrdr.ReadOuterXml())
End While
sw.WriteLine("</xml>")

sw.Close()
xrdr.Close()
testConnection.Close()
```

If you take a look at Output.xml, you should see something like as shown in Figure 12-3.

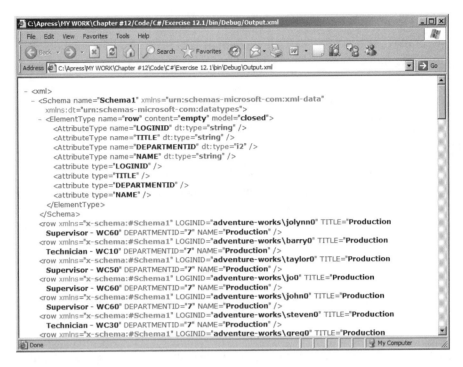

Figure 12-3. *FOR XML query's XML output using ADO.NET and XmlReader*

As you might expect, you can simply replace the command text for the `SqlCommand` in ADO.NET, and in similar fashion run either RAW, AUTO, PATH, or EXPLICIT queries. Given the size that such queries can reach, though, it's worth bearing in mind that using stored procedures gives you better manageability than storing SQL queries in your code, making the former technique the preferred way of dealing with FOR XML queries in general.

OPENXML

The OPENXML function of SQL Server's T-SQL allows an XML document to be viewed as a row set without the need for any involvement of .NET code. Once opened, this row set can immediately be manipulated using SQL statements such as SELECT, INSERT, UPDATE, and DELETE.

This tying of SQL Server to an XML document results in certain complexities. For example, what happens if the XML document inserted into a SQL Server table contains extra elements or attributes that weren't taken into account by the OPENXML command? This is referred to as *overflow*, and it results in the elements and tags in question being *unconsumed*. As you will see, the OPENXML mechanism has the ability to handle unconsumed XML by placing it in a designated column.

The OPENXML function of T-SQL is defined as follows, where parameters surrounded by square brackets (`[flags byte[in]]`) and clauses surrounded by square brackets (`[WITH (SchemaDeclaration | TableName)]`) are optional:

```
OPENXML(idoc int [in], rowpattern nvarchar [in], [flags byte [in]])
    [WITH (SchemaDeclaration | TableName)]
```

The parameters to OPENXML are defined as follows:

- idoc (input parameter of type int): A document handle referring to the parsed XML document. This document handle is created by calling the sp_xml_preparedocument stored procedure.

- rowpattern (input parameter of type nvarchar): An XPath pattern specifying the node of the XML document to be processed as a row set. For example, the following pattern indicates that the Region node is the level of the XML document to be interpreted: N'/Top/Region'.

- flags (input parameter of type byte): A flag that indicates how the XML node is to be interpreted. 1 indicates that attributes in the document become columns in the row set, while 2 indicates that elements in the document become columns. This flag can also be used to specify that data not consumed by the row set should be placed in an overflow column.

Two forms of the WITH clause can be specified with OPENXML:

- WITH SchemaDeclaration allows an XML-data schema to be specified.

- WITH TableName indicates that the schema associated with a specified table should be used to interpret the XML document specified. This is the simpler of the two variants.

In this section, let's look at how to use OPENXML in an example that requires you to add a stored procedure called RegionInsert to the Regions table in the test database. The relevant scripts containing the RegionInsert stored procedure and others can be found in the associated code download under OpenXMLSP.sql, or is reproduced in Listing 12-6 for your convenience.

Listing 12-6. *Script to Create Various Stored Procedures Using OPENXML*

```
CREATE TABLE Region
(
RegionID INT PRIMARY KEY,
RegionDescription VARCHAR(3000)
)
GO


-- XML Document is of the form
-- <Top>
--    <Region> region elements here </Region>
--    <Region> region elements here </Region>
--    ...
-- </Top>
CREATE PROCEDURE RegionInsert @xmlDoc NVARCHAR(4000) AS
DECLARE @docIndex INT
EXECUTE sp_xml_preparedocument @docIndex OUTPUT, @xmlDoc

-- 1 is ATTRIBUTE-centric mapping
INSERT Region
SELECT RegionID, RegionDescription
FROM OPENXML(@docIndex, N'/Top/Region', 1) WITH Region
```

```
EXECUTE sp_xml_removedocument @docIndex

GO

CREATE PROCEDURE RegionUpdate @xmlDoc NVARCHAR(4000) AS

  DECLARE @docIndex INT

  EXECUTE sp_xml_preparedocument @docIndex OUTPUT, @xmlDoc

  UPDATE Region
    SET Region.RegionDescription = XMLRegion.RegionDescription
  FROM OPENXML(@docIndex, N'/Top/Region',1) WITH Region AS XMLRegion
  WHERE Region.RegionID = XMLRegion.RegionID

  EXECUTE sp_xml_removedocument @docIndex

GO

CREATE PROCEDURE RegionDelete @xmlDoc NVARCHAR(4000) AS
  DECLARE @docIndex INT

  EXECUTE sp_xml_preparedocument @docIndex OUTPUT, @xmlDoc

  DELETE Region
  FROM OPENXML(@docIndex, N'/Top/Region', 1) WITH Region AS XMLRegion
  WHERE Region.RegionID=XMLRegion.RegionID

  EXECUTE sp_xml_removedocument @docIndex
```

This stored procedure contains an INSERT statement that uses OPENXML. The steps involved in the creation of the RegionInsert stored procedure are as follows:

1. Call the system-provided stored procedure, sp_xml_preparedocument, passing the XML document to be processed (@xmldoc). This stored procedure parses the XML document and returns a handle (an integer, @docIndex) that's used by OPENXML to process the parsed document:

   ```
   CREATE PROCEDURE RegionInsert @xmlDoc NVARCHAR(4000) AS
   DECLARE @docIndex INT
   EXECUTE sp_xml_preparedocument @docIndex OUTPUT, @xmlDoc
   ```

2. Call OPENXML to create a row set from the XML document. This row set can then be processed by any applicable SQL command. The following INSERT statement demonstrates OPENXML creating a row set using the schema associated with the Region table (WITH Region) and then inserting the data into that table:

   ```
   -- 1 is ATTRIBUTE-centric mapping
   INSERT Region
   SELECT RegionID, RegionDescription
   FROM OPENXML(@docIndex, N'/Top/Region', 1) WITH Region
   ```

3. Call the system-provided stored procedure, sp_xml_removedocument, in order to clean up the handle to the XML document:

```
EXECUTE sp_xml_removedocument @docIndex
```

You can add this stored procedure to the test database by executing the OpenXMLSP.sql SQL script from the code download. Once that is in place, an example of SQL code (including the XML document with data to insert) that executes the RegionInsert stored procedure is as follows (OpenXMLDemo.sql in the associated code download):

```
DECLARE @newRegions NVARCHAR(2048)

SET @newRegions = N'
<Top>
  <Region RegionID="11" RegionDescription="Uptown" />
  <Region RegionID="22" RegionDescription="Downtown" />
</Top>'

EXEC RegionInsert @newRegions
```

This calls RegionInsert to add two rows to the Region table (one with RegionID 11, and one with RegionID 22). Remember that XML is case sensitive, but SQL Server's SQL is not. When OPENXML was specified (OPENXML(@docIndex, N'/Top/Region', 1)) in the RegionInsert stored procedure, the row pattern was /Top/Region. The XML document's elements must match these exactly (<Top> and <Region>). If <TOP> or <top> had been specified as the root element name, then the insertion would have failed, as there would have been a case mismatch.

OPENXML Stored Procedures: Deletes and Updates

Another of the SQL scripts in OpenXMLSP.sql demonstrates OPENXML being used in conjunction with a SQL DELETE operation (in a stored procedure called RegionDelete):

```
CREATE PROCEDURE RegionDelete @xmlDoc NVARCHAR(4000) AS
DECLARE @docIndex INT
EXECUTE sp_xml_preparedocument @docIndex OUTPUT, @xmlDoc

DELETE Region
FROM OPENXML(@docIndex, N'/Top/Region', 1) WITH Region AS XMLRegion
WHERE Region.RegionID = XMLRegion.RegionID

EXECUTE sp_xml_removedocument @docIndex
```

Here, the FROM clause of the DELETE statement uses the OPENXML function to generate a row set named XMLRegion:

```
OPENXML(@docIndex, N'/Top/Region', 1) WITH Region AS XMLRegion
```

OpenXMLSP.sql also includes a stored procedure called RegionUpdate, which uses an XML document to provide the data used to *update* the Region table:

```
CREATE PROCEDURE RegionUpdate @xmlDoc NVARCHAR(4000) AS
DECLARE @docIndex INT
EXECUTE sp_xml_preparedocument @docIndex OUTPUT, @xmlDoc

UPDATE Region
SET Region.RegionDescription = XMLRegion.RegionDescription
FROM OPENXML(@docIndex, N'/Top/Region',1) WITH Region AS XMLRegion
WHERE Region.RegionID = XMLRegion.RegionID

EXECUTE sp_xml_removedocument @docIndex
```

The RegionUpdate stored procedure's UPDATE statement contains a FROM clause that uses OPENXML. The OPENXML function uses an XML document to generate a row set containing the entries in the Region table to be updated. The values in the Region table are matched to the values specified in the OPENXML-generated row set, XmlRegion, using the UPDATE statement's WHERE clause.

Using OPENXML with ADO.NET

So far, we've created three stored procedures that use OPENXML: RegionInsert, RegionUpdate, and RegionDelete. The Exercise 12.2 console application uses ADO.NET to demonstrate each of these stored procedure calls being executed.

The implementation of Exercise 12.2 contains a method called DemoOpenXML. That method begins by creating a SqlCommand instance that's wired to the first stored procedure we want to execute, RegionInsert:

C#

```
string strXMLDoc =
    "<Top>" + @"<Region RegionID="""11""" RegionDescription="""UpTown"""/>" +
    @"<Region RegionID="""22""" RegionDescription="""DownTown"""/>" + "</Top>";

SqlConnection sqlConn = new SqlConnection(strConnection);
SqlCommand openXMLCommand = new SqlCommand("RegionInsert", sqlConn);
openXMLCommand.CommandType = CommandType.StoredProcedure;
```

VB.NET

```
Dim strXMLDoc As String = _
    "<Top>" & _
        "<Region RegionID="""11""" RegionDescription="""UpTown"""/>" & _
        "<Region RegionID="""22""" RegionDescription="""DownTown"""/>" & _
    "</Top>"

Dim sqlConn As SqlConnection = New SqlConnection(strConnection)
Dim openXMLCommand As SqlCommand = New SqlCommand("RegionInsert", sqlConn)
openXMLCommand.CommandType = CommandType.StoredProcedure
```

Next, the application needs to create a parameter for this command's Parameters collection, setting its value to the XML document (strXMLDoc) that will be inserted using the RegionInsert stored procedure:

C#

```
SqlParameter xmlDocParm =
    openXMLCommand.Parameters.Add("@xmlDoc", SqlDbType.NVarChar, 4000);
xmlDocParm.Value = strXMLDoc;
```

VB.NET

```
Dim xmlDocParm As SqlParameter = _
    openXMLCommand.Parameters.Add("@xmlDoc", SqlDbType.NVarChar, 4000)
xmlDocParm.Value = strXMLDoc
```

The ExecuteNonQuery method of the openXMLCommand SqlCommand instance can now be called to insert the data. (ExecuteNonQuery is a good choice here because RegionInsert only inserts data and doesn't return the results of a query.)

C#

```
sqlConnection.Open();
openXMLCommand.ExecuteNonQuery();
```

VB.NET

```
sqlConnection.Open()
openXMLCommand.ExecuteNonQuery()
```

The next stored procedure to demonstrate is RegionUpdate. To facilitate this, the data associated with the parameter (the XML document) is tweaked by changing each instance of the word "town" to "state" (so "Uptown" becomes "Upstate", and "Downtown" becomes "Downstate"), courtesy of the String class's Replace method. Once the data is tweaked, the command's text is set to RegionUpdate and the command is executed using ExecuteNonQuery:

C#

```
xmlDocParm.Value = strXMLDoc.Replace("Town", "state");
openXMLCommand.CommandText = "RegionUpdate";
openXMLCommand.ExecuteNonQuery();
```

VB.NET

```
xmlDocParm.Value = strXMLDoc.Replace("Town", "state")
openXMLCommand.CommandText = "RegionUpdate"
openXMLCommand.ExecuteNonQuery()
```

The remainder of Exercise 12.2 sets the command's text to the stored procedure that handles deletion, `RegionDelete`. Once this is set, `ExecuteNonQuery` can work its magic again:

C#

```
openXMLCommand.CommandText = "RegionDelete";
openXMLCommand.ExecuteNonQuery();

sqlConn.Close();
```

VB.NET

```
openXMLCommand.CommandText = "RegionDelete"
openXMLCommand.ExecuteNonQuery()

sqlConn.Close()
```

The elegance of this technique is that .NET is blissfully unaware of how the XML document it passes to the stored procedure is eventually written to SQL Server. The stored procedure calls ultimately use `OPENXML`, but ADO.NET neither knows nor cares what's going on under the covers.

The XML Data Type: SQL Server 2005 Only

Of all the techniques you have seen so far that help you work with XML data, the common theme has been an attempt to bridge the relational table structures with a hierarchical XML structure. But in all these cases, the XML was either returned or accepted as a string that simply holds XML. That is probably the reason why, in spite of all the rich XML features in Microsoft SQL Server 2000 and 2005, a lot of developers choose to store their data directly as XML stored in `varchar` data type columns.

That approach has numerous downsides. For one, the data is not validated in any manner. Potentially someone could store data that does not validate any specified schema, because the database does not enforce those rules. Another problem is the inability to query against specific fields in that data. Probably the best you can do is string-like searching using the % characters. Yet another disadvantage that arises from the same fact that everything is stored as a string is that finding the right node to update might be difficult. The situation becomes more complex considering that you might encounter rows that do not follow a set schema so your program logic has to consider that.

Keeping all that in mind, SQL Server 2005 includes a first-class data type, like `int` or `varchar`, that allows in-place querying, processing, and storage of XML documents. This is the new `xml` data type.

Creating such a table can be achieved using the following script.

```
Create Table MyXmlTable
(
    MyXmlTableID INT IDENTITY PRIMARY KEY,
    MyXmlData XML
)
```

If you wanted the data in the MyXmlData column to be validated against a schema, you would first have to set up a schema in the database using the CREATE XML SCHEMA statement as shown here:

```
CREATE XML SCHEMA COLLECTION MySchemaCollection AS
N'<?xml version="1.0" encoding="UTF-16"?>
<xsd:schema elementFormDefault="unqualified" attributeFormDefault="unqualified"
  xmlns:xsd="http://www.w3.org/2001/XMLSchema" >
  <xsd:element name="SomeElement">
    <xsd:complexType mixed="false">
    <xsd:sequence>
      <xsd:element name="ChildElement" type="xsd:string"/>
      <xsd:element name="SecondChildElement" type="xsd:string"/>
    </xsd:sequence>
    </xsd:complexType>
  </xsd:element>
</xsd:schema>';
```

And the Create Table syntax can be modified as shown here:.

```
Create Table MyXmlTable
(
   MyXmlTableID INT IDENTITY PRIMARY KEY,
   MyXmlData XML (MySchemaCollection)
)
```

Also, to query and work with the new XML data type, you can use various new methods in the T-SQL syntax.

You could use the query method to specify specific xpath syntax and query within the XML document:

```
Select MyXmlData::query('/SomeElement/ChildElement(=42)') from MyXmlTable
```

Or you could use the value method to have a SQL Server native data type returned (rather than the previous query that will always return a varchar data type):

```
Select MyXmlData::value('/SomeElement/ChildElement(=42)', int) from MyXmlTable
```

You can also use the exist method to check for the existence of certain data within the xml column, or you can use the modify method to modify the XML contained within the xml data type column.

However, for the sake of discussion here, let's use the HumanResources.JobCandidate table in the AdventureWorks database, which has the Resume column specified as an XML data type.

Reading XML Columns in ADO.NET

So now that you have the ability to store prevalidated and easily modifiable and workable XML in the database, let's look at the other half of the story—working with such data through .NET applications using ADO.NET.

You can download this code in the associated code download under Exercise 12.3, but the important excerpts are as shown in this section.

In order to read the XML data type, you would first need to set up a SqlCommand that works with an xml column. This is no different than any other command, and is shown here:

C#

```
SqlCommand testCommand =
    new SqlCommand("Select Top 1 Resume from HumanResources.JobCandidate",
    testConnection);
testConnection.Open();
SqlDataReader rdr = testCommand.ExecuteReader();
```

VB.NET

```
Dim testCommand As SqlCommand = _
    New SqlCommand("Select Top 1 Resume from HumanResources.JobCandidate", _
    testConnection)
testConnection.Open()
Dim rdr As SqlDataReader = testCommand.ExecuteReader()
```

Once the command is set up, then you have various choices to read the data. You could simply use the ExecuteXmlReader method as shown here:

C#

```
XmlReader xrdr = testCommand.ExecuteXmlReader();
xrdr.Read();
Console.WriteLine(xrdr.ReadOuterXml());
```

VB.NET

```
Dim xrdr As XmlReader = testCommand.ExecuteXmlReader()
xrdr.Read()
Console.WriteLine(xrdr.ReadOuterXml())
```

Or you could simply read out the contents of the column as a string:

C#

```
Console.WriteLine(rdr.GetString(0));
```

VB.NET

```
Console.WriteLine(rdr.GetString(0))
```

Or you could iterate through the data reader results and work with a SqlXml data type as shown here:

C#

```
XmlReader xr = rdr.GetSqlXml(0).CreateReader();
xr.Read();
Console.WriteLine(xr.ReadOuterXml());
```

VB.NET

```
Dim xr As XmlReader = rdr.GetSqlXml(0).CreateReader()
xr.Read()
Console.WriteLine(xr.ReadOuterXml())
```

Or you could use the GetProviderSpecificValue method. Strangely enough though, the GetProviderSpecificValue method returns a string, rather than an XmlReader or something similar. That is a good thing since returning provider-specific types prevents type conversion errors or precision errors.

C#

```
Object o = rdr.GetProviderSpecificValue(0);
// Strangely enough this prints SqlString
Console.WriteLine(o.GetType().ToString());
Console.WriteLine(o.ToString());
```

VB.NET

```
Dim o As Object = rdr.GetProviderSpecificValue(0)
' Strangely enough this prints SqlString
Console.WriteLine(o.GetType().ToString())
Console.WriteLine(o.ToString())
```

Working with SQL Server XML Features: SQLXML

SQLXML, in short, is a set of components that were created to enable developers to work with XML rather than ADO.NET when querying SQL Server. You can create queries to select and update data in the database using pure XML, FOR XML, SQLXML templates, XPath, UpdateGrams and DiffGrams, and XSLT transformations, all of which I will discuss in the following sections.

As you have seen in this chapter so far, working with ADO.NET with SQL Server presents you with some powerful XML features that can be used when working in an application. Interestingly enough though, all these SQL Server–specific XML features have been accessible through a COM library called SqlXml. In fact, .NET 2.0 provides you with a fully managed wrapper around that functionality under the Microsoft.Data.SqlXml namespace.

In your applications, if you are working with .NET 1.1, you can download SQLXML 3.0 as a part of MDAC 2.8 at http://msdn.microsoft.com/library/default.asp?url=/library/en-us/dnanchor/html/anch_SQLXML.asp. For .NET 2.0, however, all you need to do is add a reference to Microsoft.Data.SqlXml.

SQLXML and ADO.NET

Having said all that, what reasons could you have for using SQLXML from .NET code—especially when ADO.NET has so many XML features? Most of the time, ADO.NET is the way to go, but you'll want to consider using SQLXML-managed classes in the following conditions:

- You're migrating to the .NET Framework from a previous version that used SQLXML in unmanaged code. In this case, it will be easier simply to migrate the SQLXML code to .NET code, rather than rewrite everything in ADO.NET.

- You want to do client-side XML formatting, which is currently not available in ADO.NET.

- You want to represent multidimensional table relations, as this cannot be done in ADO.NET.

Let's now look at the architecture of various SQLXML classes, and begin to see how you can use them.

The SQLXML Object Model

The SQLXML-managed classes themselves are implemented in the `Microsoft.Data.SqlXml.dll` assembly (typically located in the `C:\Program Files\SQLXML 4.0\bin` folder). If you're using Visual Studio .NET, you'll need to add a reference to this assembly before you can use the three classes it contains:

- `SqlXmlCommand`

- `SqlXmlParameter`

- `SqlXmlAdapter`

The SqlXmlCommand Object

A `SqlXmlCommand` object is similar to an ADO.NET `SqlCommand` object, but it's used for working with SQLXML in SQL server. As you will see, however, the `SqlXmlCommand` class is slightly more useful in certain scenarios.

The first is that it can be used to make the SQL client do more work, rather than pushing the load onto the SQL Server. When you perform a FOR XML query using the `SqlCommand` class, the work of transforming the selected row set into XML format is done in the SQL Server process on the database. When you use a `SqlXmlCommand` object and FOR XML, you have the option of saying that you want this process to occur in the data layer, and hence reduce the load on your database.

Furthermore, the `SqlXmlCommand` class allows you to write the result to a new or existing stream instance (a class derived from the `System.IO.Stream` class), an option that's not available in ADO.NET. Table 12-4 looks over a few commonly used `SqlXmlCommand` properties while Table 12-5 goes over the various methods available.

Table 12-4. *SqlXmlCommand Properties*

Property	Description
BasePath	Contains a directory path or base URL that relative filenames can be resolved from. So if you specify the XSLPath to be a.xsl, and the BasePath to be http://localhost/, then the fully resolved path will be http://localhost/a.xsl.
ClientSideXml	When set to True, this indicates that the row set returned from SQL Server should be converted to XML in the client process. By default, the conversion is done on the SQL Server.
CommandStream	Contains a stream (such as a file) that contains a query to be executed.
CommandText	Allows you to set the XML query to be executed.
CommandType	One of the SqlXmlCommandType enumeration values, which can be Sql, XPath, Template, TemplateFile, UpdateGram, or DiffGram.
Namespaces	Allows qualified XPath queries to be made. This is needed when the XML document contains namespaces, and you want to select a node from one of them.
OutputEncoding	Allows you to specify the encoding of the XML that is output and sets the encoding attribute on the XML declaration (such as encoding="UTF-8").
RootTag	Allows you to specify a root XML element that will wrap the XML returned from the query. This is especially important where the XML that is returned doesn't have a root element (a list of row elements, for example).
SchemaPath	Similar to the XslPath property, but used for XML schema files.
XslPath	Specifies the absolute or relative path to an XSL file. If a relative path is used, the BasePath is used to get the full path to the file.

Table 12-5. *SqlXmlCommand Methods*

Method	Description
ClearParameters()	Clears all parameters that have been bound to the command—useful when you want to reuse the command instance with new parameters.
CreateParameter()	Returns an instance of a new parameter object that can have its name and value set, and will be passed to the command.
ExecuteNonQuery()	Simply executes the query and returns nothing—useful for update and delete queries.
ExecuteStream()	Executes the query and returns the resulting XML as an instance of a stream object.
ExecuteToStream (Stream)	Similar to ExecuteStream(), except that it will output the resulting XML to the existing stream instance that's passed as an argument.
ExecuteXmlReader()	Executes the query and returns the result in an XmlReader instance.

Now that you know what methods and properties are available, let's look at how they can be used. You can find the code for the following example in Exercise 12.4 of the associated code download.

First, you create a new instance of the SqlXmlCommand object by passing the SQLOLEDB connection string to construct the object as follows (using the SQL Server AdventureWorks database):

C#

```csharp
private static string connectionString =
    "Provider=SQLOLEDB;Server=(local);database=AdventureWorks;" +
    " Integrated Security=SSPI";
static void Main(string[] args)
{
    SqlXmlCommand cmd = new SqlXmlCommand(connectionString);
```

VB.NET

```vbnet
Private connectionString As String = _
    "Provider=SQLOLEDB;Server=(local);" & _
    "database=AdventureWorks;Integrated Security=SSPI"

Sub Main()
    Dim cmd As SqlXmlCommand = New SqlXmlCommand(connectionString)
```

Interestingly, the connection string specified to the SqlXmlCommand object still uses the "Provider=SQLOLEDB" key-value pair. This is because SQLXML sits on top of the SqlOleDbProvider.

Next, you can specify the SQLXML query to execute in two ways. The first is to set the CommandText property to the query string:

C#

```csharp
cmd.CommandText =
"SELECT FirstName, LastName FROM Person.Contact WHERE LastName=? For XML Auto";
```

VB.NET

```vbnet
cmd.CommandText = _
  "SELECT FirstName, LastName FROM Person.Contact WHERE LastName=? For XML Auto"
```

Alternatively, you may use the CommandStream property to set a stream instance where the query to be executed is stored. In the following case, the code uses the file persons.xml to get the query, which must be a Template, an UpdateGram, or a DiffGram (we'll see how these work in the next exercise):

C#

```csharp
FileStream personFile = new FileStream("persons.xml", FileMode.Open) ;
cmd.CommandStream = personFile ;
```

VB.NET

```vbnet
Dim personFile As New FileStream("persons.xml", FileMode.Open)
cmd.CommandStream = personFile
```

If you need to do so, you can add parameters to the query using the following syntax (note the difference in syntax from a regular SqlParameter being added to a SqlCommand object):

C#

```
SqlXmlParameter parm;
parm = cmd.CreateParameter();
parm.Value = "Achong";
```

VB.NET

```
Dim parm As SqlXmlParameter
parm = cmd.CreateParameter()
parm.Value = "Achong"
```

Now that your command is set up, the next step is to run it and fetch the results. You can use any of the Execute methods described in Table 12-5 to fetch the results. For the sake of this example, let's use the ExecuteToStream method. This can be seen in the following code snippet:

C#

```
string strResult;
try
{
    Stream strm = cmd.ExecuteStream();
    strm.Position = 0;
    using (StreamReader sr = new StreamReader(strm))
    {
        Console.WriteLine(sr.ReadToEnd());
    }
}
catch (SqlXmlException e)
{
    //in case of an error, this prints error returned.
    e.ErrorStream.Position = 0;
    strResult = new StreamReader(e.ErrorStream).ReadToEnd();
    System.Console.WriteLine(strResult);
}
```

VB.NET

```
Try
    Dim strm As Stream = cmd.ExecuteStream()
    strm.Position = 0
    Using sr As StreamReader = New StreamReader(strm)
        Console.WriteLine(sr.ReadToEnd())
    End Using
```

```
Catch e As SqlXmlException
    'in case of an error, this prints error returned.
    e.ErrorStream.Position = 0
    strResult = New StreamReader(e.ErrorStream).ReadToEnd()
    System.Console.WriteLine(strResult)
End Try
```

When this is run from the SQLXML example in the code download, the following XML will be returned:

```
<Person.Contact FirstName="Gustavo" LastName="Achong"/>
```

The SqlXmlParameter Object

One of the objects you worked with in Exercise 12.4 was the SqlXmlParameter object. Just like a SqlParameter, the SqlXmlParameter object allows you to specify flexible parameterized commands.

However, an important distinction as you saw from the previous example was the syntax and usage of a SqlXmlParameter object. While a SqlParameter can be used as follows:

C#

```
SqlParameter parm = new SqlParameter();
// Set various properties on the parameter
mySqlCommand.Parameters.Add(parm);
```

VB.NET

```
Dim parm As SqlParameter =  New SqlParameter()
' Set various properties on the parameter
mySqlCommand.Parameters.Add(parm)
```

in comparison, the SqlXmlParameter object is used as follows:

C#

```
SqlXmlParameter parm;
parm = cmd.CreateParameter();
parm.Value = "Achong";
```

VB.NET

```
Dim parm As SqlXmlParameter
parm = cmd.CreateParameter()
parm.Value = "Achong"
```

Let's look at an example of how we can use templates and parameters to improve the flexibility of our SQLXML queries.

Using Templates and Parameters

The SQL queries you have used so far have been defined inline with the code, and although parameters give you a bit more flexibility in the query that is sent to SQL Server, it would be better if you could entirely separate the SQL from the code and host it in a separate file. This gives you better flexibility in a production application, a sort of hybrid approach between the convenience of changing SQL after the application has been deployed (a.k.a. Dynamic SQL) and not having to tinker with the actual database and store your queries there (a.k.a. stored procedures). This would provide for a more flexible architecture, promote reuse of XML query formats (which also improves deployment time), and even improve performance. Of course these XML files that store your queries must be secured appropriately lest any hacker gets access to them.

SQLXML provides this functionality through the use of *templates*, which allow you to create an XML document containing the details of the query that can then be passed to the command object and processed.

The following template allows us to define a query that selects products with a ProductName similar to the string that's passed in as a parameter:

```
<ROOT xmlns:sql='urn:schemas-microsoft-com:xml-sql'>
  <sql:header>
    <sql:param name="LastName" />
  </sql:header>
  <sql:query>
SELECT FirstName, LastName FROM Person.Contact WHERE LastName=@LastName For XML Auto
  </sql:query>
</ROOT>
```

The parameters must be defined in the <header> section (this is optional if you have no parameters), with a <param> element with a suitable name representing each one. (In our case, LastName is the name of the parameter.) The query to be executed is defined in the <query> element; it's a normal SQL query with the name of each parameter included in the form @*ParamName*.

How does this change our code? The new version is shown in Listings 12-7 and 12-8 or can be found in the associated code download as Exercise 12.5.

Listing 12-7. *Using Templatized Queries in C#*

```
static void Main(string[] args)
{
    FileStream xmlQuery = new FileStream("command.xml", FileMode.Open);
    SqlXmlCommand cmd = new SqlXmlCommand(connectionString);
    cmd.CommandStream = xmlQuery;
    cmd.CommandType = SqlXmlCommandType.Template;

    SqlXmlParameter parm;
    parm = cmd.CreateParameter();
    parm.Name = "@LastName";
    parm.Value = "Achong";
```

```csharp
cmd.ClientSideXml = true;
cmd.RootTag = "Person";

string strResult;
try
{
    Stream strm = cmd.ExecuteStream();
    strm.Position = 0;
    using (StreamReader sr = new StreamReader(strm))
    {
        Console.WriteLine(sr.ReadToEnd());
    }
}
catch (SqlXmlException e)
{
    //in case of an error, this prints error returned.
    e.ErrorStream.Position = 0;
    strResult = new StreamReader(e.ErrorStream).ReadToEnd();
    System.Console.WriteLine(strResult);
}
}
```

Listing 12-8. *Using Templatized Queries in Visual Basic .NET*

```vb
Sub Main()
    Dim xmlQuery As FileStream = New FileStream("command.xml", FileMode.Open)
    Dim cmd As SqlXmlCommand = New SqlXmlCommand(connectionString)
    cmd.CommandStream = xmlQuery
    cmd.CommandType = SqlXmlCommandType.Template

    Dim parm As SqlXmlParameter
    parm = cmd.CreateParameter()
    parm.Name = "@LastName"
    parm.Value = "Achong"

    cmd.ClientSideXml = True
    cmd.RootTag = "Person"

    Dim strResult As String
    Try
        Dim strm As Stream = cmd.ExecuteStream()
        strm.Position = 0
        Using sr As StreamReader = New StreamReader(strm)
            Console.WriteLine(sr.ReadToEnd())
        End Using
    Catch e As SqlXmlException
        'in case of an error, this prints error returned.
        e.ErrorStream.Position = 0
```

```
        strResult = New StreamReader(e.ErrorStream).ReadToEnd()
        System.Console.WriteLine(strResult)
    End Try
End Sub
```

As you can see from this code, the method of declaring the command has changed. First, you have to stream the command in from a stream (this could be any stream). Second, you have to specify using the CommandType property that this is a templatized query.

Next, you have to arrange to pass the parameter to the query, but unless you give it a name, it won't work. In this case, the parameter was called LastName in the template XML file, so that is what is used here. Again, you need to set the Value property, execute the query just as before, and write the result to console output. The result when this is run is shown here:

```
<ROOT xmlns:sql="urn:schemas-microsoft-com:xml-sql">
  <Person.Contact FirstName="Gustavo" LastName="Achong"/>
</ROOT>
```

This is almost the same result as the last query, but this time it's wrapped in a <ROOT> element that's added automatically when you're working with templates. If you wanted to get back the XML without this element, you'd do better to load the result into an XmlReader instance. This would require you to modify the reading portion of the previous code and replace it with the following:

C#

```
XmlTextReader rdr ;
rdr = cmd.ExecuteXmlReader() ;
rdr.MoveToContent() ;
Console.WriteLine(rdr.ReadInnerXml()) ;
rdr.Close() ;
```

VB.NET

```
Dim rdr As XmlTextReader
rdr = cmd.ExecuteXmlReader()
rdr.MoveToContent()
Console.WriteLine(rdr.ReadInnerXml())
rdr.Close()
```

If you make these changes and run the code, the following will once again be output:

```
<Person.Contact FirstName="Gustavo" LastName="Achong"/>
```

Updating with an UpdateGram

At some stage, you're going to want to update data that has been modified on the client. In SQLXML, this is typically performed using an UpdateGram when you create the update XML document yourself, but the way the SqlXmlAdapter object has been implemented means it will use the DiffGram format, as featured in ADO.NET.

An UpdateGram is very useful for operating in distributed systems and applications that can't use ADO.NET (Java applications, perhaps) because you can use HTTP and a web server to make updates to the database. An UpdateGram can be created as an XML message and sent to a .NET application that can then use the SQLXML-managed classes to update SQL Server.

The following XML file is an example of an UpdateGram that could be used to update a product with an ID of 2:

```
<ROOT xmlns:updg='urn:schemas-microsoft-com:xml-updategram'>
  <updg:sync>
    <updg:before>
      <Person.Contact FirstName='Gustavo' LastName='Achong' />
    </updg:before>
    <updg:after>
      <Person.Contact FirstName='A New Name' />
    </updg:after>
  </updg:sync>
</ROOT>
```

The UpdateGram namespace must be specified in the root of the document, and in this case it's associated with the updg prefix. The root element is the <sync> element that says you want a synchronization to take place with "before" and "after" data definitions, and contains the specific details of the modifications you want to make.

On this occasion, you wish to update the data in the column where the FirstName is Gustavo and LastName is Achong, so you need to place that information in the <before> element. The containing element for this information has the same name as the table you want to select from (Person.Contact), and the attributes you specify effectively form an AND clause in the SQL statement. If any of them cause the query to return no rows, a SqlXmlException is thrown.

The new value of the row(s) that you select should be specified in the <after> element, and again we use a child element with the same name as the table you want to update, and use attributes to indicate the new values. You want to change the FirstName column, so we specify that as an attribute.

The code to perform the update that uses this UpdateGram is shown in Listings 12-9 and 12-10 or can be downloaded as Exercise 12.6.

Listing 12-9. *Updating Using UpdateGrams in C#*

```
FileStream xmlQuery = new FileStream("updategram.xml", FileMode.Open);
SqlXmlCommand cmd = new SqlXmlCommand(connectionString);
cmd.CommandStream = xmlQuery;
cmd.CommandType = SqlXmlCommandType.UpdateGram;
cmd.ExecuteNonQuery();
xmlQuery.Close();
```

Listing 12-10. *Updating Using UpdateGrams in Visual Basic .NET*

```
Dim xmlQuery As FileStream = New FileStream("updategram.xml", FileMode.Open)
Dim cmd As SqlXmlCommand = New SqlXmlCommand(connectionString)
cmd.CommandStream = xmlQuery
```

```
cmd.CommandType = SqlXmlCommandType.UpdateGram
cmd.ExecuteNonQuery()
xmlQuery.Close()
```

The UpdateGram that's stored in an XML file called UpdateGram.xml is loaded into a FileStream instance, and this is set as the value of the CommandStream property. The CommandType property then has to be set to UpdateGram, and finally the ExecuteNonQuery method of the SqlXmlCommand object is called. When complete, the FileStream is closed.

The SqlXmlAdapter Object

The SqlXmlAdapter object is similar to ADO.NET's data adapter classes. It can be used to fill a DataSet with the results from a query, or to post changes back to the database when the DataSet is updated. There are three constructors that are used to initialize an instance of this object. The first takes a SqlXmlCommand instance as an argument, as follows:

```
SqlXmlAdapter(SqlXmlCommand)
```

The second constructor takes a string containing the query, the type of command specified in the first argument, and finally a connection string to connect to the data source:

```
SqlXmlAdapter(String, SqlXmlCommandType, String)
```

The final constructor uses a stream containing the command, rather than the string just used:

```
SqlXmlAdapter(Stream, SqlXmlCommandType, String)
```

There are no properties and only two methods associated with this class:

- Fill(DataSet) allows you to fill the DataSet passed as an argument with the XML results retrieved from the query.

- Update(DataSet) is the inverse of the Fill(DataSet) method, and allows you to update the database with the data specified in the DataSet.

The usage of the Fill and Update methods is exactly the same as the SqlDataAdapter object's Fill and Update methods. The only difference is that the command it's working with is a SqlXmlCommand. There is one minor difference in the usage of the Update method. The relevant command specified to the SqlXmlAdapter must also be specified as a schema that maps the XML UpdateGram with various tables and columns in the database.

Updating with XPath and a Schema

To make updates using the SqlXmlAdapter class, you must use XPath and a schema. In the schema, you map elements in the XML document that's returned from our query to equivalent tables and columns in a SQL Server database. This allows XPath to work on the XML data as elements and attributes, and the SQL Server client to map back to equivalent tables and columns in the SQL query that's passed to that database.

What does an XML schema look like for our tables? The schema that has been created for this sample (Exercise 12.7 in the associated code download) is shown in Listing 12-11—it's called Person.Contact.xsd.

Listing 12-11. *Schema Used to Update the Person.Contact Table*

```xml
<xs:schema xmlns:xs="http://www.w3.org/2001/XMLSchema"
           xmlns:sql="urn:schemas-microsoft-com:mapping-schema">
<!-- XML output we want to map
              <Person.Contact FirstName="Gustavo" LastName="Achong"/>
-->
   <xs:element name="Person.Contact" sql:relation="Person.Contact">
   <xs:complexType>
      <xs:attribute name="FirstName" sql:field="FirstName" type="xs:string" />
      <xs:attribute name="LastName" sql:field="LastName" type="xs:string" />
   </xs:complexType>
   </xs:element>
</xs:schema>
```

You've seen plenty of schemas before. There is also good coverage on creating schemas in Chapter 6, but because this schema has been annotated with information specific to SQL Server, an additional namespace is defined on the root element: the namespace urn: schemas-microsoft-com:mapping-schema is mapped to the prefix sql:

```xml
<xs:schema xmlns:xs="http://www.w3.org/2001/XMLSchema"
           xmlns:sql="urn:schemas-microsoft-com:mapping-schema">
```

Next, the element that will represent the elements returned from our queries has been called <products> and the <sql:relation> attribute maps this to the Products table:

```xml
   <xs:element name="Person.Contact" sql:relation="Person.Contact">
```

Next, you want to define the columns that are part of this table, and in this case you can represent them as attributes on the <products> element. The relationship between the attribute name and the column name is made by using the name attribute and the sql:field attribute. With this schema in place, you can use this in your code as shown in Listings 12-12 and 12-13.

Listing 12-12. *Using SqlXmlAdapter.Update in C#*

```csharp
SqlXmlCommand cmd = new SqlXmlCommand(connectionString);
cmd.CommandText = "Person.Contact";
cmd.CommandType = SqlXmlCommandType.XPath;
cmd.SchemaPath = "Person.Contact.xsd";
cmd.ClientSideXml = true;
cmd.RootTag = "Person.Contact";

SqlXmlAdapter da = new SqlXmlAdapter(cmd) ;
DataSet ds = new DataSet();
try
{
   // Fill the dataset
   da.Fill(ds);
   // Make some change
   ds.Tables[0].Rows[1]["LastName"] = "Unabel";
```

```
   // Update the data back to the database.
   da.Update(ds.GetChanges());
}
catch (Exception ex)
{
   Console.WriteLine(ex.ToString());
}
```

Listing 12-13. *Using SqlXmlAdapter.Update in Visual Basic .NET*

```
Dim cmd As SqlXmlCommand = New SqlXmlCommand(connectionString)
cmd.CommandText = "Person.Contact"
cmd.CommandType = SqlXmlCommandType.XPath
cmd.SchemaPath = "Person.Contact.xsd"
cmd.ClientSideXml = True
cmd.RootTag = "Person.Contact"

Dim da As SqlXmlAdapter = New SqlXmlAdapter(cmd)
Dim ds As DataSet = New DataSet()
Try
   ' Fill the dataset
   da.Fill(ds)
   ' Make some change
   ds.Tables(0).Rows(1)("LastName") = "Unabel"
   ' Update the data back to the database.
   da.Update(ds.GetChanges())
Catch ex As Exception
   Console.WriteLine(ex.ToString())
End Try
```

There is one *very* important point of consideration here. The line of code I am using to update the database looks like this:

C#

```
   da.Update(ds.GetChanges());
```

VB.NET

```
   da.Update(ds.GetChanges())
```

and *not* like this:

C#

```
   da.Update(ds);
```

VB.NET

```
   da.Update(ds)
```

Interestingly though, I didn't have to specify ds.GetChanges() to be logically correct. The final query in either case looks like the following (reformatted for readability purposes):

```
SET XACT_ABORT ON
BEGIN TRAN
DECLARE @eip INT, @r__ int, @e__ int
SET @eip = 0
UPDATE Person.Contact SET LastName=N'Unabel' WHERE  ( FirstName=N'Catherine' )
AND  ( LastName=N'Abel' ) ;  SELECT @e__ = @@ERROR, @r__ = @@ROWCOUNT
 IF (@e__ != 0 OR @r__ != 1) SET @eip = 1
 IF (@r__ > 1) RAISERROR ( N'SQLOLEDB Error Description: Ambiguous update, ➥
 unique identifier required  Transaction aborted ', 16, 1)
 ELSE IF (@r__ < 1) RAISERROR ( N'SQLOLEDB Error Description: Empty update, ➥
 no updatable rows found  Transaction aborted ', 16, 1)

IF (@eip != 0) ROLLBACK ELSE COMMIT
SET XACT_ABORT OFF
go
```

So if the final query in either case looks the same, logically both solutions would have worked—with ds.GetChanges and without. What is important to realize here is that the SqlXmlDataAdapter would have to iterate over the entire first DataTable of the DataSet to figure out the matching rows, and then formulate the previous query, rather than going over a much smaller set, which is created using GetChanges. As an exercise, you can try to execute the previous code with and without GetChanges. You'll notice that without GetChanges, it takes many hundreds of times longer to execute the same update as it would take if you would have used GetChanges.

This seemingly minor oversight can obviously have a huge impact on your performance.

Summary

This chapter, in contrast with the rest of the book, takes a SQL Server–specific viewpoint. All the features discussed here present an interesting method of architecting your applications that allows you to leverage built-in XML features of Microsoft SQL Server. Some of the discussed features such as FOR XML PATH, ROOT, and the new XML data type are specific to SQL Server 2005.

This chapter, in presenting an XML-centric view of ADO.NET, gives you an interesting viewpoint and methodology to architect your applications. XML is the all-pervasive language of the computer world, thus it is only logical that ADO.NET and Microsoft SQL Server have rich, built-in support for it.

In this chapter you read about the various flavors the FOR XML query can be used in, and how you would leverage that to build flexible ADO.NET applications. You also saw how you can use the new XML data type and build applications with ADO.NET that work with such columns.

Finally, you looked at SqlXml, which is a rather powerful library of managed code, wrapped over various COM components that offer rich XML integration and functionality with SQL Server. You also saw how you can, with relative ease, separate the XML UpdateGrams and flexible XML templates from the database or embedded SQL queries to maximize programmer time at the golf course.

When properly used, these XML features can really make a significant difference to your overall architecture. These are extremely powerful, richly supported, and, at times, much ignored features of the Microsoft data access architecture.

Continuing the theme of becoming even more Microsoft data access architecture–specific, the next chapter offers a quick rundown of what is absolutely new in ADO.NET 2.0 and SQL Server 2005.

Starting with SQL Server 2005, the database has the ability to host the CLR inside of itself. Earlier in Chapter 5, you saw a little glimpse of this when you authored a UDT and queried it using a `SqlCommand`.

The next chapter takes that discussion further and explains the ins and outs, the pros and cons, the dos and don'ts, and the nitty-gritty about the CLR in SQL Server 2005.

CHAPTER 13

■ ■ ■

The CLR in SQL Server

T-SQL is the default language supported by SQL Server. It has well-defined syntax for database features such as queries, triggers, and stored procedures; those are various tools in your arsenal that allow you to interact, modify, or manage the data inside SQL Server. While T-SQL is a rather powerful language, its nature is quite different from a typical modern-day programming language such as C# or VB.NET. For instance, when using C# or VB.NET, it is common practice to architect your solution in an object-oriented way using the rich inheritance features of such languages to express your architecture. T-SQL, on the other hand, does not offer such facilities.

However, everything has a purpose and a reason. T-SQL is the right tool for interacting with relational data. For instance, writing a join query in C# for every single row in a three table query is something that T-SQL can do much better than C# or VB.NET can. This is natural to expect since database engines are able to optimize and cache a query, its plan, and its results in many stages whereas C# or VB.NET does not have any of that.

But when working in the database, you may frequently run into situations where the unwieldiness of T-SQL in doing tasks, such as mathematical calculations or recursive operations, makes it less than a pleasure to deal with.

Note There is a new feature in SQL Server 2005 called Common Table Expressions (CTE) that does allow you to write recursive T-SQL queries on tabular data. It has a configurable recursion depth with a default value of 100 levels deep. The problem arises when you wish to write a T-SQL stored procedure that calls itself to perform an operation such as calculate factorials. When the T-SQL stored procedure calls itself, the call depth of one stored procedure calling another cannot exceed 32. In other words, it would not be possible for a T-SQL stored procedure that calculates factorials using recursion to calculate the factorial of 33. CLR, on the other hand, would have no problem doing this.

Usually, the common approach in such cases would be to extract the relevant, unprocessed data from SQL Server as result sets and process upon the data in the data layer or business layer using a higher level programming language. This, however, pays the penalty of a network roundtrip and possibly extracting more data than required.

Starting with SQL Server 2005, you have the ability to author .NET code that lives inside SQL Server. In other words, right inside the database you have the same ability to use the rich features of languages such as C# or VB.NET for specific tasks that are better suited to them.

Thus, usually when you would be forced to write this code in the business layer or data layer of your application, or simply deal with the unwieldiness of T-SQL, instead you can now write this code in a .NET language and run it directly inside SQL Server.

But before the water gets any muddier with the mention of business layer, data layer, the Common Language Runtime (CLR) in SQL Server (or SQLCLR), and T-SQL, let's get one issue straight.

Appropriate Use of SQLCLR

It's quite tempting to think that now that you can write CLR code inside SQL Server, why not just get rid of the business layer and put all your code inside SQL Server? SQLCLR is not a replacement for the business layer—it cannot get any clearer than that. Thus, just because you can write C# or VB.NET code inside SQL Server, don't expect to use SQL Server as the application server that hosts all your .NET code. The SQLCLR is there for the specific purpose of working inside the database where T-SQL might not be the right choice. The specific purpose is that *you should use SQLCLR as an alternative for logic that cannot be expressed declaratively in T-SQL*. This point is, in fact, so important that I am going to repeat it.

■**Note** You should use SQLCLR as an alternative for logic that cannot be expressed declaratively in T-SQL—not as a replacement for the business layer logic. In other words, try solving your problem using T-SQL first.

Having established that, as a rough rule of thumb you can assume that T-SQL is better for set-based operations, typical to tabular data, whereas SQLCLR is better for procedural code and recursive[1] operations. However, what truly performs better than the other is dictated by many other factors. A good comparison of T-SQL versus SQLCLR is presented in the next chapter, but the three cardinal rules are as follows:

1. Set-based operations work better in T-SQL.

2. Procedural and recursive code works better in SQLCLR.

3. These two rules can be affected by a number of factors involved, such as compiled CLR code versus interpreted T-SQL code, the overhead of loading CLR in SQL Server, data access needs within processing, library of helper functions, etc. You can see a deeper treatise on the various factors involved in the next chapter.

There are various reasons for this, and many of them stem from the fact that CLR inside the database operates under a different set of restrictions than it does on your Windows machine. The CLR on your Windows machine is run by the operating system, which works differently than when that same CLR runs inside SQL Server. The main difference is that SQL Server takes the responsibility and manages thread scheduling, synchronization, locking, and memory allocation.

---

1. Even some recursive operations can be done in T-SQL. See "Common Table Expressions" in *SQL Server Books* online.

As described in the Chapter 5 sidebar titled "The CLR Is Inside Out," another major difference between the CLR on a Windows machine and the CLR inside SQL Server is the bootstrap mechanism used to load the CLR. An application that wishes to use the CLR uses `ICorRuntimeHost`, or `CorBindToRuntimeEx`, which then in turn calls `MSCOREE.DLL` that ends up loading the runtime.

Instead, SQL Server 2005 does not load the CLR unless it needs to. This is because SQL Server follows the principle of conserving memory and lazy loading any resource that it might need. By not loading the CLR unless it needs to, it saves a few MB of memory that the CLR would have otherwise occupied. Thus, if you have one minor piece of your code that uses the CLR, you are loading the CLR and, in turn, affecting any other operation on that particular computer. Even when it does load the CLR, it does so using `ICLRRuntimeHost`, which is a new interface introduced with .NET 2.0. Next it calls, `ICLRRuntimeHost::GetHostManager`, which essentially means that the CLR now delegates operations like resource locking/thread management, etc. to the SQL Server runtime instead.

Having delegated such responsibilities to the host (SQL Server) instead brings up interesting challenges. Essentially, what this means is that individual operations running inside SQL Server can now decide to be rogue and potentially be a security threat, or bring down the server. Therefore, it becomes critical that when taking the freedom of hosting the CLR and its various operations, the SQL Server application also takes on the responsibility of doing it correctly in such a manner that individual applications should not inadvertently or surreptitiously harm the server in any manner.

SQL Server enforces this by giving you a granular level of control on the set of operations your .NET code can perform inside SQL Server. This mechanism is built on top of Code Access Security (CAS) that is a part of the CLR. The developers at Microsoft took a long and hard look at every single class in the .NET Framework, and classified them into three categories that you must specify your code to fall within. In other words, you need to tell SQL Server that your code falls into one of three categories based upon the specific operations it intends to do. If your code tries doing something other than what you had initially specified, SQL Server will block it from doing so (you will see this as an example later in this chapter).

The three levels of control are as follows:

- `SAFE`: This is the default level and most restrictive. This means that your code does not need any external resources and the operation is wholly controlled inside SQL Server. Safe code can access data from the local SQL Server databases or perform computations and business logic that does not involve accessing resources outside the local databases. A good example of this could be factorial calculation. Factorial calculation only needs an input of type integer, and then it returns another integer. To calculate a factorial, you do not need to open a file on the disk.

- `EXTERNAL_ACCESS`: This level signifies that certain external resources such as files, networks, web services, environmental variables, and the registry are accessible. Thus, if your code intends to write out some results to a file on the disk, you would need to register that code inside SQL Server under the `EXTERNAL_ACCESS` security category.

- `UNSAFE`: This level, which you should try very hard to avoid, specifies that your code is allowed to do anything. In other words, you are requesting to be free of any granular-level control, and thus giving it the same permissions as an extended stored procedure. Even though you get the same rights and permissions as an extended stored procedure, CLR still gives you certain benefits in comparison, but there could be a hole in your logic that a hacker could abuse and gain access to crucial parts of your system with. Thus, you should avoid running `UNSAFE` code inside SQL Server.

This brings up another interesting point. When you could write extended stored procedures inside SQL Server, why introduce the SQLCLR to begin with?

SQLCLR in Comparison with Extended Stored Procedures

Previous versions of SQL Server, such as SQL Server 2000, allowed you to write extended stored procedures as an alternative to T-SQL and express your code in a language such as C++. There are, however, certain differences between the SQLCLR and extended stored procedures:

- As is evident from the previous section, extended stored procedures do not give you the granular security control of specifying your code in one of three buckets (SAFE, EXTERNAL_ACCESS, and UNSAFE) that the SQLCLR gives you.

- Extended stored procedures cannot be written in a language such as C# or VB.NET, which are easier to use and, in general, safer than C++.

- SQLCLR code is much more reliable than extended stored procedures, simply because you can lock down the code to a basic set of permissions by specifying it as SAFE or EXTERNAL_ACCESS. This allows you to segregate the code that needs EXTERNAL_ACCESS into a separate entity and monitor that closely—something you cannot do in extended stored procedures.

- SQLCLR code can use the same database connection while an extended stored procedure would need to loop back and create a brand new connection to the database.

- SQLCLR has the ability to work with the new data types introduced in SQL Server 2005, such as the XML data type, or varchar(max) and varbinary(max). Extended stored procedures would need to leverage on some T-SQL code to take advantage of those new data types.

- And finally, SQLCLR can be used to write User-Defined Functions (UDFs), UDTs, aggregates, Table-Valued Functions (TVFs), triggers, and stored procedures. Extended stored procedures are only extended stored procedures.

Given the fact that the SQLCLR enjoys many advantages compared with extended stored procedures, for data access needs SQLCLR code outperforms extended stored procedures. However, for non–data access operations comparison purposes, extended stored procedures written using native code typically run faster than managed code. Also, there is some cost associated with transitioning from managed code inside a SQLCLR routine to native code when running inside the SQL Server, because SQL Server needs to do additional tracking on thread-specific settings when moving out of native code and vice versa. Thus, extended stored procedures in most cases will outperform SQLCLR code, but that does not mean that you should start writing your code in extended stored procedures. Given the other benefits, the SQLCLR is a much more attractive alternative than extended stored procedures. Needless to mention, given the various managed native code transitions involved and data access in general, managed code just might have an edge even when it comes to performance.

So without much further delay, let's try and look at some real code and demonstrative examples that run CLR code inside SQL Server 2005.

Software Requirements to Run the Examples in This Chapter

As usual, you need two things: a data source and a programming environment, usually Visual Studio 2005.

Your data source for the examples in this chapter will be a database called Test running on the local instance of SQL Server 2005. This database can be easily set up by running the following command:

```
Create database test
```

Since the content in this chapter is specific to SQL Server 2005, you cannot run the examples presented here in an Oracle database[2] or SQL Server 2000 database, etc.

Code written for SQLCLR can be authored in Visual Studio 2005 easily using a SQL Server project template. Unfortunately, this project template is available only in Visual Studio 2005 Professional and Team System Editions. However, it is almost just as easy to author the code presented in this chapter in any other edition of Visual Studio 2005, such as Standard. Let's begin by looking at an example of a SQLCLR UDF that is written without leveraging the Visual Studio 2005 SQL Server project.

Handwritten UDF

In order for you to run any CLR code inside SQL Server, you will have to compile it as an assembly and register that assembly inside SQL Server using the CREATE ASSEMBLY statement. Thus, if you are able to create an assembly similar to what a SQL Server project would produce, SQL Server would be able to register it within itself.

Therefore, in order to create a SQLCLR UDF without leveraging a SQL Server project, all you really need to do is create a class library and follow certain basic rules in the class that holds the logic of the UDF.

As it turns out, these "rules" aren't that numerous or too complex to follow. You can download the code for this example from the associated code download for this chapter under HandWrittenUDF (see the Downloads section of the Apress website at http://www.apress.com), or you could follow the steps mentioned here to create such a project:

1. So the aim of the game is to be able to create a UDF that returns an integer random number. Begin by creating a class library project, call it HandWrittenUDF.

2. Rename the Class1.cs/Class1.vb file to UserDefinedFunctions.cs/ UserDefinedFunctions.vb. Verify that Visual Studio changed the class name contained inside the file to UserDefinedFunctions. Also, verify that the scope of this class is public.

3. Wrap the UserDefinedFunctions class inside the HandWrittenUDF namespace and add a using/Imports statement bringing the relevant namespaces, including Microsoft.SqlServer.Server, in scope as shown in the following code:

---

2. It is quite possible that other major database vendors, such as Oracle and IBM, could eventually introduce their own CLR integration; chances are their implementations would be different from SQL Server anyway.

C#

```
using System;
using System.Data.SqlTypes;
using Microsoft.SqlServer.Server;
```

VB.NET

```
Imports System
Imports System.Data.SqlTypes
Imports Microsoft.SqlServer.Server
```

4. Add the code shown in Listings 13-1 and 13-2 to create a UDF called GetRandomNumber.

Listing 13-1. *Code for the SQLCLR UDF in C#*

```
public class UserDefinedFunctions
{
    [Microsoft.SqlServer.Server.SqlFunction]
    public static SqlInt32 GetRandomNumber()
    {
        Random rnd = new Random();
        return rnd.Next();
    }
}
```

Listing 13-2. *Code for the SQLCLR UDF in Visual Basic .NET*

```
Public Class UserDefinedFunctions
    <Microsoft.SqlServer.Server.SqlFunction()> _
    Public Shared Function GetRandomNumber() As SqlInt32
        Dim rnd As Random = New Random()
        Return rnd.Next()
    End Function
End Class
```

5. Build the project.

6. With the DLL built, next you need to register the assembly and the UDF contained in the assembly in SQL Server 2005. First, register the UDF inside SQL Server by running the script shown in Listing 13-3. This script can be run in SQL Server Management Studio.

Listing 13-3. *Registering the Assembly Inside SQL Server 2005*

```
Create Assembly HandWrittenUDF
from
'C:\HandWrittenUDF\HandWrittenUDF.dll'
GO
```

Do note that in my case, the DLL was present at C:\HandWrittenUDF. You might need to modify this script to point SQL Server to the correct file location on your disk.

7. Next, create a UDF from the assembly registered in step 6. The relevant script for this is as shown in Listing 13-4.

Listing 13-4. *Creating a UDF from a Registered Assembly in SQL Server 2005*

```
Create Function GetRandomNumber ()
Returns Int
As
External Name
HandWrittenUDF.[HandWrittenUDF.UserDefinedFunctions].GetRandomNumber
Go
```

8. That's it! Execute the UDF using the following statement:

```
Select dbo.GetRandomNumber()
```

You should see output similar to as shown in Figure 13-1.

Figure 13-1. *Output of the GetRandomNumber SQLCLR handwritten UDF*

Obviously, this being a random number, the exact output could differ. Also, it's quite possible that your instance of SQL Server has never been configured to work with .NET code. This, in fact, will be the case if this is the first time you are running SQLCLR code. In that case, you should get an error message as shown here:

```
Msg 6263, Level 16, State 1, Line 1
Execution of user code in the .NET Framework is disabled. Use sp_configure
"clr enabled" to enable execution of user code in the .NET Framework.
```

This problem is rather easy to fix. In order to enable the execution of .NET code inside SQL Server, just issue the following command:

```
sp_configure 'clr enabled', 1
```

This should give you a message as shown here:

```
Configuration option 'clr enabled' changed from 0 to 1.
Run the RECONFIGURE statement to install.
```

As prompted by the message, issue the RECONFIGURE command next. Now when you run the previously created UDF, you should get a random number.

If you observe the previous code, you'll notice that the only magic you did was the Microsoft. SqlServer.Server.SqlFunctionAttribute on top of a static/shared method. By doing so, you are able to create an assembly with a static/shared method that works as a UDF in SQL Server. But since this is a class library, debugging it is a whole other issue. But before I tell you about debugging SQLCLR code, let me demonstrate writing the same UDF using a SQL Server project.

SQL Server Project UDF

In the last section you saw how to create a UDF without using the built-in SQL Server project in Visual Studio 2005. Since the project was just a simple class library, the rest of the SQLCLR examples in this chapter will use a SQL Server project instead.

Because the SQL Server project is available only within Visual Studio's Professional and Team System Editions, I will provide you with the relevant SQL scripts if, in case, you decide to implement the code as class libraries in Visual Studio's Standard or Express Editions instead. These SQL scripts are also useful in an enterprise development environment where "right-click deploy" for the many procedures you will write will probably not be a viable option.

Even then SQL Server projects offer significant advantages, especially when it comes to debugging SQLCLR code. In the next section, I will demonstrate various ways to debug SQLCLR code, and you can reuse those concepts throughout all the examples presented in this chapter.

But before I can show you the various methods of debugging handwritten SQLCLR code, or code written with the help of a SQL Server project, let's quickly walk through creating a UDF that generates random numbers, using a SQL Server project instead. You can download this code from the SqlServerUDF project, or you can create it yourself by following these steps:

1. Begin by creating a Visual Studio SQL Server project in the language of your choice. This can be seen for VB.NET in Figure 13-2. Name the project SqlServerUDF.

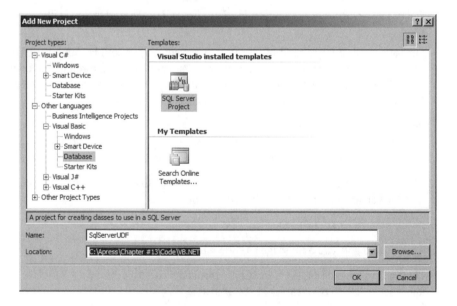

Figure 13-2. *Creating a new SQL Server project*

2. If you already have a database reference set up within Visual Studio, Visual Studio will prompt you to either pick the existing reference or create a new one. This dialog box can be seen in Figure 13-3.

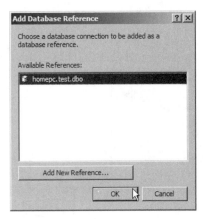

Figure 13-3. *Choosing a connection for your project*

Alternatively, if you do not have a database reference already set up in your IDE, Visual Studio will prompt you to create a new database reference. You can fill in the values and test the connection as shown in Figure 13-4.

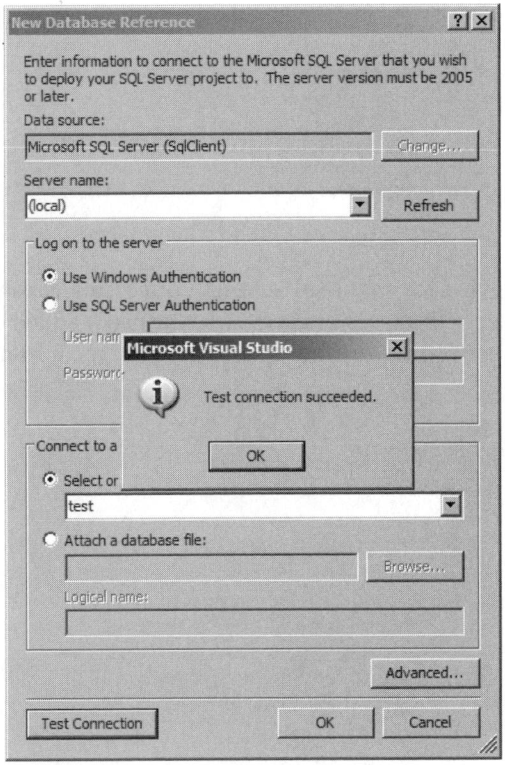

Figure 13-4. *Creating a new database reference*

When adding a new database reference, you will also be prompted with the dialog box shown in Figure 13-5.

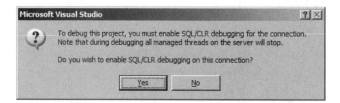

Figure 13-5. *Warning dialog box when adding a new database reference*

This warning dialog box is informing you that when you debug the CLR stored procedure, all managed threads on the server will stop. This means that you probably don't want to do this operation on a critical production server. This operation should be done on a development machine only. Click YES to accept the new database reference. You should now see a database reference added in your Server Explorer as shown in Figure 13-6. Do note that "homepc" is the name of the computer I am currently working on.

Figure 13-6. *The newly added database reference*

3. Now in the Solution Explorer, right-click on the SqlServerUDF project and, as shown in Figure 13-7, choose to add a new UDF to your project. Name the newly added UDF GetRandomNumber2.cs/GetRandomNumber2.vb. (The "2" is to differentiate it from the previous example.)

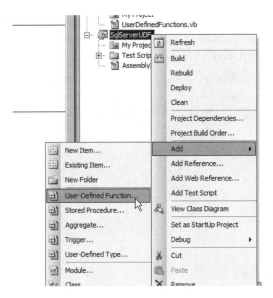

Figure 13-7. *Adding a new UDF*

4. Now modify the autogenerated code as per Listings 13-5 and 13-6.

Listing 13-5. *Creating a UDF Using a SQL Server Project in C#*

```
public partial class SqlServerUDF
{
    [Microsoft.SqlServer.Server.SqlFunction]
    public static SqlInt32 GetRandomNumber2()
    {
        Random rnd = new Random();
        return rnd.Next();
    }
};
```

Listing 13-6. *Creating a UDF Using a SQL Server Project in Visual Basic .NET*

```
Partial Public Class UserDefinedFunctions
    <Microsoft.SqlServer.Server.SqlFunction()> _
    Public Shared Function GetRandomNumber2() As SqlInt32
        Dim rnd As Random = New Random
        Return rnd.Next()
    End Function
End Class
```

This code, as you may note, with the exception of being wrapped in a partial class, is
shockingly similar to the handwritten UDF. The partial class is almost a de facto standard for all autogenerated code in the .NET Framework now. This is good thinking on

the part of Microsoft, and goes with the philosophy that now you can enhance the functionality of autogenerated code without either modifying the autogenerated file or having to inherit from the autogenerated class.

5. Now build and deploy the project. The SQL Server project also allows you to easily deploy the UDF. This is shown in Figure 13-8. If, instead, you wished to deploy the UDF using SQL statements, the instructions are exactly the same as the HandWrittenUDF.

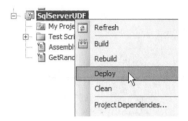

Figure 13-8. *Adding a new UDF*

6. Now simply run the following SQL command in the Test database to test the newly added UDF:

```
Select dbo.GetRandomNumber2()
```

This will give you results similar to as shown in Figure 13-1.

Thus, as you can see, the SQL Server project not only offers you a convenient method to author SQLCLR code including UDFs, but also an integrated development environment, complete with a database reference that helps you deploy the procedure right through the IDE.

Actually, it gets better than that. The SQL Server project also allows for easy debugging of your CLR code, much like debugging a Console application. Let's look at that next along with a comparison of debugging a handwritten UDF.

Debugging SQLCLR Code

The SQL Server project makes it easier for you to debug your code. Note in the last project that you had written, SqlServerUDF, Visual Studio also added a folder called Test Scripts in which there is a SQL file called Test.sql. This can be seen in Figure 13-9. Go ahead and change the last uncommented statement in that file from

```
select 'put your test script here'
```

to

```
select dbo.GetRandomNumber2()
```

Now much as you would set the start page of a website, set this script as your default debug script. You can easily achieve that by right-clicking on the script and choosing "Set as Default Debug Script." This can also be seen in Figure 13-9.

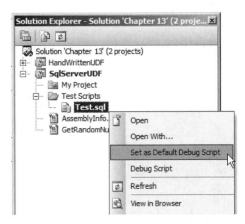

Figure 13-9. *Debugging a SQL Server project–generated UDF*

Also, right-click the SqlServerUDF project and choose "Set as Startup Project." You are now ready to debug your UDF. Now set a breakpoint at the first line in your UDF. You can start debugging at this point by stepping into the code, but to see what is going on behind the scenes, you need to make the Output window visible. To do this, select Debug ➤ Windows ➤ Output. Also, in the Output window, make sure that the filter is set to "Show output from: Debug." This can be seen in Figure 13-10.

Figure 13-10. *Enabling the Output window and setting the proper filter*

Now you can simply begin to step into the code. You'll notice that the application starts at the SQL statement, and then it behaves much like a Console application does, except you are debugging T-SQL and seamlessly hitting and stepping into SQLCLR code. If you observe the debug output closely, when the code execution skips from the SQL file to your C# or VB.NET file, you see the following message appear in the Output window:

```
Auto-attach to process '[3056] sqlservr.exe' on machine 'homepc' succeeded.
```

The exact message might be different on your specific machine, but what this message tells you is that Visual Studio 2005 automatically attached itself to a running process, specifically the sqlservr.exe process, in order to allow you to debug through the SQLCLR code.

■**Note** It might be tempting to try this on a common development database server. Do realize that in order to do so, not only will you have to set the right permissions, but also you might interfere with other developers' work working with the same database server.

If you continue debugging through the UDF, you'll notice that the Debug Output window will show you the following output:

```
'Managed': Loaded 'SqlServerUDF', No symbols loaded.
Column1
-----------
1275838787
No rows affected.
(1 row(s) returned)
Finished running sp_executesql.
The thread 'homepc [56]' (0x1614) has exited with code 0 (0x0).
The program '[3056] sqlservr.exe: HOMEPC;
.Net SqlClient Data Provider;4876' has exited with code 259 (0x103).
The program '[3056] [SQL] homepc: homepc' has exited with code 0 (0x0).
```

Thus, the output of your UDF is shown as a part of the debug output. You can use a similar mechanism to debug other kinds of SQLCLR objects such as stored procedures, triggers, etc.

While the SQL Server project makes it easier for you to debug your code in a very simple manner, debugging your HandWrittenUDF isn't very difficult either.

The basic idea remains the same: you need to attach with the sqlservr.exe process and then somehow execute the UDF. Since the project will not do this for you automatically, before running the SQL script you need to do this manually. This can be done by selecting Debug ➤ Attach to Process. In the dialog box that pops up, choose the sqlservr.exe process (you may need to check the "Show processes from all users" checkbox to see that process). With the sqlservr.exe process selected, click the Attach button to enter debug mode. This can be seen in Figure 13-11.

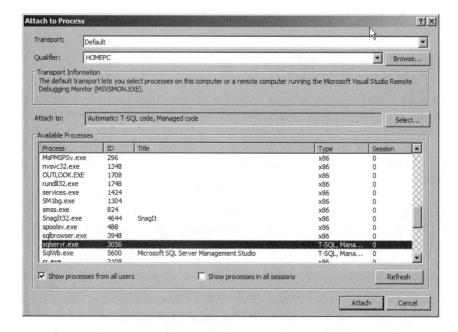

Figure 13-11. *Debugging SQLCLR code without the aid of a SQL Server project*

Now set a breakpoint in the code, and execute the following command from any application including SQL Server Management Studio:

```
Select dbo.GetRandomNumber()
```

You'll notice that the breakpoint gets hit and then you can debug much like the SQL Server project.

So, truly, whatever you can do using a SQL Server project is achievable through a simple class library project as well. Therefore, in the rest of the examples that follow in this chapter, I'll be taking advantage of the SQL Server project to demonstrate the code. You can, however, reuse the same principles presented here and the relevant SQL scripts to work with a simple class library if you wish or need to.

Writing a TVF: Table-Valued Function

A *Table-Valued Function* (*TVF*) is a UDF that returns a table instead of a scalar value. The last example you saw returned a singular scalar value as an integer. Depending on your needs, you may be presented with a case where your UDFs would need to return a table instead. In other words, your result contains tabular data with rows and columns. An example could be a TVF that returns days in a week as seven rows, and two columns, namely DayNumber and DayName.

Thus, if you wish to return the results as a table, or in the form of rows and columns, your UDF needs to have two facilities:

- It needs to be able to return a number of rows. Returning rows, as it turns out, is easy—all you have to do is return an instance of a class that implements the IEnumerable interface, instead of the scalar value, and the infrastructure will understand that you are trying to send back rows.

- It needs to have the ability to split each row into a fixed number of columns of a predefined format. Sending columns requires you to add another method, which takes the responsibility of splitting the contents of each enumerated item (row) in the IEnumerable object into columns. But how will the infrastructure know "which method is responsible for splitting a row into columns?"

In addition to implementing these two methods, you also need a way to tell the framework that the rows returned by the IEnumerable object will be split into columns by a method of a specified name. You need to specify this method name using the FillRowMethodName property of the Microsoft.SqlServer.Server.SqlFunctionAttribute attribute, which is defined on the method that works as the entry point for the TVF.

This way, SQL Server knows that it needs to call the static/shared method marked with the SqlFunctionAttribute, which acts as the stored procedure, and then it needs to split each returned row into columns using a method specified as the FillRowMethodName property on the SqlFunctionAttribute instance.

Enough of theory; let's look at this using an example. Now that you have already seen how to create either a SQL Server or a class library project, you can follow the next steps using the same concepts. The code for this example can be found in the associated code download in the SqlServerTVF project.

1. Create a new SQL Server project, call it SqlServerTVF.

2. Add a new UDF to it called NameToAscii. Put the generated class in the SqlServerTVF namespace.

3. The aim of the TVF that you are going to write in this example is for it to accept a string, and return the results as broken down into characters in one column, along with the ASCII integer code in another column. So you need something that holds the contents of one row. You could use an object, or a string, or anything else, but since you will also need to split this one row into columns afterward, let's go ahead and implement this as a class. Instances of this class will be enumerated as individual rows. Note that I am using public instance variables in the class, which is probably a bad practice on a class, but since this code is never accessed over multiple threads, and for brevity purposes, it is acceptable to take this shortcut. This class can be seen as shown here:

C#

```csharp
public class NameRow
{
    public Char CharPart;
    public Int32 IntPart;

    public NameRow(Char c, Int32 i)
    {
        CharPart = c;
        IntPart = i;
    }
}
```

VB.NET

```vbnet
Public Class NameRow
    Public CharPart As Char
    Public IntPart As Int32

    Public Sub New(ByVal c As Char, ByVal i As Int32)
        CharPart = c
        IntPart = i
    End Sub
End Class
```

4. So you want the TVF that you are writing to accept a string and return the results as broken down into characters in one column, along with the ASCII integer code in another column. To accomplish this, add a new method, which will act as the actual TVF. This is shown in the following code. Don't worry about the parameters being passed to the SqlFunctionAttribute just yet as that will be explained in just a moment:

C#

```
[Microsoft.SqlServer.Server.SqlFunction(FillRowMethodName = "FillRow",
    TableDefinition="charpart nchar(1), intpart int")]
public static IEnumerable NameToAscii(string InputName)
{
    return new NameSplitter(InputName.ToCharArray());
}
```

VB.NET

```
<Microsoft.SqlServer.Server.SqlFunction(FillRowMethodName:="FillRow", _
    TableDefinition:="charpart nchar(1), intpart int")> _
Public Shared Function NameToAscii(ByVal InputName As String) As IEnumerable
    Return New NameSplitter(InputName.ToCharArray())
End Function
```

Specifically in C#, you could use the yield keyword to simplify your code. The yield keyword gives you a convenient alternative to implementing an entire class that implements IEnumerable. Thus, by using the yield keyword, you no longer have to implement the NameSplitter class. This is, however, specific to C#. The usage is shown here:

C#

```
[Microsoft.SqlServer.Server.SqlFunction(FillRowMethodName = "FillRow",
    TableDefinition="charpart nchar(1), intpart int")]
public static IEnumerable NameToAscii(string InputName)
{
    foreach (char c in InputName)
    {
        yield return new NameRow(c, (int)c);
    }
}
```

Now, because VB.NET does not have the yield keyword, you'll need to implement a class to achieve the same functionality. The NameSplitter class is the class that implements IEnumerator and IEnumerable. This class can be seen in Listings 13-7 and 13-8.

Listing 13-7. *Implementing the NameSplitter Class in C#*

```
public class NameSplitter :  IEnumerable, IEnumerator
{
    private Int32 idx = - 1;
    private Char[] _inputName;

    public NameSplitter(Char[] InputName)
    {
        _inputName = InputName;
    }
```

```csharp
    public System.Collections.IEnumerator GetEnumerator()
    {
       return new NameSplitter(_inputName);
    }

    public object Current
    {
       get
       {
          if(( idx > - 1 ))
          {
             Char c = _inputName[idx];
             return new NameRow(c, Convert.ToInt32(c));
          }
          else
          {
             return - 1;
          }
       }
    }
    public bool MoveNext()
    {
       idx = idx + 1;
       if(( idx < _inputName.Length ))
       {
          return true;
       }
       else
       {
          return false;
       }
    }

    public void Reset()
    {
       idx = - 1;
    }
}
```

Listing 13-8. *Implementing the NameSplitter Class in Visual Basic .NET*

```vbnet
Public Class NameSplitter
   Implements IEnumerable, IEnumerator

   Private idx As Int32 = -1
   Private _inputName As Char()
   Private _current As Char
```

```vb
    Public Sub New(ByVal InputName As Char())
        _inputName = InputName
    End Sub

    Public Function GetEnumerator() As System.Collections.IEnumerator _
        Implements System.Collections.IEnumerable.GetEnumerator
        Return New NameSplitter(_inputName)
    End Function

    Public ReadOnly Property Current() As Object _
        Implements System.Collections.IEnumerator.Current
        Get
            If (idx > -1) Then
                Dim c As Char = _inputName(idx)
                Return New NameRow(c, Asc(c))
            Else
                Return -1
            End If
        End Get
    End Property

    Public Function MoveNext() As Boolean _
        Implements System.Collections.IEnumerator.MoveNext
        idx = idx + 1
        If (idx < _inputName.Length) Then
            Return True
        Else
            Return False
        End If
    End Function

    Public Sub Reset() Implements System.Collections.IEnumerator.Reset
        idx = -1
    End Sub
End Class
```

5. You would note from step 4 that the actual value being enumerated is of NameRow type. NameRow is nothing but a class I have written to hold the contents of one row. This allows for easy extraction of columnar data afterward. This class can be seen in step 3.

6. Now turn your attention to the code written in step 4. The method declaration is preceded with a SqlFunctionAttribute, marking it as a UDF. However, interestingly, there are two property values being passed as shown here:

C#

```csharp
[Microsoft.SqlServer.Server.SqlFunction(FillRowMethodName = "FillRow",
    TableDefinition="charpart nchar(1), intpart int")]
```

VB.NET

```
<Microsoft.SqlServer.Server.SqlFunction(FillRowMethodName:="FillRow", _
    TableDefinition:="charpart nchar(1), intpart int")> _
```

The first property, FillRowMethodName, identifies a method you need to write that SQL Server will call in order to split the NameRow class written in step 3 into column contents. In the previous code, the method name is FillRow. The code for FillRow can be seen in Listings 13-9 and 13-10.

Listing 13-9. *Code to Split the Enumerated Values into Columns in C#*

```csharp
public static void FillRow(object row, out char charpart, out int intpart)
{
    // break the row into its columnar parts.
    charpart = ((NameRow)row).CharPart;
    intpart = ((NameRow)row).IntPart;
}
```

Listing 13-10. *Code to Split the Enumerated Values into Columns in Visual Basic .NET*

```vbnet
Public Shared Sub FillRow(ByVal row As Object,
    <Out()> ByRef charpart As Char, <Out()> ByRef intpart As Integer)
    ' break the row into its columnar parts.
    charpart = CType(row, NameRow).CharPart
    intpart = CType(row, NameRow).IntPart
End Sub
```

Also, note the usage of the System.Runtime.InteropServices.OutAttribute, in the case of VB.NET, to clearly identify the output values that will be used by SQL Server as column values during runtime. The C# equivalent of that is the out keyword.

7. The second property, TableDefinition, identifies the structure of the output table. This is ignored by SQL Server, but it is valuable for Visual Studio so it knows how to register the type when deploying directly through Visual Studio. In this case, the table will contain two columns, charpart and intpart, of data types nchar(1) and int, respectively. Note that these data types are SQL Server data types and not .NET data types.

8. Your final code should look like as shown in Listings 13-11 and 13-12. For brevity, the yield version is shown for C#. You can find the enumerator version for C# in the associated code download. Go ahead and build the project:

Listing 13-11. *Final Code for the TVF in C#*

```csharp
using System;
using System.Data;
using System.Data.Sql;
using System.Data.SqlTypes;
using Microsoft.SqlServer.Server;
using System.Collections;
```

```
namespace SqlServerTVF
{
    public partial class UserDefinedFunctions
    {
        [Microsoft.SqlServer.Server.SqlFunction(FillRowMethodName = "FillRow",
            TableDefinition="charpart nchar(1), intpart int")]
        public static IEnumerable NameToAscii(string InputName)
        {
            foreach (char c in InputName)
            {
                yield return new NameRow(c, (int)c);
            }
        }

        public static void FillRow(object row, out char charpart,
            out int intpart)
        {
            // break the row into its columnar parts.
            charpart = ((NameRow)row).CharPart;
            intpart = ((NameRow)row).IntPart;
        }
    };

    public class NameRow
    {
        public Char CharPart;
        public Int32 IntPart;

        public NameRow(Char c, Int32 i)
        {
            CharPart = c;
            IntPart = i;
        }
    }
}
```

Listing 13-12. *Final Code for the TVF in Visual Basic .NET*

```
Imports System
Imports System.Data
Imports System.Data.Sql
Imports System.Data.SqlTypes
Imports Microsoft.SqlServer.Server
Imports System.Collections
Imports System.Runtime.InteropServices
Imports System.Threading
```

```vbnet
Namespace SqlServerTVF
    Partial Public Class UserDefinedFunctions
        <Microsoft.SqlServer.Server.SqlFunction(FillRowMethodName:="FillRow", _
            TableDefinition:="charpart nchar(1), intpart int")> _
        Public Shared Function NameToAscii(ByVal InputName As String) _
         As IEnumerable
            Return New NameSplitter(InputName.ToCharArray())
        End Function

        Public Shared Sub FillRow(ByVal row As Object, _
            <Out()> ByRef charpart As Char, <Out()> ByRef intpart As Integer)
            ' break the row into its columnar parts.
            charpart = CType(row, NameRow).CharPart
            intpart = CType(row, NameRow).IntPart
        End Sub
    End Class


    Public Class NameSplitter
        Implements IEnumerable, IEnumerator

        Private idx As Int32 = -1
        Private _inputName As Char()
        Private _current As Char

        Public Sub New(ByVal InputName As Char())
            _inputName = InputName
        End Sub

        Public Function GetEnumerator() As System.Collections.IEnumerator _
            Implements System.Collections.IEnumerable.GetEnumerator
            Return New NameSplitter(_inputName)
        End Function

        Public ReadOnly Property Current() As Object _
            Implements System.Collections.IEnumerator.Current
            Get
                If (idx > -1) Then
                    Dim c As Char = _inputName(idx)
                    Return New NameRow(c, Asc(c))
                Else
                    Return -1
                End If
            End Get
        End Property

        Public Function MoveNext() As Boolean _
            Implements System.Collections.IEnumerator.MoveNext
```

```
            idx = idx + 1
            If (idx < _inputName.Length) Then
                Return True
            Else
                Return False
            End If
        End Function

        Public Sub Reset() Implements System.Collections.IEnumerator.Reset
            idx = -1
        End Sub
    End Class

    Public Class NameRow
        Public CharPart As Char
        Public IntPart As Int32

        Public Sub New(ByVal c As Char, ByVal i As Int32)
            CharPart = c
            IntPart = i
        End Sub
    End Class
End Namespace
```

9. With the DLL built, go ahead and deploy it to the database. This can be done using the right-click deploy method for SQL Server projects or using the script shown in Listing 13-13.

Listing 13-13. *Script Used to Deploy the TVF*

```
Create Assembly SqlServerTVF
from
'C:\SqlServerTVF\SqlServerTVF.dll'
GO

Create Function NameToAscii
(
    @InputName NVARCHAR(4000)
)
Returns Table
(
    charpart nchar,
    intpart Int
)
As
External Name
SqlServerTVF.[SqlServerTVF.UserDefinedFunctions].NameToAscii
Go
```

10. With the Assembly registered and the TVF deployed, now you can easily execute it from SQL Server Management Studio using the following SQL command:

```
Select * from dbo.NameToAscii ('Sahil Malik')
```

The results produced are as shown in Figure 13-12.

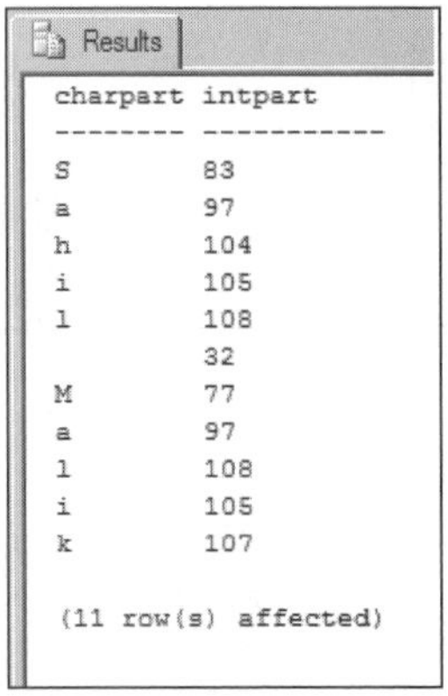

```
 Results
charpart intpart
-------- -----------
 S        83
 a        97
 h        104
 i        105
 l        108
          32
 M        77
 a        97
 l        108
 i        105
 k        107

(11 row(s) affected)
```

Figure 13-12. *Output of a simple TVF*

Now just for fun, reword the query like so:

```
Select * from dbo.NameToAscii ('Sahil Malik') order by intpart
```

The results produced are shown in Figure 13-13.

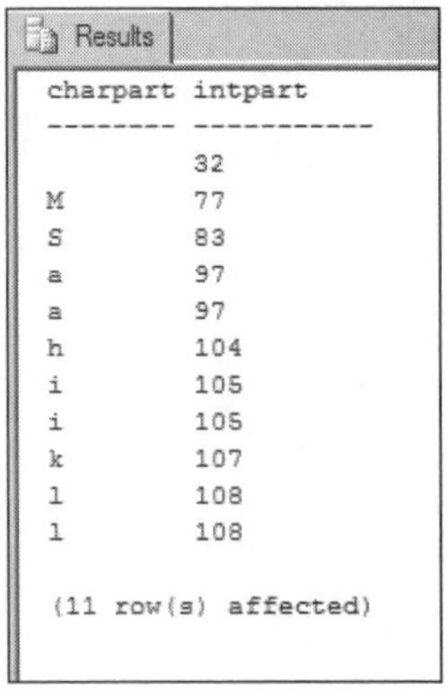

```
 Results
charpart intpart
-------- -----------
          32
 M        77
 S        83
 a        97
 a        97
 h        104
 i        105
 i        105
 k        107
 l        108
 l        108

(11 row(s) affected)
```

Figure 13-13. *Output of a simple TVF using an order by clause in the end*

Thus, as you can see, this TVF that you wrote can be used like any traditional T-SQL TVF.

The ability to write .NET code and expose it as a TVF reveals interesting possibilities. Obviously, this code executes under the permission structure set up by SQL Server, but nevertheless you could leverage this for interesting uses. Let's look at a quick sample.

Enumerating Files in a Directory Using a TVF

The ability to expose the results of your .NET code as a table introduces interesting possibilities in your system architecture. For instance, let's quickly write up a TVF that accepts a directory path and returns the list of files in that directory.

Following the steps used for SqlServerTVF, you can easily write up another TVF that reads up the contents of a directory and displays the files contained within. This code can be found in the associated code download under the SqlTVFExternalAccess project.

The code for this TVF looks like as shown in Listings 13-14 and 13-15.

Listing 13-14. *The TVF Used to Display the Files Contained in a Directory in C#*

```csharp
public partial class UserDefinedFunctions
{
    [Microsoft.SqlServer.Server.SqlFunction(FillRowMethodName = "FillRow",
        TableDefinition="FileName nvarchar(4000), FileSize nvarchar(4000)")]
    public static IEnumerable GetDircontents(string dirName)
    {
        DirectoryInfo startDir = new DirectoryInfo(dirName);
        // This implements IEnumerable, so we are done :)
        return startDir.GetFiles();
    }

    public static void FillRow(object row, out string fileName, out string fileSize)
    {
        FileInfo oneFile = (FileInfo)row;
        fileName = oneFile.Name;
        fileSize = oneFile.Length.ToString();
    }
};
```

Listing 13-15. *The TVF Used to Display the Files Contained in a Directory in Visual Basic .NET*

```vbnet
Partial Public Class UserDefinedFunctions
    <Microsoft.SqlServer.Server.SqlFunction(FillRowMethodName:="FillRow", _
        TableDefinition:="charpart nchar(1), intpart int")> _
    Public Shared Function GetDircontents(ByVal dirName As String) As IEnumerable
        Dim startDir As DirectoryInfo = New DirectoryInfo(dirName)
        ' This implements IEnumerable, so we are done :)
        Return startDir.GetFiles()
    End Function
```

```
    Public Shared Sub FillRow(ByVal row As Object, _
        <Out()> ByRef fileName As String, <Out()> ByRef fileSize As String)
        ' break the row into its columnar parts.
        Dim oneFile As FileInfo = CType(row, FileInfo)
        fileName = oneFile.Name
        fileSize = oneFile.Length.ToString()
    End Sub
End Class
```

In order for this TVF to run, it needs EXTERNAL_ACCESS permission. This is because this TVF attempts to access an external resource, namely the file system, to return a list of files contained within. There are two ways to do this. For a SQL Server project, you can set the Permission Level property of the SQL Server project to External. This is as shown in Figure 13-14.

Figure 13-14. *Setting the appropriate permission level for SqlTVFExternalAccess*

The second way of specifying the EXTERNAL_ACCESS permission level is by using a deployment script as shown in Listing 13-16.

Listing 13-16. *Specifying the Appropriate Permission Level for the TVF Using a SQL Script*

```
Create Assembly SqlTVFExternalAccess
from
'C:\SqlTVFExternalAccess\SqlTVFExternalAccess.dll'
WITH PERMISSION_SET = EXTERNAL_ACCESS
GO

Create Function GetDircontents
(
    @DirName NVARCHAR(4000)
)
```

```
Returns Table
(
    FileDirName NVARCHAR(4000),
    FileSize NVARCHAR(4000)
)
As
External Name
SqlTVFExternalAccess.[SqlTVFExternalAccess.UserDefinedFunctions].GetDircontents
Go
```

Now with this procedure deployed, you can make interesting uses of it. For instance, in the following script, I can get a list of tasks configured on my machine:

```
Select * from dbo.GetDircontents ('C:\WINDOWS\Tasks')
```

Obviously, you can enhance the TVF to do all kinds of fancy things. As an exercise, you could try a stored procedure that has the ability to store the results of a FOR XML query as an XML file on the disk.

In addition to writing UDFs and TVFs, you also have the ability to author UDTs (User-Defined Types) in SQL Server 2005 using SQLCLR. You have already seen an example of a UDT in Chapter 5, so let's take that discussion one step further and instead create an aggregate function next.

Creating Aggregate Functions

An aggregate function is a function that returns a scalar value after aggregating over a set of values. An example of an aggregate function is MAX or SUM.

Let's assume a case where you have a table created using the following script:

```
Create Table Person
(
    PersonID int identity primary key,
    PersonName varchar(200),
    PersonRole varchar(200)
)
GO

Insert into Person (PersonName, PersonRole) Values ('Sahil Malik', 'Author')
Insert into Person (PersonName, PersonRole) Values ('Erick Sgarbi', 'Reviewer')
Insert into Person (PersonName, PersonRole) Values ('Frans Bouma', 'Reviewer')
Insert into Person (PersonName, PersonRole) Values ('Jon Hassell','Lead Editor')
GO
```

Say you wanted to get the names of all the people with the "Reviewer" role. This can be easily accomplished using the following SQL query:

```
Select PersonName from Person where PersonRole = 'Reviewer'
```

In fact, this query will return results as shown here:

```
PersonName
--------------
Erick Sgarbi
Frans Bouma
```

But what if you instead wanted the names to be concatenated end to end (as shown here)?

```
Reviewers
---------------------------
Erick Sgarbi, Frans Bouma
```

What *you need* is the ability to execute a query that looks like the one shown next; but there is no method that comes with T-SQL called Concatenator, so the code shown here won't work unless you write the UDF yourself:

```
Select
    dbo.Concatenator(PersonName) as Reviewers
from
    Person
where
    PersonRole = 'Reviewer'
Group By PersonRole
```

Now, I am sure it's possible to get the concatenated results through T-SQL, and even though you should prefer to use T-SQL over SQLCLR where you can, let's use the previous use case to develop a user-defined aggregate called Concatenator that allows you to write a query as shown previously.

This is simply an exemplary sample of SQLCLR aggregate use, and it can be argued that T-SQL may have been a better choice to implement this functionality. But the whole idea is once you have seen this exemplary sample of code, the same principles can then be applied to writing an aggregate function that helps you calculate the third and a half partial derivative of semi-complex numbers on a seven-dimensional plane, or any other such reasonably complex task.

The code for this example can be found in the associated code download under the SqlServerAggregate project, or you can easily create it using what you have learned so far and with the following steps.

These steps are intentionally terse because much of the concepts required to create an aggregate are the same as creating any other SQLCLR project:

1. In order to create a SQLCLR aggregate, you either use a class library or a SQL Server project. The SQLCLR aggregate is defined in .NET code using a structure, marked with the SqlUserDefinedAggregateAttribute.

2. The basic skeleton of the SQLCLR aggregate can be created by adding a new item to the SQL Server project, and selecting a user-defined aggregate in the menu choices presented. This is shown in Figure 13-15. Name your new SQLCLR aggregate Concatenator. If you are using a simple class library, you would instead have to add a class and modify the code accordingly.

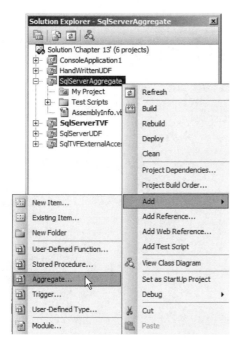

Figure 13-15. *Adding a new SQLCLR aggregate to your project*

3. As you will see in the skeleton of the code already created for you, there are four methods that exist:

   Init: This method is where you should perform the initialization.

   Accumulate: This method is where you will perform the aggregate functionality, in this case the actual concatenation.

   Merge: This is where you would write code if, in case, the aggregate is used with another aggregate.

   Terminate: This is where you would calculate the final value and send it back.

You can now go ahead and fill out the code for these four methods as per Listings 13-17 and 13-18.

Listing 13-17. *The Skeleton Code for the SQLCLR Aggregate in C#*

```
private StringBuilder sb;
public void Init()
{
    sb = new StringBuilder();
}
```

```csharp
    public void Accumulate(SqlString Value)
    {
        sb.Append(Value);
        sb.Append(",");
    }

    public void Merge(Concatenator group)
    {
        Accumulate(group.ToString());
    }

    public override string ToString()
    {
        return sb.ToString();
    }

    public SqlString Terminate()
    {
        sb.Remove(sb.Length - 1, 1);
        return sb.ToString();
    }
}
```

Listing 13-18. *The Skeleton Code for the SQLCLR Aggregate in Visual Basic .NET*

```vbnet
Private sb As StringBuilder

Public Sub Init()
    sb = New StringBuilder()
End Sub

Public Sub Accumulate(ByVal value As SqlString)
    sb.Append(value)
    sb.Append(",")
End Sub

Public Sub Merge(ByVal group As Concatenator)
    Accumulate(group.ToString())
End Sub

Public Overrides Function ToString() As String
    Return sb.ToString()
End Function

Public Function Terminate() As SqlString
    sb.Remove(sb.Length - 1, 1)
    Return sb.ToString()
End Function
```

4. Now there is still one thing left to do before this becomes a valid, workable, aggregate method. If you note, the default value of the Format property, of the SqlUserDefinedAggregateAttribute attribute, is Format.Native. This won't work. You can only use Format.Native for data types that SQL Server has the ability to read and write to a byte stream directly. In other words, for Format.Native, you do not have to implement the serialization and deserialization process. The data types that can be used with Format.Native are System.Byte, System.SByte, System.Int16, System.UInt16, System.Int32, System.UInt32, System.Int64, System.UInt64, System.IntPtr, and System.UIntPtr.

Our class, however, is returning a string, SqlString to be precise. Now, for you to be able to use Format.Native, the type has to be a blittable type, that is, no reference-type members or other non-value-based content. Thus, you will have to change the format from Native to UserDefined. In addition to changing the format from Native to UserDefined, you'll also have to implement an interface called IBinarySerialize where you'll be required to create two methods: Read and Write, to read and write from a BinaryReader and BinaryWriter, respectively.

After having made these changes, your code should look like as shown in Listings 13-19 and 13-20.

Listing 13-19. *The Full Code for the Concatenator Aggregate in C#*

```csharp
[Serializable]
[Microsoft.SqlServer.Server.SqlUserDefinedAggregate(Format.UserDefined,
    MaxByteSize=8000)]
public struct Concatenator : IBinarySerialize
{
    private StringBuilder sb;
    public void Init()
    {
        sb = new StringBuilder();
    }

    public void Accumulate(SqlString Value)
    {
        sb.Append(Value);
        sb.Append(",");
    }

    public void Merge(Concatenator Group)
    {
        Accumulate(Group.ToString());
    }

    public override string ToString()
    {
        return sb.ToString();
    }
```

```
public SqlString Terminate()
{
   sb.Remove(sb.Length - 1, 1);
   return sb.ToString();
}

#region IBinarySerialize Members

public void Read(System.IO.BinaryReader r)
{
   sb = new StringBuilder();
   sb.Append(r.ReadString());
}

public void Write(System.IO.BinaryWriter w)
{
   if (sb.Length > 0)
      w.Write(sb.ToString());
}

#endregion
}
```

Listing 13-20. *The Full Code for the Concatenator Aggregate in Visual Basic .NET*

```
<Serializable()> _
<Microsoft.SqlServer.Server.SqlUserDefinedAggregate(Format.UserDefined, _
   MaxByteSize:=8000)> _
Public Structure Concatenator
   Implements IBinarySerialize

   Private sb As StringBuilder

   Public Sub Init()
      sb = New StringBuilder
   End Sub

   Public Sub Accumulate(ByVal value As SqlString)
      sb.Append(value)
      sb.Append(",")
   End Sub

   Public Sub Merge(ByVal value As Concatenator)
      Accumulate(value.ToString())
   End Sub
```

```vb
    Public Overrides Function ToString() As String
        Return sb.ToString()
    End Function

    Public Function Terminate() As SqlString
        sb.Remove(sb.Length - 1, 1)
        Return sb.ToString()
    End Function

#Region "IBinarySerialize Members"
    Public Sub Read(ByVal r As System.IO.BinaryReader) _
        Implements IBinarySerialize.Read
        sb = New StringBuilder()
        sb.Append(r.ReadString())
    End Sub

    Public Sub Write(ByVal w As System.IO.BinaryWriter) _
        Implements IBinarySerialize.Write
        If (sb.Length > 0) Then
            w.Write(sb.ToString())
        End If
    End Sub
#End Region
End Structure
```

5. Now you can build the project and deploy it using the SQL Server project directly or by using the script here:

```sql
Create Assembly SqlServerAggregate
from
'C:\SqlServerUDT\SqlServerAggregate.dll'
GO

CREATE AGGREGATE Concatenator( @instr nvarchar(400) )
RETURNS nvarchar(MAX)
EXTERNAL NAME [SqlServerAggregate].[SqlServerAggregate.Concatenator]
GO
```

6. Now run the following SQL query:

```sql
Select
    dbo.Concatenator(PersonName) as Reviewers
from
    Person
where
    PersonRole = 'Reviewer'
Group By PersonRole
```

7. The results should look like as shown in Figure 13-16.

Figure 13-16. *Execution results of the Concatenator SQLCLR aggregate*

Now another point to note in this example is that of all the SQLCLR examples presented so far in this chapter, this is the first example that actually interacted with a table in the underlying database. Even this example, in fact, didn't quite read from the Persons table in the .NET code, but from the T-SQL query that wrapped the usage of this aggregate.

You'd think that interacting with the rest of the stored procedures, tables, etc. in the database might be something you would need to do quite frequently in your SQLCLR code. As it turns out, interacting with the database from within SQLCLR code is not at all difficult. In fact, let's next write up a quick stored procedure that calls the previous aggregate.

Writing a SQLCLR Stored Procedure

Let's kill two birds with one stone:

1. Let's look at an example that demonstrates writing stored procedures in SQLCLR code.

2. Let's use this stored procedure to call the aggregate written in the SqlServerAggregate project, thus illustrating the ability to work with the database directly from inside of SQLCLR code.

Lest there be any confusion, before I get too deep in explaining the SQLCLR stored procedure that queries the underlying database, I must make it clear that this concept of interacting with the database, from SQLCLR, is not limited to a stored procedure. In fact, you can practically copy and paste this code and use it in any SQLCLR code snippet to work directly with the database from SQLCLR code.

But before I can begin telling you about such a stored procedure, let's take a quick primer on an important and relevant concept—the context connection.

The Context Connection

Inside the SQLCLR, as usual, the basic ADO.NET principles apply. You'll need an instance of SqlConnection in order to connect with the underlying database. But think about it, the stored procedure that you are going to write is already executing inside the database. So for the SqlConnection that you create, should you be creating a brand new connection that connects right back to the database it was called from, effectively creating a "loop back" connection? That sounds incredibly wasteful. Why should you have to create a loop-back connection when, in fact, you are already inside a connection?

Well, you could certainly create a loop-back connection,[3] but if you are connecting from within the same database then you are already in a connection. Wouldn't it be nice to be able to get a hold of the same connection that the stored procedure was called upon, and simply use that connection to execute the commands?

It's for this reason that Microsoft created the concept of a *context connection*. The context connection can be created using the following connection string:

```
"context connection = true"
```

Thus, the following instance of SqlConnection holds the context connection—in other words, the same connection the stored procedure was called upon:

C#

```
SqlConnection contextConnection = new SqlConnection("context connection = true");
```

VB.NET

```
Dim contextConnection as SqlConnection = _
    New SqlConnection("context connection = true")
```

Using a context connection versus a loop-back connection has several advantages:

- By doing so, you neatly skip over the TDS protocol layer and the TCP/IP or Named Pipes protocol layer, and directly get a hold of the connection inside the database.

- You do not need to reauthenticate.

- You have the ability to latch on to a currently running transaction easily. Any external non–context connections created by specifying a full ADO.NET connection string would automatically try to enlist themselves in the active running transaction and thus be promoted to MSDTC (the exception to this rule being loop-back connections into the same SQL Server 2005 database). Such connections cannot enlist themselves in the same transaction and must use enlist=false in their connection strings to work.

However, there are certain restrictions placed on a context connection as well. These are listed here:

- Within a running instance of a SQLCLR method (procedure, TVF, UDF, aggregate etc.), you can have at most only one SqlConnection object with its State = ConnectionState.Open that was opened within the same execution scope. The execution scope begins when the code is first called, typically the first line in the method, and ends when the method completely exits, typically a return statement or the last executable line of the method. In a case where the SQLCLR method calls T-SQL from within, which in turn calls another SQLCLR method, that causes a nested execution scope in the called SQLCLR method that is different from the original execution scope in the calling SQLCLR method. In that scenario,

---

3. Such a loop-back connection cannot be enlisted in the active transaction in SQL Server 2005. More on this soon.

the nested execution scope and calling execution scope can both have one concurrently open context connection each.

- MARS does not work with context connections. (MARS is covered in depth in Chapter 11.)

- `SqlBulkCopy` cannot work with a context connection.

- Update batching does not work with a context connection.

- `SqlNotificationRequest` cannot be used with commands that execute on a context connection.

- Canceling commands is not supported. `SqlCommand.Cancel` will be ignored.

- No other connection string keywords can be specified with `context connection = true`.

In order to facilitate your working with the context inside SQL Server, ADO.NET provides an object called `SqlContext`, which can be found in the `Microsoft.SqlServer.Server` namespace.

The `SqlContext` object provides you with a `Pipe` property of `SqlPipe` data type, which is your primary means of communication with the caller application. For instance, you can do the equivalent of the T-SQL `PRINT` statement using the `SqlContext.Pipe.Send` method. If, instead, this were called from an ADO.NET application, you could intercept that message using the `SqlConnection.InfoMessage` event in the client application.

Similarly, in order to execute a set-oriented T-SQL command and send the results back to a data reader, you could use either the `SqlPipe`'s `ExecuteAndSend` method as a one-shot solution, or you could use `SendResultsStart` to begin sending results, `SendResultsRow` to send an individual row, followed by `SendResultsEnd` to complete the result set.

Let's examine what you have learned in a quick example that demonstrates both of these cases. You can create the example by following the steps here, or you can find it in the associated code download under the `SqlServerStoredProc` project:

1. In this example, let's write up two SQLCLR stored procedures. Both of the stored procedures get a hold of the context connection. The first stored procedure, `GetConcatenatedNames`, executes the `SqlServerAggregate` aggregate function you have written previously using the following T-SQL command:

```
Select
    dbo.Concatenator(PersonName) from Person
Where PersonRole = @Role
Group By PersonRole
```

The second stored procedure will return a result set using the following T-SQL command:

```
Select PersonName from Person where PersonRole = @Role
```

2. So go ahead and create a new SQL Server project, call it `SqlServerStoredProc`, and add a new stored procedure to it—call that file `GetNames.cs/GetNames.vb`.

3. Create the first stored procedure, `GetConcatenatedNames`, as shown in Listings 13-21 and 13-22.

Listing 13-21. *SQLCLR Stored Procedure GetConcatenatedNames in C#*

```csharp
[Microsoft.SqlServer.Server.SqlProcedure]
public static void GetConcatenatedNames(string role)
{
    using (SqlConnection contextConnection =
        new SqlConnection("context connection = true"))
    {
        SqlCommand contextCommand =
            new SqlCommand(
            "Select dbo.Concatenator(PersonName) from Person " +
            "where PersonRole = @Role Group By PersonRole", contextConnection);

        contextCommand.Parameters.AddWithValue("@Role", role);
        contextConnection.Open();

        SqlContext.Pipe.ExecuteAndSend(contextCommand);
    }
}
```

Listing 13-22. *SQLCLR Stored Procedure GetConcatenatedNames in Visual Basic .NET*

```vbnet
<Microsoft.SqlServer.Server.SqlProcedure()> _
Public Shared Sub GetConcatenatedNames(ByVal role As String)
    Using contextConnection As SqlConnection = _
        New SqlConnection("context connection = true")

        Dim contextCommand As SqlCommand = _
            New SqlCommand( _
            "Select dbo.Concatenator(PersonName) from Person " & _
            "where PersonRole = @Role Group By PersonRole", contextConnection)

        contextCommand.Parameters.AddWithValue("@Role", role)
        contextConnection.Open()

        SqlContext.Pipe.ExecuteAndSend(contextCommand)
    End Using
End Sub
```

4. Add a second stored procedure, GetNames, to the same class. The code for GetNames is shown as per Listings 13-23 and 13-24.

Listing 13-23. *SQLCLR Stored Procedure GetNames in C#*

```csharp
[Microsoft.SqlServer.Server.SqlProcedure]
public static void GetNames(string role)
{
    using (SqlConnection contextConnection =
    new SqlConnection("context connection = true"))
```

```
{
   SqlCommand contextCommand =
      new SqlCommand(
      "Select PersonName from Person " +
      "where PersonRole = @Role", contextConnection);

   contextCommand.Parameters.AddWithValue("@Role", role);

   contextConnection.Open();

   // first, create the record and specify the metadata for the results
   SqlDataRecord rec = new SqlDataRecord(
      new SqlMetaData("PersonName", SqlDbType.NVarChar, 200)
      );

   // start a new result set
   SqlContext.Pipe.SendResultsStart(rec);

   // send rows
   SqlDataReader rdr = contextCommand.ExecuteReader();
   while (rdr.Read())
   {
      rec.SetString(0, rdr.GetString(0));
      SqlContext.Pipe.SendResultsRow(rec);
   }

   // complete the result set
   SqlContext.Pipe.SendResultsEnd();
}
```

Listing 13-24. *SQLCLR Stored Procedure GetNames in Visual Basic .NET*

```
<Microsoft.SqlServer.Server.SqlProcedure()> _
Public Shared Sub GetNames(ByVal role As String)
   Using contextConnection As SqlConnection = _
      New SqlConnection("context connection = true")

   Dim contextCommand As SqlCommand = _
   New SqlCommand("Select PersonName from Person where PersonRole = @Role", _
      contextConnection)

   contextCommand.Parameters.AddWithValue("@Role", role)

   contextConnection.Open()

   ' first, create the record and specify the metadata for the results
   Dim rec As SqlDataRecord = _
```

```
            New SqlDataRecord(New SqlMetaData("PersonName", _
            SqlDbType.NVarChar, 200))

        ' start a new result set
        SqlContext.Pipe.SendResultsStart(rec)

        ' send rows
        Dim rdr As SqlDataReader = contextCommand.ExecuteReader()
        While rdr.Read()
            rec.SetString(0, rdr.GetString(0))
            SqlContext.Pipe.SendResultsRow(rec)
        End While

        ' complete the result set
        SqlContext.Pipe.SendResultsEnd()
    End Using
End Sub
```

5. Compile, build, and deploy the stored procedures. If you wish to deploy the stored procedure using a script, you can use the script shown here:

```
Create Assembly SqlServerStoredProc
from
'C:\SqlServerStoredProc\SqlServerStoredProc.dll'
GO

Create Procedure GetConcatenatedNames
(
    @Role NVARCHAR(4000)
)
As
External Name
SqlServerStoredProc.[SqlServerStoredProc.StoredProcedures].➥
GetConcatenatedNames
Go

Create Procedure GetNames
(
    @Role NVARCHAR(4000)
)
As
External Name
SqlServerStoredProc.[SqlServerStoredProc.StoredProcedures].GetNames
Go
```

6. Now if you run the T-SQL here,

```
exec dbo.GetConcatenatedNames 'Reviewer'
```

then you should see the following results:

```
Erick Sgarbi,Frans Bouma
```

Similarly, if you run the T-SQL here,

```
exec dbo.GetNames 'Reviewer'
```

then you should get the following results:

```
PersonName
----------------
Erick Sgarbi
Frans Bouma

(2 row(s) affected)
```

Thus, as you can see, by getting a hold of the context connection, you are able to run T-SQL commands. And with the help of SqlContext and SqlPipe, you are able to send results back to the calling client.

While it's exciting that you can execute such queries and send results back, at this point I am quite intrigued by the many questions and possibilities this brings up:

What if you had a third procedure that inserted a row?

What if the T-SQL that wrapped around that procedure inserted a row on its own, and then called your SQLCLR stored procedure in the same transaction? In the event of a rollback through SQLCLR, would the T-SQL–inserted row get rolled back?

What if the T-SQL code issued a rollback instead of the SQLCLR stored procedure? Does the SQLCLR-inserted row get rolled back?

■**Note** Another curious question jumping like a frog for attention is "What if the connection string pointed to a physically separate database, maybe even a physically separate server? What happens then?" Well, hold your horses, as you are going to find out soon.

The best way to answer such questions is to go ahead and write code and find out. So go ahead and add a third stored procedure to the SqlServerStoredProc project. The code for this stored procedure can be seen in Listings 13-25 and 13-26. Do note, however, that in this code there is a call to System.Transactions.Transaction.Current.Rollback. This facility is thanks to the fantastic integration between System.Transactions and ADO.NET. As you will see shortly, this allows the SQLCLR code to roll back the transaction it is called within.

Listing 13-25. *SQLCLR Stored Procedure InsertName in C#*

```csharp
[Microsoft.SqlServer.Server.SqlProcedure]
public static void InsertName(string personName, string personRole)
{
    using (SqlConnection contextConnection =
      new SqlConnection("context connection = true"))
```

```
    {
        SqlCommand contextCommand =
            new SqlCommand(
"Insert into Person(PersonName, PersonRole) Values (@PersonName, @PersonRole)",
            contextConnection);

        contextCommand.Parameters.AddWithValue("@PersonName", personName);
        contextCommand.Parameters.AddWithValue("@PersonRole", personRole);

        contextConnection.Open();
        contextCommand.ExecuteScalar();
        System.Transactions.Transaction.Current.Rollback();
        contextConnection.Close();
    }
}
```

Listing 13-26. *SQLCLR Stored Procedure InsertName in Visual Basic .NET*

```
<Microsoft.SqlServer.Server.SqlProcedure()> _
Public Shared Sub InsertName(ByVal personName As String, _
    ByVal personRole As String)
    Using contextConnection As SqlConnection = _
        New SqlConnection("context connection = true")
        Dim contextCommand As SqlCommand = _
            New SqlCommand( _
            "Insert into Person(PersonName, PersonRole) " & _
            " Values (@PersonName, @PersonRole)", _
            contextConnection)

        contextCommand.Parameters.AddWithValue("@PersonName", personName)
        contextCommand.Parameters.AddWithValue("@PersonRole", personRole)

        contextConnection.Open()
        contextCommand.ExecuteScalar()
        System.Transactions.Transaction.Current.Rollback();
        contextConnection.Close()
    End Using
End Sub
```

Now simply run the stored procedure using the following T-SQL script:

```
BEGIN TRANSACTION
EXEC dbo.InsertName
    @personName = N'Emily',
    @personRole = N'Project Manager'
COMMIT
```

When you run this T-SQL statement, you should get one of the following error messages:

```
Msg 1206, Level 18, State 49, Procedure InsertName, Line 0
The transaction manager has cancelled the distributed transaction.
```

or

```
Msg 266, Level 16, State 2, Procedure InsertName, Line 0
Transaction count after EXECUTE indicates that a COMMIT or ROLLBACK TRANSACTION
statement is missing. Previous count = 1, current count = 0.
Msg 3902, Level 16, State 1, Line 5
The COMMIT TRANSACTION request has no corresponding BEGIN TRANSACTION.
```

This makes sense since the transaction manager (in this case, the LTM) behind the scenes has canceled the transaction before the COMMIT statement could execute. So the second COMMIT is confused, as it does not have a matching BEGIN TRANSACTION anymore.

Now if you check the contents of the table after this code runs, you'll notice that there has been no change to the underlying table.

WHY TWO POSSIBLE ERROR MESSAGES?

Okay, this is a bit unexpected, a computer under the same set of conditions and inputs is always supposed to behave identically. Thus, given the same set of inputs, you should get the same set of outputs every time, repeatedly. So how can you get two possible inputs?

Well, I decided to give two inputs because this is something you need to be careful of when debugging SQLCLR code that involves transactions. It turns out that the fancy little tool tip that pops up in Visual Studio 2005 that allows you to browse the contents of any particular variable in debug mode has a minor issue with distributed transactions.

As you have already seen in Chapter 11, under certain circumstances, a transaction being managed by LTM is promoted to MSDTC. Well, it so happens that the tool tip that is incredibly helpful in viewing the values of various variables in debug mode actually causes the transaction to promote to MSDTC. Thus, when you are debugging SQLCLR code, or any code for that matter that involves System.Transactions, you should prefer to use the immediate window over that tool tip in order to examine the details of the transactions involved.

But I went ahead and gave you both of the possible error messages, just so there wouldn't be any confusion.

Now modify the T-SQL code so it looks like this:

```
BEGIN TRANSACTION

Insert into Person (PersonName, PersonRole)
Values ('Linda', 'Cover Editor')

EXEC [dbo].[InsertName]
                        @personName = N'Emily',
                        @personRole = N'Project Manager'
COMMIT
```

Thus, you are trying to insert one row through T-SQL, and one through SQLCLR code. As expected, the one transaction that wraps both these inserts is rolled back completely and the table is entirely untouched.

Now go ahead and comment out the SQLCLR statement that is forcing a rollback of the transaction. Rebuild and redeploy your stored procedure. This time, run your stored procedure using the following T-SQL script. Note that this time a ROLLBACK is being issued from T-SQL instead:

```
BEGIN TRANSACTION

Insert into Person (PersonName, PersonRole)
Values ('Linda', 'Cover Editor')

EXEC [dbo].[InsertName]
                    @personName = N'Emily',
                    @personRole = N'Project Manager'
ROLLBACK

Select * from Person
```

The results of this script's execution are shown here:

```
(1 row(s) affected)
PersonID    PersonName  PersonRole
--------------------------------------------
1           Sahil Malik  Author
2           Erick Sgarbi Reviewer
3           Frans Bouma  Reviewer
4           Jon Hassell  Lead Editor

(4 row(s) affected)
```

Thus, as you can see, the first insert succeeded, but the ensuing rollback rolled back both the SQLCLR and T-SQL changes. You are still left with only four rows inside the table.

Finally, change the ROLLBACK to COMMIT, and run the following T-SQL script:

```
BEGIN TRANSACTION

Insert into Person (PersonName, PersonRole)
Values ('Linda', 'Cover Editor')

EXEC [dbo].[InsertName]
                    @personName = N'Emily',
                    @personRole = N'Project Manager'
COMMIT

Select * from Person
```

This, as you would expect, ends up inserting two new rows into the database. The identities have rolled up from four to a higher number because issuing rollbacks does not cause the identities to roll back in SQL Server.

```
(1 row(s) affected)
PersonID    PersonName  PersonRole
-----------------------------------
1           Sahil Malik  Author
2           Erick Sgarbi Reviewer
3           Frans Bouma  Reviewer
4           Jon Hassell  Lead Editor
25          Linda        Cover Editor
26          Emily        Project Manager

(6 row(s) affected)
```

SqlTransaction in SQLCLR

You might have noticed that I haven't been talking about SqlTransaction in SQLCLR. Well, you can still use SqlTransaction just as you would in plain vanilla, non-SQLCLR ADO.NET. The only issue that presents itself is that you would have to be careful about transaction counts and the calling code starting any transactions before you did (much like nested transactions as mentioned in Chapter 11). Thus, using System.Transactions integration in SQLCLR presents a compelling alternative to SqlTransaction.

There are, however, situations were you should still prefer to use SqlTransaction over System.Transactions. A perfect example is, say, if you wish to use context connection only, and your transaction is not concerned with external RMs. In this scenario, you should prefer to use SqlTransaction over TransactionScope.

This is because, for the SQL Server 2005 release, the TransactionScope object will always use distributed transactions when running inside SQLCLR. This means that if there wasn't a distributed transaction already, the scope will cause the transaction to promote—even if you technically didn't need a full-fledged distributed transaction managed by MSDTC. Now because you are connecting only to the local server, this is unnecessary overhead that can be, and should be, avoided by using SqlTransaction only.

Therefore, if you are using the context connection only, you should not use TransactionScope for SQL Server 2005.

But in situations where you need to enlist external RMs in a transaction, there is no additional overhead since that transaction would have been promoted anyway.

Yet another kind of object you can write in SQLCLR is a trigger. The ability to latch on to a current running transaction, with the help of System.Transactions, proves invaluable in a trigger where you might want to validate the data and roll it back if the data is not valid. Writing a trigger in a SQL Server project is very much like authoring a stored procedure or any other SQLCLR object. Let's look at a quick example demonstrating that next.

Using Transactions in SQLCLR Triggers

Again, let's kill two birds with one stone:

- Let's write a quick sample that demonstrates writing a SQLCLR trigger.

- Let's look at how you can latch on to the current running transaction using `System.Transactions.Transaction.Current`.

The steps for authoring a SQLCLR trigger are very similar to creating any other SQLCLR project. All you have to do is, when adding a new item to the SQL Server project, select the trigger object type instead. This can be seen in Figure 13-17.

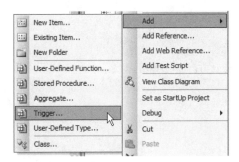

Figure 13-17. *Adding a SQLCLR trigger*

Once the trigger is added, modify its code to look like Listings 13-27 and 13-28.

Listing 13-27. *SQLCLR Trigger in C#*

```
[Microsoft.SqlServer.Server.SqlTrigger (Name="MonkeyTrigger",
   Target="dbo.Person", Event="FOR INSERT")]
public static void MonkeyTrigger()
{
    SqlTriggerContext stContext = SqlContext.TriggerContext;

    if (stContext.TriggerAction == TriggerAction.Insert)
    {
        // Check the column
        using (SqlConnection contextConn =
            new SqlConnection("context connection=true"))
        {
            SqlCommand cmd = contextConn.CreateCommand();
            contextConn.Open();
            cmd.CommandText = "Select PersonName from Inserted";

            string personName = (string) cmd.ExecuteScalar();

            if (personName.ToUpper() == "MONKEY")
            {
                System.Transactions.Transaction.Current.Rollback();
                SqlContext.Pipe.Send(
```

```
                                   "Monkey not allowed in this table, eat banana on tree");
            }
            contextConn.Close();
        }
    }
}
```

Listing 13-28. *SQLCLR Trigger in Visual Basic .NET*

```
<Microsoft.SqlServer.Server.SqlTrigger(Name:="MonkeyTrigger", _
   Target:="dbo.Person", Event:="FOR INSERT")> _
 Public Shared Sub MonkeyTrigger()
   Dim stContext As SqlTriggerContext = SqlContext.TriggerContext

   If stContext.TriggerAction = TriggerAction.Insert Then
      ' Check the column
      Using contextConn As SqlConnection = _
         New SqlConnection("context connection=true")
         Dim cmd As SqlCommand = contextConn.CreateCommand()
         contextConn.Open()
         cmd.CommandText = "Select PersonName from Inserted"

         Dim personName As String = CType(cmd.ExecuteScalar(), String)

         If personName.ToUpper() = "MONKEY" Then
            System.Transactions.Transaction.Current.Rollback()
            SqlContext.Pipe.Send( _
               "Monkey not allowed in this table, eat banana on tree")
         End If
         contextConn.Close()
      End Using
   End If
End Sub
```

As you can see from the code, a trigger is identified by the following SqlTriggerAttribute attribute:

C#

```
[Microsoft.SqlServer.Server.SqlTrigger (Name="MonkeyTrigger",
   Target="dbo.Person", Event="FOR INSERT")]
```

VB.NET

```
<Microsoft.SqlServer.Server.SqlTrigger(Name:="MonkeyTrigger", _
   Target:="dbo.Person", Event:="FOR INSERT")> _
```

This attribute signifies that the MonkeyTrigger works on the target object dbo.Person for the event "FOR INSERT". As you can also see from the code, the trigger checks if the last inserted PersonName was "Monkey". If it was, it rolls back the transaction and sends back the error message "Monkey not allowed in this table, eat banana on tree".

Once you compile and build this trigger, it can easily be deployed using the SQL Server project, or using the script shown here:

```
Create Assembly SqlServerTrigger
from
'C:\SqlServerTrigger\SqlServerTrigger.dll'
GO

Create Trigger MonkeyTrigger
 ON Person
 FOR INSERT
As
External Name
SqlServerTrigger.[SqlServerTrigger.Triggers].MonkeyTrigger
Go
```

Thus, now if you try inserting a monkey using the following script:

```
Insert into Person
    (PersonName, PersonRole)
Values
    ('Monkey','Banana eater')
```

you should get an error message as shown in Figure 13-18.

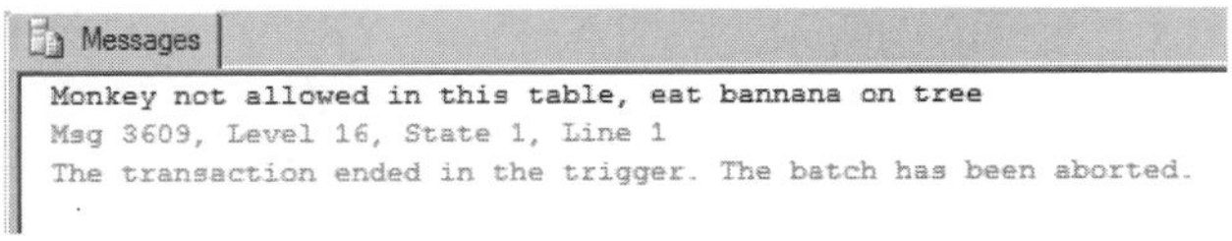

Figure 13-18. *Results of attempting to insert Monkey in the Person table*

Thus, as you can see, using System.Transactions, you are easily able to roll back the current running, implicit, or explicit transaction that the insert statement was executing under, straight from the trigger.

Now a question I had brought up earlier was "What happens when you specify a connection string, inside SQLCLR, that does not attempt to get a hold of the context connection, but instead uses a connection string similar to what you would have used in non-SQLCLR ADO.NET?" Well, stay tuned to find out. . . .

Using Non-Context Connections Inside SQLCLR

The code shown previously in Listings 13-25 and 13-26 uses the following connection string:

```
context connection = true
```

But what would happen if you specified a connection string connecting to an external database server (win2k3-smalik) as shown here?

```
Server=win2k3-smalik;Database=Test;Integrated Security=SSPI
```

Well, the best way to find out is by modifying the code to use this connection string. Go ahead and modify the connection string for the GetConcatenatedNames stored procedure as shown here, so the code for GetConcatenatedNames looks like this:

C#

```csharp
using (SqlConnection contextConnection =
    new SqlConnection("Server=win2k3-smalik;Database=Test;Integrated Security=SSPI"))
{
    SqlCommand contextCommand =
        new SqlCommand(
        "Select dbo.Concatenator(PersonName) from Person " +
        "where PersonRole = @Role Group By PersonRole", contextConnection);

    contextCommand.Parameters.AddWithValue("@Role", role);
    contextConnection.Open();

    SqlContext.Pipe.ExecuteAndSend(contextCommand);
}
```

VB.NET

```vbnet
Using contextConnection As SqlConnection = _
    New SqlConnection("Server=(local);Database=Test;Integrated Security=SSPI")

    Dim contextCommand As SqlCommand = _
        New SqlCommand( _
        "Select dbo.Concatenator(PersonName) from Person " & _
        "where PersonRole = @Role Group By PersonRole", contextConnection)

    contextCommand.Parameters.AddWithValue("@Role", role)
    contextConnection.Open()

    SqlContext.Pipe.ExecuteAndSend(contextCommand)
End Using
```

Now deploy this procedure and run the T-SQL script, shown here, to execute the procedure:

```
exec dbo.GetConcatenatedNames 'Reviewer'
```

As it turns out, you would get a System.SecurityException as shown in Figure 13-19.

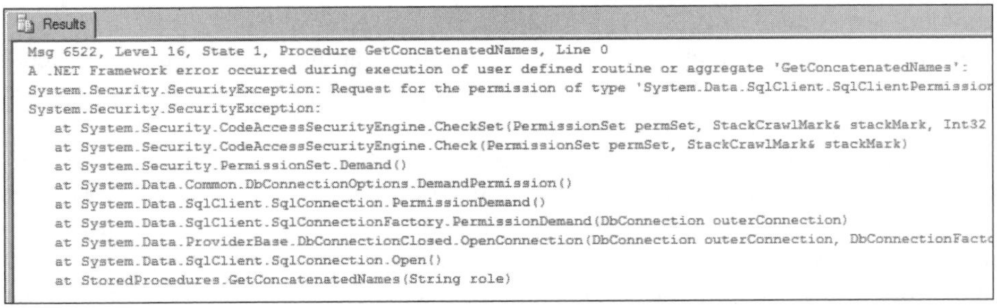

```
Results
Msg 6522, Level 16, State 1, Procedure GetConcatenatedNames, Line 0
A .NET Framework error occurred during execution of user defined routine or aggregate 'GetConcatenatedNames':
System.Security.SecurityException: Request for the permission of type 'System.Data.SqlClient.SqlClientPermission
System.Security.SecurityException:
    at System.Security.CodeAccessSecurityEngine.CheckSet(PermissionSet permSet, StackCrawlMark& stackMark, Int32
    at System.Security.CodeAccessSecurityEngine.Check(PermissionSet permSet, StackCrawlMark& stackMark)
    at System.Security.PermissionSet.Demand()
    at System.Data.Common.DbConnectionOptions.DemandPermission()
    at System.Data.SqlClient.SqlConnection.PermissionDemand()
    at System.Data.SqlClient.SqlConnectionFactory.PermissionDemand(DbConnection outerConnection)
    at System.Data.ProviderBase.DbConnectionClosed.OpenConnection(DbConnection outerConnection, DbConnectionFact
    at System.Data.SqlClient.SqlConnection.Open()
    at StoredProcedures.GetConcatenatedNames(String role)
```

Figure 13-19. *Attempting to get a context connection using Windows authentication*

While this may appear surprising, it is important to realize that your SQLCLR code is not executing as you (because the thread that was running SQL Server Management Studio is not running under the same credentials as yourself). This is because your running code gets the same access rights as the thread that was running it. And, in this case, your SQLCLR code is not running as you, but as the system account that is running SQL Server. And that system account does not have permission to connect to the specified SQL Server database.

There are three ways to solve this issue.

The *first way* is to run the SQL Server process under a specific user ID that has access to the database that you are trying to connect with.

The *second way* is to impersonate the identity you are interested in using. This can easily be done by calling SqlContext.WindowsIdentity.Impersonate on the Windows identity the code is currently running under. This also means that your client must be connected using Windows authentication in the first place, because otherwise there will be no way to get a hold of the Windows identity. By calling the Impersonate method, you are getting back a WindowsSecurityContext. By calling Impersonate, you are changing the security token of the thread. Once you are done, you can then call the WindowsSecurityContext's Undo method to revert back to the default security token.

■**Note** There is a lot more to this topic of delegation than can be mentioned in an ADO.NET book. If you are interested in further reading, I suggest you check out the following TechNet article: http://www.microsoft.com/technet/prodtechnol/windowsserver2003/technologies/security/constdel.mspx.

The *third and most obvious way* is to simply use SQL Server authentication instead.

However, creating a connection using a fully qualified connection string results in creating either a loop-back connection, if connecting with the same server, or a brand new connection, when connecting to a separate database.

One obvious downside of this, as mentioned previously, is performance—a non–context connection would usually not be as fast as getting a hold of the same connection that you were already executing upon. But in certain instances it might be necessary to create a brand new non-context connection. One such instance would be when connecting to a different server, say a different SQL Server or even Oracle database, from within SQLCLR. The second instance could be where you do not wish to enlist within the same transaction as the SQLCLR is executing upon (more on this shortly).

The point of transactions brings up another important question: "If an update is issued on the newly spawned regular connection object, does it roll back or commit with the transaction that the calling SQLCLR code was already running under?"

The good news is that the framework, with the help of System.Transactions, will be able to detect this new connection instance as an RM that is enlisting within the same transaction. The only exceptions are loop-back connections, which, in SQL Server 2005, are unable to enlist within the active running transaction. Thus, even if you were to open a connection to an Oracle database from within SQLCLR, due to the seamless integration of System.Transactions, the commands executing on the new OracleConnection will be enlisted within the same transaction as the commands on the existing SqlConnection. But since there are two connection object instances within the same transaction, the transaction will now be a distributed transaction.

There exists, however, a way to prevent this auto-enlist behavior. All you have to do is add the following to the connection string to prevent auto-enlistment:

```
enlist = false
```

■Note There is one nuance to this that you must be careful of: the same does not apply to creating a loop-back connection to the same database that you were working with in the case of SQL Server 2005. The new loop-back connection will not be able to enlist itself in the same transaction. In fact, when creating a new loop-back connection, the connection will fail if there is an active transaction, unless you add enlist = false to prevent it from trying to enlist in the same transaction.

Here is a cool thing you could not do (easily at least) before SQLCLR. In SQLCLR code, you can open a non–context connection by specifying a full connection string instead. When doing so, add enlist = false to the full connection string. This will create a brand new connection that does not enlist in the calling transaction. This way, you will be able to start a brand new and not-nested transaction from within one transaction and be able to log failures, etc.

Regular non–context connections inside SQLCLR work under a few restrictions.

First and foremost is the fact that unless you specify explicitly that you do not wish your new connection to be auto-enlisted in the transaction, the new connection will automatically enlist itself under a distributed transaction. There is no way that you can work under a non-distributed transaction even if you were looping back to the same database.

In addition to that, features such as asynchronous command execution and the SqlDependency object and the related infrastructure do not work on regular connections inside SQLCLR.

In addition to being able to leverage automatic enlistment of your new connection instances inside an already running transaction, you can use TransactionScope just as you would use it in the middle tier. The usage of TransactionScope has been explained in depth in Chapter 11. The one thing to be careful of in SQL Server 2005 is that even if you wrap only the context connection inside a transaction scope, the transaction scope will cause the transaction to promote. This will have negative performance implications; thus, if you are using context connection only, you should try and avoid using TransactionScope.

■**Note** Use `TransactionScope` only if you have to work with more than one RM. Do not wrap context connections within `TransactionScope`. This will cause context connections to promote unnecessarily.

Also, since you have the same flexibility or `System.Transactions` infrastructure available in SQLCLR as you would in the middle tier, you have the ability of not auto-enlisting inside a transaction, and programmatically deciding whether or not to enlist the new connection in the distributed transaction. In fact, you could even decide to implement your own RM and tie them up with transactions inside SQLCLR.

Summary

This chapter introduced you to a powerful new technology, SQLCLR, that opens many new doors for the architect in you.

You saw how the CLR running inside the SQL Server behaves differently from the CLR you see running on any Windows machine. You saw how it puts security requirements on your code, and how you need to explicitly decide the specific functionality your SQLCLR code will require. You saw how SQLCLR code can be written either as a SQL Server project or as a simple class library. You also saw how to write common SQLCLR objects such as UDFs, TVFs, aggregates, stored procedures, and triggers and how to debug such code.

It's true that SQLCLR gives you a lot of freedom, but with freedom comes responsibility. Like anything, it's very tempting and easy to abuse or misuse SQLCLR for purposes it isn't well suited for.

In the next and very last chapter of this book, I will discuss some of the biggest debates that surround ADO.NET. I will try and address best practices that will help you reason the correct decision in the specific circumstances.

In addition to other topics, the correct and proper use of SQLCLR will be touched upon. It's extremely important to learn the responsibilities from the next chapter along with the possibilities that you learned in this chapter.

See you in the next and very last chapter, "ADO.NET Best Practices."

CHAPTER 14

■ ■ ■

ADO.NET Best Practices

Welcome to the last chapter of this book. Up till now, you have looked at various important components of ADO.NET and data access in general. No matter what your role in an organization may be, no matter where you are in your level of career, there is a piece of application architect in you and, as an application architect, you need to make various decisions.

In the previous 13 chapters, you looked at various ways to achieve the same end by using a range of choices and tools available to you. With all of these possibilities and tools, and the freedom they give you, come responsibilities. As an application architect, you have to weigh the possibilities and intelligently decide which tool is right for which situation.

Anything that surrounds application architecture, especially data access, is subject to varying shades of gray. In other words, you can't just listen and apply any presented concept verbatim; instead, you must listen, learn, and then apply an inventive combination of solutions that were presented in this book to the specific situation you are faced with. There are various shades of gray because, depending on your needs and the underlying table structure, the decisions you need to make could change. Table structures are driven by requested requirements; hence, a table structure that works well for a reporting application does not work well for an online transaction–processing application.

Thus, if your decisions are driven by requirements, then it makes sense to start with the requirements first.

Know Your System Requirements

I can safely assume that you, my reader, are in some manner related to the software industry. So you will relate very well to what I am about to tell you.

The software industry is weird. We walk into a client's building knowing very little about the nature of their business and what they do. In addition, the client knows very little about software (but in many instances, he thinks he knows a lot). Yet, we are expected to solve their problems—and most of the time we succeed. Of course, at times, we need to solve problems that were created by other software developed in the past, primarily because of a phenomenon commonly referred to as "scope-creep." Then as the scope of the project creeps even further, someone else solves the problems we created.

Not many non–computer professionals are able to appreciate that our work involves imagining a skyscraper with all its intricate details, down to the very last brick and steel harness, and then building every part of it as only imagined, without any physical entity to touch, feel, or see whatsoever. Given that a block diagram or something similar is about as close to the physical world our ideas will ever reach, it can be quite a challenge to have a non–computer professional appreciate the nature of our work. This wouldn't be so bad except that every now and then the client wants us to build that extra room in the basement after the 120th floor has been built.

Data access and the data itself is more than just our basement. It is our foundation. And because the client is always right (isn't he?), our architecture better be firm yet flexible enough to begin with.

Another side effect of the non-physical nature of our deliverables is that failure isn't very evident to the end client until it's too late. For instance, when a patient goes to the doctor and requests a checkup, where the patient would have needed a bypass, the doctor prescribes an aspirin. Well, once the patient has had a massive heart attack, the doctor's failure is quite evident.

The problem with software is that the patient (client) comes in and insists that he be given an aspirin when even you as the doctor (software engineer) clearly know that what he really needs is a bypass. The bigger problem is that after a heart attack the patient will be dead, but after a software failure the client lives to complain and lay blame.

A classic example in terms of ADO.NET is maintaining data sanctity after a number of discrete operations. To a techie, this smells like transaction support. Everyone likes transactions, and between various interactions of the end user with a server-based, data-driven application, the sanctity of data must be kept safe. The client could request that between the two screens the end user will work through, the data should be kept integral.

Thus, you could listen to the client verbatim and make the wrong decision, implementing transactions and involving UI interaction as a part of the transactions. Or you could choose a better tool instead, implementing multiple transactions with sanity checks between each UI interaction. While either approach might be acceptable to the client, your system will not depend on exclusive locks and whims of a particular end user to be of service to other users. Thus, between two or more different ways of implementing transactions, you should consciously choose the latter because you know that for this job, you do not want tightly coupled transactions—you know better than that.

Thus, when you derive your design after your functional research, it all comes down to picking the right tool for the right job.

Picking the Right Tool for the Right Job

Data access requires you to interact with the underlying data source. ADO.NET also gives you the ability to maintain an in-memory cache of disconnected data.

So let's say that in your application you need to work with a SQL Server database, and you have a country name lookup that doesn't change over the lifetime of the application, but will be read in various screens of the application.

While there are numerous ways to approach this problem, assuming that you are writing a fully managed application, the natural choice would be to pick SqlClient over OleDb. Also, the country name lookup is a perfect candidate for storing in an in-memory cached object, rather than retrieving that from the database at every request. Do note that in both of these cases, both OleDb and hitting the database again and again would technically work and be accurate. But it wouldn't be the right solution because OleDb would suffer from a performance hit and would not give you specialized features that SqlClient would give, and hitting the database again and again unnecessarily simply would be a drag on the performance of the application.

Given your requirements, you know the job your software needs to get done. And given the gamut of tools you have to choose from within ADO.NET, you need to match the right tool with the right job.

Let's look at a few common tools with various arguments that will help you decide which alternative to pick over the other.

Data Reader or DataSet/Data Adapter?

The choice of whether to use a data reader or a DataSet should be a fairly straightforward decision, provided you know enough about the type of data you need to access and the ways in which you intend to process it. Both of these components have well-defined roles. As long as you know which roles each of these is designed for, you can choose the most effective solution for your needs. There are a number of major differences between these two components.

An important thing to keep in mind is that regardless of which solution is *faster*, it doesn't necessarily mean that either component is *better*. Each is suited for a particular task, and each will excel at that task. Conversely, each will perform poorly (if at all) when used to perform a task it isn't suited for.

Memory Consumption

One of the main differences between the data reader and the DataSet is that the data reader consumes less memory than a DataSet. Depending on the amount of data and the memory resources available, the performance advantages associated with using less memory can be enormous.

A data reader is an object that allows you to access information on only *a single row of data* at a given time. What this means is that, regardless of the size of a result set, traversing this result set with a data reader will only ever have a single record loaded in memory at a given time.

A DataSet, on the other hand, is designed specifically to be an in-memory cache of large amounts of data. In this regard, the DataSet will consume more memory than the data reader.

To summarize, if you are tight on memory, then you should consider using a data reader rather than a DataSet. However, if memory concerns are not at the top of your list of priorities, then the increased functionality of an entirely disconnected in-memory data cache may suit your needs better.

Of course, you should consider if your eventual aim for reducing memory consumption is better performance or not. If you keep a data reader open for unduly long time durations, then the connected nature of a data reader can actually impact connection-pooling performance negatively. This would be the case if you were doing time-consuming operations between each row being read out of the data reader. So for a large result set, you saved memory, but did you really garner the performance? *No you didn't!* Which is why this is a gray shade that you need to evaluate specifically for your application needs.

Traversal Direction

Whenever you plan on traversing data for a particular task, you need to consider the direction of the traversal.

If you plan on accessing data to do something simple, such as display all of the records in a result set in HTML form through an ASP.NET page, then the choice is simple. The data reader provides you with a read-only/forward-only method to access your data, designed specifically for the task of reading and traversing data in a read-only fashion, rapidly in a forward direction. So, when looking at what an application is going to need to do with the data, if you don't need to be able to write changes to an in-memory cache, or if you don't need to have indexed access to any arbitrary row at any given time, and you don't intend to do too much time-consuming processing between each row, then the data reader will definitely give you some performance benefits.

Note As you can see in Exercises 5.3 and 5.4 in Chapter 5, you can use an ArrayList or another such object in conjunction with a data reader to get around the requirement of forward-only access—this, of course, is at the cost of increased memory consumption, because the extra memory will be required for the ArrayList that will now act as your in-memory disconnected cache.

Multiple Result Sets

Both the data reader and the DataSet support the notion of multiple result sets. The DataSet supports this through using tables. The data reader enables us to access additional result sets by providing the NextResult method. Just as with row access with the data reader, accessing additional result sets in the data reader is a read-only/forward-only operation.

It is important to reiterate here that the data reader will actually only hold one row of information at any given time. This means that even though ten different result sets may be available, only one row of any given result set will be available at any given time. Once a row has been passed in a data reader traversal, that row is disposed of, and there is no way to retrieve it again without resetting the reader and starting over from the beginning.

For those of you who like using the SHAPE statement in your T-SQL statements to create hierarchical Recordsets, you can rest assured that you can still use this with the data reader. Whereas in ADO you would set a Recordset object to the individual field object of a row; instead, you now set a data reader object to the value of a column in the data reader of the parent row.

Keeping the Connection Open: Connection Pooling

As you have already seen in Chapter 4, good connection pooling is critical to the performance of your application in a highly concurrent environment. This is because database connections are expensive resources. The one big difference between a data reader and a DataSet is that a DataSet is database independent and is completely disconnected from the underlying data source. In other words, in order to retrieve data out of a DataSet, you do not need to connect with the underlying data source.

While it may be true that to fill the DataSet originally, and to update its changes back into the underlying data source, you will still need to reconnect to the data source, the entire upshot of this disconnected nature of data access is that you are able to keep the connection closed while you are actually working with the data.

But calling Close on the DbConnection object, such as SqlConnection or OracleConnection, doesn't necessarily mean that your physical network or database connection is really closed. In fact, while you weren't using it, ADO.NET took the same physical database connection and possibly served a bunch of other connection requests in the meantime.

This is in contrast with the data reader where, even if your result set had two rows in it, while you were working on the first row and hadn't explicitly closed the data reader and the connection, your connection is still open and cannot be used by anyone else. Thus, in such a situation even if the data reader is *faster* in a single-user scenario, in a highly concurrent scenario it will actually be *slower* and, hence, not a good choice.

You might raise an eyebrow here and bring up the question that a data adapter internally uses a data reader, too. But, again, even if the data adapter uses a data reader, it frees up the data reader as soon as it can. It fills up a DataSet or DataTable and returns the object. The time that it takes you to actually process upon the data is when a connection will stay closed and, hence, effectively pooled.

DataSet or Strongly Typed DataSets

DataSets out of the box suffer from one big problem: even though they try to mimic an in-memory relational data structure, they fall short on representing the actual data types contained within. Everything is an object. While that is the most portable mechanism, you would typically then need to implement checks and conditions at each point to ensure that the data contained within is not corrupted.

The other way out is to create a strongly typed DataSet. Strongly typed DataSets are as the name suggests—strongly typed, but they, too, suffer from their own set of disadvantages. The biggest problem with strongly typed DataSets is that their structure needs to be continually updated to reflect the underlying table structure. This involves code generation and recompilation.

Also, as the data structure underneath changes, the table adapters associated with the strongly typed DataSet continually get out of date as well. This is probably not an issue in a small application, but maintaining and deploying such a library of strongly typed DataSets can turn into a major headache.

Most of all, DataSets and strongly typed DataSets provide you with a ready-to-use, in-memory disconnected data cache, but at the end of the day, they contain no true knowledge of what that data truly is. It's just a dumb bucket of data. Strongly typed DataSets try to come close to the true representation of your data, but they fall short by far.

It is in these instances where you must resort to the use of a custom business object.

Strongly Typed or Not? DataSet vs. Business Object

Given the fact that for good performance for highly concurrent systems (and in order to make a distributed, disconnected architecture work) you need some kind of disconnected data cache, you can use either the disconnected data cache that comes as a part of the .NET Framework (the DataSet), or you can build your own business objects.

A *business object* is an object representation of a logical entity in the specific business domain that the program is being written for. For instance, if you are writing a program for an insurance company, an example business object could be a policy, premium, payment plan, etc. Business objects present several advantages as compared with DataSets. Some of the advantages are as follows:

1. Your customer in an insurance company understands a "policy," not a DataSet or a DataTable. This allows you to abstract and communicate what you, as a programmer, see on your screen and in your program more effectively with the end customer. This is helpful because the customer doesn't care about the technical implementation and will

not relate to a DataSet. But given a friendly printed view of a "policy" business object (say, using a Visualizer in Visual Studio 2005), the client will be able to relate with that immediately. Thus, it establishes common communication ground between the programmer and the client.

2. Catching, isolating, and debugging rogue data is easier—because the logical information for a particular business entity is all segregated as one serializable instance of the relevant business object. DataSets do not typically restrict your application data into neatly segregated logical business entities.

3a. You have the ability to encapsulate behavior of the data in the business object that contains the data itself. This approach allows you to embed logic inside business objects so it doesn't have to live in every single tier of your architecture.

3b. For situations where you might not control the end-to-end implementation, or the end-to-end implementation isn't in .NET, you can subject your objects to XMLSerialization and move away from object thinking to schema thinking. This way you can easily expose your business objects to a non–.NET world. Assuming that you need a semi-hierarchical structure specific to your business object representation, this is incredibly difficult to do using DataSets.

■Note In many situations, your architecture will make use of both 3a and 3b. A good design dictates that you should create validation logic in a pluggable manner, so your object itself can live without the logic, but can have it if need be. This validation logic can also be seen as rules, which can be categorized into two parts: rules that apply to a type, and rules that apply to an instance of the type.

---

4. You can leverage a number of third-party tools, such as LLBLGen Pro, to help you implement business objects and their translation to and from an underlying relational database structure.

5. You can implement your business objects to all have a common behavior and implementation through interfaces and inheritance. This is something that you cannot do in DataSets. Every object representation in a DataSet is nothing but a DataSet, and the DataSet is tied to a relational structure.

6. In Visual Studio 2005, you can reuse your UI logic to create Visualizers in debug mode for fast, speedy development or just have the ability to give the programmer and customer a common communication methodology.

7. Since your business objects are easy to re-create and they represent the actual program structure, writing tests in a typical test-driven development becomes much easier.

8. Your data has the ability to notify you of changes or issues—much like a living entity, something a DataSet has a tough time doing.

9. You have the flexibility of defining business objects as an aggregation of other business objects. So a policy business object can have an aggregated business object, premium, available as one of its properties. This is something that cannot be achieved using

DataSets. A DataSet can contain the data, but the data is not delineated in a semistructured hierarchical manner.

10. Once you have business objects ready, you can implement templates of your data. For instance, you could create an instance of a business object and use it as a template for all insurance policies that deal with auto insurance.

Wow, that is a handful of advantages! So business objects must be the right answer in every situation, right? Turns out, they are the right answer in many situations, and in many they are not. Here are a few disadvantages of business objects:

1. The biggest problem with business objects is that you have to write them or use some tool to author them first. Also, you have to write their translation and persistence logic. You may do a good job writing them, or you may "fall short of time" and not do such a good job. In contrast, single DataTable DataSets, or just DataTables, are easy to write persistence logic for. Writing persistence logic by hand for hierarchical DataSets is just as complex and time consuming as writing it for a business object would be.

2. As the needs of your application grow, you have to continue to author more business objects and worry about the versioning of previous business objects and their persisted instances.

3. Business objects either require you to write persistence logic for each object, or come up with a standardized mechanism to generate SQL queries. The SQL queries generated, however, are dynamic SQL. Now it may be argued that because dynamic SQL is constantly changing by nature, it suffers from the disadvantage that its query plans are not cached. But it's important to realize that for a given finite set of business objects with defined structures, the set of dynamic queries that you will generate is finite. The finite set of dynamic queries would still be larger than what you would write for a DataTable that could be a direct representation of a database table.

4. Business objects require you to write a new object for a new entity. This might not be fully true as your design might encourage reuse, but you can't beat the non–strongly typed DataSet, in which to set up the object you have to write zero code. Of course, if you pick the DataSet, you loose the advantages a business object gives you.

5. Concurrency is relatively more difficult to manage using business objects. This refers to both thread concurrency and database concurrency.

6. You have to implement ITypedList and IBindingList in order to enable data binding of your business objects.

7. You lose any enhancements Microsoft may provide you with in future versions of .NET. For instance, if you shied away from DataSets in .NET 1.1 because of its serialization problems, you probably spent a very long time getting your business objects working only to find out that Microsoft fixed it in .NET 2.0. This can be argued the other way around, however. If there is a problem in the framework, you are stuck with it until Microsoft releases a fix for it.

T-SQL vs. SQLCLR vs. Extended Stored Procedures (XP)

In Chapter 13, you read a comparison of extended stored procedures versus SQLCLR. In short, extended stored procedures do offer you better performance in all situations except data access on the same database they are called from. However, they suffer from other disadvantages, such as the inability to restrict their access rights into granular restrictions, the inability to use newer data types, and, in general, loosing all advantages that the .NET Framework can give you. You can refer back to Chapter 13 for a detailed discourse on a comparison between SQLCLR and extended stored procedures.

However, when working with operations inside a database, the conventional way of accessing and working with data inside a SQL Server database has been with T-SQL. With the introduction of SQL Server 2005, you can now, however, write your various database objects such as stored procedures, UDFs, aggregates, UDTs, etc. in a .NET language such as VB.NET or C#. The obvious question that arises is, "Under what situations should you prefer to pick SQLCLR over T-SQL and vice versa?"

Here are a few important points to consider when making this decision:

1. T-SQL can be used to perform declarative, set-based operations (SELECT, INSERT, UPDATE, DELETE) or procedural operations (WHILE, assignments, triggers, etc.). While T-SQL is better for set-based operations, it does not lend the programmer much flexibility in terms of procedural logic. In that sense, SQLCLR and the languages it will be written in (C#, VB.NET, etc.) lends the programmer a much richer set of functionality and a better language in general to express such logic in his code.

2. T-SQL is interpreted whereas SQLCLR is compiled. Interpreted code is slower than compiled procedural code.

3. T-SQL has a good library of data-centric functions. It is generally better suited to set-based operations. SQLCLR, on the other hand, is better suited to recursive calls, mathematical operations, string manipulation operations, regular expressions, XSLT, etc.

4. In situations where the end results do not depend on actual data access (for instance, returning a table with ten random numbers), SQLCLR gives you the flexibility of having your data reader start reading the first row before the entire result set has been created. In other words, SQLCLR can pipeline the results. T-SQL, on the other hand, does not have this kind of flexibility. T-SQL, however, is optimized at many levels inside SQL Server itself.

5. In T-SQL, it is very difficult to break away from a current running transaction. It is also difficult to start another transaction in another database. SQLCLR can achieve both of these easily by creating a brand new connection from within SQLCLR, and by adding enlist = false to the connection string.

6. SQLCLR has the ability to execute T-SQL from within itself; however, that SQL is treated as dynamic SQL and it is neither subject to chained security access (i.e., if a stored procedure is called from a SQLCLR stored procedure, the access rights from the SQLCLR stored procedure are not transmitted to the called stored procedure), nor is it subject to compile-time syntax checking.

7. Executing SQLCLR code will cause the CLR to be loaded by the SQL Server. T-SQL does not incur any such overhead.

8. All executing T-SQL code shares the same stack frame; however, every SQLCLR code gets its own stack frame. This results in the possibility of larger memory allocation and better concurrent performance for SQLCLR in general. There is, however, a transition overhead from native code to managed code.

Therefore, given these points, it makes sense to segregate your heavily procedural logic into separate database objects written in SQLCLR. However, for set-based operations, T-SQL is a better choice. Nevertheless, given the number of factors involved, the best judge of performance is a comparative test written for both alternatives. But just because you can now write stored procedures in CLR does not mean that you don't need to learn and use T-SQL anymore.

Transactions, Transactions Everywhere: Which Transaction to Pick

Data is knowledge, and knowledge is power. The program you are writing is not because you wanted to write a program, but because somebody needs some data to be better managed, updated, and retrieved. Thus, to protect the sanctity of the data, you need transactions. Transactions tie up a number of operations, data-related or otherwise, into one atomic unit, which either fails or succeeds as a whole.

There are many flavors of transactions to choose from. Between these various flavors, each locks certain resources and has a certain amount of management overhead. The underlying theme remains that the more there is to manage, the lower the performance will be. If you were to look at various transactions in an increasing order of management overhead and decreasing order of performance, the list would be like this:

1. Implicit transactions are automatically associated with any single SQL statement. These ensure the sanctity of the data during that statement's execution time period.

2. Another option is to wrap up a number of commands between a BEGIN TRANSACTION and COMMIT/ROLLBACK statements, thus forming a block of commands that enlist in the same transaction. This kind of transaction, simply because it needs a higher management overhead and locks more resources, is a bit more expensive. Depending on the underlying database, you also have the possibility of nested transactions. Usually, because you control the entry point and exit point of your procedural logic, it is easier to manage the transaction counts and nested transactions in this scenario.

3. The third option is to wrap up a number of DbCommand objects with the help of a DbTransaction object. The exact implementation depends on the .NET data provider, but in most common .NET data providers this translates to issuing a BEGIN TRANSACTION and COMMIT/ROLLBACK to the underlying data source. In this scenario, you have to be a bit more careful of nested transactions and transaction counts.

4. Yet another option is to automatically enlist in a single database scenario using System. Transactions. This implementation will be just as good as the wrapping .NET RM. For instance, SqlConnection supports promotable enlistment. This means that your transaction wrapped using System.Transactions will not be much more expensive than a simple SqlTransaction code block. However, if you were to do the same for Oracle, your transaction will be managed by MSDTC and will be expensive. Even in SqlConnection, the

transaction ends up promoting to MSDTC if a second RM comes into the picture. This, of course, can be controlled programmatically by not using a `TransactionScope` block, but instead manually enlisting within such a transaction (this has been covered in Chapter 11).

5. There may be a situation where you might wish to enlist in a transaction from either within SQLCLR on a separate database, or from any ADO.NET code that tries to enlist an RM that deals with a durable resource, which has nothing to do with databases in general. In this scenario, your transaction will be managed by MSDTC by default and, hence, will be rather expensive to manage.

6. The final flavor of transactions is where you need transactional sanctity over a distributed or loosely coupled system, such as a web service or message queuing architecture. In this scenario, you cannot lock the resources until the outcome of the transaction is definite. Here you need to build an architecture that loosely wraps functionality similar to a two-phase commit—except you cannot use MSDTC, `TransactionScope`, `SqlTransaction`, or anything in that family to directly wrap your entire loosely coupled transaction. Instead, what you need to do is create rollback/fail mechanisms yourself. For instance, you could implement such a transaction by storing a snapshot of previous data, which acts as your "recovery contract" and a flag on the "in doubt" rows. In the event of success, you can clear out the recovery contract and the in doubt flag and, in event of failure, you can roll back using the recovery contract and then clear out the "in doubt" on the various entities involved. The in doubt flag serves the purpose of informing other parts of the system to desist from using that data since its state is "in doubt."

So which of these six options should you pick? *The lowest one you can get away with*. In other words, you should prefer to stay away from transaction architectures designed for more than what you need. True, you can kill a mosquito with a sledgehammer, but do you really want to pay the extra price of picking up that heavy hammer and risking your friend's hand that the mosquito was sitting on?

There are, however, two choices that seem juxtaposed with each other. These are wrapping transactions in SQL or wrapping them in `DbTransaction` objects. The cardinal rule here is *prefer to wrap them in API* (i.e., `DbTransaction` objects). If a stored procedure or SQL in general needs a transaction, then it's okay to embed a transaction in there, though then you need to be careful of nested scopes. An example of where that might be a better choice would be where you need to ferry large amounts of data back to the client in order to process the next command. In that circumstance, it makes sense to keep your logic close to the data itself—in the database. The situation you want to avoid is where SQL commits or rolls back transactions started in the API or vice versa. In other words, don't mix and match.

Picking the Right Tools: The Clearly Darker Shades of Gray

Depending on the exact situation, it's not just an array of choices you need to pick from. There are situations where it isn't a matter of choice, but discipline. In spite of the many shades of gray, there are a few portions that are clearly black and should be watched out for. Thus, doing certain things is clearly good and not doing them is clearly bad. Let's look at some of these cardinal rules of working with ADO.NET.

Implementing a Data Layer

In most scenarios, implementing a data layer is a good idea. A data layer is simply a set of classes, a web service, an application server, or just any piece of code that all your data access is done through. Implementing a data layer is a good idea because of the following reasons:

1. You isolate yourself from any changes in the framework. If something changes in the framework, you only need to change your data access layer to ensure that your entire architecture doesn't change.

2. You ensure that best practices are followed by everyone. This is because in a team it might get difficult to enforce rules on everyone. If all data access is done out of one data layer, you ensure that the best practices are enforced in the data layer, and everyone automatically garners the benefit.

3. You ensure that everyone uses the same connection string defined in the configuration file, or otherwise. This helps in connection pooling all the connection requests.

4. A data layer ensures that you have one convenient place to put performance-measuring metrics and if there is a problem with your data access architecture, then you have one place to look, and one place to fix.

Closing Connections

This is one of those insidious and serious issues that tends to creep into your application architecture with the least of warning. It only raises its ugly head when the application is in production, working (or failing) under a heavy load. The reason this is a difficult problem to track is because not only will the effect not be apparent in development, where you are testing logic, not scalability, but also because generally for situations such as transactions, your data layer will either need to expose an open connection or accept an array of DbCommands with parameters in place. While the first approach relies on the end user of your data layer to make sure that any open connections are eventually closed, the second approach results in an unwieldy class structure.

Before .NET was around, programmers had to worry about memory leaks. The garbage collector makes it a lot easier by routinely performing the clean-up job for them. While you still have to be somewhat careful, the rules are much easier to live by now. If you forget to call the Dispose method on a particular object, while that isn't a very ideal situation, the object will eventually be picked up by the garbage collector, which will call the Finalize method instead. For objects that occupy a large amount of memory, the garbage collector will sense the memory pressure and be invoked more frequently as need be. However, DbConnection objects in themselves do not occupy large amounts of memory. What they do occupy is a valuable network connection resource, which the garbage collector will blissfully ignore. This results in the garbage collector firing less frequently and independent of your open connections, thus leaving the state of DbConnections open for longer than it should be.

Let's consider the situation where the garbage collector did fire between every 4 to 8 minutes and did the clean-up job that you should have done in the first place. Where you would have required the connection to be open for only a few milliseconds (typical query execution time), now your connection state remains open for a much longer time. First, when the garbage collector bumps up your unused, out of scope, but open connection objects to the second generation of garbage collection, it will stay open for 4 to 8 minutes—and then another 4 to 8 minutes[1] before it finally cleans up objects that were bumped to the second generation. Thus, where you could have closed a connection in 100 milliseconds, your connection may now remain open for 8 to 16 minutes. Four to eight minutes for each iteration of garbage collector, I might add, is a rather conservative guesstimate on 16GB RAM application servers.

Now, the garbage collector will eventually call Finalize, which eventually changes the state of the connection to "closed." But the DbConnection connection state is not the actual state of the underlying physical database connection. Even after the DbConnection is closed, the underlying network connection will still remain open for a little bit longer to serve any other immediate requests using the same connection string.

While instead of keeping a connection open for 100 milliseconds, you ended up keeping it open for 8 minutes (these are more or less the best-case scenario numbers), ADO.NET was piled up with requests to create more and more open connections, simply because the connection you should have released was still unavailable.

So what happens, essentially, is that because there is a fewer number of open available connections, more requests stand in queue; and where you needed to serve a time period of 100 milliseconds, you are now serving 8 minutes' worth of connection open requests, not to mention the backlog that might create. So the whole thing comes tumbling down like a deck of cards.

So, as a conservative guess, if your connection state remains open for 8 minutes instead of 100 milliseconds, your pool would now need to handle 4,000 times more connections than it should have. And if you had ten servers connecting to the same database, each with the same problem, you can safely assume that your database is now handling 40,000 more connections than it needs to. It is amazing that the whole application still works! It probably works because the default setting for the maximum connection pool size is 100 connections, which means starting at the 101st connection request all the way to the 4,000th connection request (possibly much more than 4,000) will have to wait in line for an available connection.

Now if you think this sounds bad, sit back in your seat, hold on to something firm and consider this—this awful scenario is based on the conservative assumption of a single leaky connection and the garbage collector firing every 4 minutes. You should consider yourself lucky if you were to get away with so little.

So thank the maximum connection pool setting that the database server didn't catch fire, commit suicide, or file for divorce, because not closing connections is truly a terrible thing to do. The short-term solution, of course, is to increase the connection pool size, but the true solution is to find the source of that leaky open connection and plug it.

And of course, let me reiterate the golden rule one last time in this book—*open a connection as late as possible, and close it as early as you can.*

Network Latency

One of the most important things to remember about large applications is that latency is your enemy. *Latency*, in our context, is the delay and lock of resources incurred while obtaining and opening a connection, executing commands, and getting the results back over a network. You want to perform this activity as *infrequently* as possible throughout an application. If you keep this in mind, performance tuning an application may be easier than expected.

In small applications or desktop applications, when accessing local data stores such as an Access database or an Excel spreadsheet, the overhead of opening and closing connections

---

1. The exact amount of time depends on a lot of factors, but this is a rough guesstimate.

may not be noticeable. However, when the component opening and closing the connection is on a different machine in a network (or worse, across the Internet) from the actual database server, the cost of opening a connection is very high.

For example, let's suppose a user of an application clicks a button to retrieve a list of orders. This opens a connection, obtains the orders, and closes the connection. Then, the user double-clicks on an order item and obtains a list of order details. This also opens the connection, obtains the result set, and then closes the connection again. Assuming the user continues with this browsing behavior for 10 minutes, the user could be consuming an enormous amount of time and resources needlessly going over the network again and again.

One way to prevent situations like this is to *anticipate the intended use of data*. You should weigh the memory cost of obtaining the information on the initial database connection against the cost of waiting until the information is needed. And then you should weigh the complexity of working with stale data and resolving the issues that may create.

DataSets are designed to be in-memory data caches. They are also designed to hold on to more than one table of information. They are an ideal candidate for storing data in anticipation of disconnected browsing behavior.

■**Note** Retrieving a large volume of data within the context of a single connection will always be faster than retrieving small portions and opening and closing the connection each time, because large-block retrieval causes less network roundtrips and incurs less latency.

Complicated Hierarchical DataSets

So you should fetch more data, possibly a related set of tables, with a number of rows. This begs the question, "Why not fetch the entire database in the DataSet, so you never have to worry about a network roundtrip ever again?"

Don't do it!!

There are a number of reasons for this:

1. You should try to work with simpler DataSets because the larger a DataSet gets, the more memory it uses.

2. As you saw in Chapter 10, saving hierarchical data is not a trivial task. You have to be careful about data relations in updates and inserts, both of which go in the reverse direction of deletes due to foreign key constraints in the database. This can cause deadlocks unless you explicitly request a pessimistic lock to begin with, which leverages deadlock resolution features in the underlying database, but is not a very efficient manner of saving data back into the database.

3. The time required to run GetChanges and Merge increases exponentially with the number of rows, tables, and relationships in a DataSet in .NET 1.1. The internal algorithm to perform these operations is vastly improved in .NET 2.0, but it still requires considerable processing. Do note here that if you have a large strongly typed DataSet with, say, 40 tables (God forbid if you ever had that many!), even if the tables are empty you still pay a significant cost.

■**Note** Having a large, complex, strongly typed `DataSet` with a large number of tables of which only two or three are filled at a given time is still a bad solution. Instead, you should have a number of strongly typed `DataSets`.

---

4. Cyclical references are bad. This is because, depending on your data, the `GetChanges`, `Merge`, and `XmlSerialization` logic can get really inefficient if your `DataSet` has cyclical references.

So what is a good size for a `DataSet`? This question is just as difficult as "How much butter on toast is enough?" While seemingly simple, the exact boundaries cannot be clearly defined.

As a rough yardstick, you can say that a large single table (why not just use a `DataTable`?), two medium-sized tables, or three small tables should be a good guideline in most situations. Though, it's perfectly acceptable to bend these rules, if you know what you're doing. Do remember, however, the structural complexity of the `DataSet` hurts performance more than the sheer size of it.

Caching Data

Every application has the possibility of benefiting from caching data. For instance, an ASP.NET application might show a banner on all of its pages, or it may need to constantly show a menu based upon a particular user's permissions. You can save a number of hits to the database by caching the data using the `HttpContext.Cache` object. It is not just about hits—typically, accessing data out of a cache based in RAM is tens of thousands to many millions of times faster than accessing it over the network, or even the Internet.

By doing so, you will significantly reduce the number of times your database will get hit for the same information. The issue is often referred to as the problem of *stale data*. Data that has been cached, say, on a web server, could have been subsequently modified in the database. You can also use objects such as `SqlDependency` to invalidate the cache if, in case, the underlying data changes or you can simply set an expiration policy.

Windows applications and services, on the other hand, do not have a built-in mechanism like ASP.NET to facilitate caching. But the good thing about .NET is that you can leverage underlying Win32 functions to build a caching API much like that exposed by ASP.NET.

Summary

Writing this book has been a lot of work. I just couldn't finish without one chapter that put all the essence and juice together. So this chapter presented a mixture of opinions and facts.

Data access is an extremely critical part of your application. It ***has*** to be done right. Lucky for you and me, it's also the easiest part to get wrong! There are certain rules to follow and certain facts to keep in mind. Certain decisions depend on the situation, and certain decisions are clearly no-brainers. This chapter demystified and shed light upon what might fall into either category. It gave pros and cons of choices between which you'll need to make a fair decision, and it clearly elucidated the potholes you need to avoid.

I've had a good time writing this book about a topic that I am so incredibly passionate about. In writing this book, at every given instant, I kept reminding myself repeatedly that my reader, who has spent his hard-earned money and many hours reading this text cover to cover, must get the worth out of it.

I'd like to thank you, my reader, for staying with me through the course of this book, and I hope you will put what you learned to good use. Sayonara!

Index